Brian A. LaMacchia
Sebastian Lange
Matthew Lyons
Rudi Martin
Kevin T. Price

F

.NET Framework Security

✦ Addison-Wesley

Boston • San Francisco • New York • Toronto • Montreal
London • Munich • Paris • Madrid
Capetown • Sydney • Singapore • Mexico City

.NET Framework Security

Many of the designations used by manufacturers and sellers to distinguish their products are claimed as trademarks. Where those designations appear in this book, and Addison-Wesley were aware of a trademark claim, the designations have been printed in initial capital letters or in all capitals.

The author and publisher have taken care in the preparation of this book, but make no expressed or implied warranty of any kind and assume no responsibility for errors or omissions. No liability is assumed for incidental or consequential damages in connection with or arising out of the use of the information or programs contained herein.

The publisher offers discounts on this book when ordered in quantity for special sales.

For more information, please contact:

Pearson Education Corporate Sales Division
201 W. 103rd Street
Indianapolis, IN 46290
(800) 428-5331
corpsales@pearsoned.com

Visit AW on the Web: www.awl.com/cseng/

ISBN **0-672-32184-X**

05 04 03 02   4 3 2 1

First printing, **May 2002**

Trademarks

All terms mentioned in this book that are known to be trademarks or service marks have been appropriately capitalized. Addison-Wesley cannot attest to the accuracy of this information. Use of a term in this book should not be regarded as affecting the validity of any trademark or service mark.

Warning and Disclaimer

Every effort has been made to make this book as complete and as accurate as possible, but no warranty or fitness is implied. The information provided is on an "as is" basis. The authors and the publisher shall have neither liability nor responsibility to any person or entity with respect to any loss or damages arising from the information contained in this book.

Executive Editor
Shelley Kronzek

Acquisitions Editor
Michelle Newcomb

Development Editor
Songlin Qiu

Managing Editor
Charlotte Clapp

Project Editor
Natalie Harris

Copy Editors
Pat Kinyon
Matt Wynalda

Indexer
Rebecca Salerno

Technical Editor
Michael Nishizaki

Team Coordinator
Pamalee Nelson

Interior Designer
Karen Ruggles

Cover Designer
Aren Howell

Page Layout
Mark Walchle

Contents at a Glance

Table of Contents

About the Authors

Brian A. LaMacchia is the Development Lead for .NET Framework Security at Microsoft Corporation in Redmond, WA, a position he has held since April 1999. Previously, Dr. LaMacchia was the Program Manager for core cryptography in Windows 2000 and, prior to joining Microsoft in 1997, he was a Senior Member of Technical Staff in the Public Policy Research Group at AT&T Labs—Research in Florham Park, NJ. He received S.B., S.M., and Ph.D. degrees in Electrical Engineering and Computer Science from MIT in 1990, 1991, and 1996, respectively.

Sebastian Lange has been working at Microsoft as Program Manager on the .NET Framework Common Language Runtime security team for over two years. He focuses on security configuration, administration, type safety verification, and secure hosting of the CLR. Prior to his work on security, Sebastian has done research and design in artificial intelligence, both in industry as well as in university. He holds a B.A. in Computer Science and a B.A. in Philosophy from Macalester College.

In his spare time, Sebastian practices a variety of musical instruments, and can be seen playing the electric viola for his band Elysian up and down the west coast.

Matthew Lyons is the QA lead for security features of the Common Language Runtime at Microsoft Corporation. He has been testing and developing against the internal workings of .NET Framework security for over two years. Before that, he spent two years testing public key cryptography and the certificate services in Windows 2000. Matt received a B.S. in Applied Physics from Purdue University in 1997 and is currently working on an M.S. in Computer Science at the University of Washington.

Rudi Martin graduated from Glasgow University (Scotland, U.K.) in 1991 with a B.S.C. in Computing Science. He spent seven years working for Digital Equipment Corporation in the operating systems group, covering areas such as file systems, interprocess communications, and transaction processing. Rudi joined the NDP group at Microsoft in 1999, where he worked in the core execution engine and the security subsystem. He worked on the OpenVMS platform, transitioned to Windows NT, and has been very busy with the Common Language Runtime security group.

Kevin T. Price has been a software architect for over seven years specializing in Web-based applications. He is presently a Senior Software Architect for CMS Information Services in Vienna, VA. Kevin has edited books on .NET as well as authored chapters in BizTalk Unleashed. The material and code samples found in his chapters reflect real-world experience. Focusing on the securing of information and platform scalability. Mr. Price has both architecture and hands-on experience using technologies including ASP, Crypto API, JSP, Java, COM/DCOM, VB, C++, .NET, and numerous other technologies related to the Internet and/or the Microsoft-based toolset.

Dedications

Brian A. LaMacchia:
As always, for Mom, Dad, and Dave.

Sebastian Lange:
*Dedicated to my parents, Barbara Lange-Gnodtke
and Karl-Heinz Lange.*

Matthew Lyons:
Dedicated to my wife, Chanda.

Rudi Martin:
*Dedicated to my parents, without whom this
definitely wouldn't have been possible.*

Kevin T. Price:
For my family.

Acknowledgments

The entire author team would like to thank Shelley Kronzek, Michelle Newcomb, Songlin Qiu, Natalie Harris, Michael Nishizaki, Pat Kinyon, and the rest of the editorial staff at Sams Publishing for their understanding and continual support during this whole process. We couldn't have done this without your help.

Brian A. LaMacchia: This book would not have been possible without the dedicated work of the current and former members of the .NET Framework security team. Their contributions over the past three years were critical to the successful completion and delivery of the .NET Framework's security system. I wish to personally thank each of them and their families for the sacrifices they made to ship a world-class product.

Sebastian Lange: Many people's support has made this book a reality. I would specifically like to thank Shajan Dasan, Jim Hogg, Gregory D. Fee, Greg Singleton, Tim Kurtzman, and John Lambert for being invaluable sources of information. I also wish to thank my family, friends, and mentors that have directly or indirectly supported my efforts throughout some difficult months: Anita Thiele, Erik Davis, Jenny Ottes-Donath, Laila Davis, Leah Bowe, Steffen and Caroline M., Thomas Elbmag Duterme, Torsten Erwin, Toni Mädler, Treçon Wolandy, Dr. Joy Laine, and Dr. Richard Molnar. Finally, thank you for your patience and support, Alexis D. Larsson.

Matthew Lyons: I would like to personally thank the whole CLR security team at Microsoft. Without their years of hard work, dedication, and sense of humor to make it through the rough times, this book wouldn't be possible. Also, thanks again to the staff at Addison-Wesley Professional and Sams Publishing for dealing with the delays and unexpected pitfalls involved with this project.

Rudi Martin: I'd like to acknowledge the help and support of the entire Common Language Runtime team at Microsoft. It was a long journey, but my traveling companions made it all worth while.

Kevin Price: I would like to thank Shelley Kronzek for considering me for this project, as well as the guys at Microsoft—Matt, Brian, Sebastian, and Rudi. A special thanks to Erik Olsen for his contributions and to my family.

Introduction

By Brian A. LaMacchia

Welcome! The book you hold in your hands is a comprehensive guide and roadmap to the security infrastructure of the Microsoft .NET Framework. The .NET Framework is Microsoft's new cross-language development environment for building rich client applications and XML Web Services. One of the key features of the .NET Framework is a robust security infrastructure that provides developers, administrators, and users with new levels of control over code that executes on their systems. Whether you are a developer, administrator, or end user, this book will help you make the most of the .NET Framework security system and create, control, deploy, and use secure .NET applications.

Demystifying .NET Framework Security

Our primary goal in writing this book is to explain the .NET Framework security system in detail and make it easy to understand. As a group, the authors have over 10 years of combined experience as members of the .NET Framework security product team at Microsoft. We have gathered together in this book our combined advice, experience, and wisdom to help you make the .NET Framework security system best serve your needs. We hope that you will find this book useful not only as an introduction to the fundamental security features of the .NET Framework but also as a frequent desktop reference as you author or administer applications.

This book is designed to serve the security needs of .NET developers, administrators, and end users. Developers who are currently writing code in one or more .NET languages (or planning to start a coding project) will find detailed instructions on how to perform security checks, how to write code conforming to the "principle of least privilege," and how to include security in your software architectures from the outset. For example, we will teach you how to use cryptographic strong names to protect your programs from outside modification and guarantee that they run with the same shared libraries with which you intended for them to run. We will also demonstrate how to create "semipublic" application programming interfaces (APIs) that can only be called by identities you specify. Debugging security exceptions and interpreting the data returned by the Common Language Runtime when your code is denied access to some protected operation are also covered in this book. Everything you need to know to develop secure components and applications is contained herein.

If you are an administrator, you will find in the following chapters detailed examples showing how to modify security policy to tighten or loosen it as needed for your particular environment. We will walk you through all the common policy modification scenarios and show you how you can configure an entire enterprise from one location through the use of the .NET Framework's security configuration tool and the Windows Active Directory. We will also explain ASP.NET configuration for deploying secure Web Services with authentication and authorization customized to fit your needs.

For end users, our primary task in this book is to demonstrate how you can control the security behavior of .NET Framework applications running on your machine. Depending on your particular situation, you may need to administer portions of your security configuration to allow or refuse rights to particular applications. You may have encountered a security exception while executing an application and want to know why that exception occurred. You might also be trying to use a Web Service and need to understand its security requirements. All of these topics are covered in this book.

What Do You Need to Know Prior to Reading This Book?

We assume that if you are reading *.NET Framework Security* that you are already familiar with the .NET Framework, the Common Language Runtime, and one or more .NET programming languages (C++, C#, Visual Basic .NET, and so on). Nearly all of the examples in this book are written in the C# programming language, so some basic familiarity with C# will help you learn the most from the sample code. Every sample in this book could just as easily been written in Visual Basic .NET, or any of the other languages that compile to MSIL and run on top of the Common Language Runtime, so what you learn from the samples will be immediately applicable in your particular programming environment.

Some specific chapters in this book assume additional topic-specific knowledge. For example, the two chapters that discuss the cryptography classes in the .NET Framework (Chapter 30, "Using Cryptography with the .NET Framework: The Basics and Chapter 31, "Using Cryptography with the .NET Framework: Advanced Topics") assume that you already have a basic understanding of cryptography. The chapters describing the security features of ASP.NET (Chapters 13 through 16) assume that the reader has previous exposure to the core features of ASP and/or ASP.NET. Chapter 18 ("Administering Security Policy Using the .NET Framework Configuration Tool") assumes basic familiarity with the Microsoft Management Console (MMC), because the .NET Framework Configuration tool is an MMC "snap-in" that works alongside other MMC-based configuration tools, such as the Device Manager.

What Software Will You Need to Complete the Examples Provided with This Book?

At a minimum, you will need to have the .NET Framework Software Development Kit (SDK) installed on your computer to compile and run the samples shown throughout this book. The .NET Framework SDK includes the Common Language Runtime, the .NET Framework class libraries, command-line compilers, and administration tools. You can install the .NET Framework SDK on any of the following versions of the Windows operating system: Windows NT 4.0 (with Service Pack 6a), Windows 2000 (at least Service Pack 2 recommended) or Windows XP Professional. The .NET Framework SDK can be downloaded for free from the Microsoft Developer Network Web site at `http://msdn.microsoft.com/net/`.

Some of the examples in this book demonstrate solutions using Visual Studio .NET. Visual Studio .NET is Microsoft's premier integrated development environment (IDE) for writing programs on top of the .NET Framework. Visual Studio .NET includes the Visual Basic .NET, Visual C# .NET, and Visual C++ .NET compilers, an integrated editor, graphical debugger, design-time wizards, and other supporting tools. Visual Studio .NET is available in three product flavors—Professional, Enterprise Developer, and Enterprise Architect. (Note that if you are a member of the Microsoft Developer Network (MSDN), your subscription may already include Visual Studio .NET.) Complete product information for Visual Studio .NET may be found on the Web at `http://msdn.microsoft.com/vstudio/`.

NOTE

Although the .NET Framework SDK is only available for Windows NT 4.0, Windows 2000, and Windows XP Professional, the .NET Framework Redistributable is available for Windows 98, Windows Millennium Edition, and Windows XP Home Edition in addition to the platforms supported by the SDK. Programs written on top of the .NET Framework require only that the Redistributable be present to run. Thus, while you need to run Windows NT 4.0, Windows 2000, or Windows XP Professional to develop .NET Framework programs, those programs can run on any of the platforms supported by the Redistributable.

Visual Studio .NET is currently available on the same platforms as the .NET Framework SDK— Windows NT 4.0 (Workstation and Server), Windows 2000 (Professional and Server), and Windows XP Professional.

How This Book Is Organized

We have arranged the content of this book into five broad sections. Each section is aimed at answering questions and providing examples for one or more of our core constituencies—developers, administrators, and end users. Because this book is intended to serve in part as a comprehensive reference guide to the .NET Framework security infrastructure, we recognize that each reader will be interested in different portions of the book and not everyone will need to read every chapter. We encourage everyone to begin by reading the three chapters that comprise Part I of the book (Chapters 1–3); they provide an introduction to the .NET Developer Platform, common security problems on the Internet, and an overview of how the .NET Framework security system addresses those concerns. After completing Part I, you should feel free to jump around and explore this book as you explore the various security features of the .NET Framework. Each chapter of the book (with a few noted exceptions) is designed to stand alone, so it is not necessary to read the book straight through.

The following is a quick summary of the contents of each of the five parts of the book:

- *Part I: Introduction to the .NET Developer Platform Security*—The first part of the book, Chapters 1 through 3, introduces the Microsoft .NET Developer Platform, describes important general features of the platform, and provides an overview of the key security feature. We recommend that everyone read the chapters in this part first to provide common background material for the topic-specific discussions in the remainder of the book.

- *Part II: Code Access Security Fundamentals*—Part II of the book details the architecture of the .NET Framework's "evidence-based security" model. Chapter 4, "User- and Code-Identity–Based Security: Two Complementary Security Paradigms," describes how the Framework's security system, which is based on *code identity*, builds on and complements the Windows NT/2000/XP security model that is based on user identity. The core elements of the evidence-based security model—evidence, permissions, stack-walking and policy objects—are detailed in Chapters 5 though 8. Chapter 9, "Understanding the Concepts of Strong Naming Assemblies," introduces *strong names*, a new technology that provides cryptographically secured unique namespaces for assemblies you author. Hosting the Common Language Runtime in your own programs is described in Chapter 10, "Hosting Managed Code." Type-safety verification, a key feature of MSIL and many languages that run on top of the .NET Developer Platform, is discussed in Chapter 11, "Verification and Validation: The Backbone of .NET Framework Security." Finally, Chapter 12, "Security Through the Lifetime of a Managed Process: Fitting It All Together," provides a "walk-through" of the security decisions and processes that occur while designing, developing, deploying, and running a .NET Framework application.

- *Part III: ASP.NET and Web Services Security Fundamentals*—Part III of this book concerns server-side security, specifically the security features of ASP.NET and Web Services. A brief introduction to the new features of ASP.NET is provided in Chapter 13, "Introduction to ASP.NET Security." Authentication and authorization in the ASP.NET model are discussed in Chapter 14, "Authentication: Know Who Is Accessing Your Site," and Chapter 15, "Authorization: Control Who Is Accessing Your Site." Channel integrity in ASP.NET, most commonly encountered on the Web through the use of the SSL/TLS family of encryption protocols, is covered in Chapter 16, "Data Transport Integrity: Keeping Data Uncorrupted."

- *Part IV: .NET Framework Security Administration*—The chapters in Part IV of this book provide a comprehensive guide to administering the .NET Framework security system and ASP.NET. Whether you administer a single machine or your enterprise's entire network, these chapters will show you how to make modifications to the default security policy that is installed by the .NET Framework to meet your particular needs. Chapter 17, "Introduction: .NET Framework Security and Operating System Security," introduces the major components of .NET Framework security policy—code access security policy, ASP.NET configuration, Internet Explorer security settings, and Windows security configuration—and how they interact with one another. Chapter 18, "Administering Security Policy Using the .NET Framework Configuration Tool," provides a comprehensive tutorial on how to modify policy using the .NET Framework Security Configuration tool MMC snap-in. Scripting and programmatic interfaces to the security configuration system are discussed in Chapter 19, "Administering .NET Framework Security Policy Using Scripts and Security APIs." Chapter 20, "Administering an IIS Machine Using ASP.NET," covers ASP.NET configuration issues, and mobile code considerations are discussed in Chapter 21, "Administering Clients for .NET Framework Mobile Code." Configuration options for isolated storage and cryptography are contained in Chapter 22, "Administering Isolated Storage and Cryptography Settings in the .NET Framework."

- *Part V: .NET Framework Security for Developers*—The final section of this book, Part V, is a guide for developers who want to write secure assemblies, author secure Web sites, create semi-trusted applications, or use cryptography and XML digital signatures in their applications. All developers should read Chapter 23, "Creating Secure Code: What All .NET Framework Developers Need to Know," for an overview of security-related tasks incumbent on developers building on the .NET Framework. Chapters 24 through 26 detail the process of architecting, building, and testing a secure assembly (a component designed to be shared and called by semi-trusted code). Included in these chapters are detailed examples showing how to make declarative and imperative security checks in your own code, implement custom permissions, work with and leverage strong names, and test the security aspects of your implementation. Security issues relevant to ASP.NET developers are the subject of Chapter 27,

"Writing a Secure Web Site Using ASP.NET," and Chapter 28, "Writing a Secure Web Application in the .NET Development Platform." Chapter 29, "Writing a Semi-Trusted Application," describes how to program defensively, including the proper use of assembly-level permission requests and isolated storage. Finally, Chapters 30 and 31 cover the cryptography features that are included in the .NET Framework, and Chapter 32, "Using Cryptography with the .NET Framework: Creating and Verifying XML Digital Signatures," discusses the classes that implement the XML digital signature standard.

Where to Download the Associated Code for This Book

The associated code files described in this book are available on Addison-Wesley's Web site at `http://www.aw.com/cseng/`. Enter this book's ISBN (without the hyphens) in the Search box and click Search. When the book's title is displayed, click the title to go to a page where you can download the code.

Conventions Used in This Book

The following typographic conventions are used in this book:

- Code lines, commands, statements, variables, and any text you see onscreen appears in a `mono` typeface. **`Bold mono`** typeface is often used to represent text the user types.

- Placeholders in syntax descriptions appear in an `italic mono` typeface. Replace the placeholder with the actual filename, parameter, or whatever element it represents.

- *Italics* highlight technical terms when they're being defined.

- The ➥ icon is used before a line of code that is really a continuation of the preceding line. Sometimes a line of code is too long to fit as a single line on the page. If you see ➥ before a line of code, remember that it's part of the line immediately above it.

- The book also contains Notes, Tips, and Cautions to help you spot important or useful information more quickly. Some of these are helpful shortcuts to help you work more efficiently.

PART I

Introduction to the .NET Developer Platform Security

IN THIS PART

1

Common Security
Problems on the Internet

By Matthew Lyons

Viruses, worms, Trojan horses, script kiddies, hackers. Late night calls to let you know that your Web site has been defaced. Is this what security means to you? Are we all doomed to follow the will of malicious teenage hackers with too much free time and not enough supervision?

It is a fact that we now live and work in a highly complex, interconnected world. There is so much complexity that it is mind boggling to attempt to fully comprehend the results that networked computing has had on our lives. While the times have changed, software practices largely have not kept up. System administrators have to worry about threats from inside their companies in addition to those from the Internet. There is a perception, though, that "security" only means installing a firewall on the network and an antivirus package on every machine. Software applications cannot be written with the assumption that they will only be run in trusted contexts. Viruses, worms, and other malicious code have shown that the same applications we rely on for day-to-day work can just as easily be the means for crippling an organization's network.

Before we can delve into the details of security in the .NET Framework, it is important to look at the key problems that need to be solved. Of all the current security problems with networked computing, there are a couple that are particularly thorny:

- How can we create and run rich, mobile applications without allowing them to access all resources on the machine?

- How can we prevent or mitigate common, yet pervasive software security problems like buffer overflows?

Problems with Securing Mobile Code

There are numerous well-supported forms of mobile code applications or components, each with its own benefits and drawbacks:

- Downloaded executables

- Source code

- Scripts

- Java applets

- ActiveX controls

Downloaded Executables

By downloaded executables, I mean files compiled to target specific architectures and operating systems. For example, `notepad.exe` is a commonly used executable file found in Windows. Downloaded executables are found all over the Internet. There are whole Web catalogs of programs for Windows, Macintosh, Linux, and other platforms. In addition, e-mail and peer-to-peer sharing mechanisms, such as Napster, have made it easy for users to share executables with each other.

Downloaded executables are good for the following reasons:

- They are very easy for end users to handle, because mobile code hosts can be configured to run them automatically.

- Executables are highly tunable by developers. They can be made to run with small footprints, fast execution, or other desired parameters.

- Executable files are well-understood entities. Some assurances about their runtime behavior can be made by using digital signatures, checksums/hashes, and virus checkers.

Executable files have the following problems:

- It can be very difficult to tell what an executable will do before it runs. From a security perspective, this is dangerous, because the code can contain some type of malicious code. Many e-mail viruses are spread by people who run seemingly harmless executable attachments.

- Executables must be recompiled for different architectures and operating systems. Thus, every version of a file you distribute must be recompiled for every target platform.

- Due to security issues with downloaded executables, it is common for companies to block some of their distribution mechanisms (such as filtering on e-mail servers).

Source Code

Source code is a common way to distribute applications in the UNIX/Linux world. Because there are numerous flavors of related operating systems with different hardware architectures and capabilities, source code can be compiled into working applications on each machine. Because Windows computers are sufficiently different from UNIX/Linux machines, tend not to have compilers on each machine, and can usually execute the same binaries, source code is a less common way to distribute applications for Windows.

Applications distributed via source code have the following benefits:

- With source code, it is easier to tell what resources are used on the computer when compared to most of the other formats mentioned. Source code can be analyzed more simply than compiled files, although it is still too daunting for average computer users.

- Application behavior can be tailored by end users to suit their specific needs. If you have the source code for an application, you can add, remove, or change capabilities, which is generally not possible with most of the other mentioned mobile code formats.

- Some kinds of application patches (for example, some security fixes) can be easily distributed with little data using source code. Source modifications are commonly shared and can be easily applied to application source code. Then, a user just has to recompile an application to get the updated behavior.

Distributing source code has the following pitfalls:

- There is no automatic execution of code. There is always a manual step of compilation before the application can be run. For many end users, this is too technically daunting to be practical.

- Compilers are not found on many machines. Thus, it is not possible to run applications on most machines by distributing source code alone.

- Even on machines where compilers exist, available headers, libraries, and versions will vary. Thus, an application that builds on one computer may not build properly on a very similar one.

- Owners of source code often do not want to give it away. Profits are difficult to make if you freely hand over all your intellectual property.

Scripts

Technically, scripts are just a certain class of source code. However, for this discussion, *source code* means files that are compiled to machine-level instructions, while *scripts* are interpreted by a scripting engine at execution time.

Scripts are text files that contain program instructions written in a specific scripting language. Some typical scripting languages are Perl, Python, ECMA Script, JavaScript, VBScript, and Tcl.

Some benefits of scripts include the following:

- Scripts are typically smaller than any of the other distribution methods listed here. A script may only be a few lines of text.

- Writing a simple application in a scripting language is typically easier than writing the same application in a compiled language.

- If scripting engine functionality is standardized across different platforms, the same script can run on multiple platforms. This is quite different from source code mentioned previously.

- Scripts are easy to read, so it is usually simple to see how they are using resources. Also, scripting engines can be specially tailored for mobile code hosts to remove potentially dangerous functionality.

Scripts have the following problems:

- Scripts require the presence of a scripting engine before they can execute. Thus, mobile code hosts will have to package the scripting engine for each scripting language they want to support.

- Scripts are interpreted rather than compiled, so they typically do not run as fast as applications using other mentioned distribution methods.

- The power of a scripting engine limits the power of scripts using that engine. Complex applications can be very difficult to write due to limitations of scripting engines.

Java Applets

Java applets came about as the power of the Java runtime was applied to Web browsers. They are somewhat like a combination between downloaded executables and scripts. They are compiled like executables, but they still run on a virtual machine, which is similar to a scripting engine.

Java applets have the following benefits:

- If Java applets are written without using platform-specific extensions, the same Java applet can run on different platforms.

- Typically, a Java virtual engine packaged with a mobile code host is written so that only safe functionality is exposed. That allows users to securely run Java applets from untrusted sources.

- The Java runtime provides a type-safe environment. This means it is possible to easily verify many security properties of Java applets. For example, we could verify that an applet doesn't perform invalid casts or access arbitrary memory.

The following are some problems with Java applets:

- Java applets can generally only be written in the Java language. While some software exists that allows developers to write them in other languages, most Java runtime environment developers are primarily trained in the Java language.

- Several Java decompilers exist that allow a user to convert a Java applet back to Java language source code. This is a threat to the applet developers' intellectual property.

- The same virtual machine that only provides safe functionality for applets also restricts their possible utility. There is no good way to differentiate between trusted and untrusted applets so that we can grant the trusted applets greater freedom.

ActiveX Controls

ActiveX controls have been around since early 1997 (`http://www.microsoft.com/com/presentations/default.asp`, presentation titled "An Overview of ActiveX"). They are basically COM controls that have been packaged in a way to ease downloading, scripting, and execution in Web browsers (though they cannot execute alone). They were developed by Microsoft as a way to make the client-side, Web programming experience powerful and simple.

Some benefits of ActiveX controls are as follows:

- They are compiled, executable files, so they have all the strengths of downloaded executables.

- Because they are COM controls at a base level, ActiveX controls can be used as components in non-Web applications in addition to Web browsers.

- They have some attempts at security built in. If a control is not marked as "safe for scripting," it cannot be used in a Web browser. This allows ActiveX controls to be safely created and deployed with functionality that is potentially dangerous for mobile code.

- Authenticode signing is often used for downloaded controls, so users can frequently tell who authored a specific control and make trust decisions based on that.

ActiveX controls have the following drawbacks:

- ActiveX controls are generally only supported by Windows operating systems.

- The "safe for scripting" determination of a control is made by developers, not users or administrators. Also, after the control is compiled, this setting cannot be changed. Thus, any "safe for scripting" control written by a careless or malicious developer cannot ever be safely used by a Web browser.

- ActiveX controls that are not Authenticode signed are usually blocked from executing. Thus, most downloaded controls are signed. However, even signed ActiveX controls usually require a manual trust decision at execution time from the user. Because most users don't comprehend the ramifications of the "run"/"don't run" decision, Authenticode security is arguably not very strong.

Writing Secure Applications

It seems like a simple statement, but software developers don't intend to write code with security problems. No one that I have worked with has admitted to intentionally writing security problems into their code. But, as we all know, software security holes appear all too often. According to the SecurityFocus vulnerability database (`http://www.securityfocus.com/vulns/stats.shtml`), around 100 security vulnerabilities have been reported each month since May of 2000. Almost everyone agrees there is room for improvement across the whole software industry.

NOTE

There are numerous places to read about software security vulnerabilities. Some industry-wide resources include the following:

- The SANS (System Administration, Networking, and Security) Institute at `http://www.sans.org`
- CERT (Computer Emergence Response Team) at `http://www.cert.org`
- SecurityFocus at `http://www.securityfocus.com`
- The CVE (Common Vulnerabilities and Exposures) Project at `http://cve.mitre.org`

In addition to these sites, some vendors provide information about security vulnerabilities and patches for their products. Some examples are

- Microsoft—`http://www.microsoft.com/technet/treeview/default.asp?url=/technet/security/current.asp`
- Apple—`http://www.apple.com/support/security/security_updates.html`
- RedHat—`http://www.redhat.com/support/alerts`
- Sun—`http://supportforum.sun.com/salerts`

Software security holes actually can be benign. They only become dangerous when exposed to untrusted code or people. If I have a computer that never connects to a network, never runs code I don't control, and is never operated by untrusted users, software security holes are probably of little concern. Of course, this is an idealized world where most of us don't live. For a majority of computer users, the rise of networked computing and the Internet has been a huge catalyst for making software security a vital concern.

The following types of software security problems have been rampant in recent years:

- Insecure default configurations
- Buffer overflows
- Canonicalization errors
- Information leaks
- Denial-of-service vulnerabilities

Insecure Default Configurations

According to the SANS Institute's list of 20 most critical Internet security vulnerabilities (Version 2.100, http://www.sans.org/top20.htm), the worst software vulnerability is that many default configurations of operating systems and applications are insecure.

Sometimes, what one person considers an insecure default configuration is considered to be adequate by someone else. In the software security community, it is preferred to limit functionality in default installations. However, some software publishers consider usability to be more important in certain cases, so additional features are enabled by default.

Some default configuration security problems include the following:

- CVE-2000-0869—SuSE Linux 6.4 has a problem with its install of Apache 1.3.12. It enables WebDAV, which allows remote users to list directory contents that shouldn't normally be possible.

- CVE-1999-0415—Certain Cisco routers enable an administrative HTTP server by default. This allows the owners *and* remote attackers to modify the router's configuration without sufficient authentication.

- Some versions of several different applications have default users and passwords. Examples include WWWBoard and Red Hat's Piranha Virtual Server. If the defaults are never changed, anyone with access to an application host can access the applications, often as administrators.

Buffer Overflows

Buffer overflows are one of the most publicized software security problems today. The Common Vulnerabilities and Exposures list (http://cve.mitre.org) contains hundreds of specific software vulnerabilities caused by buffer overflows. The list of affected products is huge. It is fair to say that few (if any) mainstream operating systems or applications are free from all buffer overflows.

A buffer overflow occurs when software allocates a slot in memory (a buffer) to hold some data and then writes more data to that slot than it has space (it overflows its buffer). These overflows can occur anywhere in memory, although they are most dangerous when they occur on the stack in architectures such as x86. Often, buffer overflows just produce access violations when they are hit accidentally while running an application. However, the results of an overflow can be unpredictable depending on where memory is overwritten, how much memory is overwritten, and what the new data is.

The first widespread buffer overflow vulnerability was the Internet Worm. It was much like Nimda and other recent worms in that it propagated quickly from server to server, although this was the first such worm, occurring all the way back in 1988. Even though this was a well-known event at the time with Internet users, buffer overflows were not widely recognized to be a security problem until the mid to late 1990s. They started to become a widespread problem after Aleph One wrote the whitepaper "Smashing the Stack for Fun and Profit" (which is available at `http://downloads.securityfocus.com/library/P49-14.txt`) in 1996. Other similar documents were written and published over the next couple of years that helped raise awareness about buffer overflows.

Buffer overflows are primarily a problem with software written in C and C++. The reason for this is that these very popular computer languages do not require strong bounds checking. More precisely, because the standard libraries do not have strong bounds checking, many programs written in C or C++ have to take care to use the library safely.

Examples of reported buffer overflows include the following:

- Microsoft Advisory MS01-033 "Unchecked Buffer in Index Server ISAPI Extension Could Enable Web Server Compromise"—This is one of the bugs in Windows that was exploited by the Nimda virus. A feature of IIS is that it allows extensions to be added to the Web server via ISAPI extensions. In this case, the Index Server's extension had a buffer overflow that was exploitable by remote users.

- CERT Advisory CA-2000-06 "Multiple Buffer Overflows in Kerberos Authenticated Services"—This was actually a set of buffer overflows in the widely used Kerberos authentication package originally written at MIT. The code for this software was open sourced and available for years before the problems were found.

- CERT Advisory CA-2001-15 "Buffer Overflow In Sun Solaris in.lpd Print Daemon"—The print daemon on multiple versions of Solaris had a buffer overflow that allowed remote users to execute arbitrary code on the system.

Canonicalization Errors

Canonicalization is the process by which paths to resources are normalized to a common format. For example, `C:\temp\abc.txt` and `C:\temp\..\temp\abc.txt` would both have the same canonical form. However, if some software treats them differently, security problems can occur. For example, take a Web server that doesn't properly canonicalize user requests. If it is only supposed to allow access to files in the `C:\wwwroot` directory, it might be easy to circumvent that restriction by issuing a request for `http://servername/../path_to_databases/creditcards.db`.

One particular problem with canonicalization errors is that they often occur outside of an application's "security" code. Unless care is taken to write secure software in an entire application, hard-to-detect problems like this can easily arise.

Some examples of reported canonicalization errors are as follows:

- Microsoft Advisory MS98-003 "File Access Issue with Windows NT Internet Information Server (IIS)"—The NTFS file system allows files to have multiple "streams," or storage areas. The default stream of a file is called $DATA. If a Web client issued a request for a page with an appended ::$DATA, the text of the Web page was shown instead of having the server process the Web page. For ASP pages with embedded passwords or other business logic, this was quite dangerous.

- CERT Vulnerability Note VU#758483 "Oracle 9i Application Server PL/SQL module does not properly decode URL"—A problem exists in the Oracle 9i Application Server that allows unauthenticated users to read arbitrary files on the host server. URLs are not properly decoded by the server, so specially formed requests bypass certain security checks in the application server.

- Microsoft Advisory MS98-004 "Unauthorized ODBC Data Access with RDS and IIS"—This defect involved Web clients sending special strings to an IIS machine with RDS (Remote Data Service) components. Essentially, the Web client could issue arbitrary commands to a database server through IIS.

Information Leaks

Information leaks come in many forms and degrees of severity. They may be as trivial as exposing the name and version of the operating system on which a Web server is running or as damaging as reading your customers' credit card numbers from a database. It can be hard to know what information someone might try to gain from an application, though as a general rule, exposing the minimum amount of information as necessary is best.

A primary reason to limit information exposure is that malicious hackers will often try to glean information about potential targets before actually launching an attack. For example, they may try to gather a list of computers or usernames on an internal network they want to attack.

Some examples of information leaks include the following:

- Checkpoint Firewall-1 Information Leak—Firewall-1 uses a piece of software called SecureRemote. SecureRemote has the ability to send an entire network topology to trusted clients. Unfortunately, the default setting of SecureRemote on Filewall-1 allowed network topology data to be sent to unauthenticated clients.

- Web server banners—Almost all Web servers will print an informational banner by default when a client makes a connection. This banner usually identifies the software package (and possibly operating system and version) of the Web server.

- CERT Advisory CA-2001-02 "Multiple Vulnerabilities in BIND"—BIND, a popular DNS server package, had a vulnerability where a remote user could discover the contents of environment variables on the server.

Denial-of-Service Vulnerabilities

Denial-of-service attacks are being seen more often as additional computers are added to the Internet. The increase in the number of computers both adds potential targets and potential attackers.

Certain classes of denial-of-service attacks are harder to defend against than others. "Standard" denial-of-service attacks are caused by one computer sending a large number or special kind of network packets to one machine. Distributed denial-of-service attacks are caused by many computers simultaneously flooding one computer with network packets. In some cases, a victim of a standard denial-of-service attack can simply ignore all requests from a certain location, thereby defeating the attack. However, there are currently few ways to fend off a distributed denial-of-service attack.

Some types of standard denial-of-service attacks are caused by software faults. For example, some network protocols involve a handshake involving a few exchanges of data. If memory is allocated at the beginning of a handshake but not released quickly, a malicious hacker could send a continuous stream of beginning hand-shakes. This could cause so many resources to be allocated by the victim that they can no longer perform standard functions.

Examples of denial-of-service vulnerabilities caused by software faults include the following:

- CERT Advisory CA-1996-26 "Denial-of-Service Attack via ping"—The "ping" utility is normally a helpful tool to help diagnose network connectivity problems. However, several vendors had problems with their TCP/IP stacks that would cause an operating system to lock up when they received certain types of packets. In particular, specially crafted packets sent by "ping" from other machines could cause denial-of-service problems. This was colloquially known as the "ping of death."

- CERT Advisory CA-2001-18 "Multiple Vulnerabilities in Several Implementations of the Lightweight Directory Access Protocol (LDAP)"—A group of researches tested multiple products that use the LDAP protocol. Many of the tested products would hang or crash when the team sent specially malformed LDAP packets.

- Microsoft Advisory MS98-007 "Potential SMTP and NNTP Denial-of-Service Vulnerabilities in Microsoft Exchange Server"—If a remote user sent specially crafted data to a Microsoft Exchange server, its mail and/or news service could be shut down.

Summary

Writing secure software and knowing what mobile code to trust are difficult problems. People have made numerous attempts at solving the problem before, and all the attempts have had their shortcomings.

Historically, attempts at secure execution of mobile code has had at least one of the following problems:

- *Too much necessary user expertise*—Source code requires too much understanding about compilers for most users to handle. Authenticode-signed ActiveX controls require users to make trust decisions on-the-fly, which most are not properly informed to decide. These mobile code options are simply too complicated or daunting.

- *Lack of user or administrator control over executed code*—Executable files can really only be checked for specific problems, such as viruses. They simply can't be secured in any real fashion in an efficient way. The "safe for scripting" option of ActiveX controls is only controlled by developers, although users and administrators can manage what controls are installed.

- *Inadequate power*—Java applets generally only run in a sandboxed environment that is too restrictive or cumbersome for many useful applications. Many scripting engines enabled for mobile code suffer from the same problem. Available mobile code formats seem like "all or nothing" propositions with respect to application power and flexibility.

Mainstream software applications and operating systems have suffered from security problems due to

- *Lack of safe programming environments*—Most C and C++ applications use standard libraries that too easily allow problems like buffer overflows. Also, there is no way to feasibly examine a C or C++ program to see if it is truly safe to run.

- *Marketing and ease-of-use pressure*—Many times, features are enabled in default installations of OSs or applications that shouldn't be. While this makes it easier for users to exploit the power of these software packages, it also makes it too easy for users to be ignorant of the security implications.

- *Ignorance and time-to-market pressure*—Some software designers or writers simply don't think about security until the specifications are generally done or most of the code is written. Security applied late in a project will likely be insufficient or incorrectly applied. Also, when qualified and careful programmers are rushed to finish their work, they make mistakes.

Before we can see how the .NET Framework addresses these issues, we must first understand how the .NET Framework functions. We will cover that in the next chapter. Then in Chapter 3, ".NET Developer Platform Security Solutions," we will see how the .NET Framework addresses today's security challenges.

2

Introduction to the Microsoft .NET Developer Platform

By Matthew Lyons

Over time, new technologies and new paradigms sweep through the computer industry. From mainframes to mini-computers to PCs to embedded computers, hardware has gotten smaller, faster, and less expensive. This has put an amazing amount of computing power at our fingertips.

While hardware has changed quite dramatically, software has undergone fewer changes, though the changes are still significant. Programming has moved from assembly-level languages to high-level languages. Reinventing the wheel has become less prevalent as components have become more readily available to purchase and use. High-quality debuggers have become an absolute necessity in software development. What Microsoft has done with the .NET Framework may not be as dramatic as these paradigm shifts, but the framework is significant in that it combines many of the benefits of previous programming successes into a single package. This alone can allow for large productivity gains over many current development environments used today.

The .NET Framework brings the following benefits together:

- Tight language interoperability—All .NET Framework compilers emit MSIL, a Microsoft intermediate language.

- Metadata—Every .NET executable or library (known as an assembly) contains not only the method bodies and signatures, but also rich information about defined data types, names of class fields, and other related information collectively called metadata.

- A just-in-time (JIT) compilation environment—Identical compiled files can run on different platforms, and JIT compilers can make platform-specific optimizations.

- Garbage collection—The .NET Framework automatically deallocates memory, eliminating memory leaks common with C/C++ programming.

- Object-oriented programming—At its core, the .NET Framework uses object-oriented programming concepts extensively.

- Code access security—A rather innovative feature in the .NET Framework is the ability to grant and enforce granular permissions based on code identity.

- Base class library—The .NET Framework provides a secure library of classes that enable critical functionality such as threading, I/O, and networking in addition to higher-level programming services such as XML manipulation, cryptography, and system management.

- Interoperability with native code—Previous investments in writing COM objects aren't lost. COM objects are treated very much like native .NET Framework objects.

TIP

Because the following terms are used extensively in this chapter and throughout the book, you should become familiar with their definitions now:

Native code—Programs or libraries that have been compiled to machine language for a specific hardware architecture, such as x86. On Windows computers, native code is generally packaged in DLL and EXE files.

Unmanaged code—Same as native code.

Managed code—Programs or libraries that have been compiled to run on the .NET Framework. Like unmanaged code, managed code is frequently packaged in DLL and EXE files.

Assembly—Logical unit of code separation in the .NET Framework. Usually a single managed DLL or EXE is an entire assembly. However, an assembly can contain multiple files.

Tight Language Interoperability

The core of the .NET Framework is the common language runtime. Tight language interoperability is what "common language" means. The real language of the common language runtime is MSIL, a stack-based intermediate language. C#, VB, managed C++, and all other .NET languages compile to MSIL instead of native machine code.

> **NOTE**
>
> For a list of other source code languages and compilers that support the .NET Framework, see http://msdn.microsoft.com/vstudio/partners/language/default.asp.

MSIL was designed to be generally language agnostic. However, some computer languages have notions that other languages do not understand. For instance, unsigned integers are not supported by all languages. To get around this problem, the .NET Framework defined the common language specification (also known as the CLS).

The CLS rules define what all .NET languages have to support, and it provides for two levels of support—consumers and producers. All .NET languages must be CLS consumers. That is, they must be able to understand and use assemblies produced by other languages. CLS producers must be able to emit assemblies that conform to all CLS rules. Not all .NET languages are required to be CLS producers.

> **NOTE**
>
> CLS rules cover numerous language features such as naming and use of pointers, arrays, and exceptions. For a list of full CLS compliance rules, see the .NET Framework SDK at http://msdn.microsoft.com/net.

When CLS compliance is guaranteed, .NET languages can inherit from and use classes from other languages. Using special calling conventions or code packaging, language interoperability in the past was generally limited to modules written in other languages. Allowing inheritance between languages is relatively new to mainstream software design.

The language interoperability benefits of the .NET Framework provide a lot of potential for programmers and organizations. Features provided by development environments should no longer be locked into one programming language such as VB or Java. Languages such as COBOL that have "gone out of style" are not obsolete. It is easier to adjust existing code bases written in different languages to use the .NET Framework than it is to completely rewrite them in a different language.

Metadata

Closely tied to MSIL is metadata. Metadata isn't a set of instructions like MSIL. Rather, it is information that describes the compiled code. It is stored in an assembly with MSIL to make one logical unit.

Here is a sampling of the information that metadata contains:

- Full assembly name (simple name, version, public key, and culture)

- Referenced assemblies

- Visibility, inherited class, and implemented interfaces of each defined class

- Information about class members such as methods, fields, and properties

Metadata allows .NET assemblies to be self-describing. This means that an assembly contains enough information to be closely inspected by other assemblies. There are unmanaged and managed APIs to view an assembly's metadata.

One other interesting benefit of metadata is that it allows the creation of custom attributes. A custom attribute allows you to store special information in an assembly. For instance, if your organization wants to store the author of an assembly in metadata, you can define an "AuthorAttribute." Then, you can simply look in assemblies for this attribute when you want to find out who wrote the assembly.

JIT Compilation

Traditional software environments have generally fallen into one of two categories: precompiled and interpreted. Precompiled environments are used by C/C++, Visual Basic, and Fortran. Source code is read in by a compiler, which then emits machine language code into a library or executable. Interpreted environments are used by Perl, Python, ASP (in IIS), and ECMA Script. Script files are text files that are treated as a set of instructions by a program (the scripting engine).

The .NET Framework has some elements of both precompiled and interpreted environments. .NET assemblies are compiled from source languages, but as mentioned earlier, they are compiled into IL instead of machine language. The IL, unlike scripting languages, is not sent to an interpreter. Also, since it isn't a machine language, it cannot be directly executed. Instead, the IL is sent to a JIT compiler. The JIT compiles each method as it is about to be executed. Unexecuted methods are never compiled.

JITted code generally runs faster than interpreted code because once it turns into machine language, it can directly execute. Interpreted languages have to convert the same source code into low-level instructions every time it executes. Note that the performance enhancements for small, short-running processes will not be very great. However, for longer-running applications such as ASP.NET applications, the speedup from JITted code can be significant.

JITted code has some benefits over precompiled code, too. First, IL is the same everywhere. Thus, the same assembly that runs on Windows should (at least in theory) run on UNIX or MacOS, as long as the common language runtime exists on each platform. Second, even if the same assembly is always run on Windows, a JIT compiler can take advantage of optimizations from different processors. A precompiled file cannot easily optimize for every different processor. However, because it takes time to start up the .NET Framework before code is compiled by the JIT, a precompiled application will start up faster than a JITted one.

Garbage Collection

Garbage collection is not a new idea by any means. It has been used in languages such as LISP and Perl for many years. However, many popular programming languages have not incorporated it. For example, C/C++ programmers have had to deal with allocating and freeing memory for decades. In addition, COM programmers have had to keep accurate ref counts to make sure COM objects were deleted at the right time. While programmer management of memory allows for quite a bit of freedom, it also has been the source of an untold number of memory leaks and premature deallocations.

Basically, in an environment that supports garbage collection, a programmer still has to say when memory should be allocated. In the .NET Framework, this occurs whenever a new object is created. However, once the programmer has finished using the object, she doesn't have to remember to explicitly free or delete it. Instead, the garbage collector will periodically sweep through all allocated objects to see which ones are no longer being used. Those objects can be freed to reclaim the memory.

Garbage collection is not a panacea for resource allocation. There are many unmanaged (non-memory) resources that a programmer will still have to manage. For instance, if an object is holding an open file handle, that handle should be explicitly closed by the programmer when the object is no longer needed.

NOTE

Sometimes, unmanaged resources used in .NET Framework classes are scarce and need to be freed as soon as possible. For these unmanaged resources, the .NET Framework created the IDisposable interface. Classes that need to quickly free unmanaged resources should implement this interface, which contains one method, Dispose. See the .NET Framework SDK for more information on how to use Dispose.

Object-Oriented Programming

At its core, the .NET Framework is built with object-oriented programming in mind. As mentioned previously, MSIL and metadata are stored in each assembly. Metadata in particular provides key object-oriented information. For instance, it shows if a given class method is public, private, or only available to subclasses.

Since what makes something "object-oriented" is somewhat controversial in the realm of computer science, here are some specific features of the .NET Framework that are generally seen as essentials that object-oriented languages must provide:

- Encapsulation—This refers to the use of classes/types to group together related data and functions. For instance, a payroll application needs to go through each employee in a company every pay period to determine how much to pay each person. To simplify the programming model, a programmer might define a class named "employee" to hold the employee name, ID, number of tax exemptions, and other employee data as well as methods that allow the application to calculate the paycheck amount for the current pay period. Without encapsulation, the programmer might have to track an employee as a separate set of data types—a string for the employee name, an integer for the ID, another integer for the number of exemptions, and so on—with a group of methods defined inside a mix of other functions. Encapsulation provides a clean and easy way to group related information and functionality so the programmer can more easily manage his codebase.

- Information Hiding—Information hiding can be seen as an extension of encapsulation where some information is deemed public and some is deemed non-public. In the case of a class for employees, a programmer would likely want to make the name and employee ID values public. However, the employee class might have internal data or methods it uses for debugging or to perform its public duties. For instance, an employee object might need to know what row in a database contains information on that employee.

- Inheritance—Inheritance allows hierarchies of types to be defined, where child types are more specialized than parent types. In the case of employees, the payroll application might want to create two subtypes of employee: hourly employees and salaried employees. This allows methods to be written that would perform differently for each type of employee. Without inheritance, the employee class would need to use something like if/then statements to differentiate between the types of employees.

- Polymorphism—This term can mean different things to different people. Generally, though, polymorphism means that a framework supports virtual calls, operator and method overloading, and other related functionality. In the case of hourly employees and salaried employees, each class may implement its own version of the method to calculate the paycheck amount for that period. However, if the payroll application just knows an object is a generic employee, it can simply call the method to calculate the paycheck amount. The runtime will determine which method implementation to call.

Code Access Security

Code Access Security (CAS) is the foundation of security in the .NET Framework. It is a key part of this book, but the following description will only cover CAS at a high level.

CAS is based on the assumption that different code should have different levels of trust. For instance, code loaded from some random place on the Internet should probably be less trusted than an application you install on your computer. Code with more trust should be allowed to do more on your computer. For instance, perhaps you want the installed application to be able to read your personal data. However, you almost certainly don't want all code from the Internet to be able to do that.

One problem with a scheme of differing trust levels is its susceptibility to luring attacks. A *luring attack* occurs when less trusted code gets code with greater trust to do something on its behalf. For example, code from the Internet may not be able to read your personal data, but perhaps it can get your installed application to do it and return the information. To prevent this problem, CAS uses a stack walk to ensure that everyone in the call chain is trusted. See Chapter 7, "Walking the Stack," for more on stack walks.

Even though CAS has a scheme for protecting against luring attacks, it is still vulnerable to type safety problems. For example, if untrusted code can read and write to arbitrary points in memory, it can simply call in to unmanaged code and bypass the security stack walk. To protect against this kind of attack, the .NET Framework verifies MSIL and its metadata against numerous rules before execution. Code that doesn't have complete trust must meet all the rules or the .NET Framework will refuse to execute it.

It is impossible for the .NET Framework creators to know what code people or organizations will want to trust. One organization may choose to distrust all code that doesn't reside in its internal network, while another organization may want to completely trust code from certain Internet sites. To accommodate this difference, CAS has a completely configurable policy system. Organizations can tailor CAS policy to their wishes and deploy that policy through the organization. However, the default policy is meant to be a generally secure and useful place to start.

Base Class Library

Just as languages such as C and VB have standard libraries, the .NET Framework has a standard library. It is often referred to as the base class library, or BCL. While it is possible to write a .NET program without ever using the BCL, it is unlikely that anyone would want to do this.

The BCL divides functionality into different namespaces. The root namespace of the BCL is named `System`. Related functionality is often grouped together in its own namespace below this, such as `System.IO` for stream-based I/O. Microsoft-specific functionality is located under the `Microsoft` root namespace (`Microsoft.Win32.Registry`, for example). To use BCL classes from the `System.IO` namespace, the following line would be required in a C# application:

```
using System.IO;
```

Some commonly used namespaces in the BCL are listed in Table 2.1. See the .NET Framework SDK for detailed information on each of these namespaces and associated classes.

TABLE 2.1   Commonly Used Namespaces in the BCL

Namespace	Description
System	Primary data types, fundamental classes, and basic services
System.Collections	Frequently used data types such as lists, queues, and hash tables
System.Configuration	Classes to read .NET application configuration files
System.Data	Classes to access different types of data sources, such as SQL servers
System.Drawing	2-D graphics APIs and access to GDI+
System.IO	Classes for reading and writing to different types of data streams, such as file streams
System.NET	Classes for using common network protocols
System.Reflection	Classes for reading type information, creating types, and invoking methods using metadata
System.Runtime.Remoting	Classes for creating distributed applications
System.Runtime.Serialization	Serialization and deserialization classes using binary or SOAP encoding
System.Security	Classes for using code access security
System.Security.Cryptography	Classes for using cryptographic services such as encryption and hashing
System.Web	Web server and client management classes
System.Windows.Forms	Classes for writing GUI-based client applications
System.Xml	XML processing using XML standards such as XML 1.0, XPath, XSLT, and DOM levels

Native Code Interoperability

Although the .NET Framework comes with a rich set of functionality, a tremendous amount of legacy code still exists. Organizations have spent millions and millions of dollars to create applications, libraries, and COM components. Rather than trying to force everyone to start from scratch, the .NET Framework was designed from the beginning to offer interoperability with existing native code.

Native code interoperability comes in two basic flavors in the runtime—COM component interoperability (known as COM interop) and calling methods in native DLLs (known as Platform Invoke, or PInvoke). COM interop enables classic COM objects to be treated just like managed objects. Since classic COM objects already have some level of metadata information through IDL definitions, the translation to using them in managed code is rather transparent. Also, managed types can be treated as classic COM objects, making COM interoperability a two-way street. The most difficult challenge with COM interop is to properly marshal data between managed and native environments. The same difficulty in marshaling data is also true for PInvoke calls. However, in both cases, many types are automatically marshaled by the .NET Framework.

One serious problem with native code interoperability is that it is not possible to apply the same security rules to native code that can be applied to managed code. Type safety cannot be guaranteed with native code, so you can't be certain what will happen when you call a certain method via COM interop or PInvoke. Because of this, only highly trusted managed code should be allowed to call native COM objects or functions via PInvoke.

Summary

The potential productivity gains for software developers writing code in the .NET Framework are impressive. I have heard numerous personal accounts regarding many saved man-hours on software projects using pre-release versions of the .NET Framework. The .NET Framework frees developers from many small details so that they can focus on the real logic of the program. However, benefits of the .NET Framework are not just for developers. Users and administrators can benefit from tighter security and less error-prone development environments. Administrators can modify security policy to meet their specific needs. Users should find .NET applications to generally be more stable due to garbage collection and interoperability rules such as the CLS. Also, code access security can protect users' private data while running mobile code.

3

.NET Developer Platform Security Solutions

By Matthew Lyons

So far, we have seen some security challenges for down-loaded mobile code and for networked computing in general. We have provided some background on the .NET Framework. Now, let's examine how the .NET platform addresses these security challenges.

This chapter's structure is similar to that of the first chapter. First, we'll examine some fundamental security benefits provided by the .NET Framework. Second, we will look at how the .NET Framework can provide mobile code download solutions that offer advantages over the traditional methods. Finally, we'll consider how the .NET Framework addresses the security challenges of networked computing.

Fundamental Security Benefits from the .NET Framework

The simplest software targets low-level hardware. Creating such software involves "writing to the bare metal." This can be rather difficult and cumbersome, but it gives the best potential performance and flexibility. Typically, such coding occurs using assembly language targeted at a specific CPU's instruction set. Unfortunately, this makes software-enforced security nearly impossible due to complexity constraints.

One of the many benefits of an operating system is that it provides security mechanisms not easily provided in small, low-level applications. For example, an operating system defines the notion of user accounts with different privileges so that some users can be restricted from reading data belonging to other users or using certain resources.

However, this is not always sufficient for our needs today. Sometimes, providing different privileges to different applications is useful, too. That is where the .NET Framework comes into play. As described in Part II of this book, "Code Access Security Fundamentals," the .NET Framework provides a way for different applications run by the same user to be automatically granted different levels of trust.

It is important to note that the .NET Framework is meant to be a layer above an operating system. This gives it the ability to leverage existing security mechanisms in addition to providing additional security enforcement through Code Access Security. Chapter 4, "User- and Code-Identity–Based Security: Two Complementary Security Paradigms," covers the difference between operating system security and .NET Framework security in more detail.

Managing Code Execution

As discussed in Chapter 2, "Introduction to the Microsoft .NET Developer Platform," the .NET Framework has several tools it uses to manage code execution. When loading an assembly, it can verify the type safety of the IL and ensure that its metadata is valid. (See Chapter 11, "Verification and Validation: The Backbone of .NET Framework Security," for more details on IL and metadata checking.) As long as no calls are directly made to native code, this alone can be a huge security win because it can prevent bad pointer manipulation. In addition, the use of garbage collection helps stop runaway resource leaks that have been the source of denial-of-service attacks in some software.

One big benefit of managed code is that bounds checking is automatically performed on array accesses. This means that buffer overflows are nearly impossible to accidentally create in managed code. This doesn't automatically make managed code secure, but it sure helps with problems we've been seeing in today's software environment.

Additional Security Enforcement

The .NET Framework is by no means the first environment to provide a managed layer (using a virtual machine or Just-In-Time compiler) for applications to target. However, it does add some unique benefits to the managed environment. Specifically, Code Access Security is a powerful tool leveraged by the .NET Framework. Stack walks, discussed in Chapter 7, "Walking the Stack," check for fine-grained permissions on each caller to ensure that maliciously written .NET applications cannot step outside their set of granted permissions. Permissions in the .NET Framework are discussed in Chapter 6, "Permissions: The Workhorse of Code Access Security."

NOTE

As you might imagine, security stack walks can hurt application performance. If the trust of all callers on the stack can be verified by fully trusted code, stack walks can be terminated early, minimizing the performance impact. Performance and security can be at odds with each other when you are writing software, and this is an example of the tradeoffs to consider. In many cases, the .NET Framework has been designed to emphasize safe programming practices, which sometimes come at the expense of better performance. Extreme caution should be taken when trying to optimize performance at the expense of security.

In addition to providing the stack-walking engine of CAS, the .NET Framework provides a flexible policy engine to ensure that administrators have the ability to express customized statements about what trust to provide to any given code. Chapter 8, "Membership Conditions, Code Groups, and Policy Levels: The Brick and Mortar of Security Policy," covers the internals of CAS policy. Without the ability to give detailed policy statements, CAS would be less useful because granularity of permission grants would be hard to achieve. Part IV of this book, ".NET Framework Security Administration," covers how administrators can tailor the .NET Framework for their particular organizations. In particular, Chapter 18, "Administering Security Policy Using the .NET Framework Configuration Tool," and Chapter 19, "Administering .NET Framework Security Policy Using Scripts and Security APIs," cover how to administer CAS policy.

Mobile Code Solutions with the .NET Framework

The .NET Framework was designed with mobile code solutions in mind. There are a couple of different ways that .NET assemblies can be used in mobile code situations. First, they can be downloaded and run just like unmanaged executables. Second, they can be loaded into a browser and run like Java applets or ActiveX controls.

NOTE

Chapter 21, "Administering Clients for .NET Framework Mobile Code," covers particular administrative concerns for mobile code, regardless of how it is executed. However, there is no chapter in this book specifically tailored at developing mobile code solutions in the .NET Framework. Developing secure mobile code on the .NET Framework has generally the same concerns as developing secure code users might install from a CD-ROM. Thus, much of Part V, ".NET Framework Security for Developers," is important for developers of mobile code.

TIP

Some software has used mobile code in the past because server-side programming does not always provide the flexibility or prewritten components needed for rich functionality. The ASP.NET programming environment has greatly improved on previous possibilities with ASP, so make sure to investigate this before deciding to use mobile code solutions. Security aspects of ASP.NET are covered in Part III, "ASP.NET and Web Services Security Fundamentals," Chapter 20, "Administering an IIS Machine Using ASP.NET," Chapter 27, "Writing a Secure Web Site Using ASP.NET," and Chapter 28, "Writing a Secure Web Application in the .NET Development Platform."

Direct Execution

In Internet Explorer, you might download and directly execute a .NET assembly when you click on an HREF link to an EXE file on a Web page. When this is done for unmanaged executables, a dialog opens asking whether you want to open or save the file. Also, depending on browser security settings, another warning dialog might appear if the EXE is not signed with a digital certificate. For managed EXEs, though, the assembly is simply executed. No warning dialogs are presented, regardless of whether or not the assembly is signed. Because the security policy is always used to evaluate trust of .NET assemblies, displaying dialogs doesn't really provide much benefit. If you mean to block execution from most sites, you can set the security policy that way before any applications are run.

Direct execution of .NET assemblies has these benefits:

- Like unmanaged executables, .NET assemblies are very easy for end users to handle. Simply click on a link and they run in a safe environment that provides semitrusted execution. Assemblies are not hindered by the Authenticode dialogs of ActiveX controls.

- Many security properties can be verified and enforced on the assembly simply because it is managed code. These properties include type safety, metadata validation, garbage collection, and automatic bounds checking on arrays.

- Because the .NET Framework is not tied to one OS, you might be able to use the same files for different platforms. Just as with Java applets, cross-platform compatibility is possible as long as native API calls are not made.

Directly running .NET assemblies has these pitfalls:

- As with Java applets and scripts, certain software must be installed first. In the case of .NET assemblies, the .NET Framework must be installed before assemblies can execute.

- As with Java applets, decompilation is quite possible with .NET assemblies.

- There is some skepticism regarding cross-platform compatibility of .NET assemblies. Portions of the .NET Framework specs have been standardized by ECMA, and there are efforts to make those portions run on other platforms. Only time will tell what level of compatibility will be possible between different .NET Framework implementations.

Browser-Hosted Controls

In addition to running directly, managed assemblies can be hosted inside a Web browser in much the same way as ActiveX controls and Java applets. Using <OBJECT> tags in HTML, types in assemblies can be referenced and used in Web pages. For version 1 of the .NET Framework, assemblies hosted in IE are partially controlled by the ActiveX settings. If ActiveX controls are barred from running in a certain Web page, so are browser-hosted .NET controls.

Browser-hosted .NET assemblies have these benefits:

- Unlike ActiveX controls, browser-hosted .NET assemblies do not pop up an Authenticode UI that requires user interaction. They just load and run in the secured environment.

- Like directly executed assemblies, browser-hosted assemblies have all the benefits provided by the .NET Framework.

- For organizations that do not permit browser-based code execution, .NET assemblies can be shut off without affecting other .NET Framework code execution paths.

Browser-based .NET assemblies have the following drawbacks:

- Browser-based .NET controls cannot be enabled if ActiveX controls are disabled. This lack of flexibility might prevent the adoption of browser-based .NET controls in some situations.

- Like directly executed .NET assemblies, browser-based .NET controls require the presence of the .NET Framework. Thus, existing clients will not be able to leverage these controls without extra work.

- Again, cross-platform assembly compatibility is still up in the air. It seems likely that some level of compatibility will be achieved, but the details are not yet known.

Networked Computing with the .NET Framework

Chapter 1, "Common Security Problems on the Internet," discussed several problems surrounding networked computing:

- Insecure default configurations

- Buffer overflows

- Canonicalization errors

- Information leaks

- Denial-of-service vulnerabilities

As we saw in Chapter 2, the .NET Framework has many interesting features for developers, administrators, and users. Those features can help solve some of these security problems. The following sections will look at how these problems are addressed.

Insecure Default Configurations

There are numerous settings that you can tweak in the .NET Framework to affect execution behavior. Among these are some key settings that help prevent security problems from arising in .NET applications. Those settings include the following:

- Default security policy (covered in detail in Chapter 8)—The .NET Framework has a set of security policies that dictate what different applications are trusted to do. For instance, code downloaded from the local intranet is not allowed to directly read or write to arbitrary locations in the file system. However, it is allowed to use a File Open dialog that allows users to pick specific files an application can read.

  The default security policy was carefully constructed to ensure that code originating from places other than the user's computer is constrained to a safe subset of functionality. Simply installing the .NET Framework on a machine should not open up the possibility of untrusted managed code performing arbitrary actions.

- ASP.NET user account (covered in detail in Chapter 13, "Introduction to ASP.NET Security")—Unlike current IIS installations, the ASP.NET worker process is not run under the SYSTEM account by default. Instead, it is run under an account with limited privileges. This is a good defense-in-depth practice that will help mitigate accidental misconfigurations of servers or bugs that may be found in the ASP.NET code in the future.

  The ASP.NET process can be configured to use the SYSTEM account if necessary. However, basic ASP.NET pages shouldn't need special privileges, so an account with limited privileges is fine.

Buffer Overflows

Fortunately, buffer overflows are much less of a problem when dealing with a managed application. String and array copying have tight bounds checking in the .NET Framework class libraries. This alone should help decrease the number of serious security holes in applications.

Note that managed applications do not completely eliminate buffer overflows. This is primarily because all managed applications run unmanaged code at some level. The .NET Framework core unmanaged code has been closely inspected for buffer overflows, so few should remain there. However, if a managed application uses the interoperability functionality to access classic COM objects or platform APIs, the unmanaged code will execute. Thus, if a managed application uses unmanaged components or API calls, buffer overflows are still possible. In these cases, careful code reviews are necessary to mitigate the risk of buffer overflows.

Using "unsafe" C# functionality or manually constructed IL can lead to unverifiable managed applications. Unverifiable applications can also have buffer overflow problems because their behavior has considerably fewer execution guarantees. However, nearly all managed code you write should be verifiable, so managed buffer overflows should be very rare.

Canonicalization Errors

Canonicalization errors are probably as easy to create in managed code as they are in unmanaged code. This is because they cannot be broadly fixed in applications by changing underlying .NET Framework behavior. They are bugs specific to each application. For instance, if some application is supposed to parse a string for specific commands to execute, the key to correctness is proper parsing logic. Bad logic will cause problems in managed and unmanaged applications.

There are some tools from the .NET Framework class library that can help prevent canonicalization errors. The `System.Text.RegularExpressions` namespace has classes to deal with regular expressions, which are very helpful when dealing with arbitrary strings. The `System.Uri` class provides a mechanism to canonicalize URIs. The `System.IO.Path` class can provide an absolute file path for any given relative file path.

Information Leaks

This is another area where the .NET Framework cannot solve an entire class of problems. Software deals with information from different sources, and determining what information can be safely shared is a complicated process. Some data, such as passwords and credit card numbers, is usually understood to be sensitive information that should not be freely handed out. Other information, such as machine names, usernames, and network topology data, isn't as widely known to be data that should be protected.

Some managed code has explicit checks to ensure that information isn't leaked. For instance, file paths (which can include usernames), private class information in assemblies, and network topology information from DNS queries are all protected by the .NET Framework when directly accessed using the .NET Framework class library. However, this information can all be accidentally handed out by a poorly written .NET component. Thus, it is really up to application writers to ensure that their applications don't cause these sorts of problems.

Denial-of-Service Vulnerabilities

Version 1 of the .NET Framework doesn't focus on fixing denial-of-service issues. Thus, it should be expected that untrusted managed code can cause .NET Framework hosts to stop responding. If you intend to use the .NET Framework in semitrusted environments such as Web-hosted applications, you will have to take care to accommodate faulty or malicious code. For example, a managed code host might want to only allow user applications to execute for a short amount of time before they are automatically killed.

Note that denial-of-service attacks should not be able to cause arbitrary code execution or information leaks. Instead, the effects should be temporary until the offending code is stopped or the host is restarted.

Summary

The .NET Framework is not the solution to all software security problems. However, it does provide some great benefits to current mainstream practices. It provides two new code download mechanisms—direct execution of assemblies and browser-hosted controls. These two mechanisms provide a unique balance of overall power and security. For general-purpose software development and deployment, the .NET Framework provides a great mechanism for developers and administrators.

The .NET Framework addresses some networked computing software problems better than others:

- The default configuration of the framework is designed to be secure, so installing the framework doesn't require additional lockdown steps.

- Buffer overruns can be nearly eliminated by using verifiable managed code.

- Canonicalization bugs in applications cannot be completely removed using the .NET Framework. However, the framework does provide functionality to help eliminate canonicalization bugs.

- The .NET Framework attempts to prevent the leaking of information known to be sensitive. Applications written on the .NET Framework can still leak information, though.

- Denial-of-service issues are simply not handled well by the .NET Framework. You need to keep this in mind if your .NET Framework hosts are designed to run partially trusted code.

Overall, we hope that you have come to see the unique power of .NET Framework security. While it isn't a panacea for security problems on the Internet, it does provide some value not available with other mainstream software development environments.

PART II

Code Access Security Fundamentals

IN THIS PART

4

User- and Code-Identity–Based Security: Two Complementary Security Paradigms

By Sebastian Lange

Security is a core component of the .NET Framework infrastructure. All managed code run on the .NET Framework Common Language Runtime (CLR) is subject to the scrutiny and restrictions that the Code Access Security (CAS) system imposes. However, this security system differs in its fundamental design from many other security systems, such as the Windows Security system. Code Access Security is based on code identity, whereas chances are, most security systems you have encountered are based on user identity. This chapter will explain this paradigmatic difference in more detail. In particular, the following key points will be covered:

- A survey of common features of computer security systems

- An explanation of what constitutes a user-identity–based security system

- A look at Windows Access protection and authorization as an example of user-identity–based security

- A definition of code-identity–based security systems

- An explanation of the scenarios that only code-identity, not user-identity, security systems could cover

- An explanation of how the .NET Framework's Code Access Security system constitutes a code-identity–based security system

- Some thoughts on how code- and user-identity–based security can complement each other

Before delving right into the differences between user and code identity security, it will be helpful to look at some general characteristics that define computer security systems. That conceptual apparatus will make it easier to compare the specific approaches to computer security.

A Little Anatomy of Computer Security Systems

Why have computer security systems in the first place? Why is it necessary to spend (sometimes considerable amounts of) money and computing time making computers more safe? And what does safety mean in this context? These are the questions that guide the fundamental constitution of any security system and will start us on our discussion of the properties that define computer security systems.

The primary function of any computer security system (and, in fact, of most security systems in general) is the protection of a resource from illicit access. Generally, resources that are in need of protection are those whose misuse could cause annoyance or even considerable loss to the user or users of a computer. For example, unrestricted access to a private medical record or the number of the bank card of a user could cause considerable problems. The following is a list of some resources to which computer security systems typically limit access:

- *Files and Folders*—Limiting access prevents information leaks and information loss.

- *Intranet and Internet access*—Limiting access to intranet and Internet locations can prevent the spreading of information not intended to leave a computer, as well as preventing the contraction of malicious or erroneous programs of unsafe or unknown origin.

- *Memory*—Protecting access of memory location of other programs prevents information loss, exposure, or undue intentional or unintentional side effects on other programs.

- *Special purpose devices*—Access to printers or special computation devices (such as a dedicated hardware instantiation of a cryptography algorithm) is limited to protect the owners of these services from costs incurred due to illicit access or misuse.

- *Global machine or domain configuration state*—Access to the registry, environment variables, machine security configuration files, and so on is limited to prevent the security system from being undermined, as well as to reduce the likelihood of having to reinstall and reconfigure a computer or network of computers due to malicious or erroneous access to the global configuration state.

The better a computer security system protects against illicit access to resources, the more safety it provides. You may now rightfully wonder exactly what defines "illicit access." Unfortunately, there can be no encompassing definition for this concept, because the right to access a resource is a privilege defined largely socially, not by hard and fast rules of computer science. For example, which user of an enterprise gets to write information to an expensive color laser printer, or what program gets to read the files and folders of the computer standing in the CEO's office, is dependent on organizational and social context. Most security systems can be configured to express what illicit access means in a particular usage context.

NOTE

See Part IV, ".NET Framework Security Administration," to find out how to administer the security systems impacting managed code.

Figure 4.1 shows the structure of security systems as we have defined them so far.

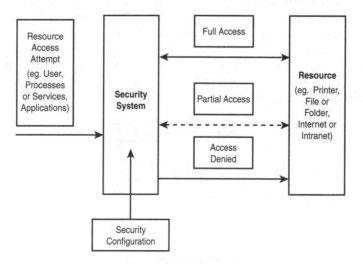

FIGURE 4.1   Control over resource access by security systems.

As you can see in Figure 4.1, attempts to access a protected resource will lead the security system to allow either full or partial access to the resource or, conversely, completely reject the access attempt. An example of partial access to a protected resource is the read-only access to a write-protected file or folder. As can be seen, security configuration settings influence the success of resource access attempts. In a sense, a security system is nothing more than a filter that sorts attempts to access resources, blocking some attempts, while partially or fully letting others pass. What then are the mechanisms that make security systems work?

Attempts to access a resource are judged by the identity of who or what makes the call to the resource. Thus, based on the identity of the caller to the resource, the security system determines, in accordance with security configuration settings, what access to the resource the caller should be given. This mechanism of mapping security configuration state and identity of the caller to a set of access rights is termed *authorization*. Before authorization can take place, however, the security system must collect information and be assured about the identity of the caller to the resource in the first place. That process is called *authentication*. Finally, for the security system to be effective at all, it must implement an *enforcement system*. An enforcement system consists of all the mechanisms that block the caller to a resource from working around the access restrictions that authentication may have placed on the caller. We can now replace the ambiguous Security System box in Figure 4.1 with something more concrete.

As can be seen in Figure 4.2, before access to a protected resource can succeed, the caller needed to be authenticated. This means that information about the identity of the caller was collected and potentially ascertained. Authentication is therefore the security system's way of making sure the caller to a resource is who he claims he is, and is used to establish an identity on which security decisions can be based. The identity information is used to determine the access rights to the resource. In other words, the security system authorizes resource access. Finally, the enforcement system blocks and prevents access to the resource that circumvents the authentication or authorization mechanisms.

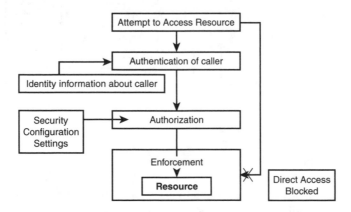

FIGURE 4.2 Resource protection through the interplay of authentication, authorization, and enforcement.

There are actually examples of such security processes at work outside the realm of computer security. One example is the process of entering the United States. At the border, your identity is established and ascertained by a thorough screening of the documents you present. If you carry a U.S. passport that fits your appearance, you will be authenticated as an American citizen. This authorizes you to stay as long as you want within the territory of the U.S., work, and take advantage of other benefits only available to citizens. If, on the other hand, you present a passport of one of the European Union countries, you are authenticated as a non–U.S. citizen from, say, Germany. Without any other identity information (such as additional visas) European Union citizenship authorizes you for a tourist stay within the territory of the U.S. for a few months, but would not give you the right to work or study. Finally, for these authorization regulations to have any value, a certain enforcement system must be in place. For example, all, not just a few, passengers on inbound international flights are required to authenticate themselves.

Much like the system protecting U.S. borders, computer security systems draw boundaries around resources, strongly regulating access to those resources. Specific security systems just differ in the type of resources they protect and the type of identity they are authenticating and authorizing against. We will now look at security systems that grant access rights to and authenticate against user identity.

A Review of User-Identity–Based Security

The computer security systems you will most likely be familiar with are based on user identity. This means that authentication takes place for particular user identities; authorization then maps user credentials to specific resource access rights based on the user credentials gleaned from authentication. Finally, the enforcement system protects resources on a per-user basis. One of the most obvious examples for such a security system is the Windows security system.

When you log on to your Windows NT, 2000, or XP machine, you are authenticating yourself to Windows. Windows asks you to prove that you are the user you claim, typically by requiring you to type in a password.

After your user identity has been established, Windows will authorize access to operating system resources, such as files or the registry, based on the administrator-defined access control settings to those resources. Finally, Windows has built-in mechanisms to maintain user isolation (data stored in your user profile directory is off limits for other nonadministrator or nonpower users) and takes care that no resources can be accessed without proper authorization.

> **NOTE**
>
> See Chapter 17, "Introduction: .NET Framework Security and Operating System Security," for an overview of the Windows Security system and its interplay with the .NET Framework security infrastructure.

Windows is a prime example of a user-identity–based security system. Security is enforced on a per-user identity basis. All user code (except for some service code) in Windows is run in a specific user context, and it is the user context in which code is running that determines the resources the code can access. However, this also means that all code run on behalf of a specific user will run with the same rights to access-protected resources. In the next section, you'll see that there are security issues that cannot be addressed with a user-identity–based model, and it will also be shown how code-identity–based security can help mitigate these problems.

Entering a New Paradigm: Code-Identity–Based Security

User-identity–based security systems have been very successful in regulating access to resources, such as the files and folders maintained by the operating system, or to a database in Microsoft SQL Server. However, there is a fundamental drawback to user-identity–based security—by design, it operates at the granularity of user identity. All code running on behalf of a user is executed with the same access rights. This does not allow for trust distinctions between code itself. You may wonder why this is necessary. Certainly in the past, when desktop machines were not interconnected to each other or to the Internet and all software needed an explicit install action on behalf of the user, it typically presented few problems treating all software running in a specific user context as having the same access rights. However, in a world that does not consist of disconnected desktop machines anymore, but in which computers are typically networked, it is not true that all code run on behalf of a user should be treated the same way. Consider the following scenarios illustrating that not all code running on behalf of a user should be treated as equal:

- An administrator has written a security configuration tool and installed it on the local hard disk. In the absence of any security system other than OS security, if both applications were run, he browses to a local intranet site containing managed control by a publisher he has never heard of. If both applications were run, they both would execute with administrative privileges, having the right to modify system files and registry settings, for instance. However, the user can have more trust in the tool he wrote and installed himself, as opposed to the application about whose origin he does not know anything. Both are given the same potential for doing harm by user-identity–based security systems because they both run on behalf of the same user.

- A user wants to run various applications from the company's intranet (such as a chess application or an accounting database). By default, he does not want code coming from the intranet to access his local hard disk to maintain privacy of the data in his user profile directory. He also regularly runs a word processor from the local computer that he wants to have access to the user profile directory in which he keeps his documents. User-identity–based security systems could not answer the demands of the user. The administrator could set up the user-identity–based security policy to fully deny all applications run on behalf of that user access to the user's profile directory or, conversely, to grant it to all programs run on behalf of the user. User-identity–based security systems, such as the Windows Access control settings, do not work at a level of granularity allowing for *some* of the user's applications to have more access rights than others.

- An administrator determines that only programs of a certain software publisher should run when executed from the intranet or Internet. User-identity–based security systems would be categorically inadequate in expressing this constraint, because the information user-identity–based security systems use to make authorization decisions is not information about code itself but the user who runs it.

These are just a few of the possible scenarios in which user-identity–based security systems turn out to be insufficient to meet a particular security configuration and enforcement requirement. In general, the main problem with user-identity based–security systems is that all code run within the same user context is executed with the same rights to access protected resources. In a world in which the trustworthiness of the origin of a particular piece of code can vary widely, this can lead either to overrestrictive security policy settings or potential security holes if only user-identity–based security is available. However, the .NET Framework ships with a code-identity–based security system (Code Access Security [CAS]) that can answer the needed security requirement. First, you may ask exactly what defines code-identity–based security systems.

Instead of information about the identity of a particular user, code identity security systems "authenticate" *code* itself by collecting information about the origin of code. For example, the .NET Framework security system collects (among other things) the following information about a piece of code:

- Site of origin

- URL of origin

- Authenticode signature (if present)

- Strong name signature (if present)
- Hash of the assembly

Information about the origin of code is referred to as *evidence*. For example, an assembly executed from the www.gotdotnet.com site would include site evidence pointing to the gotdotnet site, the specific URL of where it comes from, its hash, and, if applicable, its strong name signature value. Code-identity–based security systems, including CAS, authorize—in other words, make grants of permissions to access protected resources—based on evidence about the origin of code itself. The CAS system, for example, ships with a powerful, extensible security policy system that maps evidence to resource access permissions based on administrable policy settings. Authorization in code-identity–based security systems is always founded on information about a particular piece of code itself, not on the user context in which the code is executed. For example, CAS policy can be set such that all assemblies running from www.gotdotnet.com and signed by Microsoft get extra trust to access local resources—the user context in which the code is run does not enter the authorization decision. Finally, code-identity–based security systems, such as CAS, enforce code-identity–based authorization decisions by strictly limiting the interplay and side effects between different pieces of code. For example, the CAS system relies heavily on the code isolation mechanism implemented in the CLR called Application domains. Application domains are similar to Windows processes in the world of the .NET Framework and, by isolating code running in one Application domain from code running in another, differences of security trust allotment cannot be circumvented. To summarize, code-identity–based security systems

- *Authenticate code identity*—Information about the origin of a piece of code (such as the URL where it is run from) are collected and presented to the authorization layer.

- *Authorize code, not users, to access resources*—All trust decisions to access protected resources are made for particular pieces of code, based on security settings evolving around information about the origin of code.

- *Enforce the authorization decisions on particular pieces of code, not users*—The granularity of enforcement functions on the level of individual pieces of code (such as individual assemblies).

More specifically, the Code Access Security system shipping in the .NET Framework

- *Authenticates assemblies*—By collecting evidence about the assembly, such as the assembly's URL or strong name

- *Authorizes assemblies*—By granting assemblies a set of permissions to access protected resources (such as the file system or registry)

- *Enforces authorization decisions*—By checking that all assemblies calling to a protected resource have the appropriate permission to access that resource, as well as enforces isolation between application domains

Much of the remainder of this book is about spelling out the details of CAS authentication, authorization, and enforcement mechanisms.

You may still wonder how this security paradigm answers the challenges brought up against user-identity–based security systems previously discussed. The main advantage of code-identity–based security systems is that it no longer treats all code running on behalf of the same user as equal. In fact, code-identity–based security systems allow for a potentially indefinite discrimination of different code identities and, thus, an indefinitely fine-grained access rights allotment scheme to different pieces of code. In code-identity–based security systems, such as CAS, code is the first class citizen around which the whole model evolves. By differentiating between different assemblies based on their evidence, the CAS system can be configured to answer all the specific scenarios for which user-identity–based security systems were found lacking.

- CAS policy can be configured to treat all assemblies coming from the intranet with less trust than the assemblies residing on the local machine. In fact, as you will see in Chapter 8, "Membership Conditions, Code Groups, and Policy Levels: The Brick and Mortar of Security Policy," and Chapter 18, "Administering Security Policy Using the .NET Framework Configuration Tool," default CAS policy is designed to do just that. This capability will allow an administrator to run a trusted managed application from his local hard drive, while executing an untrustworthy control from the intranet without fearing that the control may abuse his administrative privileges.

- Again, CAS policy can also be configured to treat all assemblies running from the Internet with less trust than the assemblies installed on the local machine. Default CAS policy is already structured this way. For example, this will allow a user to run an application from the local disk with access to her profile directory, while preventing any assembly from the Internet from accessing her personal files and data. Again, code-identity–based security systems allow for the execution of code with widely different levels of trust in the same user context.

- Because evidence, information about the origin of an assembly, is the type of information CAS policy is based on, it is possible to design a CAS policy configuration that grants assemblies from trusted publishers' permissions to access protected resources, while locking down access to the same resources to all other assemblies. For example, this allows administrators to prevent any assemblies from the Internet or intranet, except for assemblies signed by trusted publishers, from running. Assemblies executing in the same user context are treated with very different levels of trust in this case.

As could be seen, code-identity–based security systems can answer some of the short-comings of user-identity–based security systems in a world where different applications or components may require different levels of trust, even if run under the same user context. You may now wonder exactly what the interplay between the two types of security paradigms should be. In particular, you may wonder whether code-identity–based security could not replace the less granular user-identity–based security paradigm.

How User- and Code-Identity–Based Security Systems Complement Each Other

User- and code-identity–based security are not contradictory, mutually exclusive mechanisms for making a computer secure. In fact, code-identity–based security can be seen as a complement to user-identity–based security in a world of highly inter-connected computing. Classical user-identity–based security schemes continue to be crucially important for security decisions in organizations where access rights to computing resources need to mirror the roles and responsibilities users have in that organization. Code-identity–based security is therefore not intended to nor likely to replace user-identity–based security. However, as has been shown, user-identity–based security systems alone cannot serve all security administration needs and scenarios. Running all code in a given user context with the same set of access rights does not honor the fact that different applications themselves, not just different users, require trust differentiations due to coming from less or more trusted origins. Code-identity–based security can therefore orthogonally complement user-identity–based security. Code run on behalf of a user is itself subject to further trust limitations depending on its origin. Where code-identity and user-identity security both protect the same resource (that is, Windows Access control and CAS protect the registry), no one security system can typically override the other. For example, managed code can only write into the registry if *both* the CAS policy system and Windows access control have granted access to the respective registry location. When code is run under both user- and code-identity–based security systems (such as Windows access controls and CAS), the access rights that piece of code possesses is the intersection of the access rights the user identity possesses and the access rights the code's origin elicits. Consequently, user- and code-identity–based security systems complement each other by placing limitations on code depending *both* on the user the code is run for as well as the origin of the code itself.

NOTE

See Chapter 17 for more information about the interaction about Windows Access protections and CAS.

Summary

Security systems are in the business of protecting resources from illicit or erroneous access. User-identity–based security systems protect resources based on the identity of the user. This leads to a situation in which all code run within the same user context has all the access rights given to that user. In a world of highly interconnected computing, where code can come from many different locations and publishers, it is necessary to limit access to resources not just based on who is running code, but also based on the origin of the code that is running. Code-identity–based security allows administrators to make such per-code trust decisions. The .NET Framework ships with a code-identity–based security system—Code Access Security—that allows administrators to fine-tune security policy based on criteria of the code itself, independent of who is running the code. Code-identity–based security systems, such as CAS, are not intended to replace user-identity–based security, such as Windows Access control settings. Rather, code-identity– and user-identity–based security together allow administrators to place the right set of limits on code, making resource access dependent *both* on who is running the code and where the code that is run comes from.

It is now time to further investigate what exactly is meant by the "origin" of managed code. The next chapter will explain in more detail the concept of managed-code evidence—the necessary input for any CAS policy decisions.

5

Evidence: Knowing Where Code Comes From

By Matthew Lyons

As explained in Chapter 4, "User- and Code- Identity–Based Security: Two Complimentary Security Paradigms," code identity security is the basis of the security system in the .NET Framework. However, what does it really mean for some program to have an identity? How can the system assign identity to a given piece of code? These are the fundamental questions that this chapter addresses.

Users generally have a username and password to authenticate themselves to a computer, but that authentication process is active. That is, users log on by typing in their names and passwords. However, code for the .NET Framework cannot simply take an active part in authenticating itself. Instead, a trusted piece of the system must provide identification on behalf of code written on the .NET Framework. That is where evidence comes into play.

This chapter will cover:

- What evidence is and how it is assigned to code
- Different sources of evidence
- Evidence classes used in the .NET Framework base class library

Evidence Explained

Evidence provides the basic building blocks for how code access security can work on .NET Framework code. An example of evidence about code is its SHA1 hash value.

This value is a cryptographically strong piece of information that is unique for different pieces of code. Thus, it is useful in providing identification.

> **TIP**
>
> For more information on cryptographic hash values, see Chapter 30, "Using Cryptography with the .NET Framework: The Basics."

There are two key points to remember about evidence:

- Evidence applies to executing code itself, not the user who is executing the code.

- Evidence is applied to the granularity of assemblies and application domains.

> **TIP**
>
> Application domains will be mentioned several times in this book. They are also referred to as *app domains*.

Evidence Applies to Executing Code

Evidence is a collection of information that is gathered about executing code, regardless of who is running it. Figure 5.1 shows an example of this. Given two users, Alice and Bob, running assembly X, the security engine (that is, the part of the CLR that is wholly charged with enforcing security) should provide the exact same evidence regarding X (with one possible exception, its security zone, which will be covered in the final section in this chapter). When Alice runs X, its SHA1 hash value doesn't differ from when Bob runs it.

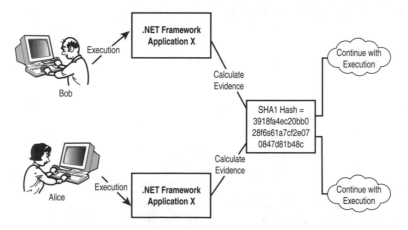

FIGURE 5.1   Evidence calculated for the same application when run by different users.

In a way, you can look at different .NET applications as different users, where evidence is the set of credentials for an application. This analogy doesn't work for all pieces of .NET Framework security, but it will help you understand the role of evidence. Evidence is how .NET Framework security differentiates one piece of code from another.

Another important piece of information regarding evidence is that it only applies to code that is executing. The .NET Framework will not precompute or cache evidence for code that is not executing. Evidence is dynamically calculated and applied when code is running. In fact, some evidence is impossible to know before code executes. For example, the URL of origin for an executing application is impossible to know beforehand since that application may exist at many different locations or be referenced by different URLs that point to the same location.

Evidence Is Applied to Assemblies and App Domains

So far, I have made the assertion that evidence is applied to running code. However, "running code" is a general concept. To be more specific about this concept, we have to understand the building blocks of a process in the .NET Framework.

In the .NET Framework, app domains are sort of like mini-processes themselves. They are the repository for loaded assemblies, and they represent a logical barrier to separate execution of code. Every .NET process contains at least one app domain, and every app domain will have assemblies loaded into it. Evidence is applied to both assemblies and app domains, so every different assembly and app domain will have individual identities.

Assemblies

An assembly is a well-defined entity in the .NET Framework. It is the primary mechanism for dividing compiled code to be loaded at a later time. It is usually, though not necessarily, a single file that contains a library or an executable file (for example, a DLL file or an EXE file). However, an assembly may contain multiple files, in which case, the primary file in the assembly is called the *manifest*.

In the .NET Framework, an assembly is referenced by using the `System.Reflection.Assembly` class. Assemblies can be loaded directly from the file system or the Global Assembly Cache. Assemblies loaded from the global cache are shared across all applications using the .NET Framework. Assemblies provided by the .NET Framework SDK will generally be located in the global cache, while assemblies for individual applications will generally be located in the individual application directories. This is similar to what Windows does with DLLs and the `%windir%\system32` directory. System libraries, such as the C runtime library, are placed there for all applications to use. However, the global cache is different in that it can simultaneously store several different versions of the same assembly. For more information on the Global Assembly Cache, see the .NET Framework SDK.

Because evidence is not precomputed by the .NET Framework, you cannot know exactly what evidence will be associated with an assembly you write. However, you can examine the evidence associated with an assembly at the time of execution by using the `System.Reflection.Assembly.Evidence` property. To obtain the evidence of an executing assembly, simply utilize the following code:

```
System.Security.Policy.Evidence ev = System.Reflection.Assembly.
➥GetExecutingAssembly().Evidence;
```

App Domains

Essentially, application domains provide in-process isolation of executing code. All .NET Framework code must run in some app domain. While it isn't obvious by running a simple "Hello World" application, a default app domain is created for every .NET Framework process. If no other app domains are created, all code runs in the default domain.

> **NOTE**
>
> The same assembly can be loaded into multiple app domains at the same time. When this happens, the compiled code in memory can be shared to reduce the working set. However, static data is not shared between app domains. If it were shared, this would mean a breakdown in the isolation that app domains are meant to provide.

App domains use the `System.AppDomain` class to represent them to managed code. The `AppDomain` class has an identical property as the `Assembly` class for handling evidence. To obtain evidence on the current `AppDomain`, you can use the following code:

```
System.Security.Policy.Evidence ev = System.AppDomain.CurrentDomain.Evidence;
```

App domains are particularly valuable for the following tasks:

- Loading assemblies that you want to unload at a later time. (In fact, the *only* way to unload an assembly is to unload the app domain containing that assembly.)

- Providing fewer rights than provided by default policy to less-trusted assemblies. (App domain policy is discussed in Chapter 8, "Membership Conditions, Code Groups, and Policy Levels: The Brick and Mortar of Security Policy.")

- Running several tasks that should be isolated from each other without using multiple processes.

Different Sources of Evidence

I mentioned earlier that evidence is a collection of information. This was meant very literally. Evidence is represented by the `System.Security.Policy.Evidence` class, and this class implements the `System.Collections.ICollection` interface. This means that it is a container class for instances of other classes. Actually, each evidence object has two separate collections to cover two different sources of evidence:

- Host-provided evidence

- Assembly-provided evidence

TIP

To gain a more practical understanding of what evidence looks like on an assembly, compile and run the program from Listing 5.1. It simply looks at the `Evidence` property on a `System.Reflection.Assembly` object.

LISTING 5.1   Program That Prints Out Its Own Evidence

```
using System;
using System.Collections;
using System.Reflection;
using System.Security;
using System.Security.Policy;

public class ShowEvidence
{
  public static void Main()
  {
    Assembly thisAssembly = Assembly.GetExecutingAssembly();
    Evidence ev = thisAssembly.Evidence;

    Console.WriteLine("Host Evidence:");
    IEnumerator enumerator = ev.GetHostEnumerator();
    while (enumerator.MoveNext())
    {
      Console.WriteLine(enumerator.Current + Environment.NewLine);
    }
    Console.WriteLine(Environment.NewLine);

    Console.WriteLine("Assembly Evidence:");
    enumerator = ev.GetAssemblyEnumerator();
```

LISTING 5.1   Continued

```
    while (enumerator.MoveNext())
    {
        Console.WriteLine(enumerator.Current + Environment.NewLine);
    }
  }
}
```

Host-Provided Evidence

Host-provided evidence is the evidence that has been discussed so far. For purposes here, a "host" is one of two things. First, a host could be something that initiates the Common Language Runtime. This is some unmanaged code that calls `CorBindToRuntimeEx` (an exported function from `mscoree.dll`). Second, a host could be a managed piece of code that can launch other managed pieces of code.

Regardless of the type of host being discussed, the Common Language Runtime provides some types of evidence by default. Table 5.2 lists those default types of evidence. Thus, a host does not necessarily have to provide any additional evidence itself. If a host does provide evidence that contradicts some evidence provided by the Common Language Runtime, then the host-provided evidence overrides the other evidence. Any host-provided evidence that doesn't override evidence provided by the Common Language Runtime is just merged into the collection of host-provided evidence.

Unmanaged Hosts

An unmanaged host is necessary to run any .NET Framework application. Certainly, something must start the Common Language Runtime. The .NET Framework ships with several different hosts. Some examples are ASP.NET, Internet Explorer, and the command-line host. All three of these hosts are capable of starting a .NET application, and all three can provide evidence about the applications they start.

The security functionality of the .NET Framework depends on another entity providing prior knowledge of managed code. The host provides the .NET Framework with information such as the root directory for an application, because the Common Language Runtime cannot determine this information. This can be done by using the `ICorRuntimeHost` interface. When a call is made to `CorBindToRuntimeEx` to start the Common Language Runtime, an interface pointer to `ICorRuntimeHost` is returned. Using that pointer, calls can be made to `CreateEvidence` and `CreateDomain`/`CreateDomainEx` to create evidence objects and apply them to an app domain, respectively.

An unmanaged host can only provide evidence on an app domain. There is no unmanaged method that loads an assembly, but the unmanaged host can transfer control to a managed piece of code that will load and provide evidence about assemblies.

To learn more about unmanaged hosts, see the .NET Framework SDK documentation under "Programming with the .NET Framework," "Hosting the Common Language Runtime."

Managed Hosts

A managed host is simply some code that loads and executes other arbitrary, managed code. Not all managed code can do this due to security mechanisms that will be explained later in this section. Suffice it to say that it takes a high degree of trust for a piece of managed code to act as a host.

Most unmanaged hosts will also have a managed piece with which to work. This is because it is simpler and more efficient to transfer control to a managed host that then launches managed user code. Thus, a likely scenario would be to have a host use its unmanaged code to set evidence on an app domain, while its managed code sets evidence on user assemblies.

Table 5.1 lists several methods a managed host might call to provide evidence on assemblies and app domains. Note that these methods often have several forms, some of which do not have arguments for passing evidence. The forms without evidence arguments simply use the default evidence provided by the Common Language Runtime.

TABLE 5.1 Methods a Managed Host Might Call to Provide Evidence About Code It Loads and Executes

Method	Description

`System.Reflection.Assembly.Load`
`System.Reflection.Assembly.LoadFrom`
`System.Reflection.Assembly.LoadWithPartialName`
	These methods load an assembly. They allow a trusted host to state additional evidence that the Common Language Runtime should take into account when determining how much trust should be granted to the assembly. Load loads an assembly from the Global Assembly Cache given its full name (friendly name, version, public key, and culture). LoadFrom loads an assembly from the file system. LoadWithPartialName loads an assembly from the Global Assembly Cache given just part of its full name.

TABLE 5.1   Continued

Method	Description
`System.Activator.CreateInstance` `System.Activator.CreateInstanceFrom`	These methods create an instance of a class from a specified assembly. Evidence can be provided to apply to the assembly that contains the given class. `CreateInstance` loads an assembly from the Global Assembly Cache given its full name (friendly name, version, public key, and culture). `CreateInstanceFrom` loads an assembly from the file system.

`System.AppDomain.CreateInstance`
`System.AppDomain.CreateInstanceAndUnwrap`
`System.AppDomain.CreateInstanceFrom`
`System.AppDomain.CreateInstanceFromAndUnwrap`
	Similar to the `Activator` methods, these methods create an instance of a class from a specified assembly. However, in this case, the instance of the class is created in the calling `AppDomain` instead of the current `AppDomain`. As before, the methods without `From` load the assembly from the Global Assembly Cache, while the methods with `From` load the assembly from the file system. The methods without `AndUnwrap` return an `ObjectHandle`, while the methods with `AndUnwrap` return an `Object`. Note that if the class of the object being created does not inherit from `MarshalByRefObject`, cross-domain access is marshaled by value, which can lead to unexpected results.

`System.AppDomain.CreateDomain`	This method creates an app domain with the specified evidence.
`System.AppDomain.DefineDynamicAssembly`	This method is used to define an assembly in a specific `AppDomain` at runtime that wasn't previously persisted on disk. When the assembly is defined, evidence is provided so that the Common Language Runtime can determine how much trust to give it when it is used.
`System.AppDomain.ExecuteAssembly`	This method is used to execute an assembly in the calling `AppDomain`. A simple managed host might create a specific `AppDomain` and call this method to execute a user assembly with specific evidence.

TABLE 5.1   Continued

Method	Description
`System.AppDomain.Load`	This method is identical in purpose to `Assembly.Load` except that the specified assembly is loaded into the calling `AppDomain`.

Assembly-Provided Evidence

While hosts provide trusted evidence regarding an assembly, an assembly is permitted to provide evidence about itself. This evidence, however, cannot override any evidence provided by a host because that would be a security hole. In fact, all default evidence classes used in assembly evidence are completely ignored by the Common Language Runtime.

Because the `Evidence` class uses generic collections to store information, it can contain any object as evidence. Consequently, an assembly could provide evidence as plain as an integer or as rich as a signed XML statement. They are all equally simple to add to evidence, though they may not all be equally useful.

> **TIP**
>
> If you want to author a class that will be assembly evidence, there are two optional interfaces to consider implementing. The first is `IIdentityPermissionFactory`. (Permissions are discussed in detail in Chapter 6, "Permissions: The Workhorse of Code Access Security.") If you have an identity permission class that corresponds to your evidence, this interface defines a standard way for the Common Language Runtime to create a corresponding identity permission object. The second interface is `INormalizeForIsolatedStorage`. (`IsolatedStorage` is discussed in detail in Chapter 29, "Writing a Semi-Trusted Application.") If you want to create an `IsolatedStorage` class that uses your custom evidence for isolation, this interface provides a way for the Common Language Runtime to compare serialized evidence objects.

Assembly-provided evidence can be used to state more information about how much an assembly should be trusted. For example, an assembly developer may have submitted his or her application to a third-party software certification lab. The certification lab could provide a signed statement that the developer could attach to his or her assembly as evidence. This statement could say that the lab certifies that the application can safely be granted a high level of trust.

Note that simply providing additional evidence on an assembly will do nothing by itself. To see the real benefits of providing assembly evidence, the Common Language Runtime will have to do something with it. That will probably mean implementing a custom membership condition and modifying the default security policy. (Both of these topics are discussed in Chapter 8.) With the signed statement example, the security policy could look for assemblies with signed statements and assign them more trust than other assemblies.

There is a good whitepaper and some example code that goes into detail about how to add assembly evidence to your assembly. It is located on `http://www.gotdotnet.com`. I encourage you to read the whitepaper and its example code if you want to provide evidence on some assembly you are writing. Basically, the steps are:

1. Create an object that represents the evidence you want your assembly to provide. This will probably be an instance of a class that you created.

2. Serialize that object to a file using the `System.Runtime.Serialization.Formatters.Binary` class.

3. Compile your .NET Framework code to a module or several modules. For the C# and VB compilers, this is done by using the `/target:module` option. Modules are much like `.lib` files used in C and C++. They are pieces of executable files or libraries.

4. Combine the module(s) and the serialized evidence into an assembly using the ALink tool (`al.exe`) from the .NET Framework SDK. ALink has a `/evidence` option that is used to point to a serialized evidence file.

Because assembly evidence is something added explicitly by developers, there is no assembly evidence by default in any assemblies. You can see this if you compile and execute the code from Listing 5.1.

Evidence and the Base Class Library

There are several evidence classes that the .NET Framework uses by default. They are listed and described in Table 5.2. All of the classes listed in Table 5.2 are contained in the `System.Security.Policy` namespace.

TABLE 5.2   Full List of Default Evidence Classes Used by the .NET Framework

Evidence Class	Description
ApplicationDirectory	This is the directory that contains the primary executing code. The .NET Framework will use this evidence along with URL evidence to determine if some assembly is in the application directory. It is very useful for ASP.NET, which sets this to the directory containing the base Web page for a Web application.

TABLE 5.2   Continued

Evidence Class	Description
Hash	This is a generic class that represents a hash value for an assembly. For multifile assemblies, this value will be the hash of the manifest file. Hashes using the MD5 and SHA1 algorithms are provided by default through this class, but it can easily accommodate other hash algorithms. Chapter 30 covers hash algorithms in the `System.Security.Cryptography` namespace and how to extend the default cryptography classes.
PermissionRequestEvidence	This evidence is a representation of assembly permission requests. Assembly permission requests can state what permissions an assembly must have in order to run, what permissions it can be granted optionally, and what permissions it should never be granted. For more information on assembly permission requests, see Chapter 6. Note that this evidence is only visible on an assembly during policy resolution. You cannot examine this evidence after an assembly has finished loading. Policy resolution is explained in Chapter 8 and Chapter 12, "Security Through the Lifetime of a Managed Process: Fitting It All Together."
Publisher	Publisher evidence gives information regarding Authenticode signatures on assemblies. The .NET Framework SDK ships with tools such as `signcode.exe` and `chktrust.exe` that can be used to sign and verify files with Authenticode signatures. For more information on Authenticode, see `http://msdn.microsoft.com/library/default.asp?url=/workshop/security/authcode/intro_authenticode.asp`.
Site	Site information gives the Web site of origin for an executing assembly. Note that this can only be determined when an assembly is directly loaded from a site. If you download an assembly from some Web site and run it from your local machine at a later time, the .NET Framework will not record the original site of origin.
StrongName	Basically, a strong name is a cryptographically strong binding of a name, version, and culture for some assembly. For more detailed information on strong names, see Chapter 9, "Understanding the Concepts of Strong Naming Assemblies."
Url	This gives the URL of origin for an assembly. Similar to Site evidence, `Url` evidence is only useful when you directly run an assembly from a network location. If you download an assembly and run it at a later time, the .NET Framework will not know the URL of origin. URLs provided as evidence should be encoded. For example, a space (" ") would be represented as `%20`. The `System.Web.HttpUtility.HtmlEncode()` method can be used to encode a raw URL.

TABLE 5.2   Continued

Evidence Class	Description
Zone	Security zone evidence is a use of Internet Explorer security zones. As mentioned earlier, this is one possible way two different users might observe different evidence for the same assembly. This is because two users may have assigned the same site to different security zones. Given the users from Figure 5.1, if Alice has the site www.microsoft.com in her trusted sites while Bob does not, an assembly loaded from the URL http://www.microsoft.com/ SomeAssembly.dll will be in the Trusted Sites zone for Alice and the Internet zone for Bob.

I have one additional note about PermissionRequestEvidence. There is another way to view permission requests on an assembly rather than looking for PermisisonRequestEvidence. The unmanaged DLL mscoree.dll exports the GetPermissionRequests function. The returned byte blobs from this API are Unicode strings containing the permission requests. Consequently, you could simply call this API to get the same information that the .NET Framework uses to create PermissionRequestEvidence. The .NET Framework SDK tool permview.exe simply calls this API to display the permission requests on a given assembly.

Summary

Because the .NET Framework assigns trust to code and not users, evidence about code is a fundamental piece of .NET Framework security. Evidence can be viewed as the credentials for .NET Framework code. Generally, the same .NET application will have the same evidence, regardless of which user executes it.

Evidence is applied to assemblies and app domains. The Common Language Runtime provides default evidence when assemblies are loaded. Hosts can provide evidence for both assemblies and app domains, and assemblies can also provide evidence about themselves. However, assembly evidence does nothing unless security policy recognizes and uses it. Unmanaged hosts can only provide evidence regarding app domains, while managed hosts can provide evidence for app domains and assemblies. Managed hosts can utilize any of the APIs listed in Table 5.1.

As shown in Table 5.2, there are numerous different kinds of default evidence, all of which are located in the System.Security.Policy namespace. However, any object can be used as evidence. Again, though, nondefault evidence types must be recognized by security policy to have an impact.

6

Permissions: The Workhorse of Code Access Security

By Matthew Lyons

So far we have covered the difference between user identity and code identity, and we have examined in detail how code identity is constructed using evidence. Identity by itself isn't enough, though. The only thing that evidence provides is authentication—a way to ensure that we have identified a piece of code. What we are still missing is a set of privileges and an authorization mechanism to map identities to those privileges. This chapter will cover the privileges, or permissions, in .NET terminology.

Roughly speaking, a permission is a fine-grained privilege that can be given to .NET code. If the .NET code is not given a certain privilege, it cannot perform an action that requires that privilege. For example, it is considered a privilege for .NET code to write to the file system. If code is not granted a permission for this, trying to write to the file system will generate a security error. No privileges are automatically granted to code.

This chapter will cover the following aspects of permissions:

- Types of permissions and their corresponding classes

- How permissions are used for authorization in the .NET Framework

- The set of permission classes built into the .NET Framework

- Permission sets and their purpose

Permissions Explained

There are a few different types of permissions in the .NET Framework. The most common form is the code access permission. The next most common type is the identity permission. Finally, a small remaining set of permissions exists, although these permissions don't have a well-defined name or type.

Code Access Permissions

Code access permissions are the permission classes that derive from the abstract class System.Security.CodeAccessPermission. These constitute the standard set of permissions dealt with in assemblies. For example, there are permission classes that represent reading/writing to certain parts of the file system, reading/writing to the event log (on versions of Windows that have an event log), and accessing a database.

Code access permission classes override the following methods from the CodeAccessPermission abstract class:

- Copy—This method simply creates and returns another permission object that represents the same privilege as the current object.

- Intersect—This method takes a permission object *p* and returns a permission object that represents the overlapping privileges of *p* and the current object. This behavior is as you would expect from set theory.

- Union—Union is similar to Intersect in that it also behaves as you would expect from set theory. Union takes a permission object *p* and returns a permission object that represents all the privileges of *p* and the current object.

- IsSubsetOf—This method takes a permission object *p* and returns a Boolean that signifies whether the current object's privileges are wholly contained by the privileges of *p*. Again, this is as you would expect from set theory.

- ToXml—When security policy is saved to disk, it must be persisted in some form. Security policy contains permissions, so the permissions must have a way to persist themselves. XML is used for this purpose, so permission classes implement ToXml to achieve this.

- FromXml—This is how permissions are re-created after they have been persisted to disk. It is worth noting that ToXml and FromXml don't deal directly with XML strings. Instead, there is a small object model based on SecurityElement objects. This eliminates the need for each permission to perform XML parsing directly.

Identity Permissions

Identity permissions are really just a subset of code access permissions, as identity permission classes also derive from `CodeAccessPermission`. However, the purpose of identity permissions is somewhat different from many other code access permissions. The purpose of an identity permission is to represent the fact that an assembly has a certain piece of evidence during policy resolution. For instance, if an assembly were loaded from the `MyComputer` zone, it would have a `Zone` piece of evidence and a `ZoneIdentityPermission`. Evidence alone isn't always enough; sometimes security decisions need to be made based on the identity of callers, not just on whether security policy allows code to access a certain resource.

Other Permissions

The remaining set of permissions is characterized by the fact that the permission classes do not derive from `CodeAccessPermission` at all. Instead, they simply implement the `System.Security.IPermission` and `System.Security.ISecurityEncodable` interfaces. There is only one permission predefined in the .NET Framework that falls into this category: `System.Security.Permissions.PrincipalPermission`.

The `PrincipalPermission` is semantically different from every other predefined permission for one reason: This permission is based on user identity instead of code identity. "Standard" code access permissions and identity permissions are both based on code identity in some way. The `PrincipalPermission`, on the other hand, uses the role-based security functionality provided in the `System.Security.Principal` namespace that checks information on user accounts. This permission can be used to check whether code calling an API is being run by a user who is in a certain predefined role or group.

How Permissions Are Used

Now that we've explored the different types of permissions, it is important to understand how they are used by the .NET Framework. There are several ways in which permissions are utilized. They can be

- Granted by the security policy
- Demanded by .NET assemblies
- Used for other security actions

Permissions and Security Policy

Chapter 5, "Evidence: Knowing Where Code Comes From," covered evidence and the authentication model for .NET assemblies. Moving from authentication to authorization requires an understanding of security policy. Chapter 8, "Membership Conditions, Code Groups, and Policy Levels: The Brick and Mortar of Security Policy," will cover security policy and permissions in fine detail, but this section provides an approximate idea of what happens.

Once .NET code starts to load an assembly and determines the evidence for that assembly, it examines the security policy on the machine. The security policy will take the evidence as input and will return a set of permissions as the output. These permissions are generally a set of "standard" code access permissions and identity permissions. You can think of the code access permissions as the list of specific privileges that the assembly can exercise. The identity permissions represent some specific authentication data that can be checked for access to certain features. Listing 6.1 shows what a set of granted permissions looks like in XML representation. See the last section of this chapter, "Permission Sets," for more details on how sets of permissions are used.

LISTING 6.1   XML Representation of a Set of Granted Permissions for a Loaded .NET Assembly

```
<PermissionSet class="System.Security.PermissionSet"
  version="1"
  Unrestricted="true">
    <IPermission class="System.Security.Permissions.StrongNameIdentityPermission,
➡mscorlib, Version=1.0.3300.0, Culture=neutral,
➡PublicKeyToken=b77a5c561934e089"
        version="1"
      PublicKeyBlob="002400000480000094000000060200000024000052534131000400000
➡100010007D1FA57C4AED9F0A32E84AA0FAEFD0DE9E8FD6AEC8F87FB03766C834C99921
➡EB23BE79AD9D5DCC1DD9AD236132102900B723CF980957FC4E177108FC607774F29E83
➡20E92EA05ECE4E821C0A5EFE8F1645C4C0C93C1AB99285D622CAA652C1DFAD63D745D6
➡F2DE5F17E5EAF0FC4963D261C8A12436518206DC093344D5AD293"
        Name="CasPol"
        AssemblyVersion="1.0.3300.0"/>
    <IPermission class="System.Security.Permissions.UrlIdentityPermission,
➡mscorlib, Version=1.0.3300.0, Culture=neutral,
➡PublicKeyToken=b77a5c561934e089"
        version="1"
        Url="file://C:/WINNT/Microsoft.NET/Framework/v1.0.3528/CasPol.exe "/>
    <IPermission class="System.Security.Permissions.ZoneIdentityPermission,
➡mscorlib, Version=1.0.3300.0, Culture=neutral,
➡PublicKeyToken=b77a5c561934e089"
        version="1"
        Zone="MyComputer"/>
</PermissionSet>
```

Permission Demands

Permission classes or objects alone don't provide much benefit. However, the addition of a permission demand adds real value to the .NET Framework.

As mentioned in Chapter 2, "Introduction to the Microsoft .NET Developer Platform," the .NET Framework is designed to prevent luring attacks, in which less trusted code uses code with greater trust to do something on its behalf. Security demands are used to stop this from happening. For example, before highly trusted code accesses a protected resource, such as the file system, the resource may demand a corresponding permission, such as a `FileIOPermission` object. When a demand occurs, all callers are checked to see whether they have the corresponding permission. If some untrusted code is on the call stack, the demand fails and a `SecurityException` is thrown. This prevents the protected resource from being accessed. For more information on how this occurs, see Chapter 7, "Walking the Stack."

Other Security Actions

In addition to permission demands, there are other security actions for which permissions are used:

- `Assert`—This is a security action that can stop a stack walk caused by a demand. Specifically, if a stack walk gets to a method with a permission `Assert`, and if the demanded permission is a subset of the asserted permission, the stack walk will terminate without throwing a `SecurityException`. `Assert` is covered in greater detail in Chapter 7.

- `Deny`—Deny is a security action that can cause a stack walk to immediately fail. If a stack walk gets to a method with a permission `Deny`, and if the denied permission is a subset of the demanded permission, the stack walk will fail and throw a `SecurityException`. `Deny` is covered in greater detail in Chapter 7.

- `PermitOnly`—PermitOnly is a security action similar to `Deny`. It can cause a stack walk to immediately fail. If a stack walk gets to a method with a `PermitOnly`, and if the demanded permission is not a subset of the permitted permission, the stack walk will fail and throw a `SecurityException`. `PermitOnly` is covered in greater detail in Chapter 7.

- `LinkDemand`—LinkDemands are similar to demands in that they check for certain permissions on a caller. However, `LinkDemands` are shallow checks. They only look at the immediate caller on the stack. Demands, on the other hand, looked at all the callers on the stack.

  LinkDemands are JIT-time checks. Say some method *A* has a `LinkDemand` for permission *p*. If method *B* calls *A*, the assembly containing *B* is checked to see whether it has permission *p* before *B* is JITted. If it doesn't have permission *p*, calling *B* will immediately result in a `SecurityException`.

LinkDemands should be used with care. Because they are shallow checks, they don't protect against luring attacks. They have a much smaller performance cost, but they don't provide the same level of security as demands. Also, because they are JIT-time actions, stack marks such as Assert, Deny, and PermitOnly don't affect them. "JIT-time" security checks occur while the JIT compiler is compiling IL to machine-level code. Runtime checks occur while the machine-level code is executing.

LinkDemands are most useful in combination with identity permissions such as StrongNameIdentityPermission. If an API has a LinkDemand for a StrongNameIdentityPermission, direct callers of the API must be signed with a particular strong name (see Chapter 9, "Understanding the Concepts of Strong Naming Assemblies," for details on strong names). Strong names are cryptographically strong parts of assembly names that software developers can control. Thus, you can expose an API on a library that only your code can call.

- InheritanceDemand—InheritanceDemands are similar to LinkDemands. They are JIT-time checks, so they don't perform a full stack walk. They do, however, verify what code can inherit from a specific class.

  As with LinkDemands, InheritanceDemands are most useful when coupled with identity permissions. If you want to have a protected, extensible way to design a component, you can use an InheritanceDemand with a StrongNameIdentityPermission or some other identity permission you can control.

- Assembly-level permission requests—Assembly-level permission requests have three parts: minimal requests, optional requests, and refuse requests. Minimal requests express basic requirements for some assembly to load. Optional requests are permissions that you would like an assembly to be granted if possible. Refuse requests are permissions that you don't want to be granted to an assembly under any circumstances.

  Assembly-level permission requests are evaluated after policy resolution has been completed. Policy resolution produces an initial grant set *A*. If *A* doesn't contain an assembly's minimal request, assembly loading immediately fails. Otherwise, *A* is intersected with the optional and minimal permissions to produce set *B*. Then the refused permissions are subtracted from *B* to produce set *C*, which is the final set of permissions granted to an assembly after it is loaded.

CAUTION

Note that if you use assembly-level permission requests and specify an optional permission request, any permissions outside the optional and minimal requests will never be given to the assembly. This is because the policy resolution's grant set is intersected with the optional and minimal sets. Thus, be sure to specify all permissions you might want to use in the minimum and optional requests if you are going to use an optional request. Using a minimal request without an optional request will not produce this behavior.

Declarative and Imperative Security

As you can see, there are several different uses of permissions in the .NET Framework. Because of the wide range of uses, there are two different ways to express security actions: declaratively and imperatively. Listing 6.2 shows the same permission demand expressed in both forms.

LISTING 6.2   Declarative and Imperative Forms of the Same Permission Demand

```
// Declarative form
[FileIOPermission(SecurityAction.Demand, Read=@"C:\Payroll.doc")]
public void MyMethod()
{
}


// Imperative form
public void MyMethod()
{
  new FileIOPermission(FileIOPermissionAccess.Read, @"C:\Payroll.doc").Demand();
}
```

The primary difference between imperative and declarative forms of security actions is that declarative forms are stored in an assembly's metadata, while imperative forms are stored in IL. JIT-time security actions (for example, LinkDemands and InheritanceDemands) and assembly-level permission requests can only be expressed in declarative forms because no IL is executing when they occur. All other security actions can be expressed in both forms.

Declarative security has several advantages over imperative security:

- All security actions can be expressed in declarative form; this is not true of the imperative form.

- Declarative security actions can be easily, statically reviewed on assemblies because they are stored in metadata. Understanding imperative security actions requires reading an assembly's IL and simulating execution, which is much more difficult.

- Declarative security actions expressed on methods will occur at the very beginning of the method. This eliminates the possibility of performing security checks too late in program logic. If protected resources are accessed before imperative security checks are performed, it is possible that, among other things, data will be leaked to the client.

- Declarative security actions can be placed at the class level. When this is done, the security action applies to every method, constructor, and property in the class. Imperative checks can only occur at the place where they are written in the source code.

Imperative security has a couple of advantages over declarative security:

- More complex security logic can be used in method bodies with imperative security. For instance, different conditional branches can perform different security actions.

- Resources that can be accessed with dynamic parameters, such as file paths, can only construct dynamic security actions using imperative security. Declarative security must work with permissions that are statically included in an assembly's metadata.

Built-in Permissions

The .NET Framework comes with numerous permissions to protect different resources. Table 6.1 lists these permissions and their descriptions:

TABLE 6.1   Full List of Permission Classes Provided by the .NET Framework

Permission Class	Description
`System.Data.OleDb.OleDbPermission`	Protects access to OLE DB data sources via classes in the `System.Data.OleDb` namespace.
`System.Data.SqlClient.SqlClientPermission`	Guards access to a SQL server via classes in the `System.Data.SqlClient` namespace.
`System.Diagnostics.EventLogPermission`	Protects reading, writing, creating, and deleting event logs using the `System.Diagnostics.EventLog` class. Note that only Windows NT–family operating systems have event logs.
`System.Diagnostics.PerformanceCounterPermission`	Safeguards use of the `System.Diagnostics.PerformanceCounter` class to access performance counters.
`System.DirectoryServices.DirectoryServicesPermission`	Controls use of the `System.DirectoryServices` namespace, which provides access to the Active Directory.
`System.Drawing.Printing.PrintingPermission`	Manages the ability of managed code to print documents.

TABLE 6.1 Continued

Permission Class	Description
System.Messaging.MessageQueuePermission	Protects the ability to use message queues via the System.Messaging namespace. Message queues are useful for cross-process and cross-machine communication.
System.Net.DnsPermission	Guards the right to access DNS servers on the network via the System.Net.Dns class.
System.Net.SocketPermission	Controls the ability to open or accept network socket connections via the System.Net.Sockets.Socket class.
System.Net.WebPermission	Safeguards the ability to access network resources with HTTP using classes in the System.Net namespace.
System.Security.Permissions.EnvironmentPermission	Manages the ability to read and write environment variables using the System.Environment class.
System.Security.Permissions.FileDialogPermission	Protects the use of the File Open/Save dialog via the System.Windows.Forms.FileDialog class. The File dialog is a good way to allow users to provide selected file system access to partially trusted code.
System.Security.Permissions.FileIOPermission	Controls access to the file system. This is primarily, but not exclusively, used in the System.IO namespace.
System.Security.Permissions.IsolatedStorageFilePermission	Guards the ability to use the .NET Framework's isolated storage functionality. Isolated storage is described in Chapter 30, "Using Cryptography with the .NET Framework: The Basics."
System.Security.Permissions.PrincipalPermission	Used to represent a name and a role that you want your code to require via role-based security in the .NET Framework.
System.Security.Permissions.PublisherIdentityPermission	Permission form of publisher evidence granted to code via the .NETFramework security policy.
System.Security.Permissions.ReflectionPermission	Protects the ability to utilize the classes in the System.Reflection namespace. These classes allow you to discover and use types, even if they are not publicly accessible. For instance, you can enumerate all fields in a type, regardless of whether the type is public.
System.Security.Permissions.RegistryPermission	Safeguards the use of the Microsoft.Win32.Registry and Microsoft.Win32.RegistryKey classes to access arbitrary registry keys and values.
System.Security.Permissions.SecurityPermission	Controls access to several different resources, including application domain, remoting, serialization, and threadingclasses. This permission has a hodgepodge of different purposes.

TABLE 6.1   Continued

Permission Class	Description
System.Security.Permissions. SiteIdentityPermission	Permission form of site evidence granted to code via the .NET Framework security policy.
System.Security.Permissions. StrongNameIdentityPermission	Permission form of strong name evidence granted to code via the .NET Framework security policy.
System.Security.Permissions. UIPermission	Manages the ability to display UI and use the system clipboard. This permission is used in several classes in different namespaces.
System.Security.Permissions. UrlIdentityPermission	Permission form of URL evidence granted to code via the .NET Framework security policy.
System.Security.Permissions. ZoneIdentityPermission	Permission form of zone evidence granted to code via the .NET Framework security policy.
System.ServiceProcess. ServiceControllerPermission	Guards the ability to use the System. ServiceProcess.ServiceController class, which works with services. Note that only Windows NT–family operating systems support services.

Permission Sets

So far in this chapter, we have discussed the power, use, and variety of permissions. However, if the same operation is to be performed on a group of permissions, it is inconvenient to type in the same thing for every permission. Permission sets eliminate this inconvenience.

The basic permission set class, System.Security.PermissionSet, is essentially just a group of permissions. For the benefit of security policy, there is another class, System.Security.NamedPermissionSet, that adds a name and description to the collection. The name gives the ability to uniquely tag and identify certain permission sets.

All of the security actions mentioned earlier can also be done with permission sets. For instance, if you want your code to demand multiple permissions, you should first create a permission set containing all the desired permissions. Then you can call the Demand method on the permission set. This is more efficient. You can also cache permission sets to reduce the number of changes needed in code that uses these permission sets.

As shown in Listing 6.1, permission sets can be represented in XML. XML representations of permission sets are used by several security tools, including the .NET Framework Configuration tool and Caspol. These tools are discussed in Chapter 18, "Administering Security Policy Using the .NET Framework Configuration Tool," and Chapter 19, "Administering .NET Framework Security Policy Using Scripts and Security APIs." Listing 6.2 shows how you can easily generate XML from a permission set.

LISTING 6.2   Creating an XML Representation of a Permission Set

```
PermissionSet ps = new PermissionSet(PermissionState.None);
ps.AddPermission(new UIPermission(PermissionState.Unrestricted));
ps.AddPermission(new FileIOPermission(FileIOPermissionAccess.Read,
➥@"C:\temp\test.txt"));
Console.WriteLine(ps.ToString());
```

Summary

This chapter discussed the three different kinds of permissions: code access permissions, identity permissions, and other permissions. Standard code access permissions directly protect resources. Identity permissions represent evidence that is granted to assemblies. Other permissions are those that don't fall into either of the other two categories. The only such permission in the .NET Framework class library is built on role-based security.

Permissions are used in several different circumstances. First, they are used by security policy to grant specific rights to code. Second, they are used in permission demands to protect against luring attacks. Third, they are used in other security actions, like Assert. Due to the variety of uses for permissions, they are represented in two different forms: declarative and imperative.

The .NET Framework comes with a wide range of default permissions. Table 6.1 lists 25 different permission classes in the .NET Framework used to protect a variety of resources.

In order to allow operations to occur on more than a single permission at a time, the .NET Framework has permission set objects. These are collections of permissions that work effectively as a single permission object.

Permissions really are at the core of Code Access Security. They represent all the nuances of different resources that you might want to protect, and they are the primary focus of stack walks. Because of this, permissions and permission sets are the most widely used security objects in the .NET Framework class libraries.

7

Walking the Stack

By Rudi Martin

IN THIS CHAPTER

- A Review of Stacks and Their Uses

- The Security Stack Walk

- Modifying a Stack Walk

- The Interaction of App Domains with Stack Walks

Walking the stack—the act of determining at runtime which methods are calling you—is a fundamental part of the .NET Framework runtime. In particular, this technique is absolutely essential to the operation of the security system. Understanding the techniques and algorithms used is vital when considering the design and implementation of secure code.

One of the advantages that a managed environment, such as the .NET Framework, enjoys is that information that would typically be discarded under a traditional, statically compiled model is still available at runtime. This includes high-level metadata detailing classes and methods that is deployed with the code itself. Such information is vital to the runtime, but would be reduced to hardwired, raw assembly code by traditional compilers (and, in a fashion, such that the original high-level structure is no longer directly derivable).

The .NET Framework uses this knowledge of the high-level structure of client code in many ways. In this chapter, we'll talk about one specific use—tracking the execution of code via examination of a stack trace. This technique is vital to the operation of the .NET Framework runtime. It is used in such varied areas as garbage collection and exception handling, but we'll concentrate on its use as a means of enforcing security policy.

This chapter aims to provide a quick refresher on the subject of stacks in general before moving on to how they can be employed for use enforcing code access security. Specifically, the goals of this chapter are as follows:

- Review the terminology and use of stacks in the execution environment.

- Show how a stack walk is performed in the .NET Framework runtime.

- Explain the use of stack walks by the security system in the .NET Framework runtime.

- Describe the advanced stack walk modification methods offered by the .NET Framework runtime security system.

A Review of Stacks and Their Uses

Stacks are a basic data type in the computing world. They store items of data in ordered lists that are typically accessed from one end only in a last-in/first-out manner. A stack is similar to an inbox tray; items are placed on the top ("pushed") and also removed from the top ("popped"). Figure 7.1 illustrates a simple stack.

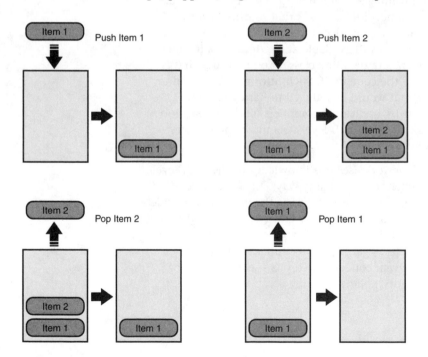

FIGURE 7.1   The workings of a simple stack.

Due to their simplicity and low-level hardware support, stacks are extensively used in most computer architectures. They provide a convenient and efficient means of storing data, usually for short-term use, such as the local variables in a method call. Such stacks are often implemented in the computer architecture using a single hardware register to keep track of the top of the stack. This is known as a stack pointer (in the Intel architecture, the actual register is called ESP). When the stack is first initialized, the stack pointer is set to the stack base—an address in memory indicating the lower boundary of the stack. As entries are pushed to or pulled from the stack, the stack pointer is raised or lowered as needed, always keeping track of where the most recent entry (the top of the stack) is located.

On most architectures, stacks grow from higher memory addresses to lower. This choice is largely arbitrary in today's systems, but it made sense before the advent of multithreading, when each program ran a single thread inside of its process space. The program itself would load into the process address space in the lower half of memory, followed by the heap—a variable-sized region used to provide long-term memory allocation. The stack base would be set at the very top of the process's virtual address range. So while the heap grew up in memory, the stack would grow downwards. This gave the greatest flexibility in memory usage and avoided the problem of trying to determine heap or stack limits in advance. The diagram in Figure 7.2 shows a typical process memory layout utilizing this simplistic scheme.

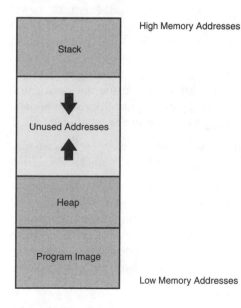

FIGURE 7.2   The use of stacks in a simple process layout.

Modern operating systems utilize multiple threads, each thread requiring its own stack (because the data stored on a stack is generally private to a particular thread of execution). Thus, more complex schemes are used than just described. A detailed description of stack management techniques is beyond the scope of this book, but we now have enough background information to proceed.

So where am I going with this? Well, the stack can be used to store more than local variables. One of its most important uses is to track the return path through nested method calls. To illustrate this, let's define a couple of simple methods:

```
public static int Foo()
{
    int result = Bar(123);
    return result + 1;
}

public static int Bar(int value)
{
    int retval = value;
    return retval;
}
```

If we were to call Foo, Foo would in turn call Bar, take the result, increment it, and return the new number (124). When Foo makes its call to Bar, the execution environment needs to record where we were in Foo when the call was made so that it's possible to resume normal execution of Foo after Bar has done its work. This is achieved by pushing the resumption address (the address of the assembly code immediately following the call to Bar) on the stack prior to making the call. After Bar has completed its work, it simply pops the return address off the stack and jumps to it, thus resuming execution in Foo where we left off.

If we were to halt Bar midway through its execution, we might see something as is shown in Figure 7.3 on the current thread's stack.

Notice how the stack forms layers of arguments, local variables, and return addresses for each method that the program is currently executing. Each of these layers is referred to as a *frame*. The layout of frames differs depending on architecture, operating system, and compiler (and sometimes even changes from method to method within a program), but the important point is that the system needs to record, at the very minimum, enough information to retrace its steps back from every nested method call that's been made.

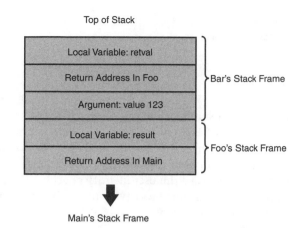

FIGURE 7.3   A typical stack trace.

You may have seen this information put to another use inside a debugger, where an examination of the stack allows the debugger to build and display the call stack (and possibly retrieve the values of local variables in each frame). To do this successfully, the debugger needs additional information from the compiler (in the form of extra debugging symbol files—`.pdb`, `.dbg`, and `.sym` files in the Windows world). Alternatively, the debugger might have to make guesses as to how the stack frames are formatted, which is why debuggers sometimes give inaccurate or incomplete call stacks.

The .NET Framework retains enough information in the runtime image, and constructs its stack frames in such a careful fashion, that it is always possible to generate a correct and complete picture of the method frames on the stack. The act of generating this picture is referred to as a *stack walk*, and it's the central part of the implementation of a number of .NET Framework features.

The Security Stack Walk

The type of stack walk that concerns us here is, of course, the security stack walk. Why would the security system need to walk the stack at all?

Let's take a simple example. Given the following code snippet from assembly `MyDatabase`,

```
public class MyDatabase
{
    public void BackupDatabase(String filename)
    {
```

```
        FileStream stream = new FileStream(filename, FileMode.Create);
        // Code to save database to newly created file…
    }
}
```

when the `BackupDatabase` method calls the constructor for `FileStream`, a security demand will be initiated to ensure that the caller has sufficient privilege to create the named file. Recall that the .NET Framework security system is primarily based on code access security. In other words, the security demand is based around the identity of the code making the call rather than the user account executing the thread. The operating system will still make the user identity checks prior to the actual file system operation, but first the runtime security system will have a chance to disallow the action based on the calling assembly.

So, assuming that within the implementation of the `FileStream` constructor a security demand is initiated for `FileIOPermission`, how does the runtime locate the calling assembly? The user identity is easy to find; it's stored in per-thread context (a collection of data kept for each thread in the process). The runtime could store the current assembly in the per-thread context as well, but this presents some problems. First, the current assembly at the time the security demand is initiated is, in fact, the assembly containing the implementation of `FileStream`, not `MyDatabase`. So the runtime would have to record not just the current assembly, but also the prior assembly as well. It soon becomes obvious that the entire list of assemblies invoked would need to be stored in the per-thread context. Second, the runtime would need to spot assembly transitions (calls from a method in one assembly into a method in another assembly) to track this information (including the return from such a call). Because method calls crossing an assembly boundary are reasonably common (at least with respect to security demands), this approach would entail undesirable performance penalties.

Instead, the security system utilizes the fact that we've already built a list of assemblies involved in the current operation—the stack itself. Determining the calling assembly is as simple as walking the stack. The frame for the `FileStream` constructor is simply ignored because it initiated the demand, but then we find the frame for `MyDatabase.BackupDatabase`. After the security system knows the method called, there is a simple mapping back to the enclosing class and then to the assembly. The assembly, being the unit of code to which the .NET Framework security system grants permissions, can then be queried to determine whether sufficient trust has been given to allow progress.

But the security system doesn't stop there. It continues on down the stack, testing each assembly it finds, until it runs out of stack frames or reaches an assembly with insufficient permissions. What's the purpose behind this behavior?

To answer this, let's look more closely at the implementation of `MyDatabase.BackupDatabase`. Notice that the method is public (and exported from a public class) and that it takes a filename that is blindly used to create the database backup file. In fact, this method represents a classic security hole, the so-called luring attack. Any untrusted assembly (say, one downloaded from the Internet with no additional credentials) can use this method to write to an arbitrary file on the user's disk. They might be limited in their ability to control the contents of that file and the operations possible will be constrained by the privileges given by the operating system to the user executing the thread, but the destructive potential is still very high.

This is actually a common security error, and it's frequently made by programmers who are not even aware that security demands are taking place or that security is an issue they need to worry about. Frequently, the mistakes can be more subtle. The author of `BackupDatabase` may prepend a directory to the filename passed in, in an effort to constrain where the backup file is written, forgetting that the caller may pass in a filename of the form `..\BadFile.dat`.

So let's assume the worst: A malicious assembly, `BadAssembly`, has a method `BadClass.TrashFile`, which makes a call to `MyDatabase.BackupDatabase` passing a filename of `c:\windows\system.ini`. How will the security system cope with this?

As before, the frame for the `FileStream` constructor will be skipped, and then the permissions for the `MyDatabase` assembly will be checked and found to be sufficient. Then the stack walk will move on to the frame for the `TrashFile` method. When the permissions for the corresponding assembly `BadAssembly` are checked and found to be insufficient, the stack walk is aborted and a security exception thrown (see the diagram in Figure 7.4).

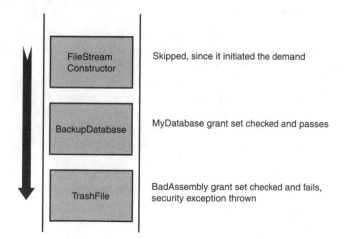

FIGURE 7.4 Catching a malicious caller using a full stack walk.

The .NET Framework security system didn't intrinsically know that BadAssembly was malicious, just that the system administrator had not placed enough trust in that assembly to allow it to perform potentially damaging actions. Equally, the security system didn't know for sure whether BackupDatabase was badly written and represented a security hole. In the absence of any other data, it made a paranoid decision that any flow of control from the untrusted to the trusted assembly represented a security risk. In the world of security, the paranoid decision is usually a good default.

Modifying a Stack Walk

So, say the author of MyDatabase comes along and, having read all about good security practices, rewrites BackupDatabase to be secure. The filename parameter is removed and the backup is written to a known location controlled solely by the MyDatabase assembly, with no input from external sources.

The security demand will still fail, if the caller of BackupDatabase is untrusted to write whatever file the underlying implementation is using. This is probably not the intended effect; the author of BackupDatabase wants to write the backup on behalf of the user, even if that user is otherwise untrusted. This is where the stack walk modification operators come in.

These operations (Assert, Deny, and PermitOnly) are methods defined on all the permission classes, as well as PermissionSet. When called, they attach their permission or permission set to the current method's stack frame in such a way that a subsequent stack walk will notice and process them. They are removed automatically when returning from the method to whose frame they are attached (including when the frame is unwound due to an exception being thrown). It's also possible to remove the attached permissions prematurely using the RevertAssert, RevertDeny, RevertPermitOnly, and RevertAll methods.

The most useful of the operations is Assert. Let's use it to solve the problem introduced in the last section. Assert allows a stack walk that has successfully traversed to the frame on which the assertion is attached to terminate early (with success). That is, it declares that further callers need not be checked (in essence, the current method vouches for the trustworthiness of its callers). Assert is a dangerous operation, and it is up to the code making use of it to either determine the trust level of its callers or ensure that no security risk is implied regardless of their trust level. When security reviews of code are being performed, calls to Assert are usually a good place to begin looking for holes.

Let's look at the modified code for BackupDatabase:

```
public void BackupDatabase()
{
    const String filename = "c:\MyDatabase\WorkArea\Backup.dat";
```

```
    new FileIOPermission(FileIOPermissionAccess.Write, filename).Assert();
    FileStream stream = new FileStream(filename, FileMode.Create);
    // Code to save database to newly created file…
}
```

When the security demand stack walk reaches the frame for BackupDatabase, the following steps will be taken:

1. The permissions for the MyDatabase assembly will be checked against the demand. It is important to do this before processing the assertion because a security hole is opened otherwise (to put it another way, the security system needs to check that you have the permissions you're attempting to assert before it allows you to assert them).

2. The security stack walker notices an assertion attached to the current method frame. It retrieves the permission associated with the assertion (in this case, a FileIOPermission for write access to the database backup file) and checks whether this satisfies the demand. If so, as in this case, the stack walk is halted immediately and successfully (no security exception is thrown).

This now makes BackupDatabase usable by anyone, regardless of his or her trust level.

Note that an assertion does not always terminate a stack walk. If the assertion is for an entirely different permission (or set of permissions) than the demand being made, it will be ignored completely. Likewise, if the assertion does not fully satisfy the demand, the overlapping portion will be removed from the demand and the stack walk continues. For example, say a demand is made for FileIOPermission, including write access to c:\a.dat and c:\b.dat, and a frame on the stack has an assertion for FileIOPermission write access to c:\a.dat. When the stack walk has reached the assertion, it will remove the asserted permission from the demand, but continue on to the next frame, now demanding FileIOPermission with write access to c:\b.dat. Assert can be looked at as taking a bite out of the demand on its way down the stack. If that bite leaves nothing of the demand behind, the walk terminates. Figure 7.5 illustrates the effect.

Deny can be thought of as the opposite of Assert. Whereas Assert causes (or can potentially cause) the early termination of a stack walk with a successful outcome, Deny will cause early termination of the stack walk with a security exception. That's to say, Deny ensures that any security demand for the associated permission or permission set that would get as far as checking your caller will result in a failure, regardless of the trust level of the caller in question.

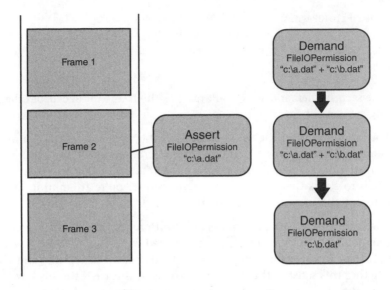

FIGURE 7.5 The effect of `Assert` on a security stack walk.

In practice, `Deny` is rarely a useful operation; any assembly denied access to a resource in this fashion is either granted the permissions to make the request directly anyway or, in the absence of such permissions, would be denied access by the security system in the normal fashion. An area where `Deny` commonly does prove its worth is in testing (especially when adding new security permissions). Take the following example, which assumes a new permission type, `MyPermission`, has been implemented:

```
// Force a security stackwalk for an instance of MyPermission.
public static void InvokeDemand(MyPermission permission)
{
    permission.Demand();
}


// Test demands on MyPermission.
public static boolean TestMyPermission()
{
    MyPermission permission = new MyPermission(PermissionState.Unrestricted);

    // Assuming this test program has been granted unrestricted MyPermission,
    // perform a positive test case first.
    try
    {
```

```
        InvokeDemand(permission);
    }
    catch (SecurityException)
    {
        return false;
    }

    // Now try a negative test.
    permission.Deny();
    try
    {
        InvokeDemand(permission);
        return false;
    }
    catch (SecurityException)
    {
     // We expect a security exception in this case.
    }

    return true;
}
```

We use Deny in this negative test case (that is, testing that MyPermission correctly throws a security exception when demanded in a situation where it is not granted). Deny is convenient for this purpose because it allows the set of permissions the assembly is granted to be effectively modified at runtime (at least from the point of view of the current thread). This allows us to place the positive and negative test cases within the same assembly.

It is reasonable to ask here whether the test is valid, given that a security demand that fails due to a Deny would seem to be a different scenario from a demand failing due to a constrained grant set. In actual fact, the difference between the scenarios is negligible to the implementer of a custom permission; the same interface methods are called with identical arguments in each case. The only real difference in code paths and algorithms is within the security system itself, which is outside the scope of testing MyPermission.

Note that we encapsulated calling Demand on MyPermission within a method (InvokeDemand). This choice was not arbitrary and, in fact, was necessary for the success of the test. Recall that a security stack walk will skip the frame of the method that initiated the demand (because making a demand against your own method is usually a worthless operation). If the frame that is skipped contains a stack walk modifier (Assert, Deny, or PermitOnly), that modifier is skipped as well. So if we'd made the demand on `MyPermission` directly from `TestMyPermission`, the `Deny` would have been skipped, and the stack walk would not have thrown a security exception.

The last of the stack walk modifiers is `PermitOnly`. This works in a negative fashion akin to `Deny` in that it attempts to terminate a stack walk early with a security exception. Whereas the permission or permission set associated with `Deny` indicates permissions that are refused and will cause an exception, the permissions associated with `PermitOnly` must satisfy the current demand to prevent a security exception being thrown. That is, the stack walk will proceed only if the demand can be entirely satisfied by the permissions associated with the `PermitOnly`.

`PermitOnly` is semantically close to `Deny` (it's really just an alternative way of specifying the accompanying permission set). So, similarly, it has little real use (beyond the testing scenario previously presented).

A NOTE ON INLINING

Because the .NET Framework security system depends so heavily on the structure of the stack for its correct operation, it's reasonable to ask whether compiler optimizations could lead to a security hole. The chief worry here is a technique known as inlining. Examining why this is not an issue will provide further insight into the workings of the security system.

Inlining is the process whereby a compiler copies the implementation of a method into a caller in lieu of actually making a call to that method. This is an optimization that trades off the speed gain realized by avoiding the overhead of making a method call versus the additional memory costs of making multiple copies of the same piece of code.

In the .NET Framework runtime, inlining is performed by the JIT when compiling a method's IL instructions into native code. The JIT is fairly aggressive and may collapse several levels of call into a single linear piece of code.

On the face of it, inlining may seem to present a problem to the security system. An inlined method no longer has its own frame on the stack, so it effectively disappears from any subsequent stack walk. This would allow a single untrusted method on the stack to disappear from sight if inlined into its trusted caller, for example.

In actual fact, the .NET Framework security system is careful to ensure that inlining does not compromise the safety of the system in this way. As previously discussed, there are two principal pieces of data the security system is searching for when walking the stack—assemblies (for their grant set) and stack walk modifiers.

When determining which assemblies are represented on the stack, the actual methods called are irrelevant and can be ignored. If a chain of three methods, all from assembly `MyAssembly`, are present on the stack, we determine whether `MyAssembly` has sufficient permissions when we encounter the first method, but can ignore the other two methods (for the purposes of assembly grant set checks). It would be pointless to check the same assembly grant set for compliance multiple times; such grant sets, once computed, are immutable.

From this it follows that only inlining that traverses an assembly boundary (where the caller and callee are in different assemblies) is interesting from an assembly grant set perspective. If the caller and callee are from the same assembly and the callee is inlined into the caller, the caller still contains the correct information for a valid security check.

The .NET Framework security system prevents the cross-assembly case from posing a security risk through the cooperation of the JIT. A simple way of ensuring safety would be to disable cross-assembly inlining altogether. However, the JIT can do better than this; it will allow a cross-assembly inline where the callee is completely trivial (defined here as the callee having no further method calls within its implementation). This allows the optimization of a large class of simple methods (most notably, property accessors) without compromising security. The algorithm applied by the JIT in future versions of the runtime might change and should not be relied on (for example, later versions of the JIT may be able to further refine the definition of "trivial callee" by differentiating calls made to security methods versus intraassembly calls).

We still have the problem of stack frames that introduce one or more stack walk modifiers (`Assert`, `Deny`, or `PermitOnly`). We can't allow any methods that introduce one of these operations to be inlined, because we lose the stack frame to which they're attached. We can't attach the operation to the caller's frame because this would affect the semantics of the modifier (recall the earlier `Deny` code example, where we relied on the demand being made from a different method than the `Deny`).

Instead, the security system again relies on the cooperation of the JIT. Because there are a limited number of method calls we care about (the `Assert`, `Deny`, and `PermitOnly` methods on the `PermissionSet` and `CodeAccessPermission` classes), the JIT simply "special cases" these and will refuse to inline any method that makes a call to one of them. This works because none of the methods are virtual and can be detected statically at JIT time.

The Interaction of App Domains with Stack Walks

In the interests of clarity, the stack walk algorithm presented thus far has been simplified somewhat. There is one further factor that can alter the outcome of a stack walk—the interaction of the app domain(s) in which the current thread is executing.

An app domain (short for application domain) can be thought of as a process within a process. Multiple app domains can exist within a single Win32 process and provide the same sort of separation between managed tasks that processes provide between unmanaged tasks. Each app domain is isolated from the others (they load their own set of assemblies and cross-domain communication requires the use of the remoting subsystem). This segregation means that should a single app domain fail, it is possible to shut down just that domain without impacting the others. The hierarchy of process, app domains, and assemblies is illustrated in Figure 7.6.

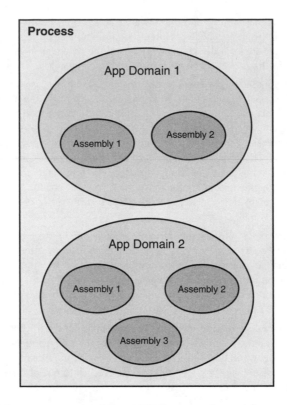

FIGURE 7.6   Major components of the .NET Framework model.

How app domains are utilized within the .NET Framework depends largely on the hosting environment. The Windows shell creates a single initial app domain and leaves the rest up to the application itself, whereas a database system might create an app domain for each user currently connected, or even each separate query.

The aspect of app domains that makes them interesting from our perspective is that it is also possible to grant them permissions in the same manner as permissions are normally granted to assemblies. For example, this facility is used by Internet Explorer when displaying a Web page containing references to managed objects. The objects themselves are granted permissions based on the identity of the assembly that owns them, but Internet Explorer also wants to assign an identity and permissions to the Web page in which they're embedded. Thus, an app domain is created for each Web page and provided with identity evidence (in the form of the Web page URL) so that the normal security policy mechanism can compute an appropriate set of granted permissions.

So how does this affect a stack walk? At any given instant, each thread running within a .NET Framework process is executing within the context of a single app domain. If a method call is made on an object that resides in a different app domain, the remoting system will transparently transition the thread into the context of that app domain (and transition the thread back again when the call completes). This transition leaves its mark on the thread's stack in much the same way that a normal method call would. An example of our revised view of a stack is shown in Figure 7.7.

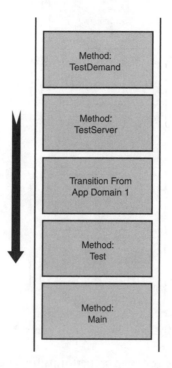

FIGURE 7.7   A typical stack with app domain transitions.

When the security system finds an app domain transition on the stack, it treats it as though it was an assembly transition. That is, the grant set is fetched and inspected to determine whether it supports the demand being made. If so, the stack walk proceeds; otherwise, the stack walk is terminated with a security exception.

Although this check is performed when an app domain transition is found (and the transition describes the app domain from which the thread came), the check performed is against the grant set of the app domain into which the thread transitioned—that is, the app domain in which the preceding frames were executing. We know the initial app domain (the one in which the thread was executing at the time the stack walk was initiated) because the .NET Framework runtime tracks the current app domain as an attribute of each thread, and the security system can query this information. Figure 7.8 is the diagram from Figure 7.7, this time with the app domains marked for each frame.

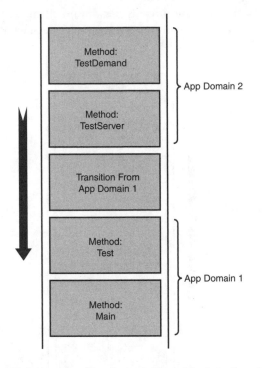

FIGURE 7.8   Integrating the app domain transition data into the stack trace.

It's important that the security system performs the check against an app domain's grant set *after* the checks against the stack frames that executed within that app domain. This is because an app domain might have a fairly restrictive grant set (in the Internet Explorer case, there's a good chance the app domain is associated with a Web page loaded from the Internet zone, whose policy is likely to assign minimal permissions to), but individual assemblies within the app domain may be granted a higher level of trust.

Consider the example of a Web page loaded from the Internet that hosts a control that needs to access the user's local file system. The control is contained within an assembly also loaded from the Internet, but it provides additional evidence (such as a strong name or an Authenticode certificate) that allows the policy system to assign it more trust (specifically, unrestricted `FileIOPermission`).

If the control tries to write a file on the user's disk and the permissions of the app domain in which the control is running were checked first, the request would always fail, because the app domain is associated with the Web page and the Web page hasn't been granted `FileIOPermission`.

Recall, however, that the stack walk algorithm will normally walk the entire stack before declaring success. So, even after we reverse the order in which the checks are performed, the file operation will ultimately still be denied. But now the control can do something about it; this is a perfect use for the `Assert` operation.

The control can simply `Assert FileIOPermission` prior to making any file system calls, preventing the lower permission level of the hosting Web page from coming into play at all, as shown in Figure 7.9.

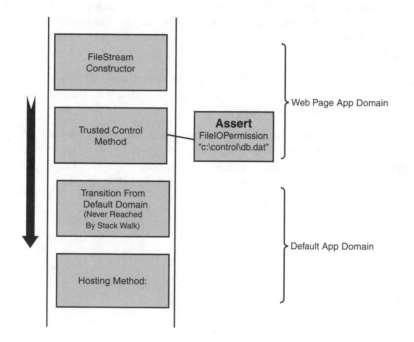

FIGURE 7.9   Overriding Web page permissions.

Note that unless the creator of an app domain explicitly associates evidence with it, app domains are considered to have no security implications whatsoever. Such app domains are not considered at all during stack walks. The default app domain created when launching an executable assembly from the Windows shell is an example of an app domain with no associated evidence and, hence, no grant set.

Summary

Stacks are used by computer systems to keep track of the execution of individual threads within the system.

Software, such as debuggers and the .NET Framework security system, can examine a stack to determine the set of nested calls that brought the thread to its current state. Each method in the chain is represented by a frame on the stack.

The .NET Framework security system checks that *every* method on the stack (or more correctly, every assembly) can satisfy the demand being made. This safeguards against the misuse of trusted but poorly written code by untrusted malicious code (luring attacks).

Stack walk modification operators (such as `Assert`) can be used by trusted code to control the stack walk. This is principally used to disable the previously mentioned safeguards (after the trusted code has ascertained that there is no security risk in doing so).

Inlining can alter the layout of a stack (by removing frames), but the .NET Framework security system ensures that this is done in a way that will never affect the outcome of a security demand.

App domains are a means of isolating several groups of assemblies within a single process. They may be granted identity and permissions in a similar manner to the assemblies they contain, in which case these grant sets are checked during stack walks (*after* the frames that executed in the context of that domain).

8

Membership Conditions, Code Groups, and Policy Levels: The Brick and Mortar of Security Policy

By Matthew Lyons

Thus far in this section of the book, we have discussed how security impacts executing code. Hosts provide evidence when code is loaded and permissions are used to determine if executing code has the right to perform some privileged action. The point of security policy is to get us from where evidence is provided for an assembly being loaded to the position where permissions can be used to cause stack walks during execution of an application.

The point at which security policy is actively being examined is known as *policy resolution*. Policy resolution is part of what happens while assemblies are loading. After evidence is provided for an assembly, the .NET Framework uses the stored security policy to compute the set of granted permissions for that assembly. After the granted permissions (otherwise known as the *grant set* or *granted permission set*) are determined for an assembly, they play a key role in stack walks and other security actions performed while code is executing.

Security policy is the mechanism by which administrators and end users can express their level of trust for different code. For example, a very cautious user may not want any code running on the intranet to execute, while another user may trust code from a few Internet sites to perform all privileged actions it might try. Security policy allows these decisions to be expressed with many levels of granularity in between.

An important concept to remember throughout this chapter is that security policy is simply a way to map intentions to something the .NET Framework can understand. The intention of the previously mentioned cautious user may be to be as safe as possible while allowing .NET Framework code to still execute. The security policy of the .NET Framework cannot understand this simple sentence, so the intention must be "translated" into terms it can recognize. Intentions must be well understood by users to be able to perform this translation properly.

This chapter will cover the following pieces of security policy:

- Membership conditions—The approach to group code into different "buckets"

- Code groups—Basic intentions that map .NET Framework code to specific levels of trust

- Policy levels—The way intentions of different parties (network administrators, a machine administrator, an end user, and a developer) are taken into account

- Default security policy—A safe, but useful set of intentions that should suffice for most users

NOTE

In the RTM release of the .NET Framework, default security policy was set to allow limited permissions for code loaded from the intranet and Internet. In mid-January, Bill Gates announced the strong commitment at Microsoft for the Trustworthy Computing initiative, which is aimed at ensuring that Microsoft as a company will meet customers' needs and expectations around privacy, reliability, and security. As a result of this, the .NET Framework team reconsidered the default security policy for the Internet zone. In order to truly emphasize the conservative "locked down" default behavior encouraged by the initiative and requested by customers, they decided to release service pack 1 (SP1) to remove the ability in default policy for code from the Internet to execute. This chapter will discuss the default security policy as reflected in SP1.

Membership Conditions

Membership conditions provide the first step in turning the evidence of an assembly into a grant set. At its most basic level, a membership condition is an object that can answer "yes" or "no" when asked if an assembly matches its membership test. For example, a membership condition object can be constructed to only answer "yes" if an assembly is being loaded from the Web site www.microsoft.com.

The following are some key points to understand about membership conditions:

- Membership conditions and evidence are closely linked.
- The .NET Framework provides several membership conditions by default.
- Membership conditions are extensible security objects, so developers can define their own.

Membership Conditions and Evidence

As mentioned in Chapter 5, "Evidence: Knowing Where Code Comes From," evidence on an assembly by itself does nothing without a membership condition that uses the evidence. This is similar to buying something using a credit card. If the merchant doesn't accept credit cards and the consumer has no other method to pay, the customer cannot buy the goods. If an assembly has evidence that no membership condition classes use, the evidence is useless.

Membership conditions have no other purpose than to match evidence provided for an assembly while it is loading. However, membership conditions can check more than one kind of evidence at once. For example, the ApplicationDirectoryMembershipCondition uses ApplicationDirectory evidence and Url evidence. Thus, each type of evidence can be examined by multiple types of membership conditions.

If a membership condition exists in policy that looks for evidence types not provided for an assembly, the membership condition simply doesn't match it. It is not an error or fatal condition.

Membership Conditions Provided by the .NET Framework

Membership condition classes are provided by default that match evidence classes provided by the .NET Framework. Table 8.1 lists the membership conditions provided by the .NET Framework. They all reside in the System.Security.Policy namespace. Note the similarity of Table 8.1 to Table 5.2, which lists all the default evidence classes.

TABLE 8.1 Full List of Default Membership Conditions Provided by the .NET Framework

Membership Condition Class	Description
AllMembershipCondition	This matches all code, regardless of what evidence is provided.
ApplicationDirectoryMembershipCondition	This looks at the ApplicaitonDirectory evidence and Url evidence. (Both kinds of evidence must be present to match the membership condition.)

TABLE 8.1   Continued

Membership Condition Class	Description
	The provided URL must be contained somewhere in the application directory. For example, if the application directory is `C:\myapp`, the URL path must start with `C:\myapp`, such as `file://C:\myapp\test.dll`.
`HashMembershipCondition`	This compares `Hash` evidence to a hash value stored in the membership condition itself.
`PublisherMembershipCondition`	This compares the Authenticode signing certificate from `Publisher` evidence to a certificate stored in the membership condition itself. The comparison of certificates is based solely on their public keys.
`SiteMembershipCondition`	This compares `Site` evidence to a site stored in the membership condition itself.
`StrongNameMembershipCondition`	This compares the `StrongNamePublicKeyBlob`, `Name`, and `Version` in `StrongName` evidence to the same kinds of values stored in the membership condition itself. The `Name` and `Version` can be `null`, but the `StrongNamePublicKeyBlob` cannot be `null`.
`UrlMembershipCondition`	This compares `Url` evidence to a URL stored in the membership condition itself.
`ZoneMembershipCondition`	This compares `Zone` evidence to an IE Security Zone stored in the membership condition itself.

Writing Custom Membership Conditions

As with many kinds of security objects in the .NET Framework, membership conditions are extensible. You can define your own membership condition that uses any default or custom-written evidence. To write your own membership condition, you need to define a class that implements the following interfaces:

- `IMembershipCondition`—Defines key membership condition methods

- `ISecurityEncodable`—Defines methods to convert objects to/from the XML representation used by .NET Framework security

- `ISecurityPolicyEncodable`—Same as `ISecurityEncodable`, but the methods to convert to/from XML also take the policy level into account

Microsoft provides an example custom membership condition with a whitepaper at `http://www.gotdotnet.com`. You might find this helpful if you want to implement your own membership condition.

TIP

If you plan on creating a custom evidence class and a corresponding custom membership condition class, you should place both classes in the same assembly. The resulting assembly will need to be added to the "policy assembly list" of security policy, so creating multiple assemblies would require you to place all of them in this list.

In addition to the assemblies that define your custom policy classes, you will need to add the transitive closure of all referenced assemblies to the policy assembly list. That is, all assemblies your custom policy classes rely on will also need to be added to the list.

The `IMembershipCondition` Interface

The `IMembershipCondition` interface defines the primary methods that a membership condition must implement. It has four methods:

- `Check`—This is the fundamental method of a membership condition. It returns `true` or `false` to note if a given assembly's evidence matches the membership condition.

- `Copy`—This simply returns a new membership condition object that is equal to the current membership condition.

- `Equals`—This determines if two membership condition objects have equivalent states.

- `ToString`—This prints out a friendly name for the membership condition. The output is used in security policy administration tools like `caspol.exe`.

The `ISecurityEncodable` Interface

The `ISecurityEncodable` interface defines methods that allow the security policy engine to serialize and deserialize membership conditions. It has two methods:

- `ToXml`—This method turns the given membership condition into a `SecurityElement`, which is the intermediary between raw XML text that represents a security object and the security object itself. It takes no arguments.

- `FromXml`—This converts a `SecurityElement` into a membership condition. The only argument is the `SecurityElement` to translate.

NOTE

The `System.Security.SecurityElement` class defines a lightweight, XML object model for security objects. It exists so that each security object doesn't need to understand XML or call into a general-purpose XML parser.

Attributes of `SecurityElement`s are name/value pairs in the XML object. Security objects generally store internal states in attributes. Children are nested XML objects inside a given `SecurityElement`. Membership conditions don't have children, but code groups (which are covered later in this chapter) do.

The `ISecurityPolicyEncodable` **Interface**

The `ISecurityPolicyEncodable` interface provides an additional way for the security policy engine to serialize and deserialize a membership condition. It has two methods:

- `ToXml`—This is similar to the `ToXml` method on the `ISecurityEncodable` interface. It converts a membership condition to a `SecurityElement`. However, this method also takes a `PolicyLevel` object as an argument in case the translation would differ depending on the `PolicyLevel`.

- `FromXml`—This is similar to the `FromXml` method on the `ISecurityEncodable` interface. As with this interface's `ToXml` method, the difference is that it takes a `PolicyLevel` as an argument.

NOTE

No default membership conditions in the .NET Framework create `SecurityElements` differently when called with the `ISecurityPolicyEncodable` methods as compared to the `ISecurityEncodable` methods. The `ISecurityPolicyEncodable` interface is provided for the possible benefit of developers writing custom membership conditions.

Code Groups

Now that we have covered membership conditions, it is logical to consider how they are used in the bigger picture. This is where code groups come into play. Code groups roughly define bindings between membership conditions and permission sets. If code matches the membership condition in a code group, it is granted a permission set.

From a high-level point of view, code groups are more than a binding between membership conditions and permission sets. They represent the intention of how much trust to grant code. For example, you may want to allow code loaded from your company's Web site to have full use of the network, but not code loaded from any other Web site. Different code groups can be constructed to express these intentions.

To understand code groups in depth, it is necessary to cover the following issues:

- Code groups are constructed from a membership condition and a policy statement.

- Code groups were designed to be placed into hierarchies.

- There are several different types of code groups provided by the .NET Framework.

- As with membership conditions, code groups are extensible security objects.

Code Group Construction

The base code group class, System.Security.Policy.CodeGroup, has one constructor. Its two arguments are a membership condition and a PolicyStatement. The membership condition argument can be either one of the default membership conditions covered earlier or a custom membership condition. The PolicyStatement is really just a dressed up PermissionSet object. It either contains a PermissionSet alone or a PermissionSet with a PolicyStatementAttribute. The attribute is one of the following values:

- All
- Exclusive
- LevelFinal
- Nothing

The meaning of the Exclusive and LevelFinal attributes will be covered later in the chapter. All means Exclusive and LevelFinal, and Nothing means neither Exclusive nor LevelFinal.

Some code group classes derived from the CodeGroup class have slightly different constructors. However, they all either have to determine the membership condition and permission set by values from the constructor or from hard-coded values in the code group itself. Also, they all need to deal with PolicyStatementAttributes in some fashion.

Code Group Hierarchies

Code groups were meant to be made into hierarchies. The reason for this is to allow complex intentions to be expressed by .NET Framework users. If a user only wants to grant certain rights to code from sites in the trusted IE security zone, he or she could create the code group hierarchy illustrated in Figure 8.1. In this example, MyPermissionSet is some user-defined permission set.

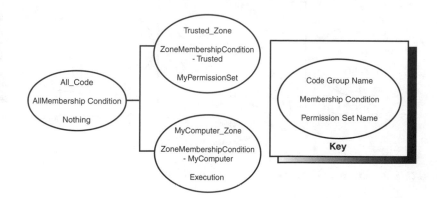

FIGURE 8.1 Example code group hierarchy.

To see what permissions an assembly should be granted from a code group hierarchy, the Common Language Runtime will call `Resolve` on the root code group object. Note that the root of the example hierarchy in Figure 8.1 matches all code and has an empty permission set. Code from a site in the trusted zone, though, will be granted the permissions in `MyPermissionSet`. Similarly, code loaded from the local computer will only have the right to execute. This occurs because the root code group will see if the assembly matches any of its children. If it does match a child code group, the child's permission set is added to the parent by unioning it (by calling `PermissionSet.Union`). This process continues until no more children code groups match.

Code group hierarchies are where the `PolicyStatementAttribute Exclusive` comes into play. If a code group has this attribute, any assembly matching the code group should not be evaluated by any other code groups in the hierarchy. The assembly should only be granted the permissions from the exclusive code group. No unions are performed from the different permission sets of matching code group. Figure 8.2 shows an example of this. If a .NET Framework user is browsing to an Internet site that tries to load assembly A from `www.goodsite.com` and assembly B from `www.badsite.com`, the following will happen:

- Assembly A will match the code groups `All_Code` and `Internet_Zone`. The resulting permission grant will contain the union of the permission sets `Execution` and `Internet`.

- Assembly B will match the code groups `All_Code` and `Bad_Site`. Because the `Bad_Site` code group is exclusive, the resulting permission grant will only contain the `Nothing` set. That will prevent the assembly from even loading. If the `Bad_Site` code group did not have the `Exclusive` flag, the resulting permission grant would have contained the ability to execute because the `All_Code` group grants that permission.

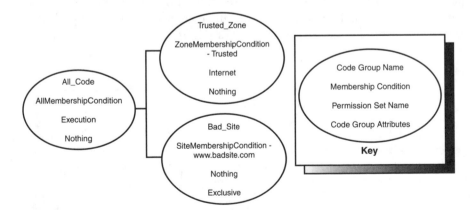

FIGURE 8.2   Example of an exclusive code group in a code group hierarchy.

NOTE

If some assembly matches two different code groups in the same hierarchy that both have the `Exclusive` flag set, this is considered an error. The Common Language Runtime will throw a `System.Security.Policy.PolicyException` while trying to load the assembly. The default security policy doesn't ship with any exclusive code groups, so this error condition can only occur via a user or administrator's change to policy.

Code Groups Provided by the .NET Framework

There are a handful of code group classes provided by the .NET Framework. Each one is designed with slightly different semantics for what permission sets are granted or how to deal with child code groups. Table 8.2 lists all of these classes with some details.

TABLE 8.2   Full List of Default Code Groups Provided by the .NET Framework

Code Group Class	Description
CodeGroup	This is the abstract, base class that the rest of the code group classes use. Because it is abstract, no code group objects can be instantiated with this type.
UnionCodeGroup	This is the "standard" code group used in the .NET Framework. It is constructed from a membership condition and a policy statement. If the membership condition matches an assembly's evidence, it grants that assembly the permission set that is part of the original policy statement. It will union the permission sets of all matching child code groups when determining the permission set grant.
FileCodeGroup	The constructor for this code group has a membership condition and a `FileIOPermissionAccess` value. If the membership condition matches an assembly's evidence, it grants that assembly file access to the assembly's directory of origin. For example, if an assembly is loaded from the directory `\\FileServer\Share\Application`, a FileCodeGroup will grant that assembly the ability to access files in the directory `\\FileServer\Share\Application` and all its subdirectories. The type of file access is determined by the `FileIOPermissionAccess` value. It merges permission sets from matching child code groups in the same manner as the `UnionCodeGroup`.
FirstMatchCodeGroup	This code group is constructed from a membership condition and a policy statement. If the membership condition matches an assembly's evidence, it grants that assembly the permission set that is part of the original policy statement. It will not union the granted permission sets of all child code groups to determine the assembly's permission set grant. Instead, it will only union the permission set of the first matching child code group with its own.

TABLE 8.2   Continued

Code Group Class	Description
NetCodeGroup	The NetCodeGroup's constructor only takes a membership condition. If the membership condition matches an assembly's evidence, it examines the assembly's evidence to find a piece of Url evidence. If Url evidence is found, the code group grants the assembly a WebPermission that allows network access to the assembly's site of origin using the same network protocol except for http, which allows connecting back to the server via http or https. For example, if an assembly is loaded from http:// www.microsoft.com/application/assembly.dll, a NetCodeGroup will grant the assembly the ability to access www.microsoft.com using only the http or https protocol. If the same assembly were loaded from ftp://ftp.microsoft.com/application/assembly.dll, it could only connect to ftp.microsoft.com using the ftp protocol. This code group merges permission sets from matching child code groups in the same manner as the UnionCodeGroup.

NOTE

The .NET Framework security administration tools only fully support the UnionCodeGroup class to create new code groups not in the default security policy. To utilize the other types of code groups, you must construct security policies programmatically, modify the security policy files manually, or deal with raw XML text in the UI administration tool. Default policy files are covered later in this chapter in the section "Working with Policy Levels", and policy administration tools are covered in Chapter 18, "Administering Security Policy Using the .Net Framework Configuration Tool," and Chapter 19, "Administering .NET Framework Security Policy Using Scripts and Security APIs."

Code Group Extensibility

Unlike membership conditions, creating a new type of code group does not require implementing a set of interfaces. Instead, a developer needs to extend the abstract class System.Security.Policy.CodeGroup. The following list of methods and properties must be overridden:

- Copy—This method makes a deep copy of a given code group. This means that any children of the target code group should be copied, in addition to any other objects being held by the code group.

- Resolve—This is the primary method that the .NET Framework will use when calling the code group. It will get called to determine the granted permissions of every loaded assembly. Its argument is an Evidence object, and its return value is a policy statement. The expected work a code group should perform begins by determining whether the evidence matches it. Presumably, this is done by calling `Check` on a membership condition passed in the constructor or created by the code group. If the assembly's evidence matches, the code group must construct a permission set to return. That permission set is combined with an optional `PolicyStatementAttribute` to form the `PolicyStatement` to return.

- `ResolveMatchingCodeGroups`—This method is used by the .NET Framework to help administrators see which code groups apply to an assembly. See the `-resolvegroup` option of the tool `caspol.exe` for an example of how this method is utilized. Its argument is an `Evidence` object, and it returns a `CodeGroup` object. This method should work similar to the first half of a `Resolve` call. If the evidence matches the code group's membership condition, check which child code groups apply. The returned `CodeGroup` object should include any matching children.

- `AttributeString`—This property returns a string representation of the `PolicyStatementAttribute` applied to that code group. For example, a code group with the flag `PolicyStatementAttribute.Exclusive` would return the `AttributeString` `Exclusive`. If a code group doesn't use a `PolicyStatementAttribute`, it should return `null`.

- `MergeLogic`—This property returns a string representation of the logic used to merge `PolicyStatements` of matching child code groups. `UnionCodeGroup`, `FileCodeGroup`, and `NetCodeGroup` return `Union`. `FirstMatchCodeGroup` returns `First Match`. No convention exists for naming merge logic that doesn't follow either of these techniques, although most code group implementers will probably want to follow `Union` logic.

- `PermissionSetName`—If a code group takes a `PolicyStatement` or `PermissionSet` in its constructor, this property returns the name of the permission set (if it has one). If the permission set has no name, it returns a null reference. For code groups that return dynamically computed permission sets (for example, the `NetCodeGroup`), a description of the permission set is acceptable.

If a code group is constructed from objects other than a membership condition and a `PolicyStatement`, all of the following methods need to be overridden. Otherwise, none of them need to be overridden.

- `CreateXml`—This method serves the same purpose as `ToXml` for membership conditions. However, because `ToXml` cannot be overridden, this method can be. The `CodeGroup` implementation of `ToXml` will call `CreateXml`.

- `Equals`—`Equals` should be overridden so that the .NET Framework understands how to check for equality of two different code group objects of the same type.

- GetHashCode—If Equals needs to be overridden, so does GetHashCode. GetHashCode is used to add code groups to data structures like hash tables. If two different code groups return the same hash code, it makes those data structures less efficient.

- ParseXml—This method is equivalent to FromXml. However, FromXml cannot be overridden, so classes derived from CodeGroup can only override this method. CodeGroup's implementation of FromXml will call ParseXml.

Policy Levels

Now we have code groups and code group hierarchies made up of membership conditions and permission sets. These aren't quite enough to understand security policy, though. Policy levels complete the picture.

This section will cover the following points about policy levels:

- The contents of a policy level

- The four different policy levels

- How to work with policy levels

Policy Level Contents

First, policy levels are represented by the System.Security.Policy.PolicyLevel class. This class has no public constructor because policy levels cannot be constructed arbitrarily. Rather, the system creates policy levels that can be enumerated by calling the method System.Security.SecurityManager.PolicyHierarchy.

Policy levels are constructed by the system using three different, but related items. The first is a list of named permission sets. The second is a code group hierarchy. The third is a list of "full trust" assemblies.

Named Permission Set List

The list of named permission sets has two kinds of permission sets. The first are immutable permission sets. These are permission sets that the system defined and cannot change. The immutable permission sets are as follows:

- Nothing—This permission set is empty. It contains no references to any individual permissions.

- Execution—This permission set only contains the Execution flag of the SecurityPermission. Code granted to just this permission set will only be able to execute. It will not be allowed to perform any trusted actions, such as reading files or accessing the network.

- `SkipVerification`—This permission set contains only the `SkipVerification` flag of the `SecurityPermission`. Code that is granted this permission is allowed to bypass type safety rules normally enforced by the .NET Framework. Code that can bypass these rules can effectively do anything, so this permission should be granted with care.

- `Internet`—This permission set contains a set of permissions you may judge appropriate for code from the Internet zone. This includes permissions to execute, store a limited amount of information on the client, display UI, access files listed by the user, and print documents.

- `LocalIntranet`—This permission set contains a set of permissions deemed safe by authors of the Common Language Runtime for code loaded from the local intranet. This includes everything from the `Internet` permission set and the ability to read some environment variables, emit assemblies using reflection APIs, use the event log, use DNS services, and assert permissions.

- `FullTrust`—This permission set is simply a permission set marked as unrestricted. It contains no references to individual permissions. Any permission that implements the `IUnrestrictedPermission` interface is completely enclosed by this permission set, even if it is not a permission that ships as part of the .NET Framework. The only shipping permissions that do not implement this interface are the identity permissions described in Chapter 6, "Permissions: The Workhorse of Code Access Security."

In addition to these immutable permission sets, there is one default mutable permission set. It is named `Everything` and contains every permission shipped with the .NET Framework. Each permission it contains is unrestricted except the `SecurityPermission`. The `SecurityPermission` in the `Everything` set is missing the `SkipVerification` flag. Thus, this permission set should cover everything except the ability to skip verification.

TIP

The `Everything` permission set can be helpful to compiler writers. It is highly desirable for compilers to emit verifiable code for the security benefits. (See Chapter 11, "Verification and Validation: The Backbone of .NET Framework Security," for details on code verification.) Running "caspol.exe -machine -chggroup MyComputer_Zone Everything" changes the default security policy on a machine so unverifiable code will fail to execute when run from the local machine.

Permission sets can be added to this list. Any added permission sets will always be mutable.

Code Group Hierarchy

The code group hierarchy in a policy level is its primary information. This hierarchy always has one root code group that can have any number of children down to any depth.

Each code group in the hierarchy is exactly the same as the code groups mentioned earlier in this chapter. The permission sets used in the code groups must come from the permission set list. That is, no permission set can be mentioned in a code group unless it is in the permission set list.

When an assembly is evaluated against a code group hierarchy, the root code group will come up with a single permission set based on that assembly's evidence. That permission set is the permission grant for the assembly according to the policy level. By default, an assembly being loaded is assumed to have no permissions. Thus, unless some permission is granted by the policy level, the assembly will not be granted that permission.

"Full Trust" Assembly List

One issue that arises during security policy resolution is that recursive loads may be necessary. Take the permission `System.Net.DnsPermission` as an example. This permission lies in the assembly `System.dll`. When a policy level is loaded, all referenced assemblies must be loaded, so if a permission set in the policy level being loaded contains the `DnsPermission`, the assembly `System.dll` must be loaded by the policy system. However, when `System.dll` is being loaded, its granted permission set must be determined, which will cause the policy levels to get loaded again. This is a never-ending cycle between policy level loading and `System.dll` grant set determination.

To break the recursive policy load problem, policy levels have a list of "fully trusted" assemblies. While policy levels are being loaded and assembly references are being resolved, any assembly in the list is assumed to have been granted all permissions. In the example with `DnsPermission`, `System.dll` is assumed to be fully trusted while the policy level is being loaded.

Whenever you create a custom security class (for example, a custom permission) that you want to add to a policy level, you *must* first add the assembly containing that class to the policy level's full trust assembly list. Skipping this step will cause policy errors whenever a .NET Framework application is launched. If you get into a state where an assembly was not added to the full trust list when it was supposed to have been, you will have to edit or erase the file containing that policy level.

The Four Policy Levels

Now that we know what a policy level contains, it may be perplexing to find out that the .NET Framework has four policy levels: Enterprise, Machine, User, and

Application Domain. To understand the reasoning for this, we should look at how the levels work together and the benefits of having four different levels.

How Policy Levels Interact

Each policy level is independent of every other policy level. The permission set list, code group hierarchy, and assembly list could be different in each level. The only way they come together is through the way their results are assessed.

During policy resolution of an assembly, the assembly's evidence is evaluated against each policy level individually. This is done in the `SecurityManager.ResolvePolicy` method. Each policy level's code group hierarchy has a permission set that it returns. The permission sets from each level are intersected by calling `PermissionSet.Intersect` to determine the overall allowable permission set for the assembly. By intersecting the permission sets from each policy level, each policy level determines a maximum permission set.

In addition to `ResolvePolicy`, which calls `Resolve` on each policy level, `SecurityManager` has the `ResolvePolicyGroups` method that calls `ResolveMatchingCodeGroups` on each policy level. The results are used by administration tools to display all the code groups that match an assembly.

Benefits of Having Four Policy Levels

The reason for having multiple policy levels addresses the problem of how to handle the intentions of disparate parties. Specifically, the network administrator, the administrator of a machine, a .NET Framework application user, and a .NET Framework developer can all apply specific policies to meet different goals. Each party is given an equal part in determining permission grants of .NET Framework assemblies. Every policy level has a "suggested" policy grant, and the system determines the lowest common denominator of all the different suggestions.

As shown in Figure 8.3, the enterprise level, which is administered by network administrators, affects all machines in a organization. The machine level, which is administered by machine administrators, affects all users on a machine. The user level, which is controlled by individual users, affects all app domains in programs run by that user. Developers control app domain policy levels for the programs they write.

The Enterprise, Machine, and User policy levels are loaded from configuration files on the machine. The purpose of the AppDomain level is to allow a developer to restrict the rights of code he or she wants to execute. It doesn't make sense for an administrator or user to be able to do anything with this level, so there are no policy files for the AppDomain level.

For an example of how these different policy levels might be used, take the case of Julie, a company X employee who browses the Web over lunch. To run managed content from the Web, she changed the default security policy to grant the "Internet" permission set to code from the Internet zone. The IT department of company X may only want its employees to be able to execute mobile code if it comes from a small list of software publishers (identified by Authenticode signatures) it deems safe. It can deploy an enterprise policy that makes this restriction on all its employees. So, when Julie executes code from one of these publishers, code runs without problem, although she is not able to run code from any other publisher. Note that she could not add software publishers, as only the least common denominator of the policy levels are taken, and the enterprise policy level was deployed by the IT department to make this restriction.

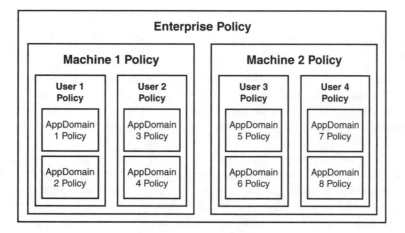

FIGURE 8.3   The scope of the four different policy levels.

The LevelFinal PolicyStatementAttribute can be used to restrict what "lower" policy levels can do. The policy levels listed from "highest" to "lowest" are Enterprise, Machine, and User. If an assembly matches a code group with the LevelFinal attribute, no lower policy levels are evaluated for that assembly. The AppDomain level is always evaluated if it exists, regardless of the LevelFinal attribute. In the previous example, if the IT department marked the code group for the safe Web sites with the LevelFinal attribute, Julie would not be able to further restrict code coming from the safe Web sites.

Working with Policy Levels

While there are four different policy levels, only three of them, Enterprise, Machine, and User, are actually persisted to files. The locations of those files are listed in Table 8.3. The AppDomain level is special in that it can only be created programmatically.

TABLE 8.3 Locations of the Policy Level Files

Policy Level	File Location
Enterprise	`<.NET Framework Version-Specific Root Directory>\config\` `enterprisesec.config`
Machine	`<.NET Framework Version-Specific Root Directory>\config\` `security.config`
User (Windows NT, Windows 2000, and Windows XP)	`%userprofile%\Application Data\Microsoft\CLR Security Config\` `<.NET Framework Version>\security.config`
User (Windows 98 and Windows Me)	`%windir%\<username>\Microsoft\CLR Security Config\` `<.NET Framework Version>\security.config`

Chapter 18 covers the use of the Common Language Runtime Configuration Tool. This GUI tool has some simple ways to modify the Enterprise, Machine, and User policy levels. In addition, it can be used to create MSI files that contain the policy level files. These MSI files can be used to deploy standard policy files to different machines.

Chapter 19 covers the use of `caspol.exe`, a tool that can script policy changes to the Enterprise, Machine, and User policy levels. This chapter also covers programmatic changes to security policy levels, including the AppDomain level.

If you want to enumerate the `PolicyLevel` objects that correspond to the different policy levels, you can simply call the `System.Security.SecurityManager.PolicyHierarchy` method. Each `PolicyLevel` object in the enumeration can be distinguished by looking at its `Label` property. This property is a nonlocalized string that contains one of the following: `"Enterprise"`, `"Machine"`, `"User"`, or `"AppDomain"`. If an application didn't set AppDomain policy, no `PolicyLevel` object exists for that level. The `PolicyLevel` objects also have the property `StoreLocation` that points to the file where the policy level was loaded, if it was loaded from a file.

NOTE

When the .NET Framework is installed, there actually are no policy files installed on the computer. Instead, the Common Language Runtime has some hard-coded defaults for the different policy levels. Whenever a managed program is executed for the first time, the security policy files are written to disk. Thus, if a policy file exists for a given policy level, the .NET Framework will use it. If no policy file exists for a given level, the hard-coded defaults are used.

As mentioned earlier in the chapter, each policy level has a permission set list, a code group hierarchy, and an assembly list. On `PolicyLevel` objects, these correspond to the `NamedPermissionSets` property, the `RootCodeGroup` property, and the `FullTrustAssemblies` property, respectively.

Default Security Policy

The .NET Framework default security policy is the culmination of the default policies of all four policy levels. Each policy level has a hard-coded default that is intended to provide a usable and secure environment.

All of the default policy levels are identical with reference to the permission set lists and assembly lists. The permission set lists contain all the named permission sets described earlier in the chapter and no other permission sets. The assembly lists contain the following assemblies:

- `mscorlib.resources`
- `System.dll`
- `System.resources`
- `System.Data.dll`
- `System.Data.resources`
- `System.Drawing.dll`
- `System.Drawing.resources`
- `System.Messaging.dll`
- `System.Messaging.resources`
- `System.ServiceProcess.dll`
- `System.ServiceProcess.resources`
- `System.DirectoryServices.dll`
- `System.DirectoryServices.resources`

In addition, `mscorlib.dll` is always considered a fully trusted policy assembly, even though it is not in the list.

With regard to the code group hierarchy, the Enterprise and User default policy levels are simple and identical. The Machine policy level has a larger, more complex hierarchy that really does the work of making default policy "locked down." There is no default AppDomain policy level. If it isn't set by an application, it doesn't exist.

Enterprise and User Policy

The code group hierarchies of these two policy levels contain a single node—the root code group. This root code group is a UnionCodeGroup with an AllMembershipCondition and the FullTrust permission set. Hence, all code matches the root code group and is granted all permissions that implement the IUnrestricted interface.

The most important point to understand with these policy levels is that when their grant sets are intersected with some permission set P, the result is P (minus any identity permissions). That is why only one of the four policy levels needs to have a more complex default. Anything restricted in that policy level will define the total default restrictions.

Machine Policy

The machine policy's code group hierarchy is primarily based on the IE security zone model. Figure 8.4 shows a graphical representation of the machine policy level's code group hierarchy. No code groups in default security policy have any PolicyStatementAttributes. Remember that these are the defaults for SP1. The default code group hierarchy of the original release is different.

The root of the code group matches all code, but grants no permissions. Below that lies a code group for every security zone. All executing code falls into only one zone, and is thus given that zone's permissions. The following is some rationale behind the decisions made in constructing the default machine code group hierarchy:

- Users have to take action to copy or install code onto their machines, so that code can be granted full trust.

- Code from an Internet site deemed "trusted" needs to be able to display basic UI, store state data, print, open files that the user specifies, and connect back (via the network) to the same site where the code originated.

- Code from your intranet should be able to do everything code from a trusted site can do. In addition, it should be able to get DNS information from the network, use the event log, have unlimited UI capabilities, emit new assemblies, read some environment variables, and read any files in the directory where the executing assembly originated.

- Code can only end up in the untrusted zone by an explicit action from an end user or administrator, so that code should not be granted any permissions.

- It isn't clear how many permissions should be given to code in the Internet zone. In order to provide "locked down" default behavior, no trust is given to that code (which prevents execution). However, many users will probably want to grant some permissions to Internet code. The "Internet" permission set provides a good example of what permissions to consider granting.

- Any system code on the local machine should be given full trust. System code is designated by the use of strong names on assemblies, which is discussed in Chapter 9, "Understanding the Concepts of Strong Naming Assemblies." Special code groups are provided for system code so that they are still given full trust if the MyComputer zone code group is locked down.

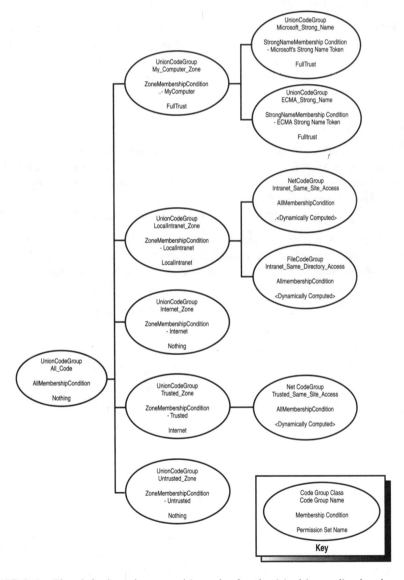

FIGURE 8.4   The default code group hierarchy for the Machine policy level.

Summary

Membership conditions are some of the basic building blocks of .NET Framework security policy. A membership condition object examines the evidence on an assembly and reports whether or not it matches. There are a set of default membership condition classes that look at the different default types of evidence. .NET Framework developers can also write their own membership conditions classes to examine default or custom types of evidence.

Code groups are objects that bind a membership condition to a permission set. When an assembly matches a membership condition, the code group grants the permission set to the assembly. Code groups are formed into hierarchies to express more complicated intentions. If an assembly matches a code group, all of its children are examined, too. For the most common code group class, the `UnionCodeGroup`, the permission sets from matching children are unioned with the parent's granted permission set. The resulting union of the root code group's permission set and all matching children's code groups is the final permission set to grant the assembly.

There are several default types of code groups. Different code groups handle the permission sets to grant and the merging logic with children differently. As with membership conditions, .NET Framework developers also have the ability to create their own code group classes.

The final piece of security policy we covered is the policy level. A policy level has three pieces—a permission set list, a code group hierarchy, and a list of assemblies. .NET Framework security policy has four levels—Enterprise, Machine, User, and AppDomain. Each policy level is controlled by different entities—network administrators, machine administrators, users, and application developers. As assemblies are loaded, they are resolved against each level to produce a set of granted permissions. The grant set from each level is intersected to produce the grant set for the entire assembly.

9

Understanding the Concepts of Strong Naming Assemblies

By Rudi Martin

Within the Windows environment today, there exists a serious code deployment problem commonly referred to as "DLL Hell." This situation arises when multiple applications share common code—usually in the form of a dynamic link library, or DLL. Each application may require features from the DLL that are specific to a particular version of that code; therefore, it is common practice for applications to ship their own copies of shared DLLs as part of their main product deployment. During product installation, these updated DLLs may overwrite any previous version already installed.

This leads to severe management problems. Installing one application may cause previously installed applications to begin failing due to version incompatibilities with the new copy of the shared DLL. Such problems are hard to isolate and track down, especially because they might not be noticed at once. Furthermore, even once the offending DLL is pinpointed, simple solutions may not be available. Simply reverting the DLL to its previous state (a nontrivial task in itself) might render the application that updated the DLL inoperative.

DLL versioning might seem to be the answer to this problem (during installation, simply select whether to keep an existing DLL or update it with the supplied copy based on the embedded version—the most recent version wins). This is problematic for a number of reasons:

- Version updates are not always backwards compatible. While every effort should be made to ensure backwards compatibility, sometimes this is an impossible goal. So installing a later version of a shared DLL might conceivably break some applications.

- It's possible that an application publisher may take a copy of a commonly shared DLL and include additional functionality before distributing the updated DLL. While this is not good practice, it does happen. This creates a branch in the DLL versioning scheme that makes identifying a highest version impossible.

- Sometimes the clash in DLLs is purely accidental. The DLLs are unrelated and merely share the same name. This can happen relatively frequently when short DLL names are chosen and installation is performed into a heavily shared area of the operating system's file system, such as the Windows system directory.

The .NET Framework solution to this problem is to allow multiple versions of a piece of code to coexist peacefully together, allowing applications to use whichever version with which they are known to work. This is known as side-by-side support, and a full description of the topic is outside the scope of this book.

Strong names play a part in the side-by-side story by providing a mechanism to name code in an unambiguous fashion, avoiding the problem of accidental name-space collision previously mentioned. They also provide a means of ensuring that no one can modify or extend the code belonging to another publisher, which serves to simplify the management of shared code and has interesting security ramifications of its own.

This chapter introduces the .NET Framework concept known as a *strong name*. Upon completion of the chapter, you should have a grasp of the following:

- Outlines of the problems strong names are designed to solve

- Concepts and terminology used when dealing with strong names

- The high-level algorithms used in the design and implementation of strong names within the .NET Framework

- The differences between strong names and Authenticode signatures

NOTE

Further information regarding the use of strong names within the programming environment can be found in Chapter 25, "Implementing a Secure Assembly."

To understand the concept of strong names, you must first look at the assembly, a new concept introduced by the .NET Framework.

Assemblies and Identity

Assemblies are the unit of code deployment in the .NET Framework, roughly analogous to the .dll and .exe files used within the Windows environment today. A single assembly can be composed of multiple files, but exactly one of these files will contain what's known as the *assembly manifest*—a database describing the overall layout of the assembly as well as various global attributes. The basic layout of an assembly is shown in Figure 9.1.

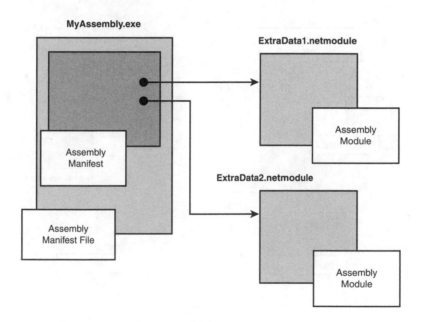

FIGURE 9.1   The structure of an assembly.

Assemblies are referenced (for example, from other assemblies and in assembly-qualified type names) through the use of names. These names can be complex entities, including a version number and culture reference on top of the text name. The text name is usually the name of the file containing the assembly manifest without the file extension. For example, an assembly contained within `MyAssembly.dll` most likely has the text name `MyAssembly`.

Strong naming is a process whereby an assembly name can be further qualified by the identity of the publisher. Thus, the likelihood of naming conflicts is greatly reduced (if we assume that a publisher can handle its own internal naming policy without conflicts). As a result, two publishers can safely distribute an assembly named `MyAssembly` without fear of ambiguity.

The identity of the publisher is used in the same way as a namespace that qualifies a classname or a file system path that qualifies a filename. This concept is illustrated in Figure 9.2.

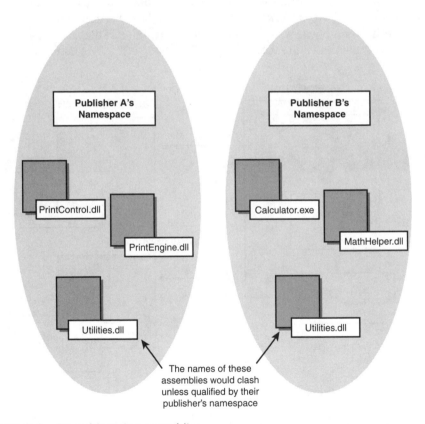

FIGURE 9.2   Disambiguating assemblies.

To encourage the use of this mechanism in scenarios where naming conflicts are most likely (the use of shared code as described earlier), installation of an assembly into the global assembly cache requires that the assembly be strong named.

The strong aspect of strong naming derives from the fact that the publisher name-space is protected—publisher B cannot publish an assembly in publisher A's name-space. This simplifies the understanding of assembly dependencies, because you now know that a copy of publisher A's assembly, even if provided to you by publisher B, cannot have been modified from its original condition. This also makes strong names useful from a security standpoint:

- The strong name can be used as input to security policy, in that permissions can be assigned to an assembly based on the identity of the assembly's publisher. This is covered in Chapter 8, "Membership Conditions, Code Groups, and Policy Levels: The Brick and Mortar of Security Policy."

- Individual methods on a class can restrict access based on the strong name of the caller's assembly. This is covered in Chapter 25.

Public/Private Key Pairs

A cryptographic technique, namely digital signing, is used to enforce this protection of the publisher's namespace. At the heart of the implementation are two related sets of binary data known as the *public* and *private* keys. As the names suggest, the public key may be freely distributed, whereas the private key is a secret known only to the publisher.

The keys are used as input to encryption and decryption algorithms—data encrypted via the public key can only be decrypted via the private key and vice versa (as illustrated in Figure 9.3). The RSA digital signing algorithm is used for this purpose.

The public key is used to represent the publisher's identity. In textual contexts, this is usually represented as a string of hexadecimal digits. For example, the following is the public key used by Microsoft for its .NET Framework components:

```
0024000004800000940000000602000000240000525341310004000000100
010007d1fa57c4aed9f0a32e84aa0faefd0de9e8fd6aec8f87fb03766c83
4c99921eb23be79ad9d5dcc1dd9ad236132102900b723cf980957fc4e177
108fc607774f29e8320e92ea05ece4e821c0a5efe8f1645c4c0c93c1ab99
285d622caa652c1dfad63d745d6f2de5f17e5eaf0fc4963d261c8a124365
18206dc093344d5ad293
```

Due to their size, such public keys can be unwieldy and difficult to use in situations were they might be manipulated by humans—within source code or configuration files, for example. For this reason, an abbreviated form, the so-called public key token, is often used. Public key tokens strike a balance between usability (they are much shorter than full public keys) and security (it is extremely difficult to find a second public key that will generate an identical public key token). Cryptographic hashing techniques are used to generate the public key token from the public key (the token is a truncated form of the SHA1 hash of the public key).

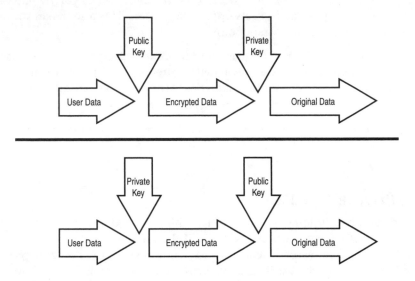

FIGURE 9.3   Public/private key pairs and algorithms.

The following is the public key token for the Microsoft public key previously given:

```
b03f5f7f11d50a3a
```

Signing and Verifying Assemblies

The publisher's public key is embedded in the assembly's metadata along with the other components of the assembly name (text name, version and culture). But it is not enough to simply supply the public key in this fashion. After all, the key is public and therefore nothing would stop another publisher from stamping its assemblies with your key. To enforce the strength of the name, you must be able to verify that the contents of the assembly were indeed generated by the advertised publisher.

It's important that the entire content of the assembly (including external modules for multifile assemblies) are covered by this verification. Otherwise, a malicious third party could modify a valid assembly and redistribute the result. Even innocuous-seeming aspects of the assembly, such as user interface resources, are potential security vulnerabilities if left open to modification by third parties. For example, simply changing the text of a dialog prompt could trick a user into revealing password information, potentially in a publicly visible manner. See Figure 9.4 for an example.

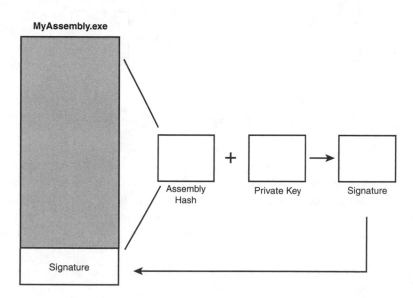

FIGURE 9.4   Deceiving the user into supplying sensitive information.

To tie together the publisher identity—the public key—and the contents of the assembly, a digital signature is computed and written into the assembly during compilation. The signature is formed by computing a cryptographic hash over the contents of the assembly (essentially, a very condensed summary of the data) and encoding the result using the publisher's private key. Figure 9.5 illustrates the signing process.

FIGURE 9.5   Computing a strong name signature.

To perform validation, the signature is decrypted using the publisher public key (found in the assembly metadata), yielding an assembly contents hash. The hash is then recomputed for the current assembly contents and the results compared. If both hashes match, you know that the current assembly contents remain identical with those from the point at which the signature was generated. Furthermore, you know that the generator of the signature was in possession of the private key corresponding to the public key found in the assembly manifest. Figure 9.6 depicts the verification process. Any attempt to modify the assembly contents will change the hash generated on verification, and storing an updated hash for the new contents requires the private key for the hash encryption phase.

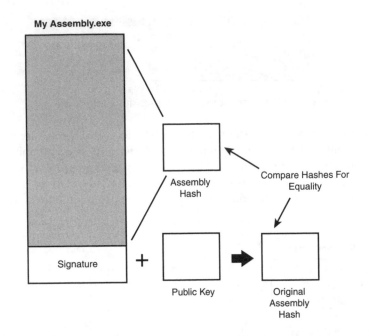

FIGURE 9.6   Verifying a strong name signature.

From this you can see that the reliability of strong name verification is dependent on two factors—the secrecy of the private key and the ability of the hash to accurately reflect the contents of the assembly. The hashing algorithm used is SHA1, which generates a 20-byte hash code. It is extremely difficult, in fact computationally unfeasible, to discover another byte sequence that will yield the same hash code under this algorithm—changing even a single bit in the input will yield a radically different hash.

In summary, the act of strong naming requires the addition of two new pieces of data to the assembly:

- The public key, which becomes visible as part of the assembly's name

- The signature, which validates the right to use the public key and allows the consistency of the assembly contents to be verified

The structure of a strong name assembly is illustrated in Figure 9.7.

The verification of any strong name assemblies is performed automatically when needed by the .NET Framework. Any assembly claiming a strong name but failing verification will fail to install into the global assembly or download cache or will fail to load at runtime.

MyAssembly.exe

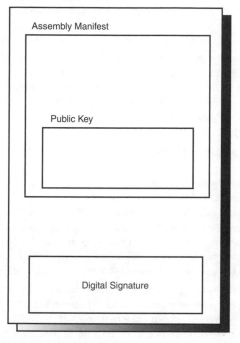

FIGURE 9.7   The strong name components on an assembly.

THE ECMA PUBLIC KEY

One public key is treated specially by the .NET Framework. This is known as the ECMA key after the European Computer Manufacturer's Association, which has determined a standard for the implementation of .NET Framework-like runtimes on other computing platforms. The ECMA key is designed to facilitate porting of the core .NET Framework class libraries to such platforms. To appreciate the problem that the ECMA solves, consider for a moment the strong names of the standard runtime libraries—mscorlib, System, System.Data, and so on. Each of these assemblies is signed with the Microsoft private key, ensuring that third parties cannot distribute altered copies that could be mistaken for the originals. This, in turn, dictates the public key (because there is a one-to-one correspondence between public and private keys). Because the public key is considered part of the assembly name, it (or rather the public key token form of it) becomes embedded in every reference from every other assembly that has a dependency.

So what happens if a publisher (let's call it Corporation X) wants to implement the core .NET Framework runtime on a new platform? It will need to implement its own versions of the standard core libraries (mscorlib, System, and so on) and while these new versions can provide all the same functionality and honor all the standardized interfaces of the Microsoft originals, no application targeted at Microsoft's runtime will actually run against them. This is because the application's assemblies will contain references to the original Microsoft core assemblies, strong named with Microsoft's public key. Corporation X cannot strong name its own assemblies with Microsoft's public key, because that would require access to Microsoft's private key—something it is not likely to be granted.

To solve this problem, the public keys embedded into the core assemblies required by the runtime are not the Microsoft public key at all. In fact, the binary blob used is not strictly a valid public key, but a simple 16-byte placeholder, the so-called ECMA key. The affected assemblies are still signed with the Microsoft private key, but the assemblies' identities are no longer pinned specifically to Microsoft. The ECMA key has the following form (as represented in hexadecimal text):

00000000000000000400000000000000

When used as a publisher identity, the ECMA key is treated as a normal public key distinct from the Microsoft public key. It has a public key token computed in exactly the same manner as for all other public keys, and identity operations are performed through byte-by-byte comparison as is normal. However, when its use is required as a cryptographic public key, as is the case during strong name signing and verification, the Microsoft runtime automatically converts the ECMA key into the Microsoft public key. Corporation X would implement its runtime to perform the conversion from ECMA key to the Corporation X public key instead.

In this fashion, assemblies using only core runtime components remain portable between differing platforms. The runtime provider for each platform can still strong name sign its core assemblies to ensure integrity without compromising such portability. The ECMA key doesn't introduce any security weaknesses because it does not allow core assemblies to be signed by an arbitrary private key. Rather, core assemblies *must* be signed by the private key of the runtime provider whose runtime is being used. Put another way, for any given implementation of the runtime, the core assemblies must be signed by the runtime provider itself.

In summary, the goal of the ECMA key is to allow a slightly more generalized strong name binding than usual, namely allowing binding to the publisher of the runtime in use, rather than to a fixed publisher.

Delay Signing Assemblies

Within a development environment, it might not always be feasible or convenient to gain access to the publisher private key to strong name the assemblies being built. This is a consequence of the need to keep the private key secure—if the key is easily available to the development team, it is increasingly difficult to ensure that the key is not compromised or even to detect such a compromise should it occur.

Consequently, many publishers will keep the private key in a secure location, possibly embedded in specially designed cryptographic hardware. Strong name signing assemblies then becomes a heavyweight process because all assembly creation within the publisher is channeled through a single location. With multiple developers building multiple assemblies many times a day, this constriction can swiftly become the chief bottleneck of the development process.

Merely removing the strong name from assemblies during development does not provide a satisfactory workaround due to the identity change involved. That is, removing the publisher public key from the assembly name changes its identity, a change with ramifications just as severe as altering any other publicly visible aspect of the assembly. For example, dependent assemblies will need to be rebuilt after the public key is added to update their references with the correct public key tokens. Even worse, some references to the development assemblies may be present in code in the form of text strings (most likely in the case of late bound references). These references will not be automatically updated via a rebuild and, due to their nature, the errors will not be revealed until runtime.

Problems such as these can pose unacceptable risks to the project—the introduction of strong names in the late stages of the development cycle can invalidate previous testing and potentially introduce or uncover hitherto unseen problems, all at the worst possible time.

A solution to this dilemma can be found by noting two important facts:

- The only publicly visible aspect of strong names—and thus the only aspect that should impact dependent assemblies—is the public key component of the assembly name.

- The cryptographic security of assemblies under development is not generally an issue; developers are building their own versions of these assemblies and are unlikely to be downloading versions from any outside source.

With these points in mind, we introduce the concept of delay signing. Delay signing is a technique used by developers whereby the public key is added to the assembly name as before, granting the assembly its unique identity, but no signature is computed. Thus, no private key access is necessary.

Although delay signing does not compute a signature for the assembly being built, it does cause the space necessary for the future signature to be allocated within the image. This makes it a simple task to compute (and, if necessary, to recompute) the signature at a later date without the necessity of a full assembly rebuild. This is advantageous because it reduces the complexity of the signing process (bearing in mind that the actual signing may be performed in a secure location where it may not be possible or desirable to re-create a full build environment). Signing in such a fashion also minimizes the differences between development and release versions of the assemblies, boosting confidence that test and quality assurance passes on the development versions haven't been invalidated by the signing process. To further aid this, utilities packaged with the .NET Framework (such as the command-line tool sn) can confirm assembly images differ only by their signatures (uninitialized, delay signed state to initialized, fully signed state) and that the resulting assemblies have self-consistent signatures.

Delay signing introduces a problem of its own, because the resulting assemblies will no longer pass strong name verification and will become essentially useless. To enable their use, the strong name verification rules need to be relaxed. Development and test machines (or any machine that is to use prerelease versions of the assemblies) can be taught to skip strong name verification for the affected assemblies. This is achieved through the use of entries in the machine's registry—manipulated through the SN management tool—that lists the assemblies or groups of assemblies to skip.

For example:

```
SN -Vr MyAssembly.dll
```

This command will turn off strong name verification for just MyAssembly.dll. To turn off strong name verification for all assemblies with the same public key token, something like the following example can be used:

```
SN -Vr *,b03f5f7f11d50a3a
```

For a full description of managing strong name verification using the SN utility, see Chapter 25.

Obviously, such a technique must be used with care to avoid opening security holes. Adding such entries to the registry removes the safeguards in place when downloading code claiming a strong name based on the publisher's own public key. Administrative privilege is required by the user to add such registry entries and, in addition, the default security policy shipped with the .NET Framework limits registry access to locally installed assemblies only.

Detailed information on building delay signed assemblies and setting up environments in which they can be used is found in Chapter 25.

Comparison with Authenticode Signatures

Authenticode signatures are another mechanism used for digitally signing files in the Windows environment (and, indeed, their use is still supported in the .NET Framework). The following section briefly outlines the chief similarities and differences of the two concepts and can be safely skipped by any reader not familiar with the concept of Authenticode.

In many ways, strong names and Authenticode certificates are alike—both seek to establish publisher identity and base part of their implementation on public/private key pair cryptography and digital signing. But there are significant differences as well.

Authenticode certificates are not considered part of the assembly name, so they play no role in separating publisher namespaces. Strong names accomplish this by submitting the publisher public key as a name component.

Strong names don't use a third-party (such as Verisign™) as part of the signing and verification algorithm. This has a number of ramifications:

- Strong names are lighter weight. The implementation is simpler, the process involved is less complex, and, at the low level, code can avoid making network connections during verification.

- There is no automatic means to associate a strong name public key with the corresponding publisher. The publisher must advertise its public key or keys in an out-of-band fashion (such as documentation shipped with the product or on the company Web site).

- No means exist to revoke the use of a given strong name public key should the corresponding private key be found to be compromised. Again, publishers must take steps themselves to inform their users of the breach of security and issue new assemblies signed with an updated key pair.

Strong name verification never results in a display of a graphical user interface requiring the user to make a trust decision. All mappings from publisher public key to trust levels are made ahead of time in the security policy database. Assemblies that are not self-consistent (in other words, the signature doesn't verify with the embedded public key) are never loaded (modulo delay signed assemblies that are registered to have their verification skipped).

Summary

Strong names are a way of distinguishing similarly named assemblies from different publishers. They also provide a mechanism for ensuring that only the publisher of an assembly can modify its content—provided the publisher can guarantee the secrecy of a private key.

The identity of a publisher is represented using a public key or, in some circumstances, the shortened form known as a public key token.

A special public key known as the ECMA key is used to name all core assemblies provided in the .NET Framework. This ensures the future portability of the Framework.

During the development process, techniques exist to allow for the signing aspect of strong naming an assembly to be skipped. This allows development in the absence of a readily available private key while maintaining the maximum testability of the assemblies involved.

Strong names are roughly similar to Authenticode signatures, but provide a more integrated, lightweight solution at the cost of some flexibility.

10

Hosting Managed Code

By Rudi Martin

U p to now, we have looked at security from the point of view of a standalone application or a control or component loaded from within another application. This chapter re-examines security from the viewpoint of a hosting application. That is, an entity that loads, executes, and controls other software components—possibly those with a trust level below that of itself.

This chapter has the following goals:

- Familiarize the reader with the concept of hosting.

- Introduce the most powerful tool the .NET Framework provides to implement a host—the appdomain.

- Describe different techniques for controlling the trust level of code loaded into a hosting environment.

- Outline the use of appdomains to secure code that runs outside the scope of the .NET Framework but manipulates managed objects.

What Does Hosting Mean?

Hosting refers to the act of loading and controlling the execution of one or more software components. In this chapter, we're going to assume the unit of software component is the assembly (after all, that's the unit to which security trust levels are assigned). We're also going to restrict ourselves to looking at hosting one or more assemblies within a single process (as we'll see, this is made secure and feasible by the nature of the .NET Framework).

Think of a host as a container for other programs, as depicted in Figure 10.1.

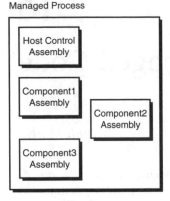

FIGURE 10.1   Hosting assemblies within a process.

Furthermore, the host typically allows components to be dynamically loaded and unloaded within this container. The security responsibilities of the host are two-fold:

- Protect the outside world (that is, other processes and the machine itself) from any malicious (or for that matter, accidental) damage from the various components loaded.

- Protect the hosted components from each other—isolate the components. This may be at the level of single components or might involve groups of components for discrete applications.

Containing Assemblies Through the Use of Appdomains

The key to achieving these goals in the .NET Framework runtime is the use of application domains (usually referred to as appdomains). These are represented by the `System.AppDomain` managed class. Each appdomain is itself a container for zero or more assemblies and, while assemblies within the same appdomain can interact freely through method calls as we've come to expect, interaction between assemblies in different appdomains is more tightly controlled. This provides the isolation needed between assemblies or groups of assemblies. Figure 10.2 illustrates the relationship between appdomains and assemblies.

Additionally, evidence can be associated with an appdomain in much the same way as it can with an assembly (allowing the appdomain to be granted a level of trust of its own). We'll look at this and why it's important later in this chapter.

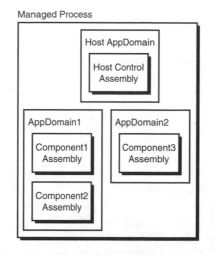

Managed Process

FIGURE 10.2 Containing assemblies within appdomains.

Appdomains are actually present in every .NET Framework process—a default appdomain is created before the first assembly is loaded. This is transparent to most managed applications; it's only when additional appdomains are needed that the explicit appdomain control is invoked. The default appdomain is fairly neutral; it has no special properties and, from a pure security point of view, is transparent (there is no evidence associated with it; therefore, the default appdomain is not granted any permissions and is not considered significant during security stack walks).

The host application need not run as managed code itself. It is perfectly possible to write an unmanaged application that starts up the .NET Framework explicitly and then interacts with managed components through the interop capabilities of the runtime (that is, treating managed objects as classic COM servers).

Explicit control of the runtime in this manner is handled through the COM interface `ICorRuntimeHost`. A full treatment of this interface (and related interfaces for controlling the garbage collector, runtime configuration, and so on) is beyond the scope of this book. To illustrate the basic concepts, the following example code starts up a runtime within the current process and explicitly creates an appdomain with a non-default application base (a file path used as a hint to find assemblies loaded within an appdomain). All error handling has been omitted for clarity.

```
ICorRuntimeHost *pCorHost;
IUnknown        *pSetup;
IAppDomainSetup *pDomainSetup;
IUnknown        *pAppDomain;
```

```
// Create a hosting environment.
CoCreateInstance(CLSID_CorRuntimeHost,
                 NULL,
                 CLSCTX_INPROC_SERVER,
                 IID_ICorRuntimeHost,
                 (void**)&pCorHost);

// Startup the runtime.
pCorHost->Start();

// Create an AppDomain Setup so we can set the AppBase.
pCorHost->CreateDomainSetup(&pSetup);

// QI for the IAppDomainSetup interface.
pSetup->QueryInterface(__uuidof(IAppDomainSetup),
                       (void**)&pDomainSetup);

// Create a BSTR (wide character string prefixed with a DWORD
// character count).
BSTR bstrDirectory = SysAllocString(L"c:\\MyDirectory");

// Set the AppBase.
pDomainSetup->put_ApplicationBase(bstrDirectory);

// Create a new AppDomain.
pCorHost->CreateDomainEx(L"My Domain",
                         pSetup,
                         NULL,
                         &pAppDomain);
```

While it is possible to code the entirety of a host in this manner (and indeed it is often necessary to code at least the initialization section of a host this way, so that runtime configuration options can be applied before the runtime first starts up), it is usually more convenient to code the majority of the host in managed code.

This is primarily due to the fact that it is easier to manipulate managed classes from the managed world itself; there are no complex marshaling or context issues to resolve.

Managed hosts use AppDomain.CreateDomain to create isolated appdomains into which to load groups of assemblies. The .NET Framework remoting services are used to communicate between appdomains, which for the most part makes the process transparent (as though objects from different appdomains were making simple method calls on one another).

By default, objects are transported across appdomain boundaries by making a copy in the target appdomain (this is done using the serialization services of the .NET Framework). This provides some level of isolation already; code in one appdomain cannot directly manipulate the state of an object in another. This technique is known as *marshal by value*. A method call from an object in appdomain A to an object in appdomain B will typically proceed as follows:

1. All the arguments to the method call are cloned in appdomain B (serialized in A and then deserialized in B).

2. The method is called in appdomain B, passing it the copied arguments. A result is computed.

3. The result is copied back into appdomain A (the result in B is no longer referenced and will be released by the garbage collector in due course).

So how do we make a call across an appdomain boundary in the first place? The key to this is that some object types are not marshal by value. Any class that derives from System.MarshalByRefObject will *not* be copied across appdomain boundaries. Instead, such objects are represented in remote appdomains by a transparent proxy object that points back to the real object in its original domain. These proxies are referred to as transparent because, from the point of view of the programmer, they look just like the real object (they have the same type and support all the same method calls).

The object we called a method on in this example was *marshal-by-reference*; we know this because an appdomain transition occurred when the method call was made (a method call on a marshal by value object returned from another appdomain will simply result in the method being invoked on the local copy).

Very importantly, the AppDomain class itself is marshal-by-reference. So when a new appdomain is created via AppDomain.CreateDomain, the appdomain object returned is in fact a proxy to the real appdomain. Method calls on this proxy will therefore take place in the newly created domain, allowing it to be controlled by the host.

A point to note here is that System.Reflection.Assembly is *not* marshal by reference. If you use AppDomain.Load to load an assembly into a new appdomain, the assembly will also be loaded into your (calling) appdomain. That is because AppDomain.Load also returns the assembly object created (and because Assembly is marshal by value, this will cause a copy back into the calling domain). AppDomain.Load is really intended only for the use of unmanaged hosts that need the assembly object returned, but aren't calling from a managed appdomain in the first place, so don't have the copy back problem.

The best way for a hosting application to control each appdomain is to load a small controlling assembly into each one. This assembly will contain a marshal-by-reference class whose methods can be used to communicate between the initial (controlling) appdomain and the hosted appdomains. The host can then instruct the control class to load hosted assemblies directly into the correct appdomain.

The following is a sample control class:

```
using System;
using System.Reflection;

public class HostControl : MarshalByRefObject
{
    // This method is called from the initial appdomain.
    public void Load(String assembly)
    {
        // This load will occur in the target appdomain.
        Assembly.Load(assembly);
    }
}
```

The server can then start up a new appdomain, load the control class into it, and then load a hosted assembly through that control class in the following manner:

```
using System;

class Host
{
    public static void Main(String[] args)
    {
        // Create a new appdomain.
        AppDomain domain = AppDomain.CreateDomain("NewDomain");

        // Create an instance of a marshal-by-reference type (our
        // control class) in the new appdomain.
        HostControl control;
        control = (HostControl)
            domain.CreateInstanceAndUnwrap("HostControlAssembly",
                                           "HostControl");

        // Instruct the control class to load an assembly in the new
        // appdomain.
        control.Load("MyHostedAssembly");
    }
}
```

When a host has no further need of the assemblies in an appdomain, it can unload that appdomain, which, in turn, unloads all the assemblies contained within (this will throw `ThreadAbortException` or `AppDomainUnloaded` exceptions on any threads executing in that appdomain). The initial (default) appdomain cannot be unloaded in this fashion.

Controlling Trust Within the Hosted Environment

A host written in this fashion already has a high degree of control over the assembly loaded in its subdomains. Such assemblies cannot enumerate the other appdomains in the process (unless the host hands them appdomain instances explicitly) and therefore cannot initiate contact with any code in any other appdomain (except any they created themselves). Together with the type safety guarantees provided by the runtime (given that all code is verifiable or trusted enough to use non-type safe code responsibly), this means that appdomains serve as a mechanism to isolate groups of assemblies even though they share the same process (and, hence, memory address space).

A host can further control assemblies by limiting the trust level associated with its code. This is useful in situations where the security policy system can't be relied on to make the right decision. This might be the case if hosted assemblies are loaded from the local machine but might well come from an untrusted source (the user has manually downloaded them from the Internet, for example). Default security policy will probably ascribe a great deal of trust to an assembly loaded from the local machine (it considers this to be equivalent to having the assembly installed and thus granted implicit trust). If the hosting environment thinks there is a likelihood that users will unthinkingly copy such assemblies directly to their disk and, in fact, knows that there is no reason to grant such assemblies more than a basic set of rights, it can manipulate the security system to lock down the level of trust provided to assemblies it loads.

There are two main methods that a hosting environment can use to achieve this result:

- Override the evidence used to resolve security policy for an assembly. This is achieved through overloads of `AppDomain.Load` and `Assembly.Load` that take an additional `System.Security.Policy.Evidence` parameter.

- Add an additional level of policy specific to a single appdomain using the `AppDomain.SetAppDomainPolicy` method. This policy level is then merged with the enterprise, machine, and user levels that are already taken into consideration by the security policy system.

Both these methods, because they modify the actions of the security system itself, require a high level of trust to implement (`SecurityPermission.ControlEvidence` to supply evidence and `SecurityPermission.ControlDomainPolicy` to add a new policy level).

Let's look at supplying additional evidence first. The following is a simple example:

```
using System;
using System.Reflection;
using System.Security;
using System.Security.Policy;

class LoadWithEvidence
{
    public static void Main(String[] args)
    {
        // Create a new evidence container and add zone evidence
        // referencing the Internet zone.
        Evidence evidence = new Evidence();
        evidence.AddHost(new Zone(SecurityZone.Internet));

        // Load an assembly with this additional evidence. Regardless
        // which zone the load really occurs from, the Internet zone
        // will be used by the security system when resolving policy
        // into a trust level.
        Assembly.Load("MyHostedAssembly", evidence);
    }
}
```

This code represents a common technique, overriding the download zone of the assembly so the policy system no longer thinks the assembly was loaded locally and amends the granted permissions accordingly. The additional evidence supplied in the call to `Load` is merged with the evidence the runtime implicitly derives for the assembly. Where there is a conflict (such as the `Zone` evidence previously supplied), the evidence provided on the call overrides the implicit evidence.

One potential problem with supplying additional evidence is the transitive loading of additional assemblies. That is, the additional evidence provided on the original load of the assembly is not applied to any load requests that assembly subsequently makes (either implicitly through early bound references or explicitly through a call to `Load` or similar methods). This is probably the behavior you want when such references are to standard libraries (such as `System.Xml`), but if the reference is to a second user assembly downloaded along with the first, this offers a simple method whereby malicious code can side-step the trust restraints you carefully set up.

Therefore, the additional evidence method should only be used when there are constraints on the loaded assembly (for example, it is loaded from a private directory with no other assemblies present).

Now let's look at the other possibility—adding a domain-specific policy level. This action can only occur once per appdomain (attempting to set it a second time will result in a `PolicyException`). Assemblies (such as your host control assemblies) can be loaded into the appdomain prior to adding the policy level, and they will have their grant sets computed normally. After the call to `SetAppDomainPolicy` is made, any further assemblies loaded will have their grant set calculated taking into account the new level. This includes any assemblies that are transitively loaded (either explicitly or implicitly) by these assemblies. So this method of trust control differs from the additional evidence technique in that respect. Because of this, you will want to pre-load any standard library assemblies that require a high degree of trust *before* making the call to `SetAppDomainPolicy`.

The following is an example of the steps a host control assembly might take to prepare a new appdomain for use by hosted assemblies:

```
// Create a new appdomain.
AppDomain domain = AppDomain.CreateDomain("NewDomain");

// Load our control class into the new appdomain.
HostControl control;
control = (HostControl)
    domain.CreateInstanceAndUnwrap("HostControlAssembly",
                                   "HostControl");

// Instruct the control class to load commonly used library
// assemblies into the new domain.
control.Load("System.Xml, " +
             "Version=1.0.5000.0, " +
             "Culture=neutral, "+
             "PublicKeyToken=b77a5c561934e089");
control.Load("System.Data, " +
             "Version=1.0.5000.0, " +
             "Culture=neutral, "+
             "PublicKeyToken=b77a5c561934e089");

// Define the set of permissions we're going to allow new
// assemblies (this will be intersected with the results from
// the other policy levels, so it's a maximum).
PermissionSet allowed;
SecurityPermission sp;
```

```
allowed = new PermissionSet(PermissionState.None);
sp = new SecurityPermission(SecurityPermissionFlag.Execution);
allowed.AddPermission(sp);

// Create a policy statement that associates the permission
// set above with an attribute describing how the policy level
// should interact with others (we'll take the default --
// PolicyStatementAttribute.Nothing).
PolicyStatement ps = new PolicyStatement(allowed);

// Create an appdomain policy level that matches all
// assemblies and assigns them the permissions we
// computed earlier (just SecurityPermission.Execution).
PolicyLevel level = PolicyLevel.CreateAppDomainLevel();
CodeGroup group;
group = new UnionCodeGroup(new AllMembershipCondition(),
                           ps);

// Add the new policy level to the target appdomain.
domain.SetAppDomainPolicy(level);

// Now we can begin loading hosted assemblies.
control.Load("MyHostedAssembly");
```

Dealing with Assembly-Sharing Issues

Both the previously described techniques have an impact on the use of shared assemblies. Shared assemblies are those that are loaded into multiple appdomains and, although they are logically distinct from one another, share the same compiled code. This is an optimization that reduces the amount of memory needed to hold the compiled versions of the assembly's methods and also the time needed to compile (JIT) them.

There are three styles of assembly sharing that can be enabled (these can all be configured through XML application configuration files, which are beyond the scope of this book):

- Share nothing except `mscorlib` (this library is always shared).

- Share only strongly named assemblies.

- Share all assemblies.

The problem we face here is that the compilation of managed code from IL to native instructions (commonly called *jitting*) is sensitive to the permissions granted to the code. Declarative actions, such as `LinkDemand` or `InheritanceDemand`, might cause some methods to be unavailable in certain trust scenarios. Therefore, it would be a potential security hole to allow two appdomains to share the code of an assembly that has been loaded with different security contexts.

Normally, this isn't a problem; loading an assembly multiple times in different appdomains will yield the same grant set each time because policy is deterministic (and reads from the policy database only once per process). After we start altering the policy system dynamically at runtime, either through additional evidence or by adding appdomain specific policy levels, we lose that determinism and conflicts can result.

Unfortunately, due to the design of assembly sharing with V1 of the .NET Framework, such a conflict cannot be resolved transparently (there is no mechanism to allow more than one version of a shared assembly to be loaded in the same process). Consequently, any attempt to load an assembly that would result in a grant set different from that of a previously loaded version of that assembly will result in an error (a `FileLoadException` will be thrown).

As a result, it's important to carefully plan how you're going to handle the loading of assemblies. A good start is to determine which standard library assemblies will be needed. These should be loaded without modified evidence or before appdomain policy is set. The remaining assemblies must then be a disjoint set; they will only be loaded as hosted assemblies and will never form part of the implementation of the host (in particular, the host's default appdomain will never load them).

Using Appdomains to Secure Unmanaged Clients

Appdomains serve another vital role in securing a hosted environment. Normally, code access security is enforced on a per-assembly basis (each assembly is assessed by the policy system to determine the level of trust to be granted and assigned permissions accordingly). But what happens when control is coming from a partially trusted environment outside the scope of the runtime?

Take the example of script running in an HTML Web page within the user's browser. This simple, non-.NET Framework aware script (JavaScript or VBScript, for example) can nevertheless instantiate and invoke method calls on managed objects because all managed objects are marked, by default, as safe for scripting (as long as the object is instantiated using the correct new `<OBJECT>` syntax, old style instantiations will treat managed objects as ActiveX controls). So what stops such a script from creating a `FileStream` object and writing to the user's disk? The demand for `FileIOPermission` wouldn't seem to help, because the real caller (the script itself) is not managed and will not appear on the stack. In fact, from the security stack walk perspective, there will appear to be no callers of the `FileStream` constructor at all, and the demand will succeed immediately (remember security stack walks are looking for negative information, that is, the first method that belongs to an assembly that is not granted the permissions demanded).

To avoid this problem, the browser (which is an example of a .NET Framework host) will create an appdomain for the Web page under which the script is running. The appdomain will have the URL of the Web page associated with it as security evidence, and this allows the .NET Framework security system to process the appdomain through security policy as if it were an assembly—granting permissions to it in the process.

As we discussed in Chapter 7, "Walking the Stack," security stack walks take appdomain transitions into account when following the call chain. So the appdomain created to run code invoked by script acts as a place holder for the trust placed in that script by the runtime. You can imagine the appdomain as being a substitute for the virtual assembly represented by the script. Figure 10.3 depicts the stack in such a situation.

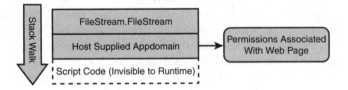

FIGURE 10.3   Using an appdomain as an assembly place holder.

Summary

In this chapter, you've learned that hosting is a technique whereby your trusted code can load and control other assemblies. This has a very practical application from the security standpoint because hosting can, through the use of isolation and more tightly controlled policy, effectively augment the basic .NET Framework security system. That is, hosts can use information not normally available to the .NET Framework to more closely tailor the security environment available to the hosted components, leading to a more secure system without compromising on flexibility.

The key points we touched on are as follows:

- The chief tool the .NET Framework provides to assist hosting is the appdomain. Use of appdomains allows software components to be isolated from each other and the outside world.

- Assemblies loaded by a host can have their trust level manipulated by the host in one of two ways—overriding the evidence provided to the security policy system or adding an appdomain specific policy level.

- When techniques such as those previously discussed are used, care must be taken to ensure that a shared assembly is always loaded with the same grant set (or else an exception will be generated).

- Evidence can be associated with an appdomain so that it will be granted permissions and act like an assembly for the purposes of security stack walks. This allows appdomains to stand in for unmanaged code that otherwise wouldn't be seen by the .NET Framework security system.

11

Verification and Validation: The Backbone of .NET Framework Security

By Sebastian Lange

Assemblies are the development and deployment unit in the world of managed code. Assemblies are also what Code Access Security (CAS) is designed around; they are the unit of security configuration and enforcement. Administrable Code Access Security policy grants permissions to assemblies. The Code Access Security infrastructure, in turn, enables APIs exposing resources such as registry or file system acccess to check all calling assemblies for having been granted sufficient permissions to access the resource. However, were it possible for assemblies, by virtue of any information or code contained in the assembly file, to circumvent the CAS policy restrictions, the CAS system would not be an effective protection against erroneous or outright malicious code. It turns out that there indeed are a number of checks that are presupposed for Code Access Security to be effective. This chapter will introduce what checks these are and how they affect program development and deployment. In particular, the following concepts will be covered:

- A brief overview of the structure and contents of assembly files

- Introduction to validation

- Why the managed PE/COFF file format must be validated and what mechanism is doing so

- What metadata is

- The metadata validation steps necessary to detect corrupted metadata that might circumvent security

- Introduction to JIT-time verification, verifiability, and type safety

- Considerations about writing unverifiable code

To understand the types of checks required to support Code Access Security, it is necessary to review what constitutes an assembly and how an assembly's content could pose a risk to security.

Review of the Anatomy of an Assembly

Managed applications minimally consist of one assembly. The .NET Framework also ships with managed code libraries for use with managed code. These libraries are all contained in various, functionally oriented assemblies. You may now wonder what exactly goes into an assembly. Figure 11.1 gives a high-level overview of what assemblies actually contain.

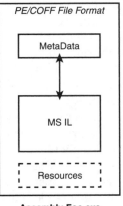

FIGURE 11.1   The constituents of an assembly.

Let's look a little deeper into each of the constituents of an assembly. *MS IL* refers to the Microsoft Intermediate Language code contained in an assembly. MS IL, or IL in short, is an object-oriented assembly language that is emitted by compilers targeting the .NET Framework. The IL for each method is Just-In-Time compiled to native code (typically x86 machine code) by the Common Language Runtime as a method is executed. Therefore, IL is not code that can be immediately executed on a given processor, but rather is code that can be quickly compiled at runtime to the native instruction set of the platform on which the Common Language Runtime is hosted.

As will be seen in the section on Verification ("IL Validation and Verification") later in this chapter, IL code may contain unsafe or dangerous constructs that could undermine Code Access Security. More general, unsafe IL may break type contracts and subvert interassembly isolation. As part of compiling IL to native code, the IL stream is checked for consistency; this process is called *IL validation*. The process of checking that IL is safe is called *IL verification* and is an integral part of the Just-In-Time compilation process from IL to native code. Both are required to guarantee the efficacy of the CAS system.

Assemblies also contain *metadata*. Metadata is a set of tables that describe an assembly's types, their methods, fields, and signatures, as well as the dependencies on other assemblies. You can think of metadata as a rich description of the type definitions and contracts, dependencies, and identity of an assembly—it is an assembly's blueprint. Compilers that target the .NET Framework must not only emit IL but also the metadata describing the compliant they are processing.

Metadata can get intentionally or unintentionally corrupted such as through a malicious user or a disk error. In that case, it would deliver wrong information about the types, fields, or methods contained in an assembly. In fact, IL verification presumes the correctness of assembly metadata. Consequently, metadata needs to be checked before it is used at runtime. The process of doing so is called *Metadata validation*, and will be covered in more detail later (see "Metadata Validation").

Resources are an optional ingredient of assemblies. They are not much different from the resources that can be contained in native executables. For example, bitmaps or localization strings could be placed in this section of assemblies. No special set of security checks is required to cover this optional part of assemblies. Indirectly, resource access and use is checked by IL verification passing over the IL code accessing the resource, as well as by metadata checks over the tables containing resource references and definitions.

All managed EXEs and DLLs are emitted by compilers in the PE/COFF (Portable Executable/Common Object File Format). This is a Microsoft-defined file format standard for Windows executable code. Managed PE/COFF files contain information about the location of metadata, entry points, as well as code to start up the CLR. Checks must be made to ensure that none of this information is corrupted. The process of making these checks is called *PE file format validation*. These checks will be the first set of validation rules we are going to focus on now.

PE File Format and Metadata Validation

Any assembly is heavily scrutinized before any contained code makes it to execution. Not only must assemblies have the necessary permissions to access resources, they must also pass a set of rigorous checks to successfully run. One set of these checks is referred to as validation. Validation encompasses three major sets of tests:

- PE file format validation

- Metadata validation

- IL validation

These checks ensure that IL verification can be carried out successfully and, ultimately, assemblies can be run within strictly enforced security constrains. All sets of tests introduced in this chapter, including PE file format validation checks, need to be met for an assembly to run in a safe manner on the Common Language Runtime. PE file format validation and metadata validation present the outer perimeter of the security apparatus protecting your machine from malicious managed code. IL validation will be explained in the "IL Validation and Verification" section later in this chapter.

PE File Format Validation

Compilers emitting managed code generate assemblies in the so-called *PE/COFF* file format. This a file format that has been specified for executable code on Windows platforms. Both managed and native code DLL and EXE files compiled to run on Windows platforms follow this standard. The following are a few of the typical ingredients of PE/COFF files:

- *Standard entry point*—The entry point invoked by Windows for all native code executables (and for managed PE files on systems before Windows XP).

- *Authenticode signature slot*—Standard location for the authenticode signature if the PE file has been signed with a publisher certificate. Both native and managed PE files can be authenticode signed.

- *Standardized resource location*—The PE file section where resources of the executable are kept.

- *A list of explicit library dependencies*—If a PE file depends explicitly on other PE files, that dependency is noted in the dependencies list.

- *PE directory slots*—The PE/COFF standard provides a limited number of slots that can be used to customize the PE/COFF file format. Slots are reserved for various types of executables. A slot holds an address pointing into the PE file where custom information (usually a custom header) can be found.

Assemblies represent a customized type of PE/COFF files—slot 14 (decimal) in the PE directory has been reserved for managed executables. Thus, whenever that slot entry is not null, you can assume to be dealing with a managed image. In turn, this slot points to a "header" containing managed executable specific information, such as the location of metadata in the PE file or the location of the strong name signature slot.

TIP

If you want to find out exactly how the assembly header for managed PE files is defined, look at the CorHdr.h include file.

This file can be found in the Include subdirectory of the FrameworkSDK directory. This file is only shipped in the .Net Framework SDK, so you will not find it on regular redistribution installations of the .NET Framework.

If you have Visual Studio installed on your system, the file can be found at %Install Drive%\Program Files\Microsoft Visual Studio .Net\Framework\Include\corhdr.h.

%Install Drive% here stands for the drive to which you have installed Visual Studio.

All managed PE files have an explicit dependency included for the mscoree.dll library—the code that has the responsibility of starting up the Common Language Runtime and provides the CLR with the header information of the managed PE file to be run.

You may now ask how mscoree.dll ever actually gets going when managed code is run in the operating system shell (when the shell acts as the host of the CLR). In versions of Windows before Windows XP, the operating system had no notion of managed PE files, so the managed PE executables contain a call to mscoree in the standard PE entry point. On the other hand, Windows XP (by looking for an entry in the PE directory slot 14) recognizes PE images representing assemblies. When Windows XP finds a managed PE executable, it calls mscoree itself, thereby ignoring the jump instruction to mscoree found in the standard PE header.

This difference between Windows XP and earlier versions of the operating system is significant. Some piece of unmanaged code is always executed (the standard PE entry point) on non-Windows XP platforms when running a managed image. Since this is the jump instruction that is supposed to start up the Common Language Runtime when managed code is hosted in the Windows shell, the CLR is not yet running to check that very PE file entry point for being well formed and pointing to mscoree.

This fact was exploited by the so called "Donut virus" that reared its head prior to the Visual Studio.NET release. This virus replaces the entry point jump instruction to point to its own code. Obviously, Windows XP machines were not affected because, as previously stated, Windows XP ignores the standard PE entry point when running a managed image in the Windows XP shell. However, earlier versions of Windows that need the entry stub to spin up the Common Language Runtime were affected. In a way, the virus had very little to do with CLR security specifically; the virus writer simply replaced a PE file entry point, and the CLR did not even need to be installed on the system. The virus thus differed little from virus corruption of any other type of PE image. However, with the support of the operating system loader in conjunction with the CLR security infrastructure, managed images can give much stronger security guarantees than native code, excluding even such PE file corruptions.

CAUTION

If you are planning to write your own host of the Common Language Runtime, be sure to either check the validity of the standard PE entry point, as jumping into `mscoree`, or calling `mscoree` yourself as the Windows XP shell host does.

It is highly recommended that you upgrade to Windows XP where possible. This will pre-empt any attempts to misuse the standard PE entry point when running managed applications in the operating system shell.

After the Common Language Runtime is spun up, it validates all major parts of the managed PE file before their use. Basically, the Common Language Runtime makes sure that all addresses, such as the one pointing to the metadata in the PE file, are not pointing outside of the PE file. This could allow malicious code to write into, or read out of, arbitrary memory locations. If such checks were not performed, malicious code could snoop around and modify the memory of other components, such the CLR itself. That would pose a clear danger to security, because assembly isolation is broken and current security policy as held in memory may be subject to being modified by malicious code.

Metadata Validation

Metadata can be seen as a thorough description of the identity and type structure that defines an assembly. The following categories of information are contained in an assembly's metadata:

- Information about the types in an assembly, including the following:

  - Their methods, including method signature, name, return types, calling convention (such as virtual, abstract, instance, and so on) and accessibility

  - Their fields, including field name, field type, accessibility, and whether the fields are static or instance fields

  - Their inheritance and dependency in relation to other types, as well as their interface implementation relation

  - Their accessibility (public, private, family access) and other modifiers, such as being sealed or abstract

- A list of other files belonging to the assembly (assemblies can consist of multiple modules)

- Identity of the assembly, including the following:

  - The name of the assembly (such as Foo)

  - The version of the assembly

  - The culture of the assembly

  - The strong name digital signature, in the form of the public key and the signature value (if present, not all assemblies must be signed by a strong name)

- Any declarative security annotations, such as an assembly's required minimum set of permissions

Therefore, metadata offers a rich set of information detailing both the way an assembly's types are defined as well as information about the assembly's identity. Metadata is a mandatory constituent of assemblies. Therefore, compilers emitting managed code must create the metadata describing the implementation they are compiling into IL. A managed image will not execute on the CLR if it lacks metadata detailing its identity and implementation.

TIP

You can programmatically browse through most of the metadata of an assembly. The process of programmatically accessing metadata and invoking members is called *reflection*. The classes provided in the System.Reflection namespace allow for easy access to an assembly's metadata. The following is a little sample program that gets the full name of an assembly from the metadata of an assembly, and then displays the name of all the types in that assembly:

```
          using System;
          using System.Reflection;
          using System.IO;
          using System.Collections;
class ReflectionTest
              {

        static void Main()
        {
        Console.Write("Type in a path to a file you want to reflect over:");
            Assembly asmbl = Assembly.LoadFrom(Console.ReadLine());
            //get and show full name of assembly
            Console.WriteLine("Full Name of assembly:"+asmbl.FullName);
            //get types of assembly
```

```
            Type[] types = asmbl.GetTypes();
            IEnumerator typeenum = types.GetEnumerator();
            //show names of the types in assembly
            Console.WriteLine("Types in Assembly:");
            while(typeenum.MoveNext())
                Console.WriteLine(((Type)typeenum.Current).FullName);
        }
    }
```

To compile and execute the assembly, save the previous code into a file called
reflectiontest.cs. Compile the code by using the C# command line compiler—csc
reflectiontest.cs. You can now run the sample program; simply type in **reflectiontest**
at the command line and, when prompted, type in the full path and name of any assembly
(such as reflectiontest itself).

Metadata is persisted in assemblies in the form of a set of cross-referenced tables. For
example, there is a table that contains all the types in that assembly. Each row in
this table points to a table containing further information about a specific type, such
as a pointer to a table containing all of the types' methods. This elaborate network of
tables describing an assembly is filled in by compilers when creating an assembly.
Let's look at an example. Suppose a class of the following structure is defined in an
assembly foo.exe:

```
public class bar
{      int i;
       float j;
       void x() {…};
       int z() {…};
}
```

foo's metadata contains a table for the types defined in foo, fields of types, and
methods defined in types, among other things. Figure 11.2 roughly shows how bar
will show up in foo's metadata:

As you can see, the structure of the class bar (its fields, scope, methods, and so on) is
recorded accurately in interconnected metadata tables. Overall, there are over three
dozen different kinds of table in metadata.

NOTE

For a complete and thorough definition of all the metadata tables, their structure, and layout,
please see the ECMA standards specification about metadata (Partition II) at
http://msdn.microsoft.com/net/ecma.

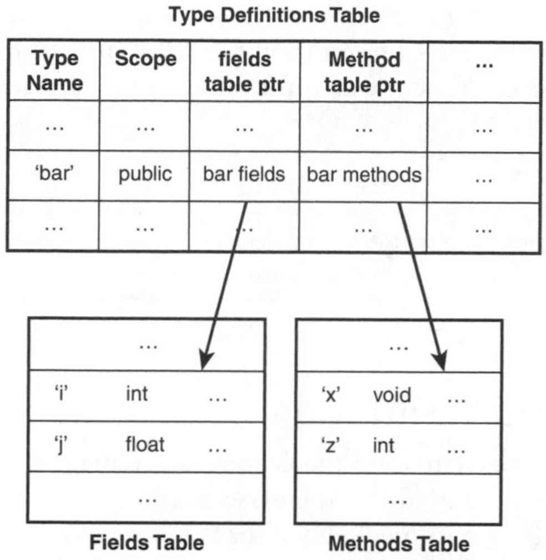

Type Definitions Table

Type Name	Scope	fields table ptr	Method table ptr	...
...	...	...	...	...
'bar'	public	bar fields	bar methods	...
...	...	...	...	...

...			
'i'	int	...	
'j'	float	...	
...			

Fields Table

...			
'x'	void	...	
'z'	int	...	
...			

Methods Table

FIGURE 11.2   Approximate metadata table entries for class bar in foo's metadata.

Metadata is used by the Common Language Runtime to access and load types, find the managed entry point to an assembly, ascertain the strong name identity of an assembly, and many other crucial functions involved in loading and executing managed code. It is information used throughout the Common Language Runtime infrastructure. As part of the CLR process of loading and accessing assembly information, metadata is checked for corruption.

NOTE

There are two types of metadata validation checks that the Common Language Runtime implements—*structural metadata validation* and *semantic metadata validation*.

Structural metadata validation refers to checks that ascertain that the metadata table structure is being adhered to. Returning to our previous example, there are metadata checks at runtime that make sure the pointer to the Fields table in the Type Definitions table, actually points into a field table—not into another table or outside of the PE image itself.

Semantic metadata validation checks are based on rules of the Common Language Runtime type system itself. Certain invariants about types and their interrelationships ought not to be broken. Therefore, such tests are not concerned with the layout of metadata in tables but whether what a specific layout represents still honors certain rules about types. An example of such a rule is the test that checks the inheritance chain of classes for circularities—preventing any subclass X of a class A to be A's superclass or a superclass of a class from which A derives.

All metadatachecks are done at runtime and preemptively—catching erroneous metadata before it is used by the Common Language Runtime infrastructure. In particular, metadata checks occur before IL verification. Let us now look at the verification checks.

NOTE

To review all the metadata tests the CLR implements, please see the ECMA Metadata Standard, Partition II, at `http://msdn.microsoft.com/net/ecma`.

IL Validation and Verification

When an assembly is executed on the Common Language Runtime, an assembly's IL is compiled on a method-by-method basis as needed just prior to method execution. This form of compilation immediately prior to code execution is aptly called Just-In-Time (JIT) compilation. As a result, IL itself never actually gets run; it is an intermediary between compilers emitting assemblies and the Common Language Runtime generating and executing native code. As a result, all IL code that gets invoked ends up being compiled into and executed as native code of the platform on which the CLR runs. However, running native code is inherently dangerous, for example,

- Unmanaged, native code has direct memory access at least throughout the process it is running in, so it can subvert the isolation of application domains (the CLR's "processes").

- Using pointer arithmetic, native code can break type contracts. For example, a class can use pointer arithmetic to read or overwrite the private fields of its superclass.

Consequently, before any IL causes native code to be run, it must pass scrutiny that would disallow exploitations of the sort previously described.

The Common Language Runtime contains two forms of checks for the IL in an assembly—IL validation and IL verification. We'll now have a look at both of these forms of tests, and then look at the repercussions of running and distributing assemblies that do not pass IL verification.

IL Validation

IL validation is the process of checking that the structure of the IL in an assembly is correct. IL validity includes the following:

- Checking that the bytes designating IL instructions in the IL stream of an assembly actually correspond to a known IL instruction. Though normally they do, not all possible combinations of bytes in the IL stream of an assembly correspond to legal, valid IL instructions.

- Checking that jump instructions do not stray outside of the method in which they are contained.

IL validity checks are always carried out by the Common Language Runtime. If an assembly contains invalid IL, the JIT compiler wouldn't know what to do with it. Consequently, any assembly failing IL validity tests is prevented from executing on the Common Language Runtime. Fortunately, IL validity is nothing you have to worry about when writing code using one of the many compilers targeting the .NET Framework. It is the compiler's job to produce valid IL sequences. Typically, failures of assemblies to meet these tests are caused by file corruptions or compiler bugs.

Let us now focus on the other IL-related set of checks carried out by the Common Language Runtime—IL verification.

Verifiability and Type Safety

Every type contained in an assembly is a form of contract. Take the following class as an example:

```
class test
{
        private int X;
        public String Z;

        private void foo() {…}
        public float bar() {…}


}
```

This class defines two fields. X is an integer and should not be accessible outside the class. On the other hand, Field Z, of type String, is publicly accessible. It is part of the public interface of class test. The class also defines two methods, foo and bar. foo is not intended to be callable from outside its enclosing class, whereas bar is declared to be publicly callable on test. The accessibility defined on fields and methods of test are part of this class's contract. It defines how state and functionality on its instances should be accessed.

It is possible to form valid IL constructs that undermine the way types have been defined and limited access to themselves. For example, valid IL allows for the use and formation of arbitrary pointer arithmetic. With that, in the previous code example, it would be possible to read or overwrite X or to invoke foo. IL that contains such constructs is called *type unsafe* and is inherently dangerous to the security of the .NET Framework. For example, such IL could be compiled into native code accessing private fields of the security infrastructure implementation, modifying the in-memory copy of security policy that determines permission allocation for newly run and loaded assemblies. The following example shows just how this could happen without IL verification:

Suppose a system assembly of the .NET Framework implementing security infrastructure defined a SecurityInfo type as follows:

```
SystemAssembly::
public SecurityInfo
{
     private bool m_fFullyTrusted;
    public IsFullyTrusted()
    { return (m_fFullyTrusted); }
    public static SecurityInfo GetSecurityInfo(Assembly a) {…}
}
```

Let's assume SecurityInfo is used to represent the security state of an assembly. The private field m_fFullyTrusted is used by the security infrastructure to denote whether the respective assembly has been granted full trust by the CAS policy system. Clearly, when security information is returned by the security system, this field should not be modifiable by any code except the security system code itself. Otherwise, an assembly could ask for its own security state and then happily grant itself full trust to access all protected resources. However, the following code is doing just that:

```
HackerAssembly::
        Public SpoofSecurityInfo
    {
        public bool m_fFullyTrusted;
    }

    Main()
    {
    SecurityInfo si = SecurityInfo.GetSecurityInfo(
        System.GetMyAssembly());
    SpoofSecurityInfo spoof = si; // typeunsafe, no cast operation
        spoof.m_fFullyTrusted=true; //fulltrust !!!
        FormatDisk();
        }
```

As you can see, the code declares its own security information type, which contains a Boolean field denoting whether an assembly has been fully trusted. Only here, the field has been declared as public. In the main function, the hacker's assembly first gets the security information about itself from the security system, by calling the static GetSecurityInfo function on the SecurityInfo class. The resulting SecurityInfo instance is stored in the variable si. However, immediately afterward, the content of si is assigned to variable spoof, which is of type SpoofSecurityInfo. But SpoofSecurityInfo made the field m_fFullyTrusted public, thus allowing the hacker assembly to grant itself full trust to access all protected resources.

In this example, the type system is being broken, an instance of SecurityInfo should never have been assigned to SpoofSecurityInfo. Verification comes to the rescue here. The following is the IL code that the IL verification checks would encounter when surveying the Main method of the hacker assembly:

```
.locals init(class SecurityInfo si, class SpoofSecurityInfo sp)
.
call class Assembly System::GetMyAssembly()
call class SecurityInfo SecurityInfo.GetSecurityInfo(class Assembly)
stloc si
ldloc si
stloc sp // type unsafe assignment here !
ldloc sp
ldc.i1 1 //true value to be stored into field
stfld int8 SpoofSecurityInfo::m_fFullyTrusted
..
```

The Verification checks built into the JIT would not allow the stloc sp instruction to pass. Verification checks would determine that the types of instances si and sp are not assignment compatible with each other and would not allow the type-unsafe IL to be compiled and executed.

IL verficiation also prevents unsafe use of pointers. If we again take the SecurityInfo class as an example, the following code, using pointer arithmetic, manages to overwrite the private state of the full trust field:

```
Main()
{
SecurityInfo si =
        SecurityInfo.GetSecurityInfo(System.GetMyAssembly());
bool* pb = (*si+4);     // unsafe assignment!!
*pb = true;     // pb now points to the private field!
}
```

The verification checks in the JIT compiler would see the following corresponding IL sequence:

```
.locals init(class SecurityInfo si, bool* pb)
..
ldloc si
ldc.i4 4
add
stloc pb // unsafe assignment
ldloc pb
ldc.i4 1 // true
stind.i1 // *pb = true
...
```

The Verification checks built into the JIT would, again, not allow the `stloc pb` assignment to pass. The verification checks would have tracked the fact that the address `si` references had been modified, thus disallowing an assignment of `si` to `pb`.

Generally, type unsafe IL breaks the CLR type system and undermines the ability to predict and mandate the behavior of types. Therefore, the Common Language Runtime does not allow any assembly with type unsafe IL constructs to be run, unless the assembly has been granted high levels of trust from the Code Access Security policy. To prevent assemblies containing type unsafe constructs from running, the Just-In-Time compilation is sprinkled with various checks that make certain no unsafe IL construct will be run unless CAS policy grants the respective assembly that tremendous privilege. A typical IL verification check is a check for the occurrence of an attempt to dereference a memory location based on an arbitrary pointer location, which could lead to the discovery of private state held in a private field.

NOTE

For a complete list of verification rules checked during JIT compilation, please see the ECMA standard, Partition III, at `http://msdn.microsoft.com/net/ecma`.

The process of checking for type unsafe constructs during Just-In-Time compilation is called *IL verification*. Unfortunately, there is not an existing algorithm that will reliably delineate all type-safe IL sequences from all unsafe IL sequences. Instead, the CLR uses a set of stringent, conservative checks that are guaranteed to only allow type-safe IL to pass, but may nevertheless fail some other more esoteric type-safe constructs. Compilers, such as the Microsoft Visual Basic compiler, that declare to emit only verifiable code, have limited their code generation to the set of type-safe IL constructs that will pass the IL verification checks built into the JIT. However, other common compilers, such as Microsoft C# or Managed C++, allow you to create unverifiable assemblies. Let us now look at some of the repercussions of creating, running, and deploying unverifiable code.

Repercussions of Writing Unverifiable Code

It is possible to have the CLR Just-In-Time compile and execute unverifiable code. However, this operation is highly guarded by the Code Access Security system. Only assemblies receiving the permission to skip verification (as expressed on a flag on the `SecurityPermission`) will be able to execute type-unsafe constructs. Default security policy only grants this right to assemblies from the local machine. Therefore, explicit administrative actions need to be taken if you want to run unverifiable code from the Internet or intranet. Unless the execution scenario for the assembly in question is strictly limited to being a desktop application run from the local hard disk, it is not recommended that you use or distribute unverifiable assemblies. In addition to potentially requiring administrators to dangerously loosen security policy, unverifiable assemblies can also be a prime target for external security exploits, because type-unsafe programming constructs are a first-rate tool to produce unwanted side effects, such as buffer overruns. Thus, whenever possible, you should stay within the realm of verifiability and avoid the creation of type-unsafe assemblies, such as through the use of [unsafe] features in C#.

NOTE

The .NET Framework SDK ships with the PE Verify tool that can be used to check on the verifiability of an assembly. If an assembly passes the checks in this tool, it is guaranteed to pass the verification checks of the CLR's JIT compiler.

Code Access Security's Dependence on Validation and Verification

Now that each of the different validation and verification technology parts of the CLR has been introduced, it is time to take a step back and review how all these checks tie back into Code Access Security. It turns out that there is a clear line of dependency between the different types of checks.

Metadata checks rely on the presence of a noncorrupted PE file. Corrupted PE files can run malicious native code before metadata checks could even begin. Therefore, there is a strong dependency between PE file format validity checks and Metadata checks. IL verification, in turn, relies both on valid IL to be present and on correct metadata. Finally, Code Access Security only works if type contracts cannot be broken, and thus depends on IL verification. Thus, .NET Framework security is the product not just of one security technology, but of a set of collections of checks all designed to enable a secure runtime environment.

Summary

This chapter introduced the various verification and validation checks presupposed by Code Access Security. All assemblies ship in the PE/COFF file format—the CLR implements a number of checks preventing security exploits through the corruption of the file.

Assemblies also carry metadata that describes the type structure and has information about the identity of an assembly. Metadata is used throughout the CLR infrastructure to successfully execute assemblies. Therefore, the CLR also implements a number of metadata checks that prevent security holes through metadata corruption.

Compilers targeting the .NET Framework translate programming language source code into an object-oriented assembly language called IL.

The CLR tests whether the supposed IL stream is well formed. It also tests whether the IL honors the ways types define access to themselves. Only assemblies having been granted high levels of permissions will be able to execute unverifiable code.

Because the Code Access Security system itself relies on not having type contracts violated, it therefore relies on IL verification.

12

Security Through the Lifetime of a Managed Process: Fitting It All Together

By Brian A. LaMacchia

This chapter concludes our discussion of Code Access Security fundamentals by showing how the features described in Chapters 4 through 11 interact when managed code is loaded and run within the Common Language Runtime. In the previous chapters, we have looked at various security features of the Runtime—verification, policy evaluation, and permission enforcement—in isolation. Now, we focus on how these individual pieces of the security system come together and interact to provide a secure environment for executing semitrusted code. After reading this chapter, the reader should be able to

- Describe the security actions that must be made by developers at code authoring time, including declarative permission requests and appropriate permission demands

- Describe the various mechanisms by which managed code can be installed onto a particular machine

- Describe the function of the `Native Image Generator` and `PE Verify` tools and their relationship to the security system

- Describe the roles the loader, the policy system, and the Just-In-Time compiler/verifier play in the CLR security system

The lifecycle of any particular managed process can be divided into three distinct stages—development, deployment, and execution. Software authors, administrators, and users make security decisions at each stage of the process that ultimately determine the permissions with which an assembly runs on a particular machine. We begin this chapter with an overview of the security decisions that face developers at code authoring time and then proceed to deployment and execution-time considerations in later sections.

Development-Time Security Considerations

The security features within the .NET Framework were designed, in part, to make it much easier for developers to write secure code. When authoring code, developers need to consider two main factors—the security requirements of the assemblies they are authoring and the sensitive resources and data (if any) that are potentially exposed by their classes to other code. The two factors are related but distinct, and it is slightly easier to understand the relationship between them if we begin with a discussion of the second factor, protecting sensitive resources, and then go back to investigate how developers indicate and declare security requirements of their assemblies.

The first security-related action a developer must perform when beginning work on a new assembly is to determine whether the assembly will expose any sensitive resources through its classes and methods? That is, will the classes and methods within the assembly expose sensitive resources to callers of those methods. If the answer to this question is yes, the assembly must be a *secure assembly*. Secure assemblies are discussed in detail in Chapter 24, "Architecting a Secure Assembly," Chapter 25, "Implementing a Secure Assembly," and Chapter 26, "Testing a Secured Assembly," but the basic issue is this—if the assembly you are authoring is going to make a new sensitive resource available to semitrusted code, your assembly must perform appropriate security checks within each method that provides access to or operates on the sensitive resource. Essentially, your new assembly is going to be a gatekeeper or guard of the protected resource, and you must treat every request for access to the resource with an appropriate degree of caution.

How do you determine whether your new assembly must be a secure assembly? This basic determination revolves around the list of resources exposed by your assembly to other code and whether those resources are sensitive or already protected. Consider the following scenario. Suppose that you want to write a method that will write a message (we'll use "Hello, World!" for historical reasons) to a file named `hello.txt` located on the C: drive of the computer. Using the .NET Framework, your code might look as shown in Listing 12.1. This program creates a `FileStream` object mapped to the `C:\hello.txt` file on the hard disk (creating the file if necessary) and writes the string `"Hello, World!"` to that file.

LISTING 12.1   Sample Hello, World! Program

```
using System;
using System.IO;

public class HelloWorld {
  public static void Main(string[] args) {
    FileStream fs = new FileStream("C:\\hello.txt", FileMode.OpenOrCreate,
➥ FileAccess.Write);
    StreamWriter sw = new StreamWriter(fs);
    sw.Write("Hello, World!");
    sw.Close();
  }
}
```

Does the program in Listing 12.1 constitute a secure assembly? That is, does this simple program require the addition of any security checks or permission demands? The answer is "No, it does not," because the program, by itself, does not expose any new sensitive resources. The only resource that is used or modified by the HelloWorld program is the c:\hello.txt file that is associated with the FileStream fs, and the FileStream class itself performs the necessary security checks to determine whether callers of its methods (including the HelloWorld program) should be granted access to the file system objects that it exposes.

The class libraries that make up the .NET Framework are secure assemblies; they implement appropriate security checks, in the form of permission demands, for the resources that they expose. Every sensitive resource that is made available to semi-trusted code through the .NET Framework class library is protected by demands for a related security permission. For example, the constructors on the FileStream class demand instances of the FileIOPermission before returning any instances of the class. Similarly, the registry-related classes demand instances of RegistryPermission, and the network-related classes demand instances of SocketPermission, WebPermission, or DNSPermission as appropriate to their function. This is one of the great advantages of writing a program on top of the .NET Framework; if all the resources that you use in your programs are already protected by appropriate permission demands, you do not need to add additional security checks to your own code. Because the HelloWorld program in Listing 12.1 only uses resources that are exposed through the class libraries of the .NET Framework, no additional security checks need to be made in our code.

NOTE

Even if your assembly does not expose any sensitive resources, if it performs any operations that affect the normal behavior of the .NET Framework security system, it must be a secure assembly. For example, if a method in your assembly calls the `Assert()` method on a permission, that modifies the behavior of the security stack walks and your assembly should be secure. Similarly, if you ever suppress the runtime security check that normally occurs when using platform invoke or COM interoperability via the `SuppressUnmanagedCodeSecurityAttribute` attribute, your assembly needs to be secure.

Even though our `HelloWorld` program does not expose any sensitive resources that require protection, it does make use of a protected resource—namely, the `FileStream` object that represents the `c:\hello.txt` file. Our program will only run successfully at execution time if it is granted sufficient access rights to write to the `c:\hello.txt` file. We can indicate this security requirement for our assembly to run through the use of assembly-level declarative permission requests. Declarative security attributes in general were introduced briefly in Chapter 6, "Permissions: The Workhorse of Code Access Security," and assembly-level requests are discussed in detail in Chapter 29, "Writing a Semitrusted Application." Basically, declarative security attributes are a mechanism for communicating assembly permission requirements to the policy system. Referring back to Listing 12.1, because `HelloWorld` will only operate correctly if it is granted write access to the `c:\hello.txt` file, we can indicate this requirement by adding the following assembly attribute to our source code:

```
[assembly:System.Security.Permissions.FileIOPermission(
➥ System.Security.Permissions.SecurityAction.RequestMinimum,
➥ Write="C:\\hello.txt")]
```

This attribute indicates that a minimum grant of the `FileIOPermission`, including write access to `c:\hello.txt`, is required for the program to run. See Chapter 29 for a complete description of the syntax and proper use of assembly-level security permission requests.

CAUTION

If you determine that your assembly will be exposing a sensitive resource, you must secure that access with appropriate permission demands. Chapters 24 through 26 describe in detail how to architect, implement, and test a secured assembly.

NOTE

There is a subtle interaction that occurs between the Runtime and your source code compiler when you use declarative security attributes within your programs. At compile time, declarative security attributes are checked for correctness by the version of the Runtime installed with your compiler and converted into a different formation before being embedded in the metadata of the output module or assembly.

The final important security-related decision that you must make at code authoring time is whether you want your assembly to have a *strong name*. As discussed in Chapter 9, "Understanding the Concepts of Strong Naming Assemblies," strong names are cryptographically protected names for assemblies. Strong names are built on top of public key cryptography. Strong names are used by the CLR to provide both integrity protection for your assemblies as well as cryptographically strong binding among assemblies. See Chapter 25 for a description on how to use the strong name tool (Sn.exe) distributed with the .NET Framework SDK to create strong name key pairs and how to build strong names into your assemblies using the `AssemblyKeyFile`, `AssemblyKeyName`, and `AssemblyDelaySign` assembly-level custom attributes.

NOTE

We recommend that all developers take advantage of the strong name features of the CLR and digitally sign their assemblies with strong names. Only strongly named assemblies can be added to the Global Assembly Cache, and strong names provide a very high degree of protection against accidental or malicious tampering with your assemblies. Also, version checking and side-by-side execution are only available for strongly named assemblies. Note that once you strong name your assembly, you will have to annotate it with the `AllowPartiallyTrustedCallersAttribute` if you want it to be callable from semitrusted assemblies. (See Chapter 25 for a detailed discussion of the `AllowPartiallyTrustedCallersAttribute`.)

Deployment-Time Security Issues

After you have finished writing, compiling, and strong name signing your assembly, you must deploy it to the machines on which you want it to run. Traditionally, deploying Windows software has consisted of

1. Combining complied code and installation instructions into an installation package

2. Copying the package onto the target machines

3. Running the package to place the included compiled code in the proper directories on the machine and perform housekeeping tasks such as registry key configuration

While this particular method of deployment is still supported, the .NET Framework also supports over-the-network deployment, dynamic loading of code, and assembly sharing through the Global Assembly Cache. Deployment scenarios and features are described in detail in the .NET Framework SDK documentation in the section titled "Deploying Applications."

The particular method you choose to deploy your application is not a security decision *per se*, but it may impact the security context in which your application runs. Specifically, as described in Chapter 8, "Membership Conditions, Code Groups, and Policy Levels: The Brick and Mortar of Security Policy," the default security policy shipped with the .NET Framework is based on the Internet Explorer Zones model, so the set of permissions granted to your assembly will vary depending on what Zone it is located in when it is loaded into the CLR. For example, assemblies downloaded as part of a Web-based application from a Web server located on your local intranet are likely to be granted fewer permissions than when installed in a directory on a local hard drive.

The primary security decision facing developers and administrators when deploying managed applications is whether to add their assemblies to the Global Assembly Cache (GAC). Assemblies that are present in the GAC are potentially accessible to any other assembly running on the machine, including semitrusted code. For example, an assembly running from a Web server in a semitrusted context can instantiate types located in assemblies in the GAC without having read access to the physical files that make up the assembly. (In particular, the `Assembly.Load()` static method always probes the GAC for the requested assembly.) For this reason, assemblies that have not been properly secured (either with appropriate security permission or by preventing semitrusted assemblies from binding to the shared assembly) should never be loaded into the GAC.

The .NET Framework includes a number of command-line tools that have security-related functions. The Code Access Security Policy tool, `Caspol.exe`, (Chapter 19, "Administering .NET Framework Security Policy Using Scripts and Security APIs") is a command-line tool that can be used to modify security policy. The Permissions View tool, `Permview.exe`, (Chapter 29) will display assembly-level permission requests and declarative demands contained within a specific assembly. The Strong Name (`Sn.exe`) and Secutil (`Secutil.exe`) utilities are useful for strong name generation, construction, and extraction. PEVerify is a standalone tool that performs type-safety verification and metadata validation checks on an assembly; it may be used to check that classes and methods within an assembly are type-safe without loading the assembly into the CLR. All of these tools are documented in the .NET Framework SDK documentation in the section titled "Tools and Debugger."

One other tool that, while not directly related to security, is impacted by security operations is the Native Image Generator (`Ngen.exe`). The Native Image Generator tool (sometimes called the "pre-JITer") creates native code from a managed assembly and caches the native code locally. When an assembly is Ngen'ed (processed by the Native Image Generator), any `LinkDemand` security checks encountered are evaluated respective to the set of permissions that would be granted to the assembly under the current security policy. If the security policy later changes, the native image may be invalidated. Specifically, if the set of permissions granted to an Ngen'ed assembly under the new policy is not a superset of those granted under the old policy, the native image generated under the old security policy will be invalidated and ignored, and the assembly will be Just-In-Time compiled at runtime. Thus, you may need to re-run the Ngen utility to regenerate native images for your assemblies after making modifications to the security policy that change the set of permissions granted to your assemblies.

Execution-Time Security Issues

Having compiled and deployed your assemblies to a target machine, the next step, of course, is to run your code within the Common Language Runtime. A lot of steps occur "under the covers" when you run your HelloWorld.exe managed executable. In this section, we're going to walk through the process by which managed code contained within an assembly is loaded, evaluated by security policy, Just-In-Time compiled, type-safety verified, and finally allowed to execute. The overall process of developing, deploying, and executing managed code is depicted graphically in Figure 12.1. We have discussed the Development and Deployment boxes previously and will focus solely on Execution in this section.

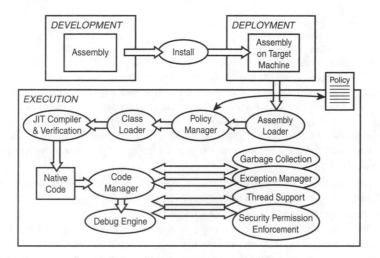

FIGURE 12.1   High-level diagram of the process of developing, deploying, and executing managed code.

The diagram in Figure 12.1 shows how an individual assembly is loaded and executed within the Runtime, but there is a key initial step that must occur before loading any assemblies. Every managed application is run on top of the Runtime within the context of a *host*. The host is the trusted piece of code that is responsible for launching the Runtime, specifying the conditions under which the Runtime (and thus managed code within the Runtime) will execute, and controlling the transition to managed code execution. The .NET Framework includes a shell host launching executables from the command line, a host that plugs into Internet Explorer that allows managed objects to run within a semitrusted browser context, and the ASP.NET host for Web applications. After the host has initialized the Runtime, the assembly containing the entry point for the application must be loaded and then control can be transferred to that entry point to begin executing the application. (In the case of shell-launched C# executables, this entry point is the Main method defined in your application.)

Loading an Assembly

Referring to Figure 12.1, the first step that occurs when loading an assembly into the Runtime is to locate the desired assembly. Typically, assemblies are located on disk or downloaded over the network, but it is also possible for an assembly to be "loaded" dynamically from a byte array. In any case, after the bytes constituting the assembly are located, they are handed to the Runtime's Assembly Loader. The Assembly Loader parses the contents of the assembly and creates the data structures that represent the contents of the assembly to the Runtime. Control then passes to the Policy Manager.

NOTE

When the Assembly Loader is asked to resolve a reference to an assembly, the reference may be either a simple reference, consisting of just the "friendly name" of an assembly, or a "strong" reference that uses the cryptographic strong name of the referenced assembly. Strong references only successfully resolve if the target assembly has a cryptographically valid strong name (that is, it was signed with the private key corresponding to the public key in the strong name and has not been tampered with since being signed). For performance reasons, assemblies loaded from the Global Assembly Cache are strong name verified only when they are inserted into the GAC; the Runtime depends on the underlying operating system to keep the contents of the GAC secure.

The Assembly Loader is also responsible for resolving file references within a single assembly. An assembly always consists of at least a single file, but that file can contain references to subordinate files that together constitute a single assembly. Such file references are contained within the "assembly manifest" that is stored in the first file in the assembly (the file that is externally referenced by other assemblies). Every file reference contained within the manifest includes the cryptographic hash of the contents of the referenced file. When a file reference needs to be resolved, the Assembly Loader finds the secondary file, computes its hash value, compares that hash value to the value stored in the manifest, and (assuming the match) loads the subordinate file. If the hash values do not match, the subordinate file has been tampered with after the assembly was linked together and the load of the subordinate file fails. (More information on cryptographic hashes and their uses may be found in Chapter 30, "Using Cryptography with the .NET Framework: The Basics.")

Resolving Policy for an Assembly

The Policy Manager is a core component of the Runtime security system. Its job is to decide what permissions should be granted, in accordance with the policy specification, to every single assembly loaded by the Runtime. Before any managed code from an assembly is executed, the Policy Manager has determined whether the code should be allowed to run at all and, if it is allowed to run, the set of rights with which it will run. Figure 12.2 provides a high-level view of the operation of the Policy Manager.

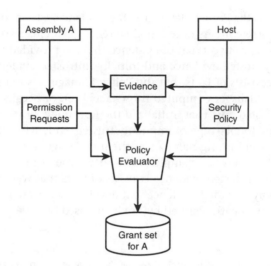

FIGURE 12.2   High-level diagram of the Policy Manager.

There are three distinct inputs to the Policy Manager:

- The current security policy

- The evidence that is known about the assembly

- The set of permission requests, if any, that were made in assembly-level metadata declarations by the assembly author

The security policy is the driving document; it is the specification that describes in detail what rights are granted to an assembly. As described in Chapter 8, the security policy in effect for a particular application domain at any point in time consists of four policy levels:

- Enterprise-wide level

- Machine-wide level

- User-specific level

- An optional, application domain–specific level

Each policy level consists of a tree of code groups and membership conditions, and it is against this tree that the evidence is evaluated. Each policy level is evaluated independently to arrive at a set of permissions that the level would grant to the assembly. The intersection of these level grants creates the maximal set of permissions that can be granted by the Policy Manager.

The second input to the Policy Manager is the evidence, the set of facts that are known about the assembly. As noted in Chapter 5, "Evidence: Knowing Where Code Comes From," there are two types of evidence that are provided to the policy system—implicitly trusted evidence and initially untrusted evidence. Implicitly trusted evidence consists of facts that the Policy Manager assumes to be true either because the Policy Manager computed those facts itself or because the facts were supplied by the trusted host that initialized the Runtime ("host-provided evidence"). (An example of the former type of implicitly trusted evidence is the presence of a cryptographically valid strong name or Authenticode signature. The URI from which an assembly was loaded is an example of the latter type of implicitly trusted evidence.) Initially untrusted evidence consists of facts that were embedded in the assembly ("assembly provided evidence") at development time by the code author; they must be independently verified before being used or believed.

> **NOTE**
>
> The default security policy that is installed by the .NET Framework never considers initially untrusted evidence, but the facility is present as an extension point. For example, third-party certifications of an assembly might be carried as assembly provided evidence.

The third and final input to the Policy Manager is the set of permission requests made by the assembly. These declarations provide hints to the Policy Manager concerning

- The minimum set of permissions that the assembly must be granted to function properly

- The set of permissions that the assembly would like to be granted but are not strictly necessary for minimal operation

- The set of permissions that the assembly never wants to be granted by the policy system

After computing the maximal set of permissions that can be granted to the assembly in accordance with the policy levels, the Policy Manager can reduce that set based on the contents of the permission requests. More details on permission request syntax and semantics can be found in Chapter 29.

> **NOTE**
>
> Permission requests never increase the set of permissions granted to an assembly beyond the maximal set determined by the policy levels.

After the Policy Manager has determined the in-effect security policy, the set of applicable evidence, and the set of permission requests, it can compute the actual set of permissions to be associated with the assembly. Recall that permissions are granted by the policy system on an assembly-wide basis; all code within an assembly is granted the same set of rights when that assembly is loaded into an application domain. After the set of granted permissions has been computed by the Policy Manager, that set is associated with the Runtime-internal objects that represent the assembly, and individual classes contained within the assembly can be accessed.

Before leaving the Policy Manager, we should mention that there are two security conditions enforced by the Policy Manager that could cause the load of the assembly to fail at this point and never proceed to the Class Loader. The first condition concerns the assembly's set of minimum permission requests. If an assembly contains any minimum permission requests, these requests *must* be satisfied by the grant set that is output by the policy system for processing of the assembly to continue. If the minimum request set is not a subset of the resulting grant set, a `PolicyException` is immediately thrown. The second condition that is checked before proceeding is that the assembly has been granted the right to execute code. "The right to run code" on top of the Runtime is represented by an instance of the `SecurityPermission` class (specifically, `SecurityPermission(SecurityPermissionFlag.Execution)`). Under default policy, the Policy Manager will check that the set of permissions granted to an assembly contains at least an instance of this flavor of `SecurityPermission`. If the right to run code is not granted for some reason, that also generates a `PolicyException` and no further processing of the assembly occurs.

Loading Classes from an Assembly

Assuming that the assembly's minimum requests have been satisfied and that the assembly is indeed granted the right to run code, control passes from the Policy Manager to the Class Loader. Classes are retrieved lazily from the containing assembly; if you access a single class from an assembly containing a hundred classes, only that single class is touched by the Class Loader. The Class Loader is responsible for laying out in memory the method tables and data structures associated with the class and verifying access (visibility) rules for classes and interfaces. After the class data structures have been properly initialized, we are ready to access individual methods defined within the class.

Just-In-Time Verification and Compilation of Methods

Referring back to Figure 12.1, after the Class Loader has finished its work, we are ready to verify the MSIL container within the assembly and generate native code from it. This is the job of the Just-In-Time compiler and type-safety verifier (also known as the JIT compiler/verifier). As with loading classes from an assembly, methods within a class are JIT verified and compiled lazily on an as-demanded basis. When a method is called for the first time within the process, the MSIL for the method is checked for compliance with the published type-safety rules and then (assuming it passes) converted into native code. The type-safety verification process is described in more detail in Chapter 11, "Verification and Validation: The Backbone of .NET Framework Security."

The JIT compiler/verifier also plays a direct role in the evaluation of class- and method-level declarative security actions. Recall that there are three types of declarative permission demands, represented by the `SecurityAction` enumeration values `Demand`, `LinkDemand`, and `InheritanceDemand`. (Examples of how to use these types of security declarations are provided in Chapter 25.) Inheritance demands, which control the right to subclass a class, and link-time demands, which restrict the right to bind to a method, are checked and enforced by the JIT as the class is being compiled. Failure to satisfy an inheritance or link-time demand will result in the generation of a `SecurityException`. Runtime demands (`SecurityAction.Demand`) are converted by the JIT compiler/verifier into a native code wrapper around the body of the method that is protected by the demand. Every call to the method must first pass through the wrapper, satisfying the security demand it represents, before entering the body of the method.

After a method has been successfully processed by the JIT compiler/verifier and converted to native code, it is ready to be executed. As the method executes, references to unprocessed methods, classes, and assemblies can occur. These references will cause the Runtime to recursively call the JIT compiler/verifier, Class Loader, or Assembly Loader and Policy Manager as necessary. These operations happen implicitly, "under the covers," as the managed code within the application executes.

Execution-Time Permission Enforcement

So far, everything that we have described in this section concerning the operation of the execution engine is largely transparent to the code author and the user.

Assembly references are resolved, assemblies are loaded, policy evaluation occurs, classes are laid out, and MSIL is verified and converted into native code, all without any external indication or control. (Of course, in the event that an error occurs at any stage in this processing pipeline, such as the failure of an inheritance demand in the JIT compiler/verifier, an exception will be generated and program execution will not proceed normally.) However, essentially all of the security processing that occurs from assembly load through JIT compilation/verification really exists primarily to set up the execution environment for execution-time permission enforcement.

Execution-time permission enforcement, the final security-related component in Figure 12.1, is the *raison d'être* of the .NET Framework security system. All of the evidence gathering, policy specification, and evaluation that has occurred up to this point was performed simply so that we can associate a permission grant set with each assembly at execution time. We need that association between assemblies and their grant sets so that we can properly perform and evaluate stack-walking security demands. As a program runs within the Runtime, security demands will generally occur as a result of one of the following three actions:

- An explicit call to a permission's `Demand()` method

- An explicit call to a method protected by a declarative security attribute specifying a demand

- Implicitly as part of a platform invoke or COM interop call, because all calls to native code through these mechanisms are automatically protected by security checks

Recall from Chapter 7, "Walking the Stack," that the goal of a stack-walking permission check is to verify that the demanded permission is within the policy grants of all the code in the call chain. For every piece of code on the call stack above the method performing the check, the Runtime security system ensures that the code has been granted the particular demanded permission by the Policy Manager. Whenever a method within a secured assembly is about to perform a potentially dangerous action, the method must first perform a security demand to check that the action is permitted by policy.

NOTE

As a practical matter, note that because the Policy Manager assigns grant sets to assemblies, a sequence of successive frames on the stack corresponding to code loaded from the same assembly will have the same set of granted permissions. Consequently, the security system needs only check permission grants at every assembly transition on the stack, not every method transition. Keep this behavior in mind when deciding how you want to organize your code into various assemblies; a poor design that includes a very chatty interface across two assemblies can slow down the performance of the security system.

Summary

In this chapter, we have demonstrated how the various components of the .NET Framework security system work together to provide a robust execution environment for semitrusted code. Assembly permission requests specified by code authors at development time can influence the permissions granted to an assembly by the Policy Manager. Similarly, the use of the Common Language Runtime's strong naming facilities when the assembly is authored provides execution-time integrity protection and can also influence the set of granted permissions. Deployment-time tools, such as PEVerify, allow administrators to check that an assembly is type-safe. When the assembly is loaded into an instance of the Common Language Runtime to execute, we showed how the Policy Manager determines the permission grants for the assembly from the set of evidence known about the assembly. Runtime security checks are performed against these granted permissions.

PART III

ASP.NET and Web Services Security Fundamentals

IN THIS PART

13

Introduction to ASP.NET Security

By Kevin Price

Now it's time to deal with a rather complex topic that has many noncomplex solutions. If there ever was an example of the phrase "ignorance is bliss," security is the winner. It seems that all is happy and running well until somebody points out a hole in your application that has exposed a Web or database server. Another developer's view on security is that it is a hopeless case. "Why should my company even worry about this—no matter what we do, someone can still get through it." These are the same people who don't bathe because they're only going to get dirty again. When it comes to securing your ASP.NET application, what you don't know or choose not to know can have devastating effects on your ability to continue to collect a paycheck, or worse. In an effort from Microsoft to help your servers stay secure, some additions were made in ASP.NET over what you may already be used to from the ASP-based application on Internet Information Server. Most of these items are quite easy to implement with little to no impact on scalability or manageability of the application. It is the intent of this chapter to present the features provided to secure your ASP.NET applications in a manner that makes you, the developer, comfortable. The purpose of this chapter is to familiarize you with the concepts of what is available in ASP.NET with regard to security. This chapter will cover an introduction to the new features provided by ASP.NET, such as forms authentication, impersonation, and Microsoft Passport.

New Security Features in ASP.NET—And How to Use Them

In the .NET platform, everything is "new." This includes the implementation of methods previously available through other means, such as IIS and DCOM, and methods introduced in .NET. In the world of authenticating users to a resource, such as a Web site, Microsoft .NET provides four options, `Basic`, `Windows`, `Forms-based` and `Passport`.

For validating user authentication and authorization when it comes to code permissions, a.k.a. code access security, there is now the simple to implement method of impersonation. While this might not be late-breaking news, what is is the fact that now a user's principals can be changed by privileged code. Impersonation, in this case, means that through the Common Language Runtime (CLR), you control the user under which code executes. Those of you familiar with Microsoft Transaction Server and Component Services for COM+ will be able to draw quick parallels. One difference that was available for the Beta releases, and not in the initial release was the use of configuration files to specify an intrinsic trust level associated with an assembly. While this feature may return in a future release, with the focus on security, it would have to implemented cautiously. For those still getting used to the new terminology, an assembly is code, usually in the form of a class or object. An assembly can (but doesn't have to) be a `.dll` file.

The following sections introduce these "new" features. In the cases covering Basic and Windows authentication, the goal is showing how to use .NET instead of IIS to perform these tasks. Forms, or Forms-based authentication, and Passport represent two truly new methods of authenticating users using built-in Microsoft functionality. The key point is that all of the features mentioned in these chapters are controlled through XML-based configuration files, such as Web.config. These are presented in the order of most likely to be used in a real-world scenario. At the end of this chapter, you will,

- Know what the features of ASP.NET security are
- How to use Forms authentication
- How to use implementation and code access security
- Know what the differences between protecting a Web service and a Web page are

Forms Authentication

By now, you should be familiar with the `web.config` file that is created by Visual Studio.NET, for each .NET Web Application you create. This is the file that controls what actions the Web site will process and what to map these events to, for example, the control of verbs for specifying if a user or group is allowed to GET or POST or has all rights. For more information on the specifics of XML-based configuration files, see Chapter 20, "Administering an IIS Machine Using ASP.NET." It is also the file that tells the Web to use Forms-based authentication. While the `web.config` file can be very useful, it is not required to be used by ASP.NET. If it is not used, the `machine.config` file will be the governing configuration of a Web site.

Forms authentication in ASP.NET is, by definition, a means by which users can be authenticated to a Web site through a Web page containing a form using cookies for state management, with regards to the authentication ticket, and storing user information in a data store. It is worth noting here that the state management used for authentication is separate from that which may be used for cookie-based session management. In the old days, this process might have been completed using an Active Server Page that made a call to `ADO` that queried a SQL Server database for a username and password, then if there was a positive result, let the user into the site and possibly personalize some information for that user based on database information that was written to a cookie. Forms authentication does not mean that the entire authentication is done on a Web page. It could be, if you like embedding users' plain-text passwords in your Web pages. In a real-world example, you would not write the plain-text password of your user to the cookie to avoid having to make a trip back to the Web server to make sure the user was authenticated from page to page. Nor in some cases would you want, or be able to use, the `Session` object to carry data. ASP.NET takes care of this by allowing you to select a "`protection level`." The protection level determines if and how the information in the cookie is treated. It can be encrypted, validated, or nothing at all. Before going too much further, let us put this in motion by creating a sample Forms-based authentication site. Some of the steps listed here may not be needed by all readers. It is more of an illustration of taking what you know and applying it to something new.

Creating the Site If You Do Not Have Microsoft Visual Studio.NET Installed
Follow the instructions in this section if you only have the .NET Framework SDK installed.

To begin, you need to make a directory that will house the application; this can be easily accomplished by clicking Start, selecting Run, typing **cmd** and pressing Enter. In the command windows, type **mkdir c:\inetpub\wwwroot\FormAuth**, and click OK. Next, open the Internet Information Services console. Then perform the following steps:

1. Right-click My Computer.

2. Select Manage.

3. Click the (+) beside Services and Applications to expand the list.

4. Click the (+) beside Internet Information Services to expand the services; you should see a screen similar to that shown in Figure 13.1.

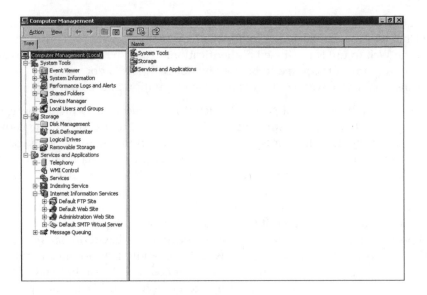

FIGURE 13.1   Computer Management console.

5. Right-click the site you want to create a virtual directory in (in this case, Default Web Site), select New, and then select Virtual Directory. This action is shown in Figure 13.2.

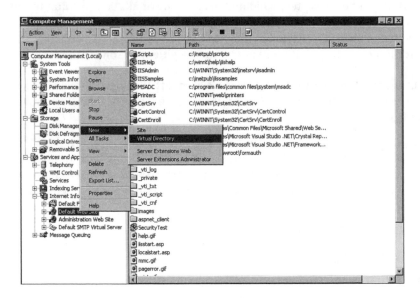

FIGURE 13.2   Selecting to create a new virtual directory.

6. Step 5 launches the Virtual Directory Creation Wizard, as shown in Figure 13.3. Click Next to proceed.

FIGURE 13.3 Virtual Directory Creation Wizard.

7. The next screen asks you for a name to give your new virtual directory. In this sample, you'll use **FormAuth**, as shown in Figure 13.4. Type this into the text box provided and click Next.

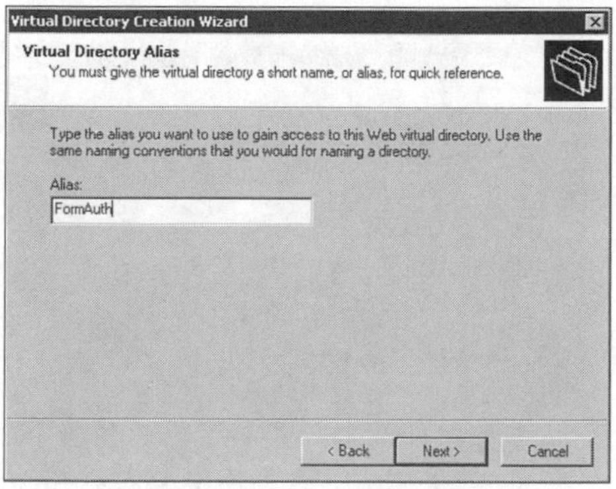

FIGURE 13.4 Virtual Directory Alias.

8. The next screen asks you for the location of the files to use. This is the physical location on a hard drive for the files. In this sample, the location is C:\Inetpub\wwwroot\FormAuth because this is the directory you created earlier. Type or browse to this location and click Next. Figure 13.5 illustrates this.

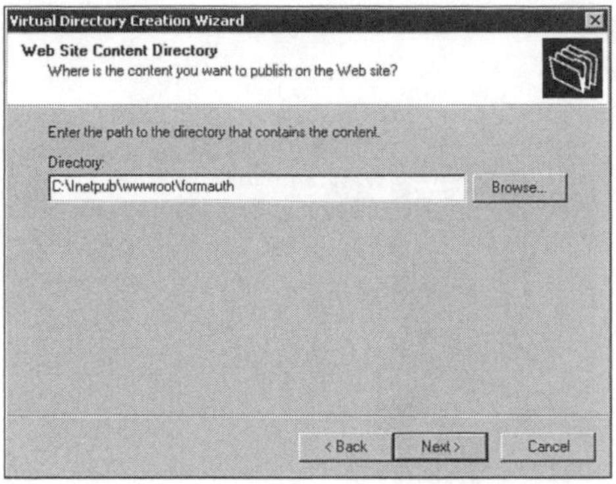

FIGURE 13.5   Web Site Content Directory.

9. The next screen is one that many developers have never stopped to read. It regards the access permissions that are needed on the site. Because you are not using ASP to call COM/COM+ objects, and because your settings here have no effect on ASP.NET, you can leave the settings as shown in Figure 13.6 and click Next. Since you are setting up forms authentication, the anonymous user needs to have access to the site. Also, the isolation settings for the site have no effect on the ASP.NET Web site.

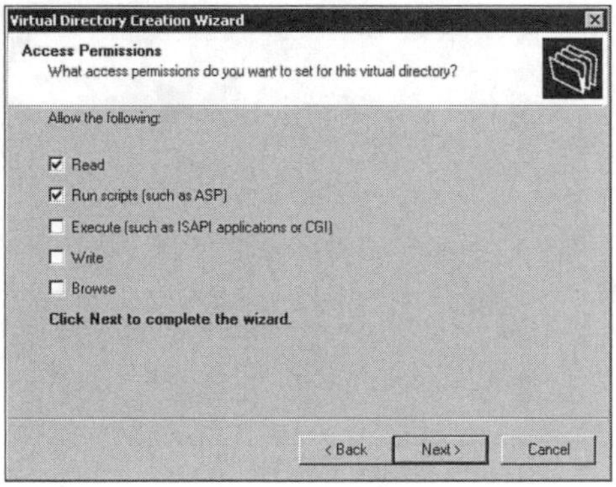

FIGURE 13.6   Access Permissions.

10. The final screen is just a confirmation that everything has been completed. Simply click Finish. This screen is illustrated in Figure 13.7.

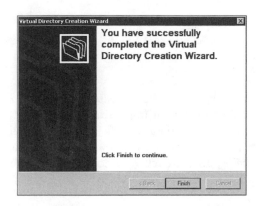

FIGURE 13.7   Wizard complete.

> **NOTE**
>
> This could have been done as well with Visual InterDev or FrontPage. It was illustrated via the previous steps to point out specifically where the access permissions come from when establishing a site.

Making the Site with Visual Studio.NET

If you followed the steps in the previous section, and made the site without using Visual Studio.NET, note that you will have to delete that virtual directory, "FormAuth," from IIS before completing the steps in this section.

From Visual Studio.NET, create a new C# Empty Web Project. To do this, select File, New, Project from the menu. Type the project name **FormAuth** in the dialog provided. Click the OK button. Where this project is stored on your hard drive will vary based on your configuration. It should look like Figure 13.8.

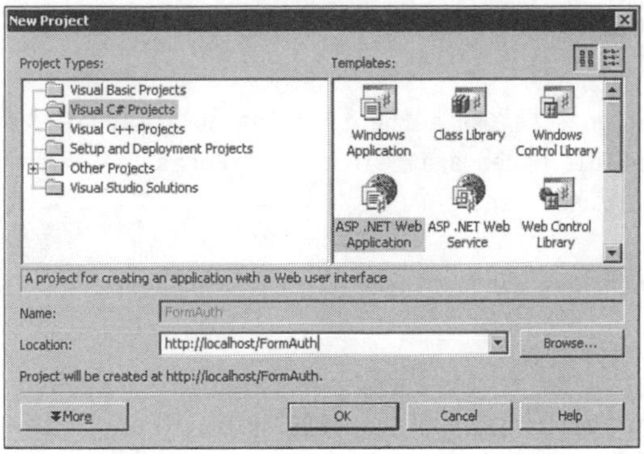

FIGURE 13.8   New Project dialog.

NOTE

If you were to select a project of type "ASP.NET Web Application", the `web.config` file will be created automatically

---

Now that the Web and project have been created, you need to create a configuration file to tell the Web that you will be using Forms-based authentication. In the IDE, add a new file to the project called **web.config**. To do this, right-click the FormAuth folder in the project view, select Add, Add New Item. From the Templates panel, in the Add New Item dialog, double-click Web Configuration File. This is shown from a Visual Studio.NET perspective in Figure 13.9.

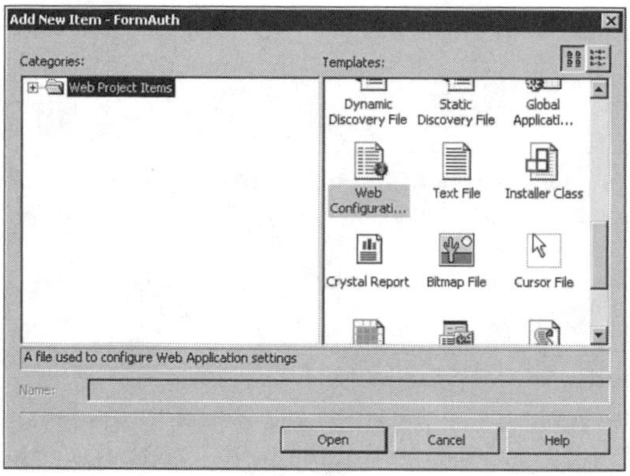

FIGURE 13.9   Add New Item dialog.

The first element you are going to alter is the authentication mode element. Listing 13.1 is an unaltered code listing from what the VS.NET Wizard–generated file produces when you add a new Web configuration file through the IDE.

LISTING 13.1   Partial `Web.config` File

```
<!-- AUTHENTICATION
        This section sets the authentication policies of the
➥ application. Possible modes are "Windows", "Forms",
        "Passport" and "None"
    -->
    <authentication mode="Windows" />
```

You are first going to change this element's value to `Forms`. The next thing to do is deny access to anonymous users. To do this, you will add the authorization element under the system.Web element. Authorization is discussed in detail in Chapter 15,

"Authorization: Control Who Is Accessing Your Site." Listing 13.2 shows the complete code for this sample's web.config file. In this sample, note the user element that contains a plain-text username and for a password, a SHA-1 hash. The password for this sample is password.

LISTING 13.2 Complete web.config File

```
<?xml version="1.0" encoding="utf-8" ?>
<configuration>
<system.Web>
    <compilation defaultLanguage="c#" debug="true" />
        <customErrors mode="Off" />
    <authentication mode="Forms">
        <forms name=".NETBOOKDEMO"
         loginUrl="login.aspx"
         protection="All"
         timeout="30"
         path="/">
    <credentials passwordFormat="SHA1" >
        <user name="user@domain.com"
password="5BAA61E4C9B93F3F0682250B6CF8331B7EE68FD8"/>
      </credentials>
      </forms>
   </authentication>
   <authorization>
          <deny users="?" />
    </authorization>
    <trace enabled="false"
     requestLimit="10"
     pageOutput="false"
     traceMode="SortByTime"
     localOnly="true" />
    <sessionState mode="InProc"
     stateConnectionString="tcpip=127.0.0.1:42424"
     sqlConnectionString="data source=127.0.0.1;user id=sa;password="
     cookieless="false" timeout="20" />
    <globalization requestEncoding="utf-8" responseEncoding="utf-8" />
</system.Web>
</configuration>
```

Notice the introduction of the forms element. This element allows you to configure the actual aspects of the form or forms that will be used on your site for authentication. Table 13.1 shows the possible attributes to include, what their values can be, and includes a brief explanation of the attribute. Table 13.2 shows specifics about the protection attribute.

TABLE 13.1   Forms Element Attributes

Attribute	Possible Values	Description
loginURL	Any valid URL, default is login.aspx	Where a user is redirected if login fails.
name	Any valid HTTP string as a name for the cookie, default is .ASPXAUTH	This is the name of the cookie that the application will use. If you intend to have more than one application running on the same server, this value should be unique.
timeout	Any valid integer, default is 30	This is how long the cookie will live on the user's machine. This is a sliding value, meaning that it expires x minutes from the last time the cookie was updated, not from when the user started the session with the site.
path	/ (default) or other string	This represents where the cookie is stored on the client.
protection	All (default), None, Encryption, Validation Note: these parameters are case-sensitive	This attribute sets the method used to protect the cookie data. The options are listed in detail in Table 13.2.

TABLE 13.2   Possible Protection Attribute Values

Attribute Value	Description
None	Does nothing. While this is the least secure, there are no performance hits.
Validation	Checks to see if the cookie has been altered since the last visit. Does not encrypt or decrypt a cookie.
Encryption	Encrypts the cookie using either DES or 3-DES (default, if available). Does not validate that contents have not been altered since last visit.
All (default)	Encrypts and validates the cookie.

To see all of this in action, have a look at the code for what is being executed. Listing 13.3 shows the complete login.aspx file.

Listing 13.3 is a sample of the cookie contents created in this sample site, once a successful login has occurred, with the protection attribute set to All and an authentication mode of "Forms". Notice that all of the user information contained within is encrypted.

LISTING 13.3   Sample Cookie Contents

```
.NETBOOKDEMO
F55C7E54A47424392E1566A04A411394C31B32791ABCC0C200B0FB93793873F980B5DFC6915335
➡F78C3D2C5E3AA8D51BD1DBF25366302DCE587BC0A805D1B1CBF26B34DADC5EEC126F5D
➡F8D47653C141E89AB3D7734BDFF1F5B985C40A2D58A1
 localhost/
1024
2515158400
33122100
43348752
29448413
*
```

Now, you have a site with no pages that no one can access, the ultimate secure site. Unfortunately, reality dictates that you must provide some content. The reason for this approach is simple. Start with the most secure you can be, without regard to the application, and work backwards. The next step will be to add a page that serves as your login page. It does not have to be elaborate, and for this example it won't be. Just a couple of simple .aspx files with the necessary text boxes and Submit button.

That is all it takes to create and enable an ASP.NET application that uses Forms-based authentication.

Using Impersonation in ASP.NET

Impersonation is the process by which an application runs as a user. In ASP, this was always on by default; in ASP.NET, it is not. As with all application development, it is important to remember that no application should ever run as an administrator—unless there is irrepressible proof that it must. Even though .NET introduces managed code, this code could still be making calls to objects and executables written prior to .NET. This opens a security risk when it becomes possible to open an unchecked buffer in an application configured to run as an administrator from a .NET-managed application. One suggestion, especially for COM- and COM+–based applications is to create a user specifically for that application and grant him or her the explicit rights needed. For example, a COM/COM+ application that writes files using the COM-based Scripting.FileSystemObject library running as an administrator means that anybody or anything that accesses that object is now an administrator, and any code running in it will run as such. Creating a user called MyApp with read/write privileges on a directory used by your application is far safer. This is also a far more intelligent decision than granting IUSR_MACHINENAME administrative rights. For certain developers, this is what has happened. Many created in-process COM objects that did not use MTS or COM+ to help manage things, like context, and ended up with a `.dll` that ran in the same process space as IIS. While a nifty performance trick, it meant that your code ran with the same rights as IIS, usually `SYSTEM`. So now your code, albeit I'm sure you did a good job, is running on the Internet with `SYSTEM` privileges. However, if your code was written as an ISAPI extension, IIS would use an impersonation token. Usually, this token was that of `IUSR_MACHINENAME` unless otherwise configured.

Thankfully, ASP.NET does not have to suffer from this. Not only does it not suffer from this kind of security issue, it has protected itself from IIS's default settings as well. The ASP.NET worker process as well runs, by default, as the ASP.NET user, which is by default a member of the Users group.

Here's why. `ASPNET_ISAPI.dll` is not just a beefed up `ASP.dll` that we all know and love. It merely passes your request to `ASP-NET_WP.exe` through a named pipe. This creates an out-of-process worker. There is a file in the `%WINDIR%\Microsoft.Net\Framework\%VERSION%\CONFIG` directory called `machine.config`. In that file, you will find an element called `processModel`. In that element, you will find the attributes `username` and `password`. This is the account that ASP.NET applications will run as. Because you don't want to place plain-text passwords in a flat file, it is advisable that you use the machine account as shown in Listing 13.4.

LISTING 13.4   Section of `machine.config`

```
userName="Machine" password="AutoGenerate"
```

So what does this do? It causes ASP.NET to run at a higher isolation level. `ASPNET_ISAPI.dll` now calls `LogonUser` and `CreateProcessAsUser` and executes with the limited permissions of `IWAM_MACHINE` or whatever account you set up in the `processModel` element. The process of modifying the remote identity of service that is set to execute as one user is referred to as *impersonation*.

Passport Authentication

Passport technology has been expanded to allow all developers to utilize this authentication technology on their sites. This feature adds a single source for authentication and user information without having to worry about integrating your code or data. The `PassportAuthenticationModule` provides a wrapper around the Passport SDK for ASP.NET applications and provides Passport authentication services and profile information from an `IIdentity`-derived class called `PassportIdentity`. As is the case with `WindowsIdentity`, the primary purpose of handling the `PassportAuthentication_OnAuthenticate` event is to attach a custom `IPrincipal` object to the context. A special `IIdentity`-derived class called `PassportIdentity` provides an interface to the Passport profile information and methods to encrypt and decrypt Passport authentication tickets. Much concern has arisen at the time of this writing as to just how secure using a public service to log in your private users really is and how much of that private user's information must be stored on the public server. In most cases, the Microsoft Passport servers need an email address and a country of origin. There is no foundation to claims that Microsoft is reading additional information placed in cookies from other sites that use Passport authentication.

To implement Passport authentication in an ASP.NET application, do the following:

1. Download, install, and configure the Passport SDK from `http://www.passport.com/business`. You must register to obtain the SDK. There is a fee involved for actually subscribing to the Microsoft Passport server. Details may be found at `http://www.passport.com`.

2. Set up Passport as the authentication mode in the application configuration file as follows:

```
<authentication mode= "Passport">
</authentication>
```

As with Forms authentication, Passport authentication provides you with a `redirectUrl` attribute that serves the same purpose as the `loginUrl` attribute on a `forms` element.

Authentication for Web Services

To look at this from the highest level, there are basically two ways to use authentication with an XML Web service created using ASP.NET; you can use what is offered within .NET or you can create custom SOAP-based security. The latter may be necessary when integrating Web services with other products that offer "Web services" such as webMethods or IBM MQSeries. Outside of .NET, there is use of firewalls, IP restrictions lists, and so forth. that can help control just who or what gets to use your Web service. For example, you may wish to establish B2B transactions with another company. Since this is a one-to-one relationship, you could establish a VPN connection between the offices and allow them access to your Web service.

NOTE

It is important to note that .NET Forms-based authentication is not directly supported by XML Web services. This does not mean that it cannot be used. Although not recommended, it can be worked around by sending a direct request to a login page setup to handle the user's credentials. Doing this, of course, most likely will require exposing the user's credentials in an HTTP Query string.

ASP.NET also provides access to remote objects, or `Remoting`. One key difference is that when using Web services, you can rely on the HTTP protocol for how to get connected. The authentication options available are those made available through Internet Information Services (IIS); Basic, Digest, Integrated Windows, and Client Certificates. For most cases, using Basic authentication over SSL will suffice. Authentication within ASP.NET is discussed in more detail in Chapter 14, "Authentication: Know Who Is Accessing Your Site." With remoting on ASP.NET, you are using an HTTPChannel or TCPChannel class. The authentication process is then handled directly in your code, if it is needed at all.

As you will find as you read this book, the methods for protecting a Web page are quite the same as those for protecting a Web service. With both, you are able to collect credential information and use it accordingly in your application. Authorization in Web services is also implanted. Details on using ASP.NET authorization can be found in Chapter 15.

Code Access Security and ASP.NET

Code Access Security is a process that allows or denies code the right to run from within a method. This could be code that you have a reference to from a third-party or code that you have written. As with any security mechanism, there is a set of guidelines to comply with that should be used to ensure that the code written uses only the permission set intended.

The first guideline is writing type-safe code. Type-safe code is code that accesses types in very well-defined, allowable ways. Type-safety really comes into play when considering the mobile environment. Code that is not type-safe may access memory blocks that it is not allowed to, resulting in a security exception on .NET. Creating type-safe code is not really a difficult task; it's really just defining your data types in a manner that the CLR will be able to verify as safe. To assist you with checking your code to verify that it is type-safe, Microsoft has provided a tool with the .NET Framework called `PEVerify`. `PEVerify` reads the assembly and verifies the information within generated `MSIL` files and associated metadata to be type-safe or not. As a rule, the `CLR` will not execute code that is not verifiably type-safe. This can be overridden, although doing so is not recommended. `JIT` compilation also relies on code to be type-safe, so by overriding this setting, you may be jeopardizing all other security settings associated with an application.

NOTE

For complete information on PEVerify and its use, type keyword **PEVerify** in the .NET documentation index.

The next guideline is familiarizing yourself with imperative and declarative syntax. Together, this is referred to as *security syntax*. The main difference in the two of these is that imperative security calls are made by instantiating a new permissions object, whereas declarative security calls are made through the attributes of an existing object. Certain calls can only be made imperatively, and certain can only be made declaratively, while most calls will support both methods. An example of when to use imperative syntax may be when you are not going to know if users need rights to access a file until they are in the application. During their work, they need no security context, nor do they need any special permission checks until they want to use your new function. When they attempt to execute the method, you imperatively check permissions to see if they can perform the task. Your code then routes the user to the appropriate response depending on the result of your permissions check. In declarative syntax, you make a request through the metadata of your application/class/method. For example, let's say you have created a permissions object called canDoEverything, and you are writing a new method that requires a validation from canDoEverything before proceeding. Declaring the canDoEverything class prior to any other method calls in your class requires that the user meet the requirements established in canDoEverything or he or she can do nothing.

Third on the list is requesting permissions for your code. Requesting permissions basically just lets the CLR know what your code needs to be allowed to do. Now here's the trick—you can ask the CLR for certain permissions that your application needs (or wants) to run but, depending on the CLR configuration, it can still say no. The actual permissions needed by your assembly can be seen using the PermView tool. This tool analyzes your code/executable and reports the permissions needed to execute it. This would allow an administrator to modify an account to suit your needs without jeopardizing the rest of the enterprise. Another fringe benefit of requesting permissions for your code is that your code only gets the permissions it needs, thus reducing the chance that if something does go wrong and someone could add some malicious code to your unchecked buffer, it would only execute with the permissions needed for the assembly, and that is, hopefully, not an administrator. Know that if you are not in control of the permissions on the box executing your code, you must trap for trying to use permissions you do have and cannot get. A message box with the text of "Security Exception – Method ~ of ~ failed" is not going to cut it.

Finally, there are secure class libraries. Basically, a secure class library is what you get if you follow the previous three guidelines. It is more an end result that states that your code is verifiably type-safe, uses security syntax, and knows what permissions it needs through making requests.

The ASP.NET application you are writing is by default set to run as the ASPNET user. While you can control what permissions this user has, it's not a bad idea to establish a separate user for an application. All code access permissions implemented in the .NET Framework can take a `PermissionState` value as an argument to their constructor. These principles can be applied from anywhere you can create a class.

Summary

In this chapter, you learned some of the new features regarding security and ASP.NET. Most of these, as shown, are built on top of the existing infrastructure with which ASP developers should be accustomed. For detailed information on the classes mentioned in this chapter, please consult the latest version of the .NET documentation of the .NET Web site on MSDN (`http://msdn.microsoft.com/net`).

14

Authentication: Know Who Is Accessing Your Site

By Kevin Price

As a developer, there have been many times when the question of how to, or even whether to, authenticate users has risen. The reasons for doing so are countless; it's how you do it that will determine its effectiveness. This chapter will introduce you to some of the new features for authentication in ASP.NET, as well as demonstrate how this works with the existing infrastructure provided in IIS.

This chapter will cover the whys and hows of using authentication in ASP.NET, as well as Internet Information Services (IIS), to establish who can access your site and to find out who has accessed your site. After reading this chapter, you will

- Understand authentication methods available in IIS

- Know how ASP.NET handles authentication

- Know how to use the CLR role-based security infrastructure to help secure your application

- Know how impersonation works now and how it can actually help you secure your site

ASP.NET Authentication and IIS Authentication

To begin, let's look at a definition of what authentication is. Microsoft defines authentication as

"...the process of obtaining identification credentials such as name and password from a user and validating those credentials against some authority. If the credentials are valid, the entity that submitted the credentials is considered an authenticated identity. Once an identity has been authenticated, the authorization process determines whether that identity has access to a given resource."

This "authenticated identity" is the basis for .NET authentication as well as IIS, Windows NT, Windows 2000, and many other platforms' means of not only determining if a user can access a resource, but also to gain information for such tasks as site personalization. Most of the functionality available to developers regarding authentication is exposed through the System.Net library.

Overview of IIS Authentication

IIS provides an interface that ties directly into the Windows operating system on which it is running. This interface allows certain types of authentication to be performed based on accounts at the operating system level. ASP.NET authentication rides on top of the existing structure already provided by Windows servers. IIS provides five ways to allow or deny a user access through a login procedure and two ways to control access based on machine settings and use of certificates. The five ways of authentication provided for in IIS are as follows:

- Anonymous
- Basic Authentication
- Digest Authentication
- Integrated Windows Authentication
- Client certificate mapping

Figure 14.1 shows the IIS dialog for selecting which authentication method to use.

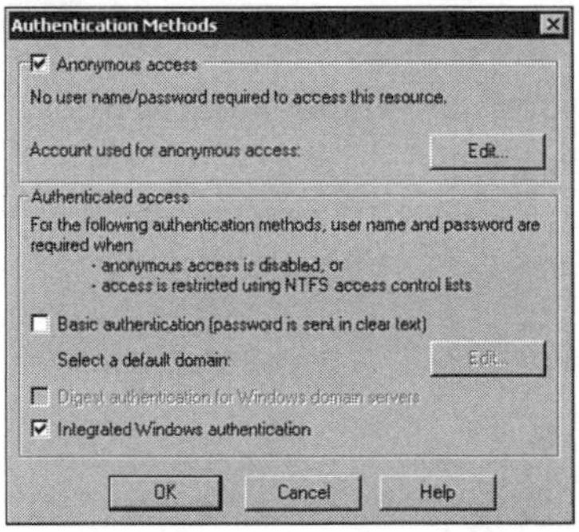

FIGURE 14.1   IIS authentication methods.

Using Anonymous Access

Anonymous access is allowed by default through a machine account named `IUSR_<your machine name here>`. This account resides the `Guests` group of your domain by default. This method allows access to certain resources without users having to identify themselves at all to the server. A few things to watch for when using the anonymous account are as follows:

- If IIS does not control the password and the password changes on the network, the service will fail. What this means is that if you were to change the password of the IUSR account and IIS was not aware of the change, the services running within IIS would fail.

- Anonymous lets anybody in unless IP/Site name or certificate restrictions are in place.

- Make sure the account used for anonymous access is a machine account so that resource access is fairly limited. Another means of handling this is to assign anonymous access to an account on the forest so that Integrated Windows Authentication can be used with SQL Server.

Using Basic Authentication

Basic Authentication is just what it sounds like—a very basic, not-so-secure way of authenticating or identifying a user. Because Basic Authentication is part of the HTTP 1.0 specification, it is by far the most widely accepted form of authentication. Most commercial proxy servers, Web browsers, and Web servers support Basic Authentication, but the information that a user types in to gain access is not encrypted at all, unless you have implemented SSL, and is basically sending plain text passwords over the network or Internet. In IIS, Basic Authentication uses a domain account list to validate user information. Therefore, any user that you want to authenticate must have a Windows account. It is strongly recommended that, unless it is absolutely necessary, that users created for this purpose are basically limited to the same rights as the "Guest" account that is created by default. Using IIS and SSL for Basic Authentication will allow you to pass credentials on Windows 2000 machines. This can be useful for delegation, but sending a plain text password without SSL for this purpose obviously creates a huge security risk. Also, if you're curious about using `Kerberos` for Windows 2000, keep in mind the following:

- `Kerberos` is only supported on Windows 2000 and later.

- To use `Kerberos`, you must have a KDC server—not something you want the whole world viewing, thus making this most useful on intranet applications.

- Whatever client you are using, it must be able to support `Kerberos` as well.

When configuring users to use Basic Authentication in a Windows NT/2000/XP network, you must grant the user a LogonMethod. Most administrators should be familiar with giving a user "Log on Locally" through the user administration interfaces; this is an example of a LogonMethod. The IIS metabase stores settings for managing clear text logons, such as with Basic Authentication. The key of MD_LOGON_METHOD can be set to the following values:

- 0, the default, for Log on Locally or MD_LOGON_INTERACTIVE

- 1, for Logon as Batch Job or MD_LOGON_BATCH

- 2, for Logon over Network or MD_LOGON_NETWORK

NOTE

The reference to editing information that is stored in the IIS Metabase is based on using the tool Metaedit 2.0 from the Windows 2000 Server Resource Kit.

This key can be set at the service, server, directory, virtual directory, and file levels. It cannot be stressed enough that this method of authentication needs to be used in conjunction with SSL if possible to make it a "secure" means of validating credentials. Depending on usage, it may be more viable for you to purchase additional machines to make up for any performance hits from using SSL. This can turn out to be a far less expense than having all of your customers' credit card information sent out by a hacker using a packet sniffer to gain login credentials on your site. If your ASP.NET application needs to run as a user validated by Basic Authentication, you will need to ensure that the web.config file indicates that Windows is the value for the authentication mode attribute. This is illustrated in Listing 14.1.

LISTING 14.1   Authentication Mode in web.config

```
<system.web>
…lots of elements
 <authentication mode="Windows" />
 … a lot more elements
</system.web>
```

NOTE

More specific information on implementing SSL on IIS is available through the Microsoft Web site at http://www.microsoft.com/windows2000/en/server/iis/htm/core/iisslsc.htm or in the Knowledge Base by searching for article Q298805.

Using Digest Authentication

Digest authentication, in a nutshell, is Basic Authentication with a twist. It creates a hash, or digest, of the user's password, the URI requested, and some padding or salt on the client and passes that to the server. Once on the server, the password portion of the hash must be decrypted and then a network login is performed. There are certain immediate pitfalls to using this type of authentication that are very similar to the issues with using Basic Authentication. The first issue is that without SSL, someone could conceivably "record" the actions of a client browser and play them back as if he or she was that user. This would give the attacker the same rights as the original user. The next thing that comes up, especially for Active Directory domains, is that if you plan to use Digest Authentication for users to come in from the outside, their passwords must be stored using reversible encryption. By default, passwords on an AD domain are one-way hashes. In addition to the points raised regarding Basic Authentication, the following must also be considered when implementing Digest Authentication:

- Digest Authentication currently only works with Microsoft Internet Explorer Version 5.0 and later.

- Digest Authentication, like Basic Authentication, works with most commercial proxy servers and firewalls.

- In Active Directory, a user account must exist for each user you want to authenticate.

NOTE

For in-depth information about the Digest Authentication Specification, refer to RFC 2617, available on the Internet at http://www.ietf.org/rfc/rfc2617.txt.

Using Integrated Windows Authentication

Now, we can have some fun. Integrated Windows Authentication is excellent for those times when you have Microsoft-based OS Servers, Microsoft-based OS Workstations, or clients and Microsoft-based Web browsers. The main reason for this is that Integrated Windows Authentication only works with Internet Explorer Version 2.0 and later. The way it works is by sending two WWW-AUTHENTICATE headers in the request when a user attempts to access a protected resource. The first WWW-AUTHENTICATE header will be the NEGOTIATE header, which will determine whether to use NTLM (NT LAN Manager) or Kerberos v5 authentication to perform the network login. If Internet Explorer recognizes the NEGOTIATE header, it will return to IIS information for both NTLM and Kerberos. If the client and the server are running Windows 2000 or later, IIS will decide to use Kerberos. If anything goes wrong, or a null result is returned, IIS and IE will default back to NTLM. Keep in mind that only when using Kerberos authentication on a Windows 2000, or later, network can security credentials be passed around, assuming it has been configured to allow this. More information about credentials and delegation is discussed later in the "Using Impersonation and Delegation in ASP.NET" section later in this chapter.

Using Client-Side Certificates

So, what to do when you have a very large client base? Use certificates. Client certificates allow you to map several users to one Windows 2000 account through certificates. A client certificate is structurally similar to any server certificate. It is used to verify credentials and establish a secure session. Although this method cannot be used to delegate, it is based on PKI (Public Key Infrastructure), meaning that the exchange will require your client's public key and the server's public key to make an exchange. In this method, your server will be issued a certificate by a CA (Certificate Authority). These will also cause the basic SSL communications to begin. The next step is to get the client certificate information and mark it as trusted. This is a very practical method on large internal networks where is it possible to be your own CA through use of Certificate Server and issue certificates to your own clients through your own server. Some of the key points to ponder when using client-side certificates for authentication are as follows:

- They don't work with all browsers.

- They require SSL or TLS.

- They provide a very strong authentication method, just not the easiest to implement.

NOTE

For a step-by-step guide to using client certificates, go to
http://www.microsoft.com/windows2000/techinfo/planning/security/
mappingcerts.asp.

Using IP Address and Domain Name Restrictions

More of a broad approach to security, rather than an authentication scheme, is the ability to configure restrictions based on a client machine name or IP address.

From the Microsoft Management Console for IIS, an administrator can determine whether to let all machines that attempt to come in through or establish certain groups that do not have permission based on either domain name or IP address. For example, you may have a situation where, on your internal network, the sales department is not allowed to see the financial department's Web site. As an administrator, you configure IIS to block the internal IP address range of the sales department on the Web server that holds the other application. What if they are on the same box? Set up virtual Webs on different ports and map those to a redirect page on the base port. Figure 14.2 illustrates the dialog for setting these parameters in IIS.

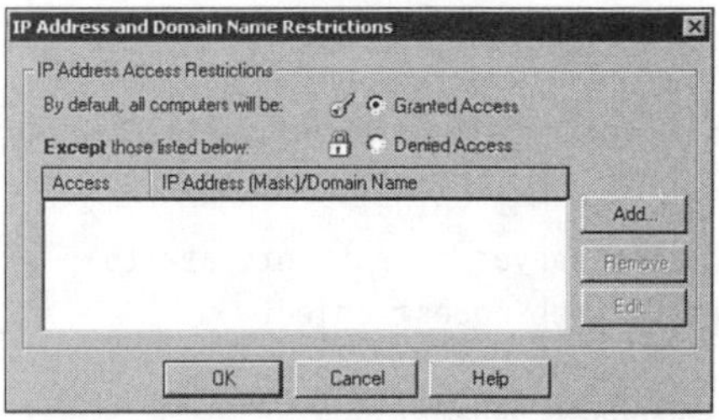

FIGURE 14.2   IP Address and Domain Name Restrictions dialog.

NOTE

The ability to restrict access by IP address and/or domain name is only available on server installations of IIS. It is not available on PWS or IIS installed on Windows NT, Windows 2000, or Windows XP Professional; however, within Windows XP, the use of IPSec can provide similar functionality.

ASP.NET Authentication Settings

Now that you have an understanding of what is available through IIS, you can look at how to use that to your advantage from ASP.NET. As previously mentioned, the functionality for HTTP client authentication is exposed through the System.Net library. Because System.Net is a vast wealth of functionality for many network functions, we will concentrate on the AuthenticationManager, NetworkCredential, CredentialCache, and WebRequest classes.

The AuthenticationManager class handles the management of the various authentication modules called during a login process. This covers a pretty important process—the actual authentication of a user. This is provided through the Authenticate() method of the AuthenticationManager class. Listing 14.2 shows the declaration syntax.

LISTING 14.2   Authenticate Method (C#)

```
public static Authorization Authenticate(
    string challenge,
    WebRequest request,
    ICredentials credentials
);
```

Notice that the declaration expects an instance of the ICredentials interface. This is exposed as the NetworkCredential class and the CredentialCache class implements ICredentials. ICredentials exposes the function GetCredentials which, as you might guess, returns a NetworkCredential object associated with a specific URL/URI and whatever authentication scheme you are using. Not clear enough, consider the snippet in Listing 14.3.

LISTING 14.3   NetworkCredentials Code Snippet—Basic/Digest Authentication

```
//Create a string to hold the URI value
String MyURI = "http://some-server-to-authenticate-to";
//Create an instance of the WebRequest object
// to handle the actual request
WebRequest WebReq = WebRequest.Create(MyURI);
//Now set the credentials for the whatever functionality
//you need to perform within this WebRequest,
//with these credentials
WebReq.Credentials = new NetworkCredential("someusername", "somepassword");
```

In Listing 14.3, if the server name were set to something real that required Basic or Digest Authentication, it would return a WebResponse object that could be traversed using the WebResponse.GetResponseStream() method to begin using information retrieved during the request. The Authenticate() method is called through hierarchy of using the NetworkCredential class.

If you slightly modify this code sample, you can make it work for NTLM or Kerberos authentication as well. Thanks to method overriding features in .NET, the code looks exactly the same, only you add a domain name to the parameter list for the NetworkCredential object. See Listing 14.4 for the complete snippet with changes.

LISTING 14.4   NetworkCredentials Code Snippet—NTLM/Kerberos Authentication

```
//Create a string to hold the URI value
String MyURI = "http://some-server-to-authenticate-to";
//Create an instance of the WebRequest object
// to handle the actual request
WebRequest WebReq = WebRequest.Create(MyURI);
//Now set the credentials for the whatever functionality
//you need to perform within this WebRequest,
//with these credentials
WebReq.Credentials = new NetworkCredential("someusername",
➥"somepassword", "somedomainname");
```

Because embedding plain text passwords is not always a good idea for creating a secure application, this same code can be slightly modified yet again to provide authentication for a user who has already logged in. For example, you may have NTLM authentication set up on a particular site; we'll call it Books for this example. According to application guidelines, people in Books can see nothing in the other department of Videos. As an administrator, you need to see it all. This can be managed easily by just letting the NetworkCredential class instantiate with the existing credentials from when you logged in. If a Books person is logged in and attempts to access a resource that is in Videos, an exception will occur that is trappable and should be handled gracefully.

Consider Listing 14.5 for how to use the default credentials of the already authenticated user.

LISTING 14.5 NetworkCredentials Code Snippet—Default User Permissions

```
//Create a string to hold the URI value
String MyURI = "http://some-server-to-authenticate-to";
//Create an instance of the WebRequest object
// to handle the actual request
WebRequest WebReq = WebRequest.Create(MyURI);
//Now set the credentials for the whatever functionality
//you need to perform within this WebRequest,
//with these credentials
WebReq.Credentials = CredentialCache.DefaultCredentials;
```

This works because the user is already logged in and his or her credentials are cached. Each time a user logs in during a session, his or her credentials can be stored in a cache, and this cache is what is accessible through the CredentialClass. This sample not only illustrates the ease with which authentication can be implemented programmatically, it is also a good illustration of inheritance for those who may be new to it.

Default IIS Settings

Out of the box, Internet Information Services comes configured for basic usage. It is not configured for scalability or security without a little user intervention. However, this configuration is quite simple and does not require recompilation of the entire server to see the changes in effect. As mentioned at the beginning of this chapter, IIS has five built-in ways of authenticating users. By default, when a new virtual Web is created, Anonymous Access and Integrated Windows Authentication are enabled. This means that, if not specified otherwise in the web.config file, .NET will execute under the ASP.NET account, unless a directory has been established that requires Integrated Windows Authentication to access resources.

How does one set up one of these Webs that has both kinds of access? Chapter 13, "Introduction to ASP.NET Security," lists the instructions for creating a new virtual directory through IIS. This directory is now established with the default settings. Because you want a secure application and a page that allows users to view public material, you will create a subdirectory for your Web from within the IIS MMC.

From Windows Explorer, or whatever your favorite method is, add a folder to the FormAuth directory created in Chapter 13. Name the folder **WinAuth**, and then complete the following steps to enable it for Integrated Windows Authentication while the parent folder of FormAuth still allows anonymous visitors.

1. From the IIS MMC, expand the Default Web Site folder as shown in Figure 14.3 to view all Web sites on the server.

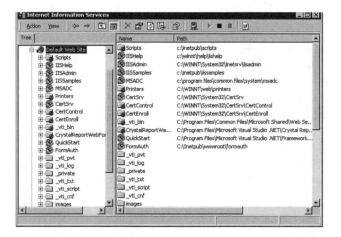

FIGURE 14.3   IIS Microsoft Management Console.

2. Click the FormAuth application icon to display its contents. If you have IIS MMC open when you make the directory, press F5 to refresh the page.

3. In the details pane, right-click the WinAuth folder icon and select Properties.

4. Select the Directory Security tab.

5. Select the Edit in the Anonymous Access and Authentication Control.

   a. Select the Directory Security tab.

   b. Select the Edit in the Anonymous Access and Authentication Control.

6. Deselect Allow Anonymous Access, as shown in Figure 14.4.

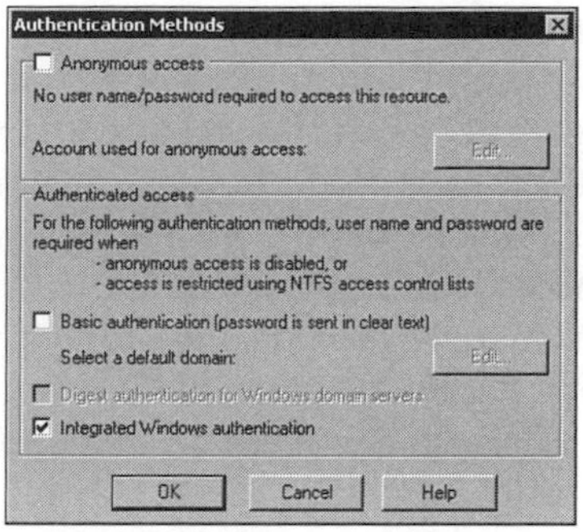

FIGURE 14.4   Virtual Web Anonymous Access settings.

7. Click OK.

You have now configured your site to use Anonymous Access for one directory, while enforcing Integrated Windows Authentication on another.

Using CLR Role-Based Security in Windows

Within the Common Language Runtime are classes that allow you to further programmatically determine which user account your code will execute under and allow things to happen outside of the rights assigned under a Windows account. In other words, it is possible to have users that are Windows users that have administrative rights within the application but are not actually in the Administrators group on Windows NT/2000/XP. The same is true of assemblies. They may have administrative logic built in, but not be part of the local administrators group.

The main reason for this starts with the principal. Basically, a principal is like a proxy that can act on behalf of a user, but also can assume the identity and role of that user. Within the .NET Framework, there are three basic principals:

- *Generic Principals*—These are users that may or may not exist within a Windows 2000 domain and, therefore, may have privileges within an application that they may not otherwise have.

- *Windows Principals*—These are Windows users within a role or group on Windows NT and/or Windows 2000. They can impersonate other users, meaning that they can access resources on behalf of another user while presenting that user's credentials.

- *Custom Principals*—This group is defined by an application, and the rules are set by that application and/or its configuration.

Now, because principals are used to determine what is in a role or what a user can do, it makes demands to determine whether or not a request can be completed. A demand will succeed only if the user is allowed to perform the task requested; otherwise, a security exception is thrown. This process is managed by the PrincipalPermission class. The PrincipalPermission class is part of the System.Security namespace. Within this are numerous members that are quite fun to play with and very informative when it comes to managing and recording who does what with what context and when they did it. Listing 14.6 demonstrates creating a new PrincipalPermission and executing a demand. Note that this call could be made imperatively by calling the IPrincipal.IsInRole method as well.

LISTING 14.6   Creating a PricipalPermission Code Snippet

```
try
{
String id = "Joe";
String role = "Sales";
PrincipalPermission PrincipalPerm1 = new PrincipalPermission(id, role);
PrincipalPerm1.Demand();
}
catch(SecurityException e)
{
… do something to handle the error
}
```

Figuring out who the Windows user is during this process can be done under one condition, the user must be authenticated by one of the methods listed at the beginning of this chapter. The following code sample in Listing 14.7 is a complete listing for the file named WebForm1.aspx.cs. This is the "code behind" file that Visual Studio.NET will compile to a DLL. I left everything completely generated as it appears in Visual Studio.NET to illustrate exactly what you may see when developing. The environment for this file to execute in is a Web with Anonymous Access turned off and only Windows Integrated Authentication turned on. This sample also shows how using the authentication mode of Windows allows ASP.NET to automatically wire the User object to your application. The complete sample is included on the book's Web site.

LISTING 14.7   WebForm1.aspx.cs (Complete)

```
using System;
using System.Collections;
using System.ComponentModel;
using System.Data;
```

LISTING 14.7 Continued

```
using System.Drawing;
using System.Web;
using System.Web.SessionState;
using System.Web.UI;
using System.Web.UI.WebControls;
using System.Web.UI.HtmlControls;

namespace Chapter14
{
 /// <summary>
 /// Summary description for WebForm1.
 /// </summary>
 public class WebForm1 : System.Web.UI.Page
 {
  private void Page_Load(object sender, System.EventArgs e)
  {
   // Put user code to initialize the page here
   if(User.Identity.IsAuthenticated)
   {
    Response.Write("Authenticated as : " + User.Identity.Name);
   }
   else
   {
    Response.Write("You are not authenticated.");
   }
  }

  #region Web Form Designer generated code
  override protected void OnInit(EventArgs e)
  {
   //
   // CODEGEN: This call is required by the ASP.NET Web Form Designer.
   //
   InitializeComponent();
   base.OnInit(e);
  }

  /// <summary>
  /// Required method for Designer support - do not modify
  /// the contents of this method with the code editor.
  /// </summary>
```

LISTING 14.7   Continued

```
private void InitializeComponent()
{
 this.Load += new System.EventHandler(this.Page_Load);
}
#endregion
}
}
```

As stated before the sample, within IIS, Integrated Windows Authentication is the
only option checked under Directory Security. Also, the web.config file is using the
default setting of Windows for the authentication element's mode attribute. Listing
14.8 illustrates this.

LISTING 14.8   web.config file (Complete)

```
<?xml version="1.0" encoding="utf-8" ?>
<configuration>

  <system.web>

    <!-- DYNAMIC DEBUG COMPILATION
         Set compilation debug="true" to enable ASPX debugging.  Otherwise,
➥ setting this value to
         false will improve runtime performance of this application.
         Set compilation debug="true" to insert debugging symbols (.pdb
➥ information)
         into the compiled page. Because this creates a larger file that
➥executes
         more slowly, you should set this value to true only when debugging
➥and to
         false at all other times. For more information, refer to the
➥documentation about
         debugging ASP .NET files.
    -->
    <compilation
        defaultLanguage="c#"
        debug="true"
    />

    <!-- CUSTOM ERROR MESSAGES
         Set customError mode values to control the display of user-friendly
```

LISTING 14.8   Continued

```
            error messages to users instead of error details (including a stack
➥ trace):

            "On" Always display custom (friendly) messages
            "Off" Always display detailed ASP.NET error information.
            "RemoteOnly" Display custom (friendly) messages only to users not
➥ running
            on the local Web server. This setting is recommended for security
➥purposes, so
            that you do not display application detail information to remote
➥clients.
    -->
    <customErrors
    mode="RemoteOnly"
    />


    <!-- AUTHENTICATION
            This section sets the authentication policies of the application.
➥ Possible modes are "Windows", "Forms",
            "Passport" and "None"
    -->
    <authentication mode="Windows" />


    <!-- APPLICATION-LEVEL TRACE LOGGING
            Application-level tracing enables trace log output for every page
➥ within an application.
            Set trace enabled="true" to enable application trace logging.  If
➥ pageOutput="true", the
            trace information will be displayed at the bottom of each page.
➥Otherwise, you can view the
            application trace log by browsing the "trace.axd" page from your
➥web application
            root.
    -->
    <trace
        enabled="false"
        requestLimit="10"
        pageOutput="false"
        traceMode="SortByTime"
  localOnly="true"
    />
```

LISTING 14.8 Continued

```
    <!-- SESSION STATE SETTINGS
         By default ASP .NET uses cookies to identify which requests belong
➥to a particular session.
         If cookies are not available, a session can be tracked by adding a
➥ session identifier to the URL.
         To disable cookies, set sessionState cookieless="true".
    -->
    <sessionState
         mode="InProc"
         stateConnectionString="tcpip=127.0.0.1:42424"
         sqlConnectionString="data source=127.0.0.1;user id=sa;password="
         cookieless="false"
         timeout="20"
    />

    <!-- GLOBALIZATION
         This section sets the globalization settings of the application.
    -->
    <globalization
         requestEncoding="utf-8"
         responseEncoding="utf-8"
    />

 </system.web>

</configuration>
```

Using ASP.NET Forms Authentication

In Chapter 13, Forms Authentication was introduced as a new feature of ASP.NET.
Now that we have covered everything behind that sample, let's look at it again and
"tweak" a few things this time. Starting with the web.config file for the FormAuth
site, Listing 14.9 shows the complete web.config file.

LISTING 14.9 web.config File for FormAuth Application

```
<?xml version="1.0" encoding="utf-8" ?>
<configuration>
 <system.web>
<authentication mode="Forms">
<forms name=".NETBOOKDEMO" loginUrl="login.aspx" protection="All"
➥ timeout="30" path="/" />
```

LISTING 14.9   Continued

```
</authentication>
<authorization>
        <deny users="?" />
</authorization>
<globalization requestEncoding="utf-8" responseEncoding="utf-8" />
 </system.web>
</configuration>
```

Now that our Web will be configured correctly, we have to make at least one page. As mentioned in Chapter 13, the element of `authentication` mode in the `web.config` file can take four possible values. Because we chose `"Forms"`, we must have a page for login and failed logins. This can be the same page. Listing 14.10 shows the default page of this site, `login.aspx`.

LISTING 14.10   login.aspx (Complete)

```
<%@ Import Namespace="System.Web.Security " %>
<html>
 <script language="C#" runat="server">

    void Login_Click(Object sender, EventArgs E) {

      // authenticate user: this samples accepts only one user with
      // a name of user@domain.com and a password of 'password'
//in a real world scenario, this would be code that hit a database of some
//sort to validate a user after validating the input to prevent against script.
      // injection and SQL injection attacks
      if ((UserEmail.Value == "user@domain.com") && (UserPass.Value ==
➥ "password")) {
         FormsAuthentication.RedirectFromLoginPage(UserEmail.Value,
➥ PersistCookie.Checked);
      }
      else {
        Msg.Text = "Invalid Credentials: Please try again";
 // unless you validate or encode *all* untrusted data before echoing it back,
 // you have a CSS attack
        Msg.Text += " You entered " + Server.HtmlEncode(UserEmail.Value) + "<BR>";
        Msg.Text += " and a password of " + Server.HtmlEncode(UserPass.Value);
      }
    }
```

LISTING 14.10   Continued

```
</script>
<body>
 <form runat="server" ID="Form1">
  <h3><font face="Verdana">Login Page</font></h3>
  <table>
   <tr>
    <td>Email:</td>
    <td><input id="UserEmail" type="text" runat="server"
➥NAME="UserEmail" /></td>
    <td><ASP:RequiredFieldValidator ControlToValidate=
➥"UserEmail" Display="Static" ErrorMessage="*" runat="server"
➥ ID="Requiredfieldvalidator1" /></td>
   </tr>
   <tr>
    <td>Password:</td>
    <td><input id="UserPass" type="password" runat="server" NAME="UserPass"
/></td>
    <td><ASP:RequiredFieldValidator ControlToValidate="UserPass" Display="Static"
ErrorMessage="*" runat="server"
➥ID="Requiredfieldvalidator2" /></td>
   </tr>
   <tr>
    <td>Persistent Cookie:</td>
    <td><ASP:CheckBox id="PersistCookie" runat="server" />
    </td>
    <td></td>
   </tr>
  </table>
  <asp:button text="Login" OnClick="Login_Click" runat="server"
➥ ID="Button1" />

   <asp:Label id="Msg" ForeColor="red" Font-Name="Verdana"
➥ Font-Size="10" runat="server" />
 </form>
 </body>
</html>
```

What happens here is that if the login fails, the user is automatically redirected to the loginURL value set in the web.config file. Ideally, users would be stored in a database, but sometimes this is just not possible. For such an event, usernames and passwords can be stored in a web.config file. Obviously, you wouldn't store the passwords as plain text, so you encrypt them. Depending on the encryption scheme used, you would get different results for a hash. All of this information is stored by adding a credentials element to the `web.config` file and storing your user information in that file. An important attribute of this element is the `decryptionKey` value. If you plan to use these pages on more than one server, the `decryptionKey` value must be the same on all machines. The default value is `autogenerate`, but it can be any string value you desire consisting of hexadecimal characters. The next attribute that must be the same across all machines is the `passwordFormat` attribute; this can be `Clear` (not a good idea), MD5, or SHA-1. The information stored is a hash of the `decryptionKey` value and the password value using the `passwordFormat` algorithm. Because you're not going to know what the value of a specific hashed password is, you need a function that can take care of this for you. Listing 14.11 demonstrates the functionality necessary to create SHA-1 hashes of a password. To try this code on its own, simply paste it into the Page_Load event for an ASPX file, save the page to a working virtual directory, and navigate to `http://localhost/<whatever filename you gave it>.aspx?password`. You should see a result similar to 5BAA61E4C9B93F3F0682250B6CF8331B7EE68FD8. Alternatively, if you set the encryption scheme to MD5, you would get a value of 5F4DCC3B5AA765D61D8327DEB882CF99. These values will differ depending on any padding that you may use to increase security.

LISTING 14.11   Sample Encryption Function

```
string s_QString = this.Page.Request.QueryString.ToString();
if (s_QString.Length > 0)
{
    string hashedPass;
    string passToHash;
    passToHash = this.Page.Request.QueryString._
➡ToString();
    hashedPass =_  ➡FormsAuthentication.HashPasswordForStoringInConfigFile(passTo-
Hash, "md5");
    Response.Write(hashedPass);}
```

This function simply displays the encrypted password, but it demonstrates how simple it is using the .NET platform to implement security features.

Another task that forms authentication handles is the creation of a cookie. After a session is started and a user is authenticated, the cookie stores encrypted information regarding that user until the browser is closed. In Chapter 13, Tables 13.1 and 13.2 illustrate the possible configuration settings for where the cookie is stored, how long it will live, encryption settings, and its name. So now we can put all of this together in a sample that will authenticate users based on entries in the `web.config` file and uses the SHA-1 algorithm for encryption.

First, we'll make an entry in the web.config file for our test user, user@domain.com. I'll use the code in Listing 14.11 to create the hashed value for the word password and add the credentials. This entry is shown in Listing 14.12. Because we will be using this method of authentication, we have to add the credentials element to our authentication element.

LISTING 14.12   User Entry in web.config File

```
<authentication mode="Forms">
    <forms name=".NETBOOKDEMO" loginUrl="login.aspx"
➥ protection="All" timeout="30" path="/">
    <credentials passwordFormat="SHA1" >
     <user name="user@domain.com"
➥password="5BAA61E4C9B93F3F0682250B6CF8331B7EE68FD8"/>
    </credentials>
   </forms>
</authentication>
```

Of course, in a real world application, we would have a relational database for such accounts. Making changes to the web.config file prompts an application to restart, this could be very inconvenient in a high-visibility application. The next step is to change the login functionality in our login page, login.aspx. Listing 14.13 shows the Login_Click function.

LISTING 14.13   New Login_Click Function

```
void Login_Click(Object sender, EventArgs E) {
    if(FormsAuthentication.Authenticate(UserEmail.Value, UserPass.Value))
    {
    FormsAuthenticationTicket fTick = new FormsAuthenticationTicket_
➥(UserEmail.Value, false, 5000);
    FormsAuthentication.RedirectFromLoginPage(UserEmail.Value,
➥ PersistCookie.Checked);
        }
    else
    {
      Msg.Text = "Invalid Credentials: Please try again";        Msg.Text += "
<BR>You entered " + Server.HtmlEncode(UserEmail.Value) + "<BR>";
      Msg.Text += " and a password of " + Server.HtmlEncode(UserPass.Value);
}
    }
```

Notice the introduction of the `FormsAuthenticationTicket` object. This is what handles communications based on the setting for the authentication mode element from which it gets its information.

> **NOTE**
>
> The .NET Platform also integrates with Microsoft Passport technologies. Working with Passport is very similar to working with `FormsAuthentication`. When a request is made to a protected resource that has a `FormsAuthentication` method of Passport, the request, if no valid Passport form is detected, is redirected to a Passport login server where, on authentication, the Ticket is passed back to the original server where it handles the rest of the transaction.

Using Impersonation and Delegation in ASP.NET

After reading Chapter 13 on getting users authenticated and reading this chapter on getting users authorized, you should have a good understanding of how to figure out getting users identities when they attempt to access a resource. One use for this information is to allow the server to impersonate the user or client. By default, in the `machine.config` file and the `web.config` file, impersonation is turned off (set to `false`). Listing 14.14 shows this element in its default setting from a `web.config` file. Enabling impersonation is quite easy; it requires you to set the impersonation attribute of the identity element to `true`. But wait, there's more. Before using this feature, there is a bit to understand about what exactly is happening here, and just how careful to be with it.

LISTING 14.14   Identity Element Snippet

```
<system.web>
    …other elements
<identity impersonate="false">
    …other elements
</system.web>
```

In Windows 2000, to configure the server to allow impersonation, the server identity must be configured as Trusted for Delegation within the Active Directory. This setting is located in the properties of a domain controller within the Active Directory Users and Computers Management Console, as shown in Figure 14.5. The check box for Trust Computer for Delegation must be checked. If a computer is not part of an Active Directory, delegation can still occur, and will by default. It's just that Active Directory gives you an easy way to disable delegation.

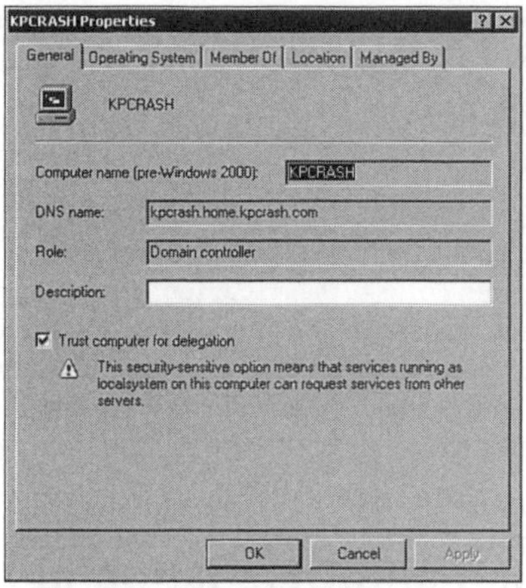

FIGURE 14.5   Domain Controller Properties page.

When it comes to configuring a user for delegation, the process is very similar.
Within Active Directory is a place where you can allow or disallow a person's right to
delegate. As with computers, if a user is not part of the Active Directory, he or she
can still delegate. This property is exposed through the user properties page of the
Active Directory Users and Computers Management Console, as shown in Figure
14.6.

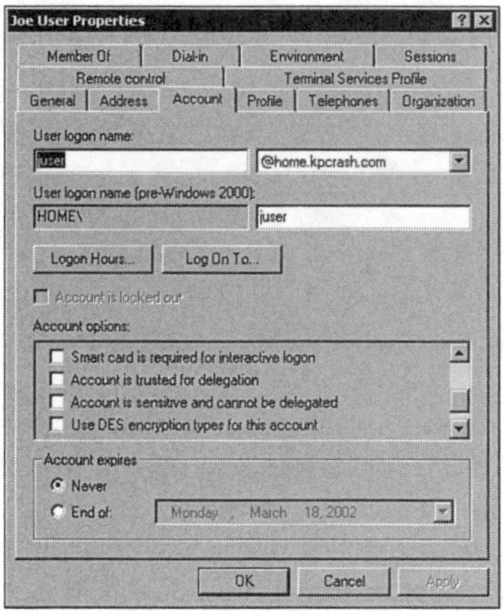

FIGURE 14.6   User Properties page.

Now that the server and the client are allowed to delegate, impersonation can take place. If you have allowed impersonation as shown back in Listing 14.14, when a user is authenticated, the ASP.NET application will run with the permissions that the authenticated user has. There is another twist—you can enable impersonation to occur as a single user. In other words, after any user is authenticated, the ASP.NET application runs as an account that you have established for this purpose. An example of this is shown in the code snippet in Listing 14.15.

LISTING 14.15   Impersonation as a User Snippet

```
<system.web>
    …other elements
<identity impersonate="true" userName="KPCRASH\juser" password="password">
    …other elements
</system.web>
```

In Listing 14.15, all authenticated users will run as user `juser`, regardless of who they are. Even if the application is on a UNC share, IIS will pass the authenticated user token unless a static account, as shown in Listing 14.15, is used. An obvious downside to this is the plain text password being stored in the `web.config` file.

In a final note on impersonation and delegation within ASP.NET, the impersonated user must have read/write access to the Temporary ASP.NET Files folder. In Windows 2000, the Authenticated Users group has read and execute permissions by default, but not write access. It is necessary before deploying any ASP.NET application that will require impersonation to either enable the Authenticated Users group to write to that directory, usually found at `%WINDIR%\Microsoft.Net\Framework\[VERSION]\Temporary ASP.NET Files\`, or enable write access to that directory on a per-user or per-group basis, depending on your specific network policies.

Summary

In this chapter, you learned what the configuration options for IIS and ASP.NET were and how to implement them. Using this information and seeing where it ties in with the new features listed in Chapter 13, you should begin to see how some of the new security features fit together to improve the processes of authentication and delegation.

15

Authorization: Control Who Is Accessing Your Site

By Kevin Price

IN THIS CHAPTER

- File and Directory Access Control Lists (ACLs)
- Using URL Authorization to Allow or Limit Access
- Using Programmatic Authorization to Determine Who Is Attempting to Access Your Site

Of the many features of ASP.NET are new objects that have been created to help simplify common Internet programming tasks, such as authorizing users attempting to access a resource on your Web site. Now that a firm representation of authentication has been presented, it is time to present what to do when users' accounts have been authenticated—they can now be authorized or at least they can learn what they are authorized to do. Authorization is not limited to determining who can access what code, it also includes managing who can access your site at all. This chapter shows techniques useful in ASP.NET applications to control who is accessing your site. ASP.NET applications can use many different sources for information regarding authorization. Some of the more commonly used sources are as follows:

- Windows Access Control Lists (ACLs)

- Web Server Permissions (IIS)

- URL Authorization (discussed later in this chapter)

- .NET Principal Objects (see Chapter 14, "Authentication: Know Who Is Accessing Your Site")

- Roles and Method Level security (discussed in Chapter 14 and later in this chapter)

- Using IIS enforcement on File and Directory Access Control Lists

- Discovering what URL Authorization can do

- Programmatically authorizing a user

File and Directory Access Control Lists (ACLs)

Just to make sure we are all on the same page, an Access Control List (ACL)—pronounced in geek circles as "ackle"—is exactly what it sounds like. An ACL is a list of SIDs or Security Identifiers; these identifiers can belong to users, resources (such as a machine), and rights. Based on user accounts, this can include machine accounts, system accounts, files, and so on. Permissions and roles are established that determine what happens when an authenticated user makes a request. Just remember that it is quite difficult to authorize a user until that user has been authenticated so that you have an identity; otherwise, you're just authorizing the anonymous user.

In Windows 2000, the most familiar ACL interface tool is the Active Directory Users and Computers applet. When you open this program—or in the Computer Management applet under Local Users and Groups—the content of the detail pane is the ACL for that domain or machine. This is where you establish groups that can do certain functions and establish default file and directory access permissions. Of course, right-clicking a file or directory and selecting properties will allow you to set rights to a specific item very efficiently. Because of the tight integration of Internet Information Services (IIS) and Windows 2000/NT, permissions that you set on the OS level can be carried over to the .NET application level as well. For example, if you set permissions on a file that only people of the Domain Users group can access, members of the Guests group (IUSR_<MACHINENAME>, for example) will not have access to the resource. To begin really understanding this process, start with Chapter 14. Now comes the part that causes some confusion. Web permissions can be set independently of NTFS permissions. Web permissions apply to all users of your site, including FTP users.

> **NOTE**
>
> Web permissions are stored within the IIS Metabase. Perhaps the easiest way to access these settings is through the MetaEdit tool available in the Windows 2000 Server Resource Kit.

NTFS permissions apply to users of a domain and the groups they may belong to and cannot be applied unless a user is authenticated. Again, if Windows authentication is used, ACL permissions override all other forms of setting permissions, including settings in config files such as web.config and system.config.

Programmatically, ASP.NET handles file and directory ACL requests through the FileAuthorizationModule class that is activated when you use Integrated Windows Authentication. It automatically performs an ACL check to see if the user has permissions to use the resource.

NOTE

Keep in mind that to use Windows ACLs on the Internet with IIS, you must be using the NTFS file system. Because Windows XP has built-in support for this, even the Home Edition, unless supporting legacy Win9x on a dual-boot machine, there really is no reason not to convert. The security features available alone are worth the reboot. Consult the Windows Help files on your specific operating system version for information on converting to NTFS and the command-line application CONVERT. Another point on this is that if Web permissions are set differently than NTFS permissions (explained in the next section), the more restrictive permissions prevail.

Using URL Authorization to Allow or Limit Access

URL Authorization is a feature that is available through modifications to the `config` file of an application or site. Using URL Authorization is rather simple; it requires the addition of at least one of two elements—allow and/or deny—to the authorization section of the `web.config` file. This section is typically found right under the `authentication mode` element. Listing 15.1 shows the configuration entry necessary to allow the user `"Administrator"` access and deny access to everyone else.

LISTING 15.1   Partial `web.config` File

```
<authentication mode="Windows" />
        <authorization>
            <allow users="Administrator" />
            <deny users="*" />
        </authorization>
```

Notice in Listing 15.1 that even though we are allowing a single user, the attribute is users. Within the elements of `allow` and `deny`, there are three optional attributes. Table 15.1 shows the possible values and how they will impact the application.

NOTE

Elements and attributes are case sensitive. .NET will throw unknown element or attribute errors if this rule is broken.

TABLE 15.1   Attributes and Values for `allow/deny` Elements

Attribute	Possible Values
roles	This is used to identify a specific role for execution. This is done through an implicit creation of the IPrincipal class. The instance created is accessible via WindowsPrincipal or GenericPrincipal.

TABLE 15.1   Continued

Attribute	Possible Values
users	The users attribute specifies the identities that have access to this resource. If it is an NT/2000 account, make sure to include the domain name in the SAM format (i.e., domain\username).
verbs	verbs defines which HTTP actions are allowed. Examples of HTTP actions are GET, POST, HEAD, and PUT.

In addition to the information in Table 15.1, the users attribute has two wildcard values. The asterisk (*) represents all users who attempt to access the site. The question mark (?) is the representative character for anonymous. In Listing 15.2, all users are allowed; but in Listing 15.3, all users except anonymous are allowed. By default, anonymous users are part of all users, but they can be blocked very easily.

LISTING 15.2   All Users Allowed Configuration

```
<authentication mode="Windows" />
        <authorization>
            <allow users="*" />
        </authorization>
```

LISTING 15.3   All Users Except Anonymous Allowed Configuration

```
<authentication mode="Windows" />
        <authorization>
            <allow users="*" />
            <deny users="?" />
        </authorization>
```

It is worth noting that during this process, .NET creates an instance of the URLAuthorizationModule class. This class inherits most of its members from object, but, like several objects derived from System.Web.Security, it also exposes a dispose method that allows you to forcibly dump the object in the event of an error or perceived security breach. It does this by setting the response's StatusCode to 401 (Unauthorized) and calling HttpApplication.CompleteRequest.

Another element that is available to the authorization element is location. The location element allows you to specify a file or directory that, when wrapped by location tags, sets permissions on that file or directory.

NOTE

One important difference between authorization and authentication is that authorization is URI-scoped, whereas authentication is application scoped. You can only have one authentication mode for an application, but you can have separate authorization settings for every URL in it if you want.

Perhaps one of the more interesting attributes is that of verbs. For example, some attacks are made on Web servers by sending a GET request filled with bogus information and/or attempts to fill the memory of a machine with virus code. To prevent this, the web.config file can support denying GET requests to certain directories. Listing 15.4 illustrates denying GET and allowing POST. From there, it is not difficult to begin blending the users and the verbs. Then, Listing 15.5 shows how to add specific users to allow and deny everyone else. Keep in mind that when using config files, rules are executed in the order listed within the web.config file, meaning that the first rule matched that applies to the situation wins.

LISTING 15.4   Deny GET and Allow POST to a Site

```
<authentication mode="Windows" />
        <authorization>
            <allow verbs="POST" users="*" />
            <deny verbs="GET" />
        </authorization>
```

LISTING 15.5   Allowing Certain Users to GET, All Users to POST

```
<authentication mode="Windows" />
        <authorization>
  <allow verbs="GET" users="Administrator"/>
            <deny verbs="GET" users="*" />
            <allow verbs="POST" users="*" />
        </authorization>
```

In Listings 15.4 and 15.5, it is important to notice that once an allow condition is met, no further checking is done.

Using Programmatic Authorization to Determine Who Is Attempting to Access Your Site

Once a user is authenticated, we will need to find out who that person is. In a real world example, code like this could be used for everything from personalization to authentication of specific files. The setup for this sample is as follows (see Listing 15.6):

- Anonymous access is disabled in IIS, Integrated Windows Authentication is enabled.

- The default authentication mode, Windows, is set in the web.config file.

- The authorization settings are not restrictive.

LISTING 15.6   default.aspx (Complete)

```
<%@ Page language="c#" Codebehind="default.aspx.cs" AutoEventWireup="false"
Inherits="Chapter15.WebForm1" %>
<!DOCTYPE HTML PUBLIC "-//W3C//DTD HTML 4.0 Transitional//EN" >
<HTML>
 <HEAD>
  <title>Authorization Sample Listing 15.6</title>
  <meta name="GENERATOR" Content="Microsoft Visual Studio 7.0">
  <meta name="CODE_LANGUAGE" Content="C#">
  <meta name="vs_defaultClientScript" content="JavaScript">
  <meta name="vs_targetSchema"
[ic:ccc]content="http://schemas.microsoft.com/intellisense/ie5">
 </HEAD>
 <body MS_POSITIONING="GridLayout">
  <%if(User.Identity.IsAuthenticated){%>
  <table>
   <tr>
    <td colspan="2">
     Welcome,
     <%=User.Identity.Name%>
    </td>
   </tr>
    <tr>
     <td>
      Your IP Address:
     </td>
     <td>
      <%=Request.UserHostAddress%>
     </td>
    </tr>
  </table>
  <%}%>
  <form id="Form1" method="post" runat="server">
  </form>
 </body>
</HTML>
```

Using the code in Listing 15.6, we can determine who is visiting the site. This information can be used throughout the application to verify credentials through the implicit `Principal` class, or in this case the `User` class, created when the user was authenticated. From the `Principal` class, we will be able to derive the `Identity` class containing all pertinent user information.

Summary

In this chapter, you learned what is available in ASP.NET to authorize users to access resources. This is vital when securing an application. The sample code snippets in this chapter demonstrate just how simple it can be to implement a multilayered security infrastructure to protect your application.

16

Data Transport Integrity: Keeping Data Uncorrupted

IN THIS CHAPTER

- Implementing SSL Encryption and HTTPS

- Encryption of Individual Data Elements—An Overview

- Remoting and Encryption via Sinks—An Overview

By Kevin Price

Chapters 13, "Introduction to ASP.NET Security," 14, "Authentication: Know Who Is Accessing Your Site," and 15, "Authorization: Control Who Is Accessing Your Site," introduced you to ways to use new features in .NET to help secure your applications. One consistently mentioned item was that all of these methods are most effective when used in conjunction with SSL. SSL provides an almost universal way to encrypt data between the client and the server. Of course, there are a couple of settings to turn on in the Internet Information Server (IIS) to enable SSL, thus allowing users to access your site over HTTPS. While this chapter may not make you an expert on certificates, SSL, and encryption, it will show you how to enable these devices as well as provide an overview to using sinks to secure remote objects and using HTTPS to secure Web services. Using these methods helps to ensure data integrity through keeping the data encrypted to prying eyes, making your site that much more secure.

This chapter covers a very important, commonly used, yet commonly overlooked aspect of securing your ASP.NET application: using data encryption to protect that data's integrity while in transfer. At the end of this chapter, you will understand

- How to implement Secure Sockets Layer (SSL)

- Configuring IIS for HTTPS connections

- Considerations for keeping your data secure during Web services transactions

- Using sinks to keep your data secure

Implementing SSL Encryption and HTTPS

As you may know, the Secure Sockets Layer (SSL) was created to provide a secure means of transferring data across a network using protocols supported by TCP/IP. HTTP, SMTP, and POP3 are examples of protocols that are capable of supporting SSL. By default, this layer operates (or listens) on port 443. The way it works is based on a rather simple principle known as public key encryption. Public key encryption relies on key pairs. With all these references to keys, it may be important to remind you that a key is merely a value used to encrypt and decrypt information. A password is an example of a key. .NET provides many key generation options that enable developers to use this technology with their own programs. One example of this is the RngCryptoServiceProvider class. Just two lines of C# code

```
System.Security.Cryptography.RNGCryptoServiceProvider rng = new
System.Security.Cryptography.RNGCryptoServiceProvider();
```

creates the instance. Two more lines of code

```
byte[] random = new Byte[128];
rng.GetBytes(random);
```

enable you to generate Random Number encryption keys. If you would like to see the results of this key in a simple display example, add the lines of code just shown to your code-behind page's Page_Load event and add Response.Write(System.Convert. ToBase64String(random));. The results will look something like bvc8wwT3tJHhTuaqP kIY1WirlANWx138FnBxb0s9umLyhe277ta4Z5nneQFTbSRzpsHHj4I2+34Z7KGi22bUVNGshXX 6nBUR4y/299MLyfjyvrTa1iq3FLQs0AXhrZpjehlpurzpGA7LKDUrN3sQ97N/qklHZzHqZuzAM 4IsViU=. To use SSL, you must first obtain a certificate from a certificate authority— VeriSign or an internal Windows 2000 certificate server, for example. This certificate will contain two keys, one public and one private. The use of these keys in SSL is referred to as asymmetric, as whatever the private key encrypts, the public key decrypts, and vice versa. (In symmetric key encryption, the same keys are used for both encryption and decryption of information.) Once you have obtained and installed the certificate, configure whatever server type you need the encrypted services running on, and that is basically it. Now that you have this new toy, what does it do? How does it do it? Why is it secure? What does a digital certificate look like? Listing 16.1 illustrates a sample digital certificate.

LISTING 16.1   Sample Digital Certificate

```
-----BEGIN CERTIFICATE-----
CBHcm91cCBDQS5jcmwwRqBEoEKGQGZpbGU6Ly9cXENFUlRTUlZcQ2VydFNydlxDZXJ0RW5yb2xsXE1
➥TIENl
cnRTcnYgVGVzdCBHcm91cCBDQS5jcmwwCQYDVR0TBAIwADBiBggrBgEFBQcBAQRWMFQwUgYIKwYBBQ
➥UHMAK
GRmh0dHA6Ly9DRVJUJUU1JWL0NlcnRTcnYvQ2VydEVucm9sbC9DRVJUJUU1JWX01TIENlcnRTcnYgVGVzd
➥CBHcm
91cCBDQS5jcnQwDQYJKoZIhvcNAQEEBQADQQAhq70nRlse0ulPstU+IWdjeNj5p
-----END CERTIFICATE-----
```

NOTE

Remember that in order to use SSL with a Web browser, that browser must support at least a 40-bit encryption algorithm and public key encryption. Most browsers (Internet Explorer, Netscape, and AOL) of version 3.0 and above support SSL.

SSL provides a protocol by which all information during a session is sent by the server and the client is encrypted. This means that when a client makes a request over HTTPS to a server, the server's public key is sent to the browser. The browser uses this key to encrypt the information before it leaves the client. Once the server gets the information, it attempts to decrypt it using its own key and finishing whatever process it was called to do, such as authenticating a user or processing a sensitive transaction.

To explain a little better how it does that, let's look at what the certificate does. The certificate contains information that guarantees that the server being visited is indeed the server it says it is. Again, a certificate will contain both a public and a private encryption key. Both the server and the client will have what are called trusted root certificates. These certificates basically indicate to the machine that if a certificate key is received and it came from a trusted source, it should be okay. Assuming that all checks out, meaning the client and server agree on a key to use, during the process (if not, your browser or managed network client should let you know), the server creates a unique session with the client and the data is encrypted using the server's key pair. As an added benefit, starting with Windows NT 4.0, a client certificate can be mapped to a specific user account. This allows the server to verify the caller's identity without sending any information to it. This feature comes in handy when you are using Web services across the Internet and need to validate a caller before allowing it access to your code.

NOTE

Remember that in order to further secure your files, you should use the NTFS file system. This is the default for Windows NT and 2000 and is even supported in XP Home Edition. If your hard drive is currently formatted using any version of FAT, you can use the Convert utility to fix this by executing the following DOS command from a command prompt window, or by selecting Start, Run and typing this in the resulting dialog box:

convert <*drive letter*> /FS:NTFS

Of course, replace the <*drive letter*> placeholder with the actual drive letter you wish to convert. Once converted to NTFS, a drive cannot be converted back to FAT without a third-party tool.

More About Certificates—Options and Installing

Since the use of certificates is becoming more and more vital, this section can serve as either a refresher or an introduction to some basics about using certificates. This is not intended to be a definitive, all-inclusive directive, but rather a tool that, from a high level, eliminates the excuse, "I don't know how to implement SSL on IIS." The purpose of this illustration is based on real-world experience with MSCE+I's, MCSD+I's, and other senior-level developers who could not correctly request and install a certificate.

Figures 16.1–16.12 illustrate the process of installing a certificate and enabling SSL on IIS using Windows 2000 and IIS 5.0. The steps for doing this on IIS 4.0 are quite similar. This is the first step to encrypting the data during an HTTPS session. First, using whatever method you are most comfortable with, open the Internet Information Services Management Console. In Windows 2000 and up, the Certificate Manager enables you to install and use certificates. This can be accessed in one of many ways. The easiest is by double-clicking your certificate file (.cer, for example) when you receive it. The associated wizard will then walk you through the steps involved in determining where to place your certificate. Another way, for the more advanced user, is to use the Microsoft Management Console (MMC). Using MMC, you can add the snap-in for certificate services and completely manage the importing, exporting, and requesting of certificates. Figure 16.1 shows this as access through the Computer Management Console.

Once you have received and installed a server certificate, IIS recognizes this and some options that were previously disabled are now available. Figure 16.2 is the result of right-clicking the Default Web Site folder and selecting Properties. Notice that the Server Certificate button is now enabled.

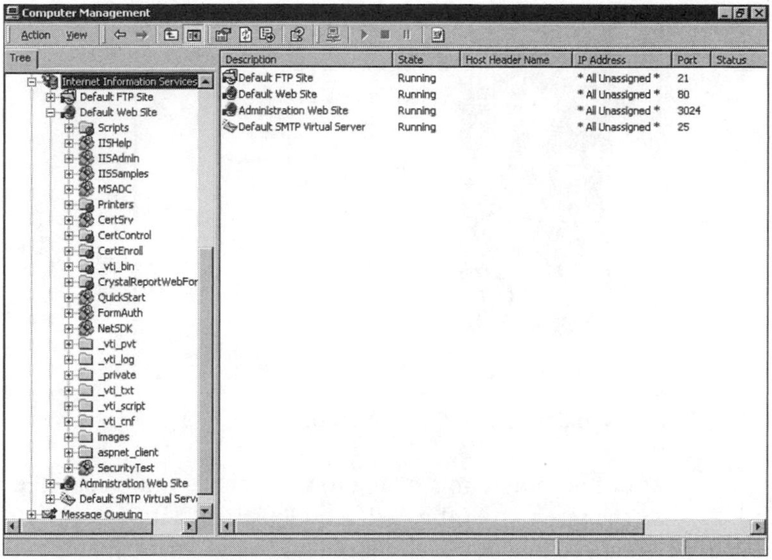

FIGURE 16.1   IIS Computer Management Console.

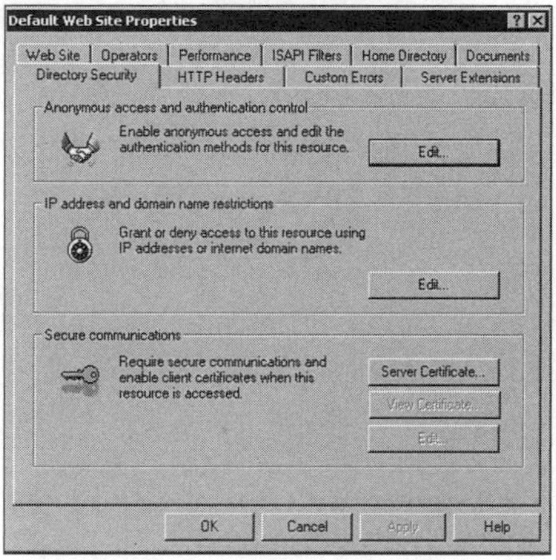

FIGURE 16.2   The Default Web Site Properties dialog.

When you click on the Server Certificate button, the Web Server Certificate Wizard is launched. Figure 16.3 shows this wizard's introductory dialog.

FIGURE 16.3   The Web Server Certificate Wizard.

Clicking the Next button brings up a dialog to select what you would like to do. Figure 16.4 shows the selection of the Assign an Existing Certificate option. Since we are importing a certificate that is already installed (read the paragraph at the beginning of this section if you missed the installation), none of the other options apply.

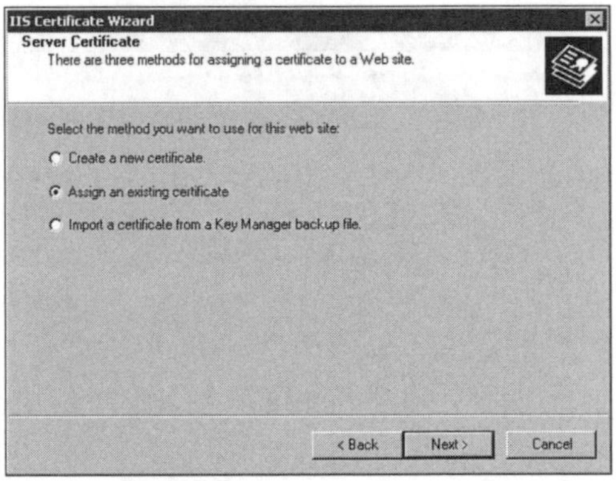

FIGURE 16.4   The IIS Certificate Wizard.

Next you will be presented with a list of the certificates installed on your machine that are available to serve as server authentication certificates. Figure 16.5 shows this dialog.

The next dialog box shown is basically a recap of the information contained within the certificate. Figure 16.6 illustrates what this might look like, based on information in a demonstration certificate.

The end result is the Completing the Web Server Certificate Wizard screen shown in Figure 16.7. Basically, the only option here is to click Finish.

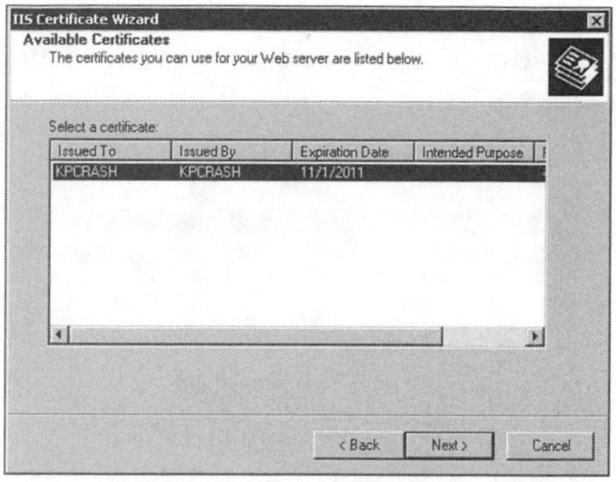

FIGURE 16.5   The Available Certificates dialog.

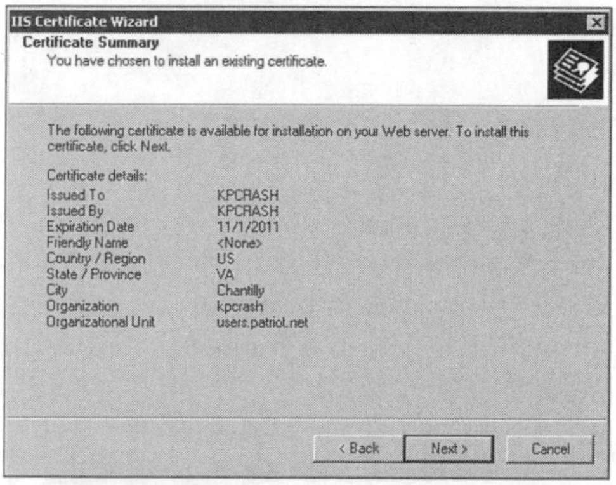

FIGURE 16.6   The Certificate Summary dialog.

FIGURE 16.7   The Completing the Web Server Certificate Wizard dialog.

Now that the wizard is complete, you will notice that the other buttons under the Directory Security tab in the Default Web Site Properties dialog are available. Figure 16.8 is basically the same as Figure 16.2, except that we have configured IIS to know that a certificate is available.

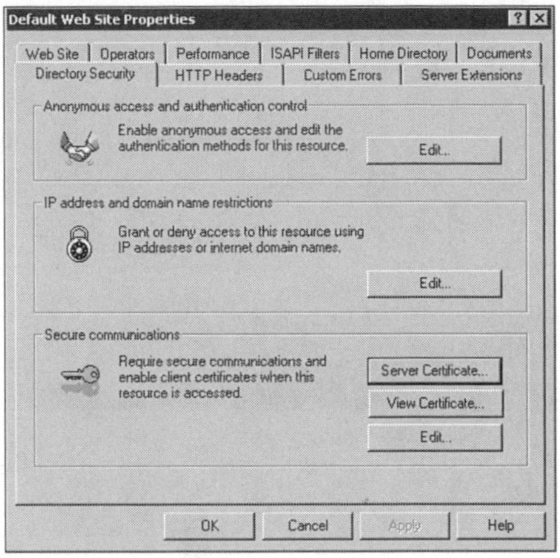

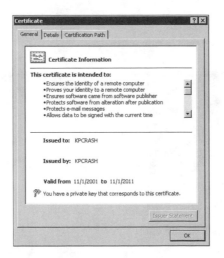

FIGURE 16.8   The IIS Properties page.

Clicking on the View Certificate button brings up a dialog similar to the one shown in Figure 16.9. (Of course, unless you got your certificate from me and are using my machine, they will not be exactly alike.)

FIGURE 16.9   The Certificate dialog.

Now that the certificate is installed and configured, the SSL Port text box is now enabled (see Figure 16.10).

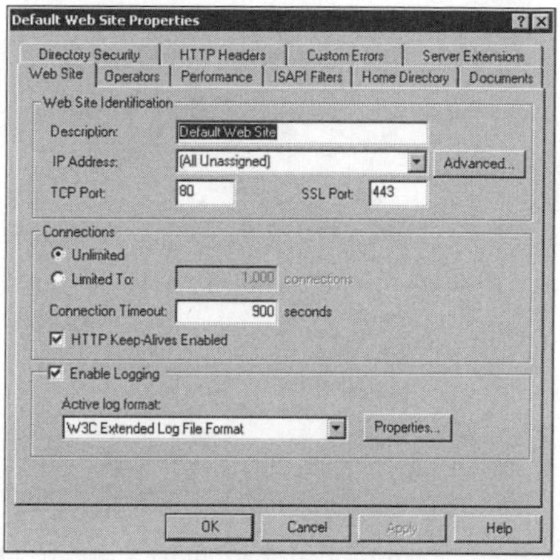

FIGURE 16.10   The Default Web Site Properties dialog with SSL enabled.

To actually enable SSL for a given site or directory, simply open the Properties for that site or virtual directory and adjust the appropriate settings on the Directory Security tab.

NOTE

It is recommended that you use SSL for every request that comes through your Web site that requires authentication. For example, in general for a publicly accessible area of your site, SSL may not be required; however, when a user reaches a form for entering sensitive information, SSL is enabled. The exception to this rule is where an entire site requires authentication to view any resource; in that case, the entire site may be protected under SSL.

Figure 16.11 shows the selections necessary on the Secure Communications dialog to establish secure connections on your IIS Web site.

Should users attempt to access the page via insecure means, they will get a message from the server similar to the one shown in Figure 16.12. You can prevent this page from being displayed by using a redirect page sending the request to the secure site.

When you request a certificate, there are a few options to consider. Depending on the use of your application and your geographical location, your answers will vary. Keys come in different lengths; 40-bit, 128-bit, 256-bit, 512-bit, and 1024-bit sizes are common. Export versions of IIS are currently limited to using the 128-bit key to encrypt and decrypt data; however, you can still use up to a 512-bit key to protect the server data. Typically, it is recommended that you use the largest key available. The certificate authority you use will be able to provide you with more information on the available key sizes.

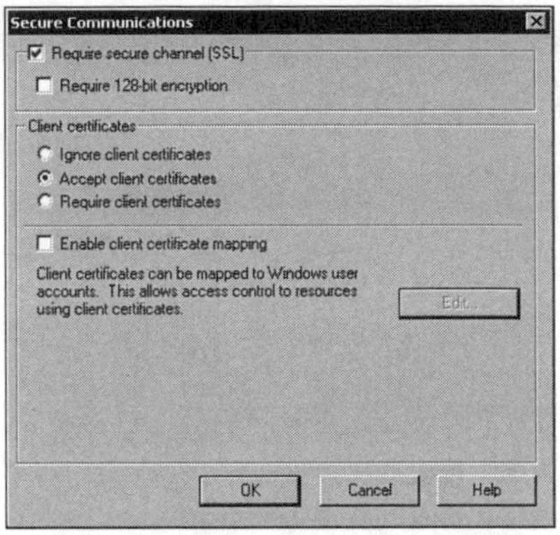

FIGURE 16.11   The Secure Communications dialog.

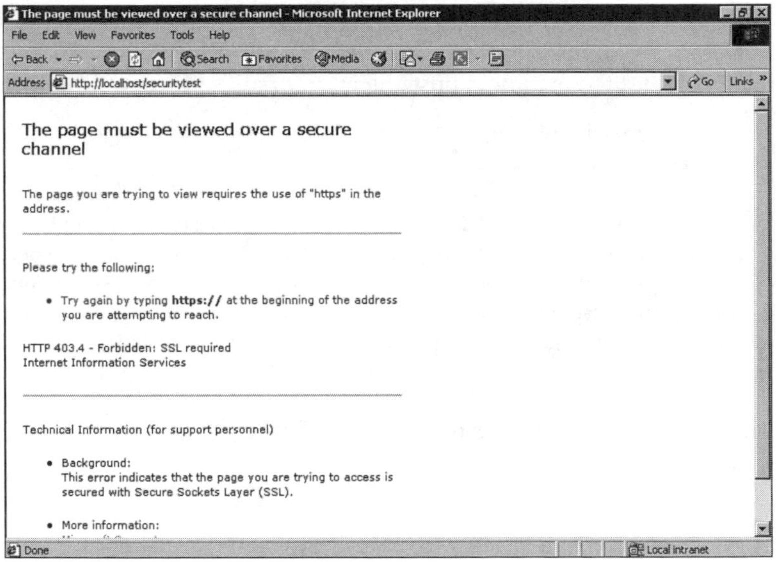

FIGURE 16.12   HTTP 403.4—Forbidden message.

For more information about the many uses of certificates in Windows, consult the online help files for the product you are curious about using certificates with.

Considerations for Web Services

As Web services and remote objects will no doubt become the pre-eminent way that distributed applications are made available, this opens up some rather large security questions, beyond just using SSL. This is where `remoting` comes into play. This section covers some advanced topics in relation to remoting and how to maintain encryption of data elements when using the remoting framework. Remoting differs from Web services in that remoting offers more features and a certain fidelity not found in Web services.

> **NOTE**
>
> The term *remoting* is used to refer to the functionality provided for by the remoting framework part of the .NET Framework. As its name indicates, remoting provides several methods and interfaces enabling developers to create secure distributed applications. If you are unfamiliar with remoting, please view the .NET Framework SDK help files on remoting before reading further.

Encryption of Individual Data Elements—An Overview

Since Web security is based on standards and specifications set forth by groups such as the World Wide Web Consortium (W3C), the concepts and practices that apply to Web security also apply to .NET security. The classes `HttpChannel` and `TcpChannel` encapsulate the functionality necessary to perform secure transactions over the Internet. `ChannelServices` allow you to send messages back and forth between the client and server, even if they are the same machine. The `CryptoStream` class provides the encryption on top of or in conjunction with `ChannelServices`. `CryptoStream` is used to hold the information while it is encrypted or decrypted through the cryptographic service providers available in .NET. To maintain the role-based security and code access security features provided in the .NET Framework, IIS must be configured in a secure manner as well. This includes using integrated Windows authentication and/or SSL. What becomes important here is not only maintaining security in the sense of trusting the code to execute, but also protecting the messages that are sent when remoting. Remoting uses the SOAP protocol to send its messages between the client and server on the `HttpChannel`. Binary information is sent over the `TcpChannel`. Both of these objects rely on streams that are passed through the `CryptoStream` class for encryption/decryption. You can find more information regarding the `CryptoStream` class in Chapter 30, "Using Cryptography with the .NET Framework: The Basics."

Remoting and Encryption via Sinks—An Overview

What happens inside a channel? Channels use channel sink objects before they send and after they receive a message. Which sink you implement depends on whether you are coming from the client side or the server side. (The base implementations are `IClientChannelSink` and `IServerChannelSink`, respectively.) Additionally, on the client, the first channel sink must implement `IMessageSink`. The combination of `IClientChannelSink` and `IMessageSink` is provided for in `IClientFormatterSink`, which formats content for an `IMessage` class. `IMessage`, of course, contains a `stream`. This stream is the message going between the client and the server. Once the stream is available, it is read into the `CryptoStream` class mentioned in the "Encryption of Individual Data Elements—An Overview" section earlier in this chapter. Once in the `CryptoStream`, data can be encrypted and/or decrypted programmatically. In a real-world example, once the user is authenticated using a certificate, the public key can be used as an encryption key within your application during the session. Chapter 28, "Writing a Secure Web Application in the .NET Development Platform," illustrates the use of remoting and encryption via sinks as well as the process of encrypting individual data elements while authenticating a user. Figure 16.13 illustrates where the `CryptoStream` fits in to this process.

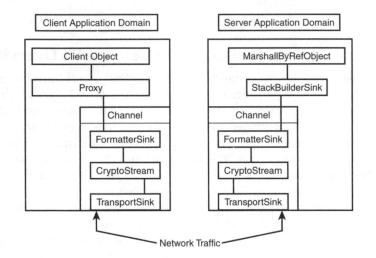

FIGURE 16.13   Using `CryptoStream` with sinks in remoting.

Summary

In this chapter, you have learned how to add SSL to IIS by requesting and installing a server certificate. You have also been introduced to low-level ways to create your own security schemes using sinks. In the next chapter, you will find more information on .NET security administration and operating system security administration. For more information on obtaining a certificate for your Web site, visit `http://www.verisign.com` or `http://www.thawte.com`.

PART IV

.NET Framework Security Administration

IN THIS PART

17

Introduction: .NET Framework Security and Operating System Security

By Sebastian Lange

IN THIS CHAPTER

- A Roadmap for Administering the Security Context of Managed Code

- .NET Framework Security and Operating System Security Settings

The most powerful and elaborate security systems are useless unless they are configured correctly. Picking the right security settings that allow managed code to execute with a minimum of constraints while protecting resources and data from illicit access can be an art. This section will show you how to view, analyze, and modify the security settings impacting assemblies executed by the Common Language Runtime (CLR).

Starting from the ground up, you will find the following key points covered in this chapter:

- A scenario-driven roadmap to administer security for managed code, including a reading guide to other chapters

- How Windows security descriptor settings impact managed applications

- How the Code Access Security (CAS) configuration state is protected using Windows ACLs

- A short review of how to view and set ACLs

- An overview of the Windows Software Restriction Policies technology

- How Software Restriction Policies and the .NET Framework security system cooperate

A Roadmap for Administering the Security Context of Managed Code

Unfortunately, there is no single tool or technology at this time that administrators can use to analyze and modify the complete security state impacting managed code. In fact, some or all of the following security technologies can get involved when managed code gets run:

- The Code Access Security policy system

- Windows Security settings

- The Internet Explorer security configuration settings

- The ASP.NET security configuration system

- Database server security

Setting relevant security state in each of these systems is covered in various chapters throughout this book. In this section, you will find quick reviews of each of these systems and where to find more information about them. Some typical runtime scenarios for managed code are then sketched out from which you can glean what security technologies you need to specially focus on for your use scenarios of managed code.

The Code Access Security Policy System

Code Access Security is a core component of the .NET Framework. It is a code-identity–based security system, which means that rights are allotted and security policy is administered based on the identity of managed code. The identity of managed code is typically determined by its place of origin, about which the host of the Common Language Runtime keeps or supplies evidence. Common forms of evidence include the hash, authenticode signature, as well as the URL of origin of a particular assembly. Administrators set CAS policy that maps assembly evidence to permissions that grant access to particular resources. The CAS system enforces that resources requiring a specific level of permissions cannot be accessed by assemblies that do not have the right level of permissions.

The CAS system is driven by a persisted security policy, offering different configuration containments (called *policy levels*) for enterprise-wide security configuration and machine-wide and per-user security settings. Security policy can be set using a GUI tool (the .NET Framework Configuration tool), a command line tool for batch scripting security changes, or by programming to the security APIs directly.

NOTE

To read more about how to administer the CAS system using the GUI configuration tool by writing batch scripts or programmatically changing security policy state, please refer to Chapters 18, "Administering Security Policy Using the .NET Framework Configuration Tool," and Chapter 19, "Administering .NET Framework Security Policy Using Scripts and Security APIs."

To find out more about the code-identity–based security paradigm, please read Chapter 4, "User- and Code-Identity–Based Security: Two Complementary Security Paradigms."

To read more about permissions and evidence, refer to Chapter 5, "Evidence: Knowing Where Code Comes From," and Chapter 6, "Permissions: The Workhorse of Code Access Security."

Windows Security

Windows security is largely based on user identity, not code identity, such as the CAS system. Windows protects resources, such as the file system and the registry, using access control permissions defined in security descriptors. Every system object (such as a file) has a security descriptor associated with it. Administrators can set a mapping between user identity or user roles to access control permissions specified in the security descriptors. This entails that the operating system security context is coincidental with user context; in other words, the rights of code to access protected system resources depends on the user on whose behalf the code is executed.

NOTE

The Windows Software Restriction Policies technology is an exception, as will be discussed in the "Windows Software Restriction Policies and .NET Framework Security" section later in this chapter.

As will be explained shortly, the CAS system does not replace or circumvent Windows security settings. Whenever managed code is executed, relevant access control permission settings are still honored.

Internet Explorer Security Settings

Whenever managed code is hosted in Internet Explorer, the IE security settings apply. Managed code gets to be hosted by IE when an HREF to a managed EXE on an HTML page occurs, or when an <object..> element refers to a managed type. In these cases, the Common Language Runtime (CLR) will be invoked by Internet Explorer, and IE security settings determining EXE download and object hosting apply.

To find out more about what IE security settings apply in managed code download or hosting scenarios, please refer to Chapter 21, "Administering Clients for .NET Framework Mobile Code."

TIP

Be sure to regularly check for and install Internet Explorer updates and patches. This will reduce the likelihood that your machines will be susceptible to security exploits that may have been found in the browser. For updates, patches, and further information, please go to `http://windowsupdate.microsoft.com`.

ASP.NET Security Settings

Whenever managed code is hosted as an ASP.NET application, the ASP.NET configuration system applies. To find out more specifics about setting the ASP.NET security levels for ASP.NET-hosted code, please refer to Part III of this book, "ASP.NET and Web Services Security Fundamentals" (Chapters 13–16) and Chapter 20, "Administering an IIS Machine Using ASP.NET."

Database Server Security Mechanisms

A common application type for managed applications is to operate over databases—as a middle-tier application or as a front-end application for data access. In fact, the .NET Framework ships with managed OLEDB and SQL data access libraries.

Whenever managed code gets run against a specific database server, such as the Microsoft SQL Server, the security mechanisms of that server will kick in and need to be appropriately configured to allow the access the application you want to run requires. You should refer to the server documentation for administration specifics.

A Different Angle: Security Systems Involved in Common Managed Code Execution Scenarios

You may still wonder what the interplay between the different systems previously discussed is in various scenarios when managed code gets run. This section contains a few key scenarios and the security systems that get involved. Obviously, this list of high-level scenarios is not complete, but it may be of help in determining the security technologies on which you should especially focus.

Managed Desktop Applications

This category contains traditional application types, such as managed word processors or a standalone accounting package. Desktop applications are usually installed from disk or CD-ROM onto the machine and provide productivity functions that stand in isolation from a network of other machines.

In this scenario, typically, only the Windows security settings and the Code Access Security settings come into play. When managed code is loaded, the Code Access Security system determines whether that code has the right to be executing to start with and exactly which resources it can access. That determination is based on the code's identity (its place of origin as expressed in the zone it comes from, its strong name signature, and the URL of origin, among other forms of evidence). If an application attempts to access a resource, such as particular file on disk, that is protected by both the CAS system as well as operating system access control settings, it requires that both systems allow access for the access operation to succeed. For example, if the managed application tries to write foo.bar into the c:\winnt directory, code access security policy needs to have granted access to that directory and file. Also, the user on whose behalf the application is running must have been granted write rights to that location by the Windows security system. If the location c:\winnt is write protected against the user executing the managed application, the fact that code access security policy had granted access to that location will be insufficient for the access to succeed. Both the user-identity–based Windows access control settings as well as the code-identity–based code access security policy are required to grant the appropriate access rights.

If you are primarily running standalone desktop applications, you should therefore familiarize yourself with the Windows ACLs model (see the "Windows Access Control Protections and .NET Framework Security" section later in this chapter), as well as the CAS administration model (see Chapters 18 and 19).

Mobile Code Applications

The Code Access Security (CAS) system allows applications to execute in partially trusted contexts. This means that applications can be run securely without endangering protected resources, such as the file system or registry. By default, all code from the intranet is executed as partially trusted, allowing users to safely execute code whose origin they may not be able to trust. That enables mobile code applications— applications that are stored on an intranet or Internet site, or even have modules on a separate site, that a user can browse to and execute. The ability to have code run in a secure, semitrusted fashion enables the intranet (or Internet if default policy is changed) as a large application repository, without requiring the user of an application to make explicit trust decisions (such as through pop-up dialogs asking whether an Authenticode Publisher can be trusted).

NOTE

All references to default policy state in this book are references to the CAS default policy shipping in the Service Pack 1 for the .NET Framework.

Mobile code applications will be run through Internet Explorer (IE) as a host to the managed application. IE security settings, such as allowing for <object..> references to managed types to be effective, will come into play. By default, mobile code applications from the intranet will be enabled to run via IE, but you may want to make some fine tuning adjustments. For more information on the IE security setting impacting managed code, see Chapter 21.

In addition to the IE security settings, the CAS policy as well as Windows access control settings will come into play. For example, if the former allows a specific mobile code application to read a file from the hard disk, but the user context has Windows access control settings not allowing such a read operation, then further security settings may need to be changed to fully enable the mobile code application in question. To find out more about Windows access control settings and managed code, see the "Windows Access Control Protections and .NET Framework Security" section later in this chapter; to read more about the CAS policy administration, please see Chapters 18 and 19.

> **NOTE**
>
> Again, by default, managed applications running from the intranet are executing in a
> constrained security context, preventing access to exploitable resources, such as the file
> system. There may be a number of mobile code applications that you want to have more
> trust to access protected resources than what is given them by default CAS policy, such as a
> mobile code from select publishers that you want to run from the Internet. Please see
> Chapters 18 and 19 for specific help on increasing the trust for a particular application.

.NET Framework Security and Operating System Security Settings

Windows security and the Code Access Security system complement and cooperate with each other. The Windows security model encompasses of two main concepts—user authentication and access control. *User authentication* is used to establish and ascertain the identity of a particular user and map that identity to a particular administrator-defined user role. On the other hand, *access control* is used to map access to system objects, such as files, directories, printing and network services, to specific user roles. Administrators can define access rights to a particular object, such as a file, for particular users or user groups in a security descriptor. Every system object has a *security descriptor* associated with it that holds the list of access permissions to that object for users or user groups. Consequently, with the exception of the Software Restriction Policies technology (see the "Windows Software Restriction Policies and .NET Framework Security" section later in this chapter for more information), Windows security settings are user-identity based. This means that the security context that Windows executes an application in is based on the user context—on who is running an application. Windows protects various resources, such as the file system, registry, and network access, using access rights checks that are configurable on a per-user or per-user–role basis. From a Windows perspective, this means that all applications (unless specific Software Restriction Policies have been set) running under the same user context will receive the same access rights appropriate to that user. For example, let us suppose user A has access rights to the Windows system directory, while user B doesn't. Application X is a system tool updating some system libraries in the system directory, while application Y is a simple word processor not accessing any protected disk locations. If user B tried to run X, he or she would get an access violation error from the operating system, while trying to run Y will succeed. Conversely, user A will be able to run both X and Y, because he or she has access rights to the system directory. From the perspective of the operating system, both X and Y (unless Software Restriction Policies provisions had been explicitly introduced) are run in the same security context; both X and Y will have exactly the same level of resource access that Windows allotted the user on whose behalf X and Y are run. No security distinctions are drawn between X and Y in terms of the allotment of different access rights to X or Y; the limiting factor is user identity, not code identity.

You may wonder exactly how the Code Access Security system fits into all of this. The .NET Framework Common Language Runtime (CLR) executes all managed code. Yet, from the perspective of the operating system, the CLR is just another application. Consequently, the CLR is subject to the access right restrictions of the user on whose behalf the CLR is executing. This means that all managed code can only access the resources that the user running the CLR is allowed to access. The CLR, and thus all managed code, does not have any way to circumnavigate access restrictions set on the operating system level. The CLR is subsumed by the Windows security system. Of course, the CLR has its own security system as well. That system is code-identity–based. This means that it is evidence about the origin of a particular assembly that determines the permissions the assembly receives to access protected resources. Unlike the Windows security system managed, then, various managed applications running on the CLR may indeed receive different levels of rights to access protected resources, irrespective of the user on whose behalf the application is run. In that way, Code Access Security and Windows security nicely complement each other; while the Windows security settings determine the access rights for the user on whose behalf managed code is run, the CAS system determines security constraints of specific assemblies based on their origin. As a result, managed applications running under the same user context may run in different CAS contexts. Let's look at an example.

Suppose user A has not been granted write access to the registry by his or her machine's administrator. User A runs two managed applications—application X is a currency converter run from an intranet location and application Y is a managed registry clean-up tool run from the local hard disk. Presuming default CAS policy is in place, X and Y are given different levels of permission to access protected resources based on their different places of origin from which they are run. X is receiving the permissions that the default policy allots to assemblies from the intranet. On the other hand, Y receives the permissions the default policy grants to assemblies running from the local machine, which is full trust to access any resource, including the registry. X, doing simple calculations and therefore staying within the bounds set both by the Windows access restrictions and the CAS policy, will execute without a hitch. Conversely, Y will cause an access violation. Although Y had been granted the right to write to the registry by CAS policy, Y still needs to execute within the constraints set for user A by the operating system. It so happened that user A had no write access to the registry, so Y will cause an access violation. For Y to run properly, the administrator needs to make sure that all users who need to run Y have the appropriate access to the registry.

> **NOTE**
>
> It is important to emphasize again that CAS settings will *not* supercede Windows access restrictions. If a user has not been granted access to a particular location by the operating system, a managed application running for that user under CAS policy granting access to that location will still fail with an access violation. Being granted the permission to access a particular resource in CAS policy does not entail that operating system access restrictions can be bypassed by the respective managed application.

There are two Windows security technologies in particular that have a bearing on managed code—Windows access control permission settings and Software Restriction Policies. The former constitutes the administrable system of resource access protection Windows contains. The latter is a code-identity–based security system for unmanaged code. You will now look at both technologies and their relation to managed code in more detail.

Windows Access Control Protections and .NET Framework Security

The .NET Framework, as any other application run on Windows, is still subject to operating system security restrictions. In this section, the specific forms of interaction between operating system access control settings and the .NET Framework security system will be explained.

A Little Sojourn into the World of Windows Access Protection

Windows protects access to system objects using security descriptors. System objects include registry keys, files, and directories and printing services, among others.

NOTE

The following is a list of the most common types of system objects Windows recognizes and for which it maintains security descriptors:

- *Files*—Such as foo.bar.

- *Folders*—Such as C:\bar, including shared folders.

- *Registry keys*—Store application and system state that is permanently persisted on the machine. The security registry state stored under the Local Machine registry directory that determines whether CAS is turned on is an example.

- *Active Directory Objects*—Active directory is an enterprise wide, scalable directory service. Objects stored within that service (such as files or directories) are system objects that can have explicit access protection settings on them.

- *Services*—Services are programs that do maintenance and other background tasks.

- *Printers*—Shared printers that need to be accessible to other users. Printer resources can be made externally accessible by assigning the right printing permissions to give the intended set of printer users access.

Whenever a new system object is created, a security descriptor to go along with the newly created object is created by the operating system as well. A security descriptor itself is nothing more than a list of access permissions to the object with which it is associated. A permission, also called Access Control Entry (ACE), maps a user identity or group to specific access rights, such as the right to read or delete the object in question. For example, the file foo.bar can have a security descriptor allowing the power user group to write to the file. In general, the type of permissions a security descriptor contains depends on the type of object with which it is associated. For example, the permissions that can be associated with a file are different from the permissions associated with a printer resource. However, all objects can have permissions of the following type:

- *Modify*—The permission that allows a user or user group to modify the system object in question.

- *Delete*—The permission that allows a user or user group to delete the system object.

- *Read*—The permission that allows a user or user group to read the system object.

- *Change owner*—This permission allows the object owner to be changed.

Permissions in security descriptors are divided into two types of lists—the Dynamic Access Control List (DACL) and the System Access Control List (SACL). The latter allows the setting of permissions that control, among other things, auditing the object in question. However, the far more frequently used permission list on a security descriptor is the DACL, which contains the permissions that regulate the actual access to the object. If you are considering modifications to the way specific system objects, such as files or folders, are accessed by a certain set of users, you will most likely just need to change the DACL settings on the object in question.

> **NOTE**
>
> For far more information about Security descriptors, please visit the MSDN site at www.msdn.microsoft.com and search for "access protection" or "security descriptor."
>
> Specifically, see http://msdn.microsoft.com/library/default.asp?url=/library/en-us/security/accctrl_2hf0.asp for more information about access control or http://msdn.microsoft.com/library/default.asp?url=/library/en-us/security/accctrl_9f8y.asp for more security related information.

Administrators can modify the access permissions for system objects with a variety of tools, depending on the type of object that needs to be administered. For example, to modify the access permissions to a specific directory, administrators can use the Windows Explorer. For more information on how to alter access protections, see the "Managing Windows Access Protections" section later in this chapter.

Permissions on system objects are user identity or group relative. This means that access protection to system resources and objects in Windows is user-identity–dependent—access rights given by the operating system to objects, such as a particular directory, are dependent on the particular user trying to access the object. This means that all applications run under the same user context will receive the same set of the access permissions; there is no Windows security relevant distinction between applications running on behalf of the same user, with the exception of Software Restriction Policies settings (see the "Windows Software Restriction Policies and .NET Framework Security" section later in this chapter).

The Interplay Between Access Protection Settings and Managed Applications

The common language runtime, which executes all managed code, is just another application from the perspective of the Windows operating system. Consequently, all managed code is subject to the same access protections set on system objects, as is any other unmanaged application running in the same user context. Let's look at a couple of examples to illustrate the interplay between Windows security descriptor settings.

EXAMPLE ONE

Suppose the system administrator has set the DACL of the directory C:\foo to be writeable only by users who are members of the system administrator group. Assembly A implements a text editor. User Joe, who does not belong to the system administrator group, executes that assembly from some directory on the local hard drive. The system administrator has not changed the default Code Access Security policy, so A will receive a permission set from the CAS system granting full trust to access all resources on Joe's machine (because in default security policy, all code originating from the local machine is granted full trust to access all protected resources). Joe executes A and, after writing a little memo, tries to save the text file into directory foo. The CAS security system checks the assembly for being granted the right to access that disk location. Because A had been granted full trust to access all protected resources, the CAS security system will let A proceed to attempt to write the text file into C:\foo. However, when A tries to do just that, a security error will be thrown by Windows because Joe does not actually belong to the system administrator group on the machine.

Here you can observe the interplay and priority of the two security systems, CAS and Windows security descriptor settings, at play. Managed applications are checked by both systems for having sufficient rights to access resources that are protected by both systems (such as the registry, file system, printers, and so on). The Windows security descriptor settings are never overwritable by CAS policy settings. Even if Code Access Security policy has granted unlimited access to a resource to code, that code still must execute in a user context that allows access to the resource in question. In this example, Joe didn't have write access to foo because foo's security descriptor DACL settings required all write access to be done by users who are part of the system administrator group. But Joe does not belong into that group, so an access violation to foo occurred when A tried to write a file into it on Joe's behalf.

Let's look at a second example.

EXAMPLE TWO

Alexis is member of the system administrator group. All security descriptors of all system objects (such as files and registry keys) give that group full access to the specific system object they protect. Alexis has not changed Code Access Security policy, so all assemblies running from the intranet have only limited access to local system objects. For example, such assemblies cannot modify the registry or write to the hard disk. Alexis is trying to execute an assembly X that she has found on the company's intranet share. X is a registry clean-up tool and, when run, will try to modify registry entries. Because Alexis is a system administrator on her machine, all programs running in Alexis' user context will be granted by Windows the rights to access and modify system objects, including registry keys. However, X will still not run successfully, but will trigger a security exception to be thrown when X attempts to write to the registry. The reason for this is that X, as an assembly from the intranet, does not receive the right by Code Access Security policy to modify the registry. It will fail with a managed security exception unless Alexis changes the CAS policy to allow X to modify the registry. Note that it was not sufficient for X to be running in a security context strong enough to permit access to the objects X tries to access. It was also necessary for X to be granted the appropriate Code Access Security permission (the RegistryPermission to be precise) to successfully do its task.

As both examples demonstrate, Windows security settings and Code Access Security settings must permit access to a resource protected by both systems. Having permissions to do so from only one system will not be enough to affect successful resource access. Rather, you can think of resource access over resources protected by both systems as having to pass two separate forms of border checks before being allowed to proceed. The Code Access Security system checks if the CAS policy allows that code to access a particular resource; if you will, it is the agency that ensures that the passport is valid and not counterfeit. On the other hand, the Windows security descriptor settings ensure that the user on whose behalf the code is run should actually be allowed to access the resource in question. You could think of that set of checks as a way to check the actual passport holder for signs of suspicion. The following is a list of the common resources that are protected both by the Code Access Security policy system as well as by Windows access protection settings:

- Files and folders
- Registry keys
- Printers

If you want an application to successfully access any of these resources, you must make sure that both Code Access Security policy and the DACL settings grant the appropriate access rights both to the assembly (or assemblies) constituting the application as well as the user or users you want to be able to run the application.

DACLs to the Rescue—How DACLs Protect the Integrity of the Code Access Security System

There is another twist to the interplay between the Code Access Security system and Windows security descriptor settings—in particular, DACL settings. As you may remember, the Code Access Security system is driven by a configurable policy state. This policy is saved in three different files, one for each administrable policy level (user, machine, and enterprise). The machine and enterprise policy levels are intended to be modifiable only by those machine users who also have the right to effect machine-wide configuration changes. Therefore, the machine and enterprise policy levels need protection against modification from any users who don't have administrator rights. Nothing is easier than using Windows security descriptor settings. In fact, the enterprise and machine policy files are stored at the following locations:

- *Enterprise policy file*—`%Windir%\Microsoft.NET\Framework\<version>\CONFIG\ enterprisesec.config`
- *Machine policy file*—`%Windir%\Microsoft.NET\Framework\<version>\CONFIG\ security.config`

<version> stands for the particular .NET Framework version installed on the machine (for example, v1.0.3705).

As you can see, the security policy configuration state for the enterprise and machine policy are saved under the Windows system directory. By default on Windows NT with NTFS, Windows 2000, and Windows XP, the security descriptor for that folder is set such that only power users and machine administrators have the right to modify content in those folders. This will prevent anyone who is not an administrator or power user to change security policy for all managed applications on the machine, or even to change the copy of the enterprise policy persisted on the machine.

CAUTION

You should make sure never to ease the DACL protections on the %Windir% folder or any of its subfolders. If anything, you should consider strengthening the access protection to these locations. For example, it would make a lot of sense to disallow power users from modifying the security configuration files. To find out how to do so, see the next section, "Managing Windows Access Protections."

Managing Windows Access Protections

You may now wonder how you can actually review and modify the security descriptor settings, specifically the DACL settings for any of the system objects previously mentioned. The following is a list pointing you in the right direction for administering access protection for the most common system objects.

For files, folders, shared files, and shared folders, the tool to administer files and folders is the Windows Explorer. You can start Windows Explorer in the following way:

1. Choose the Start button.

2. Select Run.

3. Type in **Explorer** and press Enter.

Once you have started up the Windows Explorer, you are ready to review and make security descriptor settings on files and folders. Simply right-click on the file or folder you want to review or Edit Access Protection Settings For. Choose the Properties menu option and then the Security tab.

TIP

Note that if you do not see the Security tab, it may be that you are running with the FAT32, not the NTFS file system. To be able to make access protection modification, you must switch to NTFS. The NTFS file system is not available on Windows 95, 98, and ME. However, if you are running Windows NT, 2000, or XP, you can convert from the FAT32 system to NTFS using the `Convert` command-line tool.

Type the following command at the command line to convert from a FAT32 file system to the NTFS file system (to get to the command line, select Start, Run, and type in **cmd**):

`Convert` *drive:* `/fs:ntfs`

For example

`Convert c: /fs:ntfs`

It is advisable to back up your drive before attempting this conversion.

After you have selected the Security tab, a dialog appears that will let you set the access protections on the file or folder. For example, you can add a user group and explicitly deny them any access to the file or folder.

Let's now look at how to administer access control settings for the registry.

Administering Registry Key Access Control Settings

The registry contains a tree of registry keys that are used by the Software and hardware on a computer to maintain permanent state. The registry scopes keys in a number of ways; keys used to register classes (keys in `HKEY_Classes_Root`) are separated from keys maintaining per-user state (keys in `HKEY_Current_User` and `HKEY_Users`) and global machine state (keys in `HKEY_Local_Machine`). By default (on Windows 2000 and XP installations using NTFS), all keys in `HKEY_Local_Machine` are write accessible only to users in the system administrators and power user groups. You can view and change the DACL settings on registry keys by running the Registry Editor 32 (RegEdit32) tool. To do so, simply type the following at the command prompt (to get to the command line, select Start, Run, and type in **cmd**):

`Regedt32`

RegEdit32 will present you with different windows for the different types of key scoping. Figure 17.1 shows an example screenshot of that tool. To view and modify access protection settings, as seen in the screenshot, on specific keys or key folders, simply select the respective item, click the Security menu option, and select Permissions.

The content of the Permissions window basically shows you the DACL entries of the security descriptor of the item you have selected. You are given the choice to either modify the type of access specific groups have, or add or remove user groups to the security descriptor of the key or key folder. Where possible, always reduce the write access to keys or key folders because this will minimize the potential attack surface for malicious Software. Conversely, if you expect a managed application that accesses the registry to run successfully for a user, you need to make sure that that user or the user group he or she belongs to actually has access to the required key or keys in the registry. It is necessary, but not sufficient, for Code Access Security Policy to have granted the managed application access to that portion of the registry.

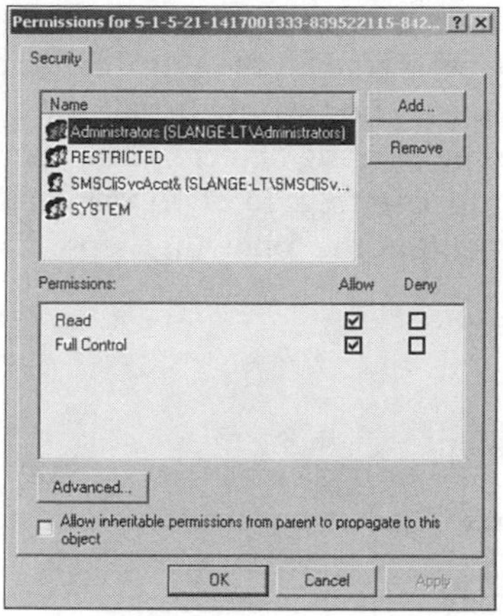

FIGURE 17.1   RegEdit32 window with Access Control Permissions window.

CAUTION

You should always be wary about adding any users and user groups to the administrators group on a machine. That group has full access to the HKEY_Local_Machine registry key repository. Among many other critical system keys, a few registry keys protecting the secure running of all managed code are also stored there. For example, the key that stores the state, whether the CLR security system is turned on or off, is stored in HKEY_Local_Machine, Software, Microsoft, .NET Framework, Security, Policy. By default, no key is present there when security is turned on. It is strongly suggested that you limit write access to the Policy folder to system administrators. One easy step to decrease surface area for security attacks is to review and, if necessary, change the DACL settings for that folder:

1. Start up regedit32 by typing **regedt32** at the command prompt.
2. Select the policy folder (full path specified in previous text).
3. Select the Security menu and click Permissions.
4. Remove FullControl (only allowing Read access) to all groups except the system administrator group.

Let us now turn to controlling printer access.

Access Control for Printers
Printers may not seem a critical system resource; after all, they are just transferring text and graphic onto paper and don't hold sensitive data. However, consider the

case of a malicious application that constantly causes print commands to be sent to the printer, causing much paper waste as well as preventing timely completion of legitimate printing jobs. For this reason, both the Windows operating system as well as the .NET Framework security system are protecting access to printing services. Thus, for a managed application to successfully initiate a printing job on a printer, the application must have been granted the printing permission by the .NET Framework. Additionally, the user on whose behalf the application is running must have been given access to the printing object by the operating system's printer access control settings. Access control settings for a printer can be viewed and modified by administrators. To do so, perform the following steps:

1. Choose the Start button.

2. Select Settings.

3. Select the Printers menu.

4. Right-click the printer object you want to administer.

5. Click the Properties tab.

6. Click the Security tab.

You can now view and modify access control settings to that printer object.

Access Control for Services

Unlike applications directly started by a user, services are programs that perform background and maintenance tasks. They are not executed within a specific user context unless otherwise configured. You can use the Computer Management tool found under the Administrative Tools folder in the Control Panel to administer services. In particular, in the Computer Management tool, select Services under the Services and Application folder. Within the Services Tool, you can administer security context settings for services, as well as start and stop services.

Access Control for Active Directory Objects

If you have Active Directory running on your system, you can modify the access control settings to individual Active Directory objects, much like you do for file and folder objects. The administrative tool to be used for this purpose is the Active Directory Users and Computers tool. You can find the tool under the Server Administrator Tools on all machines that act as domain controllers. Alternatively, you can perform the following steps:

1. Open the Start menu.

2. Select Run.

3. Type in **dsa.msc** and press Enter.

For more information on how to install and administer Active Directory, please refer to the Windows Help system.

Windows Software Restriction Policies and .NET Framework Security

Windows XP and Windows .NET Server ship with a new security technology that allows administrators to set code-identity–based security policy restrictions that are independent of user context. This technology is known as Software Restriction Policies. In this section, we'll cover a short overview of Software Restriction Policies, as well as how this technology and the code-identity–based security system for managed code cooperate.

NOTE

Again, Software Restriction Policies is a feature not available on any versions of Windows prior to Windows XP.

What Is Windows Software Restriction Policies?

Software Restriction Policies is a policy-driven technology that allows administrators to set code-identity–based rules that determine whether a native code application is allowed to execute. Following are the types of code identification that Software Restriction Policies supports by default (much like evidence in the CAS system):

- *Hash*—A cryptographically strong means to identify a set of bits, such as a file.

- *Publisher Certificate*—The X509 publisher certificate, used to make authenticode signatures of an application. Both hash and publisher certificate are a cryptographically strong (that is, hard to spoof) means of identifying an application.

- *Path*—The path (local or UNC) to a file. This can be a fully qualified path or an enclosing folder.

- *Zone*—Reusing the IE zone model, zones are a broad category of origin of a particular Windows Installer package. Internet, intranet, and MyComputer are possible zone values. Zone rules only apply to Windows Installer Packages.

NOTE

Neither path nor zones are cryptographically strong; in other words, they do not offer a strong means of identifying a particular file or set of files. For example, the Internet zone consists of *all* files found on the Internet, while a file to which a path points can be exchanged without invalidating the path value itself. Consequently, it is always advisable to base policy on the most strong types of code identification criteria that still satisfies your administrative scenario. However, path rules are sufficient as long as the folders and applications are protected by the necessary ACLs preventing users from copying over them.

Administrators can introduce rules for each of the previously mentioned code identi-fication categories. For example, administrators can set new rules for all Windows Installer packages coming from the Internet and intranet zone. At present, Software Restriction Policies only allows two outcomes for these rules—either the code fitting the rules is allowed to execute or it is not. For example, to specify that no Windows Installer packages from the Internet should be run, the administrator would add a new zone rule with zone value of Internet and set the result to a no-execute. Administrators can also specify a default rule, in case none of the more specific rules in the hash, certificate, path, or zone category match. The default rule can be set to allow all code by default to run, effectively turning the more specific rules into an exception table. Or, alternatively, the default can be such that no code gets run, which would make more specific rules an opt-in table. The former is the default rule that ships with Software Restriction Policies, but the latter can help to drastically lock down machines in very security-sensitive environments requiring knowledge and approval of all code that gets run on the system.

Software Restriction Policies always evaluates the rules that have been defined in a specific order, going from most specific to most broad. In particular, Software Restriction Policies first checks the hash rules and applies the one that it finds fitting. If no hash rules fit, Software Restriction Policies then proceeds to all certifi-cate rules. If it fails to find a rule matching the code that is being loaded, it goes on to the path rules and then the zone rules and finally, if no other rule applied, a default rule will be applied. The default rule simply states that all code by default either runs or doesn't run.

Software Restriction Policies is deeply integrated with the rest of the operating system. For it to work properly, it effectively intercepts execution and library load events and checks against its policy settings. Let's look at a small example.

Suppose that the default rule has been set to run all code. Furthermore, the adminis-trator sets a hash rule preventing execution of all files with the hash of `foo.dll`, which is a component that has been determined to be a security risk. User Joe now tries to run an application `bar.exe` from the company's intranet. `bar.exe` needs to load `foo.dll`. As part of the DLL load mechanisms, Software Restriction Policies is invoked and starts to check its most specific rules—namely, administrator-defined hash rules. A rule with the same hash as `foo.dll` is found and `bar.exe` will termi-nate without `foo.dll` being invoked. Now, suppose Joe tried to run `xyz.exe`, and `xyz.exe` does not have a dependency on `foo.dll`. Software Restrictions Policies gets invoked prior to `xyz.exe` being able to run. Software Restriction Policies first checks hash rules, finds no match, and goes on to certificate and path rules—all of which do not turn up a matching rule for `xyz.exe`. Finally, because xyz is not a Windows Installer package, Software Restriction Policies skips the zone rules and comes to the default rule, which allows all code to run. `xyz.exe` thus successfully proceeds to execute.

You may now ask how this code-identity–based security system interfaces with the .NET Framework's Code Access Security system? Will you have to set and consider two code-identity–based systems for all the managed code run on your system? We will now answer these questions.

> **NOTE**
>
> For far more in-depth coverage of the Software Restriction Policies technology, please see the whitepaper at `http://www.microsoft.com/windowsxp/pro/techinfo/administration/default.asp`.

How Does the Code Access Security System Cooperate with Windows Software Restriction Policies?

Luckily, you will not need to worry about having to make code-identity–based settings in two different security systems. The CAS system and Software Restriction Policies get out of each other's way. Whenever a managed library or executable is invoked, Software Restriction Policies will recuse itself and leave all policy decisions and enforcement actions up to the .NET Framework's Code Access Security system. Thus, when managed applications are run, Software Restriction Policies will not come into play. Conversely, when native code files are run, the CAS system does not interfere with Software Restriction Policies rules, because CAS only applies to bits run on the Common Language Runtime. In that way, you can think of Software Restriction Policies and the CAS system as nicely complementary; Software Restriction Policies offers code-identity–based settings for unmanaged, native applications, whereas CAS is the security system for managed applications. They each stay out of each other's way, so administrators will not have to worry about an overlap between the two.

> **NOTE**
>
> As you can see in Chapter 18, the CAS system is far more expressive and powerful than Software Restriction Policies. Thus, not all rules you can express in CAS can be expressed in Software Restriction Policies. The primary reason for the discrepancy in expressiveness is the fact that all managed code gets verified for adherence to type safety rules, which allows the CAS to start out with far stronger guarantees about the behavior of code. This, in turn, then allows code to run semitrusted (in a fashion that restricts access to some resources) without allowing such code to subvert the system that places the restrictions.

Administering Software Restriction Policies

You can view and administer Security Restriction Policies either for an individual machine or a whole domain. To change Software Restriction Policies just for a local machine, you can use the secpol MMC snap-in. To start this tool, perform the following steps:

1. Choose the Start menu.

2. Select the Run option.

3. Type in **secpol.msc** and press Enter.

NOTE

secpol.msc is not available on home editions of the operating system.

Select the Software Restriction Policies entry and open the Action menu. There you will find an option to create or modify policy.

To administer Software Restriction Policies for a whole domain, use the Active Directory User and Computers tool. You can start this tool in the following way:

1. Select the Start menu.

2. Select the Run option.

3. Type in **dsa.msc** and press Enter.

After the tool is started, you need to right-click the respective domain where you will find the option to change Software restriction policy.

TIP

Again, to find out more details about Software Restriction Policies, you should consult the paper at http://www.microsoft.com/windowsxp/pro/techinfo/administration/default.asp.

Summary

This chapter has served two primary functions. It has given you an overview of the different, administrable security mechanisms that can come into play when managed code gets executed. It has also offered an overview of the interaction between Windows access protection settings, Windows Software Restriction Policies, and managed code. The following are some key points to take away from this chapter:

- The .NET Framework Code Access Security (CAS) system does not replace or circumnavigate access protection settings done at the operating system level.

- There are resources, such as the registry, file system, and printers, that are protected by both the Code Access Security system and Windows access protections.

- Managed applications trying to access resources protected both by the CAS system and Windows Access protection settings must be granted the appropriate access permissions both by the CAS policy system and the Windows Access protection settings.

- The Code Access Security System is based on code-identity, whereas Windows access protections are based on user identity. As such, the CAS and Windows Access protection system complement each other.

- Windows XP and .NET Server ship with a code-identity–based security system called Software Restriction Policies. This system is only efficient over unmanaged code and does not replace or duplicate code-identity–based access protection for any managed application.

- Finally, you have been given pointers to the appropriate administration tools for the respective Windows security settings introduced in this chapter.

It is now time to show exactly how Code Access Security Policy is administered using the .NET Framework Configuration tool, as is shown in the next chapter.

18

Administering Security Policy Using the .NET Framework Configuration Tool

By Sebastian Lange

Security administration can be a fine art. Without the appropriate administrative tools, changes to security policy can be error prone and can introduce security holes. Consequently, the .NET Framework ships with a rich graphical administration tool—the .NET Framework Configuration tool. Most security administration tasks can easily be accomplished by using this tool. It will be your main aid in undertaking security policy changes as well as in analyzing the current state of security policy.

As you will have learned from previous sections of this book, the .NET Framework ships with a very expressive security model. It allows for incredible fine tuning as to which piece of code may or may not access a particular resource, such as the file system. This richness gives administrators the power to tailor security policy exactly to their needs, but also brings with it the responsibility to learn the ins and outs of the administrative tool and the security model underlying it.

In this chapter, you will find both an introduction to the features of the .NET Framework Configuration tool and general hints and tips concerning the security administration of the .NET Framework.

NOTE

From this point the .NET Framework Configuration tool will simply be referred to as "the tool". References to other tools will be made explicit.

The following are some of the key points of this chapter:

- Security administration strategies and hints
- Introduction to the basic operation of the tool
- Introduction to the security administration wizards
- Basics of directly manipulating the security policy tree
- Hints and tricks concerning user, machine, or enterprise level security policy administration
- How to model and try out policy changes without affecting your machine's own security policy
- How to test security policy changes

NOTE

To fully understand this chapter, you should have a good grasp of the security model. In particular, you may want to review Chapter 8, "Membership Conditions, Code Groups, and Policy Levels: The Brick and Mortar of Security Policy," which introduces the concepts of membership conditions, code groups, and policy levels.

Before Making Any Security Policy Change: Administration Strategies

Security breaches can be very costly, but not all such breaches are the result of actual errors in software. Many security breaches are a result of mismanagement or mistakes in security policy administration. Some of the consequences of administrative mistakes are

- Unintended side effects of security policy changes allow unsafe code to run, which can lead to the loss of files or the theft of information.
- Security policy has been too strongly tightened, preventing legitimate applications from running properly and, therefore, causing severe productivity loss.

Before dashing to make any security policy changes, you should carefully consider the following questions and heuristics. Only after such consideration should you go ahead and alter security policy. The .NET Framework Security system will only be able to enforce what security policy tells it to enforce.

Do You Have to Change Policy at All?

When thinking about changing security policy, the first question that you should ask yourself is whether you truly need to make a change at all. If an application that you expected to run causes a security exception, it may very well be that the security system is just doing its job in preventing illicit access to protected resources. Generally, there are only three main scenarios that should prompt you to change security policy:

- If an assembly can access resources that it should not have access to (it accesses the file system, registry, or even runs at all), security policy should be tightened for that assembly.

- If an assembly that should legitimately run does not execute or run properly due to security restrictions, security policy should be made less restrictive for that assembly.

- A previous change to security policy introduced an error (either opened a security hole, prevented a legitimate assembly from running properly, the enterprises security guidelines have changed, and so on), security policy should be changed accordingly.

You should think hard about changing security policy if you are motivated by a scenario different from the three defined scenarios. For example, an assembly displaying a window asking you to change security policy or trying to run an application from the Internet that throws a security exception does not necessarily represent sufficient reason to change security policy.

A special case to consider is if the security policy has not been changed at all so far, so the default security policy is still active. Default security policy has been designed to be a safe default that should suffice for most scenarios in which managed code is run. The following is a list of the main characteristics embodied by default policy:

- All assemblies running on the My Computer zone have access to all resources. This means that security is effectively not enforced for all assemblies that have been explicitly installed on the local machine.

- All assemblies from the intranet zone run in a tight security context. For example, this means that intranet assemblies must verify and have no access to the file system, registry, security system, or write access to environment variables. However, assemblies from the intranet are allowed to read certain environment variables, do unlimited User Interface interaction with the user, use the safe file storage system (Isolated Storage), and connect back to their place of origin, among other things.

- All assemblies from the Internet zone are prevented from running by default. An administrator needs to explicitly change policy to enable specific applications to run from the Internet.

- All assemblies from the Trusted site zone are executed within tight security constraints. For example, any assemblies run from a Trusted site have only limited UI access, no direct file system, registry, or environment variable access, among other restrictions.

- All assemblies from the Restricted site zone have no rights whatsoever. This means assemblies in that zone are not executed.

NOTE

Throughout this chapter *default policy* will be used interchangeably with the phrase *default security policy*.

NOTE

All references to default security policy are to the default state shipping in the Service Pack 1 for the .NET Framework.

You should go ahead and make the respective policy change only if you are certain that you want to deviate for an assembly or set of assemblies from these characteristics of default policy.

An example of a valid change to default policy is if an enterprise decided not to allow any code coming from the intranet to execute except for a few trusted applications. This requires changing the Intranet zone policy to withhold all permissions from code in that zone, while adding in policy to trust specific software publishers or strong names.

Generally, you should always remember that default policy has been carefully crafted to protect your computer's resources from illicit access by code originating from anywhere but your local machine.

NOTE

See Chapter 8 for more detail about default security policy.

Think of the Worst Case Scenario

Before making any policy change, you should not only consider whether that change will get the job done. It is also imperative to ask yourself what the worst case security vulnerability could result from your policy change. For example, if you want to enable a specific application running from your enterprise's intranet to get full access to all protected resources, you could accomplish this by giving full access to all protected resources to all assemblies from the intranet. Although this will accomplish the task, it will also enable *all other* assemblies on the intranet to run with full trust. These may be assemblies over which you exercise scant or no control. Consequently, when making security policy changes, it is essential to stay task focused *and* to consider the worst possible case that your changed security policy may encounter.

Make the Policy Change with the Least Possible Impact

To reduce the possibility of creating unintended side effects due to your policy change, you should make that change to policy that will accomplish the task at hand but affects as few assemblies as possible. For example, if you want to enable a certain assembly running from the intranet to receive full trust to access protected resources, you could do so by introducing a code group into the policy that grants that level of trust based on the Internet site at which the application is found. However, this would give all assemblies at that site the same rights that you only want to allot to a specific application. A safer way to do this would be to either use the assembly's hash or strong name as a basis to target just that specific assembly in your policy change. The more changes you make to policy, the more important this guideline becomes, because side effects can accumulate and, in combination, can open a security vulnerability.

Pre-Plan the Policy Structure of Your System

You can think of policy as a way to partition the set of all assemblies into subsections. Each of these subsections receives a specific amount of trust to access protected resources. In a way, security policy is a highly dimensional categorization mechanism that sorts assemblies into administratively defined trust categories. As you have learned earlier in this book, default policy partitions the world of assemblies along the lines of zones. You should think hard about whether you need to further partition these categories contained in default policy or introduce your own. For example, you may have a specific software publisher, such as a contractor company supplying your enterprise with custom applications, that you always want to grant full access to all resources on the system. In such a case, you should add another trust category to your policy that grants full trust to access all protected resources based on the strong name of the contractor company.

NOTE

Most likely, you would do so by adding a code group with a strong name membership condition and a full trust permission set at the root of machine policy.

Generally, you should think of all the categories of assemblies that should receive special security consideration, compare this list with the default policy, and then see if you need to make any changes.

Consider the Interaction with Operating System Settings

As you will remember from the previous chapter, the .NET Framework security system operates on top of whatever security settings the operating system enforces. Thus, managed code can only access those resources that *both* the operating system and the .NET Framework security system allow the code to access. In some cases, this will mean that changes not only to the .NET Framework security policy but also to operating system settings are needed. For example, if you change policy to allow an assembly running from the intranet to have read access to certain parts of the file system, that assembly may still be prevented from doing so, even after your policy change, for the simple reason of running into a DACL restriction. This problem usually only occurs in cases in which you attempt to relax .NET Framework security policy. Thus, prior to widening managed security policy, consider whether this also implies changes to operating system security settings.

Document Your Changes

It is good practice to maintain a log of the policy changes you have undertaken. In the case of problems with the current security policy, this may enable you to pinpoint exactly which change to the policy created the problem.

> **TIP**
>
> Below is a table of the locations of the files holding the enterprise, machine, and user policy level settings respectively. In order to maintain an accurate log of the evolution of security policy, you can make copies of these files after making policy changes. You could automate this process by writing a little script that copies these files. You can later reopen and browse these policy files using the tool (see the "Modeling Policy Changes Using Open and New" section later in this chapter).
>
> Enterprise level configuration file
>
> %WINDIR%\Microsoft.NET\Framework\v[*version number*]\Config\Enterprisesec.config
>
> Machine level configuration file
>
> %WINDIR%\Microsoft.NET\Framework\v[*version number*]\Config\security.config
>
> User level configuration file
>
> *Windows NT/2000/XP*:
>
> %USERPROFILE%\Application data\Microsoft\CLR security config\v[*version*]\Security.config
>
> *Windows 95/98:*
>
> %WINDIR%\username\CLR security config\v[*version*]\Security.config

Depending on the OS you are running on %WINDIR% will either be the \Windows or \WINNT directory into which the operating system had been installed. The %USERPROFILE% directory stands for your 'Documents and Settings'\username folder. Note that the 'Application data' folder is a hidden folder.

Introduction to the .NET Framework Configuration Tool

The .NET Framework ships with a powerful administrative tool that can be used to change settings for all configurable aspects of the .NET Framework, including security policy. The tool is a Microsoft Management Console (MMC) snap-in and will feel familiar to anybody who has used other Microsoft administrative tools, such as the IIS administration tool.

Availability of the Tool

The full tool described in this chapter ships with the .NET Framework Redistributable and SDK. It will require MMC 1.2 to run.

NOTE

The tool requires MMC (Microsoft Management Console) version 1.2 or higher. If you install the Framework on Windows 95, 98, ME, you may still not find that you have access to the tool. In that case, please download MMC from
http://support.microsoft.com/support/mmc/mmcdown.asp.

After you have installed MMC, use the Add Snap-In option under the File menu to add the Microsoft .NET Framework Configuration snap-in.

TIP

To find out whether you have the Microsoft .NET Framework SDK installed, you can do the following:

1. Click Start.
2. Click Programs or All Programs (depending on the version of Windows you are running).
3. Check the list of programs; if you find Microsoft .NET Framework SDK, the SDK has been installed and the administration tool is available on your machine.

If you do not have the right version of MMC installed on your machine, you will not be able to access all administrative features described in this chapter. However, you will still be able to do some administrative changes using the .NET Framework Wizards launcher that ships in all distribution forms of the .NET Framework. The wizard launcher can be used to start the two most common security administration wizards—the Adjust Security Wizard and the Trust Assembly Wizard. Both wizards will be described later in this chapter.

Starting the Tool

If you have Windows NT, Windows 2000, or Windows XP installed, a shortcut to the .NET Framework Configuration tool was placed in the Administrative Tools directory (see Figure 18.1).

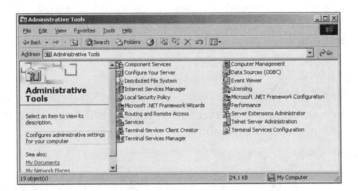

FIGURE 18.1   Shortcuts to the .NET Framework Configuration tool and .NET Framework Wizards launcher.

To start the tool, perform the following steps:

For Windows XP (Default control panel view)

1. Click the Start button.

2. Select Control Panel.

3. Select Performance and Maintenance.

4. Select Administrative Tools.

5. Choose the Microsoft .NET Framework Configuration shortcut.

For Windows NT, Windows 2000, and Windows XP (classic control panel view)

1. Click the Start button.

2. Choose Settings.

3. Choose the Control Panel.

4. Choose Administrative Tools.

5. Choose the Microsoft .NET Framework Configuration shortcut.

For Windows 95/98

1. Click the Start button.

2. Choose Programs.

3. Choose Administrative Tools.

4. Choose the Microsoft .NET Framework Configuration shortcut.

NOTE

To start the .NET Framework Wizards launcher instead of the tool, simply follow the previous directions, except for the last step; choose the Microsoft .NET Framework Wizards instead.

TIP

If you expect to use the .NET Framework Configuration tool frequently, you should place a copy of the shortcut to it on your desktop.

Overview of the Main Security Administrative Options

After the tool has been started, you will encounter the start screen shown in Figure 18.2.

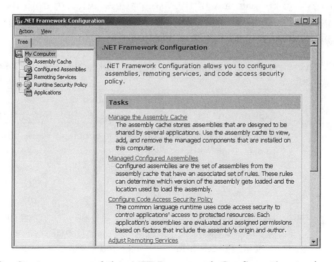

FIGURE 18.2   Start up page of the .NET Framework Configuration tool.

To access the main security administration options, right-click the Runtime Security Policy node in the tree view to the left or single-click the Runtime Security Policy node to get a task pad containing links to the main administrative options (see Figure 18.3).

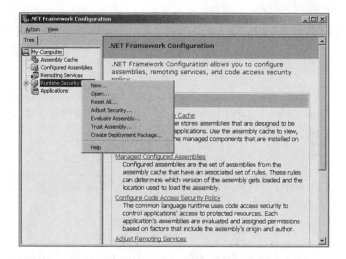

FIGURE 18.3   Accessing the main security administration options in the .NET Framework Configuration tool.

Table 18.1 gives you an overview of the use of these different options, as well as pointers to parts of this chapter or other places in this book that will give you more in-depth explanations of the respective features.

TABLE 18.1   Overview of the Main Administrative Features of the .NET Framework Configuration Tool

Feature	Explanation	Recommended Knowledge	For Further Explanation
Reset All	Resets security policy to default policy state	Knowledge of default policy, minimal knowledge of policy model	See Chapter 8 for explanation of default policy; see "Resetting Security Policy" later in this chapter
Adjust Security Wizard	Used to increase or decrease the level of trust for all code from a particular zone (such as the intranet)	Wizard is self con- tained, no or minimal background know- ledge of security policy model required	See the "Changing Trust for a Zone Using the Adjust Security Wizard" section later in this chapter

TABLE 18.1 Continued

Feature	Explanation	Recommended Knowledge	For Further Explanation
Evaluate Assembly Wizard	Used to test what permissions an assembly receives from policy or what code groups apply to it	Working knowledge of the security policy model is necessary	See Part II, "Code Access Security Fundamentals," for more background information, especially Chapters 6 and 8; also see the "Testing Security Policy Using the Evaluate Assembly Wizard" section later in this chapter
Trust Assembly Wizard	Used to increase the level of trust for a particular assembly or all assemblies signed by the same software publisher	Wizard is self contained, no or minimal background knowledge of security policy model is required	See the "Increasing Trust Just for a Selected Assembly or for All Assemblies Signed by the Same Software Publisher" section later in this chapter
Create Deployment Package Wizard	Used to wrap a policy level into an MSI file for further distribution and deployment	Good knowledge of the security policy model, depending on deployment method knowledge of Microsoft SMS or Microsoft Group Policy necessary	See the "Deploying Security Policy" section later in this chapter
New, Open Options	Used to create or open a policy level not applying to current machine, used to do modeling and testing of security policy changes	Good knowledge of security policy model	See the "Modeling Policy Changes Using Open and New" section later in this chapter

Although only the Adjust Security and Trust Assembly Wizards do not require extensive background knowledge of the security policy model, many common administration scenarios can be solved quickly and safely using either of these wizards.

Overview of the Policy Tree Manipulation Options

Besides the wizards and options already mentioned, the .NET Framework Configuration tool also includes a fully graphical, configurable representation of the security policy model. This enables you to make very fine-tuned and specialized policy changes.

As you will recall from Part II, the security policy model consists of three administrable policy levels—enterprise policy, machine policy, and user policy—also referred to as the security policy tree. If you expand the Runtime Security Policy node, you will find these three policy levels. As you may remember, each policy level consists of a tree of code groups, known permission sets at that policy level, and a list of policy assemblies. Expanding one of the policy level nodes, such as the Machine node, you will find nodes representing exactly these three constituents of a policy level. The list of known permission sets at that policy level can be viewed by expanding the permission sets node. Expanding the code group node allows you to view the code group tree of that policy level. See Figure 18.4 for an example in which the machine policy level has been fully expanded.

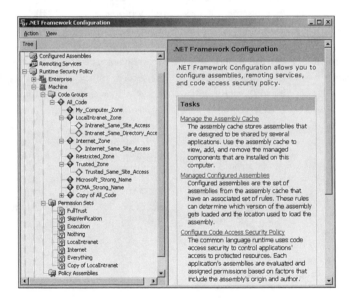

FIGURE 18.4   Policy tree view with the machine policy level fully expanded.

The right screen, here showing information about the machine policy level, will always show helpful information and a list of tasks available for the selected node in the tree view to the left (single-click a node to select it). Right-clicking any node in the tree view will bring up a menu of all the available options for that specific node. For example, if you right-click the Everything permission set under the Permission set node, you will see a number of options, such as the option to change this permission set or make a copy of it. For a thorough explanation of the various options available and their use, please see the "Manipulating the Security Policy Tree Directly—Basic Techniques" section later in this chapter.

Exiting the Tool

You can quit the tool without hesitation. All policy manipulations that you have done during your session with the tool have been saved on completion of each action. You will not have to fear any loss of your administrative work, unless the tool is forcefully shut down prior to or during the process of saving an administrative action.

TIP

In the unlikely event that all or part of a policy should ever get corrupted, you always have the option of reverting to the secure default policy by resetting all policy or a specific corrupted policy level. To reset all of security policy, right-click the Runtime Security Policy node and select the Reset All feature. To reset just one policy level, right-click a policy level node, such as Machine, and select the Reset option. For more information, please see the "Resetting Security Policy" section later in this chapter.

Increasing Trust for an Assembly or Software Publisher Using the Trust Assembly Wizard

The Trust Assembly Wizard is a feature of the tool that allows the quick, easy, and safe change of policy to *increase* the level of trust for a specific assembly or even all assemblies of a specific software publisher or strong name signer.

NOTE

This wizard is not designed to lower the level of trust for an assembly or set of assemblies. If you need to decrease the level of permissions that an assembly or set of assemblies receives, you will need to make that policy update directly in the policy tree.

If you want to decrease the level of permissions given to all assemblies from a particular zone, you can use the Adjust Security Wizard to do so (see the "Changing Trust for a Zone Using the Adjust Security Wizard" section later in this chapter).

The following are a few sample scenarios demonstrating the use of this wizard. These scenarios may also be used as recipes for similar policy change situations you need to solve. Each of the wizard options mentioned is explained in more detail later:

- *Scenario*—An assembly is installed on a shared intranet site or an intranet share. The assembly requires access to the local file system and registry, permissions that are not granted by default security policy to managed code from the intranet zone. This is evident when the assembly is run and returns security exceptions.

  Wizard action—A user or administrator can use the Trust Assembly Wizard to give full trust to access all resources on his or her machine to the assembly in question. To do so, the following wizard steps are used:

  1. Start the wizard by right-clicking the Runtime Security Policy node and selecting the Trust Assembly Wizard option.

  2. Accept Make changes to this Computer.

  3. Browse to the assembly in question and keep the This One Assembly default.

  4. Select the Full Trust option.

  5. Accept changes and finish the Wizard.

TIP

If many or all machines on an intranet need to get policy changes to trust a specific assembly or set of assemblies, it may be more efficient to develop enterprise policy and deploy it to all machines that need that policy update. See the "Deploying Security Policy" section later in this chapter.

- *Scenario*—There is a software publisher, say a contractor company supplying in-house software for your enterprise, whose assemblies you want to run without any security restrictions, independent of the location from which that publisher's assemblies are being run.

  Wizard action—The Wizard allows you to give full trust to access all protected resources based on a strong name key or a X.509v3 publisher certificate, thus uniquely identifying a specific software publisher.

  1. Start the Wizard by right-clicking the Runtime Security Policy node and select the Trust Assembly Wizard option and accept the Make Changes to This Computer option.

  2. Browse to an assembly signed by the software publisher you want to trust.

  3. On the Trust This or All Assemblies from This Publisher page, check the All Assemblies with This Public Key option, and uncheck the Version

option (if the strong name is unavailable for that assembly but a publisher certificate is present, choose the All Assemblies from the Same Publisher option).

4. Select the Full Trust option.

5. Accept the changes and select Finish.

- *Scenario*—Assemblies on the Internet by the same software publisher should get run with the level of trust that default policy grants assemblies from the intranet.

  Wizard action—The Wizard steps are identical to the previous scenario with the exception of choosing the slider position just below the Full Trust option on the Choose Minimum Level of Trust for the Trust Assembly Wizard page.

NOTE

The trust slider may not appear if security policy has changed significantly from default policy.

Generally, the Trust Assembly Wizard is an excellent tool to increase the level of trust an assembly or set of assemblies receives without causing significant side effects to other assemblies. It allows you to make very pointed trust increases without opening up the security policy unduly to other assemblies.

NOTE

If you use the Trust Assembly Wizard to increase trust for an application on the intranet or Internet, you will need to give trust to all dependent assemblies of that assembly as well. So if giving trust to a specific assembly does not seem to work, it is often the case that there are other assemblies at that location that need to be loaded and run as part of the application. You will need to run the Wizard over those assemblies as well.

Following is an explanation of all the options this Wizard has to offer on its various pages. This is the place where you should first turn if the Wizard does not seem to be operating the way you intended.

The Start Page—Choosing to Make Changes to User or Machine Policy

After starting the Wizard, either by right-clicking the Runtime Security Policy node and choosing the Increase Assembly Trust task on the task pad, the Wizard start page shown in Figure 18.5 will appear.

FIGURE 18.5   Trust Assembly Wizard start page—choosing between making changes to the machine or user security policy.

This page allows you to choose whether the policy changes you are about to make should affect user policy only or whether it should be made to all code running on the computer, by modifying machine policy. Let us now delve deeper into what these two options mean.

Making Changes to This Computer

This is the default option if available. If this option is chosen, the policy change will affect all users on the machine. For most scenarios, this is exactly what you should choose. Increasing trust for a specific application will more commonly be a setting that is independent of the user context executing the managed code.

> **NOTE**
>
> Security policy is stored in various configuration files—one for each administrable policy level. Both the machine and enterprise security policy files are stored under the Windows subdirectory, therefore, not allowing write access by default unless the current user has machine administrator or power user rights. If the operating system does not allow access to the machine level policy file because the admin tool is run under a user context that does not have machine administrator or power user rights, the option to make changes to the machine policy will not be available in the tool.

Making Changes to the Current User Policy

This option is the only one available if the tool is not run under a user context that has write access to the machine security policy file (see the previous Note). If this option is chosen, the Wizard will modify user security policy to increase the trust for an assembly in accordance with the trust level chosen in the Wizard.

However, because the user policy is already set to an unrestricted state by default, executing this Wizard over user policy will not change the trust level any assembly receives unless user policy had been modified from its default state to something more restrictive. Always remember that this Wizard is designed to *increase* the level of trust a certain assembly receives, so running this Wizard over security policy that already grants unrestricted permissions to assemblies will yield no tangible results.

Selecting the Assembly or Software Publisher to Increase Trust

After you have chosen to make a change either to user or machine-wide security policy by choosing the This Computer option, the Wizard will prompt you to select an assembly that the Wizard will base its security policy change on (see Figure 18.6).

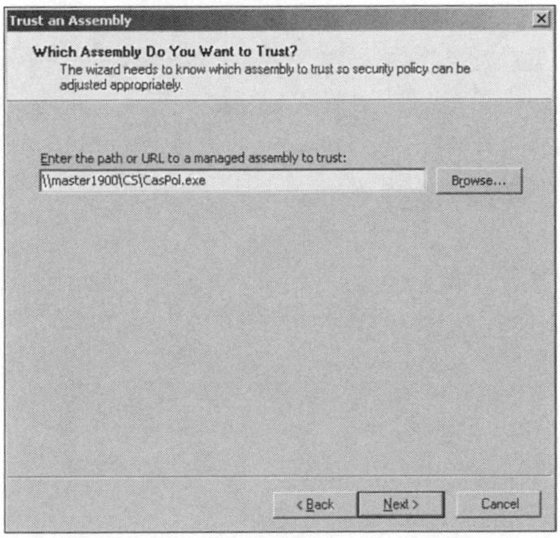

FIGURE 18.6   Selecting an assembly in the Trust Assembly Wizard.

You can either type in a valid URL to an assembly or use the Browse button to find one. The tool will test any selected file to be a valid assembly prior to making any policy change, so accidentally pointing at a native executable will not cause invalid security policy modifications. An assembly on the local machine, intranet, or even the Internet can be selected this way.

NOTE

The Wizard will not use any assembly location information in policy changes, but only cryptographically strong evidence, such as a strong name (if present), publisher certificate (if present) or an assembly's hash. Consequently, it does not matter where you locate the assembly for which (or for whose publisher) you want to increase security trust. For example, even though you know that most assemblies of a certain software publisher will run off the Internet and need an elevated level of trust because of that fact (see default policy restrictions on the Internet zone), you can point the Wizard to an assembly of that publisher located on your local hard disk.

In V1.0 of the .NET Framework, there is no easy programmatic way of determining all the assemblies belonging to a managed application consisting of and being dependent on numerous assemblies. The Trust Assembly Wizard always only works on one assembly at a time (or one publisher at a time), and you may need to run it multiple times to increase trust to all assemblies of an application that needs to run with elevated trust.

Increasing Trust Just for a Selected Assembly or for All Assemblies Signed by the Same Software Publisher

After you have selected an assembly, you are then prompted to decide whether you want to increase trust just for that assembly or the publisher of that assembly (see Figure 18.7).

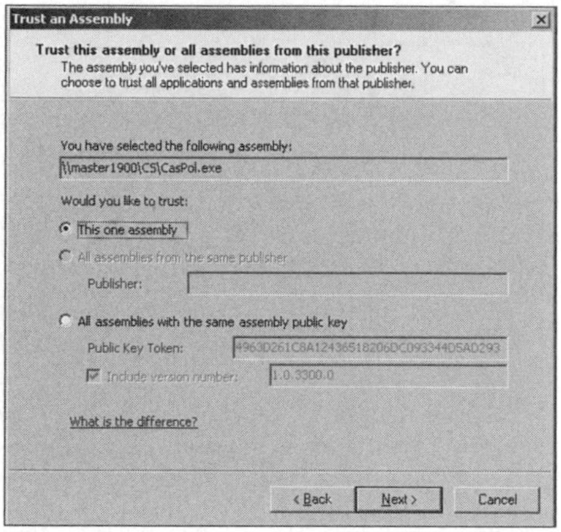

FIGURE 18.7   Trusting the assembly or all assemblies by the same publisher.

The Trust Assembly Wizard uses one of three types of assembly evidence to make policy changes:

- An assembly's strong name (default)

- An assembly's X509 publisher certificate

- An assembly's hash value

NOTE

When assemblies have neither a strong name nor a publisher certificate, the option to determine whether to trust just the selected assembly or the publisher of the assembly will not appear, because assembly hash codes are always assembly specific. Therefore, when you have selected an assembly for which the tool can only use the hash code to update policy, the Wizard page in Figure 18.7 will not appear, and you will know that the selected assembly neither had a strong name nor publisher certificate.

If an assembly is signed with a strong name, the tool will use that strong name to update policy by default. If no strong name is present but the assembly has been signed with a publisher certificate, the tool will use that information to change policy. Only when assemblies are signed neither with a strong name nor a publisher certificate will the tool use an assembly's hash code to update security policy.

> **NOTE**
>
> Hash codes result from mathematical one-way functions that have a high likelihood of mapping similar input to vastly different, far shorter values. Typical hash functions are MD5 and SHA1, which are included in the `System.Security.Cryptography` namespace. For more detail, you may want to read the relevant sections in Chapter 30, "Using Cryptography with the .NET Framework: The Basics," and Chapter 31, "Using Cryptography with the .NET Framework: Advanced Topics."

If the selected assembly is signed with a strong name and/or a publisher certificate, you have the option to trust not just the selected assembly but all assemblies of the signer. If you want to increase trust for a particular strong name, you have the option of another level of partitioning—you either trust all assemblies signed with the respective strong name (you must uncheck the Version check box to do so) or all assemblies signed with the same strong name having identical version numbers. Depending on the versioning process of an application, the latter option may help you elevate trust just for a specific application version or specific application.

Generally, you should attempt to keep the breadth of your policy changes as small as is commensurate with the administrative goals you have in mind. Thus, you should first consider whether just trusting the selected assembly is sufficient and whether just a specific version needs to be trusted, and only then open an increase of trust to all assemblies of a given publisher. If you undertake the latter, be sure you are confident that truly all assemblies from that publisher are likely to deserve the heightened trust you are about to give them.

Choosing a Level of Trust

After you have chosen whether to increase trust for just one assembly or the publisher of the assembly, you can finally select a level of trust you want the assembly or set of assemblies to be minimally receiving.

In most cases, you will be presented with the Wizard page shown in Figure 18.8.

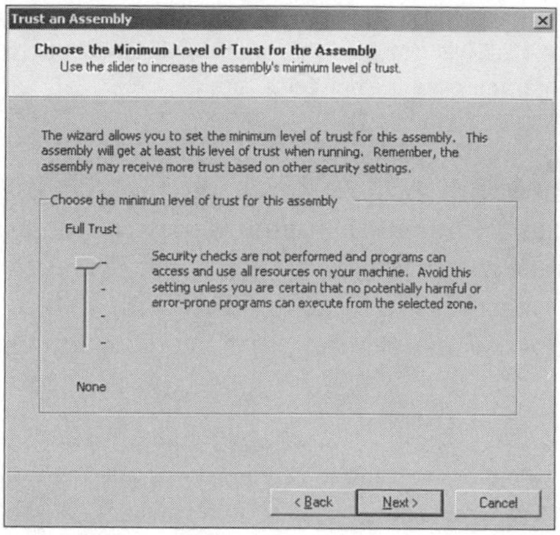

FIGURE 18.8   Increasing an assembly's minimum level of trust using the trust slider.

Each slider setting corresponds to one particular permission set that ships with the
.NET Framework. The highest slider setting corresponds to the FullTrust permission
set. In that setting, the assembly would not have any resource access restrictions
placed on it by the .NET Framework security system at all. The slider setting just
below this corresponds to the permission set given by default policy to all code
executing from the intranet. Assemblies receiving that level of permission execute in
a safe security context and are, among other things, prevented from accessing the
file system and registry on your machine. The slider setting above the bottommost
notch corresponds to the permission level generally adequate for assemblies running
from the Internet. This means that any code running with this permission level has
even fewer rights to access protected resources than code receiving intranet level
permissions—for example, code receiving the Internet level of permissions can only
do some basic user interface interaction and has no read or write access to any environment variables, in addition to the restrictions that exist for intranet code. Finally,
the lowest slider setting does not allow any permissions to code.

NOTE

The evidence about the assembly used by the Wizard (either the assembly's string name,
publisher certificate, or hash code) is tested against current security policy. If the Wizard
cannot map the result to one of the previously mentioned permission sets, the Wizard tests if
it can successfully change policy to give full trust based on the chosen evidence. If that is
possible, you will at least be presented with the option to grant full trust to the chosen assembly or set of assemblies. If policy has changed so much from default policy state that the
Wizard also cannot easily change policy to add a code group granting full trust for the chosen
evidence, the Wizard will refuse to make any policy change. If that occurs, you can either
manipulate the policy tree directly, as will be explained later in this chapter, or consider resetting the security policy to the default settings.

This Wizard is designed to allow you to state the least possible level of permissions that an assembly or publisher receives. Other parts of security policy may grant this assembly even more permissions. Consequently, choosing a specific permission level with the Wizard will not prevent an assembly from receiving more permissions than you have selected; rather, the Wizard will guarantee that it will not receive less than what you have chosen for it.

> **CAUTION**
>
> When selecting the Full Trust notch setting for an assembly or all assemblies of a given publisher, no security checks of the .NET Framework security system will be enforced on it. Please be sure that you want to grant that assembly or publisher that level of confidence. Always keep the minimum level of trust as low as is possible.

Finishing the Wizard

Finally, you must commit the policy change the Wizard is about to make. After you press the Finish button, the policy change has been persisted into policy and will be active for assemblies loaded after the policy change was made.

> **TIP**
>
> To see the exact nature of the change to the policy tree done by the Wizard, under the Runtime Security Policy node, open the machine policy level (or user policy level, if you chose to make a change for the user at the beginning of the Wizard), open the code group tree, and look for the most highly numbered code group starting with a Wizard prefix in its name.

Changing Trust for a Zone Using the Adjust Security Wizard

If an increase of trust to a specific assembly or publisher is not sufficient for the policy change scenario you have in mind, the Adjust Security Wizard offers a quick and easy way to make very wide reaching security policy changes. With this Wizard, you can change the level of trust *all* assemblies from a whole zone, such as the Internet, receive.

> **CAUTION**
>
> Because this Wizard offers such an easy way to make sweeping policy changes, it also makes it easy to open a security vulnerability. Be careful and very certain of what you are doing before setting the Internet, Intranet, Restricted Site, or Trusted Site zones to the FullTrust setting!

The following are typical scenarios in which this Wizard is used.

- *Scenario*—You or your corporation decides not to allow assemblies from the intranet zone to run.

  Wizard action:

  1. Start the Adjust Security Wizard by either right-clicking the Runtime Security Policy node or selecting the Adjust Zone Security task.

  2. Select Make Changes to This Computer (default).

  3. Select the intranet zone and reduce the slider to the Nothing position.

  4. Finish and commit the changes.

- *Scenario*—There is tight control over all code that gets installed on your intranet. You are confident that it needs more access to protected resources than what the default policy grants and, furthermore, that all installed intranet code can be trusted.

  Wizard action:

  1. Start the Wizard and select Make Changes to This Computer.

  2. Select the Intranet zone and increase the slider setting to the Full Trust position.

  3. Finish and accept the policy changes.

- *Scenario*—You decide to lower the level of trust given to all code running from the intranet just for your user context; you do not want to interfere with the settings other users have for their user security policy.

  Wizard action:

  1. Start the Wizard and select Make Changes for the Current User Only.

  2. Select the intranet zone and decrease the slider setting to the Nothing position.

  3. Finish and accept the policy change.

- *Scenario*—You decide to change default policy and enable code running from the Internet. You want this code to run within tight security constraints.

  Wizard action:

  1. Start the Wizard and select Make Changes to This Computer.

  2. Select the Internet zone and increase the slider setting to the Internet position.

  3. Finish and accept the policy changes.

The individual Wizard options are now explained in more detail.

Choosing to Make Changes to the Machine or User Policy

The first Wizard page that you will see is identical to, and serves the same purpose as, the start page on the Trust Assembly Wizard (as shown in Figure 18.5). Here, you can choose whether the Wizard should be applied to machine-wide security policy or just the user-level security policy. For most policy changes, you will want to abide by the default (by choosing Make Changes to This Computer). That option will imply a change of zone security settings for all users on that machine. However, if you choose to make user policy level changes, the zone security changes will only be applied against user security policy.

> **NOTE**
>
> If the security policy has been changed to contain a level final attribute at a policy level above the one you are applying the Wizard to, the security policy may never evaluate the policy level to which you apply the Wizard. For example, when choosing the option to make changes to your computer, the machine-wide security policy is modified. However, if the enterprise policy level contains a level final attribute, the Wizard's changes may never be effective. Thus, if applying the Wizard does not show any results, you may want to analyze policy levels above the one you applied to the Wizard for the level final code group property. (See "Manipulating the Security Policy Tree Directly—Basic Techniques" later in this chapter for more detail.)

Choosing a Level of Trust for a Zone

After selecting the scope of policy change, you will be presented with the page shown in Figure 18.9. To adjust the level of trust for a given zone, simply click the zone name and then adjust the slider.

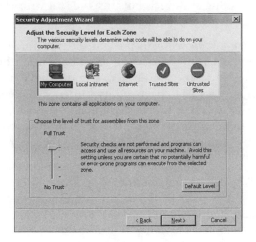

FIGURE 18.9   Changing the trust given to all assemblies from a specific zone.

Comparable to the slider settings for the Trust Assembly Wizard, each slider setting corresponds to the amount of trust the default policy gives to assemblies from MyComputer zone, LocalIntranet zone, and Restricted site zone. The Internet slider setting is the odd one out here. It corresponds to the suggested permission level for assemblies from the Internet. However, you need to explicitly enable assemblies from the Internet; default security policy does not grant any permissions to assemblies from the Internet.

- *FullTrust slider setting*—All code running with this level of trust will not be subject to security checks of the .NET Framework security system. The only security settings that act on code with this level of trust are the operating system's security settings for the user under whose context the code is running. The corresponding permission set expressing this level of trust is the FullTrust permission set.

CAUTION

The FullTrust setting is the only slider setting that does not enforce a strict security context on code running from the respective zone. It opens access to all resources not protected by operating system security settings. Please be absolutely certain that you want to give that level of trust to all assemblies from the respective zone. If you want to only give full trust to a subset of assemblies from a zone, either use the Trust Assembly Wizard or manipulate the policy tree directly (as will be explained later in this chapter).

- *2nd slider position (just under FullTrust)*—This slider position corresponds to the level of trust that the default policy grants to all assemblies from the intranet zone. This setting will not allow assemblies to access the file system or registry directly, among other things, but will still enable full user interface interaction, as well as the capability to connect back to the site of origin of the assembly. Assemblies executing at this level of trust are still strongly checked and prevented from doing substantial harm.

- *3rd slider position (just above Nothing)*—This slider setting represents the level of trust given by the default policy to all assemblies from the Internet zone. In addition to the restrictions already active in the previous slider setting, assemblies will also not be able to have full user interface access, nor will they be able to have read access to select environment variables. However, they can still connect back to their site of origin. This level of trust represents a safe security context for any assembly to run it. Access to protected resources is minimized.

- *4th slider position (Nothing setting)*—This slider setting represents the level of trust (or rather lack of) given to the restricted site zone in default policy. Assemblies will not receive any permission to access protected resources (such as the file system or registry), nor will they receive the permission to even execute. This slider position should be used if you want to exclude assemblies from a certain zone to run on your machine.

TIP

Of course, the ultimate form of computer security is not to run any code. The slider Wizard allows you to do just that for all code from a specific zone. If you have no need to run assemblies from a specific zone (such as the intranet), you should strongly consider just setting the slider for that zone to Nothing.

The Wizard will match the currently set level of trust for a given zone to a slider setting. If you want to return to the default policy setting for that zone, simply click the Default button.

NOTE

If security policy has changed significantly from the default policy, the level of permissions that a specific zone receives may not exactly match one of the four slider settings anymore. In such cases, the Wizard will not be able to display the slider and simply gives you the option to return to the default policy for the zone. If you do decide to return to the default policy setting for that zone, the slider will reappear with the setting corresponding to default policy. Be aware, however, that this will delete any policy customizations that may have been done for that zone.

After you have adjusted the trust for a zone or zones, all that remains to do is to accept these changes and finish the Wizard. Security policy is changed, persisted, and effective immediately for all assemblies loaded after the change has been made.

TIP

You can change settings for multiple zones in one Wizard session. Consequently, if you need to adjust security for two or more zones, you can get this done in one pass through this Wizard.

Manipulating the Security Policy Tree Directly—Basic Techniques

One of the key advantages of the .NET Framework security system really lies in its ability to allow for very fine-grained differentiations between assemblies, thus allowing for very fine-grained differentiation of rights to access protected resources. There is now a whole world of *semi-trust* between allowing code to run or not. Such flexibility is the result of a rich, hierarchically structured, tree-based policy system. The tool itself is simply a graphical instantiation of this model.

In this section, the elements, basic features, techniques, and hints of the tool's policy tree view are introduced. The following sections cover more complex scenarios and actions.

Policy Level Features

Security policy consists of three administrable policy levels—enterprise policy, machine policy, and user policy. You can find the policy levels by simply expanding the Runtime Security Policy Node (see Figure 18.10).

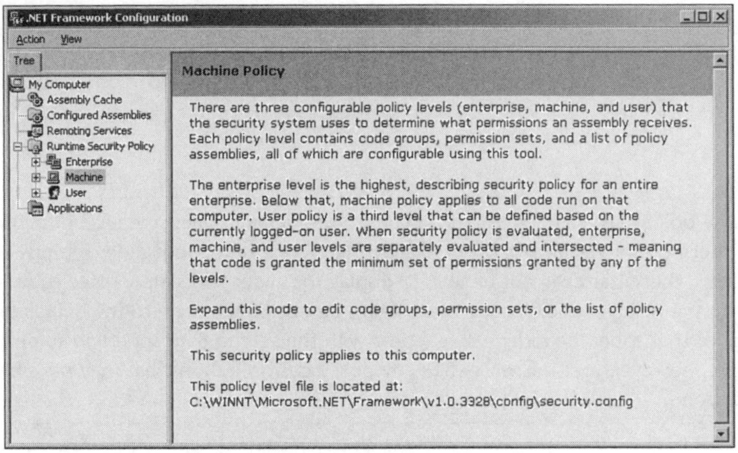

FIGURE 18.10   Security Policy Level representation in the tool.

The task window will display some general information about policy levels, followed by two important policy level specific pieces of information:

- Whether the selected policy level is used by the security system to determine the permissions an assembly gets, or whether it is a policy level that has been created or loaded in for policy modeling purposes. If the somewhat cryptic statement "This security policy applies to this computer" appears, the policy level information you see and edit will affect assemblies run on your machine.

- The location of the configuration file of the selected policy level.

TIP

Prior to major changes to a policy level, it is often worth making a backup copy of the policy level state before editing. Selecting the policy level in the tree view gives you a quick way to find out (and copy and paste) the file path to the configuration file.

The only option that right-clicking any one of the policy levels in the tree view will give you is the option to do a Reset. This will set the selected policy level back to the default policy state—the way the respective policy level was configured on install of the .NET Framework. The default policy has been designed to be a safe default and represents a good point of return if you want to start fresh in designing the policy of the respective policy level. For more information, please see the "Resetting Security Policy" section later in this chapter.

NOTE

You will only succeed in resetting a policy level if you have write access to the respective policy configuration file. Both the enterprise and machine policy configuration files are in directories to which only users with machine administrator rights have access. ACL settings typically prevent other users from access to these system locations.

Every policy level consists of three constituents:

- *Code Group Hierarchy*—The tree of code groups determines how the set of all assemblies is partitioned to give various subsets of assemblies a specific level of permissions to access protected resources.

- *Permission sets*—All the named permission sets that can be referenced in the code group hierarchy at the respective policy level. A permission set is simply a set of statements of access to protected resources.

- *Policy Assemblies*—A list of all assemblies that security objects accessed during policy evaluation depend on.

When you expand a policy level node, you will indeed find each of the three constituents of a policy level mentioned. In Figure 18.11, you can see how expanding the machine policy node revealed code groups, permission sets, and the policy assemblies list.

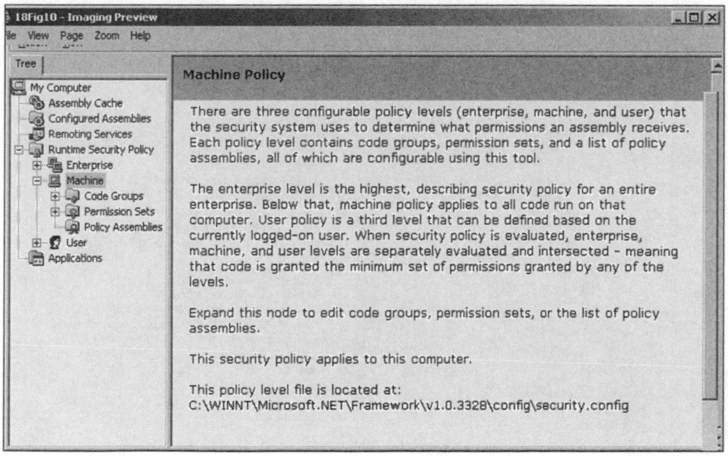

FIGURE 18.11   Accessing the constituents of a policy level.

We will now give an explanation of the available features and administrative techniques enabled on each—the features available for code group manipulation, viewing, and changing permission sets, as well as altering the policy assemblies list.

Code Group Hierarchy

Every policy level contains a tree of code groups that express the configuration state of that policy level. You can think of a code group simply as a form of conditional—it checks some condition about an assembly, such as whether the assembly came from a specific URL. If the condition is met, it then allots a permission set to the respective assembly. Each code group represents one way to slice up the set of assemblies—it "groups code," hence, its name. The code group hierarchy simply is a tree of these conditionals (for more detail on the underlying model, see Chapter 8).

When you expand the Code Groups folder, you will always be brought to the root of the code group tree—the All_Code group. It cannot be deleted, because a policy level must always contain at least one code group (see the User and Enterprise policy levels in the default Runtime Security Policy for examples). The tool offers a variety of features that help in the administration of code group hierarchies.

Creating a New Code Group

One of the most common ways to fine tune security policy is to add another code group under an already existing one. This can be used to further differentiate between assemblies if the parent code group applies. As an example, look at the way the default machine policy is set up (see the expanded code group tree under the Machine node in Figure 18.12).

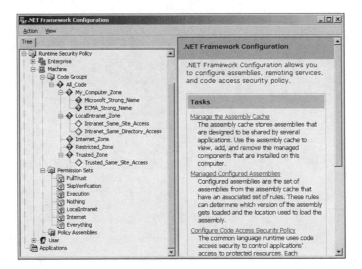

FIGURE 18.12   Machine policy code group tree in default policy expanded.

Suppose that you add a new code group under the Internet code group, let this code group check for a strong name of company *X*, and grant full trust to access protected resources. The result would be that all assemblies coming from the Internet zone would get whatever the default policy allows them *except* for all assemblies whose origin is the Internet zone *and* that are signed with company *X*'s strong name. Those assemblies would receive default policy permissions for the Internet *and* the permissions granted by the added code group, amounting to being granted full trust to access all protected resources at this policy level.

NOTE

Always remember that the permissions granted to an assembly from one policy level are *intersected* with the permissions the assembly is given at other policy levels (unless Level Final code group attributes are used).

You can create a new code group as a child code group under any code group in the code group tree. This includes the root of the code group hierarchy (the All_Code group), as well as any leaf nodes in the code group hierarchy. The tool includes a wizard that will help you create a new code group and set all its properties.

You can access the New Code Group Wizard by performing the following steps:

1. Right-click the code group under which to insert the new code group.

2. Select New.

After you have started the Wizard, you have the choice of either creating a new code group from scratch or importing one from an XML file (see Figure 18.13). The latter option will be explained in the "Dealing with Custom Code Groups" section later in this chapter, and is, as you may suspect, used to import code groups that have been custom authored into policy. The far more common option is to just create a code group from scratch by filling in all necessary properties.

All code groups have a name and optionally a description. You can leave out the description when first creating a code group, although it is a good practice to make an annotation here of what the addition of this new code group is intended to accomplish. This is an easy way to remind yourself at a later time what that policy change was intended to accomplish, greatly helping you to find potential security issues or unintended side effects. The code group name is mandatory. That name is used by the tool as a label for a code group. It can also be used to write a policy change script against (see Chapter 19, "Administering .NET Framework Security Policy Using Scripts and Security APIs"). For that reason, it needs to be unique within the policy level. The tool will reject any duplicate code group name entry within a policy level.

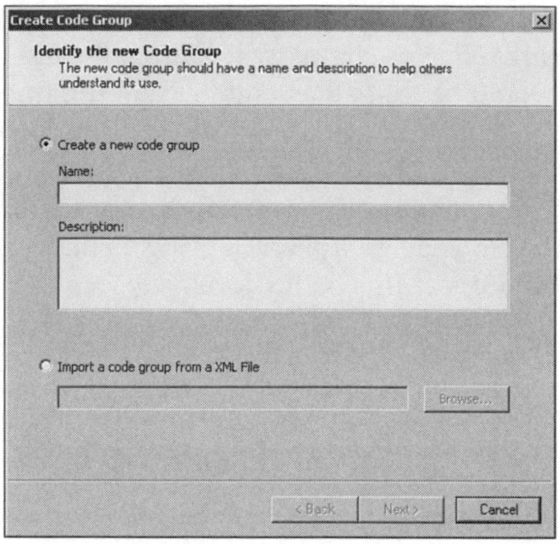

FIGURE 18.13   Choosing to create a new code group from scratch or importing one from an XML file.

Each code group also consists of a membership condition (testing an assembly for a specific piece of evidence, such as a specific site of origin) and a permission set that is granted if the membership condition applies. After selecting a name and description, the tool will ask you to select a membership condition type and, if applicable, you must supply a membership condition value (such as a specific site) for which this code group should check (see Figure 18.14).

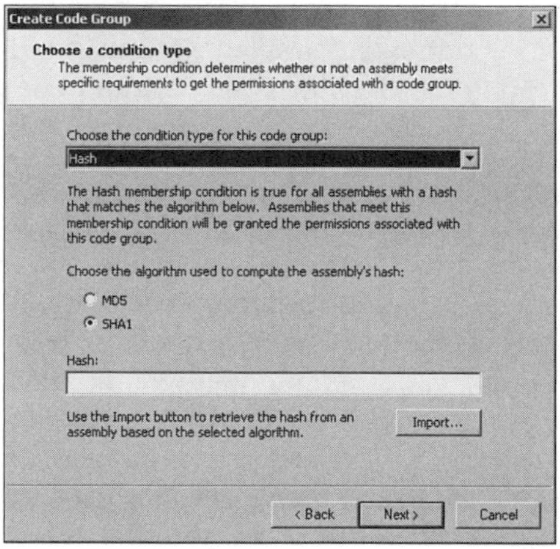

FIGURE 18.14   Selecting a membership condition for the new code group.

The following are the membership condition types available:

- *All Code*—As its name implies, all code irrespective of origin will pass this membership condition. If you choose this membership condition for your code group, the assembly reaching this code group during policy evaluation is guaranteed to receive the permission set you associate with this code group. All Code is something like a pass key for a code group's membership condition.

- *Application Directory*—This membership condition is met if an assembly comes from the same application directory as the assembly that is currently being executed. This code group can be used to distill assemblies comprising a specific managed application from other assemblies.

- *Hash*—This membership condition succeeds if the hash value of an assembly matches with one defined in the membership condition value. Hash values are highly unique identifiers for larger pieces of data or code. Code groups with hash membership conditions are used as a cryptographically strong (hard to spoof) means of identifying one specific assembly, especially if the assembly neither has a strong name nor a publisher certificate. This membership condition is used by the Trust Assembly Wizard if it cannot find either a strong name or publisher certificate on an assembly.

  The tool allows you to either type in or import a hash value from a specific assembly. The latter is suggested because typing mistakes in a hash membership condition value could easily cause hard-to-trace security policy issues. Unless you are certain otherwise, always use SHA1, because this is the preferred hash function compared to MD5.

- *Publisher*—Checks for a specific X.509v3 publisher certificate. Only code that has been authenticode signed by the publisher chosen when setting up this code group will meet this membership condition. This code group is typically used to identify a set of assemblies from a specific publisher and grant it more rights based on that information, while other assemblies, everything else being equal, would not receive that level of trust. For example, you could extend the default policy by adding a new code group under the Internet code group, with a publisher membership condition, and set the publisher certificate to a publisher you trust, and set the permission set to full trust. This would have the effect of leaving the default policy as is except for the assemblies from the trusted publisher, which get a higher level of permissions to access protected resources.

  The tool allows you to set the membership condition value in two ways. The simplest way is to point the tool to an assembly that has been authenticode signed by the publisher; use Import from Signed File for this option. Alternatively, you may have an actual certificate file handy (typically with `.cer` extension). You can point the tool at that file using the Import from Cert File option.

- *Site*—The site membership condition checks whether an assembly came from a specified site. Code groups with this membership condition are often used if all assemblies from a designated site are to receive higher levels of trust compared to assemblies from other sites.

  To specify the site that this membership condition should check for, simply type in the site name.

- *Strong name*—The strong name membership condition checks whether an assembly has been strong name signed and matches the specific strong name defined in the membership condition value. Like the publisher certificate and hash values, a strong name is a cryptographically strong form of evidence that can be used to uniquely identify an assembly or set of assemblies. Code groups with this membership are often used to mete out a high level of permissions based on this strong form of evidence. For example, if you look into the machine policy level of default policy, you will find a code group named Microsoft_strong_Name under the MyComputer zone code group. It is used to give all assemblies strong name signed by Microsoft full trust to access protected resources, enabling, among other things, the tool to continue to function, even if other code on the local machine has been constrained.

  If you want a code group to apply to all assemblies from a given strong name publisher, you only need to supply the strong name public key, either by browsing to a strong name signed file (the highly suggested method) or by typing it in yourself. If you want only one particular assembly by a given publisher to be checked, irrespective of its version, you also need to check the name and can only use the Import function to set up the public key. If you want a specific version of a specific assembly of a publisher to be checked for, also mark the Version check box. To set the correct version, you need to use the Import function to browse to the respective assembly for which you want the membership condition to check.

- *URL*—This membership condition checks whether an assembly came from the supplied URL. Code groups with this membership condition are often used to increase the level of trust given to specific intranet shares or mounted drives.

  The tool requires you to simply type in the URL value. It is important that you remember to suffix drive names and shares with the * symbols if you want the membership condition to apply to all files and subdirectories at the specified location.

- *Zone*—This membership condition checks whether an assembly comes from a given zone. For examples of how code groups with such membership conditions are used, please browse through the default policy, which is based around the concept of zones.

CAUTION

Use the site, zone, and URL membership conditions with caution because they could allow very wide broadening of security policy. You should always ask yourself whether you really can trust *all* assemblies at the specified site, zone, or URL before increasing any permissions based on these types of evidence.

- *Custom*—The .NET Framework security system is fully extensible with custom security objects. It is possible to write your own membership conditions, code groups, permissions, and so on. The custom option in the tool is used to import any custom written membership condition into security policy. To do so, you must browse to an XML file representing the XML serialization of the custom membership condition type.

TIP

If you have a lot of child code groups under a parent node and you'd like to group them into different categories for policy readability, but don't want to impact the actual security policy resolution for any assembly, simply use a code group with membership condition All Code and associated permission set to Nothing. For example, if in the default policy the Internet and intranet permission set were both under a code group Internet/Intranet Groups, which in turn is a child code group of the All_Code group, the actual results for any assembly is exactly the same as if you left the security policy in the default policy state. Code groups with an All_Code membership condition and a Nothing permission set just don't add anything to policy evaluation.

After you have chosen the membership condition for the new code group, you then need to decide what the permissions are that this code group should hand out. In a sense, by defining the membership condition, you have defined a filter that assemblies are required to pass through before being given a set of permissions. The next Wizard page will present you with two options to set that level of permissions to be handed out to an assembly if it matched the membership condition (see Figure 18.15).

You can choose a permission set that is already known and "registered" at the policy level in which you are editing. Alternatively, you can also elect to create a newly named permission set that is returned by the newly created code group. In that case, the Wizard to create a new permission set is started. The newly created permission set is available afterward for reference in other code groups as well.

TIP

When in doubt as to the level of access to protected resources that a specific named permission set stands for, use the Permission set node and inspect permission sets prior to assigning them to a code group. You may forget to double check later and, as a result, the newly created code group may grant a level of permissions that you definitely did not have in mind.

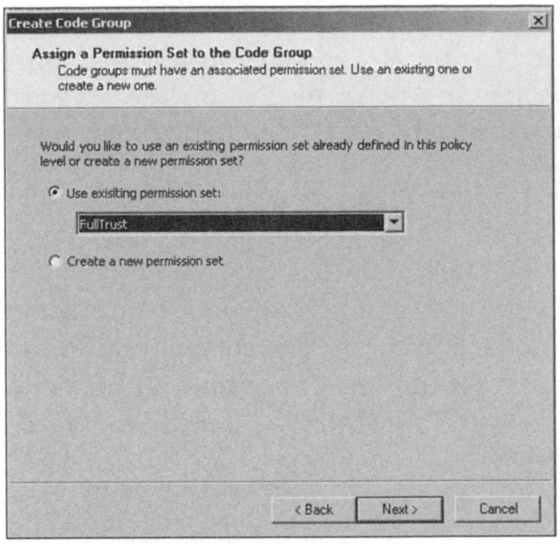

FIGURE 18.15   Selecting a permission set for the new code group.

Deleting a Code Group

Except for the root code group, you can delete any other code group in a code group hierarchy. Deleting a code group may have some strong side effects; the following are some of the possible implications:

- All child code groups are deleted also; you will lose any customizations you had done at that level in the code group hierarchy.

- Batch scripts to change security policy can break because both the code group labeling will change as well as one or more code group names may become unavailable.

- Assemblies that received the necessary permissions from the deleted code group to run properly will break.

Consequently, you should be cautious and try to be aware of all the possible side effects before deleting a code group.

If you have decided to delete a code group, you can do so by simply selecting it in the code group hierarchy and pressing the Delete key or, alternatively, right-clicking it and choosing the Delete option. Let me mention again that this will delete the whole subtree of code groups if the selected code group is a parent to other code groups.

Renaming a Code Group

Every code group has a name associated with it. This name is used both as the display name in the tool as well as a way to write a batch script to change security policy. When renaming a code group, the tool does not allow you to use a name already in use by another code group at that policy level. This would both make the tool's code group display ambiguous and any policy change scripts based on code group names indeterministic.

CAUTION

Make sure that you do not have any security policy change batch scripts that rely on the code group name you are changing. See more on administrating policy using batch scripts in Chapter 19.

To rename a code group, simply right-click it and select the Rename option. The tool will check whether the name is already in use.

Making a Duplicate of a Code Group

The tool allows you to select any code group and duplicate it, including any child code groups the code group may have. The tool will automatically rename the duplicate to avoid name conflicts by prepending a "Copy of" to the original name. You can use the Rename option to give it a more pleasing and descriptive name.

TIP

If there is a code group or subtree of code groups that is already very close to something you want to add to policy, it can be of great help to simply generate a duplicate, make the few changes necessary, and then move it to the place in the policy hierarchy where you intended to make the change.

To duplicate a code group, including all its child code groups, right-click the respective code group and select the Duplicate option.

Moving a Copy of a Code Group into Another Policy Level

Because the final permission grant to an assembly depends on the *intersection* of all permissions granted at the enterprise, machine, and user policy levels respectively (see Chapter 8), it may be necessary to copy a large part of a code group hierarchy of one level into one of the two remaining policy levels. For example, this would be necessary if user or enterprise policy are changed from granting unrestricted permissions at the root of their code group hierarchy. For such cases, the tool provides a quick and easy way to copy whole code group trees between policy levels.

Simply drag-and-drop the respective code group or tree of code groups to the desired spot in another policy level.

Moving a Code Group Within a Policy Level

Changing the position of a code group within a code group hierarchy can strongly influence security policy. For example, if you move the Microsoft_strong_Name code group in default policy from its default position under the MyComputer code group to the LocalIntranet code group, all assemblies signed with the Microsoft strong name would now only receive the FullTrust permission set either when run from the local intranet or when run from the local computer (default policy grants full trust to access protected resources to all assemblies installed on the local machine).

You can move a code group and all its child code groups to a new position in a code group hierarchy simply by dragging and dropping it.

Editing a Code Group

All properties of a code group can be viewed and changed from a code group's property page (see Figure 18.16). You can open a code group's property page by right-clicking the code group and selecting the Property option.

In addition to the membership condition, permission set, name, and description, all of which had to be defined during the creation of a code group in the tool, the Level Final and Exclusive properties can also be set.

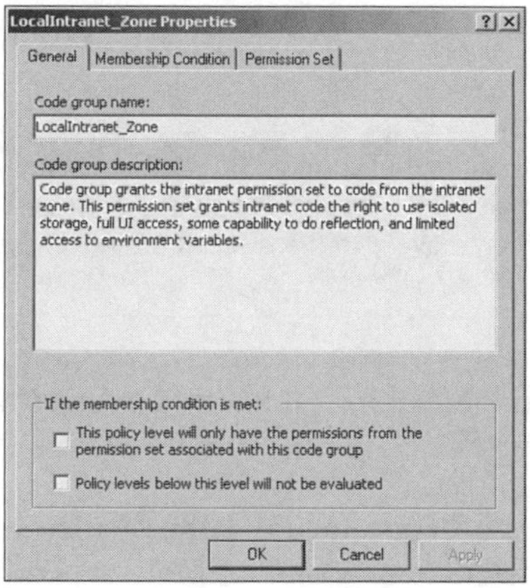

FIGURE 18.16   Editing a code group using the code group's property page.

If a code group with the Level Final property (the second check box in Figure 18.16) switched on applies to an assembly, no policy level below the one currently evaluated is taken into account in the permissions calculation for that assembly. This property is very useful when you must make certain that no administrable policy level below the one you are editing should interfere with the permission grant an assembly receives. Obviously, this will also prevent any policy customizations done in lower policy levels from being effective, so this property should be used in a very targeted and sparing way.

Security policy for an assembly is always evaluated starting with the enterprise security policy level, the machine policy level, user policy level, and then the application domain policy if it has been set programmatically by a host of the .NET Framework Runtime. Applying the Level Final attribute to a code group in user level policy will have no effect whatsoever because the Level Final attribute only applies to administrable policy levels.

Another property that can be set using a code group's property page is the Level Exclusive property (see the first check box in Figure 18.16). If a code group with this property turned on applies to an assembly (in other words, if the code group's membership condition matches the evidence of an assembly for which policy is being resolved), *no* other code group at that policy level will contribute to the permissions that the assembly receives from that policy level. As a result, this property is an "override" over all other code groups in a policy level. It can be used very effectively if you want to lower the level of trust for a select set of assemblies. For example, if you want to alter default policy to "sand box" a region on your local hard drive, you could add a code group with a URL membership condition of the hard drive path and the Internet permission set under the MyComputer code group, and then check the Level Exclusive (first check box) property for that code group.

CAUTION

The security system will throw an exception and the evaluated assembly will not run, if, at a single policy level, the assembly's evidence matches more than one code groups that have the exclusive property turned on.

This is the case because the semantics of the level exclusive property stipulates that all other code groups are excluded from contributing to the assembly's permission calculation. When more than one level exclusive code groups apply to an assembly, an inherently ambiguous state ensues, causing a security exception to be thrown.

Dealing with Custom Code Groups

With the exception of the child code groups of the intranet code group, default policy contains only so called "union code" groups. A union code group adds together all the permissions given by all applicable child code groups—hence, the name union code group. Because this is the most common form of code group, the tool has very deep support for these code groups and allows easy viewing and editing of its properties. However, the security system is fully extensible, so code groups implementing completely custom defined semantics can be used in security policy. This adds great flexibility. For example, it is possible to implement a code group that depends on the date and time to grant its permissions. On the other hand, this flexibility also means great strain on having full user interface support for editing a custom code group's properties. As a result, in version 1.0 of the .NET Framework

Configuration tool, custom code group properties cannot be edited directly in the user interface.

A custom code group is symbolized as shown in Figure 18.17.

Code group symbol

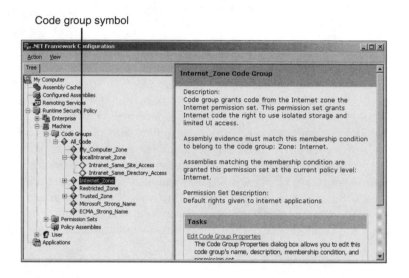

FIGURE 18.17   Non-union code group symbol in the tool.

Whenever you see this symbol in the code group hierarchy, you know that the respective code group is not a union code group. With the exception of the name and description, you cannot change any properties for these code groups on their property page, nor can you set their properties when creating them via the New option. Non-union code group property pages only include the code group's name, description, and XML serialization.

Non-union code groups are added to policy by right-clicking a desired parent code group and selecting the New option. Instead of choosing the Create a New Code Group option, you should choose the Import a Code Group from an XML File option (see Figure 18.18).

All custom code group XML serializations have the following format:

```
<CodeGroup class="fully qualified class name of code group type,
 assembly name, Version=version number,
 Culture=culture value,
PublicKeyToken=strong name public key token"
          version="1"
          Name="Code group name"
          Description="code group description"
```

```
        [Custom Code group attributes]
>

    [Custom code group XML]
</CodeGroup>
```

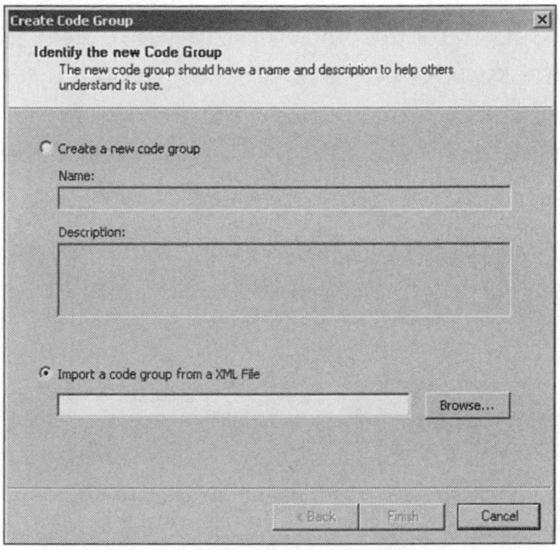

FIGURE 18.18   Creating a custom code group by importing its XML serialization.

If you try to import a custom code group and the import fails, you should check whether the file indeed follows the schema just shown. The `Name` and `Description` attributes are optional, and import of the code group should still succeed, even if both are missing.

If you want to change any properties on a custom code group, you need to delete the outdated custom code group, change the custom code group XML to the desired state, and re-import the code group serialization. You should get directions on doing so, potentially even a little tool, from the vendor distributing the custom security code group.

CAUTION

You have to add the assembly implementing the custom code group, as well as all assemblies it depends on to the policy assembly list in the policy level to which you are importing the custom code group. Please see the "Policy Assemblies" section later in the chapter.

Administrating Permission Sets

Every policy level contains a list of named permission sets. These permission sets can be referenced by one or more code groups in the code group hierarchy of that policy level. Code groups always refer to permission sets by the permission set's name. Thus, a code group will continue to refer to a permission set, even if you change all properties except for the permission set's name.

Each permission set represents a statement of trust to access a variety of protected resources. Permission sets allow for very fine-grained and granular access control to protected resources. As its name implies, a permission set is just a list of individual permissions. Each permission covers exactly one protected resource. The .NET Framework ships with a large set of built-in permission types that are used throughout the .NET Framework Base Class Library to protect resources, such as the file system and the registry.

Not surprisingly, you can find the list of known named permission sets of a policy level by expanding the Permission Set node under a policy level node (see Figure 18.19).

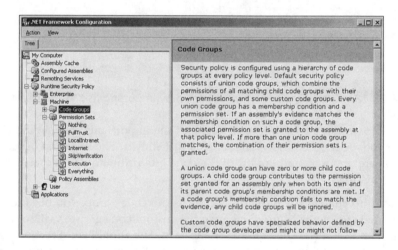

FIGURE 18.19   Finding the permission sets known at a policy level.

Default security policy ships with a number of permission sets (seen in Figure 18.19) that are used to build default policy. To find out what these permission sets contain, please see the next section, "Viewing a Permission Set." All of the permission sets shipping with the .NET Framework are immutable, with the exception of the Everything permission set.

Viewing a Permission Set
To find out what permissions a particular permission set includes, select the permission set in question.

Unless you had previously unchecked the Help topic check box (see Figure 18.20), simply click on the View Permissions link. If you always want to see the permissions for the selected permission set directly without being bothered by the Help screen, simply uncheck the Show This Help box.

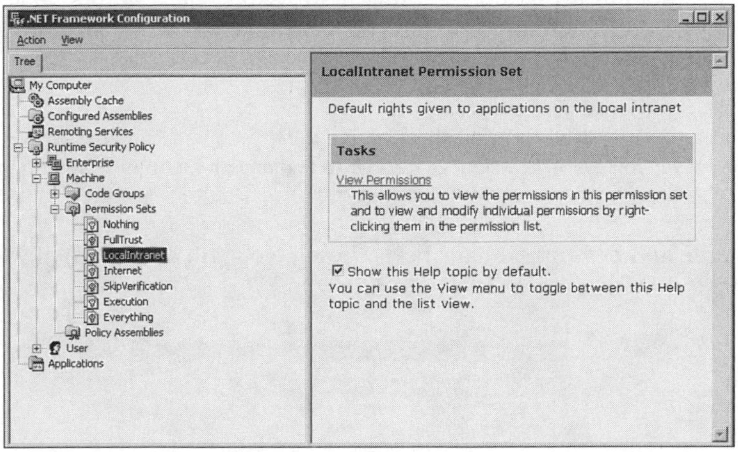

FIGURE 18.20   Viewing a permission set using the View Permissions task.

The right view will now contain the list of permissions that are part of the permission set. If the permission set does not include a particular permission type, that permission is not granted at all through that permission set. So for example, if you look at the included permission types for the LocalIntranet permission set (used by the default policy for all assemblies from the intranet), you will notice that the FileIO permission is completely lacking, which means that assemblies receiving just this permission set have no access rights to the file system.

Because each permission typically has a number of states it can be configured to, simply looking at a list of included permission types in a permission set still does not give a full picture of exactly what that permission set would grant to assemblies. For example, the inclusion of the Registry permission type in a permission set may mean that it is set to grant unlimited access rights to write and read from the registry, or it may only grant read rights to a few locations. Consequently, you have to view the state of the individual permissions included in a permission set to truly find out what the permission set grants. To do so, just right-click the permission in question and select the View Permission option.

Creating a New Permission Set
The tool includes a wizard that helps you build a new permission set from permission types that ship with the .NET Framework or even from custom written permissions.

To start that wizard, right-click the Permission set node under the policy level in which you want to create the new permission set and then select the New option.

You will first need to enter the new permission set's name and a description. Because permission sets are referenced from code groups by their name, you must enter a name that is not already used by another permission set at that policy level. Alternatively, you can import a permission set from its XML serialization.

> **NOTE**
>
> The description is optional, but you should get in the habit of including description annotations wherever you can. This will make it easier to find any problems with security policy later.

After a name and description have been chosen, you will be presented with the wizard page shown in Figure 18.21.

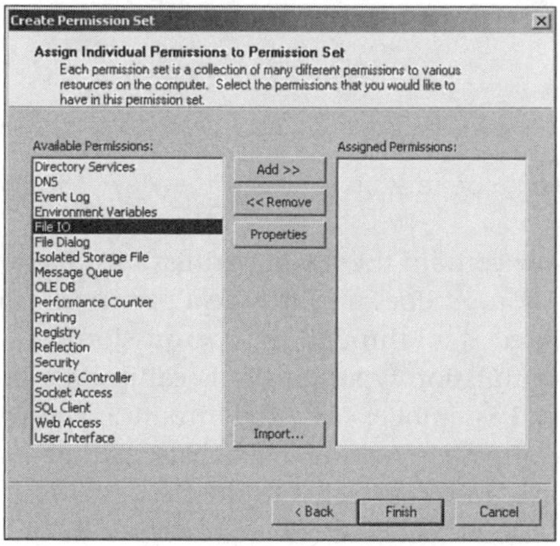

FIGURE 18.21 Adding permissions to a new permission set.

To add a permission that ships in the .NET Framework, simply select the permission in question and then click the Add button. You will be prompted to fill in the necessary properties for the permission (such as file paths and read/write rights for the FileIO permission). If you change your mind about the inclusion of a particular permission, simply use the Remove button to put a permission in the permission set back into the Available Permissions category. You can also add in a custom authored permission by using the Import button on this wizard page.

Building the right permission sets that express exactly the level of trust you need in your administrative scenarios can be an art. Think carefully about what permissions to include; the more you include, the more potential security holes you may open.

Be especially wary of giving out anything more than execution rights on the security permission, any FileIO or registry rights, and reflection emit rights.

Editing a Permission Set

It is quite easy to change an arbitrary permission set, with the exception of the permission sets shipping with the .NET Framework. Except for the Everything permission set, no permission set that ships with the .NET Framework can be edited. However, any user-defined permission set is freely changeable.

To edit a permission set (such as the Everything permission set or any user-defined permission sets), simply right-click it and select the Change Permission Set option. This will return you to the Permission Selection Wizard page (see Figure 18.21). To change the state of a permission already included in a permission set, simply select the permission and click Properties. To add or remove further permissions, use the Add and Remove buttons.

CAUTION

If you are modifying a permission set because one code group referencing it gives the wrong permissions, please make sure that no other code group in that policy level references that permission set. If so, you must be very careful that fixing a policy problem for some assemblies will not create one for another set of assemblies.

Duplicating a Permission Set

Instead of starting from scratch when creating a new permission set, you could also make a duplicate of an already existing one and modify the copy until it fits your needs. This may be much faster than using the New option if there is already a permission set quite close to the permission set you have in mind.

This option also greatly helps get around the restriction that the permission sets the .NET Framework ships with cannot be modified; simply make a copy of an immutable permission set and change the copy. This can come in handy if you want to slightly alter what the default policy grants to various zones. For example, if you do not want the Intranet zone to grant unlimited user interface rights, simply duplicate the LocalIntranet permission set, modify the UserInterface permission in it, and have the Intranet code group point at your modified permission set.

To duplicate a permission set, simply right-click it and select the duplicate option. You will probably want to change the name to something more suitable than something starting with "Copy of...".

Renaming a Permission Set

You can rename a permission set by right-clicking it and selecting the Rename option. This feature is not available for the permission sets that ship with the .NET Framework (except for the Everything permission set).

NOTE

You would break a code group if you changed the name of a permission set that is referred to by that code group. For that reason, the tool will search the code group hierarchy and only allow you to change the name of a permission set it is not referenced.

Copying a Permission Set Between Policy Levels

You can copy a permission set from one policy level's folder of known permission sets to another policy level's folder of known permission sets by dragging and dropping the respective permission sets into the target permission set folder.

NOTE

If you have copied a code group to a policy that does not contain the permission set referenced by that code group, you do *not* need to manually copy the referenced permission set over. The tool will automatically copy the referenced permission set to the target policy level's permission set folder if the referenced permission set name is not known at that policy level.

Dealing with Custom Permissions and Permission Sets

The .NET Framework security system is fully extensible and allows for, among other things, the inclusion of custom security permissions and custom security permission sets.

It may become necessary to include custom permissions in security policy when the built-in permissions do not cover a particular resource, such as an enterprise-specific database system with time share properties.

To include a custom permission in a permission set, click the Import button on the wizard page used to add permissions to a permission set (see Figure 18.21). By choosing to import a custom permission, you will need to browse to an XML file containing the XML serialization of the custom permission. The format for all custom permission XML files is as follows:

```
<IPermission class="fully qualified Class name of permission,
assembly name containing custom permission,
Version=version of assembly,
Culture=culture value,
PublicKeyToken="strong name public key token of assembly"
                              version="1"
    [custom permission attributes]
 >

    [custom permission XML]
</IPermission>
```

If the file you browse to does not have this general format, the import will fail. Please see the custom permission vendor or author's documentation for more detail on how to change permission state using the permission's XML serialization.

Not only permissions, but whole permission sets can be custom written security objects. To create a custom-named permission set in security policy, click the Import a Permission Set from an XML File button on the start page of the new Permission Set Wizard (right-click the permission set folder and select New (see Figure 18.22).

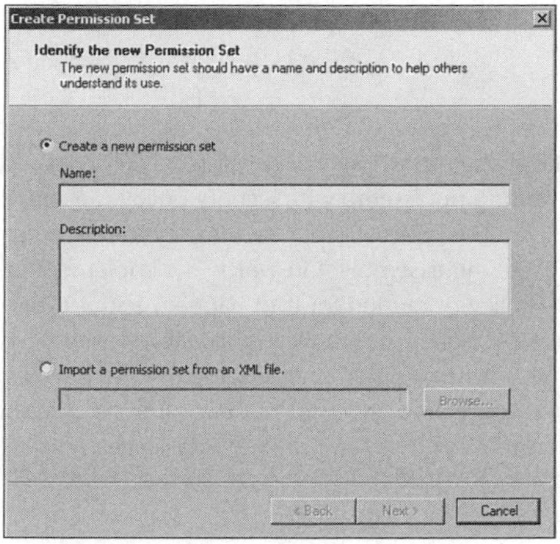

FIGURE 18.22   Creating a custom named permission set.

CAUTION

You have to add the assembly implementing the custom permission or permission set, as well as all assemblies it depends on, to the policy assemblies list in the policy level to which you are importing the custom permission or permission set. Please see the next section, "Policy Assemblies."

Policy Assemblies

Besides a code group hierarchy and the named permission sets, every policy level also contains a list of so-called policy assemblies. These are assemblies that either implement a security object (such as a membership condition, permission, permission set, or code group) directly or that these assemblies depend on. In other words, this list should contain the transitive closure of assemblies implementing custom security types.

For all security objects that ship with the .NET Framework (such as the FileIO permission type), all the right entries into this list have already been made; you do not need to worry about changing entries here if you are not using custom security objects. However, if you are adding custom security objects (such as customer membership conditions, code groups, permissions, or permission sets), you must enter the assembly or assemblies implementing the custom security object and *all* assemblies on which that implementing assembly (or assemblies) depend. Typically, the documentation from the vendor of the custom security object should let you know what these assemblies are and how to find them.

NOTE

You may ask why this list is necessary. Consider the following scenario. You have implemented a custom permission P in assembly A and have referenced P from a code group in machine policy. You are then starting up assembly B. Security policy is evaluated for B. It so happens that B's evidence matches the code group from which you reference P. The security code now tries to instantiate P accessing assembly A in which P is implemented. However in doing so, A itself causes a security policy resolution for it to happen, and it turns out that A also matches the new code group. A circular security policy evaluation dependency ensues. Assembly A waits to finish security policy evaluation until assembly A has been evaluated. To break this possible dead-lock, the policy assemblies list has been introduced, short circuiting any policy evaluation for the assemblies in that list for *that* policy level.

You can access the policy assembly list for a policy level by clicking the Policy Assemblies folder. If you are viewing this list for the first time, click the View Policy Assemblies link. You will then see the list of assemblies that are currently "registered" for the implementation of security types at that policy level (see Figure 18.23).

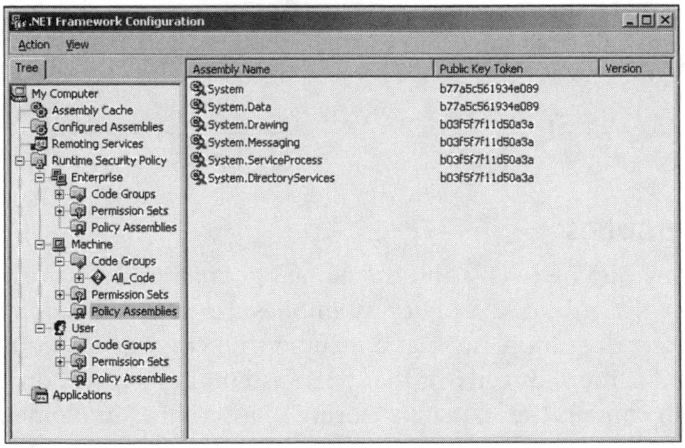

FIGURE 18.23   The Policy Assemblies list.

To add an assembly to this list, just right-click the Policy Assemblies folder and choose the Add option. You will then be able to select an assembly from the .NET Framework global assembly cache.

> **TIP**
>
> You need to have added the assembly you want to include in the Policy Assemblies list to the GAC (Global Assembly Cache) first. To do so, right-click on the Assembly Cache node in the main tree view of the tool and select the Add option. That will allow you to browse to the assembly you want to add to the cache. The assembly *must* be strong name signed for it to be added to the cache.

Adding an assembly to this list has the effect of giving it a full trust policy resolution at that policy level. If an assembly is listed in the Policy Assemblies lists of all three administrable policy levels, it will receive full trust to access all protected resources by the policy system. But again, this only is the case if it is present in all lists. If your goal is to give an assembly or set of assemblies full trust to access all protected resources, you should use the Trust Assembly Wizard or manipulate the code group hierarchy, not use this list.

If you want to delete an assembly from the Policy Assemblies list, right-click the respective assembly and select Delete.

> **CAUTION**
>
> The only reason why you should ever want to delete entries from the Policy Assemblies list is if you have excluded custom security objects from a policy level and the respective assemblies implementing the custom security object are no longer needed. If you delete assemblies that implement or are needed for the implementation of a security type at that policy level, you can cause the security system to deadlock. Be very careful when deleting any entry from this list!

Undoing a Change in the Policy Tree

You can undo the latest policy change you have made to a policy level by selecting the policy level, right-clicking it, and then choosing the Undo option. Policy changes are cached on a per-policy–level basis, so you can undo the latest change you made in machine policy, even though you have just edited enterprise policy.

> **NOTE**
>
> The tool will lose the per-policy level cache of latest policy changes when you shut it down.

Testing Security Policy Using the Evaluate Assembly Wizard

The tool provides a wizard that will help you analyze the current state of security policy with respect to any assembly. The Evaluate Assembly Wizard allows you to test the following conditions:

- What the permissions are that an individual policy level, or all three policy levels combined, will grant to a specific assembly

- What code groups are at an individual policy level or in all policy levels that apply to a specific assembly

The first feature will help you find out exactly what permissions policy will give to an assembly, and also the permissions each policy level contributes to the assembly's overall set of granted permissions. The second feature, testing what code groups apply to a specific assembly, can then be used to find exactly what subset of the code group hierarchies at each policy level contribute to the set of permissions granted from security policy. To put it succinctly, the first feature lets you know what permissions an assembly gets from the security policy, while the second feature shows you from where these permissions came.

> **NOTE**
>
> You should recall a few facts about the way the security model is designed before using this Wizard. First, the set of permissions granted at a specific policy level is *intersected* with the permissions granted at other policy levels. Also, the actual *permission grant* that an assembly receives at runtime of the assembly may differ from the set of permissions the policy hands to that assembly as shown by the Evaluate Assembly Wizard. Remember that the calculation of the assembly's permission grant set is not complete until the requested, refused, and optional permissions that an assembly has declared are taken into account. For example, although an assembly may be given full trust to access all protected resources by security policy, it may refuse to be given any access to the file system and registry and therefore would end up not receiving these permissions. If such an assembly then foolishly tried to access the file system, it would still generate a security exception, despite the fact that the administrator has set security policy such that it receives full trust, as shown by the Evaluate Assembly Wizard. Such situations are programming mistakes that an administrator will not be able to fix via a security policy change. You should contact the software vendor if that case occurs.

The following are a few scenarios that demonstrate typical situations of use for this wizard:

- You have introduced a new code group to alter the permissions a given assembly or set of assemblies receives. To ascertain that the policy change has the desired effect, you use the Evaluate Assembly Wizard to browse to an affected assembly and check the permissions that this assembly now receives after your policy change. If it is different from what you expected, reuse the Wizard to check which code groups in security policy apply, to make sure your newly introduced code group matches the assembly, and that there are no other code groups interfering with the intended results.

- An assembly generates an unexpected security exception. You use the Evaluate Assembly Wizard to find out the exact level of permissions granted by policy to the assembly, and then find out which code groups are responsible for the given permissions. This will help you greatly to pinpoint places in security policy that may need to be adjusted to enable the assembly in question.

- An assembly that should not be allowed to execute or access a variety of resources given your understanding of current security policy does so anyway. You can use the Evaluate Assembly Wizard to find out the permissions the assembly actually receives from security policy, and then reuse the Wizard to find the code groups that apply to this assembly causing the unexpected permissions grant.

To start up the Wizard, simply right-click the Runtime Security Policy node and click the Evaluate Assembly Wizard option. This will bring up the Wizard start page shown in Figure 18.24.

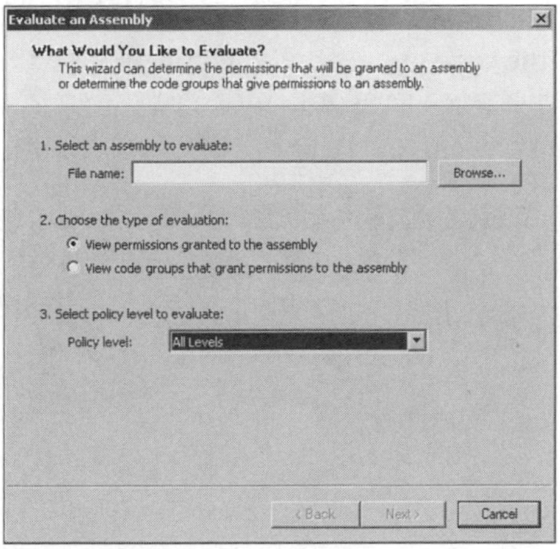

FIGURE 18.24   The Evaluate Assembly Wizard's start page.

On this page, you should first browse to or simply enter the path to an assembly you want evaluated. All of the assembly's evidence will be taken into account in the evaluation the Wizard does, so choose the assembly carefully.

NOTE

As of the date of writing of this book, it was not possible to browse to an assembly location based on the `http://` protocol.

After selecting an assembly to be evaluated, you have to select whether you want to see the permissions granted by the security policy to this assembly or the code groups in security policy that apply to this assembly. You will usually first want to see the permissions before finding out what code groups are responsible for handing them to the assembly.

Finally, you need to select whether you want to see the applicable permissions or code groups for all policy levels or just one policy level. If you choose a particular policy level, please keep in mind that all other policy levels usually contribute to the final set of permissions the assembly receives.

If you elected to see the permissions the chosen assembly receives, you will see the list of granted permissions. To view the properties of any of the granted permissions, simply select the permission whose properties you want to see and click the View Permission button. This will then show you the properties of the selected permission. Just seeing the list of permissions that have been granted tells you little as to the scope of access to resources. For example, if you see that an assembly has the registry permission, it is still unclear whether the permission state is set to give that assembly full access to all of the registry or read access to one registry location.

If you elected to see the code groups the assembly maps to, you will be presented with a condensed policy tree view containing just the code groups that match the assembly (see Figure 18.25).

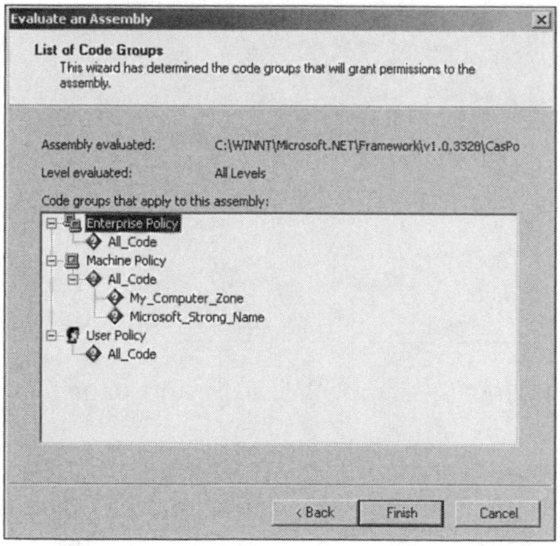

FIGURE 18.25   Browsing the code groups that apply to the selected assembly.

Unfortunately, you cannot access a code group's properties from this view. To find out exactly what the matching code groups grant to an assembly, either jot down the code group names or run a second instance of the tool in parallel and check the code group hierarchies for the respective code group properties.

Modeling Policy Changes Using Open and New

By default, your wizard actions and policy tree changes will apply to the security policy of the machine on which you are running the tool. This gives you immediate administrative access to the security configuration of this machine. However, you may not always want to directly modify the security policy applying to the computer from which you are using the tool. The following are some scenarios in which it may be advantageous to be able to modify or open security policy levels that do not directly apply to your administrative machine:

- You are about to make a very risky or pervasive security policy change and want to try it out without risking the security of your administration machine.

- You want to create a policy level to be deployed (see the "Deploying Security Policy" section later in this chapter) to other machines on the enterprise network. The policy you craft, however, is not applicable to your machine.

- You have made a backup copy of security policy configuration files prior to a set of policy changes you have made. You'd like to browse through that earlier state of policies to either debug current policy issues or simply to review how you solved some administrative task before.

- A user has unexpected security policy issues, security exceptions are triggered for an application that should run, or an application seems to access protected resources while security policy was intended to stop it from accessing protected resources. You can have the policy configuration files of the user sent to you and browse through them to find out what the policy issue may be.

The tool includes two features that help you experiment with security policy without actually having to change the security policy that applies to your machine.

By right-clicking the Runtime Security Policy node, you can either access the New or Open features.

Creating a New Policy Level

The New option lets you create a policy level in its default security policy state. You can choose either of the three administrable policy levels (see Figure 18.26), as well as a filename and path to which the policy configuration file should be stored.

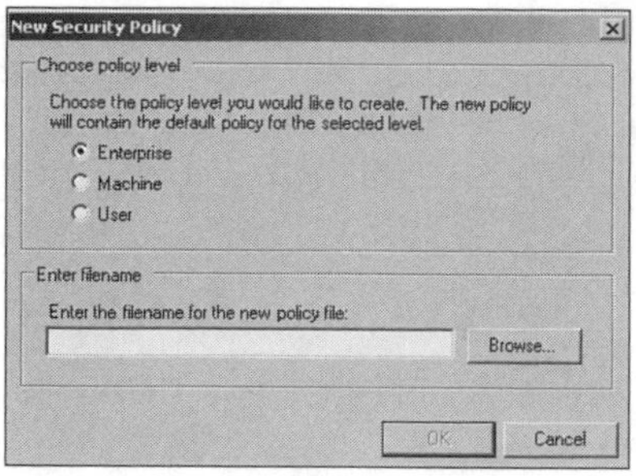

FIGURE 18.26   Creating a default policy level for modeling purposes.

All administrative features introduced in this chapter are at your disposal to modify this policy level.

You can use the Evaluate Assembly Wizard to test the effect that policy changes you made in that level have on a specific assembly or set of assemblies. You can also use this feature as a starting point for building a policy level that you will then deploy more widely (see "Deploying Security Policy," later in this chapter).

Opening a Policy Level Configuration File

Using the Open feature, you can open a policy level configuration file without changing the security policy state that applies to the machine on which you run the tool.

After selecting the Open option on the Runtime Security Policy node, you will encounter the wizard page shown in Figure 18.27.

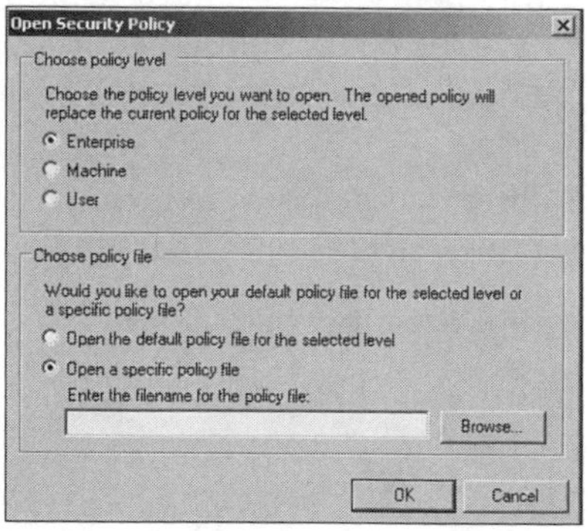

FIGURE 18.27   Opening a policy level that does not affect the security policy of the machine on which the tool is run.

You will need to select the policy level the configuration file will be loaded to. Subsequently, you either type in or browse to the configuration file you want to load.

This will load in a policy level from the selected configuration file to the policy level you have selected without any impact to the security policy for the machine from which you run the tool. All wizards and policy tree change features are at your disposal to further modify the loaded policy level. All changes to that policy level will be persisted into the selected file.

> **TIP**
>
> Because any modifications to an opened policy level are immediately persisted back to the selected configuration, you may want to make a back-up copy of the original policy level file if you see the need to return to that original state at some point.

Reverting Back to the Security Policy Levels That Apply to the Machine on Which the Tool Runs

After browsing or experimenting with policy levels that do not change the security state of the machine, you may want to again return to administering the policy levels that actually apply to the machine on which you are running the tool. To do so, simply choose the Open Default Policy Level for Selected Level option on the Open feature (see Figure 18.27). This will revert the tool back to administering the selected policy level that applies to the machine on which you are working.

Deploying Security Policy

The security policy state of the .NET Framework is persisted in three policy configuration files, one for each policy level. Per machine, you have one enterprise policy configuration file, a machine policy configuration file, and policy configuration files for each user on the machine.

> **NOTE**
>
> If the security system cannot find the configuration file for a policy level, that policy level will be set to the default policy state. One emergency technique of reverting back to default security policy, if the current policy state is hopelessly tangled, is to delete all policy configuration files.

There is no centralized infrastructure that is queried about the current policy state of an enterprise, and it becomes the administrator's responsibility to roll out the configuration files to client machines.

The tool offers some help in allowing you to quickly deploy security policy level state. The process of deploying security policy consists of two major steps:

1. Creation of a deployment package

2. Deployment of the policy using a deployment mechanism as chosen by the administrator

The tool itself offers no features that directly distribute policy, but it offers a wizard that builds the necessary deployment packages for you.

Creating Security Policy Deployment Packages

The tool ships with the Deployment Package Wizard. You can access this Wizard by right-clicking the Runtime Security Policy node. This Wizard lets you create a Windows Installer Package (a .MSI file) for a policy level currently loaded in the tool (see Figure 18.28).

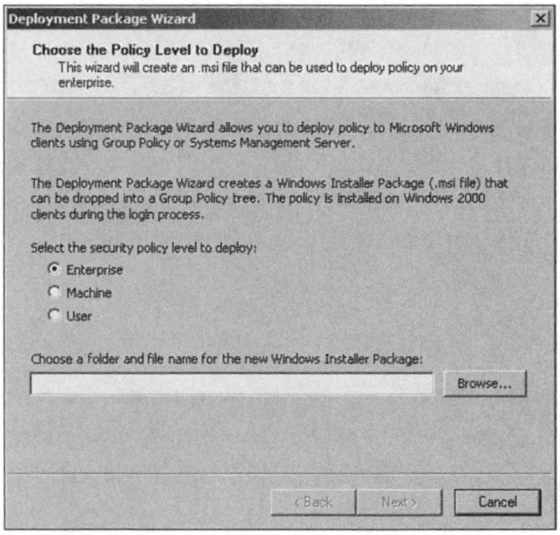

FIGURE 18.28   Creating a Windows Installer Package from a currently loaded policy level.

Simply choose which of the policy levels currently represented in the tool you want to wrap up into an installation package.

NOTE

There is no option to wrap multiple policy levels into a single deployment package. If you want to distribute multiple policy levels, you must generate multiple installer packages.

Then simply pick a filename and location to which you want to store the deployment package file. That is the file you will actually deploy to cause policy changes on other machines.

The .MSI file will contain the directory and filename information of the policy configuration file you chose to deploy. Consequently, you do not have to worry about the filenames and directories of security policy files when deploying security policy.

NOTE

If you have multiple versions of the .NET Framework installed on your enterprise and want to deploy security policy for all these versions, you will have to create separate deployment packages for each version, because security policy configuration is versioned.

Deployment Methods

The tool does not itself have infrastructure built in to actually deploy security policy across a network. However, you can use several commonly available deployment and management technologies to deploy your policy .MSI file.

TIP

For more information and details about policy administration and deployment concerning enterprise security administration, see the enterprise policy administration and deployment FAQ at `http://msdn.microsoft.com/net/security`.

If your network consists of machines running at least Windows 2000, you can use the Microsoft Group Policy editor to deploy security policy to the whole or a subset of your enterprise's intranet. To do so, you simply need to drag and drop the Windows Installer Package you created and drop it onto the group policy node representing the deployment scope of security policy.

NOTE

You will need the right administrative privileges to deploy policy via Group Policy over your intranet. Machine administrative rights on your machine will be insufficient; you must also have administrative rights on your network domain.

Another deployment method you can choose is to use SMS (Systems Management Server). If you have SMS installed on your enterprise, you could simply write a deployment script embedding the MSI file.

Finally, the Windows Installer Packages are self-contained installation units. Double-clicking an MSI file will run the installation script that will install the policy level contained in the package. If need be, you could distribute your deployment packages even via e-mail or floppy disk, although the previously discussed methods are far superior.

Resetting Security Policy

The tool allows you to reset all of security policy or individual policy levels to the default policy state. The default policy has been designed to protect against security transgressions by any code from the Internet or intranet. If you have discovered flaws in your current policy design, a return to default policy is of a good starting point for redrafting your security policy, because you are starting from a known safe origin. Of course, the drawback of resetting security policy is that you will lose any policy customizations you may have made to the affected policy levels.

TIP

You can make a backup copy of your old policy state even *after* you have reset security policy, although you must not have made any other changes after the reset. The following files always contain the security policy state just before the most recent policy change to the respective policy level.

Security Configuration Backup File locations include:

- Enterprise-level configuration file—`%WINDIR%\Microsoft.NET\Framework\ v[version number]\Config\Enterprisesec.config.old`

- Machine-level configuration file— `%WINDIR%\Microsoft.NET\Framework\v[version]\Config\ security.config.old`

- User-level configuration file

    Windows NT/2000/XP—`%USERPROFILE%\Application data\Microsoft\ CLR security config\v[version]\Security.config.old`

    Windows 95/98—`%WINDIR%\username\CLR security config\vxx.xx\ Security.config.old`

Depending on the OS you are running on, `%WINDIR%` will either be the `\Windows` or `\WINNT` directory on your system. The `%USERPROFILE%` directory stands for your `Documents and Settings\username` folder. Note that the `Application data` folder is a hidden folder.

You can use the tool's Open function to browse and access your backup copy at a later point. See the "Modeling Policy Changes Using Open and New" section earlier in this chapter.

If you want to reset all of the security policy to its default state, simply right-click the Runtime Security Policy node and select the Reset All... option.

If you want to reset only a particular policy level to its default policy state, you need to expand the Runtime Security Policy node, right-click the respective policy level, and select the Reset option.

> **NOTE**
>
> If you use the tool to do a full reset of security policy (Reset All), the tool will set the enterprise and machine policy on the respective machine to its default state, if the user in whose user context the tool is running has write access to the policy files. In addition, the user policy corresponding to the current user context is reset to its default state. No other user's policy is touched. Thus, doing a Reset All will still leave in place policy customizations that other users have done.

The .NET Framework Configuration Tool's Self Protection Mechanism

The tool is itself written in managed code. This means that it is subject to security checks within the .NET Framework security system just as any other assembly is. Although the security default policy is designed to give the tool enough trust to run properly irrespective of from where it is started, it is possible to change security policy such that the tool will not receive sufficient permissions to do its job. Consequently, the tool has a self protection mechanism built in that evaluates whether the policy change you are about to make would jeopardize the proper running of the tool during future tool sessions.

> **NOTE**
>
> Security policy changes are always only applied to assemblies that are loaded after the change was made.

Whenever the tool establishes that a policy change would prevent it from running in the future, it will warn you of that fact (see Figure 18.29).

As long as you don't quit your current tool session, you still have the chance to undo these policy changes or change policy to a state in which the tool would run properly again. When you bring security policy back into a state in which the tool could function fully, a message box will be displayed letting you know that fact. However, if you exit the tool while having persisted a policy state too restrictive for the tool to run, you will not be able to use the GUI tool at a later time to change policy back into a state in which the admin tool runs. In such cases, simply deleting all security policy configuration files by hand is a valid solution to get back to a policy state in which the administrative tool would work. The lack of the presence of a security configuration file for a specific policy level is always interpreted by the security engine as the presence of default policy for that level. As a result, if you delete all security configuration files for all three policy levels, you will set your machine back to the default security policy.

FIGURE 18.29   The tool warns of policy changes that would undermine its own functioning.

TIP

Deleting the security policy configuration files for the user, machine, and enterprise policy level will reset the machine for the respective user back to the default policy state. The policy configuration files can be found in the following locations:

- Enterprise-level configuration file—`%WINDIR%\Microsoft.NET\Framework\`
  `v[version]\Config\Enterprisesec.config`

- Machine-level configuration file—`%WINDIR%\Microsoft.NET\Framework\`
  `v[version]\Config\security.config`

- User-level configuration file

  Windows NT/2000/XP—`%USERPROFILE%\Application data\Microsoft\`
  `CLR security config\v[version]\Security.config`

  Windows 95/98—`%WINDIR%\username\CLR security config\v[version]\`
  `Security.config`

Depending on the OS you are running on, `%WINDIR%` will either be the `\Windows` or `\WINNT` directory on your system. The `%USERPROFILE%` directory stands for your `Documents and Settings\username` folder. Note that the `Application data` folder is a hidden folder.

Administrative Tactics: Scenarios, Solutions, Hints, and Tricks

This section will pull together the various tool features introduced thus far and combine them to show how various administrative scenarios might be solved. You can use this section as inspiration and starting point for tackling your own administration tasks.

The individual steps in solving specific scenarios are not covered in detail here. For a precise explanation, please refer to the respective sections in this chapter that cover the various tool features.

Also, you may want to check `http://msdn.microsoft.com/net/security` for papers on the security model and its administration. You can find further administrative recipes and important background information there.

The following are a few sample scenarios and concise solutions to common administrative scenarios. Feel free to use these as template solutions to your own tasks. All solutions presume the default security policy as their starting point.

Granting Enterprise-Wide Full Trust to an Assembly

Scenario: An assembly installed at a location not receiving full trust by default (such as any intranet location in default policy) must receive full trust to run properly. You want to guarantee that this assembly gets full trust access and protected resources across the whole enterprise network, irrespective of local machine or user policy settings.

Solution:

1. Open your current enterprise policy level (or create a new one if you want to model this policy change without directly affecting your machine's policy settings).

2. Choose the New option on the root code group.

3. On the New Group Code Wizard, choose a new name for the group code.

4. In the New Code Group Wizard, choose the strong name or hash membership condition (depending on whether the assembly you want to give full trust is strong name signed).

5. In the New Code Group Wizard, browse to and select the assembly you want to trust and select the FullTrust permission set for this code group.

6. Right-click the newly created code group and bring up its Properties page, check the Level Final flag (Policy Levels Below This Will Not Be Evaluated).

7. Bring up the Deployment Package Wizard (right-click the Runtime Security Policy node) and create a deployment package for the enterprise policy level.

8. Open the Group Policy editor and drop the newly created deployment package onto the Intranet node corresponding to your deployment target scope.

TIP

If you have a multiassembly application, you may need to repeat steps 1 through 5 for all the assemblies on which the application depends.

Granting Full Trust to All Assemblies of a Software Publisher Across an Enterprise

Scenario: All assemblies from a specific software publisher, irrespective of the location from which they are run, should receive full trust to access all protected resources.

Solution:

1. Open your current enterprise policy level (or create a new one if you want to model this policy change without directly affecting your machine's policy settings).

2. Choose the New option on the root code group.

3. On the New Group Code Wizard, choose a new name for the group code.

4. In the New Code Group Wizard, choose the strong name membership condition (you can also use the Publisher membership condition if you want to trust a publisher by its authenticode signature instead).

5. Browse to an assembly from this publisher and uncheck the name and version check boxes of the strong name. Select the FullTrust permission set and finish the Wizard.

6. Right-click the newly created code group and bring up its Properties page, check the Level Final flag (Policy Levels Below This Will Not Be Evaluated).

7. Bring up the Deployment Package Wizard (right-click the Runtime Security Policy Node) and create a deployment package for the enterprise policy level.

8. Open the Group Policy editor and drop the newly created deployment package onto the Intranet node corresponding to your deployment target scope.

Preventing an Assembly from Running Across an Enterprise

Scenario: A specific assembly should not be run anywhere on the enterprise network's client machines.

Solution:

1. Open your current enterprise policy level (or create a new one if you want to model this policy change without directly affecting your machine's policy settings).

2. Choose the New option on the root code group.

3. On the New Group Code Wizard, choose a new name for the group code.

4. In the New Code Group Wizard, choose the strong name or hash membership condition (depending on whether the assembly in question is strong name signed).

5. Browse to the assembly and, if the strong name membership condition has been chosen, uncheck the Version check box if you want to disallow all different versions of the assembly to run. Choose the Nothing permission set for this code group and exit the Wizard.

6. Right-click the newly created code group and bring up its Properties page, check the exclusive flag (This Policy Level Will Only...).

7. Bring up the Deployment Package Wizard (right-click the Runtime Security Policy Node) and create a deployment package for the enterprise policy level.

8. Open the Group Policy editor and drop the newly created deployment package onto the Intranet node corresponding to your deployment target scope.

NOTE

Microsoft Group policy will install the policy update only upon new login or reboot on client machines. If a client machine is never rebooted or logged out of, the policy change will not take effect on that machine.

For more information on enterprise administration and deployment, see http://msdn.micrososft.com/net/security.

Preventing All Assemblies of a Specific Software Publisher from Running Across an Enterprise

Scenario: All assemblies from a specific software publisher should not be run anywhere on the enterprise network's client machines.

Solution:

1. Open your current enterprise policy level (or create a new one if you want to model this policy change without directly affecting your machine's policy settings).

2. Choose the New option on the root code group.

3. On the New Group Code Wizard, choose a new name for the group code.

4. In the New Code Group Wizard, choose the strong name or publisher membership condition.

5. Browse to the assembly and, if the strong name membership condition has been chosen, uncheck the Version and Name check box. Choose the Nothing permission set for this code group and exit the Wizard.

6. Right-click the newly created code group and bring up its Properties page, check the exclusive flag (This Policy Level Will Only...).

7. Bring up the Deployment Package Wizard (right-click the Runtime Security Policy Node) and create a deployment package for the enterprise policy level.

8. Open the Group Policy editor and drop the newly created deployment package onto the Intranet node corresponding to your deployment target scope.

Reducing the Level of Trust for All Assemblies from the Intranet for a Specific Machine

Scenario: A machine administrator wants to reduce the level of trust given to all assemblies running from the intranet to the same level default policy grants to the Internet.

Solution:

Use the Adjust Security Wizard, select the LocalIntranet zone, and reduce the permission level to the second-to-last position.

Granting All Assemblies from a Specific Intranet Share or Mounted Drive Full Trust on a Machine

Scenario: All assemblies from a specific intranet share or mounted drive should run with full access to all protected resources. This setting should apply machine wide.

Solution:

1. Expand the machine policy code group hierarchy and choose to add a new code group under the root machine level code group.

2. On the New Group Code Wizard, choose a new name for the group code.

3. In the New Code Group Wizard, select the URL membership condition and type in the URL of the share name or mounted drive followed by *. The latter

is necessary and will cause all subdirectories and files at the share or drive to match the URL membership condition.

4. Choose the FullTrust membership condition and exit the Wizard.

Disallowing All Assemblies from a Specific Internet Site to Run on a Machine

Scenario: All assemblies from an Internet site should be blocked from running on a machine.

Solution:

1. Expand the machine policy node and then expand the root node of the code group hierarchy. On the LocalIntranet_Zone code group, choose the New option.

2. On the New Group Code Wizard, choose a new name for the group code.

3. In the New Code Group Wizard, select the site membership condition and type in the site whose assemblies you want to block.

4. Choose the Nothing permission set for this code group and exit the Wizard.

5. Bring up the Properties page of the newly created code group and set the exclusive flag (This Policy Level Will Only…).

"Sandboxing" a Directory on the Local Hard Drive

Scenario: For testing purposes, all assemblies from a specific subdirectory on the local hard drive should receive the same permissions that the default policy gives to assemblies from the Internet.

Solution:

1. Expand the machine policy level node. On the root code group of the machine policy code group hierarchy, select the New option.

2. On the New Group Code Wizard, choose a new name for the group code.

3. In the New Code Group Wizard, select the URL membership condition and type in `file://\\\[path]\*`, where `[path]` stands for the path of the directory (and all its subdirectories) for which you want to reduce the granted permissions.

4. Select the Internet permission set for this code group and exit the code group Wizard.

5. Bring up the Properties page for the newly created code group and set the exclusive flag (This Policy Level Will Only…).

Giving All Assemblies of a Specific Software Publisher Running from the Internet File Read Rights to a Specific Directory

Scenario: All assemblies of a specific software publisher that run from the intranet need file read permission to a specific directory on top of permissions that the default policy already grants them.

Solution:

1. Expand the Machine-level policy node, and then select New on the permission set node.

2. On the New Permission Set Wizard, choose a new name for the permission set, add the FileIO permission, check the read flag, type in the file path, and exit the New Permission Set Wizard.

3. Expand the machine level code group hierarchy and select New on the LocalIntranet_Zone code group.

4. In the New Code Group Wizard, select the strong name membership condition, browse to an assembly with the respective strong name, and uncheck both the Name and Version flags.

5. Select your newly created permission set as the permission set granted by this code group, and then exit the Wizard.

Changing One's User Level Policy to Disallow Intranet Assemblies to Do Anything But Execute

Scenario: No assemblies originating from the local intranet run in your user context should be allowed to do more than simply execute.

Solution:

1. Expand the User policy node, and select the New option on the root code group.

2. On the New Group Code Wizard, choose a new name for the group code.

3. In the New Code Group Wizard, select the zone membership condition, set to Intranet.

4. Select the Execution permission set for this code group and finish the Wizard.

5. Bring up the Properties page for the newly created code group and set the execution flag (This Policy Level Will Only...).

Summary

The .NET Framework ships with a very rich security model, allowing for very fine-grained adjustments to the permissions assemblies receive. Although the default policy state should cover many scenarios, there will still be many situations in which you need to adapt security policy to your needs. The .NET Framework Configuration tool is your main helper for doing so. Without having to understand the intricacies of the policy model, you can use the Trust Assembly Wizard to increase the level of permissions a specific assembly or all assemblies from a given publisher receive. Alternatively, you can use the Adjust Security Wizard to adjust the level of permissions all assemblies from a given zone receive, without having to delve into the details of the policy system. However, to take the fullest advantage of the .NET Framework security model, the full security policy tree and all its constituents should be administered. The .NET Framework Configuration tool is nothing less than a graphical instantiation of this rich model, allowing you to tweak and extend security policy with utmost precision. After a policy change has been made, the Evaluate Assembly Wizard will assist you in testing your work, while the Create Deployment Package Wizard will help you build self-contained installation packages from policy levels for enterprise-wide policy deployment.

19

Administering .NET Framework Security Policy Using Scripts and Security APIs

IN THIS CHAPTER

- Using Batch Scripts for Security Policy Administration
- Changing Security Policy by Programming Directly to the Security APIs

By Sebastian Lange

The .NET Framework Configuration tool introduced in Chapter 18, "Administering Security Policy Using the .NET Framework Configuration Tool," allows for easy administrative changes through the onscreen manipulation of a graphical representation of the security model. However, the .NET Framework Configuration tool does not support changing security policy *programmatically*. Changing security policy state on a machine programmatically may be required in the following scenarios:

- You want to test an application in a variety of security contexts.

- Security policy changes are time dependent, and writing a scheduled security policy batch script may be easier than writing a custom code group.

- You want to deploy an application across the network and want to run a batch script doing security policy changes as part of the application's installation process.

- You want to develop your own security policy administration or analysis tools.

The .NET Framework provides two methods for you to change security policy programmatically. You either use the Caspol command-line tool to create batch scripts for security policy changes, or you can develop directly against the security policy APIs.

Some of the key points covered in this chapter are

- How to find and start the Caspol tool

- Examples of the various options of the Caspol tool

- A set of sample Caspol batch scripts showing the batch script solutions to various administrative problems

- An overview of the security policy object model and APIs

- Examples of how to use the APIs for common security policy administration tasks

- Hints and tricks on how to use the security APIs to write security policy administration or analysis tools

NOTE

This chapter presumes that you have a good understanding of the security policy model. You may want to review Chapter 6, "Permissions: The Workhorse of Code Access Security," Chapter 7, "Walking the Stack," or Chapter 8, "Membership Conditions, Code Groups, and Policy Levels: The Brick and Mortar of Security Policy," in case some of the security model concepts in this chapter seem unfamiliar.

Also, most of the security policy change options and techniques introduced in the following sections map directly to the graphical security policy tree manipulation techniques that the .NET Framework Configuration tool offers. Please refer to Chapter 18's section "Manipulating the Policy Tree Directly—Basic Techniques" for more information on the risks and side effects of various security policy change options. Unless they are particular to the use of the Caspol tool or the security APIs, they will not be repeated here.

If you have a good understanding of the security policy model, you will find the use of Caspol and the security APIs quite intuitive. Both are just another way of providing easy access to modifying the three administrable policy levels. Because both methods of accessing a machine's policy state lack some of the safeguards and intuitive interface of the GUI tool, you should be doubly careful in considering all the effects of your policy manipulations.

Using Batch Scripts for Security Policy Administration

The .NET Framework ships with a command-line administration tool called Caspol (Code Access Security Policy tool). With it, you can undertake administrative changes of security policy via the command line. For example, the following is a Caspol command to reset the machine policy level:

```
Caspol -machine -reset
```

By adding Caspol calls into a batch file (.bat), you can effectively create indefinitely complex scripts to change security policy. The following set of Caspol commands represents a script that first turns off Caspol's prompt to the user to ascertain a policy change, resets all of security policy, and adds a new code group under the Internet code group of the machine policy. The newly created code group has a site membership condition set to www.micrsosoft.com and hands out the intranet permission set:

```
Caspol -polchgprompt -off
Caspol -all -reset
Caspol -machine -addgroup Internet_Zone -site www.micrsosoft.com LocalIntranet
```

Executing a batch file with these three commands will programmatically change security policy without requiring any user input. You can run such policy change batch scripts either as part of an installation process for an application or even add a scheduled task on a machine to periodically switch security settings if necessary.

TIP

To create a scheduled task, open the control panel, open the Scheduled Task folder, and double-click the Add Scheduled Task Wizard. Browse to the batch script containing the Caspol commands you want to run periodically and choose the times at which to run it.

The various options that you can use to string together Caspol scripts are explained in some more detail in this section.

Also refer to the SDK documentation of the .NET Framework for help and more details.

Finding and Starting the Caspol Tool

Every installation of the .NET Framework comes with a copy of Caspol. You can find it in the %Windows%\Microsoft.NET\Framework\v*[version number]*\Caspol.exe directory.

%Windows% here refers to either the Winnt or Windows directory, depending on the operating system you are running. Because the .NET Framework allows different versions of itself to coexist, most .NET Framework libraries and tools are contained in version-specific directories. By browsing to the Framework subfolder, you can see which version or versions of the .NET Framework have been installed and pick the version that you want to administer by browsing to the respective version subdirectory and calling Caspol. If you have the SDK installed, the PATH environment variable will contain the path to the latest version of the SDK on the machine. In such cases, you can type **Caspol** from anywhere in the file system. The regular redistributable installations of the .NET Framework will not modify the PATH environment variable to contain the preceding path. In that, case you will need to browse to Caspol as indicated at the beginning of this section.

> **TIP**
>
> You can change the environment variable of your system by opening the Control Panel, choosing the System icon, clicking Advanced, selecting Environment Variables and, under System Variables, select the Path variable and edit it to contain the path of the location of the Caspol tool.

Caspol will always only modify the version of the .NET Framework with which it has been installed. If you happen to have multiple versions of the .NET Framework installed on your system, you will need to run your policy change scripts for each version for which you want to change policy.

Basic Caspol Techniques

This section contains a detailed list of most of the options Caspol has to offer. They are similar in type and use to what you can do in the .NET Framework Configuration tool using the graphical security model representation it offers.

For each option, its syntax, at least one example, and the option abbreviation is given.

Format and Scope of Caspol Commands

The basic format of Caspol commands is as follows:

```
Caspol [Policy Level Directive] Option Arguments

      [ [Policy Level Directive] Option Arguments]*
```

Every line in your Caspol script will start with Caspol, invoking the Caspol tool.

The Caspol tool will execute one option and its given arguments at a time and return to the command line when finished. As the previous syntax indicates, it is possible to concatenate multiple option-arguments pairs in one Caspol call, although the suggested way of using Caspol is to call it one option-arguments pair at a time.

Because security policy consists of three administrable policy levels, most Caspol options need to be scoped to one of the three policy levels. This is done using the following option prefixes:

```
-enterprise
```

```
-machine
```

```
-user
```

For example, the first Caspol command in the following example resets the user policy level to its default policy state, while the second command resets the enterprise policy level:

```
Caspol -user -reset
```

```
Caspol -enterprise -reset
```

While the use of friendly option names makes it clearer what you are trying to do with security policy, they also can make for a lot of typing. For that reason, Caspol also understands abbreviated forms for every option it offers. For example, the policy level directives just introduced are abbreviated to -en, -m, and -u , while the reset option is abbreviated to -rs. As a result, the previous two sample commands could have just as easily been written as follows:

```
Caspol -u -rs
```

```
Caspol -en -rs
```

For every Caspol option introduced in this chapter, the abbreviations will be given, along with the full syntax of the option in question.

A few Caspol commands can also be preceded by the -all directive, meaning that the option following this directive applies to all policy levels. For example, you can reset all security policy levels, with the following command:

```
Caspol -all -reset
```

Finally, you may wonder what happens if you leave off the policy level directive before an option, such as a reset. Caspol actually always determines whether you have write access to the machine policy file. If so, it defaults all options not explicitly preceded by a policy level directive to the machine policy level. For example, if you have write access to the machine policy file (typically by having machine administrator rights), the following command will reset the machine policy level:

```
Caspol -reset
```

If the user on whose behalf Caspol is running does not have write access to the machine and enterprise policy settings, all Caspol options not preceded by an explicit policy level directive are defaulted to the user level policy. In this case, the previous command would have reset the user policy level.

> **TIP**
>
> When writing Caspol scripts, you should always precede policy change options with the policy level directive, because the script may be run in user contexts with different write access to the machine policy.

Not all Caspol options need to be preceded by a policy level directive. Mostly, these are options that refer to the security system as a whole (such as the option to turn security off) or to the functioning of the Caspol tool itself. This fact will be made explicit by the syntax notation for the respective options introduced shortly.

All policy changes made using Caspol are immediate. There is no sense of a multi-step policy change transaction. So if your script fails prior to the execution of all commands in it, the changes made by the Caspol commands that have succeeded will be present in security policy. For that reason, design scripts carefully and cautiously.

Turning the Policy Change Prompt Off

By default, Caspol requires an explicit user acknowledgment to persist policy changes into security policy. For example, after typing in the Caspol command to reset the machine policy, the user will be queried to affirm that this should really be done. This is a helpful aid in preventing usage error in case an option or an argument has been mistyped, but this would also make running an automated policy change batch script impossible. For that reason, Caspol offers the option to turn these warnings off.

Syntax:

```
-polchgprompt {off | on }
```

Abbreviation:

```
-pp {off | on }
```

Example:

```
Caspol -pp off
```

TIP

Unless you are absolutely certain that you have previously run a command, you should include the policy change prompt command as the first line in all of your scripts to make sure that it will run without requiring any user interaction. The policy change prompt setting is stored in a machine–wide registry key that sets the policy change warning for the specific version of Caspol that is run to make that change.

Showing Current Security Policy Settings

Security policy contains three administrable policy levels, each of which consists of a tree of code groups, a list of known permissions, and a list of policy assemblies.

NOTE

Please refer to Part II, "Code Access Security Fundamentals," for a detailed discussion of the security model.

To display the state of policy, Caspol ships with a variety of options that help you view parts or all of security policy.

If you want to see the tree of code groups of a policy level, or of all policy levels, use the following option:

Syntax:

```
[{-u[ser],-m[achine],-en[terprise],-a[ll]}] -listgroups
```

Abbreviation:

```
-lg
```

Example:

```
Caspol -a -lg
```

This example will show you the code group hierarchy of all administrable policy levels (user, machine, and enterprise policy level).

If you have write access rights to the machine and enterprise policy, the following command will show you the machine policy level's code groups:

```
Caspol -listgroups
```

The output of this command for the machine policy looks much like the following:

```
Security is ON
Execution Checking is ON
Policy Change Prompt is  ON

Level = Machine

Code Groups:

1.  All code: Nothing
    1.1.  Zone - MyComputer: FullTrust
        1.1.1.  StrongName -
➥002400000480000094000000060200000024000052534131000400000 1
00010007D1FA57C4AED9F0A32E84AA0FAEFD0DE9E8FD6AEC8F87FB03766C834C99921EB23BE79AD9
D5DCC1DD9AD2361321 02900B723CF980957FC4E177108FC607774F29E8320E92EA05ECE4E821C0A5
EFE8F1645C4C0C93C1AB99285D622CAA652C1DFAD63D745D6F2DE5F17E5EAF0FC4963D261C8A1243
6518206DC093344D5AD293: FullTrust
    1.1.2.  StrongName - 0000000000000000400000000000000: FullTrust

    1.2.  Zone - intranet: LocalIntranet
        1.2.1.  All code: Same site Web.
        1.2.2.  All code: Same directory FileIO - Read, PathDiscovery
    1.3.  Zone - Internet: Nothing
        1.3.1.  All code: Same site Web.

    1.4.  Zone - Untrusted: Nothing
    1.5.  Zone - Trusted: Internet
        1.5.1.  All code: Same site Web.
```

To represent a tree structure of code groups, Caspol uses both indentation as well as a sub-sectional numeric labeling system. For example, lines starting with a 1.*number* label are child code groups of the code group with label 1. Following the numeric label is the name of the membership condition, its value set for that code group, and lastly, the name of the permission set the code group hands out if the membership condition is met.

Each code group can have a description and a code group name. To display that additional information about each code group, use the following Caspol option:

Syntax:

```
[{-u[ser],-m[achine],-en[terprise],-a[ll]}] –listdescription
```

Abbreviation:

-ld

Example:

Caspol -m -ld

This example will show you the code group names and descriptions of the machine policy level.

TIP

It is strongly recommended that you use a code group's name and not the numeric label in modifying security policy. The Caspol tool will reorder the numeric label depending on what code groups have been added or deleted from the initial default policy state, while code group names remain the same unless explicitly changed by an administrative action.

The named permission set a code group references is part of a list of known named permission sets at the respective policy level. To see this list for a policy level (or for all policy levels using the -all directive), use the following command:

Syntax:

[{-u[ser],-m[achine],-en[terprise],-a[ll]}] -listpset

Abbreviation:

-lp

Example:

Caspol -all -listpset

This example will show the known permission sets at each policy level. Note that you will see the XML serialization of each permission set object known at the respective policy level. Each of the permission sets typically consists of a number of permissions configured to a specific permission state.

NOTE

Please see Chapter 6 for more details on permissions.

Finally, each policy level also contains a policy assemblies list. This list contains the transitive closure of all assemblies used to implement the code group hierarchy at a policy level.

NOTE

Please see the sections on policy assemblies in Chapters 8 and 18 for more detail.

To view this list, simply use the following Caspol option:

Syntax:

```
[{-u[ser],-m[achine],-en[terprise],-a[ll]}] -listfulltrust
```

Abbreviation:

```
-lf
```

Example:

```
Caspol -en -lf
```

This example will show you the list of policy assemblies at the enterprise policy level. Note that this list will include the assembly names as well as the assemblies' strong names.

Caspol also offers an option that combines the -listgroup and -listpset options. If you want to view both, you can just use the following option:

Syntax:

```
[{-u[ser],-m[achine],-en[terprise],-a[ll]}] -list
```

Abbreviation:

```
-l
```

Example:

```
Caspol -u -list
```

Adding a Code Group

To add a code group to the code group hierarchy of a policy level, use the following Caspol command:

Syntax:

```
[{-u[ser],-m[achine],-en[terprise]}] -addgroup

     {label_of_parent | name_of_parent} mshipcondition pset [flags]
```

Abbreviation:

-ag

Example:

```
Caspol -m -ag Internet_Zone -site www.microsoft.com LocalIntranet -n MyIntranet-
Group
```

This example adds a code group to the machine code group hierarchy under the Internet_Zone code group. The new code group has a site membership condition with membership condition value of www.microsoft.com and hands out the LocalIntranet permission set if an assembly matches that membership condition. Last, the code group has been named MyIntranetGroup. Essentially, if you were to run this Caspol line over default machine policy, it would extend policy such that all assemblies from the microsoft.com site will receive not just the Internet permission set but LocalIntranet permissions.

All items in *italics* in the previous syntax description need further definition. As you will remember from Chapter 8, the .NET Framework security system offers a number of membership condition types for building up your security policy. If the built-in membership condition types do not suffice for your needs, you could even custom author your own membership conditions. Caspol allows you to add code groups using either the membership condition types shipping in the .NET Framework or using custom membership conditions. *mshipcondition* in the previous syntax description can be replaced by any of the following switches:

Syntax for *mshipcondition*:

- -allcode—This membership condition will always be true; it is typically used for root nodes in code group hierarchies.

- -appdir—This membership condition tests whether an assembly's URL evidence matches the assembly's application directory.

- -custom *MshipXMLFile*—This membership condition switch is used to import a custom membership condition into a code group hierarchy. *MshipXMLFile* is used to point at an XML file representing the XML serialization of the custom membership condition in a specific membership condition state.

- -hash *HashAlg* {-hex hashvalue | -file assembly}—This membership condition is used to check whether an assembly has a specified hash value. *HashAlg* should be set to a proper hash algorithm name, such as SHA1 or MD5. You can then either type in the hexadecimal encoded hash value directly or (far more convenient) point Caspol at the file whose hash value you want to add to policy.

NOTE

You should not use MD5 for *HashAlg* unless you have specific requirements to use MD5. MD5 is cryptographically weaker than the various SHA hash algorithms.

When creating the hash of assembly Caspol, simply use the hash algorithm name you supplied to look up the corresponding algorithm implementation in the cryptography configuration system. This system, by default, maps standard hash algorithm names, such as MD5, SHA1, and SHA256, to their managed implementation.

- `-pub {-cert cert_file | -file signed_file | -hex certstring}`—This membership condition is used to check an assembly for a specific x.509 certificate. You can either point Caspol to a `.cer` file containing the cert you want to test for, point it at a signed assembly (probably the most common use form to supply this membership condition value), or type in the cert in hexadecimal encoding directly.

- `-site sitename`—This membership condition tests whether an assembly came from a specific site.

- `-strong –file signed_file {name | -noname} {version | -noversion}`— The –strong membership condition tests assemblies for a specific strong name signature. To set this membership condition's value, you need to point Caspol at a specific strong name signed file (such as `Caspol.exe`). Additionally, you need to specify whether the membership condition should check for a specific assembly name (such as Caspol) and version (such as 1.0).

- `-url URL`—The -url membership condition checks whether an assembly came from a specific URL address.

NOTE

To have an URL memebership condition match all files (and subdirectories) at a specific drive, folder, or site, you must append an * at the end of the drive, folder, or site value. For example, –url file://\\\h:* should be used to match all files and folders on drive h.

- `-zone zone`—The -zone membership condition tests whether an assembly comes from the specified zone. The legal values you can use for the zone membership condition are Mycomputer, intranet, Trusted, Internet, and Untrusted.

In addition to the code group membership condition, you can optionally also specify a number of flags for the new code group. The following is a list of the available options:

- -exclusive {on|off}—This flag makes a code group level exclusive. This means that if an assembly ever matches this code group, only the permission set granted by this code group determines the respective policy level's permission grant to the evaluated assembly.

- -levelfinal {on|off}—If this flag is set and the code group carrying this flag is matched, policy resolution will stop at the present policy level. No policy levels below the one in which this flag occurred are evaluated.

- -n[ame] codegroupname—This flag allows you to specify a name for the newly created code group.

TIP

It is highly suggested that you give all code groups you later may want to script to a unique name. Scripting policy changes against the numeric labels is very brittle because a simple code group addition or deletion can lead to a reordering of numeric labels.

- -d[escription] codegroupdescription—This flag allows you to add a description to a code group.

Now, let's put all this together and look at a few more examples. Note that the *Flags* and *mshipcondition* switches will also be used to change properties on a code group, so understanding how to use them will pay off when writing your scripts.

```
Caspol -m -ag Internet_Zone -strong -file Caspol.exe

➥-noname -noversion FullTrust -n CaspolSNgroup
```

The previous command will add a code group under the Internet_Zone group with a strong name membership condition. The strong name that this code group will check for is the strong name Caspol has been signed with; the code group will not check for a specific assembly name or version and grant the FullTrust permission set. The new code group has been named CaspolSNgroup.

```
Caspol -en -ag All_Code -hash SHA1 -file myassembly.exe

➥FullTrust -exclusive on -levelfinal on -n MyAssembly
```

The previous Caspol line will add a code group under the root code group of the enterprise policy code group hierarchy. The code group will check whether an assembly matches the SHA1 hash value for myassembly.exe and, if so, the code group will grant the FullTrust permission set. The code group is also marked exclusive, excluding any other code group at the enterprise policy level from contributing to the

permission set granted at that policy level. Furthermore, the code group is marked
level final, which means that no further policy levels will be evaluated. This is an
effective technique for making sure that a specific assembly or set of assemblies gets
exactly the level of permissions you want, without having user or machine policy
interfere. Finally, the code group name is set to MyAssembly.

Deleting a Code Group

The following is the syntax to delete a code group:

Syntax:

```
[{-u[ser],-m[achine],-en[terprise]}]  -remgroup {codegroup_label|codegroup_name}
```

Abbreviation:

```
-rg
```

Example:

```
Caspol -en -rg MyAssembly
```

This Caspol command deletes a code group with name MyAssembly from the enterprise policy code group hierarchy.

> **NOTE**
>
> If the code group being deleted has any child code groups, they will also be removed.

Changing the Properties of a Code Group

All properties of a code group can be altered by using the following Caspol option:

Syntax:

```
[{-u[ser],-m[achine],-en[terprise]}]
```

```
-chggroup {codegroup_label | codegroupname} {mshipcondition | pset | flags}
```

Abbreviation:

```
-cg
```

Example:

```
Caspol -en Myassembly -pub -file myassembly.exe -levelfinal off
```

When changing a code group using this option, you do not need to redefine all properties of a code group. As you can see in the previous example, the name, description, and permission set of the MyAssembly code group are left untouched. This code group is changed to check for a publisher certificate, and the level final flag is turned off.

NOTE

For a detailed description of the *mshipcondition* and *Flags* options, please see the "Adding a Code Group" section earlier in this chapter.

Adding a New Permission Set

Caspol allows you to add new named permission sets to the list of permission sets known at a policy level. Unlike the .NET Framework Configuration tool, Caspol does not have any support to help you build a new permission set. Caspol only allows you to import the XML serialization of a permission set you have already defined.

TIP

For more help on permission set XML syntax, please see the "Dealing with Custom Permissions and Permission Sets" section in Chapter 18.

Building your permission set XML is risky and very error prone. Instead, you should use the .NET Framework Configuration tool's New Permission Set Wizard to add a new permission set to a policy level. If that permission set needs to be exported across your enterprise's machines, simply open the respective policy file and copy the permission set XML the tool produced for you into a new .xml file. You can use that file with the following Caspol option.

Syntax:

```
[{-u[ser],-m[achine],-en[terprise]}] -addpset {xml_file | xml_file name}
```

Abbreviation:

```
-ap
```

Example:

```
Caspol -en mypset.xml MyPset
```

This example adds the permission set defined in mypset.xml to the enterprise policy level under the name MyPset. If the name is already defined in the XML representation of the permission set, you do not need to explicitly state a permission set name in the Caspol command.

To see examples of the XML representations of a permission set, simply list the permission sets of a policy level:

```
Caspol -m -lp
```

This will show you the XML representation of all permission sets known at the machine level.

Changing a Permission Set

To change a permission set at a policy level, you need to supply the XML representation of the permission set that should replace the permission set to be altered. Use the following command to do just that:

Syntax:

```
[{-u[ser],-m[achine],-en[terprise]}] -chgpset
```

Abbreviation:

```
-cp
```

Example:

```
Caspol -u -cp mynewpset.xml MyPset
```

This Caspol command changes the MyPset to the permission set state represented by the mynewpset.xml file.

NOTE

Please see the "Adding a New Permission Set" section earlier in this chapter for some helpful tips and notes.

Removing a Permission Set

Removing a permission set from a policy level will require you to re-import it if you need to use it later to build a new code group. Consequently, you should only remove those permission sets that you are reasonably sure you won't need at a future point. Caspol will not allow you to remove any permission set that is still referenced by a code group at that policy level. You will first either need to delete the code group or code groups referencing the permission set or change the code group(s) to reference a different permission set. When removing a permission set, you may also be able to remove assemblies from the policy assemblies list that were only added to support the implementation of a custom permission type in the deleted permission set.

NOTE

See the "Removing an Assembly from the Policy Assemblies List" section later in this chapter for more information about removing entries from the Policy Assemblies list.

The following is the syntax to remove a permission set.

Syntax:

```
[{-u[ser],-m[achine],-en[terprise]}] -rempset pset_name
```

Abbreviation:

```
-rp
```

Example:

```
Caspol -user -rempset Everything
```

This command will remove the Everything permission set from the user policy list of known permission sets.

Adding an Assembly to the Policy Assembly List

The Policy Assembly list contains all the assemblies required to implement custom security objects of a policy level. For example, if a custom membership condition was used in the code group hierarchy of the user level policy, the user level Policy Assembly list must hold the assembly (and all assemblies it depends on) that implements the new membership condition. You do not need to add anything here if you are strictly using security policy types that ship with the .NET Framework.

Syntax:

```
[{-u[ser],-m[achine],-en[terprise]}] -addfulltrust file
```

Abbreviation:

```
-af
```

Example:

```
Caspol -machine -af customperm.dll
```

This Caspol line adds the `customperm.dll` assembly to the Policy Assembly list.

> **NOTE**
>
> The name of this Caspol switch contains `fulltrust` because all assemblies added to this list are fully trusted at that policy level. This is necessary for policy resolution not to result in circularity problems. Consequently, it is important that you always add all the assemblies required to implement a custom security object used at a policy level to that policy level's list of Policy Assemblies.

Removing an Assembly from the Policy Assemblies List

After a custom security object is no longer used at a policy level, you can remove all the assemblies required to implement this custom security object from the Policy Assembly list.

> **CAUTION**
>
> Be careful which assemblies you remove from this list. If you remove any assembly that another type currently used in the security policy depends on, you may bring the security system to a halt. This is a place were you should err on the side of caution. If in doubt, leave the assembly in the list.

Syntax:

```
[{-u[ser],-m[achine],-en[terprise]}] -remfulltrust file
```

Abbreviation:

```
-rf
```

Example:

```
Caspol -u -rf MyCustomCodeGroup.dll
```

> **NOTE**
>
> This example presumes that `MyCustomCodeGroup.dll` is in the path from which Capsol is running.

Showing the Permissions or Code Groups Applicable to an Assembly

Caspol has a couple options designed to help you analyze problems with policy settings or quickly find out whether a specific policy change works as intended. You can determine the permissions applicable to an assembly or the code groups applying to it.

Use the following command to determine the permissions an assembly would be granted from one or all policy levels:

Syntax:

```
[{-u[ser],-m[achine],-en[terprise],-a[ll]}] -resolveperm file
```

Abbreviation:

```
-rsp
```

Example:

```
Caspol -m -resolveperm myassembly.exe
```

Likewise, you can determine the code groups that an assembly receives from a specific or all policy levels:

Syntax:

```
[{-u[ser],-m[achine],-en[terprise],-a[ll]}] -resolvegroup file
```

Abbreviation:

```
-rsg
```

Example:

```
Caspol -en -rsg MyAssembly.exe
```

You should use both of these options (or the equivalent options in the .NET Framework Configuration tool) if the security policy does not seem to grant an assembly the level of trust you expected.

NOTE

Sometimes, an assembly may receive a sufficient level of trust to run as expected by policy as indicated by the -rsp and -rsg resolves, but still generate a security exception. This may be the case either because the assembly itself may be annotated to require a specific level of permissions that policy is not giving it. Alternatively, it may be annotated to refuse permissions to access a resource that it later indeed tries to access. The former can be helped administratively by increasing the permissions given to the assembly in question. The latter is a programming error administrators will not be able to do anything about. Use the `permview` tool to see what permissions an assembly requires or refuses (see the SDK for more detail). Alternatively, if problems persist, it could also be that the assembly in question depends on other assemblies to whom you haven't given the required level of trust.

Turning Off Security

It is possible to switch security completely off using the Caspol tool. This switch is only available if you have write access to the local machine's registry system (usually reserved for power users and machine administrators). You should never really need to use this switch, unless you must squeeze a few more milliseconds of performance out of the .NET Framework Common Language Runtime and run on an isolated, secure machine.

CAUTION

Again, this is probably the singlemost dangerous option of Caspol. All bets are off when you have turned security to off!

Syntax:

```
-security {on | off}
```

Abbreviation:

```
-s
```

Example:

```
Caspol -s off
```

Resetting Security Policy

The default security policy has been designed to represent a known safe state that is as permissive as possible without opening undue security holes. It has been designed to protect against mobile code abusing resources on your machine, so it consigns assemblies from the local intranet to execute within a tightly protected security context, while requiring you to explicitly add permissions for any assembly you wish to run off the Internet. In case you have made administrative changes to security policy that you have become unsure of, it may often be advisable to start over with the known safe default policy settings as opposed to trying to fix policy. To return to the default policy state, simply use the following Caspol option:

Syntax:

```
[{-u[ser],-m[achine],-en[terprise],-a[ll]}] -reset
```

Abbreviation:

```
-rs
```

Example:

```
Caspol -all -reset
```

This example will return the security policy to its default policy state by resetting all policy levels.

Undoing the Latest Policy Change

Caspol creates a backup copy of the latest policy change you have made. In the case that you have mistyped some information or decided that the latest change was a mistake, you can easily revert to the policy state prior to the last Caspol command that changed security policy.

Syntax:

```
-recover
```

Abbreviation:

```
-r
```

Example:

```
Caspol -r
```

Caspol's Self-Protection Mechanism and How to Override It

Because Caspol is itself a managed application, it is subject to the .NET Framework security policy system, just like any other assembly. It is possible to change the security policy to a state in which Caspol would not run anymore. Consequently, Caspol has a self-protection mechanism built in that will check whether a specific command would prevent the Caspol tool from running again. Prefacing your policy change with the following switch will force Caspol to accept the policy change despite the fact that it may not be able to run afterwards.

Syntax:

```
-force
```

Abbreviation:

-f

Example:

```
Caspol -f -u -cg All_Code Nothing
```

This command will set the root code group of the user policy level to grant no permissions. Assuming user policy is in the default state, no assemblies—including the Caspol tool—will receive any permissions, because all policy levels are intersected. Without using the -force option, the previous command will not succeed on the default policy because the .NET Framework Configuration tool will recognize it could not run anymore. If you want the command to succeed anyway, you need to use -f[orce].

NOTE

There are a few more Caspol options that have not been explained so far. All of these are of little interest for policy scripting. The -execution directive can be used to turn off the security system's assembly load time check whether an assembly is allowed to execute; if turned off, the check will take place the first time an assembly tries to access a protected resource. The -buildcache option will cause the security system to update its policy cache for potentially better performance, while the -customuser and -customall directives can be used to model policy changes. Use the /? option to get more help, or refer to the SDK documentation of this tool.

Caspol in Action—Scripts, Hints, and Tricks

Caspol has most administrative features that the .NET Framework Configuration tool offers. By putting together the previously discussed individual Caspol commands, you can write an indefinite number of powerful scripts to change security to a new state, automating complex policy changes. The following are a few helpful hints you should consider:

- Use the policy level directives to explicitly state whether you want to make a change to the machine or user policy level. Relying on Caspol to default commands to the machine level when the user has sufficient access rights to policy is risky, because this may lead to accidental changes of user policy levels for users who do not have write access to the machine and enterprise policy levels.

- If you want the state of policy after your script to be in a fully known, predicted state, don't be afraid to do a policy reset first, giving you a known safe starting point for your script.

- Any code group changes or additions should be made using code group names and not their numeric labels. Numeric labels will get reordered as soon as a new code group is introduced or a code group gets deleted.

- Turn the policy change prompt off on your first script line unless you are absolutely certain that the machine running the script already had Caspol -pp off run on it.

- Don't remove any assemblies from the Policy Assemblies list unless you are absolutely certain they are not needed by any type used to implement the code group hierarchy or a permission set.

- Always give your newly introduced code groups a name if you expect to be scripting against them at a later point.

- Remember that removing a code group from the code group hierarchy will destroy the code group and all code groups beneath it.

- You should get in the habit of annotating your newly introduced code groups or permission sets with a description. This will make it easier to remember what you intended them to accomplish when you have to debug policy issues later.

- For importing a new permission set via Caspol, use the .NET Framework Configuration tool to build the new permission set and simply cut and paste the requisite XML from the policy file into a separate XML file.

- If you changed security policy so that neither Caspol or the GUI tool still run, just delete the policy configuration files to get back to a default policy state. See Chapter 18 for file location information.

- Don't turn off security if you have issues getting an assembly to run; do a more targeted policy update.

- Remember that a batch script is not transacted, so if any failures occur during script execution, you may end up with policy changed, but only partially to the state you intended.

- Use the GUI tool whenever you can because its graphical representation of the security system is more intuitive than dealing with a command-line representation of hierarchical code group arrangements.

- Be careful in the introduction of exclusive code groups. If more than one exclusive code group applies to an assembly, the policy system will throw an exception and the assembly will not be able to run.

- Test your scripts thoroughly before large scale deployment.

It's now time to pull together the various Caspol options previously introduced and present a few sample scripts.

The following script first turns off the policy change warning, and then resets all policy levels to their default state. After that, it restricts the permissions of all assemblies coming from the intranet:

```
Caspol -pp off
Caspol -all -reset
Caspol -m -ag LocalIntranet_Zone -strong -file myassembly.exe
        -noname -noversion FullTrust -n MySNgroup
Caspol -m -cg LocalIntranet_Zone Execution
```

First, resetting policy is of interest if you need to fully guarantee the shape of policy after your script executed, excluding any previous customizations. A code group is added under the LocalIntranet_Zone code group giving all assemblies signed with the strong name on `myassembly.exe` full trust to access all protected resources. Finally, the permission set handed out by the LocalInteraet_Zone code group is reduced to the Execution permission set, just allowing assemblies to compute without any further access to resources. In essence, the previous script cranks down the permissions for all assemblies from the intranet with the exception of the assemblies signed by the `myassembly.exe` strong name. Those assemblies would be fully trusted.

The following is another example:

```
Caspol -pp off
Caspol -m -ag LocalIntranet_Zone
        -url file:///\\mymachine\* FullTrust -n MyFullTrustShare
Caspol -m -ag Internet_Zone -site www.aw.com Nothing -exclusive on -n NoTrustToEvil
```

This example gives a share on the intranet full trust to access protected resources, while enforcing that no assemblies coming from the www.aw.com should run.

```
Caspol -pp off
Caspol -en -reset
Caspol -en -ag All_Code -pub
        -file mysignedfile.exe Internet -levelfinal on -n Trustcert
Caspol -en -ag Trustcert -strong -file myfile.exe FullTrust -n TrustCertandSN
Caspol -en -ag Trustcert -strong -file my2ndfile.exe intranet -n TrustCertandSN2
Caspol -en -ag All_Code -zone intranet Nothing -n IntranetZone
Caspol -en -ag All_Code -strong -file Caspol.exe -noname -noversion FullTrust-n
➥Caspol
Caspol -en -cg All_Code Nothing
```

This sample deletes all changes that may have been made on the enterprise policy on the client machine. Policy is then set up to give FullTrust to all assemblies signed both with the authenticode signature found on `mysignedfile.exe` and the strong name found on `myfile`, while assemblies signed with the same authenticode signature but with the strong name on `my2ndfile.exe` receive only intranet permissions. Because the Trustcert code group is level final, no policy levels below the enterprise level will interfere with the permission grant from policy for all assemblies signed with that authenticode signature. Enterprise policy is further changed to not allow any assemblies from the intranet to run (except for the assemblies signed with the previously added signatures). To continue to make the Caspol tool function when called from the intranet, a code group based on Caspol's strong name is added, while the All_Code group is changed to give the Nothing permission set instead of the FullTrust permission set. It is important that this be the last step—if you had begun your script with reducing the permissions granted by the All_Code group, further lines in the script may not have run, because at each invocation of Caspol on each separate script line, the security system checks anew whether Caspol has sufficient rights granted to it to run and access resources, such as the file system, when saving out policy changes.

Changing Security Policy by Programming Directly to the Security APIs

Instead of using a particular tool to alter or view security policy, you can also use the Security classes that ship with the .NET Framework base class library to view or change policy directly. In fact, both the Caspol tool as well as the .NET Framework Configuration tool have been implemented using these classes. To solve everyday administrative tasks, it will be very unlikely that you need to make use of these APIs, but the following are some situations in which access to these classes will be necessary:

- You want to write your own policy administration tool.

- You want to write a policy analysis tool that checks for policy invariants particular to your business or home situation.

- You want to write an alternative security scripting system.

- You want to integrate custom security objects into live policy by creating and setting state on the custom security objects programmatically, as opposed to creating an XML serialization file representing the state you want (the only way the tools currently allow you to add custom security objects).

- You are simply curious how the security model is implemented.

The rest of this chapter will introduce you to the most relevant security objects and how to use them. You can use this section as a starting point for satisfying any of the previous situations.

> **NOTE**
>
> For more information about the security objects, please consult the .NET Framework SDK. You may also want to check www.gotdotnet.com. This site contains a security section dedicated to the .NET Framework security system, and the .NET Framework security team may have posted helpful samples and papers there by the time this book appears in print.

Overview of the Security Classes Used for Policy Changes

The overall security model that you have learned about in the first section of this book (especially Chapters in 5–8) is still relevant in discussing the particular classes you can use to change security policy. Indeed, you will see that the class structure maps very well to the underlying security model to which you have been introduced.

The security classes that implement the security model can be found in the following namespaces:

- System.Security—This namespace contains the SecurityManager class from which you can access the policy levels of current security policy. Among other things, the namespace also contains the base classes for permission types, as well as the NamedPermissionSet class. You will access the latter class when viewing or modifying the known named permission sets at a policy level.

- System.Security.Policy—This namespace largely contains the classes implementing the policy system. Specifically, it contains the PolicyLevel class implementing a policy level. From the policy level class, you can access a hierarchy of code groups, a list of named permission sets (see the NamedPermissionSet type in System.Security), as well as the Policy Assemblies list. This namespace contains the base class for all code groups and some specific code group implementations. Most notably, it contains the UnionCodeGroup class that represents the code group type used to implement most of default policy. The namespace also contains the interface definition of membership conditions (IMembershipCondition) and the implementations of the standard membership condition types shipped in the .NET Framework (URL, zone, site, hash, publisher certificate, strong name, application directory and all code).

- `System.Security.Permissions`—This namespace contains the class implementations of most of the standard permissions shipping with the .NET Framework. This namespace also contains the implementation of the respective security custom attribute classes for using these permissions declaratively.

NOTE

Not all permissions shipping with the .NET Framework are contained in the `System.Security.Permissions` namespace. This namespace mostly has the implementation of the permissions protecting core runtime resources. Other permissions will be located in the namespace that implements and defines the protected resources. For example, the permissions governing access to networking resources are contained in the `System.NET` namespace. By searching the SDK for the keyword "permission," you will be able to find out all the permission types shipping in the SDK, as well as other helpful information regarding the implementation of your own permission type.

Examples of Using the Security Classes for Accessing and Changing Policy

This section will show you how to solve some of the standard policy analysis or policy change tasks. You can use the code shown in this section as a starting point. For complete coverage of the types used, please see the SDK reference documentation.

The class from which you will start all your policy change and analysis tasks is the `SecurityManager` class. Its static methods and properties provide the interface to the current security policy state of your machine. From the `SecurityManager`, you can get access to policy levels, as well as save policy changes that you have done programmatically.

Resolving Evidence Against Current Security Policy

A common task you may want to do is to find out what permissions the security policy would grant an assembly that had certain forms of evidence. You can simulate this situation by using the `SecurityManager`. The `SecurityManager` object has a static member method (`ResolvePolicy(Evidence)`) that allows you to pass in an evidence object and receive back a permission set object representing the policy resolution against the evidence you have provided. In Listing 19.1, the XML serialization of the permission set returned by the policy resolution given your evidence input is printed to the console.

LISTING 19.1   Calculating the Permissions Granted by Policy Based on Specific Evidence
Set Resolve.cs

```csharp
using System;
using System.Security;
using System.Security.Policy;
using System.IO;



class Resolve
{

    static void Main(string[] args)
    {
        Zone zoneevidence = new Zone(System.Security.SecurityZone.intranet);
        Site siteevidence = new Site("www.test.com");
        //create evidence object
        Evidence evidence = new Evidence();
        //setting assembly evidence
        evidence.AddHost(zoneevidence);
        evidence.AddHost(siteevidence);
        PermissionSet result=SecurityManager.ResolvePolicy(evidence);
        //printing the XML serialization of the returned permission set
        Console.WriteLine(result.ToXml().ToString());

        String t = Console.ReadLine();
    }



}
```

NOTE

To compile the listings given in this chapter, save the source code into a *filename*.cs file. To run the the C# compiler from the command line, type in the following:

%Windows%\Microsoft.NET\Framework\v[version number]\csc.exe filename.cs

%Windows% stands for the installation directory of Windows on your machine, version stands for the Framework version installed on your machine, and filename is the name of the file into which you saved the preceding code listing.

Resolving Evidence Against a Specific Policy Level

The `SecurityManager` class provides an enumeration of the policy levels. This enumeration, of type `IEnumerable`, is used to access and change a particular policy level. Note that this is why the `ICollections` namespace is included in this sample. The policy level enumerator returned by `SecurityManager` stores the policy levels in the following order:

1. Enterprise policy

2. Machine policy

3. User policy

4. Appdomain policy (if present)

In the following example, we move the enumerator to the machine policy level and call the `Resolve(Evidence)` method on that level to get the set of permissions that this level would grant an assembly with the provided evidence. Note that we do not get a `PermissionSet` object back but something called a `PolicyStatement`. A `PolicyStatement` is nothing more than a permission set plus a couple of attributes: the level final and exclusive attributes, to be precise.

> **NOTE**
>
> When a level final attribute is encountered, policy evaluation stops at the respective policy level; no policy levels below the one containing the level final attribute are evaluated. In order to capture the information that a level final attribute was encountered during the evaluation of a policy level, the return type of a policy resolution over a policy level needs to return more than a permission set which only consists of a list of permissions. The return type also needs to state whether the level final attribute was encountered. This is the reason why policy levels return a `PolicyStatement` rather than a simple permission set, which captures exactly that information.

The code in Listing 19.2 demonstrates how to construct an evidence set for which to do policy resolution. It then shows you how to access the machine policy level and resolve against the constructed evidence set.

LISTING 19.2   Enumeration of the Policy Levels—`Resolvelevel.cs`

```
using System;
using System.Security;
using System.Security.Policy;
using System.Security.Permissions;
using System.IO;
using System.Collections;
```

LISTING 19.2   Continued

```
class Resolve
{
    static void Main(string[] args)
    {
        Zone zoneevidence = new Zone(System.Security.SecurityZone.intranet);
        Site siteevidence = new Site("www.microsoft.com");
        //create evidence object
        Evidence evidence = new Evidence();
        evidence.AddHost(zoneevidence);
        evidence.AddHost(siteevidence);
        //getting policy levels enumerator
        IEnumerator policylevels=SecurityManager.PolicyHierarchy();
        //moving to machine policy level
        policylevels.MoveNext();
        policylevels.MoveNext();
        PolicyStatement policystatement =
            ((PolicyLevel)policylevels.Current).Resolve(evidence);
        //Printing machine policy resolution results
        Console.WriteLine(policystatement.PermissionSet.ToString());

        String t = Console.ReadLine();
    }
}
```

Building and Adding a New Named Permission Set to a Policy Level

To add a new permission set to a policy level, you need to create an instance of the
NamedPermissionSet class and add permission instances to it that represent the
specific level of trust you want this permission set to express. After you have
constructed the permission set, you simply need to call the AddPermissionSet
method on a policy level with the newly constructed permission set and save the
policy changes. Listing 19.3 demonstrates this for you. A reference to the
System.Security.Permission namespace has been added to use the
UIPermermission class without having to fully qualify the classname.

> **NOTE**
>
> The constructor of the NamedPermissionSet class requiring only a string as argument will set
> the permission set to the unrestricted state. To start with a permission set state to which you
> can still further add permissions, you need to use the overload that takes both the name and
> a PermissionState argument, where the permission state is set to nothing (Listing 19.3 is an
> example of using that overload).

LISTING 19.3   Adding a New Permission Set—AddNewPset.cs

```csharp
using System;
using System.Security;
using System.Security.Policy;
using System.Security.Permissions;
using System.IO;
using System.Collections;



    class NewPermissionSet
    {

        static void Main(string[] args)
        {
            //create new NamedPermissionSet instance
                        NamedPermissionSet pset = new
      NamedPermissionSet("ClipBoardPset",PermissionState.None);

            //expressing unrestricted permission to do UI
                                        pset.AddPermission(new
                    UIPermission(UIPermissionClipboard.AllClipboard));
            //getting policy levels enumerator
            IEnumerator policylevels=SecurityManager.PolicyHierarchy();
            //moving to machine policy level
            policylevels.MoveNext();
            policylevels.MoveNext();
            PolicyLevel machinepolicy = (PolicyLevel)(policylevels.Current);
            //add the new permission set
            machinepolicy.AddNamedPermissionSet(pset);
            //Save the changes
            SecurityManager.SavePolicy();


        }



    }
```

NOTE

The SecurityManager.SavePolicy() call will fail if the user context in which this line of code is run does not have write access to the respective policy level. If you are not certain that your code will be run on behalf of users that have the appropriate access to the policy levels, you should surround the SavePolicy call with a try-catch exception handling clause.

Removing a Permission Set from a Policy Level

Removing a permission set is simply a matter of supplying the respective permission set name and calling the RemoveNamedPermissionSet method on the policy level object. This is demonstrated in Listing 19.4:

LISTING 19.4   Removing a Permission Set—Rempset.cs

```
using System;
using System.Security;
using System.Security.Policy;
using System.IO;
using System.Collections;


    class Rempset
    {

        static void Main(string[] args)
        {
            IEnumerator policylevels=SecurityManager.PolicyHierarchy();
            //moving to machine policy level
            policylevels.MoveNext();
            policylevels.MoveNext();
            PolicyLevel machinepolicy = (PolicyLevel)(policylevels.Current);
            //remove permission set
            machinepolicy.RemoveNamedPermissionSet("ClipBoardPset");
            //Save the changes
            SecurityManager.SavePolicy();
        }


    }
```

TIP

To check the state of policy before and after running the sample code, you may want to use the -lg, -lp, and -ld options of Caspol.

Changing a Permission Set

Permission sets can easily be changed. You only need to create a new permission set and pass it into the ChangeNamedPermissionSet method on the PolicyLevel object. It will return the newly created named permission set, as shown in Listing 19.5.

LISTING 19.5   Change a Permission Set—`ChgPset.cs`

```
using System;
using System.Security;
using System.Security.Policy;
using System.Security.Permissions;
using System.IO;
using System.Collections;


  class ChangePset
  {

      static void Main(string[] args)
      {
          PermissionSet pset = new PermissionSet(PermissionState.None);
          pset.AddPermission(new UIPermission(PermissionState.Unrestricted));

          IEnumerator policylevels=SecurityManager.PolicyHierarchy();
          //moving to machine policy level
          policylevels.MoveNext();
          policylevels.MoveNext();
          PolicyLevel machinepolicy = (PolicyLevel)(policylevels.Current);
          //change permission set
          NamedPermissionSet namedpset =
              machinepolicy.ChangeNamedPermissionSet("UIPermSet",pset);
          //Save the changes
          SecurityManager.SavePolicy();
      }


  }
```

NOTE

In order for the preceding sample to work, you need to have added a permission set with name UIPermSet to the machine policy. You can do so using the .NET Framework Configuration tool (see Chapter 18 for details on how to use this tool). In the .NET Framework Configuration tool:

1. Expand the Runtime Security Policy node.

2. Expand the Machine node.

3. Right-click on the Permission Sets node and select the New option.

4. Type in UIPermSet as permission set name.

5. Set any permission state for the permission set and finish the wizard.

Now you can run the preceding example.

Adding a Code Group to a Policy Level

Listing 19.6 will add an exclusive code group under the root code group of the
machine policy level. If this sample is run over default security policy, it will have
the effect of disallowing any assemblies from the www.aw.com site to execute and
access any protected resources.

LISTING 19.6   Add a Code Group—addcg.cs

```
using System;
using System.Security;
using System.Security.Policy;
using System.Security.Permissions;
using System.IO;
using System.Collections;


class AddCodeGroup
{

    static void Main(string[] args)
    {
        //getting the policy level enumerator
        IEnumerator policylevels=SecurityManager.PolicyHierarchy();
        //moving to machine policy level
        policylevels.MoveNext();
        policylevels.MoveNext();
        PolicyLevel machinepolicy = (PolicyLevel)(policylevels.Current);
        //getting the root code group of the code group hierarchy
        CodeGroup rootcg = machinepolicy.RootCodeGroup;
        //creating a site membership condition for the new code group
        SiteMembershipCondition sitemship =
            new SiteMembershipCondition("www.aw.com");
        //get the intranet permission set from the permission set list of the machine
➥policy
        PermissionSet pset =
            machinepolicy.GetNamedPermissionSet("Nothing");
        //Creating the policy statement, including the Nothing permission set
        //making the code group exclusive
        PolicyStatement policystatement =
            new PolicyStatement(pset,PolicyStatementAttribute.Exclusive);
        //create the new code group
        //with the new membership condition and policystatement
        UnionCodeGroup newcg =
```

LISTING 19.6   Continued

```
        new UnionCodeGroup(sitemship,policystatement);
    //add the new code group under the root code group
    rootcg.AddChild(newcg);
    machinepolicy.RootCodeGroup = rootcg;
    //Save the changes
    SecurityManager.SavePolicy();
 }
```

Removing a Code Group from a Policy Level

To remove a child code group from a code group, you need to iterate through the children on that code group until you find the code group you want to delete. You then pass a reference to that code group to the RemoveChild method on the parent code group. Listing 19.7 shows you how to delete a code group under the root code group of the machine policy.

LISTING 19.7   Remove a Code Group—remcg.cs

```
using System;
using System.Security;
using System.Security.Policy;
using System.Security.Permissions;
using System.IO;
using System.Collections;


class RemCodeGroup
{
    static void Main(string[] args)
    {
        //getting the policy level enumerator
        IEnumerator policylevels=SecurityManager.PolicyHierarchy();
        //moving to machine policy level
        policylevels.MoveNext();
        policylevels.MoveNext();
        PolicyLevel machinepolicy = (PolicyLevel)(policylevels.Current);
        //getting the root code group of the code group hierarchy
        CodeGroup rootcg = machinepolicy.RootCodeGroup;
        //getting all the child code groups pf the root code group
        IEnumerator rootchildren = (rootcg.Children).GetEnumerator();
```

LISTING 19.7   Continued

```
        //finding and removing the test code group
        while(rootchildren.MoveNext())
        {
            if(((CodeGroup)(rootchildren.Current)).Name=="test")
            {
                CodeGroup codegroup = (CodeGroup)rootchildren.Current;
                //remove the code group
                rootcg.RemoveChild(codegroup);
                //save it
                SecurityManager.SavePolicy();
            }
        }

    }

}
```

The preceding code only iterates through the child code groups under the root code group of the machine policy level. You will need to extend the preceding code if you want to delete a code group at an arbitrary location in the code group tree. In that case, your code should do a recursive tree search for the respective code group. Remember that the code group tree can be irregular. Also, as will be explained in the following section, if you modify any code groups that are not direct children of the root code group, you will need to re-create the affected subsection of the tree (see the following section).

Changing the Properties of a Code Group

There is unfortunately no method you can call that will change the property of a referred code group directly. Instead, you need to perform the following steps:

1. Iterate through the code group hierarchy until you find the code group you want to alter.

2. Store a reference to that code group in a local variable.

3. Delete the code group from the parent's set of code group using the `RemoveChildCodeGroup` method.

4. Modify the properties of the locally stored code group (or simply create a new one).

5. Add the new code group to the parent's list of code groups using the add method.

6. If the parent code group is not the root code group, you will need to repeat this procedure for the parent code group (save the parent code group locally, remove it from the list of code groups of its parent, and add it back in using the AddChild method). You need to repeat this until you hit the root code group.

The reason for this elaborate set of steps is the fact that except for the root code group, you are never given a direct reference to the actual code groups constituting policy, but rather a copy of the code groups.

> **NOTE**
>
> Note that the previous steps imply that the order of child code groups does not matter. This only holds for code groups whose evaluation semantics does not rely on the order of its child code groups, such as the UnionCodeGroup used throughout default policy. For a more general solution, you need to preserve the order of code groups, so remove and add in all child code groups in the order you found them before modifying one of them.

Listing 19.8 demonstrates how to modify the properties of a child code group of the root of machine policy.

LISTING 19.8   Change a Code Group—chgcg.cs

```csharp
using System;
using System.Security;
using System.Security.Policy;
using System.Security.Permissions;
using System.IO;
using System.Collections;


class ChangeCodeGroup
{
    static void Main(string[] args)
    {
        //getting the policy level enumerator
        IEnumerator policylevels=SecurityManager.PolicyHierarchy();
        //moving to machine policy level
        policylevels.MoveNext();
        policylevels.MoveNext();
        PolicyLevel machinepolicy = (PolicyLevel)(policylevels.Current);
        //getting the root code group of the code group hierarchy
        CodeGroup rootcg = machinepolicy.RootCodeGroup;
```

LISTING 19.8   Continued

```
        //getting all the child code groups pf the root code group
        IEnumerator rootchildren = (rootcg.Children).GetEnumerator();

        //finding and changing the internet zone code group
        bool found=false;
        bool listend=false;
        while(rootchildren.MoveNext())
        {

            if(((CodeGroup)(rootchildren.Current)).Name=="Internet_Zone")
            {
                //make a copy of the code group to change
                CodeGroup codegroup = (CodeGroup)rootchildren.Current;
                //delete the code group to be changed from policy
                rootcg.RemoveChild(codegroup);
                //get the new permission set for this code group
                PermissionSet pset =
                    machinepolicy.GetNamedPermissionSet("Nothing");
                //wrapped into a policy statement, that would allow for change
                //of code group flags also
                codegroup.PolicyStatement=new PolicyStatement(pset);
                codegroup.Description="Changed code group";
                //add code group back in, this will not preserver cg order!!
                //you will have to remove and add in all children of a cg if you
                //need to preserve code group order
                rootcg.AddChild(codegroup);
                machinepolicy.RootCodeGroup = rootcg;
                //save it
                SecurityManager.SavePolicy();


            }
        }
    }


}
```

The key steps in Listing 19.8 is the removal of the code group to be changed using the RemoveChild method, the subsequent modification of the code group, and the re-addition of the modified code group to the machine policy.

Adding an Assembly to the Policy Assemblies List

As you will remember from Chapters 8 and 18, the Policy Assemblies list is used to keep a list of all the assemblies required to implement security objects that appear in the code group hierarchy or permission sets of a policy level. All assemblies in this list must be strong named and in the Global Assembly Cache (GAC). Consequently, to add a specific assembly to this cache programmatically, you will need to get the strong name of that assembly. To do so, the following sample in Listing 19.9 uses the AssemblyName's static GetAssemblyName method that returns an assembly name. The assembly name, in turn, contains the version, name, and strong name public key token of the assembly to be added to the Policy Assemblies list.

LISTING 19.9   Add to a Policy Assembly List—addtopolylist.cs

```
using System;
using System.Security;
using System.Security.Policy;
using System.Security.Permissions;
using System.Collections;
using System.Reflection;


class AddToPolicyAssemblies
{

    static void Main(string[] args)
    {
        //getting the policy level enumerator
        IEnumerator policylevels=SecurityManager.PolicyHierarchy();
        //moving to enterprise policy level
        policylevels.MoveNext();
        PolicyLevel entpolicy = (PolicyLevel)(policylevels.Current);
        //creating the strongname for the assembly to add
        AssemblyName aname = AssemblyName.GetAssemblyName("Caspol.exe ");
        //by first creating the strong name public key blob type instance
        StrongNamePublicKeyBlob spt =
                new StrongNamePublicKeyBlob(aname.GetPublicKeyToken());
        //using that and the assembly name and version
        //to create a strong name instance
        StrongName sn = new StrongName(spt,aname.Name,aname.Version);
        //adding the assembly identified by sn to the policy assemblies list
        entpolicy.AddFullTrustAssembly(sn);
        //save the changes
        SecurityManager.SavePolicy();
```

LISTING 19.9   Continued

```
    }

}
```

NOTE

Use the `RemoveFullTrustAssembly` method to remove an assembly from the Policy Assemblies list.

The two key points to remember are to first create an instance of the `StrongName` class that contains the strong name of the assembly you want to add to the Policy Assemblies list. Subsequently, you need to use the `StrongName` instance as argument to the `AddFullTrustAssembly` method, which will add the strong name reference to the policy assemblies list.

Resetting a Policy Level to Its Default State

To reset a policy level, simply call the `Reset` method on the level you want to bring back to the default security policy state. If you want to go back to the default security policy state of the .NET Framework, simply call the `Reset` method on all policy levels. After your reset calls, you still need to save the change by calling the `SavePolicy` method on the `SecurityManager` class. Listing 19.10 demonstrates how to reset the enterprise policy level to its default policy state.

LISTING 19.10   Reset a Policy Level—resetpol.cs

```
using System;
using System.Security;
using System.Security.Policy;
using System.Collections;


    class Resetpol
    {
        static void Main(string[] args)
        {
            //getting the policy level enumerator
            IEnumerator policylevels=SecurityManager.PolicyHierarchy();
            //moving to enterprise policy level
            policylevels.MoveNext();
            PolicyLevel entpolicy = (PolicyLevel)(policylevels.Current);
            //calling the reset method on the PolicyLevel object
```

LISTING 19.10   Continued

```
                //this will cause the policy level to revert its default state
                entpolicy.Reset();
                //save the changes
                SecurityManager.SavePolicy();
        }


    }
```

The main point to remember when doing a reset on a policy level is to not forget to actually save the policy changes by calling the SavePolicy method on the SecurityManager class.

Summary

The security model implemented in the .NET Framework is extremely rich. It allows for an indefinite fine tuning of permissions to access protected resources on a per-assembly basis. To change security policy into a state that correctly categorizes assemblies into various levels of trust, you have not only the .NET Framework Configuration tool at your disposal but also two ways of programmatically effecting security policy modifications. You have been introduced to Caspol, with which you can write batch scripts of high complexity. But you can go far beyond that and implement your own policy administration and analysis tools, using the policy APIs introduced in this chapter. All three forms of changing policy introduced so far—Caspol, the GUI tool, as well as the policy APIs—are just different faces of the .NET Framework Security model.

20

Administering an IIS Machine Using ASP.NET

By Kevin Price

By now, you should be aware that IIS and ASP.NET provide multiple ways to manage certain aspects of security with configuration files. While this practice may seem to hearken back to the days of .ini files, the means and scale of what can be accomplished has grown exponentially. Using configuration files takes a level of fear out of site configuration, because everything is stored in a flat text file as opposed to the Windows registry. This also has the added bonus of not requiring the server to be rebooted or restarted when a change is made; .NET automatically polls for changes and applies them as they are made to the file. Currently, the only GUI tool for editing these files is an XML editor, because that's exactly what these files are. Through the use of the intrinsic hierarchical nature of XML, configuration files can hide and/or expose functionality based on the file's contents. The main file discussed in this chapter will be the web.config file. This file is generated by default whenever a Web project is created within the Visual Studio.NET development environment. It is parsed by the CLR and can be used to determine such items as user permissions, actions, or *verbs* allowed on the Web server and remoting. By the end of this chapter, you will be able to

- Modify the web.config file to force user authentication, regardless of IIS settings

- Know the security hierarchy in relation to web.config, child directory configuration, and machine.config files

- Establish security using XML-based configuration files

XML-Based Configuration Files

First, the chapter will review the basics regarding .NET configuration files. It's like the old saying goes, "In order to break the rules, you have to know the rules." This section will provide an overview of what is essential to using the config file type to manage your applications that run under IIS, and how to control certain aspects of behavior that typically have been managed by IIS. It is important to remember that all of these files are not only case sensitive, but use what's called *camel casing*. Camel casing specifies that the first letter of the first word of each section must be lower-case and the first letter of any concatenated words must be uppercase. For example, if we were going to define a section called "My Configuration Section" the correct syntax would be `<myConfigurationSection/>`. The only exceptions to this rule are the reserved words `true` and `false`—they must always be lowercase. Additionally, any attribute values must carry what's referred to as *Pascal case*. Pascal case specifies that not only is the first letter of a word used to define an attribute uppercase, so is the first letter of any word concatenated to that name. Based on our previous example, the correct syntax would look like `<MyConfigurationSectionAttribute/>`.

> **NOTE**
>
> It is important to note up front that what is established within a configuration file, such as `web.config`, as far as file access, is only applicable to files that are processed by the `aspnet_isapi.dll` filter (such as `aspx` and `asmx`). What this means is should you attempt to use `web.config` to secure a directory of `.jpg` files and have directory browsing turned on, all users will still be able to see them. This is where IIS security comes in to play. This is discussed later in this chapter in the "IIS Security Settings—A Refresher" section.

Hierarchy of .NET Configuration Files

As far as hierarchy goes, there is none higher than the `machine.config` file. This file can be found in the `%WINDIR%\Microsoft.NET\Framework\[Framework Version]\config\` directory, where `%WINDIR%` is the directory in which your version of Windows is installed and `[Framework Version]` is the version number of the .NET Framework running on your machine; for example, `C:\WINDOWS\Microsoft.NET\Framework\v1.0.3617\config`. From that, each .NET Web application running under IIS will contain a `web.config` file in the root directory. If you remove or never have this `web.config` file, the settings contained within the `machine.config` file will take over. Under this, each child folder can contain a separate `web.config` file that provides specific settings for items and/or functionality within that directory. Figure 20.1 shows a sample of this structure. The settings that globally affect all ASP.NET applications are stored in the `system.web` *sectionGroup* of the `machine.config` file.

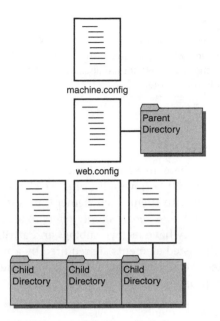

FIGURE 20.1 Configuration file hierarchy.

Within the files, there is another hierarchy that has certain elements that must be present. At the top of this hierarchy is the <configuration> tag. This defines the parent configuration element necessary in all XML-based application files for use with .NET. With ASP.NET, in the web.config file, the next section will be a <system.web> element. The system.web element is unique to ASP.NET and is the root element for ASP.NET configuration. That is not to say that you may only use a system.web element within a web.config file; you will also find one within the machine.config file that indicates the settings specific to ASP.NET on that machine. Listing 20.1 shows the beginning of a web.config file illustrating the <configuration> element as well as the <system.web> element.

LISTING 20.1 Partial web.config File

```
<?xml version="1.0" encoding="utf-8" ?>
<configuration>
 <system.web>
  <compilation defaultLanguage="c#" debug="true" />
```

These elements are also referred to as sectionGroups. Conversely, within a configuration file, the element *system.NET* refers to the configuration of network files.

Attributes and Settings

With respect to ASP.NET, there are several elements made available to you inside the system.web element. Table 20.1 shows a list of these elements and the attributes and/or subtags associated with them. Each element, unless otherwise noted, is explained following the table. A *subtag* simply refers to an element that supports a higher-level element; it may have its own subtags and attributes as well. This does not mean that all of the listed elements are required by any stretch, this is only illustrating the possibilities. Please note that, as indicated, these values are all case sensitive and are shown in proper case.

TABLE 20.1   system.web Elements

Possible Element	Attributes and Subtags
<authentication>	*mode* attribute is required, possible values are Windows, Forms, Passport, and None. Subtags depend on *mode*'s value; <forms> and <passport> are available.
<authorization>	No attributes. Has subtags of <allow> and <deny>. These subtags each carry the attributes of users, verbs, and roles.
<browserCaps>	No attributes. Has subtags of <use>, <filter>, and <result>.
<clientTarget>	No attributes. Has subtags of <add>, <clear>, and <remove>.
<compilation>	Has attributes of debug, defaultLanguage, explicit, batch, batchTimeout, maxBatchGeneratedFileSize, maxBatchFileSize, numRecompilesBeforeApprestart, strict, and tempDirectory. Has subtags of <compilers> and <assemblies>.
<customErrors>	*mode* attribute is required, defaultRedirect attribute is optional. Has the <error> subtag.
<globalization>	Has the optional attributes of requestEncoding, responseEncoding, fileEncoding, culture, and uiCulture.
<httpHandlers>	No attributes. Has subtags of <add>, <remove>, and <clear>.
<httpModules>	No attributes. Has subtags of <add>, <remove>, and <clear>.
<httpRuntime>	Has optional attributes of appRequestQueueLimit, executionTimeout, maxRequestLength, minFreeLocalRequestFreeThreads, minFreeThreads, and useFullyQualifiedRedirectUrl.
<identity>	Has three attributes—impersonate, userName, and password.
<iisFilter>	No attributes. Used only for Windows Management Interface (WMI).

TABLE 20.1   Continued

Possible Element	Attributes and Subtags
`<machineKey>`	Has three required attributes—`validationKey`, `decryptionKey`, and `validation`.
`<pages>`	Has six optional attributes—`buffer`, `enableSessionState`, `enableViewState`, `pageBaseType`, `userControlBaseType`, and `autoEventWireup`.
`<processModel>`	Has 22 optional attributes, all related to the configuration of IIS properties that are currently manageable through the IIS MMC. .NET's managed code system *does not* read these settings, so the server must be restarted for any changes to go into effect here. This element is not used under IIS 6 and is not discussed in this chapter. For more information, see the .NET Framework SDK documentation.
`<securityPolicy>`	No attributes. Has the subtag of `<trustLevel>`.
`<sessionState>`	Has a required attribute of mode. Has optional attributes of `cookieless`, `timeout`, `stateConnectionString`, and `sqlConnectionString`.
`<trace>`	Has two optional attributes, `autoflush` and `indentsize`.
`<trust>`	Has the required attribute of `level` and an optional attribute of `originUrl`.
`<webServices>`	No attributes. Has subtags of `<protocols>`, `<serviceDescriptionFormatExtensionTypes>`, `<soapExtensionTypes>`, `<soapExtensionReflectorTypes>`, `<soapExtensionImporterTypes>`, and `<wsdlHelpGenerator>`.

The `<authentication>` Element

In short, the authentication element is used to define how users are authenticated within a particular application. As for hierarchy, authentication must be initially set at the root level of an application. All subdirectories will then inherit these settings unless explicitly overridden. Depending on what you set the value of the mode attribute to will define which subtags follow. As shown in Table 20.1, the possible values are `Windows`, `Forms`, `Passport`, and `None`. By setting the value to `Windows`, the CLR will invoke an instance of the `WindowsAuthenticationModule`, which is an *authentication provider*. This provider relies on IIS to provide the correct authentication information. Hence, its availabilities and limitations are that of IIS—Anonymous, Basic authentication, Integrated Windows authentication, and Digest authentication. This method of authenticating users provides quite a great deal of information because an instance of the `WindowsPrincipal` class is created and added to the application context. All of the information contained in the NTFS ACL is then available to your application. This information is exposed in the `WindowsPrincipal` class through the `Identity` property and through the `IsInRole` method. Just as they sound, the `Identity` property will return the currently authenticated username for a context. The `IsInRole` method will return a Boolean indicator regarding the user's membership in a specific Windows user group. Windows authentication is the default method of authentication within the .NET Framework.

The next available value in the list is Forms. Setting the mode value to Forms provides a simple, yet reasonable secure means by which to authenticate users.

> **NOTE**
>
> It cannot be said enough that with all of the information given in this book, almost all of this should still be used in combination with SSL.

Using Forms authentication has all the makings of being the most widely used form of authentication available in .NET. It relies on information stored in the web.config file, not IIS. It does not require information to be stored in a relational database, and it does not require an operating system account for each user.

Forms authentication has its own attributes and subtag as well. After you have selected to use Forms authentication, the next step is to set the *name* attribute to a unique name for the cookie that will be used to store the user information. This can be any valid string of text, but by default is .ASPXAUTH. Obviously, if you plan to run more than one application from the same server, this value should be changed. The next attribute is log inUrl. This value represents a placeholder for the URL to redirect a user to where either no cookie is detected or invalid credentials have been given.

After that, there is the protection attribute. It has four possible values—All, None, Encryption, and Validation. The None option does exactly what it sounds like—nothing. This option leaves user information invalidated and unencrypted in a plain-text cookie; this is not a secure option under any circumstances. The Encryption option encrypts the cookie using either DES or Triple-DES (3DES). This decision is made based on the security-level available to the server. For example, if your server is running 128-bit encryption, you will have use of 3DES; otherwise, DES will be used. While this option does encrypt the data, it does not necessarily prevent such events as a plain text attack where a hacker has used a dictionary attack to determine what the user information inside the cookie is. To help with this is the Validation option. This option uses a Message Authentication Code (MAC) to generate a message that is appended to the user cookie. The purpose of this is to validate that the cookie has not been altered in transit. ASP.NET takes care of checking that entire process out for you when the user returns. The final option uses all of the above except for the None option. Setting this attribute to All will encrypt the data in the cookie and validate it automatically. This, in conjunction with SSL, provides a reasonably secure means of authentication.

After you have chosen the level of protection to use, you may optionally decide to set the timeout attribute. By default, this value is set for 30 minutes and represents the amount of time that can elapse between user requests and when the cookie will expire.

The final attribute is that of `path`. As in most cases related to cookies, path sets where the cookie is stored. The default value is \. Keep in mind that modern browsers are case sensitive when it comes to cookie paths and may not send the cookie back on a request with an invalid path.

The subtag of forms is `<credentials>`. This element is used for defining from where the passwords are going to come. As stated earlier, you do not need a relational database or other file to store user credential information in, but if you are going to, this is where you tell ASP.NET where to find it. `credentials` has one required attribute and that is `passwordFormat` with possible values of `Clear`, `MD5`, and `SHA1`. The value of `passwordFormat` defines which hashing algorithm is used to encrypt the passwords given. If you plan to use this element, keep in mind that the passwords must also be stored in one of these formats as well.

Next in our list is `Passport`. Passport authentication requires that you have a subscribed as a valid passport site. Specific information on how to do this can be found at `http://www.passport.com/business`. Once established, Passport authentication works very similar to Forms authentication, only you are using the Passport server to validate credentials and return a `PassportAuthenticationModule` to your server. After you have this module, you can derive the same `IPrincipal` class that the `WindowsPrincipal` class, previously mentioned, is drawn from and have access to that user's information. The passport element has one required value, `redirectUrl`. This serves the same purpose as that of `log inUrl` under Forms authentication.

The final option, `None`, is exactly that—no authentication of any kind is performed for any resource.

For code samples and detailed information regarding using the authentication element, refer to Chapter 14, "Authentication: Know Who Is Accessing Your Site."

The `<authorization>` Element

The authorization element notifies ASP.NET who is or is not allowed to perform certain actions on a particular site. There are two subtags available—`<allow>` and `<deny>`. Within these two subtags are two optional attributes, `users` and `roles`. The users attributes represents any valid users, where *user* is a name derivable from the Principal class or `Request.ServerVariables("AUTH_USER")`, and if it is an NT logon name, it should be expressed as `DOMAIN\USERNAME`. In addition to this, there are two wildcards that can be used—question mark (?) and the asterisk (*). Setting the users value to * will affect all users; setting it to ? will affect anonymous users.

The next attribute available is *roles*. The roles attribute relates expressly to groups that have been created within the domain or machine. An example of this might be the `Administrators` group or `VS Developers`.

The allow element also has a *verbs* attribute. A verb in this case is an action that can be performed against the Web server. ASP.NET recognizes four verbs—GET, POST, DEBUG, and HEAD.

Although not an incredible amount of options, the potential combinations here are endless. Creating allow and deny combinations do have a "pecking order" though; it is that of whichever rule comes first. ASP.NET will iterate through all of the allow and deny settings until it finds the first rule that matches the current user, and then that rule is applied.

For code samples and detailed information regarding using the authorization element, refer to Chapter 15, "Authorization: Control Who Is Accessing Your Site."

The <browserCaps> Element

While potentially overlooked as an aid in security, knowing what the client's browser capabilities are can help in programmatically determining what kind of security to use, as well as being useful for determining which content to provide.

This element provides a way to extract information from a browser from within the web.config file, similar to the functionality of the browscap.ini file; all of this information is also made available through the ASP.NET intrinsic Request object via the Browser class. Using browserCaps through the web.config file allows you to make runtime decisions before loading a page at all. For an example of use, look at the machine.config file in the .NET install directory. Note also that using this functionality requires some knowledge of regular expressions.

The first subtag available is <use>. use allows you to declare a variable name to the server variable you have requested. For example, Listing 20.2 shows the use element to get the server variable HOST_ADDR as a variable named HostAddress. This becomes useful when writing scripts that will parse this information or when you may be dealing with custom header information.

LISTING 20.2   The browserCaps <use> Element

```
<system.web>
    …configuration elements…
    <browserCaps>
        <use var="HOST_ADDR" as="HostAddress" />
    </browserCaps>
    … more configuration elements…
</system.web>
```

As shown in Listing 20.2, use has two attributes—var and as. The var attribute is the name of the server variable or header you want to retrieve, and as is what you intend to name this variable.

The next subtag is `<filter>`, which is just a container for the subtag `<case>`. This provides similar functionality to the switch statement or the select case statement. The filter element defines a container in which one or more cases are evaluated to determine what values to establish for certain variables you are using. If we look at the example in Listing 20.3, the HTTP_USER_AGENT header is queried and then that information is used to determine what the browser is capable of based on user knowledge.

LISTING 20.3   The browserCaps `<filter>` Element

```
<browserCaps>
     <result type="System.Web.HttpBrowserCapabilities, System.Web" />
     <use var="HTTP_USER_AGENT" />
     browser=Unknown
     version=0.0
     majorversion=0
     minorversion=0
     frames=false
     tables=false
     cookies=false
     backgroundsounds=false
     <filter>
        <case match="^Mozilla[^(]*\(compatible; MSIE
           (?'ver'(?'major'\d+)(?'minor'\.\d+)(?'letters'\w*))
           (?'extra'.*)">
           browser=IE
           version=${ver}
           majorver=${major}
           minorver=${minor}
           <case match="^2\." with="%{version}">
              tables=true
              cookies=true
              backgroundsounds=true
              <case match="2\.5b" with="%{version}">
                 beta=true
              </case>
           </case>
        </case>
     </filter>
</browsercaps>
```

Again, notice how regular expressions have been used to parse the values of version, majorver, and minorver. The result subtag has an attribute of *type* that indicates the class that will be responsible for parsing all of this information. You can create a custom class that implements the System.Web.HttpBrowserCapabilities class or, as this sample shows, just use the prepackaged model. The class shown in this code sample is the same class from which the Request class derives its information. To gather the same information directly from within an .aspx file, look at the sample in Listing 20.4. This sample is available for download from the book's Web site.

LISTING 20.4   Browser Information Through the Request Object

```
HttpBrowserCapabilities bc = Request.Browser;
 Response.Write("<p>Browser Capabilities:</p>");
 Response.Write("Type = " + bc.Type + "<br>");
 Response.Write("Name = " + bc.Browser + "<br>");
 Response.Write("Version = " + bc.Version + "<br>");
 Response.Write("Major Version = " + bc.MajorVersion + "<br>");
 Response.Write("Minor Version = " + bc.MinorVersion + "<br>");
 Response.Write("Platform = " + bc.Platform + "<br>");
 Response.Write("Is Beta Version = " + bc.Beta + "<br>");
 Response.Write("Is Crawler = " + bc.Crawler + "<br>");
 Response.Write("Is AOL = " + bc.AOL + "<br>");
 Response.Write("Is Win16 = " + bc.Win16 + "<br>");
 Response.Write("Is Win32 = " + bc.Win32 + "<br>");
 Response.Write("Does Frames = " + bc.Frames + "<br>");
 Response.Write("Does Tables = " + bc.Tables + "<br>");
 Response.Write("Does Cookies = " + bc.Cookies + "<br>");
 Response.Write("Does VB Script = " + bc.VBScript + "<br>");
 Response.Write("Does JavaScript = " + bc.JavaScript + "<br>");
 Response.Write("Does Java Applets = " + bc.JavaApplets + "<br>");
 Response.Write("Does ActiveX Controls = " + bc.ActiveXControls + "<br>");
 Response.Write("CDF = " + bc.CDF + "<br>");
```

The <clientTarget> Element

The clientTarget element is there to allow you to create aliases for user agent information. For example, if you did not want to have the entire user agent string written to a custom log file, you could create an alias that called something much simpler. Consider the example in Listing 20.5.

LISTING 20.5   `<clientTarget>` Element Snippet

```
<clientTarget>
        <add alias="ie5nt4" userAgent="Mozilla/4.0_
➥ (compatible;MSIE 5.5;Windows NT 4.0)" />
        <add alias="ie52k" userAgent="Mozilla/4.0 _
➥ (compatible;MSIE 5.5;Windows NT 5.0)" />
</clientTarget>
```

Under `clientTarget` are three subtags, `add`, `clear`, and `remove`.

The `<add>` element, as shown in Listing 20.5, has two required attributes—`alias` and `userAgent`. The value of `alias` is whatever you want to name the alias, and `userAgent` is the actual user agent string.

The `<clear>` element removes all entries related to the parent element it has. For example, if you use the `<clear>` element within the `clientTarget` element, all entries made for `clientTarget` are removed. The `<remove>` element, which has one required attribute (`alias`), will remove only the alias or aliases for which it is directed.

The `<compilation>` Element

Using the compilation element allows you to specify parameters for the compilation settings that ASP.NET will use in an application. All of the attributes listed are optional.

First, we will check out the `debug` attribute. This attribute sets whether ASP.NET will use retail or debug assemblies. The main difference being that debug assemblies usually carry a heavier load because they contain debug symbols. The default value for debug is `false`, meaning that retail assemblies are used.

Next is the `defaultLanguage` attribute. As its name implies, `defaultLanguage` is used to specify the default language used to compile dynamic compilation files, such as `.aspx`. The default value is `vb`; however, this is where the `<compilers>` and `<compiler>` subtags come in. Listing 20.6 shows how this transaction takes place.

LISTING 20.6   `<compiler>` Snippet

```
<compilation defaultLanguage="VB"
        debug="false"
        numRecompilesBeforeAppRestart="15">
```

LISTING 20.6   Continued

```
        <compilers>
          <compiler language="VB;VBScript"
            extension=".cls"
            type="Microsoft.VB. VBCodeProvider,System" />
          <compiler language="C#;Csharp"
            extension=".cs"
            type="Microsoft.CSharp. CSharpCodeProvider,System" />
        </compilers>
</compilation>
```

To use a compiler, it must be defined. This does not mean that for every application you must enter custom parameters or define every compiler on the server for each application. This is here to provide flexibility for which the compiler gets called based on a file extension, very much in the same way that IIS allows you to map file types to ISAPI filters. In addition to this, the compiler element has two optional attributes—warningLevel and compilerOptions. The compiler attributes shown in Listing 20.6 (language, extension, and type) are required.

The rest of the elements and attributes associated with the compilation element are not so tricky. In fact, there is one that will make code reviewers around the world elated. Now, you can force the use of explicit declarations from the web.config file. The explicit attribute is used for sites developed in Visual Basic and, if set to true (the default), developers working on the site will be required to declare every variable just as if they were using Option Explicit. The strict attribute, which links directly to the strict compiler option in Visual Basic, is also available in the compilation element.

The batch and batchTimeout attributes are used to determine whether batch processing is enabled and what the timeout for that process will be. batch uses true or false, and batchTimeout accepts a numeric value that represents the number of seconds that can expire before the batch aborts. Additionally, maxBatchGeneratedFileSize represents a numeric value specifying the maximum size of files generated during a batch in kilobytes. In somewhat of a misnomer, maxBatchFileSize actually determines the maximum number of pages that can be generated during a batch process.

Aptly named, the attribute of numRecompilesBeforeApprestart specifies the number of times that ASP.NET will attempt to recompile a page before restarting the application. From a security standpoint, monitoring this may tip you off to an attack if an application that has not changed in months suddenly starts restarting with no user intervention.

Finally, the <assemblies> subtag allows you specify additional resources that may be used during the compilation of your application. This works somewhat like adding a reference to an application. Under the assemblies subtag are the <add>, <remove>, and <clear /> subtags. These function the same as for the clientTarget element, except that the add subtag has a required attribute named assembly. When you add or remove an assembly, it is important to remember that you are setting the assembly parameter to the assembly's name and not the path to the .dll.

The <customErrors> Element

In IIS, you can configure custom error pages for response codes given by the Web server. For example, you can modify the default page for 404–Not Found to be a special page on your site that can give some additional guidance to the user. In ASP.NET, there is the customErrors element that provides the same service.

The customErrors element has one required attribute, mode. There are three possible values for mode—On, Off, and RemoteOnly. When set to On, custom errors are shown to the user; Off shows the detailed error message coming from the CLR or your code. If On is enabled, you can use the defaultRedirect to specify a particular URI for handling error messages or if you do not specify a defaultRedirect page, a generic page, the "friendly error message" page in Internet Explorer, will be displayed to the user. The other option is RemoteOnly. This displays the custom error pages to all visitors other than those from localhost or the local machine. This way, developers can see what the real error messages are without relying on recounts from end users.

The available <error> subtag has two optional attribute—statusCode and redirect. The statusCode value represents the number associated with an HTTP response code, such as 404 or 500. The redirect value is there in case you want to send the user to a different page other than the one specified in the defaultRedirect attribute. For example, you may not want to send a user receiving a 404 error to the same page as a user getting a 403. Listing 20.7 shows a sample of this usage.

LISTING 20.7   customErrors Snippet

```
<customErrors defaultRedirect="myerror.htm"
        mode="RemoteOnly">
        <error statusCode="404"
                redirect="NotFound.htm"/>
<error statusCode="403"
                redirect="Unauthorized.htm"/>
</customErrors>
```

The `<globalization>` Element

Again, the self-naming elements are abundant in .NET. In short, globalization allows you to configure the globalization settings for an application. All of the attributes are optional and are not dependent on each other at all.

`requestEncoding` allows you to set what the encoding of each request must be. This value, however, will be overridden should the request contain an `Accept-Charset` header. The default value is `UTF-8`, but it can be any valid encoding definition, such as `ISO-8859-1`. `responseEncoding` works the same way, only affecting the HTTP response. Unless you want plenty of headaches or have some truly valid reason, the `requestEncoding` and `responseEncoding` attributes should have the same value. The `fileEncoding` attribute allows you to extend this value to `.aspx`, `.asmx`, and `.asax` files as well.

The `culture` and `uiCulture` attributes are there to enable addition of a culture to incoming Web requests. Their values must be a valid culture string as accepted by the `System.Globalization.CultureInfo` class. Listing 20.8 shows a sample of preparing the Web server to receive requests in the "Spanish-Spain" culture.

LISTING 20.8   globalization Snippet

```
<globalization
culture="es-ES" />
```

The `<httpHandler>` Element

For those of you familiar with the concept of an ISAPI filter, the `httpHandler` is not that far of a stretch. Basically, an assembly that implements `IHttpHandler` or `IHttpHandlerFactory` is announced here so that requests are handled by it first. The uses for this are endless, especially when it comes to custom logging, or scanning for malformed URL requests, such as the URLScan filter from Microsoft does.

`httpHandler` has three subtags—`<add>`, `<remove>`, and `<clear />`. As stated previously, the `clear` subtag serves only to clear any instances of anything related to the parent container—in this case, `httpHandler`. When you add an `httpHandler`, you must also specify the verb(s) `GET`, `POST`, or `PUT`; you want to watch the *path* or URL to monitor (ex. `*.aspx`) and the `type` attribute that defines the object's name. Optionally, you may set the `validate` attribute that will not load the assembly until a match is found. Consider the snippet in Listing 20.9.

LISTING 20.9 httpHandler Snippet

```
<httpHandlers>
         <add verb="GET" path="*.aspx" type="MyHandler.New,MyHandler" />
         <add verb="*" path="*.myNewFileExtension"_
➥ type="MyHandler.Fin,MyHandler.dll" />
</httpHandlers>
```

What's happening here is that we are now mapping the .aspx extension to go through the MyHandler assembly—probably not the best idea, but used to get the point across. The next entry maps any document with the extension of .myNewFileExtension to the MyHandler.Fin assembly.

> **NOTE**
>
> Even though these settings may exist, IIS still commands the file extension mapping arena. As always, if you create a custom filter for a custom extension, that must be mapped separately in IIS.

The <httpModule> **Element**

While close to an httpHandler, the httpModule is more of a plug-in than a pre-processor. The sample shown in Listing 20.10 covers a lot of ground in relation to httpModule.

LISTING 20.10 httpModule Snippet

```
<httpModules>
         <add type="System.Web.Caching.OutputCacheModule"
             name="OutputCache" />
         <add type="System.Web.SessionState.SessionStateModule"
             name="Session" />
         <add type="Selector, selector.dll"
             name="Selector" />
</httpModules>
```

In this example, modules are being added. The type attribute accepts the assembly's path, relative to the application's location on the server. The name attribute is how you refer to the assembly from your applicaton. As with httpHandler, there are the <remove> and <clear /> subtags as well. The remove element takes a parameter of name, which corresponds to the name attribute given an assembly when it was added. The clear element, as usual, removes all instances of all modules from the application.

The modules shown in Listing 20.10 illustrate some of the uses for `httpModule` classes. By definition, an `httpModule` class is one which implements `IHttpmodule` and handles events. The items shown in Listing 20.10 handle caching and session state. Custom modules could be created to implement a custom encryption scheme across an application or server.

The `<httpRuntime>` Element

The `httpRuntime` element brings a bit of the IIS metabase out into the open. While some of the attributes associated with this element are quite familiar to those used to administering IIS, others are more advanced and lean themselves more towards improving site performance. The attributes available are as follows:

- `appRequestQueueLimit`—This attribute defines the maximum number of requests that ASP.NET will queue for the application. This should only come into play if the application is not handling requests as fast as the requests are coming in. If and when this number is reached, the server will return a 503–Server Too Busy response to clients until space is made available. This is a good place to handle this event with the `customErrors` element discussed previously in this chapter.

- `executionTimeout`—As in ASP, this number represents the maximum time allotted for a page to execute in seconds.

- `maxRequestLength`—This attribute, simply put, limits the number of bytes allowed in a file upload request. Use this number wisely because this is a very popular way for hackers to launch denial of service (DOS) attacks against Web servers.

- `minFreeLocalRequestFreeThreads`—The number specified in this attribute will ensure that ASP.NET keeps a minimum number of threads open not only for processing new requests, but also child requests that may spawn at the same time. You may want to use caution when setting this to prevent chance of attack through malicious code that would create an endless or recursive loop within the application—leading to DOS. The main difference between this attribute and `minFreeThreads` is that `minFreeThreads` does not consider local or child requests. The `minFreeThreads` attribute keeps a minimum number of threads open for new requests coming into the server.

Using the attribute `useFullyQualifiedRedirectUrl`, if set to `true`, will cause all redirects to be the fully qualified address of the user being sent to. This may be necessary if you have mobile clients. If set to `false`, users will be sent relative links. The snippet in Listing 20.11 shows a sample of using these attributes together.

LISTING 20.11 `httpRuntime` Snippet

```
<httpRuntime maxRequestLength="4000"
      appRequestQueueLimit="5000"
        useFullyQualifiedRedirectUrl="true"
        executionTimeout="45"
     minFreeLocalRequestFreeThreads="100"
/>
```

The `<identity>` Element

The `<identity>` element controls under what user the application runs. It has three attributes—`impersonate`, `userName`, and `password`. Listing 20.12 shows setting the `impersonate` value to `true` and having the application run as user `Test` with a password of p2s4w5r6d.

LISTING 20.12 `identity` Element Snippet

```
<identity
impersonate="true"
username="Test"
password="p2s4w5r6d" />
```

Notice that the user information is not encrypted in any way. Even without this level of security, using this element can still serve to limit access of an application by allowing the anonymous Internet user to impersonate a local account, thus giving enhanced functionality without creating additional risk.

The `<machineKey>` Element

The machineKey element serves a vital purpose to sites using Forms authentication. It allows you to configure the keys used to encrypt and decrypt the data stored in user cookies. As an added feature, this element can be set at the machine (`machine.config`), site, and application levels, but does not change if set at the directory level—such as trying to have different subdirectories in an application use different keys. Being able to set this at the machine and/or application level becomes important when establishing a Web farm because the keys are going to need to be consistent across all of the machines. If you are unfamiliar with generating truly random number sequences, Microsoft has provided the `RNGCryptoServiceProvider` class. As you may have guessed, the `RNG` is for Random Number Generation. Using the class to generate a key is rather simple, as shown in Listing 20.13. This code listing is available for download from the Sams Web site.

LISTING 20.13   GetRNG Function

```
public string GetRNG()
   {
   //Create a byte array to hold the numbers
   byte[] bRNG = new Byte[64];
   //Get an instance of the RNG Crypto Provider
   RNGCryptoServiceProvider rng = new RNGCryptoServiceProvider();
   //Call the GetNonZeroBytes method to get all non-zero results
   rng.GetNonZeroBytes(bRNG);
   //Convert the byte array to a string
   String results = BitConverter.ToString(bRNG);
   //return the string
                     results = results.Replace("-", "");
   return results;
  }
```

The results of this function executed from an .aspx page should look something like Listing 20.14.

LISTING 20.14   GetRNG Results

```
8DB4729D44C0B79AAB0897726B4CB3F982
D6AAC47DB649DB6F6BEE71CB08468254EF
3EA33AC6BD8B3F2BC0FA967E7257A7E7E4
1E2957D9624B9E04B1E3B6FD566B4D25C7
```

This result is a much harder key to guess than pretty much anything you or I could come up with off the top of our heads.

The machineKey element has three required attributes—validationKey, decryptionKey, and validation. Each of these attributes has a set number of options with not too much space to play, except if you manually set one of the key values.

The validationKey attribute can equal either AutoGenerate or a manually assigned value. If you are using a Web farm, as stated before, use the manually assigned value and generate it using something like the GetRNG function in Listing 20.13. Keep in mind that the key must be at least 40-characters (20 bytes) long and not more than 128-characters (64 bytes) long; Listing 20.14 demonstrates a 64-byte result. The default value for validationKey is AutoGenerate. The decryptionKey attribute must follow the same rules as validationKey because it is established to specify the encryption used for data validation. It may be confusing to see the word validation thrown around so much, especially considering that the next attribute is named validation. So after explaining what the validation attribute does, Listing 20.15 will demonstrate the use of this element. The validation attribute specifies which encryption algorithm will be used to validate the data coming in from the user cookies. Its value can be SHA1, MD5, or 3DES.

LISTING 20.15   machineKey Element Snippet

```
<machineKey
 validationKey="AutoGenerate"
 decryptionKey="2964C6F5C2969FC203A226CD567A17D0FE5AAE8251E58907FF1AEAB04D291_
➡ C8559418336DD9FE5311A32A6801B4DF8E5283A3878249E5FD03CE52238979A3D65BB1ABF
➡ 840A19C96B43ABBE254D1F514ED25E70CD3C0B6BC76E6CA8D7BE76F19DC7D226FD73C3F
➡ 32993E04CA072674D7B3C15BB61756FE59EE74D83432C34CB94"
 validation="SHA1" />
```

What's happening in Listing 20.15 is that information going into the user cookie is encrypted using an automatically generated key. This data is then protected by a MAC (see earlier section on Forms authentication, "The <authentication> Element") using the decryptionKey. The validation attribute is setting which algorithm will be used to hash the information coming in to make sure it has not been tampered with.

The <pages> Element

The pages element allows you to define page specific items at an application level. In ASP 2.0/3.0, you could define certain items, such as enabling of session state, within the page or through the IIS MMC application. With ASP.NET, these settings can be controlled through the web.config file. Using the configuration file in this manner is somewhat similar to using a style sheet to control the way a site looks. The main benefit is that you can change the style in one place and have it affect the whole site.

The first attribute we will look at is the autoEventWireup setting. There are only two possible values for this—true or false. Setting this attribute to true tells .NET that any page events (Page_Load for example) are automatically enabled. This means that you can "assume" that if your code calls one of these events, it will be there. Setting autoEventWireup to false does not automatically map or enable page events.

The second attribute is buffer. Think of this exactly the same way you may think of Response.Buffer in ASP—it's the exact same thing. The possible values for this attribute are true and false. As a quick reminder, buffering in this context is referring to whether or not ASP sends the page as it is being processed (false) or after the page has completely processed (true).

> **TIP**
>
> In ASP.NET, the buffer property of `Page.Response`, which inherits `HttpResponse`, has been deprecated. Current practices recommend using the `BufferOutput` property of the `HttpResponse` class.

Perhaps one of most improved options in ASP.NET brings us to the next attribute—`enableSessionState`. Though claims of improved performance appear to be `true`, one of the overlooked features is the `ReadOnly` setting available for this attribute. In addition to `true` and `false`, `ReadOnly` allows you to specify that an application can read information stored in the session but cannot change it. From a security standpoint, this could save many headaches in corporate intranets using shared information across applications. It can also prevent certain spoofing techniques used by hackers who attempt to change session or cookie variables by interrupting the streams of data transferring between the client and server. This brings up the point again of why to use SSL if at all possible or applicable.

The fourth attribute available is `enableViewState`. This Boolean indicates whether a page maintains its view state after being sent to the client. As a refresher, view state allows ASP.NET to know whether a form is being sent to the client for the first time or it is being submitted.

In another reference to what could be called "server-side style sheeting," the `pageBaseType` attribute allows you to define a `code-behind` class that all `.aspx` pages will inherit by default. It seems to take server-side includes (SSI) to the next level because you do not need to add any code to the page you are working on to have the functionality provided for in the class. Also, unlike present technology for includes and style sheets, this functionality stays at the server, reducing the amount of non-browser related information sent to the client. The attribute of `userControlBaseType` works the same way, only in relation to a user control that all pages inherit by default.

The `<securityPolicy>` Element

The `securityPolicy` element allows you to specify a configuration file to associate with different named levels of security for an application. These named levels are `Full`, `High`, `Low`, and `None`. Only `High` and `Low` will allow you to specify a configuration file to use because `Full` indicates a full trust of the application and `None` signifies no trust level.

Under `securityPolicy` is one subtag—`<trustLevel>`. The `trustLevel` element has two required attributes—`name` and `policyFile`. The value of `name` must be one of the named values mentioned previously, and `policyFile` indicates the filename to use as the configuration for that level. Listing 20.16 shows a sample security configuration file. Listing 20.17 shows a snippet of using the securityPolicy element in a web.config file.

LISTING 20.16   FullTrust Security Configuration File

```
<configuration>
  <mscorlib>
    <security>
      <policy>
      <PolicyLevel version="1">
        <SecurityClasses>
          <SecurityClass Name="StrongNameMembershipCondition"
➥Description="System.Security.Policy.StrongNameMembershipCondition,
➥ mscorlib,➥Version=1.0.3300.0, Culture=neutral,
PublicKeyToken=b77a5c561934e089"/>
<SecurityClass Name="UrlMembershipCondition"
➥Description="System.Security.Policy.UrlMembershipCondition, mscorlib,
➥ Version=1.0.3300.0, Culture=neutral, PublicKeyToken=b77a5c561934e089"/>
          <SecurityClass Name="SecurityPermission"
➥Description="System.Security.Permissions.SecurityPermission, mscorlib,
➥ Version=1.0.3300.0, Culture=neutral, PublicKeyToken=b77a5c561934e089"/>
        <SecurityClass Name="UnionCodeGroup" Description="System.Security
Policy.UnionCodeGroup, mscorlib, Version=1.0.3300.0, Culture=neutral,
➥ PublicKeyToken=b77a5c561934e089"/>
          <SecurityClass Name="IsolatedStorageFilePermission"
➥Description="System.Security.Permissions.IsolatedStorageFilePermission
➥, mscorlib,
➥ Version=1.0.3300.0, Culture=neutral, PublicKeyToken=b77a5c561934e089"/>
          <SecurityClass Name="AllMembershipCondition"
➥Description="System.Security.Policy.AllMembershipCondition, mscorlib,
➥ Version=1.0.3300.0, Culture=neutral, PublicKeyToken=b77a5c561934e089"/>
          <SecurityClass Name="NamedPermissionSet" Description=
➥"System.Security.NamedPermissionSet"/>
          <SecurityClass Name="FirstMatchCodeGroup"
➥Description="System.Security.Policy.FirstMatchCodeGroup, mscorlib,
➥ Version=1.0.3300.0, Culture=neutral, PublicKeyToken=b77a5c561934e089"/>
        </SecurityClasses>
        <NamedPermissionSets>
          <PermissionSet class="NamedPermissionSet"
                         version="1"
                         Unrestricted="true"
                         Name="FullTrust"
```

LISTING 20.16 Continued

```
                                Description="Allows full access to all
➥ resources"/>
            <PermissionSet class="NamedPermissionSet"
                        version="1"
                        Name="SkipVerification"
                        Description="Grants right to bypass the verifier">
                <IPermission class="SecurityPermission"
                            version="1"
                            Flags="SkipVerification"/>
            </PermissionSet>
            <PermissionSet class="NamedPermissionSet"
                        version="1"
                        Name="Execution"
                        Description="Permits execution">
                <IPermission class="SecurityPermission"
                            version="1"
                            Flags="Execution"/>
            </PermissionSet>
            <PermissionSet class="NamedPermissionSet"
                        version="1"
                        Name="Nothing"
                        Description="Denies all resources, including
the right to execute"/>
            <PermissionSet class="NamedPermissionSet"
                        version="1"
                        Name="ASP.NET">
                <IPermission class="IsolatedStorageFilePermission"
                            version="1"
                            Allowed="DomainIsolationByUser"
                            UserQuota="1048576"/>
                <IPermission class="SecurityPermission"
                            version="1"
                            Flags="Execution"/>
            </PermissionSet>
        </NamedPermissionSets>
        <CodeGroup class="FirstMatchCodeGroup"
                    version="1"
                    PermissionSetName="Nothing">
            <IMembershipCondition class="AllMembershipCondition"
                                version="1"/>
```

LISTING 20.16 Continued

```
                    <CodeGroup class="UnionCodeGroup"
                            version="1"
                            PermissionSetName="ASP.NET">
                <IMembershipCondition class="UrlMembershipCondition"
                                      version="1"
                                      Url="$AppDirUrl$/*"/>
                    </CodeGroup>
                    <CodeGroup class="UnionCodeGroup"
                            version="1"
                            PermissionSetName="ASP.NET">
                <IMembershipCondition class="UrlMembershipCondition"
                                      version="1"
                                      Url="$CodeGen$/*"/>
                    </CodeGroup>
                    <CodeGroup class="UnionCodeGroup"
                            version="1"
                            PermissionSetName="FullTrust">
                <IMembershipCondition class="UrlMembershipCondition"
                                      Url="$Gac$/*"
                                      version="1"/>
                    </CodeGroup>
                    <CodeGroup class="UnionCodeGroup"
                             version="1"
                             PermissionSetName="FullTrust"
                             Name="Microsoft_Strong_Name"
                             Description="This code group grants code signed
with the Microsoft strong name full trust. ">
                    <IMembershipCondition
                      class="StrongNameMembershipCondition"
                                         version="1"

PublicKeyBlob="00240000048000009400000006020000002400005253413100040000001000
10007D1FA57C4AED9F0A32E84AA0FAEFD0DE9E8FD6AEC8F87FB03766C834C99921EB23BE79AD
9D5DCC1DD9AD236132102900B723CF980957FC4E177108FC607774F29E8320E92EA05ECE4E82
1C0A5EFE8F1645C4C0C93C1AB99285D622CAA652C1DFAD63D745D6F2DE5F17E5EAF0FC4963D2
61C8A12436518206DC093344D5AD293"/>
                    </CodeGroup>
                    <CodeGroup class="UnionCodeGroup"
                             version="1"
                             PermissionSetName="FullTrust"
```

LISTING 20.16   Continued

```
                            Name="Ecma_Strong_Name"
                            Description="This code group grants code signed
                                        with the ECMA strong name full trust. ">
                <IMembershipCondition class="StrongNameMembershipCondition"
                                        version="1"
                        PublicKeyBlob="00000000000000000400000000000000"/>
                </CodeGroup>
            </CodeGroup>
            <FullTrustAssemblies>
                    <IMembershipCondition class="StrongNameMembershipCondition"
                                        version="1"
                            PublicKeyBlob="00000000000000000400000000000000"
                                        Name="System"/>
            </FullTrustAssemblies>
        </PolicyLevel>
        </policy>
    </security>
  </mscorlib>
</configuration>
```

LISTING 20.17   securityPolicy Element Snippet

```
<securityPolicy>
<!--the value of policyFile for Full will always be "internal" -->
   <trustLevel name="Full" policyFile="internal" />
   <trustLevel name="High" policyFile="my_hightrust_web.config" />
   <trustLevel name="Low"  policyFile="my_lowtrust_web.config" />
   <trustLevel name="None" policyFile="noaccess.config" />
</securityPolicy>
```

The `<sessionState>` Element

As mentioned earlier in the section, "The <pages> Element," the use of session state is not to be feared or ridiculed in ASP.NET. The sessionState element allows you to define where session information is stored. This is both an enhancement to functionality as well as administration, because currently in IIS 5, there is nowhere to configure such settings.

There is one required attribute, mode. The mode attribute must have one of the following values—Off, Inproc, StateServer, or SQLServer. The rest of the attributes associated with this element are optional, depending on what mode's value is. If you set the value of mode to `Off`, session state is disabled completely for that application. Setting it to `Inproc` specifies that session information is stored on the local server—basically, the way it works in ASP. Additionally, at this point, you may want to configure the `timeout` attribute, which specifies the number of seconds of inactivity before the session times out. Also available is the `cookieless` attribute that, setting to `true` or `false`, indicates whether to use cookies to store session information.

Should you want to configure your application to store session information on a remote server, the `StateServer` value must be given to mode. After this is set, a `stateConnectionString` attribute must be added and given a value of the protocol, name, or IP address and port. For example, `tcpip=192.168.0.2:42424`. For this to work, the ASP.NET State Service must be running on the remote machine. At the time of this writing, this is installed with the Enterprise Architect and Premium versions of .NET.

The final option is using SQL Server to manage session state. Setting mode to `SQLServer` requires that you also set the `sqlConnectionString` attribute to a valid SQL Server database connection string. To most developers, this is nothing new, but from a security standpoint, it raises an issue. Because the `web.config` file is not encrypted, the user information used to log in to SQL Server is available in plain text. By design, ASP.NET will not serve any file with the `.config` extension; however, it may still be possible for someone internally to get this information and use it for malicious purposes. If the application is running as a specific user or running as the currently logged-in user in an application using Windows authentication, you may be able to use `"TRUSTED_CONNECTION=YES"` in the connection string eliminating any specific user information. Use of this will depend on whether that user has privileges within SQL Server.

To establish the database to use for this option, locate the `InstallSqlState.sql` file. By default, this file should be located in the `%WINDIR%\Microsoft.NET\Framework\[version]` directory. Executing this file in SQL Server will create the `ASPState` database and associated stored procedures in the `TempDB` database. Listing 20.18 shows a complete `web.config` file that could be the basis for any ASP.NET Web site configured to use SQL Server to store session information. The complete code listing is available in the code downloads for this chapter on Sams Web site.

LISTING 20.18   sessionState Enabled web.config File

```
<?xml version="1.0" encoding="utf-8" ?>
<configuration>
 <system.web>
  <compilation
   defaultLanguage="c#"
    debug="true"
```

LISTING 20.18   Continued

```
    />
  <customErrors
    mode="RemoteOnly"
    />
  <authentication
    mode="Windows"
    />
<!--Setting the identity to impersonate=true
    requires the currently logged in user
    to have an account on SQL Server →
  <identity
    impersonate="true"
    />
  <sessionState
    mode="SQLServer"
    cookieless="true"
    timeout="20"
    sqlConnectionString="server=(local);TRUSTED_CONNECTION=YES"
    />
  <trace
    enabled="false"
    requestLimit="10"
    pageOutput="false"
    traceMode="SortByTime"
    localOnly="true"
    />
  <globalization
    requestEncoding="utf-8"
    responseEncoding="utf-8"
    />
  </system.web>
</configuration>
```

The `<trace>` Element

The trace element allows you to define listeners that collect, route, and store messages generated during tracing an application. While an entire chapter could be devoted to tracing applications, this section offers to give an overview of what is available in .NET for configuring tracing at the application level through the web.config file.

The `trace` element only has one attribute—`autoflush`. The `autoflush` attribute is a Boolean indicating whether the trace output buffer is automatically flushed. The default value is `false`.

Additionally, the `trace` element has one subtag, `<listeners>`, which allows you to add or remove different listeners to the tracing of the application, specify the type of listener, and specify the path to where the trace messages are logged.

The `<trust>` Element

Not to be confused with the trust settings in the `securityPolicy` element, the `trust` element allows you to trust applications other than your own. It uses the default security configuration files provided by .NET. For an example of one of these files, see Listing 20.17 earlier in this chapter.

The `trust` element carries a required attribute of `level`. As with the `securityPolicy` element, `level` may be one of four named values—`Full`, `High`, `Low`, or `None`. These levels relate to the Code Access Security applied to the application. The optional attribute of `originUrl` allows you to specify from where the trusted request can come. Listing 20.19 shows a sample of trusting an outside application. For this example, we'll say that your company is `YourCompany.com` and you trust an application from `SomeOtherCompany.com` (both hopefully fictitious sites).

LISTING 20.19   trust Element Snippet

```
<trust level="High"
originUrl="http://www.someothercompany.com/default.aspx" />
```

The `<webServices>` Element

In its simplest explanation, the `webServices` element allows you to configure the settings associated with Web Services created in ASP.NET. This section will assume a certain amount of knowledge regarding Web Services and Simple Object Access Protocol (SOAP).

> **NOTE**
>
> For an in depth understanding of SOAP, check out the online documentation at MSDN (`http://msdn.microsoft.com/SOAP`) or *Applied SOAP: Implementing .NET XML Web Services* by Kenn Scribner and Mark Stiver.

While the `webServices` element has no direct attributes, it does have six subtags, each having a rather direct purpose and explanation. The first subtag we will examine is the `<protocols>` element. The purpose of this element is to define which protocols ASP.NET can use to decrypt information sent from a client in an HTTP request. This is extremely important because the request can contain not only the Web Service's name, but also any parameters necessary for execution. Having the wrong protocols enabled will only serve to create application errors that can easily be prevented. The protocols element has no attributes, but it does have one subtag—<add>. The add element has one required attribute of name. If a protocol is not defined here, it is not used. There is no need for a remove or clear element as with other elements listed previously. The name attribute of the add subtag may have one of four values. These values are the currently supported protocols by Microsoft for handling HTTP requests. They are HttpSoap, HttpPost, HttpGet, and Documentation. Note that the Documentation option is not indicative of a native HTTP standard protocol. Documentation allows direct requests to an .asmx file to be responded to with an ASP.NET-generated documentation page. This is what happens by default when you build a Web Service in Visual Studio.NET.

The next element to review is the serviceDescriptionFormatExtensionTypes subtag. This element has a subtag of <add> with a required attribute of type. The value of type must be the name of the class you want to use as a ServiceDescriptionFormatExtension. In short, a ServiceDescriptionFormatExtention allows you to add an extensibility element to a Web Service in addition to those defined by the Web Services Definition Language (WSDL).

Speaking of WSDL, the next element we will look at is the wsdlHelpGenerator subtag. This provides a container for the developer to enter a URI of a page that provides descriptive information regarding a Web Service. This page is accessed when a user attempts to navigate directly to the .asmx file, thus overriding the default generated page created when the Documentation protocol is enabled.

The next and final three elements available are related to SoapExtensions. A SoapExtension, other than inheriting the SoapExtension class, allows the developer to extend or monitor SOAP messages and modify them if necessary. Microsoft has provided an excellent code sample in the .NET documentation showing a SoapExtension that traces the SOAP messages in a request and logs the request and response output. The documentation URL for this sample is ms-help://MS.VSCC/MS.MSDNVS/cpref/html/ frlrfSystemWebServicesProtocolsSoapExtensionClassTopic.htm. The soapExtensionTypes, soapExtensionReflectorTypes, and soapExtensionImporterTypes elements allow you to add specific classes to run under certain events. soapExtensionTypes allows you to define SoapExtensions that are called with every request to a Web Service. soapExtensionReflectorTypes is there to define any SoapExtensions you may want to call when a service description is generated for a Web Service, for example, when a user navigates directly to the .asmx file. Finally, soapExtensionImporterTypes allows you to define classes that will be called when a Web Service must call a proxy class or stub. This can occur under circumstances where COM+ compatibility is required from within a Web Service.

Using Custom Attributes and Settings

Here is where we will see a sample of the extensibility available in ASP.NET through the use of XML. You can use custom attributes from within the `web.config` file for just about any purpose. Two things to keep in mind are that every time one of these values is called, the `web.config` file must be read; this could lead to a performance question. The other is that this is a plain-text file, so make sure that you have set the ACL permissions correctly depending on your situation. Listing 20.20 shows a `web.config` file using a custom attribute of `"welcomeMessage"`.

LISTING 20.20   `web.config` File with Custom Attribute

```
<?xml version="1.0" encoding="utf-8" ?>
<configuration>
 <appSettings>
  <add key="welcomeMessage" value="Welcome to ASP.NET " />
 </appSettings>
</configuration>
```

Notice the use of the `appSettings` element to store a new key called `"welcomeMessage"`. This could just as easily be used to store a database connection string or parameters for a specific Web control on your page. Listing 20.21 shows how to access this value from your `aspx.cs` page. These samples are included in the code downloads available from the book's Web site.

LISTING 20.21   Code Showing `appSettings` Value

```
using System;
using System.Collections;
using System.ComponentModel;
using System.Data;
using System.Drawing;
using System.Web;
using System.Web.SessionState;
using System.Web.UI;
using System.Web.UI.WebControls;
using System.Web.UI.HtmlControls;
using System.Web.Configuration;
using System.Configuration;
using System.Collections.Specialized;

namespace Ch20CustomConfig
{
 /// <summary>
```

LISTING 20.21   Continued

```
/// Summary description for WebForm1.
/// </summary>
public class WebForm1 : System.Web.UI.Page
{
 private void Page_Load(object sender, System.EventArgs e)
 {
  Response.Write(ConfigurationSettings.AppSettings["welcomeMessage"]);
 }

 #region Web Form Designer generated code
 override protected void OnInit(EventArgs e)
 {
  //
  // CODEGEN: This call is required by the ASP.NET Web Form Designer.
  //
  InitializeComponent();
  base.OnInit(e);
 }

 /// <summary>
 /// Required method for Designer support - do not modify
 /// the contents of this method with the code editor.
 /// </summary>
 private void InitializeComponent()
 {
  this.Load += new System.EventHandler(this.Page_Load);
 }
 #endregion
 }
}
```

What Listing 20.21 shows is just how simple it is to access your custom attributes stored in a web.config file. Using Windows Integrated authentication and the inherited User object, you could easily add the user's name to this message after he or she is authenticated.

IIS Security Settings—A Refresher

At its lowest level, IIS, like any other Web server, is basically a file server. A client, usually a Web browser, makes a request and the server sends the file. What happens between these two actions can vary widely. Looking at IIS in this way, it becomes easy to understand that the basis for IIS Security is the way you have configured file access permissions on your server. Only through proper file access configuration will any of the features of IIS, and for that matter ASP.NET, be as effective as they were intended. Right-clicking a file, directory, or drive and selecting Properties from the menu allows easy access to the settings referred to in this paragraph. Files and directories should only have users and groups allowed to perform any action—read, write, or execute—if they need it. Setting a global policy that allows everyone full access to every resource unless otherwise noted is not a good policy.

The next consideration is the permissions required by the files themselves. These settings are most easily accessed through the IIS Management Console. What is meant here is that at the directory level, you should not over allow on permissions. If you have a directory that is full of static HTML pages, that directory should have read access only to all users and groups with the possible exception of authors changing content, automated or otherwise. In a directory containing either all Active Server Pages and/or a mix of Active Server Pages and static content, the only permissions needed are read and script. Unless you have a directory that contains active .dll and/or .exe files that should execute on the server, you should have read and execute permissions enabled. This setting has confused some developers as they place COM/COM+ objects in a directory on the Web server and mark it with execute. This is not necessary because COM/COM+ objects can live anywhere on a Web server. This is mostly intended for directories where ISAPI extensions exist and are called through the URL.

The final basic consideration for refresher is authentication. While the use of authentication with ASP.NET is adequately explained in Chapter 14, it can never be underrated how helpful it can be in securing a site by requiring users to log in. Be it through Integrated Windows authentication or a SQL Server database containing encrypted user information accessed over SSL, keeping users out of your site is often more important than letting users in.

Summary

Knowing what is available to manage through the web.config file is essential to securing ASP.NET applications. It enables you to have one more tool that will help secure not only applications, but Web servers as well. Some of the information given here relies on or is enhanced by the security settings of IIS as well as the operating system. Using this information to correctly secure your Web site will prevent many a stressful event due to lack of planning with regard to securing your application.

21

Administering Clients for .NET Framework Mobile Code

IN THIS CHAPTER

- Default Security Policy and Mobile Code
- Limitations on Calling Strong Named Components
- Running Mobile Code in Internet Explorer

By Sebastian Lange and Matthew Lyons

Securely running mobile code is one of the most difficult problems on the Internet. As discussed in Chapter 1, "Common Security Problems on the Internet," mobile code comes in many different forms, including executables, source code, scripts, Java applets, and ActiveX controls. Generally, you can think of mobile code as any data sent to computers and run in some automated fashion. A very common way this happens is your Web browser. Many Web pages have some kind of embedded, mobile code these days to perform tasks like data validation when filling in a form. In addition to Web browsers, there are applications like virus scanners that automatically pull down updates from the Internet.

The .NET Framework provides the potential for rich mobile code scenarios on client machines. To properly administer clients that use the .NET Framework for mobile code scenarios, you need to understand how default security policy and strong named components affect those scenarios. In addition, you should know how mobile code is dealt with in Internet Explorer, because the .NET Framework provided code to tightly integrate assemblies with Internet Explorer.

If you haven't read Chapter 18, "Administering Security Policy Using the .NET Framework Configuration Tool," and Chapter 19, "Administering .NET Framework Security Policy Using Scripts and Security APIs," yet, you should do so before actually trying to administer .NET Framework clients. This chapter will discuss security policy changes that you might consider, but it won't discuss how to actually perform those changes.

Default Security Policy and Mobile Code

Running mobile code on clients is initially bound by the default policy distributed by the .NET Framework. You should evaluate if the provided default policy is appropriate for your organization and then apply any changes that are deemed necessary. The provided security policy is very restrictive by default, so this chapter will cover various ways to properly expand the permissions granted to mobile code.

Default Security Policy's Impact on Mobile Code

In the RTM (the original V1.0 release prior to any Service Packs) release of the .NET Framework, default security policy was set to allow limited permissions for code loaded from the intranet and Internet. In mid-January, Bill Gates announced the strong commitment at Microsoft for the Trustworthy Computing initiative, which is aimed at ensuring that Microsoft as a company will meet customers' needs and expectations around privacy, reliability, and security. As a result of this, the .NET Framework team reconsidered the default security policy for the Internet zone. To truly emphasize the conservative "locked down" default behavior encouraged by the initiative and requested by customers, they decided to release Service Pack 1 (SP1) to remove the ability in default policy for code from the Internet to execute.

> **NOTE**
>
> The remainder of this chapter will assume you have either applied SP1 to your .NET Framework clients or that you installed a version of the .NET Framework that includes SP1.

There are four security zones from where mobile code may originate: Intranet, Internet, Trusted, and Untrusted (also called Restricted):

- Code from the Internet and Untrusted zones will not be able to execute at all by default. Thus, if a client attempts to load code from such a site, that code will fail to load due to security restrictions.

- Code from the Trusted zone will be given permissions represented by the built-in `Internet` permission set and the ability to use the network to connect back to its site of origin. The `Internet` permission set is a very limited set of permissions that includes the ability to display UI, print documents, use isolated storage, and use a file open dialog.

- Code from the Intranet zone will be given permissions represented by the built-in `LocalIntranet` permission set and the ability to use the network to connect back to its site of origin. The `LocalIntranet` permission set allows everything that the `Internet` permission set allows plus the ability to use the NT event log, DNS servers, classes from the `System.Reflection.Emit` namespace, and the `USERNAME` environment variable.

How to Expand Mobile Code Scenarios

If you want to enable mobile code to run in more scenarios than allowed by default security policy, one thing you can do is add Web sites to the Trusted zone. Figure 21.1 shows the dialog used to add sites to the Trusted zone. You can get to this dialog by running Internet Explorer, opening the Tools menu, choosing the Internet Options menu item, clicking on the Security tab of the resulting dialog, picking the Trusted sites zone, and clicking the Sites button.

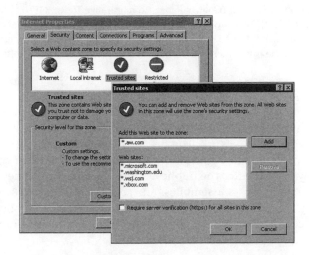

FIGURE 21.1   Dialog used to add Web sites to the Trusted sites zone.

If a Web site is moved from the Internet zone to the Trusted zone, default security policy will allow mobile code loaded from that site to execute. To understand how to distribute Trusted zone changes to clients on a network, see the Internet Explorer Administration Kit (IEAK).

NOTE

The IEAK kit allows enterprise administrators to customize Internet Explorer settings, enabling administrators to deploy custom browser packages to client machines.

For more information on the IEAK, please see `http://www.microsoft.com/windows/ieak/default.asp`.

Another possibility for expanding mobile code scenarios is to change the default security policy. There are generally three different kinds of changes you might want to make. First, you can expand the permissions granted to a given zone. Second, you can explicitly grant permissions to all code from a software publisher. Third, you could explicitly grant permissions to one specific application.

If you choose to change permissions granted to a specific zone, you need to be very careful, because this is the least granular choice. However, this change is probably the easiest to perform because you don't need to add any code groups. Instead, you should just pick the code group for the zone in question and change the permission set. For example, you might want to change the code group for the Internet zone to use the Internet permission set.

> **TIP**
>
> You can use the .NET Framework Configuration tool's Adjust Security Wizard to change the permission level managed code from the Internet receives. To do so, first start up the .NET Framework Configuration tool (Control Panel, Administrative Tools, .NET Framework Configuration shortcut). Then right-click the Runtime Security Policy node and select the Adjust Security Wizard. Select to make changes to "this computer" and select the Internet zone. Finally, push the trust slider to the notch above No Trust. For more information, please see Chapter 18.

The .NET Framework provides the ability to grant specific permissions to assemblies from a specific software publisher. There are two ways to identify a software publisher in the .NET Framework. The first way is to pick an X.509 certificate the publisher uses for signing its applications and use a PublisherMembershipCondition. The second way is to identify the public key from a strong name key pair that the publisher uses for signing its assemblies. A StrongNameMembershipCondition can be used to identify this public key to the .NET Framework security policy. In either case, you can add a code group with the identifying information that grants a specific permission set to the publisher.

The last way to expand trust for mobile code is to identify a specific assembly or set of assemblies that you want to run. For each assembly, you should add a code group that identifies the SHA1 or MD5 hash value and gives the desired permissions. A HashMembershipCondition can perform the identification in .NET Framework security policy.

> **NOTE**
>
> You could also use the site or zone membership conditions to expand trust for specific sites or whole zones. Generally, this is not suggested, because sites and zones are very broad evidence categories and many assemblies unknown to you may satisfy the site or zone membership

condition. The membership conditions based on strong name, hash, and publisher certification are the only cryptographically strong means we ship to identify specific sets of managed code in security policy.

Limitations on Calling Strong Named Components

In many cases, mobile code should be granted fewer permissions than full trust. However, this decision limits what libraries mobile code can call. The `System.Security.AllowPartiallyTrustedCallersAttribute`, nicknamed APTCA, is the cause of these restrictions. If code has been granted less than full trust, it cannot call into an assembly signed with a strong name unless that assembly is also marked with APTCA.

APTCA was created so that malicious semi-trusted code has fewer vectors of attack on a client. A given client will probably have many assemblies installed in the Global Assembly Cache, and each assembly could expose a vulnerability. Because the default behavior of strong named assemblies is to deny access to semi-trusted code, a developer will have to at least consider whether a given assembly should be used by partially trusted code.

Because APTCA is involved with the "contract" between managed code libraries and semi-trusted code, you should consider how security policy is involved with this. When you plan on giving trust to mobile code, you should look at what assemblies that mobile code will use. If any of those libraries have a strong name and do not contain APTCA, you have to grant full trust to the mobile code if you want it to run successfully. If this is too dangerous, your clients simply will not be able to run that particular mobile code.

Running Mobile Code in Internet Explorer

Internet Explorer is the most popular Web browser on Windows operating systems. It has many different forms of mobile code available to it while executing. To add managed code to the list of mobile code formats Internet Explorer supports, the .NET Framework provides a MIME filter that Internet Explorer uses to determine whether downloaded executable code is managed or unmanaged.

NOTE

The setup process of the .NET Framework registers a MIME filter. This filter will recognize managed code images that are included on a Web page either in an object tag (`<object ...>`) or referred to by an HREF when they are clicked in a Web page hosted in Internet Explorer. After a managed image is recognized, the CLR is invoked and the managed image is executed.

Managed code executed from Internet Explorer is subject to the same security policy as code executed from other hosts. However, there are a couple of properties about managed code in Internet Explorer that are interesting. First, there are some ties between ActiveX control execution and managed code execution. Second, there are two different ways that managed code can execute in Internet Explorer.

If you want to find further information about how Internet Explorer interacts with the .NET Framework, look up Internet Explorer in the index of the .NET Framework SDK.

ActiveX Controls and Managed Controls

If you have performed administrative tasks involved with Windows client machines, you may be familiar with how ActiveX controls work within Internet Explorer. There are several Internet Explorer settings that control how ActiveX controls work. These settings include the following:

- Whether to download unsigned ActiveX controls

- Whether to download signed ActiveX controls

- Whether to allow scripting with ActiveX controls marked safe for scripting

- Whether to allow scripting with ActiveX controls not marked safe for scripting

- Whether to run ActiveX controls and plug-ins

There are no unique settings to dictate whether to download or run managed controls within Internet Explorer. However, managed controls share the same setting with Internet Explorer for running ActiveX controls and plug-ins. Managed controls will only run if ActiveX controls are set to run and if ActiveX controls marked safe for scripting can be scripted in the zone where the managed control is loaded. If ActiveX controls are set to not run or script, managed controls will not work, independent of .NET Framework security policy.

One other notable difference between ActiveX controls and managed controls is the fact that ActiveX controls can display an Authenticode dialog like the one shown in Figure 21.2. Managed controls will not display such a dialog when they execute.

The Authenticode security mechanism was built with the premise that users could decide whether code was signed and/or by whom it was signed. However, many users do not really have the knowledge to make a well-informed decision. They just know to click Yes to run the code. Instead of using this paradigm, the .NET Framework relies on predetermined policies to make the decision of whether to execute code and how much trust to provide. Authenticode's trusted publisher list is a step in this direction, but not as expressive as the .NET Framework security policy.

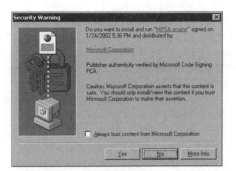

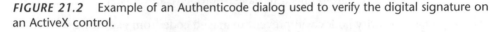

FIGURE 21.2   Example of an Authenticode dialog used to verify the digital signature on an ActiveX control.

One similarity that can be drawn between ActiveX controls and managed controls is the similarity between "Safe for Scripting" and APTCA. In the ActiveX world, "Safe for Scripting" is used to designate that a control is safe to be run in hostile environments. In the .NET Framework, APTCA is used to designate that a control is safe to be run by code with less than full trust. They basically mean the same thing. One important distinction between "Safe for Scripting" and APTCA is to see how security policies handle them. Default ActiveX policy decisions are directly based on the "Safe for Scripting" marking, but APTCA is completely unrelated to .NET Framework security policy. The .NET Framework model is cleaner in that developer decisions (that is, whether to use APTCA) are completely isolated from administrative decisions (that is, what permissions to grant to code).

Different Ways to Run Managed Code in Internet Explorer

There are two different ways to run managed code in Internet Explorer—an <object> tag to a managed control and an HREF to a managed executable. An <object> tag is used to embed controls in a Web page, and an HREF executable is meant to launch a new managed application.

Note that neither way to run managed code will display any UI to the user. Thus, they won't see any Open/Save/Cancel dialog for HREF exes or Authenticode dialogs in either case. .NET Framework security policy is predefined to prevent malicious code from being able to perform any dangerous actions. Thus, displaying UI doesn't really help increase security and generally just gets in the way.

If you are concerned about the spread of viruses or worms through Internet Explorer, it would take one of two things to make this fear a reality. The first possibility is that an exploitable security hole would have be found in the .NET Framework. It would be foolish to say that no such bug will ever be found, although the use of managed code in the .NET Framework should greatly decrease problems like buffer overruns.

The second possibility is that security policy would have to be changed to grant an inappropriate level of trust for managed code from the location of a malicious assembly. As mentioned earlier, the default security policy starting at SP1 denies the ability to execute for managed code running from the Internet zone. Consequently, unless you modify default policy, malicious code would have to come from your intranet or a trusted site.

Summary

The .NET Framework provides the ability to create rich client applications, but there is some information that you need to have to properly administer those applications:

- Default security policy will prevent managed code from executing in the Internet zone. You may need to modify this policy to run applications important to your organization.

- The absence of the `AllowPartiallyTrustedCallersAttribute` will prevent the ability for semi-trusted code to call many managed code libraries installed on client machines. If an application needs to use one of these libraries, it will need to be granted full trust to run properly. If that decision is inappropriate, the application simply cannot be executed.

- Managed code has been tied into Internet Explorer in ways both similar to and different from ActiveX controls. Understanding how they are related is important for properly controlling your clients.

22

Administering Isolated Storage and Cryptography Settings in the .NET Framework

By Sebastian Lange

The .NET Framework contains two technologies that fall outside the administrative capabilities of the .NET Framework Configuration tool as well as Caspol, but which may occasionally require administrative changes—Isolated Storage and cryptography. Isolated Storage provides for a safe data and file storage system not requiring direct access to the file system, while the .NET Framework cryptography resources offer easy access for managed code to cryptography algorithms, such as RSA and DSA, as well as XML digital signatures. Administrators can set various parameters for both technologies. In this chapter, you will find the following key points covered:

- Review of the Isolated Storage system

- How to access and use the Isolated Storage administration tool

- Some help in writing your own Isolated Storage administration code against the Isolated Storage API set

- How to effectively use the IsolatedStoragePermission to define the degree of access managed code needed for the Isolated Storage system

- Overview of the cryptography configuration system

- Overview of the default settings for the cryptography configuration system

- Advice on how to change the `machine.config` file to include new cryptography resource mappings

If you find yourself in one of the following situations, you have come to the right portion of this book:

- A managed application has run out of Isolated Storage space.

- You want to clean out all state persisted by applications not having direct access to the file system (typically applications from the Internet or intranet).

- You want to write your own Isolated Storage administration tool.

- You have acquired a new managed cryptography library replacing part or all of the resources in the .NET Framework and want instantiations of common cryptography algorithms to go through the new library.

- You have written your own cryptography algorithm implementation and want that to be used by default as opposed to an algorithm implementation shipping in the .NET Framework `System.Security.Cryptography` namespace.

- Your enterprise has purchased a dedicated cryptography device (such as a hardware cryptographic accelerator), and this machine offers access to its services via a managed wrapper. You want the device's wrapper class and not the cryptography algorithm implementation in the .NET Framework's `System.Security.Cryptography` namespace used by default.

- You are simply curious what the Isolated Storage system and cryptography configuration system are all about.

As you will see, we have left behind the realm of GUI supported administration. However, both the Isolated Storage and cryptography configuration systems are very straightforward, and changes are very tractable and simple to make.

Administering Isolated Storage

The .NET Framework ships with a safe state storage system that can be used even by code that could not be trusted to access protected resources, such as the registry and the file system, directly. This allows a semitrusted application to still keep state, such as user preferences or user data, for later uses of that application. If there would not be such a system, any code running without access to the file system and registry would have no way of programmatically and seamlessly persisting state on the client machine, which would severely limit the usefulness such applications would have.

For example, not even the equivalent of a `notepad.exe` could have been written without saving some user data, namely a text file, to the user's machine. An assembly gains access to Isolated Storage through the Isolated Storage APIs that can be found in the `System.IO.IsolatedStorage` namespace. All data written and accessed through Isolated Storage is isolated by user context. Thus, Isolated Storage could not be used to share state between users. Rather, Isolated Storage data is written into the User Profile location of the respective user context in which Isolated Storage is exercised. In addition to this fundamental form of isolation, an application writing or accessing data through the Isolated Storage system has a couple of choices in how its data will get further isolated:

- *Isolation by User and Assembly only*—The most specific Assembly evidence, such as the assembly strong name, is used to create an Isolated Storage location for the respective assembly. Only instances of that assembly will be able to access and modify the contents of that Isolated Storage location.

- *Isolation by User, Application Domain, and Assembly*—In addition to the assembly evidence, the most specific appdomain evidence (such as a site name) is used to create an isolation context. Only instances of that assembly running in an appdomain with the same evidence (such as running from the same site) are allowed to access and modify data in that Isolated Storage context.

The order of specificity of evidence the Isolated Storage system looks for on an assembly or appdomain is as follows (most specific to least specific):

1. Authenticode signature (presence of publisher certificate)

2. Strong name

3. URL

4. Site

5. Zone

Let's look at an example. Suppose there is a widely used, shared component A that needs to save some state. A is authenticode signed. A is used in application B as well as in another application—C. To avoid collision of data access and modification between B and C, component A elects to write out data using the `User`,`Application` Domain and Assembly isolation option. This will direct all data access requests through Isolated Storage to a location in the User Profile directories that is specific both to A's publisher certificate (remember A is authenticode signed) as well as A's appdomain's URL (basically the URL from which either application B or C are running). This will avoid collision of data access between applications B and C.

> **NOTE**
>
> What actually happens on disk in the User Profile directory is that a directory is created that has a name consisting of the hash value over the assembly's evidence and, if application domain isolation is chosen, appdomain evidence. Only assemblies whose evidence, in combination with their app domain's evidence generates the same hash value, will be mapped back by the Isolated Storage system to that same location in the User Profile directories to create, modify, or access data or files persisted there.

In addition to the type of isolation, assemblies using Isolated Storage may also choose whether they want that data to roam with the User Profile or remain on the client machine where it has been created. Depending on that choice, the Isolated Storage system maps data access either to the roaming profile section of the User Profile or just to the local User Profile directory.

Isolated Storage is safe to use even for semitrusted applications because

- File location is strictly bound to assembly and possibly appdomain identity
- There are no pathnames or URLs involved
- Amount of file space resources available can be restricted by the administrator
- Assemblies cannot break out of per-user data and file isolation
- Assemblies cannot access data or files of another assembly, yielding protection against cross assembly information leaks

> **NOTE**
>
> Please see the .NET Framework SDK for more detail on Isolated Storage. Type `Isolated Storage` into the index of the SDK documentation viewer to view further background information.

Using `Storeadm.exe` to Administer Isolated Storage

Unlike the .NET Framework garbage collection system, the Isolated Storage system does not currently automatically reclaim unused Isolated Storage data. If a user wants to clean up Isolated Storage data, he or she needs to do so by using the `Storeadm` tool. This tool allows you to remove *all* roaming or *all* non-roaming Isolated Storage data saved in your User Profile.

> **TIP**
>
> Because the `Storeadm` tool only cleans out Isolated Storage for the user on whose behalf it is run, you cannot clean out Isolated Storage for all users on the machine. To do so, you can

write an MSI file that invokes the `Storeadm` tool for the roaming and non-roaming stores. That MSI file can then be deployed via Group Policy to all users on the machine (or even all users in an enterprise) and will run during the next login of the user. If you choose to do this, do not forget to switch off the user feedback on the `Storeadm` tool by setting the `/quiet` switch.

Finding and Invoking `Storeadm.exe`

The Isolated Storage administration tool, `Storeadm.exe`, ships with the .NET Framework SDK. It is located in the SDK directory, under the bin subdirectory (`....\FrameworkSDK\Bin\Storeadm.exe`).

TIP

To find out whether you have the .NET Framework SDK installed, open your Programs folder under the Start menu and see if you can find an entry for Microsoft .NET Framework SDK. Alternatively, select the Search option under the Start menu and search for a folder with name `FrameworkSDK`. The latter will show you where on your hard disk the SDK, and therefore `Storeadm`, has been installed. You can also search for the tool file directly by searching for `Storeadm.exe`.

Viewing Current Content of Isolated Storage

Before you start deleting the content of Isolated Storage, you should have a look to see what has been stored in it. You may discover that an application you use often has persisted important state that you do not want to delete just yet.

As previously mentioned, there are two forms of Isolated Storage that a managed application can choose. It can either write data or files into the roaming or the stationary Isolated Store. You can view either of the stores by using or not using the `/Roaming` option on the `Storeadm` tool.

To list the content of the non-roaming isolated storage, use the following command:

```
Storeadm /List
```

If `Storeadm` returns without printing out anything, the isolated store is empty and there is nothing in the non-roaming store you need to delete.

To list the content of the roaming isolated store for the current user context, use the following line:

```
Storeadm /Roaming /List
```

Again, if no content is printed out and `Storeadm` returns "empty handed," this means there is nothing in your roaming store as yet.

If there is content in Isolated Storage, the tool will show you the XML representation of the evidence used to isolate various stores, as well as the size in bytes of the respective store.

Typically, you will encounter strong name, publisher certificate, or URL types of evidence used to demarcate stores from each other. The following sample output of Storeadm shows an assembly store being isolated via a URL with a current size of 8,192 bytes.

```
Record #1
[Assembly]
<System.Security.Policy.Url version="1">
   <Url>file://C:/Documents and Settings/slange/My Documents/Visual Studio
➥Projects/ConsoleApplication1/bin/Debug/ConsoleApplication1.exe</Url>
</System.Security.Policy.Url>

        Size : 8192
```

> **NOTE**
>
> Note that the current size will not be available for roaming stores. The output for roaming stores will therefore exclude the store size.

Again, all data displayed is particular to the user context in which Storeadm is run.

Removing Content from Isolated Storage

You can delete all data from roaming Isolated Storage or from the non-roaming Isolated Storage. The Storeadm tool does not allow you to delete the data representing a specific assembly.

> **NOTE**
>
> Although Storeadm does not allow you to remove part of the content of Isolated Storage, it is still possible to programmatically do so. Please see the "Using the Isolated Storage APIs to Administer Isolated Storage" section later in this chapter as well as the .NET Framework SDK for some help.

The following are a few sample scenarios in which you may want to run the Storeadm tool to remove all data in the roaming or non-roaming stores:

- You want to clean out all persisted state of applications that have used your Isolated Storage (this is analogous to deleting all cookies that may have been dropped on your behalf by Internet sites you have visited).

- You are running low on disk space and know that you are not running critical Internet or intranet applications that need to use already persisted data.

- Current state persisted in Isolated Storage contains information that consistently causes an application not to function correctly (such as wrong or garbled personal settings that the application does not allow to be re-edited).

You can delete the local Isolated Storage content with the following command:

```
Storeadm /remove
```

To delete the content of the roaming Isolated Storage, use the following command:

```
Storeadm /roaming /remove
```

Isolated Storage content that has been removed cannot be retrieved again. You should err on the side of caution before summarily deleting all persisted state of all assemblies having used either the roaming or non-roaming Isolated Storage.

Using the Isolated Storage APIs to Administer Isolated Storage

In case you want to delete data in local or roaming Isolated Storage, or simply want to write a GUI tool representation of Isolated Storage content, you can do so using the Isolated Storage APIs shipping in the .NET Framework. The `System.IO.IsolatedStorage` namespace contains a number of classes that can be used to view and modify Isolated Storage properties and state:

- `IsolatedStorage` class—This is the abstract base class from which all Isolated Storage implementations must sub-class. It is conceivable to implement Isolated Storage not just over a file system, but other data or state storage systems as well (such as the registry). This class will serve as the base class for all these implementations. It is a class that you do not need to worry about if all you want to do is write your own code to administer the file-based Isolated Storage shipping in the .NET Framework.

- `IsolatedStorageFile` class—This class is the centerpiece of the Isolated Storage file system that ships in the .NET Framework. You can use this class to enumerate all stores under the current user context, delete stores or files in stores, as well as finding out the current size and maximum allowed size of a given store.

- `IsolatedStorageScope` enumeration—This enumeration is used to specify the isolation scope of a store.

Viewing All Stores of a User

The IsolatedStorageFile class contains the static GetEnumerator method. This method will return an enumeration of the stores of the current user. Each member of this enumeration is an instance of type IsolatedStorageFile. This class also contains a number of properties that are helpful in determining the size, scope, and evidence used to isolate the specific store. The following code sample in Listing 22.1 shows all the local stores of the current user as well as the scope, size, maximum allowed size, and the isolation evidence of every store of the current user. If you want to list all the roaming stores, you need to use the following line in Listing 22.1 for the user store enumeration:

You will also need to trap access to the CurrentSize property when accessing roaming stores, because the current store size is not defined for roaming stores.

LISTING 22.1   Viewing All Stores of the Current User—viewstores.cs

```
using System;
using System.IO;
using System.IO.IsolatedStorage;
using System.Collections;

public class EnumerateIsoStores
{

    public static int Main()
    {
        bool fRoaming = false;
        IsolatedStorageScope scopeRoaming = (IsolatedStorageScope.User|
                                    IsolatedStorageScope.Roaming);

        IsolatedStorageScope scopeLocal = (IsolatedStorageScope.User);

        IEnumerator allstores = IsolatedStorageFile.GetEnumerator(fRoaming ?
scopeRoaming : scopeLocal);
        long fullsize = 0;
        // Display the size and isolation properties of all iso stores of the
current user
        while(allstores.MoveNext())
        {
            //save current store in local var
            IsolatedStorageFile store = (IsolatedStorageFile)allstores.Current;
```

LISTING 22.1   Continued

```
            //print out scope
            Console.WriteLine("Scope:"+store.Scope.ToString());
            //print out what assembly evidence is used to isolate store
            Console.WriteLine("Store - Assembly
➥ID:"+store.AssemblyIdentity.ToString());
            //print out domain evidence if store is also isolated by domain
            if((store.Scope & IsolatedStorageScope.Domain) != 0)
                Console.WriteLine("Domain:"+store.DomainIdentity.ToString());

            try{
                //print current size of store if present
                Console.WriteLine("Store Size:"+store.CurrentSize);
            } catch(Exception) {
                Console.WriteLine("Current Size is not defined");
            }
            Console.WriteLine("----------------------------------------------");

            if (!fRoaming)
                //count up size of store
                fullsize += (long)store.CurrentSize;
        }

        Console.WriteLine("The total size = {0} \npress ENTER to exit",
                    (fRoaming) ? "undefined" : System.Convert.ToString(full
➥size));
        String t = Console.ReadLine();
        return 0;
    }

}
```

NOTE

To enumerate and access stores belonging to other assemblies, the
`IsolatedStoragePermission`'s `AdministerIsolatedStorageByUser` flag needs to have been
granted to the assembly trying this access. It is, for example, not possible to run the previous
code, as shown in Listing 22.1 from the local intranet under the default policy settings. Policy
would need to be changed to grant this permission to the assembly containing the code of
the previous sample.

Removing All Stores of a User

You can remove all local stores or all roaming stores from Isolated Storage by calling the static `Remove` method on the `IsolatedStorageFile` class. Listing 22.2 deletes all roaming isolated stores.

LISTING 22.2   Removing All Stores of the Current User

```
using System;
using System;
using System.IO;
using System.IO.IsolatedStorage;
public class deleteallroamingstores
 {

    public static int Main()
    {
        Console.WriteLine
            ("Deleting all roaming iso stores of current user...");
        IsolatedStorageFile.Remove
            (IsolatedStorageScope.User|IsolatedStorageScope.Roaming);
                Console.WriteLine("press ENTER to exit");
        String t = Console.ReadLine();
        return 0;
    }

 }
```

NOTE

You can also delete individual files and folders from a store. The `IsolatedStorageFile` class contains the `DeleteFile` and `DeleteDirectory` that can be used for that purpose. Please refer to the .NET Framework SDK for more detail.

Using the `IsolatedStorageFilePermission` to Govern Code Access to Isolated Storage

The .NET Framework ships with the `IsolatedStorageFilePermission` that determines all access to isolated file storage. If code does not receive this permission, it cannot create, modify, or read from Isolated Storage files. By default policy, this permission is given both to code running from the local machine as well as the local intranet. If you configure the policy to allow for code from the Internet to run (using the Internet permission set on the Internet code group), all assemblies from the

Internet also receive rights to create and access Isolated Storage. There are a couple of properties that can be set on this permission:

- `UserQuota`—The size of the current user's local Isolated Storage for the respective assembly. If code exceeds this size due to writing to Isolated Storage for that user, an exception will be thrown. This quota expresses the maximum store capacity for this assembly in bytes.

- `UsageAllowed`—This property determines the isolation and access scope allowed to code receiving this permission. For example, it is possible to mandate that code receiving this permission should only be able to use user+domain+ assembly isolation and not also user+assembly isolation.

Using this permission, you can mandate how any code should access the Isolated Storage file system. For example, the Internet permission set currently sets a quota limit of 10Kb of data. There is nothing magic about this number. If you know that many Internet applications you allow to run will need more storage space in Isolated Storage, you should consider increasing the user store quota for Internet assemblies to a reasonable limit. You will typically notice this necessity either by seeing Internet code surface with an `IsolatedStorageException` or another error message to the same effect. You may want to proactively increase the maximum allowed storage for the user's local Isolated Storage to the amount of data and file storage you feel comfortable giving to Internet code. By contrast, the default policy sets no true quota limit for intranet applications (limit is set to 9,223,372,036,854,775,807 bytes, to be specific). If you find that you do not want any intranet application to take up all your hard disk space maliciously or as a result of programming error, you may consider lowering this limit substantially.

Because the `IsolatedStorageFilePermission` is a security permission type that you can freely use in security policy, there is nothing that binds you to having different Isolated Storage usage limits only at the per-zone level. You could easily use a more complex Isolated Storage access rights allotment scheme. For example, you can introduce a few code groups at the root of the machine policy (presuming default policy state) that will grant unlimited quota rights to isolated file storage based on strong names and authenticode signatures. This would allow you to grant more disk resources to applications that have been signed by publishers you trust highly.

Administering Cryptography Settings

The .NET Framework ships with a rich, fully extensible library of cryptography algorithm implementations. The .NET Framework ships with

- *Hash algorithms*—Included are the standard implementations of hash algorithms, such as SHA1, MD5, but also SHA256 and SHA512, in the `System.Security.Cryptography` namespace.

- *Symmetric algorithms*—The .NET Framework contains the standard implementations of DES and Triple DES, among other symmetric ciphers in the `System.Security.Cryptography` namespace.

- *Asymmetric algorithms*—The .NET Framework ships with the standard implementations of RSA and DSA, also in the `System.Security.Cryptography` namespace.

- Class collection for doing XML digital signatures in the `System.Security.Cryptography.XML` namespace.

- Finally, included in the .NET Framework are also a few classes to do rudimentary processing and work with x.509v3 publisher certificates, contained in the `System.Security.Cryptography.X509Certificates` namespace.

NOTE

To find out more about each of the cryptographical resources appearing in the previous bulleted list, please refer to Chapter 30, "Using Cryptography with the .NET Framework: The Basics," Chapter 31, "Using Cryptography with the .NET Framework: Advanced Topics," and Chapter 32, "Using Cryptography with the .NET Framework: Creating and Verifying XML Digital Signatures."

All of the cryptographic algorithms in `System.Security.Cryptography` are organized into a strict class hierarchy. For example, all hash algorithms derive from the abstract base class `HashAlgorithm`. All implementations of the SHA1 algorithm have to derive from the abstract base class `SHA1`, which in turn derives from `HashAlgorithm`. This strict ordering from most generic cryptographic algorithm category to specific implementation is done for all symmetric and asymmetric algorithms as well. This class structure provides an easy and well-defined way to extend the cryptography library with other cryptographic algorithm implementations, but it also provides the backdrop for the cryptography configuration system.

The cryptography configuration system provides the following main features:

- Every abstract base class for hash algorithms and symmetric and asymmetric algorithms can be queried for a default implementation instance.

- You can query the cryptography configuration system directly to return a cryptography algorithm instance to you simply by supplying a friendly name.

Let us look at a few examples of these features. It is possible to ask the `SHA1` base class to return a default instance of a `SHA1` implementation. Unless cryptography configuration has been changed, this call will return an instance of the

SHA1CryptoServiceProvider class, which in the default cryptography configuration settings has been deemed the standard SHA1 implementation. The following line of code shows how the default SHA1 implementation is created:

```
SHA1 sha1alginstance = SHA1.Create();
```

A developer will not need to know exactly which SHA1 algorithm instance is returned (all SHA1 implementations have to implement a set of members defined by the SHA1 base class as well as the HashAlgorithm superclass). Nor will the developer need to know the syntax of how to instantiate that class. He or she asked the SHA1 base class for a SHA1 instance and got it.

The second feature is quite similar, although here the developer needs to supply the friendly name of an algorithm for which he or she wants to have an instance. The following line of code shows how you can get your hands on the default Triple DES implementation without having to explicitly know which algorithm in the cryptography library of the .NET Framework to instantiate:

```
SymmetricAlgorithm 3des = CryptoConfig.CreateFromName("TripleDES");
```

Both features allow for the notion of a default implementation for cryptography algorithms. This provides developers with a way to work at a level that is abstracted away from a particular algorithm implementation. You may wonder why this is useful. The answer is that this allows you to seamlessly shift to a new library of cryptography algorithm implementations or the managed wrappers accessing newly purchased dedicated cryptography hardware without breaking any code. In either case, only a change to the default mappings of the respective cryptography algorithms is necessary.

Overview of the Cryptography Configuration Settings

The cryptography configuration system provides two types of mappings:

- From friendly names to classnames that can be instantiated (this mapping is used by both features mentioned in the previous section)

- From friendly names to the respective algorithm's assigned ASN.1 Object Identifier (OID) number

---

NOTE

ASN.1 is a binary serialization format that is used by some cryptographic object standards, such as X.509v3 certificates. In ASN.1, each cryptographic algorithm is associated with one or more Object Identifiers (OIDs). An OID is a dotted sequence of numbers; for example, the OID that represents the SHA1 algorithm is "1.3.14.3.2.26." The configuration system provides

name-to-OID mappings as part of the support for certain signature and key exchange formatting algorithms, such as RSAPKCS1. The only time you should have to change the OID
mapping rules is when you add new cryptographic algorithms to the .NET Framework and
want to use those algorithms with an existing ASN.1-based formatter.

The CryptoConfig class provides static methods for both of the previously discussed
mapping forms. For example

```
AsymmetricAlgorithm rsainstance = CryptoConfig.CreateFromName("RSA");
```

The CreateFromName method looks up the friendly name in the "name to classname"
table of the cryptography configuration system. The corresponding classname is used
to load and instantiate that class by calling the default constructor of that class. The
resulting instance is then returned by the configuration system.

Similarly, the following example illustrates how to obtain an OID string corresponding to a friendly name by calling the static MapNameToOID method on the
CryptoConfig class:

```
String oidstring = CryptoConfig.MapNameToOID("SHA1");
```

Corresponding to these two mappings of friendly algorithm names (such as RSA) are
two cryptography configuration tables that are part of the configuration system that
hold these mappings.

One table simply has columns for friendly names and corresponding fully qualified
classnames. The other table has columns for friendly names and the corresponding
OID numbers. The cryptography system ships with reasonable default values for
both of these tables (see the "Default Mappings" section later in this chapter), but
you can change the table to fit your or your organization's needs (such as changing
the friendly name to classname mapping on installation of a dedicated cryptography
device doing RSA encryption/descryption).

Default Mappings

Table 22.1 shows the default mappings between friendly algorithm names and classes
in the .NET Framework. As will be shown in the "Modifying Cryptography
Configuration" section later in this chapter, you can modify these mappings to set
the default implementations of cryptography algorithms to other implementations
in the .NET Framework cryptography library or to external implementations.

TABLE 22.1   Default Mappings Between Friendly Cryptography Algorithm Names and Classnames

Friendly Name	Class Name
System.Security.Cryptography. HashAlgorithm	System.Security.Cryptography. SHA1CryptoServiceProvider
SHA	System.Security.Cryptography. SHA1CryptoServiceProvider
SHA1	System.Security.Cryptography. SHA1CryptoServiceProvider
System.Security.Cryptography.SHA1	System.Security.Cryptography. SHA1CryptoServiceProvider
MD5	System.Security.Cryptography. MD5CryptoServiceProvider
System.Security.Cryptography.MD5	System.Security.Cryptography. MD5CryptoServiceProvider
SHA256	System.Security.Cryptography.SHA256Managed
SHA-256	System.Security.Cryptography.SHA256Managed
System.Security.Cryptography.SHA256	System.Security.Cryptography.SHA256Managed
SHA384	System.Security.Cryptography.SHA384Managed
SHA-384	System.Security.Cryptography.SHA384Managed
System.Security.Cryptography.SHA384	System.Security.Cryptography.SHA384Managed
SHA512	System.Security.Cryptography.SHA512Managed
SHA-512	System.Security.Cryptography.SHA512Managed
System.Security.Cryptography.SHA512	System.Security.Cryptography.SHA512Managed
RSA	System.Security.Cryptography. RSACryptoServiceProvider
System.Security.Cryptography.RSA	System.Security.Cryptography. RSACryptoServiceProvider
System.Security.Cryptography. AsymmetricAlgorithm	System.Security.Cryptography. RSACryptoServiceProvider
DSA	System.Security.Cryptography. DSACryptoServiceProvider
System.Security.Cryptography.DSA	System.Security.Cryptography. DSACryptoServiceProvider
DES	System.Security.Cryptography. DESCryptoServiceProvider
System.Security.Cryptography.DES	System.Security.Cryptography. DESCryptoServiceProvider
3DES	System.Security.Cryptography. TripleDESCryptoServiceProvider
TripleDES	System.Security.Cryptography. TripleDESCryptoServiceProvider

TABLE 22.1 Continued

Friendly Name	Class Name
Triple DES	System.Security.Cryptography.TripleDESCryptoServiceProvider
System.Security.Cryptography.TripleDES	System.Security.Cryptography.TripleDESCryptoServiceProvider
System.Security.Cryptography.SymmetricAlgorithm	System.Security.Cryptography.TripleDESCryptoServiceProvider
RC2	System.Security.Cryptography.RC2CryptoServiceProvider
System.Security.Cryptography.RC2	System.Security.Cryptography.RC2CryptoServiceProvider
Rijndael	System.Security.Cryptography.RijndaelManaged
System.Security.Cryptography.Rijndael	System.Security.Cryptography.RijndaelManaged

As you can see in Table 22.1, there is often a many-to-one mapping between friendly names and classnames representing the default implementation of the respective algorithm. One example is the TripleDes algorithm; supplying either 3DES or Triple DES to the CreateFromName method on the CryptoConfig class will yield an instance of the TripleDESCryptoServiceProvider class. Table 22.1 also makes clear how various abstract base classes map to default implementations. The classname of the abstract base class is simply used as the friendly name in Table 22.1, the right column corresponding to the default implementation for that base class. For example, calling the Create() method on the HashAlgorithm class will return an instance of the SHA1CryptoServiceProvider class, as can be seen in the first line of the table. The base class simply calls the cryptography configuration system with its own classname as friendly name and sees if it can receive back a default implementation mapping. Thus, if you want to change the default implementation for hash algorithms, you only need to change the mapping for the friendly name System.Security.Cryptography.HashAlgorithm to a different classname from what is defined in the default mappings.

NOTE

A typical consumer of the cryptography configuration is, in fact, Caspol, the administration tool introduced in Chapter 19, "Administering .NET Framework Security Policy Using Scripts and Security APIs." When you use the -hash *algorithmname* membership option, Caspol just calls the crypto configuration system with *algorithmname* to get back an algorithm instance mapping to the friendly hash algorithm you supplied.

Table 22.2 presents the default mapping for OIDs and friendly names.

TABLE 22.2   Default Mappings Between Friendly Cryptography Algorithm Names and OIDs

Friendly Name	OID
SHA1	1.3.14.3.2.26
System.Security.Cryptography.SHA1	1.3.14.3.2.26
System.Security.Cryptography.SHA1CryptoServiceProvider	1.3.14.3.2.26
System.Security.Cryptography.SHA1Managed	1.3.14.3.2.26
SHA256	2.16.840.1.101.3.4.1
System.Security.Cryptography.SHA256	2.16.840.1.101.3.4.1
System.Security.Cryptography.SHA256Managed	2.16.840.1.101.3.4.1
SHA384	2.16.840.1.101.3.4.2
System.Security.Cryptography.SHA384	2.16.840.1.101.3.4.2
System.Security.Cryptography.SHA384Managed	2.16.840.1.101.3.4.2
SHA512	2.16.840.1.101.3.4.3
System.Security.Cryptography.SHA512	2.16.840.1.101.3.4.3
MD5	1.2.840.113549.2.5
System.Security.Cryptography.MD5	1.2.840.113549.2.5
System.Security.Cryptography.MD5CryptoServiceProvider	1.2.840.113549.2.5
System.Security.Cryptography.MD5Managed	1.2.840.113549.2.5
TripleDESKeyWrap	1.2.840.113549.1.9.16.3.6

Supplying any of the names in Table 22.2 to the static MapNameToOID function on the CryptoConfig class will return a string containing the respective OID number shown in the table.

Modifying Cryptography Configuration

The default settings introduced in the previous section should suffice for most use cases of the cryptography library of the .NET Framework. Typical scenarios in which you may want to change these settings include:

- You have purchased a dedicated cryptography device for which you have a managed class wrapper from which to access the device.

- You have written or obtained cryptography algorithm implementations other than the ones in the .NET Framework class.

- You have good reason to change the default implementation for a base class to another class in the .NET Framework (for example, you may want to make SHA256Managed instead of SHA1CryptoServiceProvider the default hash algorithm).

When custom cryptography configuration settings are introduced into `machine.config`, the cryptography configuration system will first try to locate any mapping request in those user-supplied settings. However, if no match is found, the cryptography configuration system will try to find a match in the default mappings (see the "Default Mappings" section earlier in this chapter). Thus, the default mappings will always be available as fallback, and you only need to introduce mappings that either override default mappings or are not contained in the default mappings table.

To modify the mappings, perform the following steps:

1. Find or create the `machine.config` file.

2. Add your configuration mappings into the `machine.config` file.

3. Save the `machine.config` file.

4. Test your changes.

These steps will now be explained in more detail.

Finding `machine.config`

Cryptography configuration settings are part of the machine-wide configuration state that can be defined for the .NET Framework in the `machine.config` file. The file can be found at

`%WINDIR%\Micrsosoft.NET\Framework\v[.NETversion]\Config\machine.config`.

Depending on which operating system you are running, `%WINDIR%` will be the directory where the operating system had been installed, most commonly `c:\Windows` or `c:\WINNT`.

> **NOTE**
>
> The fastest way to find this file is by using the Search option under the Start menu, and typing in the filename **machine.config**.

Because `machine.config` is located under the Windows operating system directory, it receives the same ACL protections that other system resources have on a specific machine. By default, only machine administrators and power users will be able to change files under this directory, so `machine.config` is typically not modifiable by users without machine administrator rights.

This file is an XML file that is read by various core technologies of the .NET Framework. You can insert the cryptography configuration section into this file, which must adhere to a cryptography configuration XML schema (see the "Schema for Adding XML Configuration Settings" section later in this chapter). The default mappings (see the "Default Mappings" section earlier in this chapter) are not explicitly written into this file, but are implicit in the cryptography configuration system implementation. Consequently, you should not be surprised to find no cryptography configuration settings in this file when you edit it the first time. When reading the `machine.config` file, the cryptography configuration system goes through the following sequence of steps to determine what mappings should apply:

1. Locate `machine.config`; if not located, go to step 4.

2. Find the `<cryptographysettings>` element in the `machine.config` file under the explicitly versioned `<mscorlib>` element matching the version of the .NET Framework CLR currently running. If successful, apply those settings; otherwise, go to step 3.

3. Find the `<cryptographysettings>` element in the `machine.config` file under the `<mscorlib>` that has not been explicitly versioned. If found, apply those mappings. If no mapping match is found, proceed to step 4; otherwise, return the requested mapping.

4. Apply the default mappings, as implemented in the cryptography configuration system itself.

These steps basically mean that you can configure cryptography mappings for different versions of the .NET Framework. If no cryptography configuration settings can be found in the `machine.config` file or the `machine.config` file does not exist, the cryptography configuration system will apply the default mappings as described earlier. For the v1.0 release of the .NET Framework, you will not have to worry about versioning your cryptography settings and should just include your cryptography configuration settings under the general `<mscorlib>` element as determined by the schema in the following section.

Adding Cryptography Settings

You will need to hand edit the `machine.config` file to change cryptography configuration mappings and then save the changed file. There is currently no tool support to help you change the cryptography default mappings. Listing 22.3 shows the general schema for adding cryptography settings to the `machine.config` file. All italicized items are explained after the schema definition. All items in bold belong to the metalanguage, defining properties of the schema and not being a literal part of the XML file. This means that the following symbols are just used to group and describe the schema in question; they will never appear in the actual XML files. The (and) symbols group schema expressions. The + symbol states that an expression can occur one or more times. // denotes a comment. All these symbols are used to talk about the specific symbols occurring in the cryptography configuration XML. They are used to define the grammar of all possible XML representations for cryptography configuration XML.

LISTING 22.3   The Cryptography Configuration XML Schema

```
<configuration>
//other configuration settings, ignore, do not modify!
   <mscorlib>
      <cryptographySettings>
         <cryptoNameMapping>
            <cryptoClasses>
               (
               <cryptoClass
                 classreferencename="classnameinassembly, assemblyname
                  Culture=
                        culturevalue, PublicKeyToken=strongnamepublickeytoken,
                    Version=assemblyversion"/>
            )+
             </cryptoClasses>
            (
             <nameEntry name="friendlyname" class="classreferencename"/>
            )+
         </cryptoNameMapping>
          (
          <oidMap>
                <oidEntry OID="OIDvalue"   name="friendlyname"/>
             </oidMap>
            )+
         </cryptographySettings>
      </mscorlib>
//other settings, ignore!
</configuration>
```

The cryptography settings need to be inserted under the <mscorlib> element in the
machine.config file. If no <mscorlib> element is in the machine.config file, you
need to add that element yourself somewhere as a child element under the
<configuration> element. All cryptography configuration information must be
enclosed by the <cryptographySettings> element that is directly enclosed by the
<mscorlib> element. The schema contains sections both for the friendly name to
class mapping, delineated by the <cryptoNameMapping> and <oidMap> elements,
respectively. The <cryptoNameMapping> section contains the <cryptoClasses>
section. This section defines the class references for instantiating default implementations. An indefinite number of classes can be included in that section. Each class
reference is expressed by a <cryptoClass> element, whose attributes determine the
class reference. That reference is named by *classreferencename*, which is used as a
shortcut within the configuration file. You should not confuse *classreferencename*
with the friendly name (*friendlyname*). Each class reference is just the fully qualified

type name of the class (please see the .NET Framework SDK for more help on this topic).

After the classes have been defined in the <cryptoClasses> section, an indefinite number of mappings between friendly names and classes occurs. Each mapping is represented by a <nameEntry> element, whose name attribute holds the friendly name (*friendlyname*), while the class attribute holds the name of the class reference (*classreferencename*) defined in the <cryptoClasses> section. Following the name mapping section (<cryptoNameMapping> element scope) is the OID mapping, as represented by the <oidMap> element. Each OID mapping is denoted by an <oidEntry> element, whose OID attribute contains the OID string and whose name element contains the friendly name (*friendlyname* reference). There can be an indefinite number of defined OID mappings.

All this may sound terribly complicated, but it is actually quite straightforward. The abbreviated example in Listing 22.4 will cause any requests to the default implementation of RSA or AsymmetricAlgorithm to be satisfied with an instance of a new RSA class implemented in the RSAAssembly. An OID mapping is also defined for this implementation.

NOTE

It is very important to note that the settings in Listing 22.4 will only override the RSA, System.Security.Cryptography.RSA, and System.Security.Cryptography.AssymetricAlgorithm entries of the default mappings defined in the configuration system. All other default mappings will still apply.

The fully qualified type names of classes shipping in the .NET Framework can be found in the .NET Framework SDKs class reference documentation for the respective class.

LISTING 22.4   Example of Cryptography Configuration Settings in machine.config

```
<configuration>
//various other config settings in machine.config
   <mscorlib>
      <cryptographySettings>
         <cryptoNameMapping>
            <cryptoClasses>
               <cryptoClass NewRSA="RSADeviceClass, RSAAssembly
                  Culture='en', PublicKeyToken=a2b42345f64568d,
                  Version=1.0.0"/>
            </cryptoClasses>
            <nameEntry name="DeviceRSA" class="NewRSA"/>
            <nameEntry name="RSA" class="NewRSA"/>
```

LISTING 22.4   Continued

```
        <nameEntry name="System.Security.Cryptography.RSA" class="NewRSA"/>
        <nameEntry
            name="System.Security.Cryptography.AsymmetricAlgorithm"
➥class="NewRSA"/>
        </cryptoNameMapping>
        <oidMap>
            <oidEntry OID="1.1.11.1.41.1"  name="NewRSA"/>
        </oidMap>
    </cryptographySettings>
  </mscorlib>
</configuration>
```

Testing Cryptography Configuration Changes

After you have made your cryptography configuration changes, you should quickly
test whether your settings map as expected. Because you have to hand edit XML to
set state for the cryptography configuration system, it is easy to introduce an error.
To test successful name mappings, simply use the CreateFromName method on the
CryptoConfig object with the friendly names corresponding to name mappings you
have changed or altered. Or to find out whether OID mapping changes were successful, simply use the MapNameToOID method on the CryptoConfig class. Listing 22.5
shows an example of testing whether the cryptography configuration changes introduced in Listing 22.4 were successful.

LISTING 22.5   Testing Whether Cryptography Configuration Changes Were Successful—
cryptcfgtest.cs

```csharp
using System;
 using System.IO;
 using System.Security.Cryptography;

 public class TestCryptoMapping
 {

     public static int Main()
     {
        //try and find a mapping for name "DeviceRSA" in crypto config
        RSA rsadev = (RSA)CryptoConfig.CreateFromName("DeviceRSA");
        //if not found print out error message
         if(rsadev==null)
            Console.WriteLine(
                            "DeviceRSA not found in Crypto config!");
```

LISTING 22.5   Continued

```
          //if found print out type name
                //of the class returned by crypto config
          else
          Console.WriteLine((rsadev.GetType()).AssemblyQualifiedName);

      //try and find an Oid mapping in the crypto config settings
      string Oid = CryptoConfig.MapNameToOID("NewRSA");
      //if not found print error message
       if (Oid==null)
          Console.WriteLine(
                            " NewRSA not found in Crypto config!");
      //else print out return val from crypto config settings
       else
          Console.WriteLine("Crypt Config returned:"+Oid);
      Console.WriteLine("Press ENTER to continue...");
       string dummy = Console.ReadLine();
       return 0;
    }


}
```

The preceding sample code tests both whether the DeviceRSA name mapping works and, if so, what class gets returned from the cryptography configuration system. It also checks whether a mapping to an OID number for the NewRSA name exists.

Summary

Neither Isolated Storage or cryptography configuration settings are likely to be on your list of areas requiring frequent administration. For this reason, there is very little tool support for setting state for either of these technologies, and you should have a good understanding of the contents of this chapter before making any administrative modifications in either area. Isolated Storage will require you to write your own administrative code, using the API set introduced in this chapter, if you want to do more than erasing all Isolated Storage state for a user. Likewise, cryptography configuration settings will require you to write an XML representation of the mappings you want the cryptography configuration system to make. Because both writing code and creating XML are error prone, you are well advised to take your time and thoroughly test each change.

PART V

.NET Framework Security for Developers

IN THIS PART

23

Creating Secure Code: What All .NET Framework Developers Need to Know

IN THIS CHAPTER

- Security and the Developer
- Structure of the .NET Framework Security System
- Limitations of the .NET Framework Security System

By Rudi Martin

So far, we have dealt with the .NET Framework security system primarily from an abstract, conceptual level or from the point of view of an administrator. The following chapters (23 through 26) focus on a developer-oriented approach. This encompasses the entire development life cycle: from initial architecture and design to implementation, testing, and maintenance.

We'll discuss the mechanics of designing and writing your own secure code: common strategies, pitfalls, and trade-offs. Where appropriate, we'll discuss details of the .NET Framework's own security design and implementation.

This chapter will concern itself principally with describing what exactly we mean by security and defining the bounds of the .NET Framework security system. You will gain insight into the following topics:

- What constitutes "secure" code

- How security enforcement is split between the .NET Framework and the operating system

- What the .NET Framework security system can and cannot do to protect your applications

Security and the Developer

What do we mean when we refer to "secure code?" In essence, the ultimate purpose of security is to allow "good" code to execute while denying access to "bad" code. Unfortunately, there are no algorithms that let us differentiate "good" code from "bad." Suppose, for example, that a request is made to append data to a file. Is this an attempt to inject a virus, or is it merely new output being added to some log file?

No security system can judge the intent behind such an action; even humans sometimes have difficulty discerning the true purpose of a piece of code. Instead, the security system concentrates on evidence about the user or code that it knows is factual or can be validated: usernames validated by passwords, strong names or Authenticode signatures, code download URLs, and so on. These allow the security system to characterize the user or code based on identity—either specifically, as with usernames or digital signatures, or more broadly, as with user groups or Internet zones based on download URLs.

Together with policy information from the system administrator, this allows the security system to assign levels of trust to users and code. In this way, we manage to sidestep the problem of needing to understand intent; instead of asking "Is that operation bad?" we now ask "Is that operation risky?" and "Do we trust this user/code to perform such risky operations?"

To get back to our original question—What is secure code?—secure code is about responsibilities. The extent of those responsibilities depends on the level of trust your code will be granted. Highly trusted code will have the ability to perform very dangerous operations (such as formatting the user's hard disk) and may even be able to circumvent the security system itself. Such code needs to be written very carefully to avoid mistakes that could open up serious security holes. Code with low levels of trust, on the other hand, has fewer responsibilities: Such code is "sandboxed" into a low risk environment where access to dangerous facilities such as file access is denied. Code at the lowest levels of trust couldn't open up a security hole even if it tried.

The responsibilities of trusted code are twofold:

- Protect access to operations that could compromise the system. These operations are typically focused around system resources: files, the registry, access to the desktop display. The code that implements access to such resources must validate the caller's level of trust. Typically, it does so by associating a permission with the resource and demanding that permission of any caller (the caller's level of trust is modeled as a set of permissions that are granted by system policy).

- Ensure that the levels of trust granted aren't open to misuse by callers of lesser (or undetermined) trust. This is the hard one and constitutes the source of the majority of security holes. Breaches of this responsibility can range from the blatant—exporting a public method that writes to an arbitrary file on behalf of an untrusted caller—to the subtle—leaving a sensitive member field marked protected so that an untrusted caller can subclass the type and gain access. Failure to uphold this responsibility will allow code of lower trust to break out of its sandbox and enjoy a greater level of trust than the system administrator was willing to grant it.

Protecting access to resources will require direct interaction with the APIs of the security system. The managed libraries that come with the .NET Framework contain abstractions for most common system resources (along with the necessary access protection), so typically developers will only need to worry about new resources specific to their system. For instance, a banking application may define a new permission to control access to the bank's accounts database.

```
public ResultSet QueryAccountsDatabase(String query)
{
    new AccountAccessPermission("Accounts",
                                DBAccess.ReadOnly).Demand();
    …
}
```

Ensuring that trust is not leaked to untrusted code is a much more pervasive problem. Solutions to potential holes may or may not involve the security infrastructure directly. Secure coding practice can fundamentally impact the codebase (especially when performance is taken into consideration). For instance, access to some resource may depend on the acquisition of a token, allowing the relatively heavyweight security access checks to be performed at one choke point and leaving the high-frequency access paths free of overhead (similar to the model used for file access). Implementing such a scheme has the potential of affecting the implementation, and possibly even the design, of all other dependent software components.

From this, two important points should be apparent:

- Security should be a part of the product life cycle from the very beginning. You should design the techniques and protocols that will ensure that your code is secure before moving into the implementation phase. The cost of retrofitting correct (and efficient) security is too high, both in terms of code destabilization and in terms of risk. A security change introduced at a late stage typically won't have had the breadth of exposure that a design-time change would have: Less thought will have gone into verifying its correctness, programmers will be less likely to understand its importance, and test coverage may well be compromised (code security is much harder to test than most features, since negative testing plays such an important role). While early planning and testing is important for any aspect of software design, it's particularly important for security because the problems can be so subtle and hard to find and the consequences of not finding a problem before shipping are so dire. In fact, the cost of a security flaw being unearthed once the product has reached customers is usually many times greater than the cost of any other type of software defect.

- Good, secure code design and implementation is the responsibility of everyone working on the product, not just a focused security group. While having specific individuals who focus on security is a good idea in most cases, it's important that all developers have an understanding of the basic rules and where their responsibilities lie. When just one subtle error can compromise the security of an entire system, it is unrealistic to expect that a subset of the developers will have the resources and expertise to locate all such errors in a reasonable time frame. It makes much more sense to teach every developer the basics of secure coding and have them evaluate and fix their own code than to try and teach a small number of security experts about every aspect of the system you're building.

The .NET Framework does provide one tool for limiting the impact that trusted but potentially flawed code can have on the system. Strong named assemblies (those being the most likely to be shared amongst applications) which have not been explicitly marked with the `System.Security.AllowPartiallyTrustedCallersAttribute` custom attribute will not allow any untrusted callers at all. This allows developers to restrict access to potentially buggy or poorly designed code until such time as that code can be reviewed and tested thoroughly. At this point, the attribute can be added to the assembly and access opened to callers with a lower level of trust. For further discussion of the mechanics of `AllowPartiallyTrustedCallersAttribute`, see Chapter 25.

Structure of the .NET Framework Security System

Now that we've covered the basics of security responsibilities, let's see what the .NET Framework provides in the way of support.

Figure 23.1 shows how the runtime acts as a layer between the client code and the operating system, adding (from the perspective of security) the concept of code-identity–based security checking.

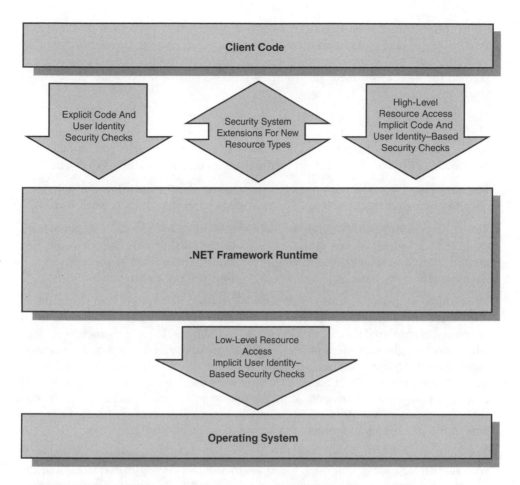

FIGURE 23.1   .NET Framework layering from the security perspective.

Notice that the lowest, most fundamental level is the operating system itself. This is not just a case of the .NET Framework utilizing general operating system services as part of its implementation (though it certainly does this). Rather, we mean to show that the security checks and constraints put in place by the framework are in addition to those provided by the operating system.

Say a developer writes the following code fragment:

```
FileStream file = new FileStream("c:\foo.dat", FileMode.Open, FileAccess.Read);
```

Execution of this code will cause the .NET Framework security system to initiate a demand for FileIOPermission with read access to c:\foo.dat. The demand will walk the stack and verify that every assembly involved in the call chain has been granted the aforementioned permission. That takes care of the code access security check.

The implementation of the FileStream constructor will at some point call the Win32 function CreateFile to let the operating system access the file. At this point, the user credentials of the process or thread will be checked against the protections on the file (using Win32 ACLs). So user identity checks are performed as well.

Therefore, for the FileStream operation to succeed, the file must be accessible to both the user making the call and the managed code with which the call is made.

Registry access is the other major area where the same dual access check behavior is exhibited. In future versions of the framework, it is possible that managed wrappers around other access-controlled operating system resources (such as processes or shared memory) will become available and follow the same pattern.

The framework sometimes checks code access to operating system resources that don't have any corresponding notion of user access checks. Examples include the use of environment variables and the ability to manipulate UI elements such as dialog windows. This gives a system manager or user much greater control over a managed application than the traditional unmanaged world allows. For example, default security policy prevents a downloaded Internet applet from determining the user's account name from the environment. The operating system would allow such access since environment variables are essentially private to a process, and it seems reasonable that a process should always be allowed to access its own data.

The next category of security checking is for resources that are entirely managed, with no unmanaged counterpart. Examples include access to isolated storage or the reflection subsystem, and the ability to control the .NET Framework security system itself (using, for instance, SecurityPermission.ControlEvidence or PrincipalPermission).

PrincipalPermission is interesting in that it provides the basic infrastructure to implement security access checks that are based on arbitrary data associated with the thread of execution as opposed to the identities of assemblies on the current call stack. This is similar to the way in which the operating system tracks user identity using tokens, and is referred to as role-based security within the managed world. Role-based security is a fundamental part of ASP.NET's security implementation.

The .NET Framework class libraries provide a rich set of resource access APIs that already implement the required security checks. In the preceding examples, we already touched on some of them: file, registry, reflection, and so on. It's important to note that this alone is not enough to ensure secure code, however. Such resources must always be treated responsibly to avoid creation of security holes. For instance, if a trusted method opens a file and then passes the file handle out to an untrusted caller, it's important to realize that access to the handle is not guarded by any further security checks (all security checks are centered on handle creation for performance reasons), so you might be introducing a security hole.

Sometimes it might be necessary to explicitly call the security system in order to secure some aspect of your code. The .NET Framework exposes a number of APIs to demand and manipulate permissions, permission sets, policy, and the like. For instance, a new public method that exposes functionality to access the unmanaged world might incorporate the following code to ensure that callers have the required level of trust:

```
new SecurityPermission(SecurityPermissionFlag.UnmanagedCode).Demand();
```

The .NET Framework security system provides the ability to extend the code access security model as well. If your application creates a new resource to which code access should be restricted, it is a simple matter to implement a new permission to represent the level of access granted and the corresponding policy extensions to decide under what conditions that access should be granted. Since the .NET Framework is based on an object-oriented model, extending the system in this manner is usually just a case of subclassing a type or implementing an interface.

To recap, the .NET Framework security system provides basic infrastructure in terms of code access and role-based security (the means to represent levels of trust and then check those levels at runtime). On top of this, the framework libraries provide common permission types (`FileIOPermission`, for example) and enforce access checking on the resources they expose. Underlying all of this, the operating system continues to enforce the same access controls it always has. Users of the framework can leverage existing permissions to provide their own access control or implement entirely new permissions and policies.

Limitations of the .NET Framework Security System

While the .NET Framework offers a very flexible environment in which to secure your code and takes every opportunity to make such implementations as simple and foolproof as possible, it will not do all of your work for you. The designers and implementers of code must be aware of the security subsystem's limitations.

For instance, the security system cannot divine the intent of code. It doesn't know "good" code from "bad" code. It merely knows how to take a set of administrator-supplied rules (policy), apply it to known facts about an assembly (evidence), and generate the set of permissions that describe the level of trust now assigned to that assembly (the grant set). Demands are applied mechanically against the assemblies of the methods on the call stack, without the security system ever really understanding what operations are being performed. The name FileIOPermission is suggestive of its function to a human reader, but to the security system it is just another abstract permission, policing access to another abstract resource.

It is all too easy to forget this and assume that the security system will cope with breaches that, in reality, it's not even aware have happened. For example, consider the following snippet of code:

```
class PrivateFlags
{
    public int _flags;

    [PrivateFlagsPermission(SecurityAction.Demand, Unrestricted=true)]
    public void SetPrivateFlags(int flags)
    {
        _flags = flags;
    }
}
```

It's obvious to a human reader that a mistake has been made; the author intended the _flags field to be private and accessible only via the SetPrivateFlags method when the caller possesses the requisite permission. But the security system understands none of this; it doesn't see a link between the public field and the protected accessor of that field at all.

There are times when the security is paranoid on your behalf, in order to catch common coding errors. This was covered in Chapter 7, "Walking the Stack," where we showed that the default action of a security demand is to check *every* caller on the stack for the required permissions. As careful as this is, it is not foolproof. It assumes that data from untrusted callers will be passed via method parameters in a call, for instance. So it will not spot untrusted data read from a file or over a network. And that is a fundamental limitation of the security system, because it does not (and cannot) understand what is really being implemented. It is the responsibility of the application designers and implementers to consider these aspects of security and to ask themselves, "How do I validate the data I'm reading from this file or validate the trust level of the provider?" The security system can't ask this question for you, though it may provide the tools with which to implement the answer.

The other fundamental limitation of the .NET Framework security system is that it is constrained to the framework itself. The trust level of unmanaged code outside the framework is unknowable to the security system (since unmanaged code does not come packed up in assemblies, it cannot apply the policy system to it). Unmanaged code is not constrained by the requirements of type safety, whereas verifiable managed code must meet these requirements and, in doing so, limit itself to a "sandbox" from which it cannot escape.

Consequently, access to unmanaged code from the managed world is controlled by a very high-level permission in the .NET Framework: `SecurityPermission.UnmanagedCode`. Holders of this permission are very highly trusted by necessity, since code with this permission can subvert the security system itself. Remember that the .NET Framework runtime is implemented as user mode code inside the same process in which managed code is run. The security of the model relies on access to the process address space being rigidly controlled by the runtime (this is where type safety comes in). This rigid control cannot be enforced on code running raw, unmanaged instructions (the operating system only protects processes from each other; it enforces no in-process rules).

Naturally, unmanaged code is still under the control of operating system security; if a request to delete a file is made, that request will be validated against the user account under which the process is executing. The .NET Framework is trying to solve a larger problem, though. It is trying to constrain not just the user, but the code that the user runs. If a script file downloaded from the Internet tries to delete a file, it is not enough that the user is allowed to perform the operation; the code must have that privilege as well. After all, many viruses will destroy the user's own files, a perfectly allowable operation under the operating system's rules. So you can see that unmanaged code, given that it is not constrained by the .NET Framework, must be used very carefully if you want to avoid nullifying all the additional protection the framework was designed to provide.

The same is true of data that comes from outside the boundary of the framework (that is, from outside the process). The framework cannot validate raw data read from a file or a network connection for correctness, since it doesn't understand what the data means in the first place. Even for structured data (a serialized object read from a file, for example) it can only validate that the protocols of that structure have been adhered to; higher-level inconsistencies may still exist.

Security is more fundamental than a simple enumeration of the places where security demands will be initiated. A security weakness could stem from an action as seemingly benign as passing an instance of a particular type of object out of a public API. Often, the simplest and safest approach to security is prohibitively expensive (in terms of performance), requiring subtler schemes and protocols that you must adhere to carefully in order to avoid problems.

Summary

So what have we learned?

First, security is a fundamental concept, not a bolt-on module of code. A basic understanding of security is required of everyone working on a project, not just a security team; otherwise, security holes *will* result. If code is to be granted trust by a system administrator, it must earn that trust by not compromising system security.

Second, the runtime security is in addition to, not an alternative to, operating system security.

Finally, the runtime provides a rich set of resource access methods with prepackaged security checks, plus the ability to add more checks and even create new types of checking. None of this automates the security process, however, or absolves the developer from the need to understand basic security principles.

24

Architecting a Secure Assembly

By Rudi Martin

As discussed in the previous chapter, it's important to begin planning your security story *before* writing any code. This chapter will give you an idea of some broad strategies that you can employ in order to design security into a product from day one.

Given the wide diversity of applications that can be implemented under the .NET Framework, and the subtlety and complexity of designing a watertight security model for any piece of code that's even mildly complex, this chapter cannot provide exhaustive coverage of its subject. Rather, it should serve as a starting point for your own investigations.

The goals of this chapter are somewhat broad and a little fuzzy. Don't worry, we'll get a lot more specific in the next chapter, when we start to look at implementation details. For now, the principal aim is to give you an idea of where to begin thinking about the problem and to introduce you to the correct mindset—something that's just as important, if not more important, than the code itself.

Those who are architecting, designing, implementing, or testing a secure piece of software will benefit from reading this chapter.

Thinking Like a Security Expert: How to Improve the Security of Your Designs from Day One

You are now in a daunting position: You need to design for security in a new software component you're about to develop, but the concept of security is a slippery one. How exactly do you "design for security?" Where do you even begin?

Remember our discussions of trust and responsibility in the previous chapter? When we look at the problem in those terms, we see that our principal concern is interacting with code of a lower (or undetermined) level of trust. The system administrator will handle assigning trust through the use of a security policy. The .NET Framework security system will take care of sandboxing each unit of code (that is, each assembly) into the appropriate trust level. It's your responsibility to ensure that an untrusted party cannot leverage your trust level for its own means by using your code as a proxy in order to effectively work outside the sandbox set for it.

This implies that most of the design for a secure system will focus on the boundaries of your code: the public classes, interfaces, and methods plus input files, network connections, and any other means by which information and/or commands may be passed to your code. Only your interactions with code of lesser trust need to be scrutinized: When interacting with code of higher trust, it is that code's responsibility to ensure that the rules aren't broken.

Now let's get into the right frame of mind. The right mindset for security can be summed up in two words: paranoia and conservatism. These qualities won't necessarily make you the most popular developer around, but then again neither will a security breach in your product.

Paranoia: Designing Defensively for the Worst-Case Scenario

Paranoid developers believe that everyone is out to get them and is trying to find security weaknesses in the product that will grant a toehold into the system itself. While for the most part this is not the case, paranoia is nevertheless a pragmatic standpoint for a designer to take. Code that is not malicious will never exploit a security hole and therefore the only interesting code from the security perspective is malicious code.

It pays to assume the worst-case scenario: Not only are all people malicious hackers, but they're smart, malicious hackers with full access to your source code. It's a good idea to be paranoid for a number of reasons:

- There are a lot of very smart hackers out there. Just because they're destructive and malicious doesn't mean that they can't think intelligently. Consider buffer overrun attacks. Some of these attacks (which rely on overflowing internal buffers in an application so that the hacker can write data into another part of the program) are very elegantly constructed indeed, and require a great deal of time, effort, and knowledge to construct.

- It is very hard to keep secrets. Any security mechanism that relies on simple obscurity (a secret key built into the application, for instance) is doomed to failure. Some hackers are smart enough to find out secrets from the application itself, via reverse engineering. (In fact, finding keys within a program is actually reasonably easy due to properties of the key itself.) Your company may sell the source to external parties or there may be lapses in internal security (either unintentional or malicious). There are so many holes through which this information can leak, it's hard to plug them (and know they're plugged) with any degree of confidence.

All this doesn't mean that you shouldn't make it difficult for hackers to understand what's going on, of course. Just don't *rely* on it for any part of your security story.

- Once someone has found a security hole, information about the attack spreads quickly. Hackers (at least a certain class of them) like to publicly boast of their exploits. Therefore, details of their attacks very often become available on mediums such as the Internet within a very short period of time. This means that it only takes one smart hacker to identify a weakness and you'll have a hundred hackers trying to exploit it. As some email viruses in the last couple of years have shown, elaborate and carefully constructed attacks can be mutated into new attacks with relatively little imagination or skill.

In practice, what does this mean to you? The key points to remember are listed here:

- Think of every point of entry into your code (public method, input file, and so on) as a potential vulnerability. Consider how the API might be abused (hackers might not call a method in the way you intended it to be called; they're not under any obligation to follow the rules, after all).

- When looking for attacks, always assume that the hacker has access to at least as much information as you. If there's an embedded secret such as a key, assume that the hacker will find it. Likewise, a bizarre sequence of events or preconditions (certain error paths being taken, for example) that happen to lead to lowered security, no matter how Byzantine, must be considered important. If you found it, so will a hacker.

Conservatism: Limiting the Scope of Your Design to Reduce the Likelihood of Security Flaws

The key ideas here are that "less is better" and that the safest answer is always "no." Whereas paranoia makes you suspicious of every transaction with the outside world, conservatism will compel you to limit such interactions whenever possible. This has two benefits:

- The safest way to eliminate bugs is to eliminate code. By removing code, you remove its ability to introduce defects into your product. The same holds true for security.

- Because the number of areas with potential vulnerabilities is reduced, you can focus your attention on the remaining areas during design, implementation, and testing. Thus, vulnerabilities in those areas are more likely to be found and fixed earlier in the product life cycle.

Of course, balance is necessary if your code is to prove useful: The most secure piece of software would refuse to interact with the world in any way at all, but that is unlikely to be practical. Instead, the idea is to prune away avenues of attack that your product does not really need. How severely you do this depends on the product itself. For example, an application likely to be granted a low level of trust (a control designed to be downloaded from the Web, for instance) or one that does not use security-sensitive resources (such as a package of mathematical transforms) has less need of such conservatism than a component that manages file system operations on the user's computer.

One way to approach the problem is to look at the class hierarchy your software exposes. Start at the top (the larger units of code) and work down:

- Assemblies—If your product is designed to be installed locally (that is, onto the user's hard disk) and contains a mixture of assemblies to install into an application directory (under Program Files, for example) and into the Global Application Cache (GAC), consider moving as many assemblies as possible into the application directory. Only install assemblies into the GAC when they need to be shared among multiple applications.

- Classes—By default, classes should not be marked public. Only expose those classes that need to be exposed. Remember, it's much easier to make these classes public at a later stage than it is to make them private (and potentially break third party applications) when a security vulnerability in them is discovered.

  Another technique is to seal classes that are not intended for subclassing. Many attacks in the code access security world depend on the attacking code being derived from a poorly written class (see Listing 24.1). This technique is obviously at odds with some object-oriented programming practices—many times code is derived from a class just to add additional context that the caller wants to associate with each instance. The designer of the code needs to weigh the vulnerability of the class versus the likelihood of useful subclassing possibilities.

  An alternative to sealing a class is supplying a class-level security inheritance demand. This is a form of declarative security that ensures that code derived from the given class comes from an assembly granted the requisite permissions (see Listing 24.2). This is covered in greater detail in the next chapter.

- Methods and fields (and other class members)—Again, lower the visibility of these as much as possible. It's often tempting to make class members internal (using the C# terminology) so that other classes in the same assembly can access them directly. On the face of it, this is not an issue, because no wider access is granted. However, it does make the job of tracing potential code paths through the code base that much harder, so it's wise to leave such members marked private until wider access is explicitly needed.

Another common strategy is to make all fields private and allow access only through a property. This has a couple of advantages (apart from allowing the implementation of the field to change in the future): You can set different levels of access for getting and setting the field, and the property can use Code Access Security to control access. (Fields cannot be directly protected in this way.)

Be careful when creating virtual methods. Malicious code may override them with unexpected results (see Listing 24.1 for an example). If there is no real need to customize the behavior of the method based on the class, remove the virtual keyword. Otherwise, a couple of alternative options exist. If the method is virtual only for internal reasons (you have a type or types deriving from a base type and need to customize the behavior of this method, but don't need to expose this to outside code), the method can be sealed in the most commonly derived types. This will prevent code derived from these types from providing a new implementation of the method. Alternatively, you can use a method-level inheritance demand (similar to the class-level demand described previously) to ensure that only code with the given permissions can override this method. See Listing 24.2 and the next chapter for more details.

LISTING 24.1   A Poorly Written Base Class and a Derived Class Taking Advantage of It

```
using System;

public class Base
{
    protected String secretData = "This might contain a password";

    public virtual void SetSecretData(String data)
    {
        secretData = data;
    }
}

public class Derived : Base
```

LISTING 24.1   Continued

```
{
    // First problem: sub classes can access protected members.
    public String GetSecretData()
    {
        return secretData;
    }

    // Second problem: if the data is ever explicitly set, it can be
    // intercepted by a malicious subclasser because the set method is
    // virtual.
    String mySecretData;
    public override void SetSecretData(String data)
    {
        mySecretData = data;
    }
}
```

LISTING 24.2   Various Techniques for Securing a Base Class

```
using System;
using System.Security.Permissions;

// The following code secures the Base class in a number of different ways.
// In practice, it's not necessary to use all of these techniques at once,
// they're shown here just for illustrative purposes.

// We assume you've created a permission -- SecretDataAccessPermission -- to
// control access to the sensitive data. Alternatively, one of the standard
// code access security permissions (e.g. FileIOPermission) could be used if
// it makes sense with respect to the resource being protected.

// Prevent this class being subclassed by code without the requisite
// permission.
[SecretDataAccessPermission(SecurityAction.InheritanceDemand,
                            Unrestricted=true)]

// Or seal the class to prevent any subclassing at all.
public sealed class Base
{
    // Make internal data private.
    private String secretData = "This might contain a password";
```

LISTING 24.2   Continued

```
// Require implementors of SetSecretData to possess the required
// permission.
[SecretDataAccessPermission(SecurityAction.InheritanceDemand,
                            Unrestricted=true)]

// In this case we can secure SetSecretData by simply removing the
// virtual keyword. If this method was instead inherited from a
// parent class and was required to be a virtual override, it can
// still be secured by adding the keyword 'sealed', so that
// subclassers cannot re-implement the method.
public void SetSecretData(String data)
{
    secretData = data;
}
}
```

The techniques demonstrated in Listing 24.2 cover the most common ways that your code is controlled by the outside world, but don't forget that other modes of information transfer often exist. These include mediums such as the file system (your application reading settings from a .ini file) or the network (a server taking requests from a client).

Remember that these sources are beyond the scope of the .NET Framework security system: It can't guarantee that they're safe and/or tamper free. Paranoia tells you that hackers will modify the data in any way possible to cause undesirable effects—maybe in ways that don't seem to make sense. For instance, well-behaved data sources might always format the data in a specific way, but unless you verify this at the receiving end, a hacker can leverage the resulting unpredictable behavior as part of an attack. Don't forget that even if a protocol isn't published, a hacker can still reverse engineer it.

Actions that you can take to curtail this sort of mischief include

- Limiting where the input comes from. An initialization file may need to come from a specific directory (maybe protected with an operating system access control list) or network requests might be allowed only from specific hosts. For instance, you may require that an initialization file be read from the system directory (where everyone can read the file, but only an administrator can write it).

- Verification of the sender/creator of the data. The data may be digitally signed with the private key of the sender. This allows your code (together with the corresponding public key) to validate the sender's identity. Your code can then determine whether to trust the sender not to have sent malicious data.

- Verification of the data itself. This is the most flexible option, but also the hardest to implement. In anything except the simplest protocol, the ways in which data can be maliciously altered are almost innumerable. It's very easy to define verification rules that appear to work (since most test cases won't be trying to maliciously compromise the system), but proving that they work is harder. Exhaustive testing is also difficult, especially given that most test cases should result in a failure condition.

Take the seemingly simple example of verifying a filename. (This example is valid for the case where the filename is passed as a parameter to a public method as well.) If the filename is just taken as is, there could be many different effects: The file might be nonexistent where the code does not expect it to be and the resulting error path might expose vulnerabilities in code that hasn't been as highly tested or inspected. If a verification check is added for file existence, a hacker might provide one of the Windows "special" device names (CON, PRN, and so on) in order to launch a denial-of-service attack or elicit other strange effects. If these names are filtered out, the hacker might try names of well-known system files, trying to gain information about them or destroy them. (The knowledge of a file's existence on the user's hard disk is enough to serve as part of some attacks.) Your code attempts to block this by always prepending a known directory to the filename. The hacker responds by using a filename of the form ..\windows\system.ini.

As you can see, verifying something as seemingly simple as a filename can be a difficult and error-prone task. In general, data validation should be used as a last resort and the data itself should be kept as simple as possible to aid in its validation.

Another way to look at cutting down the number of vulnerable entry points into your code is to set up specific security "choke points." These are avenues into your code that utilize the .NET Framework security primitives to demand a specific level of trust and open the gateway to a larger set of APIs that no longer need to revalidate that trust.

The way this typically works is that the caller of your code needs to acquire some sort of "handle" (an instance of an object, possibly opaque to the caller). Creating this handle will initiate a security demand to determine whether the caller has the permissions your code deems necessary to perform operations on the handle.

From this point on, the caller provides the handle on every operation. (The operations are usually methods on the handle's class.) Because the .NET Framework guarantees that callers can't generate their own instance of the handle without going through the security choke point we referred to earlier, there is no need to revalidate the caller's permissions on each call. This has benefits both to security—it reduces the number of places where a bug in the code could introduce a security hole—and to performance.

The code in Listing 24.3 demonstrates this technique. An instance of the DatabaseHandle class is required to perform operations against the database, so we can control access to the operations simply by controlling the creation of the DatabaseHandle object itself. All other operations (such as GetStatus) can remain unburdened by additional security, making them both faster and less likely to present a security threat. The creator of a DatabaseHandle then has the responsibility of making sure that the object is never passed to caller with lower trust.

LISTING 24.3   Defining a Security Choke Point

```
using System;
using System.Security.Permissions;

// Define a class that will represent controlled access to a database.
public sealed class DatabaseHandle
{
    // Prevent construction without arguments by making the default
    // constructor private.
    private DatabaseHandle()
    {
    }

    // The following the only way to create a DatabaseHandle.
    // So we can concentrate our security here.
    public DatabaseHandle(String someData)
    {
        // We're using FileIOPermission here just for convenience,
        // you'll probably want to define your own permission to
        // cover controlling access to a database.
        new FileIOPermission(PermissionState.Unrestricted).Demand();

        // Now we've checked the caller (and all their callers too)
        // have the necessary permission, we can get on with the
        // business of setting up the database connection and other
        // housekeeping tasks.
    }

    // All further (non-static) methods in this class don't need to
    // recheck the trust level of the caller, since they're based on
    // an instance of this class that was obtained through the
    // constructor above.
```

LISTING 24.3   Continued

```
    public String GetStatus()
    {
    }

    // Be careful with static methods, they don't depend on an object
    // instance. If the method is security sensitive, secure it
    // separately.
    public static void SetDefaultOptions(int optionflags)
    {
        new FileIOPermission(PermissionState.Unrestricted).Demand();
    }
}
```

The FileStream class in the .NET Framework is an example of this technique. The constructor for the class initiates a demand for FileIOPermission, but none of the other methods on the class needs to recheck this.

There are a couple of caveats regarding this technique. One is that it only works if you expect your callers to have a certain level of trust. If you expect to be called by absolutely anybody, you need to use a technique that doesn't demand high-level permissions. (At the same time, you probably shouldn't be exporting anything like arbitrary file access to such people.)

The other point to consider is that this pushes more responsibility onto your callers. You've already verified that they have the requisite level of trust to perform the operation, but by giving them a handle as described earlier, you've opened up the possibility that they'll mistakenly give that handle out to code of a lower level of trust. This would be like your code handing out a FileStream object to an untrusted caller. It's hard to set any firm rules when trying to take this into account, but in general you have to consider the sophistication of the callers you expect to have. Are they likely to be people familiar with fundamental security principles?

This becomes another exercise in risk assessment; you must balance the risk of a trusted caller accidentally misusing your interface versus the reduction in risk that concentrating security into a choke point gives your code.

If All Else Fails

Unfortunately, your code is likely to ship with security weaknesses. Like eliminating all bugs from a complex product, finding all the security flaws is a gargantuan task, and mistakes are likely to be made.

Proper design can help mitigate these potential disasters; code can be sectioned off so that a breach in one area doesn't compromise the entire system. But it's always wise to have something up your sleeve if the unthinkable happens. If a security vulnerability is found and exploited and your code is out in the field, you'll need to offer a fix very quickly indeed.

This can be problematic: Finding the vulnerability, designing, implementing, and testing a fix can certainly take more than a few hours. In this situation, it would be nice to have some workarounds for the customer (short of uninstalling your software altogether). Here are some ideas that might help:

- Supply a rip cord. The idea here is to provide a means to turn off part of the functionality of your software (the part where the vulnerability is discovered) without impacting unrelated parts of your product. The rip cord could be configured through a registry setting or a config file, for instance.

  Say that your software processes transactions sent and received using HTTP. A vulnerability is discovered whereby a request coming from the Internet can compromise a server. A possible rip cord here is to allow disabling of Internet requests (allowing only local and intranet requests to be serviced). This would remove the possibility of an Internet-based attack, and for some customers, this would be impact free (assuming they are performing intranet-only transactions). This would give you some time to design a proper solution.

- Offer further configuration options. For instance, if your software is producing digital signatures using a particular signing algorithm and key size, you might want to provide configuration options that allow these to be changed. That way, if a vulnerability is discovered in the algorithm (or if the key size becomes insufficient) you have a way of updating customer systems without requiring a patch.

  These configuration options don't need to be documented, or even officially supported. They're just an option you can keep in your back pocket. That way, the maintenance cost is kept low. There's no need to design a fancy way to manage these options or spend time making them user friendly in any way.

A word of caution here: Remember to review and thoroughly test any such options that are implemented. It would be terribly unfortunate were such a technique itself to serve as the vector for an attack!

Don't Throw It All Away

One final piece of advice: All the planning that happens during the design phase will be for naught if it isn't communicated to the developers implementing and testing the code. Remember that this includes people who might be brought in much later in the product life cycle—people who have no prior knowledge of the security protocols being used.

It's obviously essential to document the design philosophy from the security perspective, as well as the specific protocols being used (the use of choke-point handles, for instance). But developers are notoriously bad at reading documentation, so extra effort is needed.

The most important information should be included with the sort of materials used to bring developers up to speed on a project (information on the source code control and build system for the project, for example). You should make an effort to include relevant details in the source code, where developers are most likely to see and read it.

Probably the most effective technique here is to keep it simple. Security, like synchronization in a multithreaded environment, is incredibly easy to mess up once it gets complicated. If you have a complex scheme with different rules for different scenarios and many special cases, it's likely that your code will have many subtle preconditions that could be broken without anyone noticing. Furthermore, the more complex the rules, the less likely that all the developers will know and abide by them.

Summary

So what are the key points to take away from this chapter?

- The most crucial aspect of securing a piece of software is the boundary between your code and code of lesser (or unknown) trust. This boundary can consist of public methods or other forms of communication such as files or network connections. Knowing this allows you to focus your efforts to secure your code on the places where it really matters; maximizing the use of your resources.

- Be paranoid in your dealings with untrusted code. Assume that all code of lower trust is malicious and will try to use your interfaces in ways that don't match their intended purposes. This is important because the 99% case (well behaved, benign code) is not the security threat. The attacks on your code base will be launched by malicious hackers that do not feel any need to follow the rules or use programming interfaces in the manner that you intended. By realizing this, and looking at your interfaces with the rest of the world through the eyes of a hacker, you stand a much higher chance of spotting vulnerabilities in your code that much earlier.

- Assume that all hackers have full access to your source code. Securing code by making vulnerabilities hard to find will not work. By examining your design from this perspective, you are more likely to architect code that is secure at a fundamental level (i.e., enforced security). Remember that a maze might seem complex to navigate, but very often is reduced to triviality by tracing a route backwards from the end target. Hackers almost invariably have this kind of technique at their disposal.

- Be conservative in your approach to exporting potentially sensitive interfaces to untrusted code. It's easier to add than to remove when it comes to such things, and the less you expose, the less that can go wrong. Applying this thinking has benefits at many levels: Reduced code and complexity lead to shorter design, implementation, and testing times and hence to enhanced coverage of the remaining features. Ultimately, this will lead to a more secure (and generally robust) product.

- Consider securing access to sensitive resources through a security choke point. Such a scheme will isolate the trickier security code in one area and might provide performance benefits. This technique has been applied to many areas of software development in the past and has proven its benefits many times over.

- Consider setting up rip cords or configuration options that allow you to quickly secure software that is under attack at customer sites. Just don't let these become security vulnerabilities in themselves. Careful use of such techniques gives you a reasonable contingency plan in the face of security breaches in the field, and may buy you some time in the repair of such breaches.

- Document the security aspects of the software design and make sure that this information is communicated effectively across the entire development team. A little up-front work here will save a lot of heartache later. It's important to adhere to this practice since the other techniques described previously, even if applied rigorously during the design process, are liable to fall by the wayside during the implementation phase unless some means to effectively communicate them forward is used.

25

Implementing a Secure Assembly

By Rudi Martin

In previous chapters, you've looked at high level architectural and design issues crucial to producing secure code. Now we're going to delve down deeper into the low-level details of actually implementing such code. This chapter is focused on writing code that explicitly interacts with the .NET Framework security system (the implicit facets of writing code that doesn't give away trust can't really be dealt with at such a low level—they're very dependent on the exact nature of your product).

This chapter seeks to acquaint you with three broad areas of coding with the .NET Framework security system:

- *Working with the basic representations of trust (permissions and permission sets)*—The difference between imperative and declarative security operations and how to use them.

- *Implementing your own permission type*—The difference between code access security and non-code access security permissions will be explained here, as well as the role of permission attribute classes in declarative security.

- *Strong naming your assemblies*—Including key pair generation, the mechanics of applying a strong name to various types of assemblies and how to set up a system to deal with delay signed assemblies.

A couple of notes before we begin:

In the following sections, we will often refer to standard .NET Framework permission types (RegistryPermission and the like). The majority of these permissions live within the System.Security.Permissions namespace in the mscorlib assembly, so we'll omit this information for brevity. If we refer to any type or enumeration based in a different namespace and/or assembly, this will be noted in the text.

Often, in the interest of using a well understood example, we'll look at code snippets that demand FileIOPermission and other standard permissions. Use of the standard permissions in this manner will be reasonably uncommon—the low level access routines in the .NET Framework already demand such permissions. Even if you're providing an intermediate layer above these, the stack walk mechanism will take care of checking the permissions of both your code and your caller. The only occasions in which it becomes necessary to think about demanding standard permissions yourself are when using the Assert operation (discussed in Chapter 7, "Walking the Stack") or calling methods decorated with declarative LinkDemands (discussed in the following sections).

Using Existing Security Mechanisms

Before we dig down into the mechanics of requesting security services, let's recap a little of what we know about security permissions.

Permissions describe a level of access to a resource. In general, for each resource type to be protected, there is a corresponding permission type. The .NET Framework provides many pre-baked permissions for such standard resources as files, registry keys, and environment variables, as well as abstract resources, such as the ability to manipulate the security system itself or execute unmanaged code. Permission types can also be implemented by your own code or third parties to cover new resources or situations where security is appropriate.

While some permission types are binary in nature (they can only be granted or not granted, nothing in between), others are much more detailed. For example, the standard permission type FileIOPermission can specify exactly which files are affected and which type of access is granted (read, write, and so on) in each case. This subsidiary information is known as *permission state*. The amount of additional state a permission type possesses is obviously specific to the function of the permission (and to the resource it's guarding).

All permissions, however, do share two special states—empty and unrestricted. These correspond to the logical extremes of the access possible—no access at all versus complete and unqualified access. We now see that binary permission types are simply those that have no other states than these.

If permission types describe the scope of access possible to a resource, an instance of a permission type describes a specific concrete level of access. The permission state is encoded as member data in the permission object (in whatever manner the implementation of the permission type sees fit). Note that the existence of a particular permission instance (`FileIOPermission` for read access to `foo.dat`, for example) does not imply that the permission is granted or demanded in any way. It merely describes a possible permission state, in much the same way that a filename describes a file without saying what action is to be performed on it.

Often, you may want to perform the same operation with multiple permission instances at the same time (for clarity or for performance). This can be accomplished through the use of permission sets, embodied by the `System.Security.PermissionSet` class. This class is a container for multiple permission instances and supports exactly the same sorts of operations that a single permission instance would.

The operations that can be performed on permissions or permission sets include demand (asking whether the associated permission(s) are granted) and security stack walk modifiers (`Assert`, `Deny`, `PermitOnly`—see Chapter 7). Code cannot ask to be granted permissions; the set of granted permissions for each assembly is calculated automatically by the security system the first time a security demand is made against that assembly. An assembly can request to be granted less permissions than the security system and the current security policy would normally give out, and the mechanism for doing this will be discussed in the section titled "Using Assembly-Level Declarative Security," later in this chapter.

There are two distinct ways in which security requests can be invoked within the .NET Framework runtime—declarative and imperative. For some operations (`Demand`, `Assert`, and so on), both techniques offer identical semantics, while others (`LinkDemand` and `InheritanceDemand`) are only available declaratively. There are also other tradeoffs in the use of declarative versus imperative; we'll compare and contrast these techniques in the following sections.

Using Imperative Security

Imperative security operations are those initiated explicitly in the caller's source code via a standard method call. The instance will be a security permission or permission set, while the method describes the operation desired. The following example shows one way of checking that your callers have permission to call unmanaged code:

```
new SecurityPermission(SecurityPermissionFlag.UnmanagedCode).Demand();
```

If the call succeeded, no value is returned; execution simply proceeds as normal to the next line. If, however, the operation failed (in the sense that one of your callers did not have the permission requested), a `SecurityException` is thrown. We'll discuss these exceptions in greater depth in the "Implementing Your Own Permissions" section later in this chapter.

The instance of `SecurityPermission` that we made the call on can simply be discarded afterward; it's no longer needed. In the interest of performance, demands or other security operations on common code paths can cache specific permission instances and use them over and over again. This is legal (and thread safe) because the permission instance is never altered in any way by any of the security operations—it merely serves as a read-only copy of the permission state that is being demanded, asserted, and so on.

`SecurityPermission` is a standard .NET Framework permission type that is actually a grab bag of various binary "sub permissions" that relate to the system itself (for example, the ability to skip IL verification, control the policy system, override security evidence for an assembly, and so on). The `SecurityPermission` class allows these various states to be set directly on construction of an instance via the `SecurityPermissionFlag` enumeration; all the subpermissions required can simply be `OR`'d together to achieve the desired result. This is common for permission types; much of their state is settable from constructor args, allowing the sort of simple, single line invocation seen in previous examples.

Other, more complex, permissions may require additional fields or properties set after initial object creation and before an operation is invoked:

```
FileIOPermission perm = new FileIOPermission(PermissionState.None);
perm.SetPathList(FileIOPermissionAccess.Read, "foo.dat");
perm.SetPathList(FileIOPermissionAccess.Write, "bar.dat");
perm.Demand();
```

Here we created a permission instance with no state whatsoever, and then added read and write access to separate files before finally invoking a `Demand` on the resulting fully formed permission. These setup steps can be arbitrarily complex; the permission objects are normal managed objects, just like any other in the .NET Framework. This demonstrates one of the strengths of imperative security requests—flexibility. Most of the important details of the request can be computed dynamically at runtime, something (as we shall see) that is not possible declaratively. The following is an example of state being set up dynamically:

```
public void AccessFile(String filename, bool create)
{
    FileIOPermission perm;
    perm = new FileIOPermission(PermissionState.None);
    if (create)
        perm.SetPathList(FileIOPermissionAccess.Write, filename);
```

```
    else
        perm.SetPathList(FileIOPermissionAccess.Read, filename);
    perm.Demand();
    ...
}
```

The details of how permission state is set will vary depending on the implementation of the permission type, but all implementations should follow the general model previously described. In addition, all permission types should provide a constructor that takes the `PermissionState` enumeration. This has two values—`None` and `Unrestricted`—and allows the permission to be created with either no or full access, respectively.

```
new FileIOPermission(PermissionState.Unrestricted).Assert();
```

`PermissionState.None` is generally only useful as a base state for a permission (when you intend to set other state through fields or properties). That's because operations on empty permissions are typically no-ops (an empty permission is always considered granted).

Operations on sets of permissions are constructed in much the same manner as the single permission case. Simply create an empty `PermissionSet`, instantiate individual permission instances as before, and include them in the set with `PermissionSet.AddPermission`. The desired operation (`Demand`, `Assert`, and so on) can then be performed on the permission set instance itself, which will automatically take care of the business of applying the operation to each of the embedded permissions (and generally in a far more efficient manner than performing the operation manually on each permission). The following are a couple of examples demonstrating how to compose complex permission sets:

```
PermissionSet pset = new PermissionSet();

EnvironmentPermission eperm;
eperm = new EnvironmentPermission(PermissionState.Unrestricted);

pset.AddPermission(eperm);

FileIOPermission fperm;
fperm = new FileIOPermission(PermissionState.None);
fperm.SetPathList(FileIOPermissionAccess.Read, "foo.dat");
fperm.SetPathList(FileIOPermissionAccess.Write, "bar.dat");

pset.AddPermission(fperm);

pset.Demand();
```

Permission sets also have the notion of the unrestricted state (there's a constructor overload on `PermissionSet` that takes the same `PermissionState` enumeration as the individual permissions). It means more or less the same thing but at a higher level—unrestricted access to all resources (that is, all permissions with their state set to unrestricted).

However, it does not make sense to include all permission types in this unrestricted set. Examples of this are the identity permissions—permissions that represent the right to be known by specific pieces of identity evidence, such as the `StrongNameIdentityPermission` granted to assemblies signed with a strong name. These don't fit well into a model using unrestricted sets; no assembly is granted all identities, so demanding a set containing all of them would be guaranteed to fail.

Therefore, permissions are divided into two sets—those which can be considered part of the unrestricted set (the normal permissions) and those that are not (such as the identity permissions). These two types of permissions are distinguished by whether the `IUnrestrictedPermission` interface is implemented by the permission type; if so, the permission is considered part of the unrestricted set and will be implicitly included every time a `PermissionSet` is created with `PermissionState.Unrestricted`. The `IUnrestrictedPermission` interface will be discussed further in the "Implementing Your Own Permissions" section later in this chapter.

Using Declarative Security

Whereas imperative security is performed through the use of method calls in the code, declarative security is specified in the metadata. Specifically, this means adding attributes to classes and methods. These attributes have the same source code format as custom attributes; they use the same syntax that your language would for those entities. For example, in C#

```
[ReflectionPermission(SecurityAction.Demand, ReflectionEmit=true)]
public void CreateAssembly()
{
    ...
}
```

Here, `ReflectionPermission` actually refers to the `ReflectionPermissionAttribute` class (any permission that can be used declaratively must implement a complementary permission attribute class; by convention, the attribute classname is the same as the permission classname with an `Attribute` suffix). C# allows the `Attribute` suffix to be omitted for readability.

Security attribute classes always have a single constructor that takes one argument—an enumeration of type `SecurityAction`. This enumeration indicates the type of operation to be performed with the permission or permission set specified with the rest of the attribute declaration. Consequently, the action corresponds to the final method call made in imperative usage (that is, `SecurityAction.Demand` is equivalent to `permission.Demand()`).

After the action code, a number of name/value pairs can be specified. Each of these corresponds to a field or property that will be set to the given value in the permission prior to enacting the action. This allows complex state to be set up in the permission (such as indicating specific files and access modes in a `FileIOPermission`).

```
[FileIOPermission(SecurityAction.Assert,
                  Read="c:\\foo.dat",
                  Write="c:\\log.txt")]
```

The previous declarative statement could be written imperatively as follows:

```
FileIOPermission perm = new FileIOPermission(PermissionState.None);
perm.SetPathList(FileIOPermissionAccess.Read, "c:\\foo.dat");
perm.SetPathList(FileIOPermissionAccess.Write, "c:\\log.txt");
perm.Assert();
```

Note that the state of the permission is initially empty. That is, at least one state item should be supplied to make the statement useful. The following demands nothing at all (an empty `RegistryPermission`):

```
[RegistryPermission(SecurityAction.Demand)]
```

This demand will always pass, regardless of the permissions granted to the calling assemblies. The following will demand the highest possible level of access to the registry:

```
[RegistryPermission(SecurityAction.Demand, Unrestricted=true)]
```

The `Unrestricted` property is common to all permissions; it is the equivalent of specifying `PermissionState.Unrestricted` to the permission constructor in the imperative case:

```
new RegistryPermission(PermissionState.Unrestricted).Demand();
```

We have stated that declarative security can be applied to methods or classes. When applied to a method, the action (`Demand`, `Assert`, and so on) is performed just prior to the execution of that method (the exceptions are `LinkDemand` and `InheritanceDemand`; we'll cover those in the sections titled "Using Declarative `LinkDemand`" and "Using Declarative `InheritanceDemand`"). A declarative attribute on a class is, with one exception, simply shorthand for the same attribute applied to every method defined by that class. This includes constructors, properties (getters and setters), and events (add and remove). The exception is InheritanceDemand, which has different semantics at the class and method level and will be discussed in the "Using Declarative InheritanceDemand" section later in this chapter.

```
[SecurityPermission(SecurityAction.Demand, ControlThread=true)]
class MyThreadPackage
{
    public void Foo() {}
    private void Bar() {}
    protected void Baz() {}
}
```

In this example, all three methods (Foo, Bar, and Baz) will demand SecurityPermission's ControlThread (we commonly refer to this as SecurityPermission.ControlThread). The implicit default constructor supplied by the compiler will also demand this permission. Hence, the mere act of creating a new MyThreadPackage instance will demand the permission (later in this section, we'll discuss an important caveat about the use of this technique with value types).

The level of control over declarative security placed on "special" methods (property getters or setters and implicit event methods) will differ from language to language. In C#, declarative security must be applied directly to property setters or getters and will not work (or even compile) when applied to the property itself:

```
String MyProperty
{
    [MyPropertyPermission(SecurityAction.Demand, ReadAccess=true)]
    get { return m_string; }

    [MyPropertyPermission(SecurityAction.Demand, WriteAccess=true)]
    set { m_string = value; }
}

// The following will not compile.
[MyPropertyPermission(SecurityAction.Demand, Unrestricted=true)]
String BrokenMyProperty
{
    get { return m_string; }
    set { m_string = value; }
}
```

When dealing with events, the add and remove methods are implicitly defined by the compiler, so declarative security must be specified on the event itself, using the method qualifier on the attribute:

```
[method: MyPermission(SecurityAction.Demand, Unrestricted=true)]
public event EventHandler MyEvent;
```

The attribute will be applied to both add and remove methods; there is no way to limit the action to one of the methods or apply different attributes to each.

There are some important caveats when applying declarative security to classes:

- In most cases, declarative security for a given action specified at the method level will completely override and replace declarative security for the same action specified at the class level. This is not the case for InheritanceDemand (whose semantic varies depending on the placement) and LinkDemand (which we'll discuss later in the "Using Declarative InheritanceDemand" and "Using Declarative LinkDemand" sections, respectively). This means that if a Demand is made at both class and method level, the method will demand only the permissions specifically attached to that method.

  A special case of this is using a null declaration on the method to cancel the effect of a class level declaration for one or more methods.

  ```
  [SecurityPermission(SecurityAction.Demand, ControlThread=true)]
  class MyThreadPackage
  {
      public void Foo() {}
      [SecurityPermission(SecurityAction.Demand)]
      private void Bar() {}
      protected void Baz() {}
  }
  ```

  In this code, the class level demand for SecurityPermission.ControlThread is cancelled for the Bar method only.

  However, different actions can coexist peacefully between the levels. A Demand at the class level will not replace an Assert at the method level; both will be evaluated prior to the execution of the method.

  Note that multiple security attributes can be applied to a single class or method (and they will merge as expected). This can be used to work around cases where two distinct demands are being made at the class and method levels, and both are required on the method:

```
[RegistryPermission(SecurityAction.Demand, Unrestricted=true)]
class RegistryClass
{
    public void Foo() {}

    [RegistryPermission(SecurityAction.Demand, Unrestricted=true),
     SecurityPermission(SecurityAction.Demand, UnmanagedCode=true)]
    public void Bar() {}
}
```

This works even if the two demands are for the same permission type. That is, the following two demands are equivalent:

```
[FileIOPermission(SecurityAction.Demand,
                  Read="c:\\foo.dat",
                  Write="c:\\bar.dat")]
```

```
[FileIOPermission(SecurityAction.Demand,
                  Read="c:\\foo.dat"),
 FileIOPermission(SecurityAction.Demand,
                  Write="c:\\bar.dat")]
```

- A class level demand is sometimes assumed to protect instantiation of an instance of that class (due to the constructor, even if implicit, being automatically decorated with the demand). This assumption does not always hold for value types (structs, in C# parlance). Instantiating simple value types (that is, without supplying any parameters) won't invoke a constructor; the initial state (zeroed memory) is assumed to be sufficient. So the following structure can be created (and manipulated, because fields never have declarative security applied) by untrusted code:

```
[SecurityPermission(SecurityAction.Demand, UnmanagedCode=true)]
public struct DangerousStructure
{
    public IntPtr pointerToData;
    public int lengthOfData;
}
```

The only guarantee you get with value types is that the initial state is all zeros. This fact can be used to police whether a given value type instance was created in a "blessed" manner (that is, through a secured method):

```csharp
public struct DangerousStructure
{
    // A field indicating whether an instance has been initialized
    // through a "secured" method -- Allocate below. This field is
    // private so that it can't be set directly and will be
    // initialized to false by the runtime at instance creation time.
    private bool authenticated;

    // Allocate an instance of this structure that is authenticated.
    [SecurityPermission(SecurityAction.Demand, UnmanagedCode=true)]
    public static DangerousStructure Allocate()
    {
        DangerousStructure ds = new DangerousStructure();
        ds.authenticated = true;
        return ds;
    }

    // Check whether a given instance was authenticated (i.e.
    // allocated through Allocate).
    public bool IsAuthenticated()
    {
        return authenticated;
    }

    public IntPtr pointerToData;
    public int lengthOfData;
}
```

- Declarative security on a class will not propagate to any nested types (or their methods) defined within that class.

```csharp
[EnvironmentPermission(SecurityAction.Assert, Unrestricted=true)]
class Outer
{
    void OuterFoo() {}

    class Inner
    {
        void InnerFoo() {}
    }
}
```

In this example, the `Assert` will propagate to `OuterFoo`, but not to `InnerFoo`. To work around this, the attribute needs to be manually propagated:

```
[EnvironmentPermission(SecurityAction.Assert, Unrestricted=true)]
class Outer
{
    void OuterFoo() {}

    [EnvironmentPermission(SecurityAction.Assert, Unrestricted=true)]
    class Inner
    {
        void InnerFoo() {}
    }
}
```

Demands of any sort (declarative or imperative) should not be relied on when applied to a static class constructor. Such one-time constructor calls are initiated automatically by the runtime, and the state of the stack at the time can be non-deterministic (or, at least, hard to predict). It's even worse for the declarative `LinkDemand` operation (we'll look at this in detail in the "Using Declarative LinkDemand" section later in this chapter, but part of the semantics of its operation is that the `LinkDemand` is evaluated at the point the caller is compiled from IL to native code). Take a look at the following code:

```
using System;
using System.Security.Permissions;

class Test
{
    public static void Main(String[] args)
    {
        Console.WriteLine("In Main");
    }

    [SecurityPermission(SecurityAction.LinkDemand, UnmanagedCode=true)]
    static Test()
    {
        Console.WriteLine("In static class constructor");
    }
}
```

Even when run from a network share (default security policy will deny
SecurityPermission.UnmanagedCode to such assemblies), the code will execute
successfully (both messages will be output). This is because the LinkDemand is ignored
completely; there is no managed caller of the static class initializer at all—it is called
implicitly by the runtime, and is compiled to initiate the demand. While the results
of performing a normal Demand are somewhat less dramatic, it is still unwise to rely
on the state of the stack during such operations.

Because static class constructors are run only once, and logically this is done on
behalf of all code that will ever use the class, it is doubtful that any meaningful
demands could be made anyway. Any malicious assembly could simply wait until
another, more trusted assembly accesses the class and then proceeds unhindered.

There are a couple of security actions available declaratively that are not available
imperatively. These are InheritanceDemand and LinkDemand, and the following
sections will look at them in more detail.

Using Declarative InheritanceDemand

As we've previously mentioned in passing, InheritanceDemand is the one declarative
action whose semantics differ when used at the class versus method level.

When applied to a class, InheritanceDemand controls subclassing of that class. That
is, an assembly attempting to derive from the decorated class must be granted the
permissions specified by the attribute. If assembly A has the following declaration:

```
[EnvironmentPermission(SecurityAction.InheritanceDemand, Unrestricted=true)]
public class Base
{
}
```

And assembly B has:

```
class Derived : Base
{
}
```

Then assembly B would have unrestricted EnvironmentPermission demanded of it.
The check is performed once, at the point when class Derived is first used in any
way (via a method call, field access, reflection, and so on). If the check fails, a
SecurityException will be thrown.

The effect of an InheritanceDemand is transitive, that is, all subclassers of the attributed class will be checked, regardless of whether the subclassing was direct or indirect. So if assembly C contains the following code,

```
class MoreDerived : Derived
{
}
```

then C is also subject to the check for EnvironmentPermission.

The second form of InheritanceDemand occurs when the attribute is applied to a virtual method (it has no meaning when applied to a non-virtual method).

```
[MyPermission(SecurityAction.InheritanceDemand, Unrestricted=true)]
public virtual void SetPassword(String password)
{
    m_password = password;
}
```

Here, the attribute controls the overriding of the SetPassword method. Only assemblies granted unrestricted MyPermission will be allowed to override the implementation of SetPassword. Like an InheritanceDemand applied to a class, this check is performed once at the point at which the class containing the overriding definition of SetPassword is first used.

InheritanceDemand is also applied transitively when used on a method. So an overriding implementation of SetPassword that's defined in any subclass, direct or indirect, will trigger the check.

InheritanceDemand, in both its forms, is useful when it's impractical to seal a class (or mark a method as final)—perhaps because your own internal code needs the flexibility of subclassing and/or overriding.

Using Declarative LinkDemand

LinkDemand can be seen as a special form of Demand. It performs the same basic operation (checking the given permissions against the grant set of the caller) but with two important differences:

- Only the immediate caller is checked, not the entire stack of callers. So given three assemblies, A, B, and C, defining methods Foo, Bar, and Baz respectively, if Foo calls Bar calls Baz and Baz is decorated with a LinkDemand, only assembly B (containing method Bar) will be checked for the permissions demanded. Under a full Demand, assembly A would be checked as well.

- The check is made only once per call site of the decorated method, not every single time the method is invoked. By *call site*, we mean the position in the IL of a calling method where the actual invocation of the protected method takes place (this will be a call or callvirt instruction). The check actually takes place during the JIT (Just In Time compilation) of the calling method. Consequently, given the following definitions:

```
[MyPermission(SecurityAction.LinkDemand, Unrestricted=true)]
public String Foo()
{
    return "Hello World!";
}

public String Bar()
{
    return Foo() + Foo();
}
```

When the method Bar is compiled (this is commonly referred to as jitting within the .NET Framework), the check for MyPermission will be performed twice for Bar's assembly—once for each invocation of Foo. The jitting of Bar will probably occur on the first invocation of the method, but further invocations will not cause any additional checks (because there's no need to compile the method more than once).

One important aspect of the implementation of LinkDemand checks in .NET Framework Version 1 is that a failing check will cause an immediate security exception. Ideally, the JIT would detect the failure and generate code to throw the same exception *at the time the method (and, more specifically, the point in that method) is invoked.* The current implementation means that you cannot call a method that might possibly call another method it does not have access to, regardless of whether the code would have really attempted the second call. Additionally, the JIT often compiles methods well ahead of their actual use for the purpose of inlining. This has a noticeable effect in a couple of cases:

- The stack trace in the security exception may stop short of the real location of the failure (because we haven't actually called the method decorated with the LinkDemand yet, and the JIT may perform multiple levels of inlining in advance of calls).

- Exception handlers that attempt to catch any resulting security exceptions may not work, for the same reason: We may not have entered the try section of code prior to a call to the decorated method.

Take the following example:

```
using System;
using System.Security;
using System.Security.Permissions;
```

```
class LinkDemandTest
{
    public static void Main(String[] args)
    {
        try
        {
            ProtectedMethod();
        }
        catch (SecurityException)
        {
            Console.WriteLine("Caught security exception");
        }
    }

    [SecurityPermission(SecurityAction.LinkDemand, Unrestricted=true)]
    static void ProtectedMethod()
    {
    }
}
```

When run in a restricted environment (such as from a network share), an unhandled
exception message will be displayed on the console (that is, our handler is never
invoked).

It's rare that such behavior will impact your code to any degree (usually code is
written expecting to be granted a certain level of permissions, and failure to get
them is catastrophic, not something to be worked around via the use of exception
handling). If you want to ensure that deterministic evaluation of LinkDemands are
made, use an intermediate method to make the dangerous call, and force the JIT to
suspend inlining for that method using the
System.Runtime.CompilerServices.MethodImpl custom attribute:

```
using System;
using System.Security;
using System.Security.Permissions;
using System.Runtime.CompilerServices;

class LinkDemandTest
{
    public static void Main(String[] args)
    {
        try
        {
            CallProtectedMethod();
```

```
        }
        catch (SecurityException)
        {
            Console.WriteLine("Caught security exception");
        }
    }


    [MethodImpl(MethodImplOptions.NoInlining)]
    static void CallProtectedMethod()
    {
        ProtectedMethod();
    }


    [SecurityPermission(SecurityAction.LinkDemand, Unrestricted=true)]
    static void ProtectedMethod()
    {
    }
}
```

The demand is evaluated at the JIT of the caller rather than the callee for two reasons. First, it would be easy to circumvent LinkDemand in the alternate scenario; simply wait for trusted code to invoke the target method (and thus, JIT the method and trigger the demand) and then invoke the method at will without ever having had the demand directed at your assembly. Second, at the time we JIT the caller, the runtime has precise information about the identity of the calling and callee methods (and thus their respective assemblies). This implies that we have no need to walk the stack to determine the caller, which saves a lot of time.

This brings us to a particularly important point—the dangers of using LinkDemand. LinkDemand is tempting because of its performance characteristics; it's evaluated infrequently relative to the number of times the decorated method is called, effectively amortizing the cost of the check. Even when the check is performed, it does not involve a costly stack walk. But this comes with a subtle cost; LinkDemand is not always intuitive in its operation and inadvertent security holes can result.

The two main points to remember are

- Because only the immediate caller is checked, it is easy to wrap the functionality of a protected method and re-export it to potentially untrusted callers. This allows such callers to side-step the security by using your assembly as a trusted proxy. The following code is an example of this sort of security hole:

```
[MyPermission(SecurityAction.LinkDemand, Unrestricted=true)]
public String Foo(String[] args) { … }
```

```
public String FooWrapper(String[] args)
{
    return Foo(args);
}
```

There are two cases to bear in mind here. You must document clearly when your public methods are decorated with LinkDemand rather than Demand (so that others do not inadvertently open up access to your methods), and you must pay special attention to which methods you call using a LinkDemand (to avoid creating such wrappers yourself).

If it becomes necessary to build such a wrapper, one method of maintaining security is to simply add the LinkDemand to the wrapper itself:

```
[MyPermission(SecurityAction.LinkDemand, Unrestricted=true)]
public String Foo(String[] args) { … }

[MyPermission(SecurityAction.LinkDemand, Unrestricted=true)]
public String FooWrapper(String[] args)
{
    return Foo(args);
}
```

In the absence of good documentation for assemblies and methods you rely on, the PermView utility supplied with the .NET Framework SDK, along with the /decl command line option, will allow the viewing of all declarative security present in the target assembly. Compile the following code into an assembly called PropertiesAndEvents.exe:

```
using System;
using System.Security.Permissions;

class Hello
{
    String m_datum;

    String MyProperty
    {
        [EnvironmentPermission(SecurityAction.Demand, Unrestricted=true)]
        get { return m_datum; }
        [RegistryPermission(SecurityAction.Demand, Unrestricted=true)]
        set { m_datum = value; }
    }
```

```
    public delegate void EventHandler();

    [method: FileIOPermission(SecurityAction.Demand, Unrestricted=true)]
    public event EventHandler MyEvent;

    public static void Main(String[] args)
    {
    }
}
```

The `PermView` utility can then be used as follows:

```
PermView /decl PropertiesAndEvents.exe

Microsoft (R) .NET Framework Permission Request Viewer. Version 1.0.3612.0
Copyright (C) Microsoft Corporation 1998-2001. All rights reserved.

Method Hello::get_MyProperty() Demand permission set:
<PermissionSet class="System.Security.PermissionSet"
               version="1">
   <IPermission class="System.Security.Permissions.EnvironmentPermission,
➥mscorlib, Version=1.0.3300.0, Culture=neutral, PublicKeyToken=
➥b77a5c561934e089"
               version="1"
               Unrestricted="true"/>
</PermissionSet>

Method Hello::set_MyProperty() Demand permission set:
<PermissionSet class="System.Security.PermissionSet"
               version="1">
   <IPermission class="System.Security.Permissions.RegistryPermission,
➥mscorlib, Version=1.0.3300.0, Culture=neutral, PublicKeyToken=
➥b77a5c561934e089"
               version="1"
               Unrestricted="true"/>
</PermissionSet>

Method Hello::add_MyEvent() Demand permission set:
<PermissionSet class="System.Security.PermissionSet"
               version="1">
   <IPermission class="System.Security.Permissions.FileIOPermission,
➥mscorlib, Version=1.0.3300.0, Culture=neutral, PublicKeyToken=
➥b77a5c561934e089"
```

```
                    version="1"
                    Unrestricted="true"/>
</PermissionSet>

Method Hello::remove_MyEvent() Demand permission set:
<PermissionSet class="System.Security.PermissionSet"
                   version="1">
   <IPermission class="System.Security.Permissions.FileIOPermission,
➥mscorlib, Version=1.0.3300.0, Culture=neutral, PublicKeyToken=
➥b77a5c561934e089"
                    version="1"
                    Unrestricted="true"/>
</PermissionSet>
```

- At the JIT time of the caller, information about the callee is sometimes not as precise as we'd like it to be. This is true for all virtual calls (which include calls through interfaces or on abstract classes/methods). In these cases, the runtime will know which slot in the vtable or interface table the final method will reside in, which is enough to compile the calling code, but the actual choice of target method is deferred until runtime (and may indeed vary on every call). For this reason, it is very hazardous to place a LinkDemand on a virtual (or override) method or a method implementing an interface or an abstract method.

In the following example, the first call invokes the LinkDemand as expected; the second does not.

```
public interface IFoo
{
    String Foo(String[] args);
}

public class MyClass : IFoo
{
    [MyPermission(SecurityAction.LinkDemand, Unrestricted=true)]
    public String Foo(String[] args) { … }
}

public class Test
{
    public static void Main(String[] args)
    {
        MyClass mc = new MyClass();
```

```
        // Call method on class directly.
        mc.Foo(args);

        // Call method through interface.
        ((IFoo)mc).Foo(args);
    }
}
```

One workaround to this problem is to attach the same LinkDemand to all possible routes to the method. For example, in the previous example, we could add the LinkDemand to the method declaration in IFoo:

```
public interface IFoo
{
    [MyPermission(SecurityAction.LinkDemand, Unrestricted=true)]
    String Foo(String[] args);
}
```

Likewise, LinkDemands can be propagated from abstract methods to their implementations and virtuals to their overrides. But such schemes can be complex, error prone, and may not give satisfactory semantics (for example, it is rarely acceptable—or even possible—to propagate a LinkDemand from a method implementing an interface to the interface definition itself). In such cases, it may be time to think about using a Demand instead. This will incur a performance penalty, but will be evaluated at runtime, when there is no ambiguity as to which method is being called.

Link demands on methods that are being invoked via reflection (for example, Type.InvokeMember or MethodInfo.Invoke) must have the demands emulated by the reflection subsystem. That's because at the JIT time of the caller, the runtime has no idea which method is going to be invoked (that's the entire point of late binding in the first place). In Version 1 of the .NET Framework, the emulation is not precise; the permission set demanded is checked against the grant set of all assemblies on the stack rather than just the assembly of the method that initiated the reflection call. This behavior should not be relied on; in future releases, the semantics of link demands, whether invocation is late or early bound, are likely to converge.

Building Declarative Actions Against Permission Sets

It is occasionally necessary to specify multiple permissions to which a single declarative action will apply on a given method or class. This can be achieved via multiple single permission attributes as follows:

```
[RegistryPermission(SecurityAction.Demand, Unrestricted=true),
 FileIOPermission(SecurityAction.Demand, Unrestricted=true)]
public void Foo()
```

However, the runtime also presents another method of achieving the same result. `PermissionSetAttribute` (as usual, this can be abbreviated in C# to `PermissionSet`) will allow the specification of an entire permission set in one attribute declaration. There are four ways the set can be specified:

- If the `Unrestricted` property is set to true, the unrestricted permission set is created. You'll recall that this is the set of all permissions that implement the `IUnrestrictedPermission` interface (that is, most non-identity permissions).

  ```
  [PermissionSet(SecurityAction.Demand, Unrestricted=true)]
  ```

- The `XML` property can be set to a string containing the XML serialized encoding of the permission set. This is the same encoding that can be seen by calling `ToString` on a permission set instance. Remember to escape any characters your compiler treats specially (such as quote or backslash).

  ```
  [PermissionSet(SecurityAction.Demand,
                 XML="<PermissionSet class=\"System.Security.PermissionSet\"
  ➥version=\"1\"><IPermission class=\"System.Security.Permissions.
  ➥FileIOPermission, mscorlib, Version=1.0.3300.0, Culture=neutral,
  ➥PublicKeyToken=b77a5c561934e089\" version=\"1\"
  ➥Unrestricted=\"true\"/>
  ➥<IPermission class=\"System.Security.Permissions.RegistryPermission,
  ➥mscorlib, Version=1.0.3300.0, Culture=neutral, PublicKeyToken=
  ➥b77a5c561934e089\" version=\"1\" Unrestricted=\"true\"/>

  ➥</PermissionSet>")]
  ```

- The `File` property can be set to the name of a file containing the same kind of XML encoding described for the `XML` property. The file contents may be encoded in ASCII, UTF8, or Unicode; the runtime will automatically detect which format is used.

  ```
  [PermissionSet(SecurityAction.Demand, File="c:\\PermSet.xml")]
  ```

- The `Name` property can be set to the name of a well known permission set (one of the built-in ones, such as Nothing, Everything, or LocalIntranet, or any named permission set configured into security policy).

  ```
  [PermissionSet(SecurityAction.Demand, Name="LocalIntranet")]
  ```

Using Assembly Level Declarative Security

Until now, you've looked at declarative security applied to classes and methods. It is also possible to apply security attributes at the assembly level. However, the set of actions applicable at this level is entirely different from the actions discussed so far. That is, you cannot demand or assert permissions for every method over an entire assembly (in practice, it is unlikely this would be a useful operation anyway).

Rather, there is a set of actions specific to the assembly level. These all provide extra data for policy resolution (the mechanism whereby the .NET Framework security system grants permissions to an assembly). Because assemblies cannot be trusted to assign their own trust level, these requests can at most reduce the set of permissions that policy would grant. This can be useful for testing, self-documenting trust requirements, and limiting the impact of security bugs in the assembly code.

There are three such security actions:

- `RequestMinimum`—This specifies the set of permissions the assembly considers essential for its operation. If the policy system is unwilling to grant all of these, the assembly is not loaded at all. On a failure to load the assembly for this reason, a `System.Security.Policy.PolicyException` will be thrown. The default is to require no permissions at all (that is, the `PolicyException` will never be thrown).

- `RequestOptional`—These are permissions the assembly would like, but are not essential for operation. This allows for the possibility of code that attempts an operation one way (say, storing data in a file) and then detects any security violation by catching the security exception and backs off to an alternative solution requiring less trust (such as storing the data as in-memory arrays). The default is to request unrestricted permissions—that is, anything the policy system will give the assembly is accepted. In actual fact, the policy system will ask *only* for the permissions in this set (together with any permissions in the `RequestMinimum` set). This attribute can be used to limit the grant set of an assembly to a specific set of permissions (if that set is required rather than optional, `RequestMinimum` with the set and then `RequestOptional` with the empty set):

```
[assembly: FileIOPermission(SecurityAction.RequestMinimum,
➥Unrestricted=true)
 PermissionSet(SecurityAction.RequestOptional, Name="Nothing")]
```

- `RequestRefuse`—This allows you to list permissions that should specifically *not* be granted to the assembly. This is sometimes easier than explicitly listing the permissions that are desired.

So let's take an example. Say the assembly you've just written absolutely needs to access the registry and environment variables, would like to access files but can live without it, and wants to make sure it can never expose any abuses of unmanaged code. The following attribute should fit the bill (like any assembly level attribute, this should be placed near the top of one of your source files, after any using declarations):

```
[assembly:
 RegistryPermission(SecurityAction.RequestMinimal, Unrestricted=true),
 EnvironmentPermission(SecurityAction.RequestMinimal, Unrestricted=true),
 FileIOPermission(SecurityAction.RequestOptional, Unrestricted=true),
 SecurityPermission(SecurityAction.RequestRefuse, UnmanagedCode=true)]
```

Implicit Declarative Demands

There are two situations in which declarative demands are implicitly added to a method by the runtime—P/Invoke and interop methods. P/Invoke (Platform Invoke) methods are calls from managed code into unmanaged code. They must be declared on the managed side so that the runtime knows how to marshal (convert) the types of the arguments and result back and forth between the two worlds. Interop methods are calls on classic COM objects (sometimes called servers) and thus represent a more structured means of calling into unmanaged code. COM interop can also be used to call from the unmanaged world into the .NET Framework runtime, but we're not concerned with method calls going in that direction in this section (primarily because unmanaged callers are usually considered to be fully trusted).

Take the following example of a P/Invoke declaration:

```
[DllImport("Kernel32.dll")]
public static extern int GetTickCount();
```

Any time the GetTickCount method is called, a demand for SecurityPermission.UnmanagedCode is made. This is because any use of unmanaged code is potentially a security hole (unmanaged code is outside the jurisdiction of the runtime, so can potentially subvert it). Because the runtime cannot determine which unmanaged APIs are "safe," it demands this permission for all of them.

Interop calls from managed code to an unmanaged COM server are the other route into unmanaged code, and these methods are similarly protected via a demand for SecurityPermission.UnmanagedCode. Both the creation of the server instance object and any method calls against that instance are protected. In the following code, two demands are made (assuming ComServer is an unmanaged COM class):

```
ComServer server = new ComServer();
server.DoStuff();
```

By default, the implicit demands described here are per-call, full-stack walking demands. This is nice and secure (it will catch cases where code unthinkingly wraps a public managed method around a dangerous unmanaged method, such as `CreateFile`). But there is certainly a high performance penalty here. This may not be an issue depending on the nature of your application and the frequency with which calls to unmanaged methods are made.

If performance does turn out to be critical, there exists a technique whereby the full demand can be mutated into a link demand. Because this is checked less frequently and does not involve a stack walk, the average performance overhead will approach zero as the method is repeatedly called. This does mean, however, that special care must be taken when calling such methods to ensure that your code cannot be coerced into performing unmanaged operations on behalf of an untrusted caller.

The mechanism that allows the demands to be modified into link demands is a custom attribute—`System.Security.SuppressUnmanagedCodeSecurityAttribute`. For P/Invokes, the attribute can be added to either the specific P/Invoke method or the class in which the P/Invoke is defined (in which case it applies to every P/Invoke method in that class):

```
[DllImport("Kernel32.dll"), SuppressUnmanagedCodeSecurity]
public static extern int GetTickCount();
```

The story is slightly different for interop calls. Here, the switch can only be made at the interface level (all interop calls are dispatched through interfaces, because the method implementation is in unmanaged code). `SuppressUnmanagedCodeSecurity` can be applied to the interface definition to make all calls through that interface use a link demand. If the attribute is applied to an interface method, it will be ignored.

```
[SuppressUnmanagedCodeSecurity]
public interface IComServer
{
    ...
}
```

A non-obvious side effect of applying `SuppressUnmanagedCodeSecurity` to an interface is that the runtime cannot tell at JIT time whether the interface implementation will really be managed or unmanaged. Therefore, the link demand for `SecurityPermission.UnmanagedCode` will be evaluated regardless. This is not an issue with the default full stack walk, because the evaluation of the demand is made at runtime and the implementation is known at that point. In the following example, both calls to `Foo` will result in a link time demand at JIT time:

```
[SuppressUnmanagedCodeSecurity]
public interface IFoo
{
    void Foo();
}

class Test
{
    IFoo obj1 = new UnmanagedFoo();
    IFoo obj2 = new ManagedFoo();
    obj1.Foo();
    obj2.Foo();
}
```

If the interface used in interop calls has been generated via the tlbimp utility, the suppress attribute can be automatically added by specifying the /unsafe switch to the tlbimp command line:

```
tlbimp /unsafe ComServer.tlb
```

The SuppressUnmanagedCodeSecurity attribute will only modify the behavior of implicit demands made for P/Invoke and interop calls; no other declarative security is affected.

Allowing Untrusted Callers

As has been discussed previously, one of the principal problems when trying to secure code is managing interactions with code of unknown or lower trust levels. To try and reduce the probability of bugs in an assembly's code leading to such security holes, the runtime adds additional security demands to certain methods if the following conditions all hold:

- The defining assembly is strong named (these are considered to be critical assemblies because strong naming is a prerequisite of installation into the Fusion Global Assembly Cache (GAC), and security policy may well base trust decisions on strong names).

- The assembly is not marked with the System.Security.AllowPartiallyTrustedCallersAttribute custom attribute. This attribute should only be used when it has been determined that all code in the assembly has been thoroughly reviewed for security holes in the face of attacks from malicious untrusted callers. The syntax of the attribute (in C#) is as follows:

```
[assembly: AllowPartiallyTrustedCallers]
```

- The method in question is publicly visible (the containing class is public and the method itself is public, protected, and so on). Only publicly visible methods have implicit security checks added because they're the only available entry point for callers from another assembly.

If all the previous conditions are satisfied, the runtime adds a link demand for the unrestricted permission set (that is, all permissions that implement IUnrestrictedPermission, sometimes referred to as full trust). This link demand is special in that if at JIT time the runtime can determine that the caller is actually from the same assembly as the callee, the link demand will be skipped. This ensures that the assembly can't be called from untrusted assemblies (anything below full trust), but that intra-assembly calls will always succeed, even if the assembly itself isn't granted full trust.

Consequently, given the following example (assuming the assembly is strong named and does not possess the AllowPartiallyTrustedCallers attribute)

```
public class PublicClass
{
    public void PublicMethod() {}
    private void PrivateMethod() {}
}

class PrivateClass
{
    public void PublicMethod() {}
    private void PrivateMethod() {}
}
```

only PublicClass.PublicMethod will be decorated with the implicit link demand for full trust. If this method is called from anywhere inside the same assembly, the link demand will be ignored.

A more precise check would be to compare the trust level of the caller to the callee and fail only when the caller is less trusted. However, this is an expensive operation (involving many set operations on the respective grant sets). Therefore, the link demand for full trust is seen as a compromise between efficiency, flexibility, and safety.

Note that, due to these simplified rules, a partially trusted, signed assembly (one downloaded from the Internet via Internet Explorer, for example) cannot have callers from partial trust assemblies. This is particularly likely to cause problems if a single application is written as a set of assemblies with intra-assembly communication via method calls. The only resort in these cases is to review the assemblies for security correctness and add the `AllowPartiallyTrustedCallers` attribute to each assembly. This may not be all that difficult, given that assemblies designed to operate in partial trust scenarios are unlikely to manipulate security sensitive resources heavily.

As previously mentioned, link demands on methods that are invoked via late bound mechanisms (reflection) will be converted into full stack walking demands (in Version 1 of the .NET Framework, at least). This applies to the implicit link demands described in this section as well.

An `Assert` can be used to simulate the correct link demand behavior in these cases:

```
public void CallSomeMethod()
{
    // Assume that we've already located the method to call prior to
    // now, and the target MethodInfo has been placed in a static
    // variable. We believe the method is safe to call, but resides
    // in an assembly that does not allow untrusted callers. We
    // presume this assembly will be granted full trust, but our
    // callers may not. Since we're guaranteeing the safety of this
    // operation, it seems unfair to require full trust of our callers.
    // Therefore we'll assert full trust prior to making the call to
    // the target method. This will halt the stack walk initiated by
    // the reflection system.
    new PermissionSet(PermissionState.Unrestricted).Assert();
    s_targetMethod.Invoke(null, new Object[]);
}
```

Identity Demands and Their Uses

One particularly useful form of a security demand is a demand for an identity permission. You'll recall that identity permissions are those granted to an assembly based on the evidence used to establish trust in the policy database. For each piece of evidence used (download URL, strong name, Authenticode signature, and so on), a corresponding identity permission is granted.

It's not usually all that useful to perform a full stack walking demand for an identity permission (there are limited scenarios where you'd expect to see the same identity all the way down the stack). But it's certainly possible, as the following code snippet shows:

```
try
{
    new ZoneIdentityPermission(SecurityZone.MyComputer).Demand();
    Console.WriteLine("All assemblies located in the MyComputer zone");
```

```
}
catch (SecurityException)
{
    Console.WriteLine("Assembly from different zone found");
}
```

Where identity demands really become useful is when using declarative link demands. This is because only the immediate caller is checked (and, as an additional benefit, the cost of the check is low and amortized toward zero the more times the method is called).

One particularly useful example of this technique is to perform a link demand for a strong name identity permission on a public method. This gives the ability to export methods that are only callable from your other assemblies—something akin to a version of internal that crosses assembly boundaries.

The following is an example of a method that can only be called by an assembly with the given strong name:

```
[StrongNameIdentityPermission(SecurityAction.LinkDemand,
                    PublicKey="0x00000000000000000400000000000000")]
public void MyInternalMethod()
```

The PublicKey property contains the full public key encoded in hex format. The ECMA public key has been used in the previous code for brevity; most public keys are a lot longer. Use the secutil utility to determine the hex string format of a public key for a given assembly:

```
secutil -hex -s mscorlib.dll
```

The strong name identity demand can be made more specific with name and/or version information:

```
[StrongNameIdentityPermission(SecurityAction.LinkDemand,
                    PublicKey="0x00000000000000000400000000000000"),
                    Name="MyOtherAssembly",
                    Version="1.0.0.0"]
public void MyInternalMethod()
```

Remember that when using such specific identities, the assembly declaring the method may be unable to call the method itself. This can be worked around using an internal method (used within the assembly itself) and a public wrapper with the link demand (to be used between assemblies):

```
[StrongNameIdentityPermission(SecurityAction.LinkDemand,
                             PublicKey="0x00000000000000000400000000000000"),
                             Name="MyOtherAssembly"]
public void MyInternalMethod()
{
    MyInternalMethodImplementation();
}

internal void MyInternalMethodImplementation()
{
    ...
}
```

Note that this technique has the limitation that only one identity can be checked (if you specify two identity demands for a given method, both demands must be satisfied for access to succeed, which is unlikely to be the semantic you're after). This is one reason for omitting the name and version information in a strong name identity demand; the strong name will usually remain the same throughout a given product, without being available to code from another company.

If a set of specific assemblies must be identified, one possible workaround is to use a wrapper technique similar to that described earlier in this section, but with separate wrappers for each individual calling assembly.

Implementing Your Own Permissions

From time to time, it will be necessary to implement your own custom permissions. This will most likely come about because your code has created a new form of resource to which access must be policed.

For example, you might be controlling access to some new external hardware device. For the purposes of illustration, we're going to assume the device is a toaster. The managed code that will provide access to the toaster needs to provide methods to determine the presence of bread, its current "toasted" level, eject the bread, and so on.

Listing 25.1 is a simplified model of the Toaster class, along with some possible security declarations we may use to control access to the toaster resource.

LISTING 25.1   Outline of the Toaster Class

```
// Enum describing the level of toasting of a piece of bread.
public enum ToastLevel
{
```

LISTING 25.1   Continued

```
    Uncooked,
    LightBrown,
    MediumBrown,
    DarkBrown,
    Burnt
}

public class Toaster
{
    // Constructing a toaster object implies gaining exclusive
    // access to the actual toaster hardware (in a real example,
    // we'd write a finalizer method to deal with releasing the
    // hardware resources when we're finished with the managed
    // object). A more complex example might allow the toaster
    // to be accessed in a read-only mode, in which case the
    // permission required on the constructor could be dynamically
    // computed, and we'd move from declarative to imperative
    // security.
    [ToasterPermission(SecurityAction.Demand, ExclusiveAccess=true)]
    public Toaster()
    {
    }

    // Read-only property telling us whether any bread is currently
    // in the toaster.
    [ToasterPermission(SecurityAction.Demand, Information=true)]
    public bool ContainsBread
    {
        get {}
    }

    // Read-only property telling us the current cooked status of
    // the bread in the toaster.
    [ToasterPermission(SecurityAction.Demand, Information=true)]
    public ToastLevel Toastedness
    {
        get {}
    }

    // Method to eject the bread from the toaster.
    [ToasterPermission(SecurityAction.Demand, Eject=true)]
```

LISTING 25.1   Continued

```
    public void EjectBread()
    {
    }


    // Method to eject the bread from the toaster once it has reached
    // the supplied level of toastedness.
    public void EjectBread(ToastLevel level)
    {
        // Need both the Eject permission and the right level of
        // Toastedness permission (not everyone is allowed to produce
        // burnt toast).
        ToastedPermission tp;
        tp = new ToastedPermission(PermissionState.None);
        tp.Eject = true;
        tp.ToastLevel = level;
        tp.Demand();
    }
}
```

This example is obviously rather contrived, but it demonstrates the basics. We'll be using it as the basis for much of our discussions in the following sections.

An important point to note at this stage is that the .NET Framework (at least in Version 1) does not support extension of the security system from partial trust code. That is, to create our new permission, the assembly that provides the implementation must be granted full trust. Of course, this does not restrict which assemblies can use or be granted the new permission. What this means in practice is that you should code new permissions expecting them to be installed onto the user's machine as opposed to an Internet downloadable control or a network shared component.

We're going to implement a code access security (CAS) permission for our toaster project. This is the most common type of .NET Framework permission (all the permissions we've used so far in this chapter are CAS). Code access security permissions are simply those that are granted based on the identity of the assembly and, as such, are granted on a per-assembly basis. They're the ones the runtime checks by (typically) walking the stack and finding the assemblies for each method in the call chain.

The .NET Framework also supports non-code access security permissions (non-CAS). The implementation of individual non-CAS permissions defines how and to whom such permissions are granted. For example, the .NET Framework defines role-based permissions that record role identities at a thread level. When a demand for one of these permissions occurs, the implementation of the demand looks at data stored in thread local storage to determine the result, rather than walking the stack.

From the implementation point of view, the difference between CAS and non-CAS permissions is simply down to a matter of inheriting from the right class. All permission types need to implement the `IPermission` interface; this defines the methods that the runtime uses to interact with the permission internally, as well as the `Demand` method with which we're familiar. In addition, CAS permissions need to derive from `System.Security.CodeAccessPermission`. This provides the implementation for `IPermission.Demand`, handling all of the stack walking aspects. `CodeAccessPermission`'s implementation of `Demand` will delegate the actual work of comparing permission instances and so on to the other methods of `IPermission` (for which you provide the implementation).

`CodeAccessPermission` also provides methods such as `Assert` and `Deny`; these are stack walking operations and, as such, make no sense for non-CAS permissions and are not included in `IPermission`.

So let's start a skeleton implementation of our `ToasterPermission`, presented in Listing 25.2.

LISTING 25.2   Basic Outline of the `ToasterPermission` Class—`ToasterPermission.cs`

```
[Serializable]
sealed public class ToasterPermission : CodeAccessPermission,
                                        IUnrestrictedPermission
{
    // Permission state fields. Normally we'd make these private
    // and provide public property accessors, but for simplicity's
    // sake we'll just make them public (none are read-only anyway).

    // The ability to exclusively control the toaster.
    public bool ExclusiveAccess;

    // The ability to read toast state information.
    public bool Information;

    // The ability to eject toast.
    public bool Eject;

    // The maximum level to which auto-eject can be set for the
    // toaster.
    public ToastLevel ToastLevel;
```

LISTING 25.2   Continued

```
// Provide the usual constructor taking a PermissionState (for
// consistency with other permission types).
public ToasterPermission(PermissionState state)
{
    if (state == PermissionState.Unrestricted)
    {
        ExclusiveAccess = true;
        Information = true;
        Eject = true;
        ToastLevel = ToastLevel.Burnt;
    }
}
}
```

NOTE

Beginning with Listing 25.2, we'll be building up a fully functional permission class. The full source code for the finished class can be downloaded as `ToasterPermission.cs` from the publisher's Web site.

The `Serializable` attribute marks this class as serializable via the standard .NET Framework binary serializer. This is a requirement when implementing custom permissions (the runtime internally serializes/deserializes permission instances in a number of cases). For most permission types, simply supplying the `Serializable` attribute is sufficient; the binary serializer will automatically determine the correct way to serialize your data. If your state data has special requirements, merely making direct copies of the fields won't capture the correct state; you may implement the `ISerializable` interface to better control the process. This topic is outside the scope of this book.

We seal the class because there is no real reason to allow anyone to derive from us, and sealing will prevent the possibility of any derivation-based security attacks. This is a good practice in general, and it's not confined to the implementation of permission classes.

We derive from `CodeAccessPermission` because we're implementing a CAS style permission. `CodeAccessPermission` implements `Ipermission`, so we don't explicitly reimplement it here (although we will need to implement some of the `IPermission` methods that `CodeAccessPermission` doesn't provide for us).

We implement `IUnrestrictedPermission` to indicate that this permission is considered part of the unrestricted permission set (that is, part of full trust and not an identity permission). If we wanted to ensure that `ToasterPermission` is never to be granted automatically and unthinkingly by the security policy system (that is, it would have to be granted with an explicit rule in the policy database), we could skip the implementation of `IUnrestrictedPermission`. We discuss this interface later in this section.

We provide the usual constructor (taking a `PermissionState` as argument) for consistency with other permission types. We could also provide alternative constructors to set the state to varying levels of access, but this permission is simple enough that this is not really a requirement.

So far, all we have in the body of `ToasterPermission` are the state fields necessary to indicate the levels of access we determined to be meaningful earlier. We now need to implement the methods the runtime security system will use to manipulate and query an instance. Let's look at the definition of `IPermission` first:

```
public interface IPermission : ISecurityEncodable
{
    IPermission Copy();

    IPermission Intersect(IPermission target);

    IPermission Union(IPermission target);

    bool IsSubsetOf(IPermission target);

    void Demand();
}
```

The `IPermission` interface itself implements another interface—`ISecurityEncodeable`. Ignore this for now; we'll explain it in detail later in this section.

The `Copy` method simply creates a clone of the current permission instance and returns it. This is necessary because several .NET Framework runtime security APIs return permission instances from the assembly grant set; copies must be returned or the caller can simply alter the permission and thereby modify the grant set itself. For that reason, the implementation of `Copy` should perform a deep copy—that is, any permission state data that is itself an object reference should be recursively cloned as well.

This is a simple method for us to implement, given that our state data is not all that complex. We present a possible implementation in Listing 25.3.

LISTING 25.3   Implementing `IPermission.Copy`

```
public override IPermission Copy()
{
    ToasterPermission perm;

    // Create a vanilla permission with no state.
    perm = new ToasterPermission(PermissionState.None);

    // Copy state fields from the current instance into the
    // new instance.
    perm.ExclusiveAccess = ExclusiveAccess;
    perm.Information = Information;
    perm.Eject = Eject;
    perm.ToastLevel = ToastLevel;

    // Return the new copy.
    return perm;
}
```

The `Intersect` method returns a permission that is the result of computing set inter-section between the current permission and the one provided as an argument. That is, the permission returned will represent all the common state between the two input instances. If there is no common state, `null` can be returned (rather than a permission instance with no state set). It is not absolutely necessary to return `null` in these circumstances, but doing so can lead to performance improvements during evaluation of demands.

The exact definition of common state is up to the permission type to decide (the definition should obviously give deterministic, intuitive results that a user or system administrator can understand).

For `ToasterPermission`, it's easy to define the meaning of common state for our Boolean state fields; if both permission instances have the same field set to `true`, that aspect of the permission state is shared (this works because the various state fields are totally independent of each other; one can imagine a more complex permission where the algorithm would have to take into account subtle interactions between the fields).

The `ToastLevel` state field is not quite so straightforward; given two values of the enumeration, how do we compute a third value that represents the common aspects of the two? The approach here is to consider the fact that we deem the enumeration to be an ordered list. That it is the ability to set the auto-eject level to `Burnt` is considered a more privileged operation than setting it to `Uncooked`. In such scenarios, the common state is the highest level of access that both permissions are granted. For ToastLevel, this is simply the lower value of the two enumerations (by default, C# will number enumerations from 0 in ascending order).

Listing 25.4 gives a possible implementation of Intersect.

LISTING 25.4   Implementing IPermission.Intersect

```
public override IPermission Intersect(IPermission target)
{
    // An input of null is a special case (it represents a
    // permission with no state). There is obviously no common
    // state in such cases and we should return null to represent
    // this.
    if (target == null)
        return null;

    // Cast target into a ToasterPermission for ease of use.
    // Note that this will throw an InvalidCastException if
    // someone mistakenly passes us the wrong permission instance.
    ToasterPermission other = (ToasterPermission)target;

    ToasterPermission result;

    // Create a vanilla permission with no state.
    result = new ToasterPermission(PermissionState.None);

    // Consider shared state for each state field in turn.
    result.ExclusiveAccess = ExclusiveAccess && other.ExclusiveAccess;
    result.Information = Information && other.Information;
    result.Eject = Eject && other.Eject;

    // Shared state for ToastLevel is the lesser of the two.
    result.ToastLevel = ToastLevel < other.ToastLevel ?
        ToastLevel : other.ToastLevel;

    // Return the shared state instance.
    return result;
}
```

The next method to consider is Union. This is similar to Intersect but computes the permission instance containing all state from both inputs. It can be thought of as adding two permissions together. When we compute the union of the ToastLevel state fields, we will pick the most permissive (highest value) of the pair.

Our implementation is given in Listing 25.5.

LISTING 25.5   Implementing IPermission.Union

```
public override IPermission Union(IPermission target)
{
    // An input of null is a special case (it represents a
    // permission with no state). We can just return a copy of
    // the current permission in this case.
    if (target == null)
        return Copy();

    // Cast target into a ToasterPermission for ease of use.
    // Note that this will throw an InvalidCastException if
    // someone mistakenly passes us the wrong permission instance.
    ToasterPermission other = (ToasterPermission)target;

    ToasterPermission result;

    // Create a vanilla permission with no state.
    result = new ToasterPermission(PermissionState.None);

    // Consider shared state for each state field in turn.
    result.ExclusiveAccess = ExclusiveAccess || other.ExclusiveAccess;
    result.Information = Information || other.Information;
    result.Eject = Eject || other.Eject;

    // The union of state for ToastLevel is the most permissive
    // of the two.
    result.ToastLevel = ToastLevel < other.ToastLevel ?
                        other.ToastLevel : ToastLevel;

    // Return the shared state instance.
    return result;
}
```

IsSubsetOf returns a Boolean result indicating whether the current permission is a subset of the permission given as an argument. To be a subset, every piece of state in the current permission must also be present in the target permission. Where we have state such as ToastLevel, the current permission should have a ToastLevel less than or equal to the target permission. (Note that equality part; a permission is considered to be a subset of another if both are identical).

IsSubsetOf is the principal means that CodeAccessPermission uses to determine if a given assembly grant set satisfies a demand permission set. If every permission in the demand permission set is a subset of the corresponding grant permission, the demand set can be considered granted.

Listing 25.6 gives a possible implementation.

LISTING 25.6   Implementing IPermission.IsSubsetOf

```
public override bool IsSubsetOf(IPermission target)
{
    // An input of null is a special case (it represents a
    // permission with no state). We can only be a subset if
    // we're in a similar empty state.
    if (target == null)
        return !ExclusiveAccess &&
               !Information &&
               !Eject &&
               ToastLevel == ToastLevel.Uncooked;

    // Cast target into a ToasterPermission for ease of use.
    // Note that this will throw an InvalidCastException if
    // someone mistakenly passes us the wrong permission instance.
    ToasterPermission other = (ToasterPermission)target;

    // For each state field that's in a non-empty state, check
    // that the state is mirrored (or present at a greater
    // permissive state) in the target.

    if (ExclusiveAccess && !other.ExclusiveAccess)
        return false;

    if (Information && !other.Information)
        return false;

    if (Eject && !other.Eject)
        return false;

    if (ToastLevel > other.ToastLevel)
        return false;

    // Checked all state, we must be a subset.
    return true;
}
```

There is no need for us to provide an implementation of Demand, the last method in
IPermission. CodeAccessPermission has already provided an implementation for us
(that knows how to walk the stack and call back into our implementation of
IsSubsetOf for each assembly grant set).

However, if we were implementing a non-CAS permission and, therefore, did need to
provide an implementation of Demand, we would very likely use something like the
code presented in Listing 25.7.

LISTING 25.7   Implementing IPermission.Demand

```
public override void Demand()
{
    // Use permission specific means to determine what permission
    // state is granted. In role based security for instance, the
    // current thread would be queried for the account of the user
    // in control. This information could then be mapped to the
    // permission state granted to that user.
    MyPermission granted = GetGrantedState();

    // Check that the demand made is a subset of what's been granted.
    // If not we inform the security system by throwing a security
    // exception.
    if (!IsSubsetOf(granted))
        throw new SecurityException("Insufficient permissions",
                                    typeof(MyPermission),
                                    ToXml().ToString());
}
```

Note that when throwing a security exception from Demand (to indicate insufficient
granted permissions to satisfy the request), the SecurityException constructor may
be given additional parameters to help the user diagnose security failures. The first
parameter is a string specifying the exception message (you may want to make this
string localized for various cultures in your implementation, perhaps by using the
.NET Framework resource manager facility). The second parameter is the
System.Type of the demand (in our example, we assumed this was a permission type
called MyPermission). The third and final parameter is a string, which by convention
contains the XML serialized state of the demand (we'll see the ToXml method again
later). These pieces of information can be retrieved from the exception either
through the use of ToString (in which case the additional data is merged in which
the usual stack trace information) or individually through the Message,
PermissionType, and PermissionState properties, respectively.

Getting back to our toaster example, you'll recall that `ToasterPermission` also claimed to implement the `IUnrestrictedPermission` interface. This is a very simple interface:

```
public interface IUnrestrictedPermission
{
    bool IsUnrestricted();
}
```

The sole method, `IsUnrestricted`, should return `true` if the permission instance is in the unrestricted state (that is, the most permissive state it can be in) and `false` at all other times. For `ToasterPermission`, this equates to all of our Boolean state fields being set and `ToasterLevel` being set to its highest state—Burnt.

Listing 25.8 gives an implementation of `IsUnrestricted`.

LISTING 25.8   Implementing `IUnrestrictedPermission.IsUnrestricted`

```
public bool IsUnrestricted()
{
    return ExclusiveAccess &&
           Information &&
           Eject &&
           ToastLevel == ToastLevel.Burnt;
}
```

We still have a couple methods to implement; remember the `ISecurityEncodable` interface implicitly brought in by `IPermission`?

```
public interface ISecurityEncodable
{
    SecurityElement ToXml();
    void FromXml(SecurityElement e);
}
```

The purpose of these methods is to translate instances of your permission back and forth between an XML serialized format used to persist the permissions to disk. For example, declarative security stored in the metadata of an assembly is stored in this format.

Rather than translating directly from the permission instance to a string (or vice versa), an intermediate form is used—`System.Security.SecurityElement`. This structure represents a single node that can be linked into a tree structure (each node has a single parent and zero or more children, with the exception of the root node, which has no parent).

Let's consider the following piece of XML:

```
<Foo bar="1" baz="true">Hello World<SubFoo/></Foo>
```

This can be represented by two `SecurityElements`. The top level `SecurityElement` has the following values associated with it:

- A tag—in this case, the string `"Foo"`.

- Zero or more attributes—in this case, `"bar"` and `"baz"`. Each attribute has a string value; `"1"` and `"true"` in the example, respectively.

- An optional text string—`"Hello World"`, in this case.

- Zero or more child `SecurityElements`—in this case, we have one child (tag `"SubFoo"`, no attributes, text, or children of its own).

Given the following declarative description of permission state

```
[FileIOPermission(SecurityAction.Demand,
                  Read=@"c:\foo.dat",
                  Write=@"c:\bar.dat")]
```

the XML produced would be as follows:

```
<IPermission class="System.Security.Permissions.FileIOPermission, mscorlib,
➥Version=1.0.3300.0, Culture=neutral, PublicKeyToken=b77a5c561934e089"
                version="1"
                Read="c:\foo.dat"
                Write="c:\bar.dat"/>
```

Some parts of this encoding are dictated by the .NET Framework runtime—the tag of `IPermission`, the attributes `class` (set to the assembly qualified type name of your permission), and `version` (set to `"1"`). The other attributes (`Read` and `Write` in this case) are defined by the permission type itself. Note that, by convention, these attributes are capitalized to distinguish them from the runtime attributes.

You'll notice that no text or child elements are used; permissions rarely have any truly complex state to encode, and attributes usually suffice.

Regardless of how you choose to encode your permission state, `SecurityElement` provides a slew of methods to create nodes, manipulate attributes and text, and link children. The following is a simplified view of the `SecurityElement` class:

```
public class SecurityElement
{
    // Construct a SecurityElement with no associated text.
    public SecurityElement(String tag) {}
```

```
// Construct a SecurityElement with the specified text.
public SecurityElement(String tag, String text) {}

// Get or set the tag name.
public String Tag { get {} set {} }

// Get or set a hash table of the element attributes. Keys are the
// attribute names, values are the attribute values (always a
// string).
public System.Collections.Hashtable Attributes { get {} set {} }

// Get or set the text for an element.
public String Text { get {} set {} }

// Get an array list of the children of the current element.
public ArrayList Children { get {} set {} }

// Add an attribute with the given name and value.
public void AddAttribute(String name, String value) {}

// Add a child SecurityElement.
public void AddChild(SecurityElement child) {}

// Compare elements for equality; tags, text, attributes and
// children must all match to be considered equal.
public bool Equal(SecurityElement other) {}

// Check whether a given tag string is legal.
// To be valid, tag must be non-null and contain none of the
// following characters: ' ', '<', '>'.
public static bool IsValidTag(String tag) {}

// Check whether a given text string is legal.
// To be valid, text must be non-null and contain none of the
// following characters: '<', '>'.
public static bool IsValidText(String text) {}

// Check whether a given attribute name is legal.
// To be valid, name must be non-null and contain none of the
// following characters: ' ', '<', '>'.
public static bool IsValidAttributeName(String name) {}
```

```
// Check whether a given attribute value is legal.
// To be valid, value must be non-null and contain none of the
// following characters: '<', '>', '"'.
public static bool IsValidAttributeValue(String value) {}

// Escape invalid characters ('<', '>', '"', ''', '&') in
// attribute values or text. Such values will always be returned
// unescaped, therefore no Unescape method is exported.
public static String Escape(String str) {}

// Return the string (XML) form of the element.
public override String ToString () {}

// Return the value for the named attribute.
public String Attribute(String name) {}

// Search for a child element by tag name.
public SecurityElement SearchForChildByTag(String tag) {}

// Search this element and all children (recursively) for the
// named tag. If found, return the associated text.
public String SearchForTextOfTag(String tag) {}
}
```

ToasterPermission's implementation of the ISecurityEncodeable might look something like the code in Listing 25.9.

LISTING 25.9   Implementing ISecurityEncodable Methods

```
// Convert the current permission to a SecurityElement (or tree
// of elements).
public override SecurityElement ToXml()
{
    // Create new element, tag name must always be "IPermission",
    // element text is not needed.
    SecurityElement elem = new SecurityElement("IPermission");

    // Determine assembly qualified full type name of our permission
    // class (the security system uses this to locate and load the
    // class).
    String name = typeof(ToasterPermission).AssemblyQualifiedName;

    // Add attributes for the class name and protocol version
```

LISTING 25.9   Continued

```
        // (currently always "1") to the element.
        elem.AddAttribute("class", name);
        elem.AddAttribute("version", "1");

        if (IsUnrestricted())
        {
            // Create an abbreviated encoding for unrestricted
            // instances of this permission.
            elem.AddAttribute("Unrestricted", Boolean.TrueString);
        }
        else
        {
            // Encode each state field as an attribute of the element.
            // Only bother adding elements for state in the non-default
            // state, this makes the encoded format more compact.

            if (ExclusiveAccess)
                elem.AddAttribute("ExclusiveAccess", Boolean.TrueString);

            if (Information)
                elem.AddAttribute("Information", Boolean.TrueString);

            if (Eject)
                elem.AddAttribute("Eject", Boolean.TrueString);

            if (ToastLevel != ToastLevel.Uncooked)
                elem.AddAttribute("ToastLevel", ToastLevel.ToString());
        }

        // Return the completed element.
        return elem;
    }

    // Convert a SecurityElement (or tree of elements) to a permission
    // instance.
    public override void FromXml(SecurityElement e)
    {
        // Check whether we have an unrestricted instance.
        String unrestricted = e.Attribute("Unrestricted");
        if (unrestricted != null &&
            Boolean.Parse(unrestricted))
```

LISTING 25.9   Continued

```
    {
        ExclusiveAccess = true;
        Information = true;
        Eject = true;
        ToastLevel = ToastLevel.Burnt;
        return;
    }

    // Ensure we start from a clean base state.
    ExclusiveAccess = false;
    Information = false;
    Eject = false;
    ToastLevel = ToastLevel.Uncooked;

    // Check the value of each attribute which encodes a state
    // field.
    String value;

    value = e.Attribute("ExclusiveAccess");
    if (value != null)
        ExclusiveAccess = Boolean.Parse(value);

    value = e.Attribute("Information");
    if (value != null)
        Information = Boolean.Parse(value);

    value = e.Attribute("Eject");
    if (value != null)
        Eject = Boolean.Parse(value);

    value = e.Attribute("ToastLevel");
    if (value != null)
        ToastLevel = (ToastLevel)Enum.Parse(typeof(ToastLevel),
                                            value, true);
}
```

There are a number of interesting points to note about the implementation just given:

- We optimize the encoding of the unrestricted state to a single attribute—
  "Unrestricted" = "true". This is convention followed by all the built-in .NET
  Framework runtime permissions and helps keep the encoding compact.

- Another method of keeping the encoding compact is to add attributes only for state fields that are in their non-default state. (When decoding the permission again, it's important to remember to clear any existing state in the permission instance back to its default state for this to work.) Also note that the `FromXml` code is robust in that it takes the value of the attribute into consideration (not just the existence of the attribute), so adding an attribute, such as `Information=false`, to the XML will have the expected effect. Even though we never encode state in this fashion in `ToXml`, this will make the XML form of the permission easier to edit by hand.

- We make extensive use of the `ToString` and `Parse` methods provided by runtime primitive types to encode and decode state field values. This simplifies the code and allows for flexibility in input formats (such as case insensitivity) which, again, can ease editing of the XML by hand.

That should complete our implementation of `ToasterPermission`. At this point, it should be possible to compile the permission and try a few simple tests (constructing instances with different state, encoding them to XML and checking the results by hand, and so on). It should also be possible to demand permission instances (because we implemented `IUnrestrictedPermission`, `ToasterPermission` will be granted to assemblies with full trust, but no other assemblies).

To use the new permission declaratively, we'll need to create a custom attribute class for it.

Implementing a Security Custom Attribute

The .NET Framework runtime uses a custom attribute class to encode permission instances for a couple reasons. First, it can leverage the existing syntax, compiler support, and user understanding of custom attributes. Second, the extra level of indirection (the custom attribute code itself) allows the permission author a great deal of flexibility. This second point needs some explanation.

Although the syntax of a security custom attribute mirrors that of any other custom attribute, they're treated somewhat differently by the compiler and the runtime. Whereas a standard custom attribute is encoded directly into the assembly metadata at compilation time, a security custom attribute is actually instantiated (that is, the runtime is started up and an actual instance of the custom attribute is created). A special method on the security custom attribute is then called to create a permission instance. It is this permission instance that is serialized (via the `ToXml` method we looked at earlier) and placed into the metadata.

This additional step (creating a security custom attribute instance during compilation) allows the attribute author to perform non-trivial processing at compile time.

For example, public key information could be extracted from a certificate file and placed in the resulting permission.

For more trivial permissions (such as our `ToasterPermission`), the implementation of the attribute class is more straightforward. The attribute serves as a container for all the permission state data, which is then used to re-create the desired permission instance.

One very important restriction is imposed on permissions that are to be used declaratively (as a result of the use of security custom attribute classes and their compile time instantiation). No permission (or permission attribute) class can be used in the same assembly in which it is defined. Otherwise, the runtime will attempt to load and use an assembly that the compiler has not finished emitting yet, with unpredictable results. Commonly, the permission and associated permission attribute class are defined in a separate assembly of their own, away from all the other code in the project.

The runtime locates the permission assembly in the same manner it would any other assembly (which is different from the search rules used by the compiler to locate references). So, when compiling an assembly that uses one of your new permissions declaratively, the permission assembly should be either placed in the current directory (easy for quick and dirty testing of new permissions) or installed into the Global Assembly Cache (GAC).

The code present in the security custom attribute implementation will be granted permissions in the same manner as any other assembly. Because the assembly will usually be loaded from the local computer, the assembly will typically be granted full trust. Because this might be undesirable in certain circumstances (if source code is being automatically generated from instructions from an untrusted source, for example), there is a mechanism to lock down permissions for security custom attribute code. If the environment variable `_ClrRestrictSecAttributes` is defined to a nonempty value, and then all code run during a compilation will be restricted to `ExecutionPermission` only. For example

```
set _ClrRestrictSecAttributes=1
csc TestPermission.cs
```

Implementing a security custom attribute is relatively simple; an attribute class is created in much the same way as for a standard custom attribute (we'll see an example soon). Security custom attributes derive from one of two security classes (`System.Security.Permissions.SecurityAttribute` or `System.Security.Permissions.CodeAccessSecurityAttribute`) rather than `System.Attribute`. The intent was that attributes for CAS permissions derive from `CodeAccessSecurityAttribute` and non-CAS from `SecurityAttribute`. However, due to a bug in compiler support, inheriting your non-CAS permission attributes from

SecurityAttribute may not work in all languages. For V1 of the .NET Framework, it's recommended that all security attributes derive from CodeAccessSecurityAttribute. This may look odd, but will not have any impact on the functionality of your attributes.

There are three main components of a security custom attribute:

- A single constructor that takes a SecurityAction as an argument and simply delegates to the base constructor (you can also implement any other initialization code here as well if you want).

- A set of fields and/or properties that the caller can use to set state in the permission. These should closely mirror those in the permission implementation itself (down to having the same name, if possible).

- A method called CreatePermission. It is this method that the runtime will call to create the fully formed permission. The implementation will typically use the information stored in the previously mentioned fields to set the state in the final permission object.

During compilation of a declarative security attribute based on your permission, the runtime will create an instance of your attribute class (causing the constructor to run), set all the fields or properties referenced in the declarative security statement, and call the CreatePermission method. Note that the SecurityAction passed to the constructor is not actually intended for use by the permission attribute or permission—the constructor argument was just a convenient place to record it (from a custom attribute syntax point of view). In actuality, the runtime parses out the action prior to even calling the attribute constructor and stores it in the assembly metadata separately.

Let's look at the implementation of a security attribute to complement our ToasterPermission, given in Listing 25.10.

LISTING 25.10 Implementing a PermissionAttribute Class—ToasterPermissionAttribute.cs

```
[Serializable,
 AttributeUsage(AttributeTargets.Method |
               AttributeTargets.Constructor |
               AttributeTargets.Class |
               AttributeTargets.Struct |
               AttributeTargets.Assembly,
               AllowMultiple = true,
               Inherited = false)]
sealed public class ToasterPermissionAttribute : CodeAccessSecurityAttribute
```

LISTING 25.10   Continued

```
{
    // State fields to mirror those in actual permission.
    public bool ExclusiveAccess;
    public bool Information;
    public bool Eject;
    public ToastLevel ToastLevel;

    // Nothing to do in constructor but pass action code back up to
    // the base implementation.
    public ToasterPermissionAttribute(SecurityAction action)
        : base(action)
    {
    }

    // Create a permission instance with the current state set in the
    // attribute.
    public override IPermission CreatePermission()
    {
        ToasterPermission perm;

        // The runtime automatically provides a property which
        // indicates whether an unrestricted instance is required.
        if (Unrestricted)
            return new ToasterPermission(PermissionState.Unrestricted);

        // Create an instance with default (empty) state.
        perm = new ToasterPermission(PermissionState.None);

        // Copy state across.
        perm.ExclusiveAccess = ExclusiveAccess;
        perm.Information = Information;
        perm.Eject = Eject;
        perm.ToastLevel = ToastLevel;

        // Return the finished permission.
        return perm;
    }
}
```

NOTE

The code for the `ToasterPermissionAttribute` class given in Listing 25.10 is available for download from the publisher's Web site as `ToasterPermissionAttribute.cs`.

As for permission classes, security attribute classes should be marked as serializable and public. It's also a good practice to seal them; there is no real reason to allow anyone to subclass this type.

The `AttributeUsage` attribute is a standard feature of all custom attributes (whether security or standard). Its primary role here is to inform the compiler where use of the attribute is legal (all the places we'd expect for declarative security—methods, classes, value types, and assemblies). It also notes that multiple instances of the same attribute can appear on a single method, class, and so on (which is obviously important for declarative security) and that the attributes are not inherited through the class hierarchy (that is, an attribute on a base class doesn't imply that same attribute on any derived class). Note that the `AttributeUsage` annotation is used only by the compiler; it is ignored by the runtime. Therefore, widening the list of attribute targets or marking the attribute as inherited will not enable any extended functionality (for example, making fields a valid attribute target will not enable declarative security on fields).

We provide state fields in the attribute class that mirror the permission class. This is sensible in that it hides the distinction between the two classes to users of your permission (users have no need to understand the complexities of the actual implementation). This illusion is heightened by the fact that the C# compiler will allow the `Attribute` portion of the custom attribute name to be omitted if no ambiguity results (it is not confused by the presence of a real class with the same name—that is, the permission class itself—because the permission class does not derive from `System.Attribute` and is not considered a viable alternative).

The implementation of `CreatePermission` is straightforward and merely consists of taking the state data the user set and constructing a matching permission object from it. If you encounter an error at this point, simply throw an exception; the compiler should handle this by displaying the exception name and any exception message embedded within a compiler error message.

You should now be in a position to test your permission declaratively. First, build your permission and permission attribute classes into a single assembly. Next, create a test assembly referencing your permission assembly and containing declarative security statements. After compiling the test assembly, use the `PermView` command to examine and check the declarative security embedded in the assembly.

```
PermView /decl TestAssembly.exe
```

Alternatively, you can add `Console.WriteLine` statements within your implementation of the custom attribute and observe the progress of the various method calls during the compilation process. Remember to remove these output statements from the final product (C#'s conditional compilation feature can be useful here).

Working with Strong Names

We have previously discussed strong names and their uses (see Chapter 9, "Understanding the Concepts of Strong Naming Assembles"), and now it's time to look at the nitty-gritty details of actually applying them to your project. There are several aspects to this:

- Creation of a public/private key pair

- Adding the strong name to your assemblies

- Optionally full signing or re-signing assemblies during the latter stages of building/creating setup kits

- Managing keys within your development environment

We'll cover these topics in detail in the following sections.

Strong Name Key Pair Generation

Strong names are based on the use of a public/private key pair. The public key provides a well known identity (roughly corresponding to a publisher), while the private key remains a secret used to generate a digital signature.

The first step in strong naming an assembly is to create such a key pair. It is wise to bear in mind that this key pair is long lived; because the public portion provides identity, regenerating the key pair will change the name of any assembly bearing that strong name. At that point, any dependent assemblies (your own or a third party's) that have references to the changed assembly will need to be recompiled at the very least (the act of rebuilding automatically updates early bound assembly references with the new name). If assemblies are dependent on yours in a late bound manner (that is, they use methods such as `Assembly.Load` to force explicit loads), actual source code changes will be required (because the code needs to explicitly provide public key information in such cases). Additionally, other changes, such as security policy updates, may be required (if your strong name is used as a basis of granting trust; this is particularly important, because it implies changes on customer machines).

Basically, the public key is a highly visible part of your assembly (there are even managed APIs to read it), so changing it should be considered a breaking change on par with updating public classes and methods (if not more so).

The key pair itself is a stream of binary data that can be considered opaque (as we shall see later in this section, there are limited operations that can be performed on this data, such as extracting the public key). The data is not random; the keys are related to each other and have certain mathematical properties. Consequently, key creation is non-trivial and requires external utilities.

The first possibility is to use the SN utility provided with the .NET Framework SDK. SN is a command-line–based strong name utility, providing many simple management operations. In this case, we're interested in the -k option (note that all SN options are case sensitive). The following will create a key pair in the file KeyPair.snk:

```
SN -k KeyPair.snk
```

There is no requirement for a specific extension on strong name files, although snk is common. However, be aware that files containing both key pairs and individual public keys are commonly created. So either use different extensions for the two or choose a descriptive filename, as just demonstrated. (A quick tip here: in V1 of the .NET Framework, key pair files will be 596 bytes long, public key files will be only 160 bytes, allowing for quick identification by hand.)

Using SN in this manner will cause the Windows Cryptographic API (CAPI) to call into a Cryptographic Service Provider (CSP) to actually generate the key pair. For V1 of the .NET Framework, only one key type is supported—the algorithm must be RSA signing (CALG_RSA_SIGN in CAPI terms) with a key length of 1024 bits. SN will attempt to use the default CSP providing RSA services; if no specialized hardware/software CSPs have been installed for this purpose, Microsoft provides a default implementation that will work just fine.

Certain CSPs (particularly those based on cryptographic hardware) will not export a full key pair for security reasons (they never expose private keys outside of their implementation, which reduces the risk of the key being compromised). If you have configured such a CSP as the default RSA provider, SN will refuse to generate a key pair for you.

This leads us on to the second method of key pair creation. Because the file format used by the .NET Framework for key pairs is exactly that output by a CSP (from the CAPI API CryptExportKey, for example), you can create them yourself either by writing code that directly talks to CAPI or through the use of management utilities that may have come with the CSP/crypto hardware. Such topics are beyond the scope of this book (and very dependent on the actual software/hardware in use).

In general, the key pairs provided by Microsoft's default software-based CSP are satisfactory (mathematically speaking, they are as hard to compromise as key pairs from any other provider). But because the full key pair is exported to disk (and must be kept around, to sign each new build of your assemblies), it is difficult to guarantee that the private key is not compromised. If the private key becomes known, there can be a number of problems:

- It may not be immediately obvious that the key has been compromised because the key data can be passively scanned.

- The attacker can now create assemblies that claim to be published by you. This allows maliciously altered versions of your own assemblies to be distributed (with some sort of Trojan virus added perhaps), or allows the individual to take advantage of security policy that grants additional permissions to assemblies based on strong name.

- The cost to repair the damage to a compromised private key is high. A new key pair will have to be generated and, as explained previously, this will result in a renaming of all of your assemblies and the corresponding incompatibilities with existing assemblies.

For additional security, it is advisable to use a hardware CSP that generates key pairs within itself and refuses to export them (such devices often have tamper proof implementations that will destroy the keys if any attempt to physically access them is made). When using this approach, you cannot use SN to create the key pair (at least in Version 1 of the .NET Framework). Again, you will need to either call CAPI directly (look at the API CryptGenKey) or refer to utilities/documentation that came with the cryptographic hardware.

CAPI generalizes the handling of key pairs that can't be directly expressed outside the CSP by using named key containers. The key container name serves as a way to reference a given key pair within a CSP. So you (through CAPI) can ask a CSP to encrypt an array of bytes using the key pair in container Foo. This way, the CSP never needs to reveal the private key; it takes the plain text data in, encrypts it internally, and passes the encrypted data back out again.

For this reason, most of the strong name management supported in the .NET Framework can reference key pairs via either filenames or key container names.

When the key pair is kept highly secret (locked away in a piece of hardware) as previously described, it often becomes a problem to sign assemblies during the day-to-day development of assemblies. Typically, there will be only one machine capable of performing the signing operation, and it may well be placed well away from the normal development environment (for security reasons and to protect it from environmental dangers that could lead to the loss of the keys contained).

This is the reason that delay signing is supported under the .NET Framework. You'll recall that this involves setting the identity of the assembly as normal (using the public key) but deferring the generation of a digital signature until much later in the build (or product) cycle.

So in delay signing scenarios, we won't be dealing with a full key pair, but rather just the public key. Public keys are always represented in files; the runtime does not support the use of key containers for such entities. You can use SN to generate public key files from key pairs; the syntax differs slightly depending on how the key pair is stored.

If the key pair was exported to a file (such as when using SN -k KeyPair.snk), the following command will generate a public key into the file PublicKey.snk:

```
SN -p KeyPair.snk PublicKey.snk
```

If, however, your key pair resides in a key container (called MyContainerName for instance), use the following instead:

```
SN -pc MyContainerName PublicKey.snk
```

Note that the file format of public key files is *not* exactly the same as the CAPI output format, so it's advisable to always use SN to manipulate these files. Sadly, the file formats for public keys and key pairs are not self-describing (at least in V1 of the .NET Framework). So careful naming of the key files is advisable to avoid confusion (many utilities will give strange errors when handed the wrong format file). Again, you can use the file sizes to differentiate the two by hand (596 bytes for key pairs, 160 bytes for public keys).

Building Strong Names into Your Assemblies

Now you have a key pair or a public key; how do you apply this to your assembly and form a strong name?

When building an assembly from source code, the answer is custom attributes. In one of your source files, place the following assembly level attribute near the top of the file (this is using C# syntax):

```
[assembly: System.Reflection.AssemblyKeyFile("KeyFile.snk")]
```

where KeyFile.snk is the filename of your key pair or public key. If you're actually using a key pair file, that's all you need to do. The compiler will extract the data and sign the assembly during compilation. If you're using a public key file, however, add the following attribute as well:

```
[assembly: System.Reflection.AssemblyDelaySign(true)]
```

This informs the compiler that the file referenced in the previous attribute contains only a public key, and the full signing process should not be attempted.

If you have neither a key pair nor a public key file, but instead have the full key pair in a key container, use the following attribute in place of the previous two:

```
[assembly: System.Reflection.AssemblyKeyName("MyContainerName")]
```

One problem with the use of custom attributes in this manner is that build environment–specific information (that is, filenames) needs to be placed in the source code. One solution is to use a build script to generate a source file on-the-fly containing only the necessary attributes. The following is an example Perl script that relies on the presence of an environment variable named BUILDROOT to identify the root directory of your source tree. It generates a file called StrongNameAttributes.cs in the current directory, which can then be tagged onto the list of source files to be compiled for your assembly.

```perl
my $RootDir = $ENV{"BUILDROOT"} or
    die("Environment variable BUILDROOT needs to be set\n");

my $KeyPairFile = "$RootDir\\BinaryFiles\\KeyPair.snk";
my $SourceFile = "StrongNameAttributes.cs";

open(OUTFILE, ">", $SourceFile) or
    die("Failed to create $SourceFile, $!\n");

print(OUTFILE "[assembly: System.Reflection.AssemblyKeyFile(@\"
➥$KeyPairFile\")]\n");

close(OUTFILE);
```

Other utilities that create assemblies may take command-line attributes instead. For example, TlbImp uses one of the following forms (for delay sign, full sign from file, and full sign from key container, respectively):

```
TlbImp /publickey:PublicKey.snk /delaysign Foo.tlb
TlbImp /keyfile:KeyPair.snk Foo.tlb
TlbImp /keycontainer:MyContainerName Foo.tlb
```

ILASM, on the other hand, uses the following scheme, all based on the use of the /key option. The argument to /key is taken as a filename unless it begins with the @ character, in which case it's taken as the name of a key container (minus the @). If given a filename, ILASM attempts to guess whether the contents represent a public key or key pair by looking at the contents and then delaying signing or full signing

as appropriate. The method it uses to make this guess is heuristic, but given the
current implementation of the .NET Framework and CAPI, it should be right 100
percent of the time. The `ILASM` versions of the previous `TlbImp` examples would look
like the following:

```
ILASM /key:PublicKey.snk Foo.il
ILASM /key:KeyPair.snk Foo.il
ILASM /key:@MyContainerName Foo.il
```

The final example we'll look at is adding a strong name to an assembly generated via
managed code (reflection emit). The technique followed varies depending on
whether a public key or key pair is being provided, but in all cases, we modify the
`System.Reflection.AssemblyName` passed to
`System.AppDomain.DefineDynamicAssembly`.

First, let's look at delay signing an assembly. This is triggered by adding a public key
(represented as a byte array) to the `AssemblyName`. Because you probably have the
public key stored as a file on disk, you'll need to read this into memory first. Listing
25.11 gives an example implementation.

LISTING 25.11   Delay Signing an Assembly via Reflection Emit

```
using System;
using System.Reflection;
using System.Reflection.Emit;
using System.IO;

public class StrongNameEmit
{
    public static void Main(String[] args)
    {
        // Build a new assembly name.
        AssemblyName name = new AssemblyName();

        // Add simple name.
        name.Name = "NewAssembly";

        // Read the public key from disk. The file format is exactly
        // the same as the in memory format, so just slurp the entire
        // file into a byte array.
        FileStream fs = File.OpenRead("PublicKey.snk");
        Byte[] key = new Byte[fs.Length];
        fs.Read(key, 0, key.Length - 1);
        fs.Close();
```

LISTING 25.11   Continued

```
        // Add the public key to the name (since we're not supplying
        // a private key, the assembly will be only delay signed at
        // this stage).
        name.SetPublicKey(key);

        // Define a dynamic assembly with the given name.
        AssemblyBuilder ab;
        AppDomain domain = AppDomain.CurrentDomain;
        ab = domain.DefineDynamicAssembly(name,
                                          AssemblyBuilderAccess.Save);

        // Add a single module (this is a single file assembly).
        ModuleBuilder mb = ab.DefineDynamicModule("ModuleOne",
                                                  "NewAssembly.exe ");

        // Persist the assembly to disk.
        ab.Save("NewAssembly.exe ");
    }
}
```

Fully signing an emitted assembly is similar, but you will need to construct a
System.Reflection.StrongNameKeyPair object to encapsulate the form in which the
key pair will be made available to the runtime.

StrongNameKeyPair has three different constructors:

- Given a FileStream, the entire contents of the file are read into memory and
  assumed to represent a key pair.

- Given a byte array, the array is directly treated as a key pair.

- Given a string, the string is assumed to be the name of the key container
  holding a key pair.

After the StrongNameKeyPair has been constructed, it can be attached to the
AssemblyName using the KeyPair property. The modified code for full signing (assuming FileStream input of the key pair) is given in Listing 25.12.

LISTING 25.12   Full Signing an Assembly via Reflection Emit

```
using System;
using System.Reflection;
using System.Reflection.Emit;
```

LISTING 25.12   Continued

```
using System.IO;

public class StrongNameEmit
{
    public static void Main(String[] args)
    {
        // Build a new assembly name.
        AssemblyName name = new AssemblyName();

        // Add simple name.
        name.Name = "NewAssembly";

        // Open the key pair file on disk. The StrongNameKeyPair
        // constructor will read the file contents for us (though
        // we are still responsible for closing the stream).
        FileStream fs = File.OpenRead("KeyPair.snk");

        // Create a StrongNameKeyPair to describe the key pair input
        // method.
        StrongNameKeyPair keypair = new StrongNameKeyPair(fs);
        fs.Close();

        // Add the key pair to the name (since we're supplying a full
        // kwy pair, the assembly will be fully signed).
        name.KeyPair = keypair;

        // Define a dynamic assembly with the given name.
        AssemblyBuilder ab;
        AppDomain domain = AppDomain.CurrentDomain;
        ab = domain.DefineDynamicAssembly(name,
                                    AssemblyBuilderAccess.Save);

        // Add a single module (this is a single file assembly).
        ModuleBuilder mb = ab.DefineDynamicModule("ModuleOne",
                                            "NewAssembly.exe ");

        // Persist the assembly to disk.
        ab.Save("NewAssembly.exe ");
    }
}
```

Note that when reading a key pair from a file, the file read operations are performed during the construction of the `StrongNameKeyPair` object, not during the strong naming of the assembly (which occurs during the `AssemblyBuilder.Save` method call). Therefore, the `FileStream` object may be safely closed directly after the `StrongNameKeyPair` object is created. When passing a byte array, the array is buffered in the `StrongNameKeyPair`, so the original array may be safely modified before the call to `Save`.

Coping with Signature Invalidation During the Build Process

One problem that may crop up when building strongly named assemblies is accidental invalidation of the signature (leading to failures when trying to load the assembly or install it into the GAC). Just about any change to the assembly data will cause an invalidation, the only exceptions being the following:

- Any data in the image security directory (this allows Authenticode certificates to be added to a strongly named assembly without problems)

- The file header checksum (to allow updates such as we've just described)

- The signature blob itself (obviously we can't include this data when we're trying to compute the signature value in the first place)

All files in a multifile assembly are included in the signing process. This includes non-code files, such as linked resources.

The common reasons for modifying the image after the build step include stripping debugging information, rebasing images, and adding/modifying resource data.

There are several strategies that may be employed to work around such issues:

- *Avoid the modifications entirely*—Rebasing, for example, is generally less effective for a purely managed assembly that contains only a single unmanaged reference for the operating system loader to fix up (managed code handles code fixups in a different manner to the OS).

- *Full sign as the last stage of the build/setup process*—Generate delay signed images during compilation, perform any assembly post-processing steps, and then full sign the assemblies as a final step. This fits in well with a model where access to the private key involves heavyweight process and full signing is performed rarely (that is, day-to-day development uses delay signed assemblies).

- *It is possible to re-sign already fully signed assemblies as many times as desired (providing access to the private key is possible)*—This works well if access to the private key is cheap.

SN can be used to fully sign a delay signed assembly (or re-sign a previously fully signed assembly). If you have the key pair in a file, use the following syntax:

```
SN -R MyAssembly.dll KeyPair.snk
```

Recall that SN options are case sensitive, so it's important to use -R rather than -r. If your key pair resides within a key container, use the following instead:

```
SN -Rc MyAssembly.dll MyContainerName
```

Using Delay Signed Assemblies

If your development environment is going to use delay signed assemblies (perhaps because access to the private key is secured and full signing is a heavyweight process), your target execution environments need some preparation.

This is because delay signed assemblies look identical to fully signed assemblies that have been tampered with as far as the .NET Framework is concerned. Not having had a signature computed is the same as having a bad signature. For such assemblies to be successfully loaded or installed in the global assembly cache, the runtime must be forewarned that the signature is expected to be bad.

This is achieved by creating special entries in the registry listing assemblies and groups of assemblies that will have their strong name signature verification skipped. The easiest way to create these entries is via the use of SN. SN has a set of operations (all starting with -V) that allow management of the verification entries.

To register an assembly to be skipped, use SN -Vr:

```
SN -Vr MyAssembly.exe
```

The full path to the assembly must be given. However, the assembly file is used only to discover the two pieces of information SN is interested in—the simple string name of the assembly (probably MyAssembly in the previous example) and the public key (actually its condensed form, the public key token). You can move the assembly after registration and verification skipping will continue to work.

Alternatively, you can instruct SN to enable verification skipping for all assemblies using a given public key token. Use the notation *,public key token, where the public key token is given as a hexadecimal string:

```
SN -Vr *,b03f5f7f11d50a3a
```

Note there are no spaces around the , character.

The previous commands may be followed by a comma-separated list of usernames (in fully qualified domain\username format). This restricts the operation of the settings to the specified users. That is, signature verification will only be skipped for the named assemblies when run under the account of one of the listed usernames.

```
SN -Vr Foo.dll domain1\john,domain2\bill
```

To find out which assemblies are currently covered by your settings, use SN -Vl:

```
SN -Vl
```

```
Microsoft (R) .NET Framework Strong Name Utility  Version 1.0.3612.0
Copyright (C) Microsoft Corporation 1998-2001. All rights reserved.


Assembly/Strong Name                    Users
=============================================
*,B03F5F7F11D50A3A                      All users
Foo,1E7130EED55A0CC0                    domain1\john domain2\bill
MyAssembly,3D61F69268DA82E1             All users
```

To unregister an assembly, use SN -Vu, specifying the assembly name the same way as you would for SN -Vr:

```
SN -Vu MyAssembly.exe
SN -Vu *,b03f5f7f11d50a3a
SN -Vu Foo.dll
```

There is never any need to specify a list of usernames when unregistering assemblies. There can be only one entry for a given assembly name, so the unregister request is unambiguous. To quickly remove all settings, use SN -Vx:

```
SN -Vx
SN -Vl
```

```
Microsoft (R) .NET Framework Strong Name Utility  Version 1.0.3612.0
Copyright (C) Microsoft Corporation 1998-2001. All rights reserved.


No verification entries registered
```

One point to bear in mind is that the .NET Framework runtime reads these settings from the registry at process startup and will not see any updates after that point. For a managed program to start using new settings, the process will need to be stopped and restarted.

Obviously, switching off strong name verification in such a manner has serious security ramifications. It is not advisable to turn off checking for images you've received from untrusted sources (such as the Internet). The runtime won't be able to tell the difference between an assembly from the advertised publisher and one that just claims to be from that publisher. Conversely, you should never ship delay signed assemblies to customers or expect them to configure their machines to run your assemblies in the ways described in this section. You should always fully sign strong named assemblies prior to shipping.

Setting up verification skipping entries is allowed by Administrators only (the settings in the registry are ACL protected), which prevents malicious, untrusted code from changing the settings for your machine under your feet.

Summary

So, what have you learned in this chapter? First, you saw how permissions or permission set instances can be created and then acted on by a security operation either declaratively or imperatively:

- Imperative operations look like normal method calls. They are the most flexible form of security request because all parameters of the call can be dynamically computed.

- Declarative operations are specified in the form of attributes attached to the assembly, classes, or methods. They are less flexible than imperative calls because all parameters values are statically computed at compile time. However, there are a couple of operations available declaratively that aren't available to imperative calls—LinkDemand and InheritanceDemand. LinkDemand, in particular, provides a more performant means of establishing a caller's trust level, at the cost of being harder to use correctly without introducing security holes in your code.

- Declarative security at the method level overrides any at the class level (with the exception of LinkDemand and InheritanceDemand).

- Declarative security at the assembly level offers distinct functionality from that at the class or method level. The operations supported allow the assembly to modify (but never expand) the set of permissions granted by the security policy system.

- Implicit declarative security is added to P/Invoke calls or methods that call out to unmanaged COM servers. This security can be modified from the default, full stack walking demand, into a cheaper link demand by using the System.Security.SuppressUnmanagedCodeSecurityAttribute custom attribute (on classes/methods for P/Invoke and interfaces for interop).

- Strong named assemblies without the assembly level custom attribute `System.Security.AllowPartiallyTrustedCallersAttribute` will have an implicit link demand for full trust applied to all their public methods (when called from an external assembly). This reduces the possibility of trusted code written without regard to security being the cause of a security hole.

- Declarative link demands for `StrongNameIdentityPermission` provide a simple and cheap way of restricting access to your public APIs to other assemblies you own.

We then looked at the process of creating your own custom permissions:

- Permissions must all implement the `IPermission` interface. This implies implementation of the `ISecurityEncodable` interface as well.

- Permissions can be CAS (code access security, assigned to specific assemblies) or non-CAS (assigned based on permission implementation). CAS permission must derive from `System.Security.CodeAccessPermission`. This base class contains all the stackwalking logic plus the logic necessary to associate sets of granted CAS permissions with each assembly.

- Permissions may optionally implement the `System.Security.Permissions.IUnrestrictedPermission` interface. Doing so will cause the permission to be considered part of the unrestricted (full trust) permission set (which is the norm for most non-identity permissions).

- To be used declaratively, permissions must have an accompanying permission attribute class. Such classes are instantiated at compile time to translate security custom attributes into actual permission instances (which are then serialized and written into metadata).

- Permission and permission attributes should be defined in a different assembly than any code that uses them declaratively.

- Permission attribute code may be restricted to `ExectionPermission` rights by creating a non-null value for the environment variable `_ClrRestrictSecAttributes` during compilation.

Finally, we looked at the use of strong names within the build environment:

- The use of strong names requires a public/private key pair. Currently, this key pair is always based on 1024-bit keys using the RSA signing algorithm.

- Key pairs can be created in software using the `SN` utility and Microsoft's default Cryptographic Service Provider (CSP) or in specially designed hardware using the management utilities provided by the hardware vendor.

- Correspondingly, key pairs can be specified as files or key container names. The latter method allows code to reference key pairs without ever seeing the value of the private key.

- Strong names are added to source code via custom attributes that reference the key pair file or container name. For delay signing, a file containing just the public key is referenced.

- Other utilities, such as `TlbImp` or `ILASM`, take the key information as command-line parameters. Reflection emit (dynamic generation of assemblies) allows modification of the `System.Reflection.AssemblyName` class to specify a full or partial strong name.

- Strong named assemblies cannot be modified in any manner (aside from adding an Authenticode signature) without destroying the strong name signature. Your build environment can cope with this by delaying the signing of assemblies to the last possible stage.

- Delay signed assemblies can be installed and loaded without error on development machines by adding verification skip entries to the registry with the `SN` utility.

26

Testing a Secured Assembly

By Matthew Lyons

In the .NET world, most applications do not need to explicitly write security measures. They get it "for free" from the .NET Framework class library. However, the default security provided by the .NET Framework class library isn't always sufficient. Perhaps an application will need to access a resource that wasn't exposed by the .NET Framework. Another possibility is that the .NET Framework class library did not expose resources in a way that an application needed. In these cases, a .NET developer will write a custom permission or use the default permissions provided by the .NET Framework in his or her own class library.

If you have simply used the .NET Framework class library in an assembly without any security stack operations or custom permissions, you can skip this chapter. However, if you have used any custom permissions or security operations (such as `Assert`, `Demand`, and `LinkDemand`) in your assembly, this chapter is for you.

Testing a secured assembly has many concepts in common with testing any .NET Framework assembly. For example, correctness, performance, localization, usability, and reliability testing apply to a secured assembly just like they do for assemblies not applying any specific security measures. However, there are four unique steps for testing a secured assembly:

1. Define what is being protected as specifically as possible.

2. Understand how resources are being protected.

3. Test any custom permissions that are used to protect resources.

4. Test the protected code that directly accesses the resources.

Determining What Is Being Protected

The first step in testing a secured assembly is to consider two points. First, you must understand what is conceptually being protected. Second, you must understand where your assembly is referencing those conceptual resources. This step is equivalent to understanding a software application's requirements before writing code for it. While it is tempting to try and jump to testing custom permissions or protected methods and properties, skipping this step can produce an end result that may not be what was really necessary.

Conceptual Resources

Unless you have detailed specifications for your secured assembly, this question can be the most difficult part of the whole process, because it involves defining abstract concepts for a work in progress. What is *really* trying to be protected by the secure class library? The answer to that question will be your targeted conceptual resource. A conceptual resource is some resource that can be programmatically accessed independent of other resources.

TIP

If specifications were not written for a secured assembly before it was coded, it is still valuable to write them afterwards. It is better to write specifications later than not at all, because the process of writing them can bring up issues missed during coding and testing alone.

If specifications were written once and left alone, that is not enough. Specifications should be treated as "living documents." They should be revisited periodically to change, add, and remove material to reflect the expected state of the software. As products change from version to version, it is likely that the security expectations will change as well.

As an example of a conceptual resource the .NET Framework protects, think about the file system. The FileIOPermission protects access to anything that can be treated as a file. This includes not just a text file on a C: drive, but all different kinds of file systems, files across the network, and anything that can be mounted on a drive letter. Understanding this brought up an interesting point when the .NET Framework creators looked at how the FileIOPermission interacts with NTFS (the Windows NT file system). NTFS supports the concept of streams in files, which are independent storage locations within a file. While there are some benefits to using streams, they have also been criticized as an unnecessary complexity that is mostly employed by hackers to hide data. To simplify file system access, the FileIOPermission was written to explicitly deny the use of streams.

Once you have a notion of the conceptual resource to be protected, it is good to consider the security implications. As was found with NTFS streams, you may find corner cases where specific design decisions should be made to boost or simplify security. Testing a specification itself is a well-known test opportunity that applies in the .NET world, too.

In addition to thinking about what *is* being protected, it is important to think about what *is not* being protected. For example, while the FileIOPermission should protect access to files on a drive mounted from the network, it should not be responsible for guarding access to the same file server using raw sockets on any given port. Also, it can only protect the file system via managed classes. If an assembly is allowed to execute unmanaged code, it can call Win32 APIs to perform file manipulations. Thus, there are limits to what a secured assembly can protect. While the goal is to be the "gatekeeper" to resources, there are often more "gates" to resources than you may be able to protect.

Access Points in a Secured Assembly to a Resource

This substep is mostly bookkeeping. Essentially, it should involve documenting the specific methods and properties that will be accessing the resource to protect. This information will be critical to have during later steps. An example of what to document is shown in Table 26.1.

TABLE 26.1   Access Points to the File System in the .NET Framework Classes (Not an Exhaustive List)

Class/Method	FileIOPermission **Type**
System.IO.Directory.Exists()	Read access to the directory being checked
System.IO.Directory.Delete()	Write access to the directory to be deleted and all its children
System.IO.FileInfo.DirectoryName()	PathDiscovery access to the directory where the file exists
System.Reflection.Assembly.Location()	PathDiscovery access to the location of the assembly file
System.Reflection.Emit.AssemblyBuilder.Save()	Write and Append access to the filename of the dynamic assembly to be saved

As you can see from Table 26.1, the FileIOPermission is not used exclusively in the System.IO namespace. Similarly, all access to given resources may not occur in individual namespaces. Remember to look at all the classes in a secured assembly for possible access points to resources.

Determining How Resource Protection Is Implemented

The most straightforward way to protect a resource is by explicitly using permissions. Permissions explicitly protecting resources in the secure class library code will look something like the following if used imperatively:

```
new FileIOPermission(FileIOPermissionAccess.AllAccess,

➥@"C:\mydir\myapp.xml").Demand();
```

or something like the following if used declaratively:

```
[FileIOPermission(SecurityAction.Demand, All=@"C:\mydir\myapp.xml")]
```

In all cases of explicit protection, there will be some kind of Demand, LinkDemand, or InheritanceDemand in the code. Demands may occur either imperatively or declaratively. LinkDemands and InheritanceDemands will only be found in declarative form.

In my experience, most permissions protecting a resource will be used explicitly. However, it is possible that you will want to implicitly protect some resource. In this case, you would rely on a different secure assembly to explicitly protect a resource. For example, see Figure 26.1. Suppose you are writing a secured assembly, PrinterTestPage, that can print out test pages on a given printer so that you know it is configured properly. PrinterTestPage may want to use the System.Drawing.Printing.PrintDocument class internally to access printer resources. The PrintDocument class uses the System.Drawing.Printing.PrintingPermission to guard access to the printer resources. Thus, PrinterTestPage is implicitly relying on the PrintingPermission through the PrintDocument class to guard access to the printers.

After a few more words on implicitly protected resources, they won't be mentioned any more in this chapter. This is because you do not need to test the secured assemblies you are using with implicitly enforced permissions. In the printing example, this means you do not need to ensure that the PrintDocument class is using the PrintingPermission properly. That is the job of the supplier of the PrintDocument class.

One goal for testing permissions used implicitly should be to ensure you provide proper documentation. If someone using your secured assembly is not expecting to need a specific permission, but your library implicitly uses it, you are really just asking for support calls. Developers commonly reuse code, so any documentation you provide should spell out all the necessary permissions to use the classes you provide.

Another goal for testing implicitly enforced permissions should be to ensure that your secured assembly uses the other secure classes properly. In the printing example from Figure 26.1, this means to make sure PrinterTestPage uses the PrintDocument class in a correct, straightforward manner according to its documentation. This step is generally done via a source code review. Reading the source code for your secured assembly will show the exact use of any internal classes.

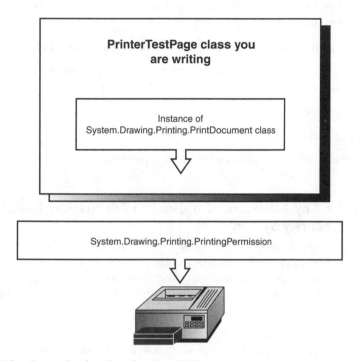

**PrinterTestPage class you
are writing**

Instance of
System.Drawing.Printing.PrintDocument class

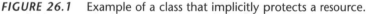

System.Drawing.Printing.PrintingPermission

FIGURE 26.1   Example of a class that implicitly protects a resource.

> **CAUTION**
>
> If you see any permission Asserts, SuppressUnmanagedCodeSecurity attributes, or LinkDemands during a source code review of your secured assembly, take note. All of these constructs will prevent a complete stack walk from happening. If care isn't taken, this can open up the possibility of a luring attack. As mentioned earlier in the book, a luring attack is where code with little trust uses code with more trust to perform an action it wouldn't normally be able to perform alone.

Testing Any Applied Custom Permissions

There are many permissions defined in the System.Security.Permissions namespace of the .NET Framework class library, although it is expected that they will not meet all the needs of future secure class libraries. Thus, the security system of the .NET Platform was designed to be extensible so that permissions could be added by .NET developers.

If a secured assembly is going to use a custom permission, it is crucial to test the permission class in addition to the secured methods and properties in the secured assembly. After the permission class is added to the security policy, it becomes a trusted piece of the system. If it is designed poorly, this permission could open serious security holes.

The following are major considerations when testing a custom permission:

- Testing the key methods of a custom permission that interface with the security system

- Testing imperative use of a custom permission

- Testing declarative use of a custom permission

- Other miscellaneous issues with custom permissions

Testing the Key Methods of a Custom Permission That Interface with the Security System

When a custom permission is written, is it generally written as a class that inherits from `System.Security.CodeAccessPermission`. There are a few key methods that the custom permission class overrides from the `CodeAccessPermission` base class. These methods are called by the security system of the CLR to enforce the permission. These methods are as follows:

- `Union`—Creates a new permission that covers all of the two original permissions. (In Figure 26.2, the union of Permission 1 and Permission 2 is the sum of all areas A, B, C, and D.)

- `Intersect`—Creates a new permission that covers the common subset of the two original permissions. (In Figure 26.2, the intersection of Permission 1 and Permission 2 is area C.)

- `IsSubsetOf`—Returns `true` or `false` to show if one permission is a subset of another. (In Figure 26.2, Permission 3 is a subset of Permission 2.)

- `Copy`—Creates a new permission that is identical to the original permission.

- `ToString`—Prints out a textual representation of a permission.

- `ToXml`—Creates an XML representation of a permission.

- `FromXml`—Changes an XML representation of a permission to a permission object itself.

When testing these methods, it is important to use a wide representation of possible permission objects. This means using `null` (when possible), an empty permission, an unrestricted permission, and a variety of states in between. If all states of a permission can be easily enumerated (for example, the permission state is really just represented by a few Boolean flags, such as `SecurityPermission`), go ahead and use all possible states. If the permission has an infinite number of possible states (for example, `FileIOPermission`), at least try to get a good representation of different permission states for testing.

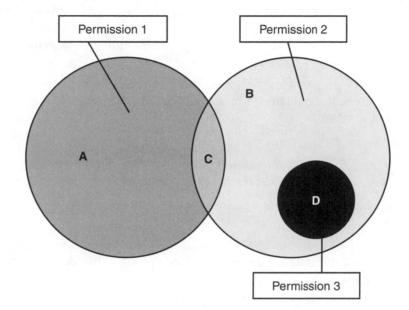

FIGURE 26.2   A Venn diagram that represents three permission objects with overlapping states.

Union
There is one primary principle to test with `Union`. If C is the union of A and B, `A.IsSubsetOf(C)` and `B.IsSubsetOf(C)` should both be `true`. In addition, there are a few secondary principles that ensure precise behavior for boundary conditions.

- The union of A and B should never return references to the A or B objects themselves. It should always return `null` or create a new custom permission object to return.

- The union of A and `null` should be a copy of A.

- The union of A with an empty custom permission (for example, one created with `PermissionState.None`) should be a copy of A.

- The union of A with an unrestricted custom permission (for example, one created with `PermissionState.Unrestricted`) should be an unrestricted custom permission.

- If A and B are different types (that is, they are instances of different classes), A.Union(B) should throw an exception unless an explicit design decision was made to allow this for the custom permission.

Intersect

There is one primary principle to test with Intersect. If C is the non-null intersection of A and B, C.IsSubsetOf(A) and C.IsSubsetOf(B) should both be true. Just as with Union, there are a few secondary principles that ensure precise behavior for boundary conditions.

- The intersection of A and B should never return references to the A or B objects themselves. It should always return null or create a new custom permission object to return.

- The intersection of A and null should be null.

- The intersection of A and an empty custom permission (for example, one created with PermissionState.None) should be an empty custom permission.

- The intersection of A and an unrestricted custom permission should be a copy of A.

- If A and B are different types, A.Intersect(B) should throw an exception unless an explicit design decision was made to allow this for the custom permission.

IsSubsetOf

IsSubsetOf is generally tested by testing the other key methods of a custom permission. However, there are some interesting cases to make sure to test directly. The examples use some given custom permission object A and an unrestricted custom permission object B.

- A.IsSubsetOf(B) should return true.

- B.IsSubsetOf(A) should return false.

- A.IsSubsetOf(null) should return true if A is an empty permission (for example, one created with PermissionState.None).

- If A and C are different types, A.IsSubsetOf(C) should throw an exception unless an explicit design decision was made to allow this for the custom permission.

Copy

Essentially, testing Copy just requires creating a range of different kinds of permissions, making copies of them via this method, and ensuring the copy is identical to the original. Note that you cannot ensure permission objects are identical by calling the `Equals` method, because permission objects do not override that method. Instead, you can determine equality of two permissions A and B by calling `A.IsSubsetOf(B)` and `B.IsSubsetOf(A)`. If A and B are identical permissions, both calls should return `true`.

CAUTION

Calling `A.Equals(B)` doesn't tell you if the internal permission states of A and B are identical. `A.Equals(B)` tells you if A and B are references to the same object in memory. To see if internal states of A and B are identical, you should call `A.IsSubsetOf(B)` and `B.IsSubsetOf(A)`. If both calls are `true`, A and B are identical permissions.

`ToString`
This method is less critical than the rest of the methods listed here because no runtime decisions are based on the output. However, `ToString` is often used in debugging, so it is important to get it right.

The output of this method is highly dependent on the custom permission itself, so there is little guidance to give for testing. Returning anything non-`null` should be safe, but you should try viewing the output for several different permission objects and ensure that they make sense.

`ToXml` **and** `FromXml`
Guidance for testing `ToXml` and `FromXml` is put together because testing them is best done together. There is little need to examine the `SecurityElements` returned by `ToXml` or constructing strange `SecurityElements` to pass to `FromXml` because the custom permission should only have to consume `SecurityElements` in `FromXml` that it produced via `ToXml`.

Generally, the best way to test these methods is the following:

1. Create an instance of the custom permission.

2. Call `ToXml` on that custom permission object.

3. Call `FromXml` on the `SecurityElement` returned by `ToXml`.

4. Compare the original custom permission object to the one resulting from the call to `FromXml`.

The original custom permission object and the resulting custom permission object should be identical. As in the case of testing `Copy`, testing equality should be done using `IsSubsetOf`. So, if B is the result of calling `ToXml` followed by a call to `FromXml`, `A.IsSubsetOf(B)` and `B.IsSubsetOf(A)` should both return `true`. The real key to testing `ToXml` and `FromXml` is to use a wide variety of different custom permission states.

Testing Imperative Use of a Custom Permission

When you know the key methods of a custom permission work correctly, you have gone a long way to making sure the permission can be used properly. However, a permission used declaratively executes a somewhat different code path compared to when it is used imperatively. Thus, it is important to ensure to test the permission in both cases.

Testing imperative use of a custom permission consists of creating objects of your custom permission class and calling the following methods on those objects:

- Assert
- Deny
- PermitOnly
- Demand

You should be able to reuse the same permission states for these methods that were used for the previously tested methods. Using a wide variety of permission states will ensure robustness of the custom permission.

Assert

To test that Assert works properly for the custom permission, a good test framework to make is shown in Listing 26.1. Following this paragraph are the main scenarios to try using that framework. The individual scenarios refer to two custom permission states A and B where A.IsSubsetOf(B) is true. Also, a third custom permission, state C, is used where A.Intersect(C) returns an empty custom permission.

- Assert A and Demand A should not throw a SecurityException.
- Assert A and Demand B should throw a SecurityException.
- Assert A and Demand C should throw a SecurityException.
- Assert B and Demand A should not throw a SecurityException.

LISTING 26.1   Test Framework for Imperatively Testing the Assert Method of a Custom Permission

```
class AssertTest {
  public void TestDriver() {
    // Make calls to RunTest per recommendations
  }
  private bool RunTest(CustomPermission permToAssert,
      CustomPermission permToDemand,
      Bool fShouldThrowSecurityException) {
    new CustomPermission(PermissionState.Unrestricted).Deny();
```

LISTING 26.1   Continued

```
  try {
    RunTestSubA(permToAssert, permToDemand);
  }
  catch (SecurityException) {
    if (fShouldThrowSecurityException)
      return true;
    else
      return false;
  }
  if (fShouldThrowSecurityException)
    return false;
  else
    return true;
}
private void RunTestSubA(CustomPermission permToAssert,
    CustomPermission permToDemand) {
  permToAssert.Assert();
  RunTestSubB(permToDemand);
}
private void RunTestSubB(CustomPermission permToDemand) {
  permToDemand.Demand();
}
}
```

CAUTION

If Assert and Demand are called in the same method, the Assert will not affect the resulting stack walk. After calling Assert, the test must call another method that calls Demand. This is because when a call is made to Demand, the stack walk begins with the frame above the frame containing the Demand. See Chapter 7, "Walking the Stack," for more details on stack walking.

This same principle also applies for Deny and PermitOnly. Calls to Deny and PermitOnly will not affect calls to Demands in the same method.

Deny

For Deny, see Listing 26.2 for a testing framework. Following this paragraph are the main scenarios to try in that framework. The individual scenarios refer to two custom permission states A and B where A.IsSubsetOf(B) is true. Also, a third custom permission state, C, is used where A.Intersect(C) returns an empty custom permission.

- Deny A and Demand A should throw a SecurityException.

- Deny A and Demand B should throw a SecurityException.

- Deny A and Demand C should not throw a SecurityException.

- Deny B and Demand A should throw a SecurityException.

LISTING 26.2   Test Framework for Imperatively Testing the Demand Method of a Custom Permission

```
class DemandTest {
  public void TestDriver() {
    // Make calls to RunTest per recommendations
  }
  private bool RunTest(CustomPermission permToDeny,
      CustomPermission permToDemand,
      Bool fShouldThrowSecurityException) {
    permToDeny.Deny();
    try {
      RunTestSubA(permToDemand);
    }
    catch (SecurityException) {
      if (fShouldThrowSecurityException)
        return true;
      else
        return false;
    }
    if (fShouldThrowSecurityException)
      return false;
    else
      return true;
  }
  private void RunTestSubA(CustomPermission permToDemand) {
    permToDemand.Demand();
  }
}
```

PermitOnly

For PermitOnly, see Listing 26.3 for a testing framework. Following this paragraph are the main scenarios to try in that framework. The individual scenarios refer to two custom permission states A and B where A.IsSubsetOf(B) is true. Also, a third custom permission state, C, is used where A.Intersect(C) returns an empty custom permission.

- PermitOnly A and Demand A should not throw a SecurityException.

- PermitOnly A and Demand B should throw a SecurityException.

- PermitOnly A and Demand C should throw a SecurityException.

- PermitOnly B and Demand A should not throw a SecurityException.

LISTING 26.3 Test Framework for Imperatively Testing the PermitOnly Method of a Custom Permission

```
class PermitOnlyTest {
  public void TestDriver() {
    // Make calls to RunTest per recommendations
  }
  private bool RunTest(CustomPermission permToPermitOnly,
      CustomPermission permToDemand,
      Bool fShouldThrowSecurityException) {
    permToPermitOnly.PermitOnly();
    try {
      RunTestSubA(permToDemand);
    }
    catch (SecurityException) {
      if (fShouldThrowSecurityException)
        return true;
      else
        return false;
    }
    if (fShouldThrowSecurityException)
      return false;
    else
      return true;
  }
  private void RunTestSubA(CustomPermission permToDemand) {
    permToDemand.Demand();
  }
}
```

Demand

Testing Demand was included while testing Assert, Deny, and PermitOnly, so no additional work should be necessary.

Testing Declarative Use of a Custom Permission

Declarative testing is similar to imperative testing. However, in this case, there is an expanded set of uses to try with the permission:

- Assert

- Deny

- `PermitOnly`

- `Demand`

- `LinkDemand`

- `InheritanceDemand`

`Assert`, `Deny`, `PermitOnly`, **and** `Demand`

`Assert`, `Deny`, `PermitOnly`, and `Demand` are generally the same imperatively as they are declaratively. Thus, the previous scenarios for `Assert`, `Deny`, `PermitOnly`, and `Demand` can be used for testing the custom permission declaratively. Also, the test frameworks can be easily modified to change the imperative calls to declarative calls. Listing 26.4 shows how this would be done for `Assert`. Note that the exact declarative representation of a permission depends on its attribute class, so this example will need to be modified to match your custom permission attribute class. Also, instead of constructing permissions in the `TestDriver` method and calling `RunTest` many times, several `RunTest` methods will be necessary because each one will need a different declarative security attribute.

The reason to test `Assert`, `Deny`, `PermitOnly`, and `Demand` declaratively in addition to imperatively relates to how the permissions are constructed. For imperative security, the test code creates the custom permission object itself. For declarative security, the custom permission object is created using the custom permission's attribute class. Thus, a bug in the declarative attribute class will only show up when using the custom permission declaratively.

LISTING 26.4   Test Framework for Declaratively Testing the `Assert` Method of a Custom Permission

```
class AssertTest {
  public void TestDriver() {
    // Make calls to RunTestX per recommendations
  }
  [CustomPermission(SecurityAction.Deny, Unrestricted=true)]
  private bool RunTest1(CustomPermission permToAssert,
      CustomPermission permToDemand,
      Bool fShouldThrowSecurityException) {
    try {
      RunTestSub1A(permToAssert, permToDemand);
    }
    catch (SecurityException) {
      if (fShouldThrowSecurityException)
        return true;
```

LISTING 26.4   Continued

```
      else
        return false;
    }
    if (fShouldThrowSecurityException)
      return false;
    else
      return true;
  }
  [CustomPermission(SecurityAction.Assert, Flags=SomeFlagsToTest)]
  private void RunTestSub1A(CustomPermission permToAssert,
      CustomPermission permToDemand) {
    RunTestSub1B(permToDemand);
  }
  [CustomPermission(SecurityAction.Demand, Flags=SomeOtherFlagsToTest)]
  private void RunTestSub1B(CustomPermission permToDemand) {
    return;
  }
}
```

NOTE

The two exclusive uses of permissions in declarative security, LinkDemand and InheritanceDemand, are described in more detail in Chapter 6, "Permissions: The Workhorse of Code Access Security."

LinkDemand

What follows are the key scenarios to check for a LinkDemand. All the scenarios will refer to method a in class A located in assembly 1, methods b1 and b2 in class B located in assembly 2, and an instance P of your custom permission.

TIP

If you are using default security policy, your secured assembly X.dll should be granted unrestricted use of your custom permission if X.dll is located on your local machine.

If you want to ensure some assembly is not granted some custom permission state P, then use an assembly permission request like the following:

```
[assembly:CustomPermission(SecurityAction.RequestRefuse, State=P)]
```

You will need to modify the State=P portion of this assembly permission request to fit your specific custom permission. See Chapter 6 for more details of assembly permission requests.

- A.a() has a LinkDemand for P. Assembly 1 *is* granted P when it is loaded, and assembly 2 *is not* granted P when it is loaded. B.b1() calls B.b2(), which calls A.a(). A SecurityException should be thrown inside B.b1() at the point when it calls B.b2().

- A has a LinkDemand for P. Assembly 1 *is* granted P when it is loaded, and assembly 2 *is not* granted P when it is loaded. B.b1() calls B.b2(), which creates an instance of A and calls A.a(). A SecurityException should be thrown inside B.b1() at the point when it calls B.b2().

- A.a() has a LinkDemand for P. Assembly 1 *is* granted P when it is loaded, and assembly 2 *is* granted P when it is loaded. B.b1() calls B.b2(), which calls A.a(). No SecurityException should be thrown in any of these calls due to the LinkDemand.

InheritanceDemand

What follows are the key scenarios to check for an InheritanceDemand. All the scenarios will refer to method a in class A located in assembly 1, method b in class B located in assembly 2, methods c1 and c2 in class C in assembly 3, and an instance P of your custom permission. Class B inherits from class A, and method b is an overridden version of method A.a().

- A.a() has an InheritanceDemand for P. Assemblies 1 and 3 *are* granted P when they are loaded, and assembly 2 *is not* granted P when it is loaded. C.c1() calls C.c2(), and C.c2() creates an instance of B. A SecurityException should be thrown when C.c1() calls C.c2().

- A has an InheritanceDemand for P. Assemblies 1 and 3 *are* granted P when they are loaded, and assembly 2 *is not* granted P when it is loaded. C.c1() calls C.c2(), and C.c2() creates an instance of B. A SecurityException should be thrown when C.c1() calls C.c2().

- A has an InheritanceDemand for P. Assemblies 1, 2, and 3 *are* granted P when they are loaded. C.c1() calls C.c2(), and C.c2() creates an instance of B and calls B.b(). No SecurityException should be thrown in any of these calls due to the InheritanceDemand.

Other Miscellaneous Issues with Custom Permissions

There are two issues that might be worthwhile investigating while testing a custom permission. The first issue is use of globalized data in the permission. By globalized data, I mean data that is different in different cultures, such as dates and character sets. The second issue is remoting across AppDomains.

Globalized Data

If the custom permission you need to test consists only of a group of Boolean flags, skip this section. However, if the permission is more complex and uses strings or dates, it is worthwhile to take note here.

When testing a custom permission, it is important to really examine the whole realm of possible inputs to the permission. If the permission stores state in the form of a string (for example, the FileIOPermission) and that string ever left managed code, there is a chance that there could be a string parsing problem in the unmanaged code. Strings and dates (among other types) are also related to cultures. It is worthwhile to try giving data formatted for other cultures to the permission. A data parsing problem in a permission could easily open up a security hole in the system.

Remoting Across AppDomains

Stack walks will not propagate in remoting across machine boundaries. However, they will propagate within a process across AppDomains. Because of the complexity of remoting and serialization of permissions, it would be useful to at least try a scenario involving a stack walk across AppDomains for your custom permission. If your permission is incorrectly serialized or deserialized across the AppDomain boundary, it could turn out to be a problem if complex applications tried to use your custom permission or any secured assemblies using your custom permission. Listing 26.5 shows an example of stack walking across app domains. Note that this requires multiple assemblies, so the example is broken into two source files.

LISTING 26.5   Example of Cross-AppDomain Stack Walking

```
// This section should be compiled into its own assembly
// If the source code is saved to "testhelper.cs", compile it via
// "csc /target:library testhelper.cs"
using System;
using System.Security;

public class CrossDomainTest : MarshalByRefObject {
  public void DemandPermission(PermissionSet p1) {
    p1.Demand();
  }
}


// This section should be compiled into a different assembly
// If the source code is saved to "testdriver.cs", compile it via
// "csc /r:testhelper.dll testdriver.cs"
using System;
using System.Security;
```

LISTING 26.5   Continued

```
using System.Security.Permissions;
using System.Security.Policy;

public class CrossDomainTestDriver {
  private AppDomain MyTestDomain;

  public static void Main(String[] args) {
    try {
      CrossDomainTestDriver ADtest = new CrossDomainTestDriver();
      ADtest.RunTest();
    }
    catch (Exception e) {
      Console.WriteLine("Unexpected error occurred");
      Console.WriteLine(e.ToString());
    }
  }

  private void RunTest() {
    MyTestDomain = AppDomain.CreateDomain("test", null,new AppDomainSetup());
    CrossDomainTest TestObj = (CrossDomainTest)MyTestDomain.
➥CreateInstance("TestHelper", "CrossDomainTest").Unwrap();
    CustomPermission cp = new CustomPermission(PermissionState.Unrestricted);
    PermissionSet p1 = new PermissionSet(PermissionState.None);
    p1.AddPermission(cp);
    try {
      p1.Deny();
      TestObj.DemandPermission(p1);
      Console.WriteLine("Fail: A security exception should have been
➥thrown");
    }
    catch(SecurityException se) {
      Console.WriteLine("Pass: A security exception was received appropriately");
      Console.WriteLine(se.ToString());
    }
  }
}
```

NOTE

See the .NET Framework SDK documentation for more information on remoting and serialization.

Testing the Methods and Properties That Should Be Protected

This fourth step for testing a secured assembly is the culmination of work for the first three steps:

1. Define what is being protected as specifically as possible.

2. Understand how resources are being protected.

3. Test any custom permissions that are used to protect resources.

This step asks how well the assembly design was implemented in the secured assembly. To address this point, it is especially important that you have the list of methods and properties being protected from the first step.

To test the methods and properties that should be protected, there are two primary actions that must occur. First, the methods and properties should be checked to see if they implement the minimum specified security checks. Second, those same methods and properties should be checked to make sure there aren't additional, unintentional (or undocumented) permission requirements.

Checking Minimal Protection on Methods and Properties

Checking if a documented method is properly protected is generally a straightforward process for Demands. You can just modify a small, positive test case that you already have. Listing 26.6 shows a complete example for the System.IO.File.OpenRead() method.

LISTING 26.6   Test for Minimal Permission Demands on System.IO.File.OpenRead()

```
using System;
using System.IO;
using System.Security;
using System.Security.Permissions;

public class FileIOTest
{
  public static void Main() {
    try {
      if (RunTest()) {
        Console.WriteLine("Pass: File.OpenRead properly protected");
      } else {
        Console.WriteLine("Fail: File.OpenRead not properly protected");
      }
    }
```

LISTING 26.6   Continued

```
    catch (Exception e) {
      Console.WriteLine("Unexpected error occurred.");
      Console.WriteLine(e.ToString());
    }
  }

  public static bool RunTest() {
    new FileIOPermission(FileIOPermissionAccess.Read, @"C:\test.txt").Deny();
    try {
      FileStream fs = File.OpenRead(@"C:\test.txt");
      return false;
    }
    catch (SecurityException se) {
      return true;
    }
  }
}
```

For code in the secured assembly protected by LinkDemands or InheritanceDemands, checking for minimal protection is a little more complex. LinkDemands and InheritanceDemands check permission grants on assemblies that call the protected code. Thus, you will need to ensure your test assemblies explicitly do not have the required permissions. Also, because these kinds of errors are generated at JIT time instead of runtime, the test code will need an extra level of indirection to properly catch any SecurityExceptions. Listing 26.7 shows an example of how this might be done.

LISTING 26.7   Example of How to Test Minimal Protection of a Method with a LinkDemand

```
// This example assumes Foo.LinkDemandProtectedMethod() has a LinkDemand for
//   some FileIOPermission
// The expected output on the command line for this scenario is the following:
//   Inside Main
//   Caught exception in Main
//   System.Security.SecurityException: Request for the permission of type
//   System.Security.Permissions.FileIOPermission, mscorlib,
//   Version=1.0.????.0, Culture=neutral, PublicKeyToken=b77a5c561934e089
//   failed.
//   at TestLinkDemand.CallProtectedMethod()
//   at TestLinkDemand.Main()
```

LISTING 26.7   Continued

```
using System;
using System.Security;
using System.Security.Permissions;

[assembly:FileIOPermission(SecurityAction.RequestRefuse, Unrestricted=true)]
public class TestLinkDemand {
  public static void Main() {
    Console.WriteLine("Inside Main");
    try {
      CallProtectedMethod();
    }
    catch (Exception e) {
      Console.WriteLine("Caught exception in Main");
      Console.WriteLine(e.ToString());
    }
  }

  public static void CallProtectedMethod() {
    Console.WriteLine("Inside CallProtectedMethod");
    Foo f = new Foo();
    f.LinkDemandProtectedMethod();
    Console.WriteLine("Finished calling LinkDemandProtectedMethod");
  }
}
```

Testing a class or method protected by an InheritanceDemand is very similar to testing protection by LinkDemands. In the code from Listing 26.7, two changes would need to be made. First, a class would need to be defined that overrides the protected class or method. Second, the call to f.LinkDemandProtectedMethod would need to change to a call to the overridden class or method you just defined in the first step.

Testing If Undocumented Protection Exists on Methods and Properties

After you know that the necessary permission requirements are in place, you should ensure that there are not additional permission restrictions. In the case of testing Demands, you can simply replace calls to Deny with calls to PermitOnly and reverse your expected outcome. Listing 26.8 shows these changes made on Listing 26.6.

LISTING 26.8   Test for Undocumented Permission Demands on
System.IO.File.OpenRead()

```
using System;
using System.IO;
using System.Security;
using System.Security.Permissions;

public class FileIOTest
{
  public static void Main() {
    try {
      if (RunTest()) {
        Console.WriteLine("Pass: File.OpenRead properly protected");
      } else {
        Console.WriteLine("Fail: File.OpenRead not properly protected");
      }
    }
    catch (Exception e) {
      Console.WriteLine("Unexpected error occurred.");
      Console.WriteLine(e.ToString());
    }
  }

  public static bool RunTest() {
    new FileIOPermission(FileIOPermissionAccess.Read, @"C:\test.txt").
➥PermitOnly();
    try {
      FileStream fs = File.OpenRead(@"C:\test.txt");
      return true;
    }
    catch (SecurityException se) {
      return false;
    }
  }
}
```

If both the Deny case and the PermitOnly test cases pass, you know that the secure
library method needs the correct permissions and only the correct permissions to
access the protected resources.

For testing LinkDemands and InheritanceDemands, you can modify the minimal
permission test cases to replace the RequestRefuse request with a RequestMinimum

request. Listing 26.9 shows an example of how Listing 26.7 could be modified to perform this testing.

LISTING 26.9 Example of How to Test for Undocumented Protection of a Method with a LinkDemand

```
// This example assumes Foo.LinkDemandProtectedMethod() has a LinkDemand for
//   some FileIOPermission
// The expected output on the command line for this scenario is the following:
//   Inside Main
//   Inside CallProtectedMethod
//   Finished calling LinkDemandProtectedMethod
using System;
using System.Security;
using System.Security.Permissions;

[assembly:FileIOPermission(SecurityAction.RequestMinimum,
➥Read=@"C:\test.txt")]
// The next two assembly permission requests are necessary to execute and get
// a grant set only containing the right to execute and the right to read
// "C:\test.txt".
[assembly:SecurityPermission(SecurityAction.RequestMinimum, Execution=true)]
[assembly:PermissionSet(SecurityAction.RequestOptional, Name="Nothing")]
public class TestLinkDemand {
  public static void Main() {
    Console.WriteLine("Inside Main");
    try {
      CallProtectedMethod();
    }
    catch (Exception e) {
      Console.WriteLine("Caught exception in Main");
      Console.WriteLine(e.ToString());
    }
  }

  public static void CallProtectedMethod() {
    Console.WriteLine("Inside CallProtectedMethod");
    Foo f = new Foo();
    f.LinkDemandProtectedMethod();
    Console.WriteLine("Finished calling LinkDemandProtectedMethod");
  }
}
```

CAUTION

The examples in Listings 26.8 and 26.9 may not work for you because you may have other test code that needs additional permissions to run. For example, your test may try to log results to a file but fail to do so because the necessary `FileIOPermission` was excluded in the assembly requests. If you run into this problem, try separating the core test code that calls the secured assembly methods/properties into a separate assembly. Then you can place the assembly permission requests on just the small test assembly instead of the entire test code.

Summary

Testing secured assemblies shares many aspects with testing any .NET Framework assemblies. For example, performance may be a concern for all assemblies you need to test. However, there are some extra steps to perform when testing secured assemblies. These steps are as follows:

1. Determine what is being protected.

2. Determine how resource protection is implemented.

3. Test any applied custom permissions.

4. Test the methods and properties that should be protected.

If all four of these steps are performed successfully, you have gone a long way to ensure your secured assembly is safe to use.

27

Writing a Secure Web Site Using ASP.NET

IN THIS CHAPTER

- Designing a Secure Web Site
- Implementing a Secure Web Site

By Kevin Price

By now, you should be familiar with the concepts involved in setting up a basic, secure Web site using Windows 2000 and Internet Information Services (IIS). To review the basics, see Chapter 16, "Data Transport Integrity: Keeping Data Uncorrupted." In this chapter, you learn how to use the following techniques to write a secure Web site using ASP.NET.

- Use Advanced IIS Security tools to secure your site

- Use Authentication to allow or deny users

- Use Authorization to determine which users can execute code used in the site

- Implement your secure Web site

- Learn tactics used by hackers to attack your Web site

In this chapter, we will analyze the fictitious "SecureOffice" Web site. Before its creation, however, we will step through the decision-making process to look at our "requirements" and determine exactly which new features from ASP.NET we should use.

SecureOffice is a simple Web site that allows users to log in and read their material online. The goal of this Web site is to enable network users to log in, using their Windows 2000 credentials, and have access to certain company documentation that they have created. The hardware scenario is one server, protected by a firewall with port 80 open for inbound and outbound TCP; and port 443 open for HTTPS. Our user base should be considered basic, meaning they can open a browser and navigate through an application, but explaining security to them would be a lost cause. The key selling point is that you can create a secure site and have it up and running quickly.

> **NOTE**
>
> It is well beyond the scope of this book to discuss how to configure every possible option for whatever firewall you may be using. Please consult the documentation that came with your product regarding limiting port access. Also keep in mind that no Web site needs NetBIOS ports (135-139) exposed on an external interface.

Given that extensive set of requirements, pun intended, knowing that the data might contain proprietary information and your reputation is at stake, let's begin.

Designing a Secure Web Site

Before we dive into a bunch of code, let's look at our options and take this step by step.

The first step is establishing a Web server. We'll skip the formalities of how to create a development, staging, and production environment and just imagine that they are all in place. One of the tools that is a part of Microsoft's Security Toolkit is URLScan. This ISAPI filter checks incoming requests for a variety of malformations and decides whether to allow the request to proceed or to reject it. Although it is no substitute for keeping up with whatever service packs, hotfixes, or bulletins that are sent out by Microsoft, it is an effective tool at reducing the number of ways potential hackers can get in. URLScan works with IIS 4, 5, and 5.1 and is easy to install and configure.

> **NOTE**
>
> You can get the latest copy of URLScan, as part of the IIS Lockdown Tool, free from the Microsoft Web site. The direct URL is `http://www.microsoft.com/Downloads/Release.asp?ReleaseID=33961`. The information only Web page is `http://www.microsoft.com/technet/security/urlscan.asp`. Installation of the URLScan filter is done easily through the IIS Lockdown Wizard. Not only will it set up the configuration file for you based on the type of server you are running (BizTalk, Exchange, and so on), but it also registers the filter with IIS.

The `urlscan.ini` file stores the configuration for the filter, so from within that file we want to make sure a few things are enabled—just to make sure. Discretion is always the better side of valor. Table 27.1 shows the values within the `urlscan.ini` file that we are going to pay special attention to, what their values will be, and why they are set that way.

TABLE 27.1   Selected `urlscan.ini` Properties

Property Name	Value	Reason
UseAllowVerbs	1	This prevents certain kinds of requests from coming through. For this, we will enable GET, POST, and HEAD—nothing else.
UseAllowExtensions	0	Setting this to 0 means that it will use the settings in the DenyExtensions section of the URLScan.ini file. It is in this section that we will deny access to file extensions to which no user will have access, for example, .asa, .config, and so on.
NormalizeURLBeforeScan	1	Forces normalization (canoncalization) of the URL before determining to allow or deny the request.
VerifyNormalization	1	This just canoncalizes the URL again to make sure nothing changed from the first check (Buffer attacks can happen this way).
EnableLogging	1	Have a log file to find out if any bad requests come though, and who made them.

As shown in Table 27.1 and implemented in Listing 27.1, these settings will be important in securing the ASP.NET application. By setting explicit verbs in the AllowVerbs section, we are preventing actions associated with the HTTP verbs that do not relate to what is explicitly needed by the application. At no point will anything other than GET, POST, or HEAD be used, so get rid of everything else.

In the DenyExtensions section, we can add any variety of file extensions that we do not want the Web server to provide direct access to. In this application, access is going to be denied to any .exe, .dll, .cmd, or .com file located anywhere on the Web server.

CAUTION

The URLScan filter is not directory specific by default; it is server specific. After it's installed, the default behavior is to protect the entire machine. Unless there is some incredibly overwhelming need, there is no need to ever modify this behavior.

Using NormalizeURLBeforeScan, we can prevent attacks associated with malformed URL requests, such as those associated with Nimda and CodeRed. What this does is force a URL to be canonicalized—that is, fully determined—prior to attempting to execute the request.

VerifyNormalization is just a double-check on NormalizeURLBeforeScan to make sure that nothing has changed during the canonicalization process. This further protects against buffer overflow attacks.

Finally, `EnableLogging` is just good practice to see if your server is being attacked and what additional measures, if any, you should take to protect it. Such measures can include further file extension blocking or allowing additional verbs should your site deploy a software package that uses them, such as SharePoint Portal Server.

Listing 27.1 shows the complete `urlscan.ini` file with generated comments from the IIS Lockdown Wizard. This listing is shown merely as an example of how the `urlscan.ini` file looks and can be configured. It become important when using the URLScan filter to know what is available for you to change and the consequences of doing so. In this listing, notice the sections that correspond with the items in Table 27.1 and how they are set. Also in this listing, notice the `.config` addition to the Infrequently User Scripts section. This prevents users from being able to browse your `web.config` or `machine.config` file.

LISTING 27.1   `urlscan.ini`—Complete

```
[options]
UseAllowVerbs=1
➥; if 1, use [AllowVerbs] section, else use [DenyVerbs] section
UseAllowExtensions=0
➥; if 1, use [AllowExtensions] section, else use [DenyExtensions] section
NormalizeUrlBeforeScan=1
➥; if 1, canonicalize URL before processing
VerifyNormalization=1
➥; if 1, canonicalize URL twice and reject request if a change occurs
AllowHighBitCharacters=1
➥; if 1, allow high bit (ie. UTF8 or MBCS) characters in URL
AllowDotInPath=0
➥; if 1, allow dots that are not file extensions
RemoveServerHeader=0
➥; if 1, remove "Server" header from response
EnableLogging=1
➥; if 1, log UrlScan activity
PerProcessLogging=0
➥; if 1, the UrlScan.log filename will contain a PID (ie. UrlScan.123.log)
AllowLateScanning=0
➥; if 1, then UrlScan will load as a low priority filter.
PerDayLogging=1
; if 1, UrlScan will produce a new log each day with activity in the form
➥ UrlScan.010101.log
RejectResponseUrl=
; UrlScan will send rejected requests to the URL specified here.
➥ Default is /<Rejected-by-UrlScan>
```

LISTING 27.1   Continued

```
UseFastPathReject=0
; If 1, then UrlScan will not use the RejectResponseUrl or allow IIS
➥ to log the request

; If RemoveServerHeader is 0, then AlternateServerName can be
; used to specify a replacement for IIS's built in 'Server' header
AlternateServerName=

[AllowVerbs]

;
; The verbs (aka HTTP methods) listed here are those commonly
; processed by a typical IIS server.
;
; Note that these entries are effective if "UseAllowVerbs=1"
; is set in the [Options] section above.
;

GET
HEAD
POST
;OPTIONS ; FrontPage Server Extensions requires OPTIONS.  If you need to enable
        ; it, uncomment the OPTIONS verb and set "AllowLateScanning=1" in the
        ; [Options] section above.  Additionally, after changing this file and
        ; restarting the web service, you should go to the "ISAPI Filters" tab
        ; for the server's properties in MMC and ensure that UrlScan is listed
        ; lower than fpexedll.dll.

[DenyVerbs]

;
; The verbs (aka HTTP methods) listed here are used for publishing
; content to an IIS server via WebDAV.
;
; Note that these entries are effective if "UseAllowVerbs=0"
; is set in the [Options] section above.
;

PROPFIND
PROPPATCH
MKCOL
```

LISTING 27.1   Continued

```
DELETE
PUT
COPY
MOVE
LOCK
UNLOCK

[DenyHeaders]

;
; The following request headers alter processing of a
; request by causing the server to process the request
; as if it were intended to be a WebDAV request, instead
; of a request to retrieve a resource.
;

Translate:
If:
Lock-Token:

[AllowExtensions]

;
; Extensions listed here are commonly used on a typical IIS server.
;
; Note that these entries are effective if "UseAllowExtensions=1"
; is set in the [Options] section above.
;

.asp
.htm
.html
.txt
.jpg
.jpeg
.gif

[DenyExtensions]

;
; Extensions listed here either run code directly on the server,
; are processed as scripts, or are static files that are
```

LISTING 27.1   Continued

```
; generally not intended to be served out.
;
; Note that these entries are effective if "UseAllowExtensions=0"
; is set in the [Options] section above.
;
; Also note that ASP scripts are allowed to run with the below
; settings.  If you wish to prevent ASP from running, add the
; following extensions to this list:
;    .asp
;    .cer
;    .cdx
;    .asa
;

; Deny executables that run on the server
.exe
.bat
.cmd
.com

; Deny infrequently used scripts
.htw     ; Maps to webhits.dll, part of Index Server
.ida     ; Maps to idq.dll, part of Index Server
.idq     ; Maps to idq.dll, part of Index Server
.htr     ; Maps to ism.dll, a legacy administrative tool
.idc     ; Maps to httpodbc.dll, a legacy database access tool
.shtm    ; Maps to ssinc.dll, for Server Side Includes
.shtml   ; Maps to ssinc.dll, for Server Side Includes
.stm     ; Maps to ssinc.dll, for Server Side Includes
.printer ; Maps to msw3prt.dll, for Internet Printing Services
.config  ; Disables someone trying to browse the web.config file

; Deny various static files
.ini     ; Configuration files
.log     ; Log files
.pol     ; Policy files
.dat     ; Configuration files

[DenyUrlSequences]
..  ; Don't allow directory traversals
./  ; Don't allow trailing dot on a directory name
```

LISTING 27.1   Continued

```
\   ; Don't allow backslashes in URL
:   ; Don't allow alternate stream access
%   ; Don't allow escaping after normalization
&   ; Don't allow multiple CGI processes to run on a single request
```

If you don't believe this is worth the minor effort of installation and configuration, trust me—it is. Listing 27.2 shows a few actual entries from my Web server's urlscan.log (urlscan.112401.log) file for the date that this chapter was written. What is most disturbing about these entries is that patches are available, and the administrators of these site have either chosen to ignore them or do not know that they are sending these kinds of requests. An e-mail was sent to the administrator or Web master for each of these sites. In most cases, the response was an apology. What this shows are requests attempting to access executable files to execute malicious code on the Web server.

LISTING 27.2   urlscan.112401.log Entries

```
[11-24-2001 - 11:50:27] -------------- Initializing UrlScan.log -----------
[11-24-2001 - 11:50:27] -- Filter initialization time: [11-20-2001 - 22:45:30]
[11-24-2001 - 11:50:27] Client at 209.249.70.152: URL contains extension '.exe'
➥, which is disallowed. Request will be rejected.  Site Instance='1',Raw
➥ URL='/scripts/root.exe'
[11-24-2001 - 11:50:33] Client at 209.249.70.152:
➥URL contains extension '.exe', which is disallowed.
Request will be rejected.  Site Instance='1', Raw URL='/MSADC/root.exe'
[11-24-2001 - 11:50:42] Client at 209.249.70.152:
➥ URL contains extension '.exe', which is disallowed.
Request will be rejected. Site Instance='1',Raw URL='/c/winnt/system32/cmd.exe'
```

Now that the basics of what requests can and can't come through are covered, it's time to request the certificate for SSL, get it installed, and restart IIS to make sure that any changes made in the urlscan.ini file are active.

> **NOTE**
>
> At this point, knowledge of how to acquire and install certificates for IIS is assumed. If you are unfamiliar with installing certificates, please refer to Chapter 16 in the "More About Certificates—Options and Installing" section.

At this point, all I have done codewise is create a new C# ASP.NET Web Application in the Visual Studio .NET IDE. This was done to create the directories in IIS and create the template `web.config` file that we will be modifying throughout the following sections of this chapter. The next step in creating our application is to determine how users will gain access to the site. To determine this, the next few sections center on the different authentication choices provided by ASP.NET.

Authentication Choices

The second step in the process is to determine how to authorize users attempting to access the site. The first thing that the user will do is browse to the URL for this site. At this point, they must be authenticated because there is no mention in the requirements of allowing anonymous access to anything. IIS provides the following options for authentication:

- Anonymous—Does nothing for authentication.

- Basic Authentication—Nothing is encrypted.

- Forms-based Authentication—Encryption depends on settings in `web.config` file; within IIS, anonymous access is allowed.

- Digest Authentication—Hash value is created on the client and sent to the server; the password itself is not sent.

- Integrated Windows Authentication—Provides a hash-based exchange between Internet Explorer and Windows. User's password is not sent over the Internet.

Because everything is running on a Windows 2000 network, we will use Integrated Windows Authentication. Why? Integrated Windows Authentication allows us the most secure login available without deploying additional software on the client; it will also enable us to impersonate or delegate quite easily should that become necessary.

Impersonation on this site will further reduce the risk of attack because the code will only execute as the authenticated user. In addition, we have already incorporated some additional security settings for IIS. Even with such advanced technology embedded into the operating system and Web server, the goal remains the same: Keep the data encrypted at all times between the client and the server. It is not possible to stress the importance of this enough. As a general rule, go with this: If you don't want everybody in the known world to see something you are typing, it better be encrypted. Using encryption via SSL is better than relying on the fact that your company is too small for anyone to care about. In addition, the outside world might not necessarily be the biggest concern. Many attacks on information come from within. Listing 27.3 shows the authentication element's value in the `web.config` file for the SecureOffice site.

LISTING 27.3   Authentication Element Setting

```
<authentication mode="Windows"/>
```

Authorization Choices

Now that we have an authentication mechanism established, it's time to determine who can do or see what is on the site. The choices are File Authorization, where the OS and File ACLs control who can access what, and URL Authentication where access is more controlled by where a user is coming from. Because no administrator really wants to keep track of all the possible IP addresses users could be coming in with from home dial-up accounts, we rely on File Authorization. To enable this, we add an authorization element to the web.config file, and within that add a deny element. Another step we take is the creation of a "SecureOfficeUsers" group. This helps in managing users within the company that have access to the application. Listing 27.4 shows the complete entry.

LISTING 27.4   Authorization Element

```
<authorization>
    <allow roles="KPCRASH\SecureOfficeUsers"/>
    <deny users="?" />
</authorization>
```

In Listing 27.4, note the deny element's users attribute value. The ? represents anonymous users, and for this application, they are not allowed to do anything. The configuration options for authorization also enable you to control verbs in relation to users and groups; this is discussed in Chapter 15, "Authorization—Control Who Is Accessing Your Site." For this site, we rely on the settings in the urlscan.ini file to control the verbs allowed. During the process of authorization, an instance of the WindowsIdentity class is created. Using this class, you can gather information about the user. Listing 27.5 shows a sample of what can be retrieved with our current Web configuration.

LISTING 27.5   default.aspx.cs

```
using System;
using System.Collections;
using System.ComponentModel;
using System.Data;
using System.Drawing;
using System.Web;
using System.Web.SessionState;
```

LISTING 27.5   Continued

```
using System.Web.UI;
using System.Web.UI.WebControls;
using System.Web.UI.HtmlControls;
using System.Security;
using System.Security.Principal;
using System.Threading;
using System.Net;
using System.Security.Permissions;

namespace SecureOffice
{
 /// <summary>
 /// Summary description for _default.
 /// </summary>
 public class _default : System.Web.UI.Page
 {
  private void Page_Load(object sender, System.EventArgs e)
  {
   WindowsIdentity wi = (WindowsIdentity)this.User.Identity;
   //This is just here to show checking a role.
   string wp_InAdmin = User.IsInRole("HOME\\Domain Admins").ToString();
   //We could also check here to make sure they are in the
   //SecureOfficeUsers group, but if they weren't, they would
   //not be seeing this page.
   //Note, the values that are available through
   //the WindowsIdentity
   string wi_Name = wi.Name;
   string wi_Type = wi.AuthenticationType;
   string wi_Auth = wi.IsAuthenticated.ToString();
   string wi_Anon = wi.IsAnonymous.ToString();
   string wi_Guest = wi.IsGuest.ToString();
   string wi_System = wi.IsSystem.ToString();
   string wi_Token = wi.Token.ToString();
   //Write everything out to a web page.
   Response.Write("Principal Value:");
   Response.Write("<BR>");
   Response.Write("Is in Administrators " + wp_InAdmin);
   Response.Write("<BR><BR>");
   Response.Write("Identity Values:");
   Response.Write("<BR>");
   Response.Write("Name: " + wi_Name);
   Response.Write("<BR>");
```

LISTING 27.5   Continued

```
Response.Write("Type: " + wi_Type);
Response.Write("<BR>");
Response.Write("IsAuthenticated: " + wi_Auth);
Response.Write("<BR>");
Response.Write("IsAnonymous: " + wi_Anon);
Response.Write("<BR>");
Response.Write("IsGuest: " + wi_Guest);
Response.Write("<BR>");
Response.Write("IsSystem: " + wi_System);
Response.Write("<BR>");
Response.Write("Token: " + wi_Token);
Response.Write(wi_Name.GetHashCode().ToString());
}

#region Web Form Designer generated code
override protected void OnInit(EventArgs e)
{
 //
 // CODEGEN: This call is required by the ASP.NET Web Form Designer.
 //
 InitializeComponent();
 base.OnInit(e);
}

/// <summary>
/// Required method for Designer support - do not modify
/// the contents of this method with the code editor.
/// </summary>
private void InitializeComponent()
{
 this.Load += new System.EventHandler(this.Page_Load);
}
#endregion
}
}
```

NOTE

This entire code sample is available for download from the Sams Web site.

At this point, in the real world, we would turn on some basic functionality to show users which files they could see, and allow them to view them. This could be taken many different directions, but the base groundwork has been firmly demonstrated in code listings of this chapter. When SSL is enabled on the site, all data will be encrypted during transit, keeping the chance of a replay attack (see the section, "Possible Attack Scenarios," later in this chapter), from happening.

Channel Options

When your application cannot use Web Services, but has assemblies that will access information via SOAP, .NET makes available the `HttpChannel` and the `TCPChannel` classes. These classes encapsulate the functionality necessary to perform secure SOAP transactions over the Internet. `ChannelServices` are what allow you to send messages back and forth between the client and server, even if they are from the same machine.

HttpChannel

The `HttpChannel` class combines the `HttpClientChannel` class and the `HttpServerChannel` class. This becomes convenient in developing Web sites because messages can be exchanged using the `HttpChannel` from an `.aspx` file to gather data necessary to the application. To do this, basically you would have an instance of `HttpChannel` make a request to a URI, the request would then go through the SOAP formatter, and out to the server via HTTP/HTTPS. The response would come back to the client via HTTP/HTTPS, run back through the SOAP formatter, and be made available to the client's programming logic.

TcpChannel

`TcpChannel`, like `HttpChannel`, combines the `TCPClientChannel` class and the `TCPServerChannel` class. The main difference is that the `TCPChannel` class uses binary sockets for data transfer for those wanting to employ a "roll-your-own" means of working with the data. Both classes contain the `bindTo` property, which allows the channel to attach itself to a specific IP Address on a server. Use of this aids in security through allowing selected channel traffic to only travel on a specified NIC (Network Interface Card).

NOTE

More information regarding the HTTPChannel and the TCPChannel is available in Chapter 16.

A real-world example of where these classes might come into play is in handling the negotiations to get data from a database that might not be exposed to the Internet, or in performing basic authentication to another machine, on another network, in order to call Web services.

Possible Attack Scenarios

In this section, we will touch upon some of the possible attack scenarios behind the reasons for using the combination of security features discussed in the previous sections, as well as some that are not.

Within the world of hacking, there are people that literally have nothing better to do than scan ranges of IP addresses, check which ports are open on them, and determine what they can do on that port. The techniques used to do this are not kept secret; they are published on several Web sites, `http://www.hackers.com`, for example. Along with this are the very public announcements about security holes found in products such as IIS that spawn a wave of copycats who try to launch attacks on top of someone else's.

One common misperception is that a firewall is bulletproof. Although not having one is just asking for trouble, it is not and cannot be aware of all the software running behind it, nor all the possible security risks associated with them. This is where proactive system administration comes in. Checking the Microsoft Security Web site (`http://www.microsoft.com/security`) is an excellent resource for keeping track of what's going on with flaws, updates, and fixes available for Microsoft products.

Invalid Data Attack

In this attack, a hacker attempts to gain information or access through adding commands in the URL. An example of this was shown in Listing 27.2, `URL='/c/winnt/system32/cmd.exe'`. In this attempt, the hacker was trying to take advantage of a buffer overflow, which might execute arbitrary code. By appending the URL with the direct path to where the `cmd.exe` file might be, the user could then pass information through the request that might execute within that command window. This form of attack is also referred to as a "malformed URL attack." Another example of this is shown in Listing 27.6.

LISTING 27.6   Malformed URL Request Example

```
URL='/_mem_bin/..%255c../..%255c../..%255c../winnt/system32/cmd.exe'
```

Replay Attack

With a replay attack, the attacker uses a program that sniffs and records the network traffic going between a client and a server. With this, the attacker can "play back" the information sent by the client to try and gain access. There are ways to combat this, however—employing encryption with an adequate (40-bits, at least) key length is one way, provided a timestamp and a TTL setting is used. This prevents playbacks because for the data to be sent back to the server it cannot be decoded. This is made available in .NET through the use of HttpChannel and TCPChannel. These classes enable you to establish secure client/server connections using the CryptStream class to keep the data encrypted while in route. Also, support for SSL is built into the HttpChannel class. Another way is through the deployment of IPSec policies; however, at the time of this writing, IPSec has some performance questions as well as some incompatibility issues with certain firewalls and VPNs.

Brute Force Attack

During a brute force attack, usernames and passwords are guessed until access is achieved, or the hacker gives up. Usually, if a hacker doesn't at least get a username, they can't try the password for that user. This kind of attack is what leads system administrators to rename the administrator account, disable the guest account, and remove WINS bindings from the TCP/IP stack. Most hackers can quickly determine the operating system of a Web server through the request headers. When that is established, you can "test" the common usernames set up for that OS. In Windows, "Administrator," "Guest," and NULL are all popular accounts that hackers try to use to get in. If a hacker does guess an administrator's password, they can then download the entire System Accounts Manager (SAM) database and use a dictionary attack to gain the passwords of everyone on the machine they have attacked.

Preventing brute force attacks is not difficult. The first thing is to create an incredibly hard-to-guess Administrator password. Hint: "Password" is known; they try that. Other rules with passwords have to do with not using any of the following:

- Your name

- Pet names

- Kids' names

- Significant other's name

- Common English words

- Phone numbers

- Birthdates

If this list has removed all the passwords you can think of, try this: Using a hash algorithm (MD5, SHA-1), think of something that is easy for you to remember. Then take the first 12 characters of the hash and use that. From personal experience, I can tell you that the number of people who don't follow these rules are the majority—by a lot.

Implementing a Secure Web Site

At this point, the site is designed, the security fundamentals—such as SSL, authentication, and authorization—are established, and everything has been tested. Now it's time to go over what is involved in implementing the secure Web site. Some of the items in the following paragraphs might seem to be a review of the steps that were completed previously, but in this section we will be discussing these items on a more global level.

First and foremost, implement the certificate to enable SSL. Then configure IIS to force SSL on the directory in which your application resides. Also, note that in the web.config file, you can make an entry for impersonation to be on by default. To increase security, it is recommended that you only impersonate what has to be. In other words, when a file is accessed, does it need permissions of another user, or is the ASP.NET account allowed to access it? If the first case holds true, you need to use impersonation; otherwise, it should not be needed. It is probably quite rare that an entire site needs to be run as the Administrator; however, it might be frequent to use this impersonation element to run an entire site with an account that has very limited permissions.

Protected Modules

Starting with Microsoft Transaction Server, the concept of allowing modules to have a "run as" environment has been possible. The .NET Framework has provided several enhancements to this, even to the point of how accessible impersonation now is through code.

When you have created code that might access a protected entity, it becomes important to secure that code to prevent it from being misused. Listing 27.7 shows a code snippet that uses the FileIOPermission class to grant all permissions to files in the c:\inetpub\wwwroot directory. If the Demand method fails, an exception is raised.

LISTING 27.7   FileIOPermission Snippet

```
try
{
FileIOPermission fP = new FileIOPermission(FileIOPermissionAccess.AllAccess,_
➥ "c:\\inetpub\\wwwroot");
fP.Demand();
}
catch(SecurityException SecErr)
{
Response.Write(SecErr.ToString());
}
```

In the previous sample, AllAccess was granted; in practice it is important to grant only what is absolutely necessary. Should you need to have code execute as a specific user regardless of who is logged into the site, you can always implement impersonation.

Using Application Logs to Uncover Security Breaches

At the beginning of this chapter, the URLScan ISAPI filter was explained to show how to block users from issuing malicious requests to your Web server. IIS also provides extensive information in its log files that can be analyzed to detect bogus requests and attempted brute force attacks on your Web server by those who attempt to constantly hit the Web site with bogus credentials. An example of this would be a multitude of listings with the same username attempting to gain access several times in a very short time period.

In applications that you create with ASP.NET, you can create an additional logging file that can keep track of data that is processed internally by your application. While some may initially gripe that this can cause a performance hit, that issue is minimal compared to tracking exactly what your application is doing.

TIP

While creating your own application log requires write access to a folder, it does not require execute permissions. Unless you plan to publicly distribute what you are logging, the ASP.NET user does not need read access either. Whenever creating customized logging functionality, never give the folder the files that are written to execute permissions because this can lead to serious security issues.

With ASP.NET, you can still write to the computer's event log; the only caution there is to not write so much that the event log is full of debugging information instead of really important information about your application, such as attempted security breaches.

NOTE

Additional information on this topic may be found at http://www.microsoft.com/technet/security/tools/iis5chk.asp?frame=true.

Summary

In this chapter, we have covered designing and implementing a secure Web site using ASP.NET. At this point in the book, you should understand how to use authentication and authorization not only from the web.config file but also from within IIS to prevent unauthorized access to your site. Also, you should understand how different attack scenarios operate and how to prevent them. In the next chapter, we will cover creating and deploying a full secure application.

28

Writing a Secure Web Application in the .NET Development Platform

By Kevin Price

The goal of this chapter is to answer the question of what to do when your application uses the Internet but isn't just a Web site or isn't a Web site at all. It will also show you how to use encryption features from within ASP.NET to help secure your application. These applications are where you can exercise a great deal of control over the security of your application, because in some cases, you control the client completely. There are also applications that are both—browser-based and have B2B or B2C type transactions that take place on the back-end. In this chapter, you will learn the following:

- How to encrypt data within ASP.NET

- The differences between ASP.NET using .NET remoting and Web Services

- How to incorporate authentication when using IIS is not possible

- How to authorize users when IIS is not available

- How using Channels keeps data secure

Inevitably, there will come a time when the project at hand is not entirely using the Microsoft .NET platform, or even entirely Microsoft-based technologies. This is one of the arenas that gets seldom covered and, if so, is usually garbled with philosophical rhetoric instead of what to do. With the advent of SOAP, services that are exposed via the Internet have a means to communicate; this is always the first step in managing a relationship. Now that they can exchange data, they can almost interoperate. What makes this possible is what the services are programmed to do. Because services, and pages for that matter, can contain code that accepts parameters that could execute commands on a remote machine, security is of the highest priority. Although Microsoft has provided such tools as the .NET Framework Wizards and Microsoft .NET Framework Configuration applet, there may be a time when you need to adjust security dynamically.

ASP.NET with Remoting Versus Web Services

According to Encarta, the first definition of the word "remote" is as follows:

"re·mote [ri mot] adjective

1. far away: situated a long way away"

(Source: Encarta.com online dictionary)

The Case for Using ASP.NET with Remoting

First, let us look at remoting as a standalone item. Just the name sort of lends itself to being, well, alone. Why should we even consider remoting when DCOM has been faithfully there in Windows DNA for so long, especially considering that there is no built-in security in the `TCPChannel` class? DCOM has been a standard in Microsoft computing for years, yet with .NET, it has been dropped, completely—or has it? The new kid on the block is called remoting. Remoting addresses some of the problems with DCOM while providing more of a "different" way of doing things instead of just a "new" way of doing things. Remoting provides communication between `AppDomains` and client/server components. DCOM introduced us to a way of invoking methods on other Windows machines that weren't necessarily part of the same Windows domain. Security was quite tight and difficult—at least not easy—to set up. There was also a performance question with DCOM in that, being based on COM, it had to use the counter callback reference to see if an instance existed. In DCOM, this was achieved by pinging the server by the client to see if the object was available. As of this writing, .NET remoting has come under some scrutiny by those who may not understand exactly what is available in .NET and start pouncing immediately on what they do not see. Remoting relies on an `Application Domain` as opposed to a Windows Domain. This level of granularity can actually be more secure because it gives you a higher level of control over specific assemblies. It is difficult to prepare an "apples-to-apples" comparison because they both approach the same problem from different angles. The improvements in .NET come from the acceptance of open specifications, such as SOAP. webMethods b2b Server and IBM server products have had this type of functionality for years in the Java Community. The basic premise stays the same, even though the names may have changed.

The concept of neither remoting, nor DCOM for that matter, strays too far from the basics of client/server programming. The main differences are that the client is not necessarily a client application such as a Web browser or custom fat-client form, and that by using .NET, you can actually "self-document" what it is that you are exposing—not to mention the lack of "dll hell." When using remoting with ASP.NET, you are provided access to a way of blending the best of distributed computing with the presentation benefits of ASP.

Enough theory, let's look at the players in remoting. Because all of this starts with an Application Domain, we will look at the AppDomain class. Application Domain and AppDomain are synonymous. An AppDomain is a virtual, isolated (secure) environment established for the execution of a process. An AppDomain also has the ability to separate managed applications at runtime. AppDomain implements the IEvidenceFactory and MarshalByRefObject classes. The IEvidenceFactory gets an object Evidence. The Evidence class, an ICollection, contains information about an object. This information is related to what is relevant to an object, such as URI, code signing information, site name, and so on. The CLR will use this information to make decisions about security and permissions at runtime. Table 28.1 shows the default elements available to the Evidence class.

TABLE 28.1   Default Evidence Elements

Element	Description
Application Directory	The directory in which the application is installed
Hash	A cryptographic hash or key
Publisher	An Authenticode signature of the publisher of the code
Site	The site publishing the software, such as http://www.samspublishing.com
Strong name	A cryptographically generated strong name for the assembly
URL	The URL where the software can be located, such as http://www.samspublishing.com/myservices.asmx
Zone	Relates the Security Zones available, such as Internet Zone, Intranet Zone, and so on

MarshalByRefObject is the base class that components running within an AppDomain, on different machines, communicate with by using application proxies. If more than one AppDomain exists on the same machine, they communicate directly with each other. The use of MarshalByRefObject over implicit marshalling by value (MarshalByValObject) is more efficient when using MarshalByRef. Only a proxy to the application is passed, whereas when using MarshalByVal, an entire copy of the application being called is passed to the client.

Listing 28.1 shows a simple implementation of the `AppDomain` class to set the current security policy on the application to that of the calling user. The first line of code shows the declaration of the class implementing `MarshalByRefObject`.

LISTING 28.1   AppDomain Snippet

```
public class SnippetClass : MarshalByRefObject
    {
        public void myFunction()
        {
AppDomain.CurrentDomain.SetPrincipalPolicy
➥(PrincipalPolicy.WindowsPrincipal);
        … more code…
```

What that one simple line of code does is to establish a context for everything that happens after it. Because this is an ASP.NET application, it's quite easy to catch the `IIdentity` implementation in the form of a `WindowsIdentity` class. Listing 28.2 shows the creation of this class.

LISTING 28.2   Creation of the `WindowsIdentity` Class

```
WindowsIdentity wi = (WindowsIdentity)this.User.Identity;
```

From this point, one more line of code will get you the calling user's information in the form of a `WindowsPermission` class implementation. Listing 28.3 shows this.

LISTING 28.3   `WindowsPermission` Creation

```
WindowsPrincipal wp = new WindowsPrincipal(wi);
```

NOTE

In Chapter 27, "Writing a Secure Web Site Using ASP.NET," Listing 27.5 contains a complete code sample showing the properties that can be retrieved using the `WindowsIdentity` class.

In closing arguments, remoting provides a secure, reliable means by which to allow code to execute behind the presentation layer that is provided for by ASP.NET. While ASP.NET can handle the execution, remoting within ASP.NET provides a more robust means of handling permissions and security for individual assemblies through containing them in the `AppDomain`. In addition, the authentication and authorization methods discussed in Chapter 14, "Authentication: Know Who Is Accessing Your Site," and Chapter 15, "Authorization: Control Who Is Accessing Your Site," apply to both ASP.NET using remoting and Web Services.

Now that we've looked at the highlights of remoting, what about Web Services? With what is available through remoting, why use Web Services? Here's why. Using ASP.NET with remoting to control who can execute code and what code can execute is an excellent use of managing the presentation layer of an application. Web Services come into play when there is an absence of or an unknown presentation layer.

The Case for Using Web Services

Web Services is being touted as one of the most exciting new features of .NET, and with good reason. Like remoting, when it comes to executing code, gathering data, or any other valid use for distributed computing, Web Services can be used to enhance an application by providing a secure means of execution. As an added bonus, Microsoft has made sure that Web Services have at least three means of exchanging information—XML, SOAP, and binary. At the basic level, Web Services return data in an XML document format. As stated numerous times over the last several months, using XML allows data to be read into classes via parsing. This is a very generic, often scalable means of transferring data from different servers. This is because of the close relation between parsing an XML document and the use of a forward-only cursor in a database. At the next level, there is the HTTPChannel class, which allows secure communication, through SSL support, by exchanging SOAP messages with other servers. Finally, there is the TCPChannel class. This class allows for every exchange of information possible with the HTTPChannel and intense flexibility through the creation of custom serializers. More information on channels can be located in Chapter 16, "Data Transport Integrity: Keeping Data Uncorrupted." The code sample in Listing 28.4 illustrates using a Web Service to verify a hash value that has been passed. It also illustrates creating a method that is capable of creating hashes. In the real world, functionality like this could be used for custom authentication schemes, file decryption techniques, or for generating a value to be added to a SOAP header.

LISTING 28.4   CryptText Web Service

```
using System;
using System.Collections;
using System.ComponentModel;
using System.Data;
```

LISTING 28.4   **C**ontinued

```csharp
using System.Diagnostics;
using System.Web;
using System.Web.Services;
using System.NET;
using System.Security.Cryptography;
///This is here for the Unicode functionality
using System.Text;


namespace Chapter28
{
/// <summary>
/// Summary description for CryptText.
/// </summary>
public class CryptText : System.Web.Services.WebService
{
 public CryptText()
 {
  //CODEGEN: This call is required by
  // the ASP.NET Web Services Designer
  InitializeComponent();
 }
 public static Byte[] ConvertStringToByteArray(String s)
 {
  ///<summary>
  ///This function is quite important when working with
  ///hashing routines.
  ///</summary>
  return (new UnicodeEncoding()).GetBytes(s);
 }
 public static string ConvertByteArrayToString(Byte[] b)
 {
  ///<summary>
  ///This function is quite useful as well
  ///when working with hashing routines.
  ///</summary>
  string s_tempStr = "";
  s_tempStr = BitConverter.ToString(b);
  s_tempStr = s_tempStr.Replace("-", "");
  return(s_tempStr);
 }
```

LISTING 28.4   Continued

```csharp
#region Component Designer generated code

//Required by the Web Services Designer
private IContainer components = null;

/// <summary>
/// Required method for Designer support - do not modify
/// the contents of this method with the code editor.
/// </summary>
private void InitializeComponent()
{
}

/// <summary>
/// Clean up any resources being used.
/// </summary>
protected override void Dispose( bool disposing )
{
 if(disposing && components != null)
 {
  components.Dispose();
 }
 base.Dispose(disposing);
}

#endregion

[WebMethod]
 ///<summary>
 ///Create a large byte array to hold the string
 ///coming in
 ///</summary>
public String EncryptedString(String sToEncrypt)
{

 //Create buffers for the byte arrays needed
 //by the CSP
 Byte[] bOfString = ConvertStringToByteArray(sToEncrypt);
 byte[] results;
 //Create an instance of the
 //MD5 CSP
```

LISTING 28.4 Continued

```
MD5CryptoServiceProvider md5 = new MD5CryptoServiceProvider();
//Generate the hash
results = md5.ComputeHash(bOfString);
//Return the string equivalent to
//the caller
return (ConvertByteArrayToString(results));
}
[WebMethod]
/// <summary>
/// Check hash will compare hash value sent
/// to an unhashed value. Note that as this is
/// a web service, everything must start out
/// as a string
/// </summary>
public String CheckHash(String sToHash, String sentHash)
{
//Same as above
Byte[] bOfHash = ConvertStringToByteArray(sToHash);
byte[] hashedValue = (new MD5CryptoServiceProvider()).ComputeHash(bOfHash);
//Instead of returning the string of a hash
//compare it
string sCheckHash = (ConvertByteArrayToString(hashedValue));
if(sentHash != sCheckHash)
{
 return("The hashes did not match values sent were
➥ " + sCheckHash + " and " + sentHash );
}
else
{
 return("The hashes match");
}

 }

 }
}
```

When using the CryptText Web Service (refer to Listing 28.4), there are a few things
to remember. The first is that it is based in XML, meaning that all data coming in is
going to be a string, so functions must exist to handle this. The next thing is just

how easy it is to implement the `MD5CryptoServiceProvider`. While this service contains very few lines of code, it performs a very valuable service, quite similar in theory to how digest authentication works. The last thing to take away from this sample is the use of Unicode to keep internationalization options open. This comes in to play frequently when creating true world-wide Web sites.

Authentication and Authorization Without IIS

When using ASP.NET, remoting, or any technology that relies on authentication, it seems common that somewhere there will be a relational database (SQL Server 2000) that contains user information for purposes of authenticating users to a site. While this practice is somewhat understandable for those who don't want to issue a network account to every user who visits their site, probably because the site and the rest of the network are on the same subnet, it raises some security issues of its own. In fact, "issues" may not quite describe it—burning red flags of despair probably comes closer. Regardless, because ASP.NET has introduced new methods of authentication, discussed in Chapter 14, they rely on the use of Internet Information Services (IIS). This section will address what is possible to do when you cannot use one of these new methods that easily encrypt everything for you or when porting an existing system to the .NET platform where you cannot replace the entire existing infrastructure.

Using a SQL Server Database for Authentication

This practice is as old as the Internet itself—using a database to validate user login information, setting some session or hidden variables, and personalizing or allowing access based on the results. What is disturbing is that while some sites do not support SSL for handling this information, the information is stored in plain text within the database. While the code samples in the section are not intended to be the "be all and end all" of how .NET can help, at least the minimal implementation involved will increase security exponentially compared to using nothing at all. For this section, we will go on the assumption that you do not want to create an NTLM account for each and every user that could access the Web site. This is often the case for large portals and e-commerce sites. To start with, let's create the `Users` table. Note that the sample is for demonstration purposes and is in no way intended to represent a live production site.

Listing 28.5 shows the `Users` table created to hold the basic user information; the database in this sample is named `NetSecurityDemo`, but this could be in any database.

LISTING 28.5   Users Table Script

```
if exists (select * from dbo.sysobjects where id = object_id(N'[dbo].[Users]')
➡ and OBJECTPROPERTY(id, N'IsUserTable') = 1)
drop table [dbo].[Users]
GO
CREATE TABLE [dbo].[Users] (
    [UserID] [uniqueidentifier] DEFAULT NEWID() ,
    [UserLogonName] [varchar] (20) NULL ,
    [UserPassword] [varchar] (128) NULL ,
    [UserFirstName] [varchar] (32) NULL ,
    [UserLastName] [varchar] (50) NULL ,
    [CreateDate] [datetime] DEFAULT GETDATE()
) ON [PRIMARY]
GO
```

You may also want to add a user to see this work; Listing 28.6 is an INSERT statement for Joe User. This user has a UserLogonName of juser and a password of password. For the purposes of this example, the password has already been encrypted with the code in Listing 28.4. The resulting value is B081DBE85E1EC3FFC3D4E7D0227400CD. Listings 28.4 (as CryptText.asmx.cs), 28.5, and 28.6 are all available for download from the book's Web site.

LISTING 28.6   Insert User Statement

```
insert into users
(userlogonname, userpassword, userfirstname, userlastname)
 values
('juser', 'B081DBE85E1EC3FFC3D4E7D0227400CD', 'Joe', 'User')
```

NOTE

Notice in Listing 28.5 that the UserPassword field is given space for a potential 128 charac-ters. This is based on the fact that once padded and encrypted, the password may be consid-erably longer than originally typed. As a general rule, this table was designed calculating a factor of four (4) for storing padded and encrypted strings; a factor of two (2) is usually suffi-cient if the data is merely encrypted. This may not be apparent at first because byte array sizes may not equal the length of a string in characters.

From the ASP.NET side, I have created one page—default.aspx. This page handles the basic login functionality and returns a simple result. Listing 28.7 shows the basic HTML page that the user will see. Listing 28.8 shows the functionality within this page.

LISTING 28.7   `default.aspx`

```
<%@ Page language="c#" Codebehind="default.aspx.cs"
➡ AutoEventWireup="false" Inherits="Chapter28.WebForm1" %>
➡ <!DOCTYPE HTML PUBLIC "-//W3C//DTD HTML 4.0 Transitional//EN" >
<HTML>
 <HEAD>
 <title>WebForm1</title>
 <meta name="GENERATOR" Content="Microsoft Visual Studio 7.0">
 <meta name="CODE_LANGUAGE" Content="C#">
 <meta name="vs_defaultClientScript" content="JavaScript">
 <meta name="vs_targetSchema"
➡ content="http://schemas.microsoft.com/intellisense/ie5">
 </HEAD>
 <body MS_POSITIONING="GridLayout">
  <form id="Form1" method="post" runat="server">
  <asp:Label id="lblLoginName" style="Z-INDEX: 101; LEFT: 40px;
➡POSITION: absolute; TOP: 44px" runat="server" Width="91px"
➡ Height="16px" Font-Names="Tahoma" Font-Size="Small">
➡Login Name:</asp:Label>
  <asp:TextBox id="txtLoginName" style="Z-INDEX: 102; LEFT: 150px;
➡ POSITION: absolute; TOP: 47px" runat="server" Width="141px"
➡ Height="20px" Font-Names="Tahoma" Font-Size="Smaller"></asp:TextBox>
  <asp:Label id="lblPassword" style="Z-INDEX: 103; LEFT: 42px;
➡ POSITION: absolute; TOP: 84px" runat="server" Width="74px"
➡ Height="13px" Font-Names="Tahoma" Font-Size="Small">Password:
➡</asp:Label>
  <INPUT style="Z-INDEX: 104; LEFT: 130px; WIDTH: 170px;
➡ POSITION: absolute; TOP: 86px; HEIGHT: 18px" type="password"
➡ size="23" name="txtPassword" id="Password1" runat="server">
  <asp:Button id="btnSubmit" style="Z-INDEX: 105; LEFT: 40px;
➡ POSITION: absolute; TOP: 123px" runat="server"
➡ Width="85px" Height="21px" Text="Submit"></asp:Button>
  <asp:Label id="lblResults" style="Z-INDEX: 106; LEFT: 46px;
➡ POSITION: absolute; TOP: 162px" runat="server" Font-Names="Tahoma"
➡ Height="38px" Width="268px"></asp:Label>
  </form>
 </body>
</HTML>
```

LISTING 28.8   default.aspx.cs

```csharp
using System;
using System.Collections;
using System.ComponentModel;
using System.Data;
using System.Data.SqlClient;
using System.Drawing;
using System.Web;
using System.Web.SessionState;
using System.Web.UI;
using System.Web.UI.WebControls;
using System.Web.UI.HtmlControls;

namespace Chapter28
{
 /// <summary>
 /// Summary description for WebForm1.
 /// </summary>
 public class WebForm1 : System.Web.UI.Page
 {
  protected System.Web.UI.WebControls.Label lblLoginName;
  protected System.Web.UI.WebControls.TextBox txtLoginName;
  protected System.Web.UI.WebControls.Button btnSubmit;
  protected System.Web.UI.HtmlControls.HtmlInputText Password1;
  protected System.Web.UI.WebControls.Label lblPassword;
  protected System.Web.UI.WebControls.Label lblResults;
  //Create a private variable to use
  //as a security check. This variable
  //can only be modified from with this code
  private static bool doSubmit;

  private void Page_Load(object sender, System.EventArgs e)
  {
   // No initialization code needed for this page
  }

  #region Web Form Designer generated code
  override protected void OnInit(EventArgs e)
  {
   //
   // CODEGEN: This call is required by the ASP.NET Web Form Designer.
   //
```

LISTING 28.8   Continued

```csharp
 InitializeComponent();
 base.OnInit(e);
}


/// <summary>
/// Required method for Designer support - do not modify
/// the contents of this method with the code editor.
/// </summary>
private void InitializeComponent()
{
 this.btnSubmit.Click += new System.EventHandler(this.btnSubmit_Click);
 this.Load += new System.EventHandler(this.Page_Load);

}
#endregion
//Trap the button click event
private void btnSubmit_Click(object sender, System.EventArgs e)
{
 //Check to make sure we have something to work with
 if(txtLoginName.Text.Length == 0 || Password1.Value.Length == 0)
 {
  lblResults.Text = "Invalid Login Attempt";
  doSubmit = false;
 }
  //If so, attempt to authenticate the users credentials
 else
 {
  lblResults.Text = "";
  doSubmit = true;
  isAuthenticated();

 }
}
private String makePassword()
{
 //Make the hash that will be compared
 //as the password. If you wanted to
 //limit this to a specific domain name, or machine
 //you could append that information to the
 //string value passed to the Encrypted String method
 Chapter28.CryptText ct = new Chapter28.CryptText();
```

6 of 816

LISTING 28.8   Continued

```
  return ct.EncryptedString(Password1.Value.Trim());

}
private bool isAuthenticated()
{
 //Internal security check
 if(doSubmit)
 {
  //Connect to the database and compare
  //information submitted
  try
  {

    SqlConnection conn = new SqlConnection();
    conn.ConnectionString = "server=(local);database=NetSecurityDemo;
TRUSTED_CONNECTION=Yes";
    SqlCommand cmd = new SqlCommand("SELECT UserLogonName,
UserPassword FROM USERS WHERE UserLogonName = '" +
txtLoginName.Text.Trim() + "'", conn);
    SqlDataReader dr = null;
    conn.Open();
    dr = cmd.ExecuteReader();
    //Check to see if there are any results
    //before proceeding
    if(!dr.Read())
    {
     lblResults.Text = "Name not found in database";
     conn.Close();
     return false;
    }
    String hPassword = makePassword();
    if(dr.GetString(1).Trim() == hPassword)
    {
     lblResults.Text = "Login OK";
     conn.Close();
     return true;
    }

    else
    {
     lblResults.Text = "Login Failed";
```

LISTING 28.8   Continued

```
      conn.Close();
      return false;
    }
  }

  catch(Exception err)
  {
   lblResults.ForeColor = System.Drawing.Color.Red;
   lblResults.Text = err.ToString();
   return(false);
  }
 }
 else
 {
  lblResults.Text = "Method Failed Security Check";
  return false;
 }
 }
}
}
```

Though database-based authentication may be subject to replay attack, this can be augmented with session information that times out quickly, within 20 minutes, to help prevent attacks. Also, in Listings 28.4, 28.7 and 28.8, as well as all of the listings in this chapter, SSL can be implemented.

Using JSP to Call a Web Service

As an example of the true versatility of Web Services, Listings 28.9, 28.10, and 28.11 show the use of JavaServer Pages to invoke the Web Service using the result to determine whether or not to allow the user. Listing 28.9 is a modification to the CryptText service from Listing 28.4. By adding a reference to System.Data.SqlClient and the doLogin method, we can call this from any HTTP client and get the same results.

NOTE

To execute this sample in its entirety, you must have a Web server with some sort of processor for JavaServer Pages, such as Apache's Tomcat Server or JServ from Allaire. This sample was written using Windows XP Professional, Sun's Java Development Kit (JDK) 1.3, Apache's Tomcat Server Version 4, Microsoft VisualStudio.NET, and Microsoft SQL Server 2000, Developer's Edition.

LISTING 28.9   doLogin Method for CryptText Web Service

```
[WebMethod]
  public bool doLogin(String sUserName, String sPassword)
  {
   try
   {

    SqlConnection conn = new SqlConnection();
    conn.ConnectionString = "server=(local);database=NetSecurityDemo;
➥TRUSTED_CONNECTION=Yes";
SqlCommand cmd = new SqlCommand("SELECT UserLogonName, UserPassword
➥ FROM USERS WHERE UserLogonName = '" + sUserName.Trim() + "'", conn);
    SqlDataReader dr = null;
    conn.Open();
    dr = cmd.ExecuteReader();
    //Check to see if there are any results
    //before proceeding
    if(!dr.Read())
    {
     conn.Close();
     return false;
    }
    String hPassword = EncryptedString(sUserName.Trim()
➥ + sPassword.Trim());
    if(dr.GetString(1).Trim() == hPassword)
    {
     conn.Close();
     return true;
    }

    else
    {
     conn.Close();
     return false;
    }
   }

   catch(Exception err)
   {
    return(false);
   }
  }
```

As you may notice, this is very much like the code from Listing 28.9. This was done intentionally to show the two different means of implementation. Next, Listings 28.10 and 28.11 show the default login page for our JSP login and the processing page used to call the Web Service.

LISTING 28.10 index.jsp

```
<html>
<head>
<title>Login Page</title>
<body bgcolor="white">
<form method="POST" action="login.jsp">
  <table border="0" cellspacing="5">
    <tr>
      <th align="right">Username:</th>
      <td align="left"><input type="text" name="j_username"></td>
    </tr>
    <tr>
      <th align="right">Password:</th>
      <td align="left"><input type="password" name="j_password"></td>
    </tr>
    <tr>
      <td align="right"><input type="submit" value="Log In"></td>
      <td align="left"><input type="reset"></td>
    </tr>
  </table>
</form>
</body>
</html>
```

LISTING 28.11 login.jsp

```
<%@ page contentType="text/html;charset=WINDOWS-1252"%>
//Note:* is used for compression of space in code sample
//as always, import only what you must have to make the
//code execute
<%@ page import="java.NET.*"%>
<%@ page import="java.io.*"%>
<%
try
{
```

LISTING 28.11   Continued

```
//First get the variables passed from login.jsp
String user = request.getParameter("j_username");
String pass = request.getParameter("j_password");
//Create a URL object to use for the request
URL url = new URL("http://localhost/Chapter28/CryptText.asmx/doLogin?
➥sUserName=" + user + "&sPassword=" + pass);
//Read the response stream to look for a result
BufferedReader in =
➥ new BufferedReader(new InputStreamReader(url.openStream()));
String str;
while ((str=in.readLine()) != null)
  {
//since the method we are calling returns a boolean
//check for true
  if(str.indexOf("true") != -1)
 out.println("Login Succeeded");
  else
   out.println(str);
  }
//Cleanup
  in.close();
}
catch (Exception e)
{}
%>
<HTML>
<HEAD>
<META HTTP-EQUIV="Content-Type" CONTENT="text/html; charset=WINDOWS-1252">
<TITLE>
Calling .NET from JSP
</TITLE>
</HEAD>
<BODY>

</BODY>
</HTML>
```

As Listings 28.10 and 28.11 have indicated, the programmatic ways of gathering
basic user information for the purposes of authorization and authentication do
extend beyond just ASP.NET and IIS. This is the reason for using eXtensible Markup

Language (XML) to store information. From here, authorization may be extended by mapping a database-based account to a generic network account that has permissions for delegation.

Summary

In this chapter, options were offered that covered certain scenarios, such as using JavaServer Pages and needing to authenticate users, where using the operating system alone or using Internet Information Services for authentication was not available. Authorization in these scenarios comes programmatically from what you do with the user information after you have the credentials.

29

Writing a Semi-Trusted Application

By Matthew Lyons

Chapter 25, "Implementing a Secure Assembly," covered working with permissions in different forms and using strong names in your assemblies. These topics focus directly on interacting with the .NET Framework security system, which is most often done in fully trusted assemblies. Chapter 27, "Writing a Secure Web Site Using ASP.NET," and Chapter 28, "Writing a Secure Web Application in the .NET Development Platform," covered writing secure Web sites and Web applications with ASP.NET and the .NET Framework. This chapter covers security aspects of assemblies that are important for all .NET Framework assemblies, even those that are only semi-trusted by users.

> **NOTE**
>
> A semi-trusted application means that some program will be restricted in some way by the .NET Framework. For example, it might not be able to directly call into an unmanaged library, such as a Windows system DLL. Even though a semi-trusted application has restrictions, there are important details of security to remember when writing such an application.

There are several interesting aspects of security that apply to .NET applications. First, some class libraries may not be usable by semi-trusted applications due to protections from the .NET Framework. Second, you can make certain assurances about what permissions will be granted to your application. This is useful if you know your application must have a certain permission or should never be granted some other permission. Third, there are some important aspects to consider for sensitive data used by your application. For example, you will see how you can store data that cannot be accessed by other semi-trusted .NET applications. Fourth, it is beneficial to understand what happens with code execution in certain security-sensitive cases. If you don't understand how some .NET Framework features work, you can inadvertently expose security problems. Finally, code should be aware of permissions and security actions that happen. If you are oblivious to the fact that your code might be denied access to some resources, your applications may appear brittle and buggy to users.

NOTE

Microsoft has published a whitepaper on secure coding guidelines for the .NET Framework. Some information presented in that whitepaper is covered in this chapter. If you want to see all of Microsoft's suggestions for secure coding in the .NET Framework, you can find this whitepaper at `http://msdn.microsoft.com/library/en-us/dnnetsec/html/ seccodeguide.asp`.

Restrictions on Libraries That Can Be Called

As mentioned in Chapter 25, there is an attribute in the `System.Security` name-space named `AllowPartiallyTrustedCallersAttribute`. For the sake of brevity, this attribute will be called APTCA throughout this chapter. The motivation behind APTCA is to limit the vectors of attack for malicious, semi-trusted code. Any managed code library with a strong name cannot be used by semi-trusted code unless that library is marked with APTCA.

In addition to APTCA, many managed code libraries have permission requirements that your applications will have to meet. If you are unaware that your application will need a certain permission, it is quite possible that you could hit a `SecurityException` while executing.

Assemblies with APTCA

Because a strong named, managed code library without APTCA will block access to semi-trusted code, it is important to ensure that all libraries your applications use are marked appropriately. Users and administrators can limit the trust given to applications they run, so you cannot always assume your applications will be granted full trust.

TIP

If your application receives a `SecurityException` with the description "Security Error" at an odd point in your application, you may have run into the

AllowPartiallyTrustedCallersAttribute (APTCA) restriction. If your application was not granted full trust, check what assemblies you are calling. One of them may have a strong name but not have APTCA.

In the initial release of the .NET Framework, the following assemblies are marked with APTCA:

- `mscorlib.dll`

- `System.dll`

- `System.Data.dll`

- `System.Xml.dll`

- `System.Drawing.dll`

- `System.Windows.Forms.dll`

- `System.Web.Services.dll`

- `Microsoft.VisualBasic.dll`

- `IEExecRemote.dll`

- `Accessibility.dll`

If you plan on using any assemblies not on this list, you should check if that assembly is marked with APTCA. You can see if an assembly is marked with APTCA using the `ildasm` tool that comes with the .NET Framework SDK. If you run `ildasm.exe <assembly file>`, it will display information about the given assembly. If you then double-click the MANIFEST portion of the display, it will show you what attributes were applied to the assembly. Figure 29.1 shows this for the `System.Data.dll` assembly. Notice that `System.Security.AllowPartiallyTrustedCallersAttribute` is listed.

Libraries with Known Permission Requirements

There are some security restrictions besides APTCA that may come with certain managed code libraries. If you plan on writing an application that accesses protected resources, you should understand the security requirements.

The easiest way to learn security requirements for accessing protected resources is to read the documentation for the managed code libraries you call. For example, look at the .NET Framework SDK documentation for the method `System.IO.File.OpenRead`. In the "Requirements" section, it mentions that the `FileIOPermission` is necessary to use the method. Other methods that access protected resources have similar documentation.

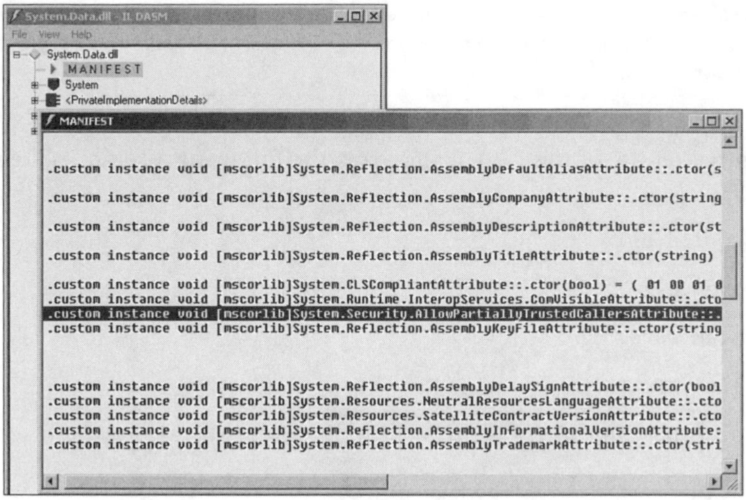

FIGURE 29.1 Manifest information for the System.Data.dll assembly.

Unfortunately, there is no way to reliably, programmatically determine all security permissions an application might need. If you don't have adequate documentation for an assembly you want to use, you can look at the disassembly of that assembly using ildasm.exe. You might be able to find the information you need searching for declarative and imperative security actions in method information.

Making Permission Requests

Chapter 25 showed how to use permission requests in the "Using Declarative Security" section. So, this section will only cover when to use permission requests instead of the technical details of how to do it.

Ideally, you should have a list of permissions that you know your application must have to properly function. If you have the documentation for managed libraries you use, you should be able to gather this information while developing the application. When you have the list of required permissions, you should use it in a minimal permission request. This has two primary benefits. First, it is a statement to users and administrators that your application needs certain permissions to run properly. Second, it gives you a guarantee that if your assembly is running, you were granted all permissions in your minimal set.

When determining the minimal permissions your application will need, remember to take APTCA into account. If you plan to use any assemblies that are not marked with APTCA, your minimal permission request should be for full trust (that is, an unrestricted permission set). This is because without full trust, your application will throw a SecurityException at the point when you first access the non-APTCA assembly.

In addition to minimal permission requests, you can make optional and refuse requests. Optional requests state that your application could use a given request, but it is not necessary for your application to function. Refuse requests state that you never want to be granted a permission, regardless of a given security policy setting.

You can use refuse requests to limit the liability of your application. For example, if you plan on writing an application on the .NET Framework that just displays stock quotes, you could use a refuse request to make sure that it cannot write to the file system. No matter when you did in that application, any direct attempt to open a file to write data would cause a `SecurityException`.

Protecting Data

Data protection is something of which you should be aware. If you deal with any data that is sensitive in nature, the .NET Framework can help you protect it. In addition, there are some coding principles you should follow to prevent trivial discovery of sensitive data. Depending on where the sensitive data is—persisted to disk, stored in memory, or sent on the network—there are different approaches to protecting that data.

Data Persisted to Disk

Some data you want to store in your application may need to be protected. For example, if you want to store a credit card number or if you want to store data that is used to authenticate users (passwords, tokens, and so on), you probably don't want to just create a file named `secrets.txt` and write out the data. This allows malicious code or malicious users to easily discover the critical data.

To limit who can read data an application persists to disk, the .NET Framework provides two sets of functionality—isolated storage and cryptography classes. Isolated storage provides storage capabilities to semi-trusted .NET Framework applications that other semi-trusted .NET Framework applications cannot read. Cryptography is a general field of study in computer science that allows for clever obfuscation of data. The .NET Framework has a rich set of cryptography classes that allow you to encrypt data, among other things.

Isolated Storage

Isolated storage is provided by the .NET Framework as a mechanism for semi-trusted applications to store data that other semi-trusted applications cannot read. Just as Web sites use cookies on a client machine to store data such as user preferences, .NET Framework assemblies can store data in isolated storage on a client machine. Also, just as Web sites should not be able to access cookies for other Web sites, semi-trusted applications should not be able to read for isolated storage for other semi-trusted applications.

Note that isolated storage only protects data from other semi-trusted applications, such as applications granted only the LocalIntranet or Internet permission sets. Applications that are granted unrestricted `FileIOPermissions` will be able to read your isolated storage data. This is because isolated storage is contained somewhere on the hard drive, so the application can search for it and will be allowed to read any files it finds. This is also true for cookies because they are stored on the hard drive. Basically, remember that any application that is given unrestricted access to a hard drive can read anything it finds (as long as the operating system doesn't block it due to ACLs or some other protection mechanism).

Isolated storage is provided by the types located in the `System.IO.IsolatedStorage` namespace. In that namespace, there are two primary classes that do the work—`IsolatedStorageFile` and `IsolatedStorageFileStream`. `IsolatedStorageFile` defines a scope of containment for isolated storage. An `IsolatedStorageFile` then contains any number of `IsolatedStorageFileStreams`.

To use isolated storage, you start by calling the static method `IsolatedStroageFile.GetStore`. The most interesting parameter of this method is the `IsolatedStorageScope` parameter. Table 29.1 lists the most useful values for this parameter. You will generally want to pass null for the second and third parameters to indicate that you want to use the scope of the current application domain and assembly evidence. If you pass anything except null, you will have to be granted the `IsolatedStorageFilePermission` with the flag `AdministerIsolatedStorageByUser`. This permission is not given in the `Internet` or `LocalIntranet` permission sets.

TABLE 29.1   Different Ways to Utilize Isolated Storage Using `IsolatedStorageScope` Parameters

`IsolatedStorageScope` **Values**	**Description**
User | Assembly	Isolates storage on the basis of a specific assembly for a given user. This scope will use the same storage for an assembly no matter what application calls it. That is, an identical assembly can be used by multiple applications, but this scope will cause all of those applications to share the same storage.
User | Assembly | Domain	Isolates storage on the basis of a specific assembly in a specific application for a given user. This scope will provide different storage for an assembly if is in different applications.
User | Assembly | Roaming	The same as User | Assembly, except that the data stored on the client will roam if the user is using a roaming profile.
User | Assembly | Domain | Roaming	The same as User | Assembly | Domain, except that the data stored on the client will roam if the user is using a roaming profile.

After you have an `IsolatedStorageFile` object, you can just read or write data from `IsolatedStorageFileStream` objects as long as you don't exceed the quota listed in the `IsolatedStorageFilePermission` granted to your assembly. Listing 29.1 shows an example of code that saves and loads data in isolated storage.

LISTING 29.1   Example of Using `IsolatedStorage`

```
using System;
using System.IO.IsolatedStorage;
using System.IO;

class IsolatedStorageExample
{
  public static void Main()
  {
    IsolatedStorageFile isf = IsolatedStorageFile.GetStore(
➥IsolatedStorageScope.Assembly | IsolatedStorageScope.User, null, null);
    IsolatedStorageFileStream isfs = new IsolatedStorageFileStream("file1",
➥FileMode.OpenOrCreate, isf);
    StreamWriter sw = new StreamWriter(isfs);
    sw.WriteLine("This data is contained in isolated storage.");
    sw.Close();

    isfs = new IsolatedStorageFileStream("file1", FileMode.Open, isf);
    StreamReader sr = new StreamReader(isfs);
    Console.WriteLine(sr.ReadToEnd());
    sr.Close();
  }
}
```

There are more things you can do with the `IsolatedStorageFile` and `IsolatedStorageFileStream` objects. For example, you can create directories or enumerate files with `IsolatedStorageFile` objects. See the .NET Framework SDK for a complete listing of methods on these objects.

Cryptography

While isolated storage can hide your data from other semi-trusted applications, it can't do anything about protecting the data if it is discovered by a fully trusted application or malicious user. That's where cryptography can help you. For example, you could encrypt data with a password provided by an application user. That way, even though the sensitive data might be discovered, nothing could actually understand what it found unless it had the password.

Cryptography functionality is provided in the System.Security.Cryptography name-space. Chapter 30, "Using Cryptography with the .NET Framework: The Basics," Chapter 31, "Using Cryptography with the .NET Framework: Advanced Topics," and Chapter 32, "Using Cryptography with the .NET Framework: Creating and Verifying XML Digital Signatures," go into great detail about using the cryptography classes in the .NET Framework.

Data Stored in Memory

Something you may not think about at first is that data you store in memory while executing may be valuable. You cannot determine what other code will be running in your process when you write an application, so some precautions might need to be taken when you are executing.

There are two types of protection that you can take for in-memory data. The first is to properly design your application to disallow other semi-trusted code from trivially reading or writing data in your classes. The second is to hold truly secret data in memory as little as possible and to clean it up when disposing of it.

Application Design—Visibility, Inheritance, and Boxing

Depending on what your code does, it may actually be run in process with other semi-trusted .NET Framework code. Because of this, proper application design can affect the security of your application. Three specific things to look at are visibility, inheritance, and boxing.

Visibility of fields, properties, methods, classes, and so on in your application's code could potentially be a security problem. For example, if you have a field in a public class that is supposed to hold a user's password, and that field is public, other semi-trusted code can easily read the password from that field. If some element in your code doesn't need to be public, don't make it public. If it doesn't need to be visible to subclasses, make it completely private.

One caveat with visibility is that even properly designed visibility of types in an application cannot protect against code that is granted the ReflectionPermission with the MemberAccess flag or the SecurityPermission with the SerializationFormatter flag. Any applications granted the ReflectionPermission with the MemberAccess flag can read and write to private fields, call private methods, and create instances of private classes. Applications that were granted the SecurityPermission with the SerializationFormatter permission can read or write private fields of classes if they can serialize them to a data blob, change that data blob, and deserialize it back to the class. These are considered powerful permissions, so they aren't granted to any Internet or intranet code by default.

Inheritance can have detrimental effects on security if it isn't considered while designing an application. All security-sensitive parts of your code need to make sure that they recognize two things. First, if your classes don't prevent subclassing, malicious code may subclass you. Second, objects returned from methods may be subclasses of the type in the method signature. Inheritance is simply a language feature. However, if you have a class that is security sensitive, think about what happens if someone subclasses it and overrides critical methods. Can malicious code bypass security checks? Similarly, consider what happens if someone subclasses some classes that you use. If you aren't careful, subtle security issues can arise.

One final issue to consider regarding securely storing data in memory is boxing. Boxing allows value types, such as structs, enumerations, and integral types, to be treated as objects. The .NET Framework will covert value types to the `object` type and vice versa when necessary. For example, you can assign an integer to an `object` value and the .NET Framework will perform the conversion. This can actually be a security problem in classes with fields of the `object` type. If you have an object field that is storing a value type, and you hand out that object to some other code, the field's contents can be changed at will by anyone who has that object. Listing 29.2 shows an example of such a problem.

LISTING 29.2   Security Problem with Object Fields and Boxing

```
using System;
using System.Reflection;

public class ClassWithObjectField
{
  private object badField;

  public ClassWithObjectField (int value) {
    badField = value;
  }

  public ClassWithObjectField (Uri value) {
    badField = value;
  }

  public Object SomeValue {
    get {
      return badField;
    }
  }
}
```

LISTING 29.2   Continued

```
  public void PrintValue() {
    Console.WriteLine(badField);
  }

  public static void ChangeInt(ref int i) {
    i = i * 2;
  }

  public static void ChangeUri(ref Uri u) {
    u = new Uri("http://www.msn.com");
  }

  public static void Main() {
    ClassWithObjectField intTest = new ClassWithObjectField(123);
    ClassWithObjectField uriTest = new ClassWithObjectField(new
➥Uri("http://www.microsoft.com"));

    Console.WriteLine("Initial values");
    intTest.PrintValue();   // Prints "123"
    uriTest.PrintValue();   // Prints "http://www.microsoft.com"

    object intObject = intTest.SomeValue;
    typeof(ClassWithObjectField).GetMethod("ChangeInt").Invoke(null,
➥new Object[] { intObject });
    object uriObject = uriTest.SomeValue;
    typeof(ClassWithObjectField).GetMethod("ChangeUri").Invoke(null,
➥new Object[] { uriObject });

    Console.WriteLine("After attempt to modify values");
    intTest.PrintValue(); // Prints "246"
    uriTest.PrintValue(); // Prints "http://www.microsoft.com"
  }
}
```

Basically, through all parts of software construction, it is important to think about how malicious code might attack your application. There are implementation details covered throughout the book, but don't forget security during the design phase!

Clearing Memory After Use

If you have to use secret data (like an encryption key) during execution, it is best to wipe your copy of the data before releasing it. Under normal circumstances, there aren't any threats about this. However, there are two cases where leaving the data can be scary. The first is where your data crashes and a debugger holds onto the dying process or saves the process memory to disk. In this case, the secret can be easily found. The second case to consider is where a totally separate process is running and reading memory from other processes. While both cases are not main-stream scenarios, they could unintentionally expose secret data in memory.

There are some mitigating factors related to clearing memory in semi-trusted .NET applications:

- Only non-verifiable managed code or unmanaged code could directly perform this type of attack.

- This requires a situation where highly trusted malicious code runs on the same machine as the application dealing with the valuable data.

- Finding secrets in memory is not always easy to do, even if an application has the means to search.

Unfortunately, there is one major problem with clearing memory in a semi-trusted application. Once a managed variable holds a value, you can never directly clear the memory or know when it has been reliably cleared. Remember that the .NET Framework uses garbage collection. At any given time, a collection may occur that could move the variable in memory. The old location for the variable will still contain a copy of the data. Because of the problems involved with trying to clear managed memory, if you need to store a secret in memory that you want to clear out, you will need to do it in unmanaged code.

Because of the mitigating factors involved with discovering secrets in the memory space of other processes, you probably don't need to do worry about this in most cases. Just remember that there is a remote threat of secrets being discovered when they are stored plainly in memory.

Data Sent on the Network

One other situation during which your data can be exposed is when you send it on the network. This has been known for a long time, but passwords and other impor-tant data are still sent plainly on the network with commonly used applications. Sometimes this is part of a protocol, like Telnet. For any new applications, though, this should be avoided.

Generally, the only way to solve the problem of sending data on the network is by using cryptography in some fashion. The .NET Framework has built-in support for SSL when using the `System.Net.WebRequest` and `System.New.WebResponse` classes. See the .NET Framework SDK for more details on this. In addition to SSL, you could use classes from the `System.Security.Cryptography` namespace to encrypt data to go onto the network. However, you should be *very* careful if you don't use a standard protocol. You could easily open yourself up to attacks with a mistake in the protocol design or implementation. This is a field where experts often propose designs that are later found to have weaknesses, so don't assume you can just put some protocol together and have it be used securely.

Being Careful About What Code Gets Executed

Beyond simply protecting data your application uses, there are some special cases where you may end up executing code that you didn't intend to execute. Those special cases include the following:

- `LinkDemands` and inheritance
- Virtual, internal methods
- Delegates and stack walks
- Loading assemblies on behalf of other code
- Exceptions and filters
- Race conditions

`LinkDemands` and Inheritance

It is of the utmost importance to remember that `LinkDemands` trigger when a method is JITted, not while a method is actually executing. Thus, applying `LinkDemands` to interfaces, classes, and virtual methods has a big caveat. If there is an inheritance hierarchy where `LinkDemands` are not applied uniformly for a given method, malicious code can downcast an object to a class or interface that doesn't have a `LinkDemand` on that method. By doing so, that code can avoid a security check by executing a base class method.

If you are using `LinkDemands` on any interface, unsealed class, or virtual method, you should be careful to uniformly apply those `LinkDemands` across the entire hierarchy.

Virtual, Internal Methods

When a method is marked as internal, you might intuitively feel that you have complete control over the code you run when that method gets executed. However, if that method is also marked as virtual, it can still be overridden on subclasses. Thus, if you accept objects from outside your code, and if you execute virtual, internal methods on those objects, you must assume that those methods were overridden. In some cases, this might be by design. However, this could also lead to security holes if trust decisions are based on the output of the virtual, internal method.

You should avoid marking methods as virtual and internal unless you plan on leveraging both the fact that it is virtual and internal. From our experience, this has been done more often accidentally than from intentional design.

Delegates and Stack Walks

Delegates are much like function pointers in C/C++. They are used most often to enable events in the .NET Framework. However, managed code can perform security stack walks when running delegates as a result of permission demands, while unmanaged code has no such mechanism with function pointers. If your application needs to run a delegate on behalf of other code, those stack walks will happen on your application's current call stack instead of the call stack from whatever code handed the delegate to your application. Thus, haphazard use of delegates could lead to luring attacks.

There are two limiting factors that prevent code with very low trust from picking malicious methods and getting them run successfully by code with more trust. First, if the delegate was defined in an assembly with low trust, a stack walk will include that assembly with low trust on the stack. This will stop malicious code from simply defining arbitrary methods to use as delegates. Second, a method's signature must match the defined delegate signature. That means the malicious code must find a dangerous method with a precise signature before it can treat it as a delegate.

The best way to protect your application from running malicious delegates is to carefully define any delegate signatures you use. You probably want to include a class that you define in the argument list. This will prevent any signature matches from happening with methods shipped as part of the .NET Framework. It would be unfortunate, for example, if you defined a delegate with a single integer argument. If you did that, malicious code could register the method `Environment.Exit` for you to run. Thus, malicious code could get you to terminate your own application prematurely.

One other action you should consider before running delegates is to use a permission `Deny` or `PermitOnly`. For example, if you only want to allow the delegates you call to display UI, you could use the following statement:

```
New UIPermission(PermissionState.Unrestricted).PermitOnly();
```

This would prevent any stack walks from succeeding if a demand occurred for a permission other than the `UIPermission`.

Loading Assemblies

Loading assemblies on behalf of other code is something you may not realize could be dangerous. As long as you just load an assembly from the global assembly cache or a specific path, you should be fine. However, there are some assembly loading methods you should be careful using:

- Any form of `Assembly.Load` or `AppDomain.Load` that loads an assembly from a byte array

- Any form of `AppDomain.DefineDynamicAssembly`

- Any methods that load an assembly and have an `Evidence` argument

When an assembly is loaded from a byte array, the .NET Framework cannot tell some types of evidence about that assembly, such as from what zone the assembly originated. Because of this, the .NET Framework grants the same permissions to the byte array assembly as were granted to the assembly loading the byte array assembly. For example, if you write assembly A that loads assembly B from a byte array, assembly B is granted the same permissions as assembly A. Therefore, you don't want to load arbitrary assemblies from byte arrays on behalf of unknown code. You might end up providing an easy way for malicious code to gain permissions.

The results are very similar for defining a dynamic assembly on behalf of another assembly. If your code immediately runs the dynamic assembly, it will have the same permissions granted to it as your code was granted. Thus, you need to be as careful with dynamic assemblies as you are with loading assemblies from byte arrays.

The third category to watch is any method that loads or defines an assembly while providing evidence about that assembly. You should be careful not to provide evidence that grants the code an inappropriate amount of trust. For example, if you provide zone evidence that says the assembly comes from the MyComputer zone, the assembly you load will be given full trust when used with default security policy.

Exceptions and Filters

User-filtered exception handlers are a feature of the .NET Framework that may be unexpected if you have only used C#. They are not used by C#, but VB.NET does take advantage of this feature using the `When` keyword. Their purpose is to determine whether to handle an exception at a given level or to pass it up to the next protection block.

When using a `try/finally` scheme for exception handling, you need to realize that user-filtered exception handlers may run between your try block and finally block. This can cause problems if you change sensitive global state in the `try` block that gets reverted in the `finally` block. For example, if you impersonated a different user in a `try` block and planned on reverting back to the original user in the `finally` block, semi-trusted code you didn't write could execute as the impersonated user. Listing 29.3 shows an example of the execution order when user-filtered exception

handlers are implemented. The example is written in VB.NET because C# does not
have user-filtered exception handlers. To get a feeling for how these filters could
cause security issues, pretend the subroutine Main is code with very low trust and
CallTwo is your application code.

LISTING 29.3   User-Filtered Exception Handlers and try/finally Blocks

```
Imports System

Public Class VBTest
  Public Shared Sub Main
    Try
      Console.WriteLine("Try 1")
      CallTwo
    Catch When (RetTrue("1"))
      Console.WriteLine("Catch 1")
    Finally
      Console.WriteLine("Finally 1")
    End Try
  End Sub

  Public Shared Sub CallTwo
    Try
      Console.WriteLine("Try 2")
      ThrowException
    Finally
      Console.WriteLine("Finally 2")
    End Try
  End Sub

  Public Shared Sub ThrowException
    Throw New Exception("Exception")
  End Sub

  Public Shared Function RetTrue(s as String) As Boolean
    Console.WriteLine("Inside When " + s)
    Return True
  End Function
End Class
```

The console output from Listing 29.3 is printed in the order "Try 1," "Try 2," "Inside
When 1," "Finally 2," "Catch 1," "Finally 1." The unexpected situation here is that

the outer exception handling block gets to execute code at "Inside When 1" before the inner exception handling block runs the "Finally 2" clause.

There are two ways to fix a situation where your code has a try/finally scheme with a security problem. The first solution is to change your finally block to a catch block and rethrow the exception at the end of the catch block. The second solution is to wrap your try/finally blocks with another try block and add a catch block to the outer try that simply rethrows the exception.

Race Conditions

Race conditions in software are the cause of many bugs, both security related and non-security related. There are numerous ways that a race condition could cause a security problem. Rather than trying to compile a list that would probably be incomplete, my recommendation is that you make sure to plan for multithreaded callers in your application. In addition, you should write multithreaded tests for your application. If you aren't sure how to deal with multithreading in the .NET Framework, look for "multithreaded programs" in the index of the .NET Framework SDK.

Being Aware of Permissions at Runtime

There is quite a bit of code you can write that shouldn't need to directly deal with Code Access Security. However, there are some cases where your application should be aware of what might be happening with regards to Code Access Security. First, if your application is designed to behave differently depending on what permissions it was granted, you can use the SecurityManager.IsGranted method to easily check for certain granted permissions without needing to perform a stack walk. Second, if your application is working with protected resources, you need to plan what should happen if a SecurityException is thrown.

Using SecurityManager.IsGranted

If you have designed your application to work differently depending on what permissions it was granted, you probably used an optional assembly permission request to state what permissions your assembly would like to use. However, optional permission requests can't tell you which permissions your assembly was actually granted. You could simply demand permissions to see what you were granted, but this doesn't limit the check to the one specific assembly. The System.Security.SecurityManager class has a method named IsGranted that will return true or false to tell you if your calling assembly was granted a specific permission.

If you really want to check all the callers on the stack, you can always put a permission demand inside a try block and catch any SecurityExceptions that occur.

Remember, a stack walk is a heavyweight mechanism that can truly enforce security. `SecurityManager.IsGranted` is lightweight in comparison, but it is not suitable for enforcing security.

Dealing with `SecurityExceptions`

Your application should be aware of when `SecurityExceptions` can be thrown. Whenever you access a protected resource, there is a possibility that a demand will fail. In such a case, if you do not catch the `SecurityException` yourself, it will bubble up to a higher level. If your caller doesn't catch the exception, the application's process will get taken down or a user will get a dialog box saying your application performed some invalid action. To avoid this situation, it is best to be conservative and set exception handlers at high level points in your application, such as the `Main` method for single-threaded applications.

Summary

This chapter covered several issues to consider when writing a semi-trusted application. These topics include the following:

- *Restrictions on libraries that can be called*—APTCA and permission requirements limit what library code your application can use.

- *Making permission requests*—Assembly permission requests can help determine what permissions are granted to your code. In addition, they can give information about security requirements of your assembly to users and administrators.

- *Protecting data*—When dealing with data in your application, you need to consider how it is handled when persisted to disk, when stored in memory, and when sent over the network.

- *Being careful about what code gets executed*—There are many different implementation details of writing .NET Framework applications that can have security implications. Security needs to be considered throughout the whole software design and implementation process.

- *Being aware of permissions at runtime*—Applications should be prepared to deal with `SecurityExceptions` and plan on being granted different permissions at different times.

TIP

There is a tool from Microsoft called FxCop that can help you automatically search for known security issues in your .NET Framework applications. It also has many other checks for design guidelines, such as naming conventions. You can find this tool at `http://www.gotdotnet.com/team/libraries/`. Note that FxCop is by no means a substitute for proactively thinking about security through all parts of building .NET Framework applications.

30

Using Cryptography with the .NET Framework: The Basics

By Brian A. LaMacchia

This chapter introduces the cryptography libraries and functions included in the .NET Framework in the `System.Security.Cryptography` namespace. On completion of this chapter, the reader should be able to

- Describe the contents of the `System.Security.Cryptography` namespace in the .NET Framework and the cryptographic object models.

- Demonstrate how to encrypt and decrypt data using symmetric (shared-key) and asymmetric (public key) algorithms.

- Demonstrate how to provide message integrity and authentication services through the use of digital signatures.

- Demonstrate how to compute cryptographic hashes and keyed hashes of data buffers and streams.

- Demonstrate how to combine cryptographic transforms using multiple wrapped instances of the `CryptoStream` class.

- Show how to generate cryptographically strong pseudo-random numbers and how to derive secret key material from passwords.

Chapter 31, "Using Cryptography with the .NET Framework: Advanced Topics," continues the discussion of cryptography in the .NET Framework and builds on the concepts introduced in this chapter.

Cryptography is the science of keeping messages secure. When discussing "message security," we typically are interested in one or more of the following three features:

- *Confidentiality*—Keeping the contents of a message private so that only authorized parties can read it

- *Integrity*—Ensuring that the contents of a message have not been tampered with while it is in transit from sender to recipient

- *Authentication*—Ensuring that a message claiming to have been sent by a party actually originated with that party

As you program and develop applications with the .NET Framework, you may want these features for all or portions of your data. For example, you may want to use cryptography to secure your data from unauthorized access or detect if the data has been changed without authorization. The .NET Framework includes a comprehensive set of object classes that can be used to perform cryptographic operations.

Setting the Stage: Key Definitions and Scenarios in Cryptography

Before describing the contents of the .NET Framework's cryptographic libraries, we briefly review and define some of the basic concepts of cryptography: symmetric algorithms, asymmetric algorithms, cryptographic hash functions, and digital signatures. We introduce these concepts in the context of basic two-party communication scenarios requiring one or more features of message security (confidentiality, integrity, and authentication).

> **NOTE**
>
> Cryptography is a rich and active field of ongoing research. It is impossible to provide a strong introduction to the theory and practice of modern cryptographic techniques in only two chapters, so we do not attempt to do so here. We assume that the reader is already familiar with cryptography; our goal in these two chapters is to demonstrate the features available in the .NET Framework to the knowledgeable reader.

To assist in our scenario descriptions, it is helpful to introduce some characters. A large assortment of common characters have grown up over the years in the field of cryptography to help explain scenarios, and the two most common characters are Alice and Bob, shown in Figure 30.1.

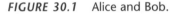

FIGURE 30.1   Alice and Bob.

Alice and Bob are two parties who want to communicate information over an open channel, such as an insecure network. In our first scenario, Alice wants to communicate some sensitive information to Bob in such a way that no one listening to the channel can learn the sensitive information. Alice wants to keep her message secret from everyone but Bob. In particular, Alice knows that Eve, an eavesdropper, has access to the network Alice must use to talk to Bob, so Eve will be able to listen to every communication between Alice and Bob. Figure 30.2 depicts Alice, Bob, and Eve in this scenario; the message M represents the sensitive information Alice wants to communicate to Bob. (Like Alice and Bob, Eve is a common character in cryptography scenarios and always represents an eavesdropper who can passively listen to communications.)

Ensuring Confidentiality with Symmetric Algorithms

Alice wants to send Bob the sensitive information in such a way that Eve cannot learn it, *even though Eve will hear everything Alice says*. How can Alice accomplish this task? Cryptography provides multiple possible answers. For example, if Alice and Bob have previously met and agreed on a *shared secret key* known only to the two of them, Alice can use this shared secret key to encrypt message M that she wants to send to Bob. Figure 30.3 shows Alice encrypting message M using the secret key K and then sending the encrypted message to Bob. The encrypted message is represented as E(M,K), the result of encrypting message M using the secret key K using encryption algorithm E. On receipt, Bob uses his own copy of the secret key K to decrypt the encrypt message, applying decryption algorithm D, to obtain message M.

The algorithms used by Alice and Bob in Figure 30.3 used the same secret key K as input to both the encryption and decryption functions, and the encryption used in this scenario is known as a *secret key cipher* or a *symmetric algorithm* ("symmetric" because Alice and Bob use the same key K to encrypt and decrypt). The K key must be kept secret between Alice and Bob to preserve the secrecy of any information encrypted using K. In the .NET Framework, these types of encryption and decryption algorithms are represented by the `SymmetricAlgorithm` class and its subclasses; these classes are described in detail in the "Using Symmetric Algorithms" section later in this chapter.

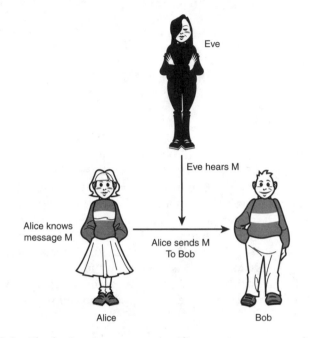

FIGURE 30.2   The basic secrecy scenario: Alice wants to communicate information to Bob without Eve learning the contents of the communication.

Symmetric algorithms are a key tool in the cryptographer's toolbox, but using them properly requires that Alice and Bob already possess a shared secret key K before any information can be encrypted. Pre-shared secrets are acceptable in situations where Alice and Bob have some out-of-band mechanism for sharing the key (perhaps they met previously in person), but if Alice and Bob have never met before, they will not share *any* secret information between them that could be used as a secret key or to generate a secret key. For such scenarios, we turn to the other major class of encryption algorithms in the cryptographer's bag of tricks—asymmetric algorithms.

Ensuring Confidentiality with Asymmetric Algorithms

Asymmetric algorithms differ from symmetric algorithms in that an *asymmetric algorithm* uses different keys to perform encryption and decryption operations. In Figure 30.3, Alice used secret key K to encrypt the message she sent to Bob, and Bob used the same key K to decrypt the encrypted message. With an asymmetric encryption algorithm, the encryption and decryption keys are different (but mathematically related). Each party wanting to receive encrypted communications generates a pair of keys: a *public key* that is used to encrypt information to the party and a *private key* that is used to decrypt encrypted messages. Asymmetric algorithms are also known as *public key algorithms*. Figure 30.4 depicts a sample scenario in which Alice uses an asymmetric algorithm and Bob's public key to encrypt information for Bob.

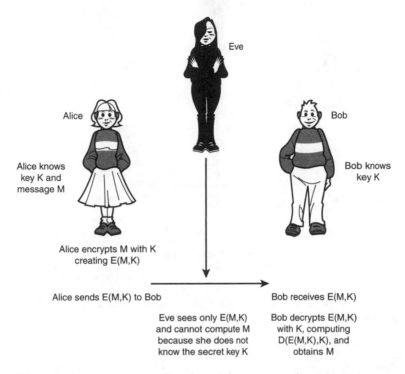

FIGURE 30.3   Using a symmetric algorithm cipher to securely communicate a message from Alice to Bob.

On receipt, Bob decrypts the information he received from Alice using his private key. Notice that in contrast to the symmetric encryption sample shown in Figure 30.3, Alice and Bob do not share any common secret key. Anyone wanting to send Bob encrypted information can do so if he or she holds a copy of Bob's public key and, because the public key is not used for decryption, it need not be kept secret. Indeed, it is common for users' public keys to be made available through an online directory or other database so that potential correspondents can easily find copies of them.

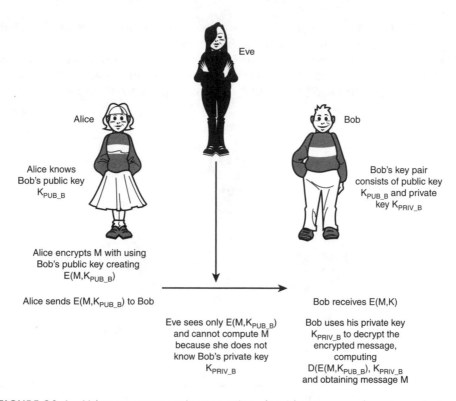

Alice

Eve

Bob

Alice knows
Bob's public key
K_{PUB_B}

Bob's key pair
consists of public key
K_{PUB_B} and private
key K_{PRIV_B}

Alice encrypts M with using
Bob's public key creating
$E(M,K_{PUB\_B})$

Alice sends $E(M,K_{PUB\_B})$ to Bob

Bob receives $E(M,K)$

Eve sees only $E(M,K_{PUB\_B})$
and cannot compute M
because she does not
know Bob's private key
K_{PRIV_B}

Bob uses his private key
K_{PRIV_B} to decrypt the
encrypted message,
computing
$D(E(M,K_{PUB\_B}), K_{PRIV\_B}$
and obtaining message M

FIGURE 30.4   Using an asymmetric encryption algorithm to securely communicate a
message from Alice to Bob.

NOTE

When Alice and Bob use a symmetric algorithm to communicate securely, they mutually agree
on a secret key to use and know that each other has a copy of that key. The situation is different when using asymmetric algorithms because Bob generates his pair of public and private
keys without input from anyone else. When Alice obtains a copy of Bob's public key, she
needs to know that the public key claiming to belong to Bob really does and matches Bob's
private key. For example, if Alice downloads a copy of a public key claiming to belong to Bob
from an online directory, she needs to obtain sufficient evidence to convince her that the
public key really does belong to Bob.

There are many different techniques for conveying trust information about Bob's public key to
Alice. Ultimately, the specific evidence that is necessary to convince Alice to use the public key
depends on Alice's particular trust policy. The situation is very similar to the operation of the
CLR Security Policy described in Chapter 8, "Membership Conditions, Code Groups, and
Policy Levels: The Brick and Mortar of Security Policy." The policy system decides what permissions to assign to an assembly based on presented evidence. Trust management systems for
public key cryptography, including *public key infrastructures* (PKIs), are an active area of

research and development. An in-depth discussion of various PKIs is outside the scope of this book. When dealing with asymmetric algorithms, we will assume that parties using public keys have been successfully convinced of the identities of the owners of their corresponding private keys.

Classes implementing asymmetric algorithms in the .NET Framework are represented by the `AsymmetricAlgorithm` class and subclasses of it. The section, "Using Asymmetric Algorithms," later in this chapter, discusses asymmetric algorithms in greater detail.

Using Cryptographic Hash Functions for Message Integrity and Authentication

Encryption algorithms are the bread-and-butter of cryptographers and, when used properly, can keep your data secret from unauthorized parties. However, encryption algorithms themselves do not provide the two other key features of message security—integrity and authentication. To provide these features, we need to discuss another fundamental building block used in security protocols—the cryptographic hash function. *Cryptographic hash functions* accept as input an arbitrary amount of binary data and compute from that data a "hash value"—a fixed-length value that is mathematically related to the input data. Hash functions are sometimes called "message digest algorithms" because they compute a "digest" (the hash value) of whatever data they are given.

> **NOTE**
>
> Obviously, any function that maps a binary string to a fixed-length value could be considered a hash function, but for a hash function to be useful cryptographically, it must additionally be a *one-way* function that is *collision-resistant*.
>
> - A *one-way* function is a function that is easy to compute but computationally unfeasible to invert. Let H(x) be a hash function, M an input message, and h = H(M) the hash value of M. Then we say that H(x) is a one-way hash function if it is (a) easy to compute h given M, but (b) for any given h', hard to find an M' that satisfies H(M') = h'.
> - A *collision-resistant* function H(x) is a function for which it is computationally unfeasible to find a pair of distinct inputs M and M' that have the same output H(M) = H(M').
>
> These two properties distinguish cryptographic hash functions from other types of checksums, such as CRC-32 or the algorithm for computing the check digit for a credit card number.

For a good cryptographic hash function that generates hashes of length n bits, the probability that any input message has a particular hash value h is 2^{-n}. This makes hash values extremely useful when trying to detect whether a message M has been tampered with in transit. If $h = H(M)$ is the hash value of M, changing a single bit of M has a 50/50 chance of independently changing each bit in the hash value h. (The "Using Cryptographic Hash Functions" section later in this chapter discusses the classes implementing cryptographic hash functions in the .NET Framework; the base class for all hash function implementations is the `HashAlgorithm` class.)

Cryptographic hash functions are the cryptographer's weapon of choice to protect the integrity of data in transit. Unlike message secrecy, in which Alice and Bob are concerned about protecting their data from Eve the eavesdropper, in a message integrity scenario, the threat is that data in transit will be modified by a malicious, active attacker. Figure 30.5 shows a typical message integrity scenario and introduces a new character—Mallet. Mallet represents an active adversary that not only listens to all communications between Alice and Bob but can also modify the contents of any communication he sees while it is in transit. When Alice sends message M to Bob, Mallet intercepts M and may choose to change any of the bits in the message, creating message M'. Mallet then forwards M' to Bob. Bob receives M' and must determine whether M' differs from the original message M Alice sent.

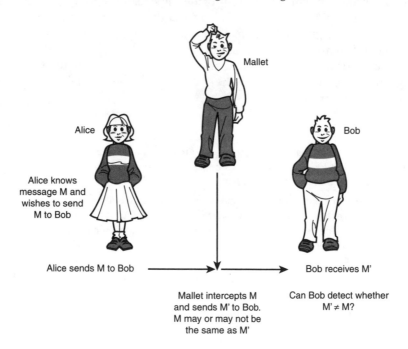

Mallet

Alice

Bob

Alice knows
message M and
wishes to send
M to Bob

Alice sends M to Bob ⟶

Bob receives M'

Mallet intercepts M
and sends M' to Bob.
M may or may not be
the same as M'

Can Bob detect whether
M' ≠ M?

FIGURE 30.5   The basic integrity scenario: Alice wants to communicate information to Bob so that any tampering performed by Mallet will be detected.

Cryptography hash functions are a fundamental building block of message integrity protocols, but they are not by themselves sufficient because Mallet can also calculate hash values. If Alice sends Bob the message M plus the result of hashing M, H(M), Mallet could replace M with M' *and* calculate a new hash value H(M'). Bob would receive M' and H(M') and believe that the message was unaltered.

What can Alice do to guarantee that any tampering by Mallet of her message will be detectible by Bob? One possibility, if Alice and Bob share a secret key for a symmetric encryption algorithm, is to send the message M and its hash to Bob encrypted. Figure 30.6 shows this approach. First, Alice generates the message M that she wants to send to Bob. Alice then calculates the hash of M, H(M), using an agreed-upon cryptographic hash function. Alice concatenates the message with its hash, creating M ‖ H(M), and then encrypts the entire package to Bob using the shared secret key K. (The operator ‖ denotes concatenation.) The message that Alice sends, and that Mallet sees, is E((M ‖ H(M)), K).

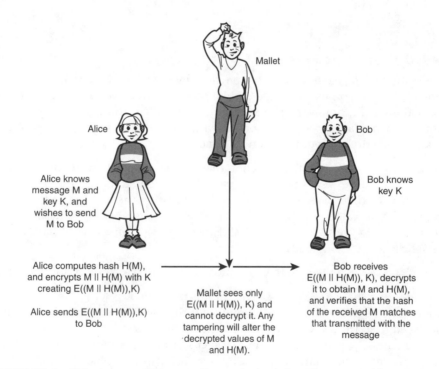

Mallet

Alice

Bob

Alice knows
message M and
key K, and
wishes to send
M to Bob

Bob knows
key K

Alice computes hash H(M),
and encrypts M ‖ H(M) with K
creating E((M ‖ H(M)),K)

Alice sends E((M ‖ H(M)),K)
to Bob

Mallet sees only
E((M ‖ H(M)), K) and
cannot decrypt it. Any
tampering will alter the
decrypted values of M
and H(M).

Bob receives
E((M ‖ H(M)), K), decrypts
it to obtain M and H(M),
and verifies that the hash
of the received M matches
that transmitted with the
message

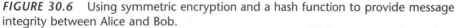

FIGURE 30.6   Using symmetric encryption and a hash function to provide message integrity between Alice and Bob.

Now, Mallet cannot tamper with Alice's message without being detected with high probability, because Mallet sees only ciphertext and does not know the secret key K. If Mallet changes any of the bits in the ciphertext corresponding to the encryption of message M, those changes will impact Bob's decryption of the received message.

Bob will decrypt the message from Alice and see an M' different from M, which (again, with high probability) will not have the same hash value M. (Depending on the type of encryption used, Bob may also see a modified hash value H(M″) which corresponds to neither M nor M'.) As a result, Bob will detect the tampering. This technique, *hash-and-encrypt*, is used in the sample functions shown in Listings 30.8 and 30.9 to protect a file stored on disk from tampering.

NOTE

The key to making the protocol depicted in Figure 30.6 work is that Alice protected the hash of the message using a piece of secret information shared with Bob, namely their secret encryption key. If Mallet can break the encryption, he could see the plain text M, change that message into M', change the hash value from H(M) to H(M'), and re-encrypt the altered package M' ‖ H(M') for Bob.

Keyed Hash Functions

The protocol depicted in Figure 30.6 provides message security and integrity but depends on encryption to provide both of those features. We can remove the encryption requirement, however, by changing the type of hash function we use in the protocol. By replacing the hash function with a keyed hash function, we can provide message integrity without also requiring encryption.

A *keyed hash function* is a hash function that computes a hash value for some data mixed with a secret key. That is, the hash value computed for some data depends on both the data and the secret key; change a bit in either the data or the key value, and the output value will change. Implementation classes for keyed hash functions are described in the "Using Keyed Hash Functions" section; all keyed hash functions are subclasses of the KeyedHashAlgorithm class.

Figure 30.7 shows a message integrity protocol based on a keyed hash function.

Alice and Bob share a secret key K, but in this protocol, K is a key for the keyed hash function H, not a symmetric encryption algorithm. For message M, Alice computes the keyed hash H(M,K) corresponding to her message and secret key and sends Bob both the message and the hash value. Mallet sees both the message and the hash value on the network, but he cannot make undetectible modification to either of them. If Mallet wants to change M into M' undetected by Bob, he must also change the hash value H(M,K) into H(M',K). However, Mallet does not know K, so he cannot easily recompute the hash value to account for his changes in the message. Any tampering with message M will be easily detected.

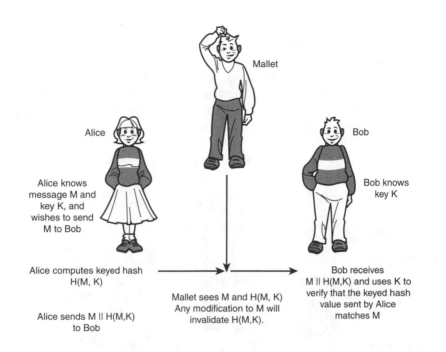

FIGURE 30.7   Using a keyed hash function to provide message integrity between Alice and Bob.

The keyed hash function Alice used in Figure 30.7 not only allows Bob to verify the integrity of message M, but also authenticates that M was generated by Alice. Assuming that only Alice and Bob know secret key K, only Alice could have generated the hash value H(M,K) and sent it to Bob. When a shared secret exists between two parties, it may also be used to provide data origin authentication (the message must have originated with Alice because only she and Bob hold secret key K). Bob knows that the message he received originated with Alice because their shared secret was used with the message to produce the keyed hash value.

Digital Signatures: Authentication and Integrity Using Asymmetric Algorithms

It is also possible to use asymmetric algorithms to provide authentication services, in particular, digital signatures. We saw how the asymmetry between the public and private keys in a key pair can be used to allow anyone to encrypt a message to Bob that only Bob can decrypt (refer to Figure 30.4). In that scenario, any party wanting to encrypt information to Bob used Bob's widely available public key to perform the encryption. Bob decrypted such encrypted information by applying his private key to the encrypted messages. We now demonstrate data origin authentication using an asymmetric algorithm that works by leveraging the asymmetry in reverse. Figure 30.8 shows a simple digital signature protocol between Alice and Bob; Alice sends Bob message M along with a digital signature for M that she creates using the hash of M and her *private key*. (The digital signature is denoted SIG(H(M), K_{PRIV_A}) because it depends both on the content of the message and Alice's private key.) Bob (or anyone) receiving the message can verify the signature by applying Alice's *public key*, K_{PUB_A}, to the signature to obtain the signed hash value. Bob then computes his own hash of M and compares his result with the signed hash value. Any discrepancy indicates that the message has changed since it was signed by Alice.

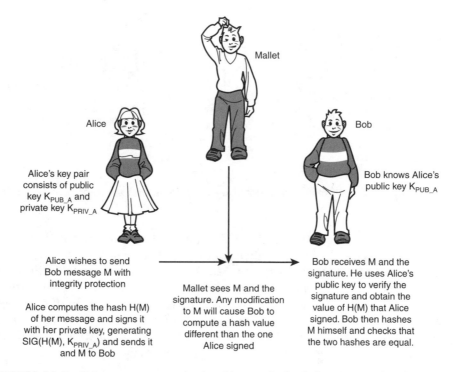

Mallet

Alice

Bob

Alice's key pair consists of public key K_{PUB_A} and private key K_{PRIV_A}

Bob knows Alice's public key K_{PUB_A}

Alice wishes to send Bob message M with integrity protection

Alice computes the hash H(M) of her message and signs it with her private key, generating SIG(H(M), K_{PRIV_A}) and sends it and M to Bob

Mallet sees M and the signature. Any modification to M will cause Bob to compute a hash value different than the one Alice signed

Bob receives M and the signature. He uses Alice's public key to verify the signature and obtain the value of H(M) that Alice signed. Bob then hashes M himself and checks that the two hashes are equal.

FIGURE 30.8   Using an asymmetric algorithm and a hash function to digitally sign a message from Alice to Bob.

NOTE

Asymmetric algorithms tend to have size limits on the amount of data that can be signed or encrypted using a particular key pair; typically these limits are associated with the size of the public key parameters. Thus, in Figure 30.8, the signature is computed using the hash of message M instead of M itself. Signing a hash of the message still preserves the integrity of the message and avoids the length limits inherent in the algorithm. Asymmetric algorithm size limits are discussed in more detail in the section, "Using Asymmetric Algorithms," later in this chapter.

Whether an asymmetric algorithm can be used for encryption or generating digital signatures depends on the particular algorithm in question. Both asymmetric algorithms that ship with the .NET Framework SDK, the RSA public key cipher (named after its inventors, Ron Rivest, Adi Shamir, and Leonard Adleman) and the Digital Signature Algorithm (DSA), can be used to create and verify digital signatures. However, only the RSA algorithm supports encryption.

This concludes our brief review of asymmetric algorithms, symmetric algorithms, cryptographic hash functions, and digital signatures. In the next section, we begin a detailed discussion of the classes and objects in the .NET Framework that implement these algorithms.

The Cryptographic Object Model of the .NET Framework

One of the first things a developer will notice of any reasonable cryptographic library is an abundance of different algorithms that perform equivalent functions. Nothing is static in the field of cryptography. Over time, new algorithms are invented and old algorithms are broken, so any application using cryptography needs to be able to adopt these new algorithms and retire the old ones over time. Consequently, a good cryptographic library has to have easy extensibility by third parties (to accommodate new algorithms) as one of its fundamental design goals if it is to be useful over time. Users must be able to add new and improved algorithms to the system in a way that makes them available seamlessly to current and future applications. Additionally, a cryptographic library must also be able to accommodate multiple implementations of a particular cryptographic algorithm coexisting on the same machine. For example, a Web server handling e-commerce transactions is likely to include a hardware accelerator for improving the performance of cryptographic operations (for example, establishing SSL/TLS connections).

The .NET Framework cryptographic object model was designed to facilitate the addition of new algorithms and implementations in an interoperable manner. In the model, a category of algorithms, such as "symmetric algorithms," is represented by a single abstract base class. Figure 30.9 shows a portion of the object hierarchy for secret key ciphers such as Triple DES, Rijndael (AES), and RC2. Individual algorithms in the category are represented by abstract algorithm classes, which are subclasses of the base class, and algorithm implementation classes are subclasses of the abstract algorithm classes. In Figure 30.9, the `SymmetricAlgorithm` class is the abstract base class for all symmetric key ciphers (for example, `Rijndael`). Each algorithm is then represented by an abstract subclass of `SymmetricAlgorithm`—`TripleDES`, `Rijndael`, `RC2`, and so on. Each of these classes is then subclassed by one of the implementation classes—`TripleDESCryptoServiceProvider` (an implementation of `TripleDES` using CryptoAPI), `RijndaelManaged` (a managed code implementation of `Rijndael`), or `RC2CryptoServiceProvider`.

NOTE

The Rijndael algorithm was chosen as the winner of the Advanced Encryption Standard (AES) contest sponsored by the U.S. Government's National Institute of Standards and Technology (NIST) as the replacement for DES, the Data Encryption Standard. Throughout the .NET Framework, we refer to the algorithm by its original name.

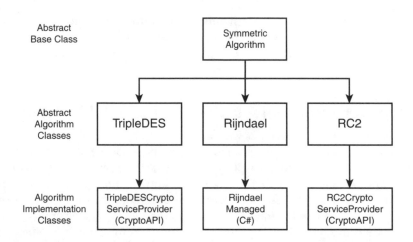

FIGURE 30.9   The Crypto object model.

For secret key ciphers, the abstract base class `SymmetricAlgorithm` defines the top of the object hierarchy. The `SymmetricAlgorithm` class defines methods and properties that are common to all algorithms in this class, and every class representing a secret key cipher is a subclass of `SymmetricAlgorithm`. For example, a symmetric algorithm is defined only for certain key lengths, so the `SymmetricAlgorithm` class defines an abstract `LegalKeySizes` property to represent the set of valid key sizes (in bits) for a cipher. The specific properties defined by each abstract base class are described in more detail in the later sections of this chapter.

Individual algorithms are represented in the model as subclasses of the abstract base class. These abstract algorithm classes have two functions. First, where possible, they expose algorithm-specific details, such as key and block sizes, by providing implementations of properties and methods defined by the abstract base class. For example, the Rijndael algorithm is defined for key sizes of 128, 192, and 256 bits, so the `Rijndael` class provide an implementation of the `LegalKeySizes` property that returns these specific values. The second function of an abstract algorithm class is to define properties and methods that are common to every implementation of the algorithm they represent but do not apply to other algorithms. The `IsWeakKey` method on the `TripleDES` abstract algorithm class is an example of such a method. This method checks potential TripleDES keys against a list of known weak keys (specific keys that should not be used with the TripleDES algorithm because there are known attacks against them).

Implementations of a particular algorithm are supplied in subclasses of the corresponding abstract algorithm class. So, for example, an implementation of the TripleDES algorithm is provided by a specific class, `TripleDESCryptoServiceProvider`, that is a subclass of the `TripleDES` class. The naming convention used for algorithm implementation classes included in the .NET Framework is to concatenate the name of the algorithm class with a string identifying the source of the implementation. A `CryptoServiceProvider` suffix denotes an implementation based on the Microsoft Cryptographic Service Providers (CSPs) that ship as part of the Windows CryptoAPI library of functions; RC2, DES, and TripleDES are implemented on top of CryptoAPI in the .NET Framework. A `Managed` suffix denotes an algorithm implemented in managed code (a language that runs on top of the Common Language Runtime, such as C#). The Rijndael algorithm is implemented in C#, so its implementation class is denoted `RijndaelManaged`.

Although the crypto object model contains a large number of abstract classes, its design has a number of advantages for developers. First and foremost, is it very easy to extend the model to add your own (or a third party's) algorithms and implementations. Have a hardware cryptographic accelerator on your system that implemented Rijndael? Create a subclass of the `Rijndael` class that interfaces to your hardware device, and now any managed code can use your device. Want to add a new algorithm to the .NET Framework, say the RC6 secret key cipher? Create an abstract `RC6` class that subclasses `SymmetricAlgorithm`, and then create an implementation class (`RC6Managed`, perhaps) that subclasses RC6. We discuss extending the cryptographic framework in more detail in the next chapter.

We have focused in this section on the portion of the object hierarchy that relates to secret key ciphers, but equivalent object hierarchies also exist for public key algorithms (rooted at the `AsymmetricAlgorithm` class) and cryptographic hash functions (rooted at the `HashAlgorithm` class). The following is a quick summary of the three algorithm-related hierarchies that are included in the .NET Framework crypto object model:

- HashAlgorithm (abstract)
  - SHA1 (abstract)
    - SHA1CryptoServiceProvider (an implementation of SHA-1 using CryptoAPI)
  - SHA1Managed (an implementation of SHA1 in C#)

- SHA256 (abstract)
  - SHA256Managed (an implementation of SHA256 in C#)
- SHA384 (abstract)
  - SHA384Managed (an implementation of SHA384 in C#)
- SHA512 (abstract)
  - SHA512Managed (an implementation of SHA512 in C#)
- MD5 (abstract)
  - MD5CryptoServiceProvider (an implementation of MD5 using CryptoAPI)
- KeyedHashAlgorithm (abstract)
  - HMACSHA1 (an implementation in C#)
  - MACTripleDES (an implementation in C#)
- SymmetricAlgorithm (abstract)
  - TripleDES (abstract)
    - TripleDESCryptoServiceProvider (an implementation of TripleDES using CryptoAPI)
  - RC2 (abstract)
    - RC2CryptoServiceProvider (an implementation of RC2 using CryptoAPI)
  - DES (abstract)
    - DESCryptoServiceProvider (an implementation of DES using CryptoAPI)
  - Rijndael (abstract)
    - RijndaelManaged (an implementation of Rijndael in C#)
- AsymmetricAlgorithm (abstract)
  - RSA (abstract)
  - RSACryptoServiceProvider (an implementation of RSA using CryptoAPI)
  - DSA (abstract)
    - DSACryptoServiceProvider (an implementation of DSA using CryptoAPI)

Given all the crypto classes that exist in the .NET Framework, plus the ability to arbitrarily extend the object model with new algorithms and implementations, you might be thinking right now, "How can a program ever know what new implementations of an algorithm exist on a system?" Or, equivalently, "How does a program know what the user's preferred secret key cipher is?" Developers have to be able to answer these questions easily to make their programs robust to changes in the object hierarchy, which is why the .NET Framework also includes a configuration system for the cryptography classes. The key feature of the crypto configuration system is that it defines a "default implementation type" for each abstract base class and abstract algorithm class in the crypto object model. Every abstract class in the crypto object model defines a static `Create()` method that, when called, creates an instance of default implementation for the abstract class. This allows a developer to ask for an instance of "the default implementation of the SHA-1 algorithm"

```
SHA1 sha1 = SHA1.Create();
```

without having to know the specific name of the class that implements SHA-1. Of course, if you know that you want an instance specifically of the CryptoAPI-based implementation of SHA-1, you can create that instance directly:

```
SHA1CryptoServiceProvider sha1 = new SHA1CryptoServiceProvider();
```

In the remainder of this chapter and the next, example code demonstrating cryptographic functions will use the static `Create()` methods (and, implicitly, the cryptographic configuration system) whenever possible. If the example demonstrates a property of the abstract base class, such as the `ComputeHash(byte[])` method of the `HashAlgorithm` class, we will just use an instance of the default `HashAlgorithm`:

```
HashAlgorithm hash = HashAlgorithm.Create();
hash.ComputeHash(someByteArray);
```

Unless you have a particular reason to request a specific implementation of an algorithm, we suggest that you always create cryptographic objects using `Create()`. This will allow your programs to take advantage of newer algorithm implementations as they are developed and made available through the cryptographic configuration system.

Operating on Streams: `CryptoStreams` and `ICryptoTransforms`

A common scenario for developers is the application of cryptographic transforms to a stream of binary data, such as encrypting data about to be written to an on-disk file or a network connection. The .NET Framework cryptography classes make it very easy to perform these sorts of operations using the `CryptoStream` class and objects implementing the `ICryptoTransform` interface. We first describe the `ICryptoTransform` model block transforms and then show how these transforms can be "wrapped" around any stream in the .NET Framework using the `CryptoStream` class.

Figure 30.10 shows the basic model of an `ICryptoTransform`. An `ICryptoTransform` represents any blockwise mathematical transformation, such as encryption or decryption by a symmetric key cipher. By "blockwise," we mean that the transform takes in input blocks of fixed size and turns them into output blocks of fixed size. All of the secret key ciphers supported natively in the .NET Framework are block ciphers that operate this way: DES, Triple DES, and RC2 operate on input blocks of 8 bytes (producing 8 bytes of output), and Rijndael/AES operates on input blocks of 16 bytes (producing 16 bytes of output). Although it has "crypto" in its name, the transformation represented by an `ICryptoTransform` need not be an encryption or decryption function. Within the .NET Framework, we also model operations such as cryptographic hash functions, Base64 encoding and decoding, and even specialized padding and formatting operations, such as PKCS#1 padding `ICryptoTransforms`.

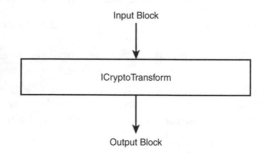

FIGURE 30.10   The `ICryptoTransform` interface.

Every `ICryptoTransform` exposes four read-only properties, detailed in Table 30.1. These properties describe how the transform operates and under what conditions the object can be reused. Because `ICryptoTransforms` are most often used in conjunction with the `CryptoStream` class, these properties exist primarily to help `CryptoStream` tailor itself to the particular transform. You will only need to deal with these properties if you call an `ICryptoTransform` directly or implement a new `ICryptoTransform`.

TABLE 30.1   `ICryptoTransform` Properties

Property	Type	Description
InputBlockSize	Integer	Size of input block in bytes.
OutputBlockSize	Integer	Size of output block in bytes.

TABLE 30.1   Continued

Property	Type	Description
`CanTransformMultipleBlocks`	Boolean	If `true`, multiple blocks of input data can be passed to the `TransformBlock` method in a single call.
`CanReuseTransform`	Boolean	If `true`, the transform can be reused on another data stream after the `TransformFinalBlock` method has been called.

In addition to its four properties, each `ICryptoTransform` implements two methods—`TransformBlock` and `TransformFinalBlock`. These two methods perform the actual cryptographic transformation represented by the `ICryptoTransform`. The difference between the two methods is that the `TransformFinalBlock` method signals that the last block of data from the input stream is being processed and that the `ICryptoTransform` should do whatever final processing is required to finish the stream. (For example, depending on the length of the input, the last block to be transformed may be a "short" block and not contain a full `InputBlockSize`'s worth of data, thus necessitating that some padding data be added.)

All objects that represent secret key ciphers include methods for creating related `ICryptoTransform` objects. In particular, every `SymmetricAlgorithm` includes two methods, `CreateEncryptor()` and `CreateDecryptor()`, that create encryption and decryption `ICryptoTransforms` from the key material, initialization vector, and operation modes specified by the object. Every `HashAlgorithm` also implements the `ICryptoTransform` interface, as do encoding and decoding objects such as `ToBase64Transform` and `FromBase64Transform` (which encode and decode binary data as ASCII strings in the Base64 format).

Now that we know an `ICryptoTransform` represents a blockwise cryptographic transformation, how can the `ICryptoTransform` be used to transform a stream of data? Transformations on streams are performed by "wrapping" an `ICryptoTransform` around the input stream using the `CryptoStream` class. A `CryptoStream` is itself a stream, but its contents are generated by applying an `ICryptoTransform` block-by-block to other input data. Figure 30.11 graphically depicts the flow of data read from a `CryptoStream` in read mode.

To create a `CryptoStream`, you must specify three arguments—the underlying stream, the `ICryptoTransform` to be applied to the input data, and an enum value, either `CryptoStreamMode.Read` or `CryptoStreamMode.Write`, to indicate whether the `CryptoStream` is going to be used in read mode or write mode. A `CryptoStream` must be used exclusively in either read mode or write mode, and its behavior changes depending on the mode in which it is operating. In read mode, reading bytes from a `CryptoStream` causes data to be read from the underlying stream, transformed by the specified ICryptoTransform, and then returned as the results of the read request. In write mode, writing bytes to the CryptoStream causes that data to be transformed by the specified ICryptoTransform and then written to the underlying stream. In both cases, the CryptoStream will buffer input and output bytes as necessary to use the ICryptoTransform properly.

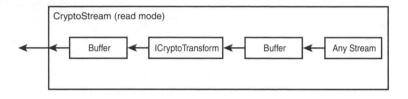

FIGURE 30.11   How CryptoStream works in read mode.

CryptoStreams are pretty easy to use, but keep in mind the following requirements when using them. First, the underlying stream inside a CryptoStream must be a descendant of the System.IO.Stream class, which is the base class for all stream-like classes in the .NET Framework. Additionally, the subclass of System.IO.Stream must support reading if the CryptoStream is in read mode (and writing if the CryptoStream is in write mode). CryptoStreams are not seek-able; you cannot read or set the Length or Position of a CryptoStream, because the class only supports sequential access to the underlying data. Finally, note that whether a CryptoStream is in read or write mode is independent of whether its ICryptoTransform is performing an encryption or decryption operation. We tend to think of stored data as being encrypted and then naturally associate "read from file" with decryption and "write to file" with encryption, but, as you will see in the examples in the next section, all four combinations can arise in your programs.

> **NOTE**
>
> A Stream class supports reading if the value of its CanRead property is true. Similarly, a Stream supports writing if the value of its CanWrite property is true.

Using Symmetric Algorithms

Having introduced the cryptographic object model and the operation of CryptoStreams and ICryptoTransforms, we now move on to detailed discussions and examples of using each of the base types defined within the model: symmetric algorithm, cryptographic hash functions, keyed hash functions, random number generators, and asymmetric algorithms. We begin with the secret key ciphers, represented by the SymmetricAlgorithm class and its descendants. Secret key ciphers are most commonly used for bulk encryption—scenarios that require encrypting or decrypting large amounts of data. We start with a discussion of the structure of an object that derives from `SymmetricAlgorithm`, describe how to create individual instances of `SymmetricAlgorithm`, and then present examples showing how to use a `SymmetricAlgorithm` for encryption and decryption.

The `SymmetricAlgorithm` Base Class

An instance object of a `SymmetricAlgorithm` descendant class represents a particular algorithm and choice of operating parameters. There are four major parameters defined for every `SymemtricAlgorithm`, denoted by the instance properties `Key`, `Mode`, `IV`, and `Padding`:

`Key`—This property holds the secret key value that will be used to encrypt or decrypt data. The `Key` property is initialized to a random value when the object is created.

`Mode`—This enumeration, of type `CipherMode`, defines the chaining mode of operation of the cipher. The chaining mode of an algorithm determines whether and how the encryption of one block of data influences the encryption of the next block of data. The default value for the `Mode` property is "cipher block chaining," `CipherMode.CBC`, which is the strongest generally available mode of operation. Unless you explicitly have a reason to choose another chaining mode, you probably want to use cipher block chaining.

> **NOTE**
>
> There are five defined values for `CipherMode`: electronic codebook (ECB, no chaining between blocks), cipher block chaining (CBC), cipher feedback mode (CFB), output feedback mode (OFB), and cipher text stealing (CTS). Every algorithm implementation that ships as part of the .NET Framework supports both ECB and CBC, and the `*CryptoServiceProvider` implementations additionally support CFB with a feedback size of 8 bits. OFB and CTS are not supported by any of the implementations included in the .NET Framework but can be supported by third-party implementations.

`IV`—This property holds the *initialization vector (IV)*, which is used when the algorithm is operated in a chaining mode, such as CBC. When an algorithm is operating in a chaining mode and encrypts the first block of data, the feedback values of the "previous block" are provided by the initialization vector. The `IV` is the same size as a single block of data and is initialized to a random value when the object is created. Initialization vectors need not be kept secret but should always be randomly chosen before encrypting a stream of data.

> **CAUTION**
>
> In particular, do not set your initialization vectors to a known value, such as all zeros, before use. This weakens the security of your application.

`Padding`—This enumeration, of type `PaddingMode`, describes how the cipher should pad a short final block (that is, what happens if the last block of data to be encrypted is less that `BlockSize` bytes). Unless you have a specific reason for requiring a particular padding mode, stick with the default value, `PaddingMode.PKCS7`.

> **NOTE**
>
> PKCS7 padding mode fills the remainder of the block with bytes whose value is equal to the number of bytes needed to pad; that is, if three bytes of pad are needed, the pad string is 03 03 03. This has the advantage that when decrypting the last block it is immediately evident how many bytes of padding need to be removed. With zero padding (the other padding option) there is a possibility of error on decrypt if the last plain text bytes to be encrypted were zeros.

Specific algorithms can, of course, have additional operating parameters, but in general, these four are the only ones you will need to access.

Creating Instances of `SymmetricAlgorithm` Classes

To create an instance of a class that implements a particular symmetric algorithm, simply call the static `Create()` method on the abstract class representing the algorithm. This statement creates a new object that implements the Rijndael algorithm and assigns it to the variable `rijndael`:

```
Rijndael rijndael = Rijndael.Create();
```

The object will be a member of the default implementation class for the Rijndael algorithm, which is the `RijndaelManaged` class by default. Recall that by convention, cryptographic objects are created with default parameter values set to the strongest available settings. For `SymmetricAlgorithm` descendant classes, instance objects will be initialized with a random secret key and random initialization vector, and will be configured to operate in cipher block chaining (CBC) mode with PKCS7 padding for short final blocks. For ciphers that support multiple key lengths, the largest legal key size will be used by default. Table 30.2 lists the default and legal key sizes for the symmetric algorithm implementations that ship as part of the .NET Framework.

TABLE 30.2   Symmetric Algorithm Key Sizes

Cipher	Default Implementation Class	Legal Key Sizes	Default Key Size
DES	`DESCryptoServiceProvider`	64 bits	64 bits
TripleDES	`TripleDESCryptoServiceProvider`	128, 192 bits	192 bits
RC2	`RC2CryptoServiceProvider`	40–128 bits	128 bits
Rijndael	`RijndaelManaged`	128, 192, 256 bits	256 bits

The supported key lengths for `DESCryptoServiceProvider`,
`TripleDESCryptoServiceProvider`, and `RC2CryptoServiceProvider` depend on the "high encryption" version of CryptoAPI being installed on the platform. If you are running Windows XP, Windows 2000 with Service Pack 2 or later, or Internet Explorer 5.5 or later, you already have the high encryption version of CryptoAPI installed on your machine. For other versions of Windows, you will need to install a "high encryption" update (a "high encryption" flavor service pack for Windows NT 4, and a "high encryption" update for older versions of Internet Explorer). See `http://www.gotdotnet.com/team/clr/cryptofaq.htm` for details on where to download the high encryption update appropriate for your version of Windows.

The key length for DES and TripleDES includes the parity bits that are defined as part of the key but do not contribute to the overall strength of the algorithm. DES, for example, is defined to use 56-bit keys, but 56-bit keys are expanded to 64 bits by adding a parity bit per byte. CryptoAPI treats DES as a 64-bit algorithm and ignores every eighth bit of the input (recalculating the parity bits as necessary), and the `DESCryptoServiceProvider` class acts similarly. TripleDES has "two-key" and "three-key" flavors, which thus use 112 and 168 bits of key material. As with DES, CryptoAPI assumes TripleDES keys as though they include the parity bits, so it accepts 128- and 192-bit keys for use with TripleDES. The `TripleDESCryptoServiceProvider` follows this convention as well.

The `RijndaelManaged` class is implemented entirely in managed code (C#) and is available on every platform on which the .NET Framework has been installed. `RijndaelManaged` is also the default implementation class for `SymmetricAlgorithm`. Thus, in the following statement

```
SymmetricAlgorithm symAlg = SymmetricAlgorihtm.Create();
```

the *symAlg* variable will be assigned to an instance of `RijndaelManaged`. (This mapping can be overridden by modifying the crypto configuration system.)

After you have created a `SymemtricAlgorithm` object for the cipher, key, and IV you want to use, the next step is to create `ICryptoTransform` objects that represent encryption and decryption operations using that cipher/Key/IV combination. `ICryptoTransforms` are created using the `CreateEncryptor()` and `CreateDecryptor()` methods:

```
ICryptoTransform rijndaelEncryptor = rijndael.CreateEncryptor();
ICryptoTransform rijndaelDecryptor = rijndael.CreateDecryptor();
```

The resulting `ICryptoTransforms` implement encryption and decryption using the current values of the Key, IV, Mode, and Padding properties of the `rijndael` object. The `ICryptoTransforms` are self-contained and once created are not affected by changes in these property values on the `SymmetricAlgorithm` object that was used to create them.

Encrypting and Decrypting with `ICryptoTransforms` **Created from a** `SymmetricAlgorithm`

After you have an `ICryptoTransform`, it can be combined with any stream using the `CryptoStream` class to transform data read from or written to the underlying stream. We now present some examples showing how to use the `rijndaelEncryptor` and `rijndaelDecryptor` `ICryptoTransforms` we just created with `CryptoStream` to perform encryption and decryption of memory buffers and on-disk files.

Encrypting an In-Memory Buffer

Our first code sample, shown in Listing 30.1, demonstrates simple encryption of an in-memory plain text buffer. Suppose you have an array of plain text bytes that you want to encrypt in memory using `rijndaelEncryptor`. An easy way to do this is to create a `MemoryStream` to hold the output ciphertext bytes, "wrap" the `rijndaelEncryptor` around the `MemoryStream` using `CryptoStream`, and then write the plain text bytes into the `CryptoStream`. The code in this listing performs the encryption; we'll assume that the plain text already exists in a byte array called `plain textArray` and that we ultimately want the encrypted ciphertext in a byte array called `ciphertextArray`.

> **NOTE**
>
> Source code in electronic form for all code listings in this chapter may be downloaded from the publisher's Web site for this book.

LISTING 30.1   Encrypting In-Memory Plain Text Creating In-Memory Ciphertext

```
// create the MemoryStream that will hold our output:
MemoryStream ciphertextStream = new MemoryStream();
// create the CryptoStream. Bytes written to this stream will be encrypted
// by the rijndaelEncryptor and then written to the ciphertextStream
CryptoStream cryptoStream = new CryptoStream(ciphertextStream,
➥ rijndaelEncryptor, CryptoStreamMode.Write);
// Now, write the all the plain text bytes to the cryptoStream to encrypt them
cryptoStream.Write(plain textArray, 0, plain textArray.Length);
// We have no more bytes to encrypt, so tell the cryptoStream that it
// has seen the last block of input
cryptoStream.FlushFinalBlock();
// read the output ciphertext from the ciphertextStream
byte[] ciphertextArray = ciphertextStream.ToArray();
// close the CryptoStream
cryptoStream.Close();
```

That's all there is to it! When the bytes in plain textArray are written to the cryptoStream, they are automatically encrypted by the rijndaelEncryptor transform and written out to the ciphertextStream. Note that the call to cryptoStream.FlushFinalBlock() is important; it tells the cryptoStream that we have finished using the stream and any remaining bytes buffered inside the CryptoStream need to be processed. In this case, that final processing will be to pad out the last block of input data to a multiple of the block size of Rijndael (128 bits or 16 bytes), encrypt it, and write it out to the ciphertextStream.

Encrypting an In-Memory Buffer to an On-Disk File

Let us now change the scenario slightly and show how to modify the code in Listing 30.1 to persist the ciphertext to an on-disk file. All we need to do is change the destination stream, ciphertextStream, from a MemoryStream to a FileStream associated with the desired on-disk file. CryptoStream does not care about the type of stream to which it is writing; so long as it is a descendant of the System.IO.Stream class and supports writing operations, CryptoStream will work with it. Listing 30.2 contains a modified version of the previous program that persists the ciphertext in the file C:\ciphertext.bin (root directory of the C: drive, which is usually the primary partition of your computer's hard disk drive).

LISTING 30.2   Encrypting In-Memory Plain Text and Writing the Ciphertext to a File

```
// we have to escape backslashes in C# strings
String filename = "C:\\ciphertext.bin";
// create the FileStream that will hold our output:
FileStream ciphertextStream = new FileStream(filename, FileMode.Create);
// create the CryptoStream wrapping this FileStream
// with the rijndaelEncryptor CryptoStream
CryptoStream = new CryptoStream(ciphertextStream,
➡ rijndaelEncryptor, CryptoStreamMode.Write);
// Write the plain text bytes to the cryptoStream
cryptoStream.Write(plain textArray, 0, plain textArray.Length);
// We are now done writing, so flush the last block out
cryptoStream.FlushFinalBlock();
// close the CryptoStream
cryptoStream.Close();
```

Notice that we do not need to explicitly close the underlying FileStream ciphertextStream; when the Close() method is called on a CryptoStream instance, the underlying stream is automatically closed too. If you want to write some bytes out to the underlying stream after the CryptoStream is finished, you can do so after calling the CryptoStream's FlushFinalBlock() method.

Encrypting and Decrypting an On-Disk File to a Second File

The examples in Listings 30.1 and 30.2 demonstrate simple uses of CryptoStream to encrypt files, but they simplify the key management by assuming that you have an instance of SymmetricAlgorithm with the proper key and IV already set. In the next example, we create two methods, EncryptFile and DecryptFile, that convert between unencrypted and encrypted files. Both methods will always use Rijndael and take as input an encryption/decryption key suitable for use with Rijndael (that is, 16, 24, or 32 bytes in length). Initialization vectors will be randomly generated on encryption and persisted with the encrypted file as the first 16 bytes of the file; on decryption, we will read the IV from the ciphertext before decrypting the rest of the file. Both methods take two additional inputs—the names of the source and destination files. For EncryptFile, the source is plain text and the destination is ciphertext; the reverse is true for DecryptFile. Listing 30.3 contains the source code for the EncryptFile method; the source for DecryptFile is shown in Listing 30.4.

LISTING 30.3   Encrypting an On-Disk File to a Second File with Random IV Generation

```
public static void EncryptFile(byte[] key, String sourceFile,
➥ String destFile) {
  // initialize with random key and IV
  Rijndael aes = Rijndael.Create();
  // set the key to the passed-in arg
  aes.Key = key;
  // create FileStreams for source and dest
  FileStream inStream = new FileStream(sourceFile, FileMode.Open);
  FileStream outStream = new FileStream(destFile, FileMode.Create);
  // We want to write the IV out to the destFile unencrypted,
  // so in this case we can wrap a CryptoStream around the *sourceFile*
  // and read encrypted bytes from it
  CryptoStream encryptedInStream = new CryptoStream(inStream,
➥ aes.CreateEncryptor(), CryptoStreamMode.Read);
  // Write the IV out to the ciphertext file as the first bytes in the file.
  outStream.Write(aes.IV, 0, aes.IV.Length);
  // Now we're ready to encrypt. Read the bytes from the CryptoStream
  // in a loop until there aren't any more (end-of-file), writing to
  // the output file as we go. We need a buffer to hold what we're going to
  // read, and bytesRead tells us how many bytes in buffer are
  //valid ciphertext.
  int bytesRead;
  byte[] buffer = new byte[1024]; // read 1K at a time
  do {
      bytesRead = encryptedInStream.Read(buffer,0,1024);
      outStream.Write(buffer, 0, bytesRead);
```

LISTING 30.3   Continued

```
  } while (bytesRead > 0);
  // Done!  Close() the streams we used.
  inStream.Close();
  outStream.Close();
  return;
}
```

Notice that when we create the aes object using `Rijndael.Create()`, the object is generated with a random initialization vector; each file we encrypt with this method will use a different random IV. (In fact, encrypting the same file twice will yield two different ciphertext files because the IVs used for the two files will be different.) The method uses a `CryptoStream` in "read" mode because it is slightly more convenient in this case where we are writing both the unencrypted IV and ciphertext to the same output file.

Decrypting a file is also straightforward; the only tricky part is that we have to read the IV from the file before creating the `CryptoStream` and `ICryptoTransform`.

LISTING 30.4   Decrypting an On-Disk File to a Second File

```
public static void DecryptFile(byte[] key, String sourceFile,
➥ String destFile) {
  // initialize with random key and IV
  Rijndael aes = Rijndael.Create();
  // Create an array to hold the IV read from the file:
  byte[] realIV = new byte[aes.IV.Length];
  // create FileStreams for source and dest
  FileStream inStream = new FileStream(sourceFile, FileMode.Open);
  FileStream outStream = new FileStream(destFile, FileMode.Create);
  // We want to read the IV out to the sourceFile unencrypted,
  // so in this case we can wrap a CryptoStream around the *destFile*
  // and write encrypted bytes into it. The output bytes will be decrypted
  // First, read the IV in
  inStream.Read(realIV, 0, realIV.Length);
  // set the key and IV of the aes object
  aes.Key = key;
  aes.IV = realIV;
  // Create the CryptoStream
  CryptoStream decryptedOutStream = new CryptoStream(outStream,
➥ aes.CreateDecryptor(), CryptoStreamMode.Write);
  // Now we're ready to decrypt.
  int bytesRead;
```

LISTING 30.4   Continued

```
byte[] buffer = new byte[1024]; // read 1K at a time
do {
  bytesRead = inStream.Read(buffer,0,1024);
  decryptedOutStream.Write(buffer, 0, bytesRead);
} while (bytesRead > 0);
// We've read everything, so now call FlushFinalBlock() to write out any
// remaining bytes
decryptedOutStream.FlushFinalBlock();
inStream.Close();
decryptedOutStream.Close();
return;
}
```

Performing Multiple Cryptographic Transforms Using Cascaded CryptoStreams
For our final example in this section, we demonstrate how CryptoStreams themselves can be cascaded to perform multiple ICryptoTransforms in sequence. We
modify the task presented in Listings 30.3 and 30.4 slightly. We want to encrypt and
decrypt files on-disk, using random initialization vectors, but we additionally require
that the encrypted ciphertext be stored Base64-encoded. Base64 is an encoding algorithm that represents binary data in a subset of the ASCII character set that is suitable for printing or sending through text email systems. It is commonly used today
when sending attachments in MIME email messages and is also used in XML Digital
Signatures (see Chapter 32, "Using Cryptography with the .NET Framework: Creating
and Verifying XML Digital Signatures"). Base64 encoding works by converting three
bytes of data into four encoded bytes, where each of the encoded bytes is one of the
following 64 characters: a–z, A–Z, 0–9, /, or +. (Additionally, the equal sign character,
=, is used for padding any short blocks.)

The ToBase64Transform and FromBase64Transform classes in
System.Security.Cryptography are ICryptoTransforms that implement Base64
encoding and decoding. To Base64 encode our ciphertext, all we need to do is pass
the ciphertext through a second CryptoStream that uses a ToBase64Transform.
Listing 30.5 shows the modified code for EncryptFile using a Base64 encoding.
(Note that we do not Base64 encode the initialization vector in this example.)

LISTING 30.5   Encrypting and Base64-Encoding an On-Disk File with Random IV
Generation

```
public static void EncryptFile(byte[] key, String sourceFile,
➥ String destFile) {
  // initialize with random key and IV
  Rijndael aes = Rijndael.Create();
```

LISTING 30.5   Continued

```
aes.Key = key;
FileStream inStream = new FileStream(sourceFile, FileMode.Open);
FileStream outStream = new FileStream(destFile, FileMode.Create);
CryptoStream encryptedInStream = new CryptoStream(inStream,
➥ aes.CreateEncryptor(), CryptoStreamMode.Read);
   // We want to Base64-encode the ciphertext that comes out
   // of encryptedInStream, so we simply wrap a second CryptoStream
   // around it that uses a ToBase64Transform. When we read from
   // b64EncodedInStream, we will read transformed bytes that came
   // from encryptedInStream, which in turn are encrypted bytes that
   // came from inStream (the sourceFile)
CryptoStream b64EncodedInStream = new CryptoStream(encryptedInStream,
➥ new ToBase64Transform(), CryptoStreamMode.Read);
   // Write the IV out
outStream.Write(aes.IV, 0, aes.IV.Length);
   // Now we're ready to encrypt.
int bytesRead;
byte[] buffer = new byte[1024]; // read 1K at a time
do {
   // read from the wrapping CryptoStream!
   bytesRead = b64EncodedInStream.Read(buffer,0,1024);
   outStream.Write(buffer, 0, bytesRead);
} while (bytesRead > 0);
   // Done! Close all streams
inStream.Close();
outStream.Close();
return;
}
```

Bytes read from the b64EncodedInStream are produced by Base64-encoding bytes read from the underlying stream encrytpedInStream. The bytes produced by encryptedInStream are, in turn, produced by encrypting the bytes read from *its* underlying stream (inStream). Thus, this routine cascades two distinct data transformations, represented by the two ICryptoTransforms.

Decrypting a Base64-encoded ciphertext file produced by EncryptFile is similarly straightforward; a version of DecryptFile that undoes the Base64 encoding before performing the decryption is shown in Listing 30.6.

LISTING 30.6   Base64-Decoding and Decrypting an On-Disk File

```
public static void DecryptFile(byte[] key, String sourceFile,
➥ String destFile) {
  // initialize with random key and IV
  Rijndael aes = Rijndael.Create();
  // Create an array to hold the IV read from the file:
  byte[] realIV = new byte[aes.IV.Length];
  // create FileStreams for source and dest
  FileStream inStream = new FileStream(sourceFile, FileMode.Open);
  FileStream outStream = new FileStream(destFile, FileMode.Create);
  // First, read the IV in
  inStream.Read(realIV, 0, realIV.Length);
  // set the key and IV of the aes object
  aes.Key = key;
  aes.IV = realIV;
  // Create the CryptoStreams. We need two: one to undo the Base64 encoding
  // and one to decrypt. We wrap the b64DecodedOutStream around the
  // decryptedOutStream because we want to do the Base64 decoding
  // before decrypting
  CryptoStream decryptedOutStream = new CryptoStream(outStream,
➥ aes.CreateDecryptor(), CryptoStreamMode.Write);
  CryptoStream b64DecodedOutStream = new CryptoStream(decryptedOutStream,
➥ new FromBase64Transform(), CryptoStreamMode.Write);
  // Now we're ready to decrypt.
  int bytesRead;
  byte[] buffer = new byte[1024]; // read 1K at a time
  do {
    bytesRead = inStream.Read(buffer,0,1024);
    // Write to the Base64 decoder
    b64DecodedOutStream.Write(buffer, 0, bytesRead);
  } while (bytesRead > 0);
  // We've read everything, so now call FlushFinalBlock() to write out any
  // remaining bytes
  b64DecodedOutStream.FlushFinalBlock();
  inStream.Close();
  b64DecodedOutStream.Close();
  return;
}
```

The Base64 encoding is removed by passing the data through a
FromBase64Transform object in the b64DecodedOutStream CryptoStream. The

unencoded bytes are then automatically passed on to the second (inner) `CryptoStream`, `decryptedOutStream`, which then writes the decrypted plain text out to the desired file.

This concludes our introduction to using symmetric ciphers in the .NET Framework. Symmetric ciphers are one of the fundamental building blocks of cryptographic protocols, and we will use them extensively throughout the remainder of this chapter and the next in conjunction with hash functions and asymmetric algorithms.

Using Cryptographic Hash Functions

We turn our attention now to the portion of the .NET Framework object model that represents cryptographic hash functions. Cryptographic hash functions are represented by the `HashAlgorithm` class and its descendants. In this section, we describe the hash algorithms that are included in the .NET Framework class library, how to create a `HashAlgorithm` object corresponding to the algorithm you desire, and how to compute hashes using these objects over static and streaming data.

Creating `HashAlgorithm` Objects

The .NET Framework includes "in-the-box" support for the hash algorithms commonly used today in cryptographic protocols. Table 30.3 lists the hash algorithms that are supported in the .NET Framework class libraries, along with their implementation classes.

> **NOTE**
>
> In keeping with the naming convention introduced for symmetric ciphers, implementations that are built on top of the Win32 CryptoAPIs are named *CryptoServiceProvider, and implementations that are written in managed code are named *Managed.

TABLE 30.3 Hash Algorithms Included in the .NET Framework

Hash Algorithm	Hash Size in Bits	Implementation Class(es)
MD5	128	MD5CryptoServiceProvider
SHA-1	160	SHA1CryptoServiceProvider
		SHA1Managed
SHA-256	256	SHA256Managed
SHA-384	384	SHA384Managed
SHA-512	512	SHA512Managed

By far, the most common hash function in use today is SHA-1, the Secure Hash Algorithm developed by the U.S. National Security Agency (NSA) and National Institutes of Standards and Technology (NIST) as part of their Digital Signature Standard (DSS). SHA-1 is a 160-bit hash algorithm, meaning that for any size input, it generates a 160-bit output. MD5 (short for "Message Digest Algorithm 5") is an older hash function designed by Ron Rivest that is still widely used today. SHA-256, SHA-384, and SHA-512 are new hash functions designed by NSA and NIST to complement Rijndael, the AES cipher. They are sized so that their output values are twice the length of the allowable key sizes in Rijndael.

> **NOTE**
>
> The reason SHA-256, SHA-384, and SHA-512 are sized as they are is so that a brute force attack against them will be comparable to a brute force attack against Rijndael with a 128-, 192- or 256-bit key. A brute force attack against Rijndael takes exponential time proportional to the key length, for example, $O(2^{128})$ operations to brute force a 128-bit key. A birthday attack against SHA-256—that is, the average time it would take to find a colliding pair of inputs x, y with SHA-256(x) = SHA-256(y)—is also exponential proportional to half the key length, for example, $O(2^{256/2}) = O(2^{128})$.

Computing Hash Values Using the `ComputeHash()` Methods

The .NET Framework makes it very easy to compute hash values of streams and arrays of bytes. If you just want to compute the hash of some binary data, all you need to do is create an appropriate `HashAlgorithm` object corresponding to the algorithm you desire and call the `ComputeHash()` method on that object. The following computes the SHA-1 hash of an array of bytes stored in the `myMessage` variable:

```
SHA1 sha1 = SHA1.Create(); // create a new SHA1 hash object
byte[] hashValue = sha1.ComputeHash(myMessage);
```

> **NOTE**
>
> Note that although hash algorithms are typically defined to work binary data of any length, the implementations provided in the .NET Framework only work for inputs that are a multiple of 8 bits in length (for example, consist of an whole number of bytes).

You can also compute the hash of a portion of an array by using the `ComputeHash` overload that accepts an array offset and count:

```
byte[] hashValue = sha1.ComputeHash(myMessage, offset, count);
```

There is also an overloaded ComputeHash method for hashing the contents of a stream of bytes. The stream must support reading, and hashing will begin from the current position of the stream and proceed until no more bytes are available. The following is a code snippet to hash the contents of the file "c:\hashinput.txt":

```
FileStream inputFile = new FileStream("c:\\hashinput.txt", FileMode.Open);
SHA1 sha1 = SHA1.Create();
byte[] hashValue = sha1.ComputeHash(inputFile);
inputFile.Close();
```

You can call ComputeHash() multiple times on the same hash object to compute multiple hashes; HashAlgorithm objects automatically reset their internal state after computing a hash value and are immediately ready to be used again. The HashSize property on a HashAlgorithm returns the size, in bits, of the hashes computed by the object. There is also a Hash property on the object that returns the most recently computed hash value.

Our next example program shows how a single HashAlgorithm object can be reused to compute multiple hash values. The program shown in Listing 30.7 takes as input a single command-line argument, a directory path, and prints out the SHA-256 hash value for every file within the directory. (This program ignores subdirectories, although it would be easy to modify it to recursively compute the hash of every file in the input directory or one of its subdirectories.) The PrintByteArray method is a subroutine that prints byte arrays as a hexadecimal string with spaces inserted every eight characters for readability.

LISTING 30.7   Compute and Print the SHA-256 Hash of Every File in a Directory

```
using System;
using System.IO;
using System.Security.Cryptography;

public class HashDir {

  // This routine pretty-prints a byte array
  public static void PrintByteArray(byte[] array)  {
    int i;
    for (i = 0; i < array.Length; i++) {
      Console.Write(String.Format("{0:X2}",array[i]));
      if ((i % 4) == 3) Console.Write(" ");
    }
    Console.WriteLine();
  }
```

LISTING 30.7   Continued

```
public static void Main(String[] args) {
  if (args.Length < 1) {
    Console.WriteLine("Usage: hashdir <directory>");
    return;
  }
  // Create a DirectoryInfo object representing a directory
  DirectoryInfo dir = new DirectoryInfo(args[0]);
  // Get FileInfo objects for every file in the directory
  FileInfo[] files = dir.GetFiles();
  // Initialize a SHA-256 hash object and output variable
  SHA256 sha256 = SHA256.Create();
  byte[] hashValue;
  // Loop over the files, computing & printing hash values
  foreach (FileInfo fInfo in files) {
    // Create a fileStream for the file
    FileStream fileStream = fInfo.Open(FileMode.Open);
    // Compute the hash of the fileStream
    hashValue = sha256.ComputeHash(fileStream);
    // Write the name of the file to the Console
    Console.Write(fInfo.Name+": ");
    // Write the hash value to the Console
    PrintByteArray(hashValue);
    // Close the file
    fileStream.Close();
  }
  return;
  }
}
```

Notice that all of the file hashes are computed using a single SHA256 hash object and repeated calls to its ComputeHash method.

Computing Hash Values of Streaming Data Using a CryptoStream

The ComputeHash methods on HashAlgorithm objects provide the easiest way to calculate hashes for fixed streams and arrays of bytes, but if you want to hash data as it is being generated, these methods are not useful. To hash data generated over time, you will need to use a HashAlgorithm object in conjunction with a CryptoStream. The HashAlgorithm class implements the ICryptoTransform interface so that every object that is a descendant of HashAlgorithm can be "wrapped" around a stream, just like an encryption or decryption transform.

HashAlgorithms work a little differently as ICryptoTransforms than the other trans-forms we have looked at already in that they do not actually modify the data being passed through them. When you use a HashAlgorithm object as an ICryptoTransform, you pass the to-be-hashed data through the transform to build up the hash state within the HashAlgorithm object, but the output of the transform itself is the input unchanged. The value of the Hash property of the HashAlgorithm contains the hash of the content that has passed through the CryptoStream and is constantly updated as data is written to or read from the stream.

NOTE

Notice that the InputBlockSize and OutputBlockSize of a HashAlgorithm are both one byte. This is because the HashAlgorithm is a "pass-through" transform when used in this mode.

Why do HashAlgorithms pass the source data through themselves unmodified when used as an ICryptoTransform, instead of returning the hash value as the output of the transform? The goal behind this particular design choice is to simplify common security protocol operations that mix hashing and other transforms together. One such common operation is "hash-and-encrypt," in which to-be-encrypted plain text is hashed, the hash value is then appended to the plain text, and then the resulting plain text and hash are encrypted values. By including the hash of the plain text in the encryption stream, the intended recipient of the ciphertext can easily verify whether the ciphertext was tampered with after leaving the sender. Any change in the ciphertext will change the resulting decryption output, and the included hash value will no longer match the hash of the decrypted ciphertext. The version of EncryptFile shown in Listing 30.8 is a modification of the code in Listing 30.3 that implements a form of hash-and-encrypt; it hashes the input plain text using the SHA256 algorithm and then encrypts both the plain text and the hash value using Rijndael. (As in Listing 30.3, we also use a random initialization vector that is prepended to the output ciphertext.)

LISTING 30.8   Hash-and-Encrypt a Source File to a Target File, Appending the Hash Value to the End of the Encrypted File

```
public static void EncryptFile(byte[] key, String sourceFile,
➡ String destFile) {
  // initialize with random key and IV
  Rijndael aes = Rijndael.Create();
  aes.Key = key;
  FileStream inStream = new FileStream(sourceFile, FileMode.Open);
  FileStream outStream = new FileStream(destFile, FileMode.Create);
  SHA256 sha256 = SHA256.Create();
```

LISTING 30.8   Continued

```
// Hash the input file as we read from it,
// encrypt as we write to the output file
CryptoStream hashedInStream = new CryptoStream(inStream,
➥ sha256, CryptoStreamMode.Read);
CryptoStream encryptedOutStream = new CryptoStream(outStream,
➥ aes.CreateEncryptor(), CryptoStreamMode.Write);
// Write the IV out
outStream.Write(aes.IV, 0, aes.IV.Length);
// Now we're ready to hash and encrypt.
int bytesRead;
byte[] buffer = new byte[1024]; // read 1K at a time
do {
  // read from the wrapping CryptoStream!
  bytesRead = hashedInStream.Read(buffer,0,1024);
  encryptedOutStream.Write(buffer, 0, bytesRead);
} while (bytesRead > 0);
// Done encrypting, we can close the input stream
inStream.Close();
// Write the hash value out to the encryption stream
encryptedOutStream.Write(sha256.Hash, 0, sha256.Hash.Length);
encryptedOutStream.FlushFinalBlock();
outStream.Close();
return;
}
```

In this example, note that we have not wrapped one CryptoStream around the other, but rather the hashing CryptoStream around the input stream and the encrypting CryptoStream around the output. For hash-and-encrypt, this particular configuration is easier to work with than the double-wrapping used in Listing 30.3 because we want to hash just the input plain text but encrypt both the plain text and the resulting hash value. So the first CryptoStream, hashedInStream, uses a SHA256 hash algorithm object as its ICryptoTransform and wraps it around the plain text stream in read mode, and the second CryptoStream wraps the encryption transform around the desired output stream in write mode. The hash of the input plain text is automatically calculated as we read bytes from hashedInStream; all we need to do is write it to the encryptedOutStream after all the ciphertext hash been written.

Decrypting the ciphertext file produced by this version of EncryptFile is a little trickier than producing it, because we need to separate out the encrypted hash value and verify it. In the example method shown in Listing 30.9, we decrypt the ciphertext into a MemoryStream so that we can access the entire decrypted file as a buffer (the msArray variable). After we have the buffer, we can then compute the hash of the plain text portion of the buffer (hashValue) and compare it to the hash value stored in the buffer (msHashValue).

LISTING 30.9   Decrypt and Verify the Hash of a Hashed-and-Encrypted File

```
public static void DecryptFile(byte[] key, String sourceFile,
➡ String destFile) {
  // initialize with random key and IV
  Rijndael aes = Rijndael.Create();
  // Create an array to hold the IV read from the file:
  byte[] realIV = new byte[aes.IV.Length];
  // create FileStreams for source and dest
  FileStream inStream = new FileStream(sourceFile, FileMode.Open);
  FileStream outStream = new FileStream(destFile, FileMode.Create);
  // First, read the IV in
  inStream.Read(realIV, 0, realIV.Length);
  // set the key and IV of the aes object
  aes.Key = key;
  aes.IV = realIV;
  MemoryStream ms = new MemoryStream();
  CryptoStream decryptedOutStream = new CryptoStream(ms,
➡ aes.CreateDecryptor(), CryptoStreamMode.Write);
  // Now we're ready to decrypt.
  int bytesRead;
  byte[] buffer = new byte[1024]; // read 1K at a time
  do {
    bytesRead = inStream.Read(buffer,0,1024);
    decryptedOutStream.Write(buffer, 0, bytesRead);
  } while (bytesRead > 0);
  // We've read everything, so now call FlushFinalBlock() to write out any
  // remaining bytes
  decryptedOutStream.FlushFinalBlock();
  inStream.Close();
  decryptedOutStream.Close();
  // Now, compute the hash value of everything but the hash in ms
  SHA256 sha256 = SHA256.Create();
  int hashSizeInBytes = sha256.HashSize/8;
  byte[] msArray = ms.ToArray();
  byte[] msHashValue = new byte[hashSizeInBytes];
  Array.Copy(msArray, msArray.Length - hashSizeInBytes,
➡ msHashValue, 0, hashSizeInBytes);
```

LISTING 30.9   Continued

```
  byte[] hashValue = sha256.ComputeHash(msArray, 0,
➥ msArray.Length - hashSizeInBytes);
  // compare hashValue and msHashValue
  for (int i=0; i< hashSizeInBytes; i++) {
    if (msHashValue[i] != hashValue[i]) {
      Console.WriteLine("Hash values differ!
➥ Encrytped file has been tampered with!");
      return;
    }
  }
  return;
}
```

If the ciphertext file has not been modified since it was created, this routine will
decrypt the ciphertext into the plain text file silently. If, however, a modification has
been made to the ciphertext file, then the computed hash value will not match the
stored hash value and `DecryptFile` will print out a warning.

"Hash-and-encrypt" is one mechanism for providing authentication and integrity
services for plain text. If the computed hash matches the stored hash, the recipient
knows two facts about the plain text. First, the plain text originated with an entity
that holds a copy of the encryption key; otherwise, the ciphertext would not be
decodable by the receiver. Second, the ciphertext was not modified after being
encrypted by the sender. In the next section, we describe another technique for
providing authentication and integrity for data that does not require an explicit
encryption step.

Using Keyed Hash Functions

Keyed hash functions are a subset of cryptographic hash functions that provide data
authentication services in addition to integrity protection. As their name implies,
keyed hash functions work by mixing a shared secret key with the to-be-hashed
message to generate a hash value. That is, the hash value $h = f(M, k)$, where f() is the
keyed hash function, M is the to-be-hashed message (of arbitrary length), and k is
the secret key. Changing either the message or the secret key will change the
computed hash value.

Keyed hash functions are represented in the .NET Framework as subclasses of the
`KeyedHashAlgorithm` abstract class, which itself is a subclass of `HashAlgorithm`.
Because every `KeyedHashAlgorithm` is a `HashAlgorithm`, a `KeyedHashAlgorithm` object
has `Hash` and `HashSize` properties and can be used as an `ICryptoTransform`.
Additionally, a `KeyedHashAlgorithm` has a `Key` property for setting and retrieving the

secret key associated with the instance object. As is the case with `SymmetricAlgorithms`, a random `Key` value will be generated when a `KeyedHashAlgorithm` object is constructed if you do not specify the key to use. Table 30.4 lists the keyed hash functions that are included in the .NET Framework class library; of course, additional algorithms can be added by subclassing `KeyedHashAlgorithm`.

TABLE 30.4   Keyed Hash Algorithms Included in the .NET Framework

Hash Algorithm (Implementation Class)	Legal Key Sizes (Bytes)	Output Hash Size (Bytes)
HMAC-SHA1 (HMACSHA1)	All key sizes are legal. Recommended size is 64 bytes.	20
MAC-3DES-CBC (MACTripleDES)	24	8

Keyed hash functions are often constructed from other hash algorithms or block ciphers; the two such algorithms included in the .NET Framework are representative of these construction techniques:

- HMACSHA1—HMAC, short for *hash-based message authentication code*, is a general method for constructing a keyed hash algorithm from a hash algorithm. The HMACSHA1 class implements the HMAC construction using SHA-1 as the underlying hash function; HMAC using SHA-1 is frequently used as a keyed hash algorithm. The HMAC construction mixes a secret key with the message data, hashes the result with the hash function, mixes that hash value with the secret key again, and then applies the hash function a second time. The output hash will be 20 bytes in length—the size of a SHA-1 hash. The secret key input to HMAC-SHA1 can be of any length, but if it is more than 64 bytes long, it will be hashed (using SHA-1) to derive a 64-byte key. (The internal construction of HMAC limits the key size to 64 bytes.)

- MACTripleDES—MACTripleDES is a keyed hash algorithm constructed from a block cipher, in this case TripleDES. MACTripleDES simply encrypts the to-be-hashed message with TripleDES using cipher block chaining (CBC) mode, zero padding for short blocks, a user-supplied secret key, and an initialization vector of all zeroes. The keyed hash of the message is the final block of the encrypted ciphertext and is 8 bytes in length. The secret key must be 24 bytes in length because it is used as a key for three-key TripleDES.

Computing a keyed hash value in the .NET Framework is almost identical to computing a non-keyed hash value, except for the additional `Key` property. The following code shows how you compute the HMAC-SHA1 keyed hash of an array of bytes stored in the `myMessage` variable with key `myKey`:

```
HMACSHA1 hmacsha1 = new HMACSHA1();
hmacsha1.Key = myKey;
byte[] hashValue = hmacsha1.ComputeHash(myMessage);
```

You can also specify the key value as an argument to the object constructor:

```
HMACSHA1 hmacsha1 = new HMACSHA1(myKey);
byte[] hashValue = hmacsha1.ComputeHash(myMessage);
```

There are also overloaded versions of ComputeHash that accept an array offset and count:

```
byte[] hashValue = hmacsha1.ComputeHash(myMessage, offset, count);
```

Additionally, you can use a KeyedHashAlgorithm object as an ICryptoTransform within a CryptoStream.

In the EncryptFile method of Listing 30.8, we used a "hash-and-encrypt" operation to provide authentication and integrity protection for the contents of a file. Keyed hash functions also provide authentication and integrity services; we can use an HMAC-SHA1 keyed hash to provide the same guarantees as "hash-and-encrypt" without using encryption. Listings 30.10 and 30.11 show the source code for two methods, EncodeFile and DecodeFile, which produce and consume authenticated and integrity-protected files. The EncodeFile routine takes as input three arguments: a secret key, a source filename, and a target filename. EncodeFile computes the HMACSHA1 keyed hash of the source file and then writes the concatenation of the hash value and the contents of the source file to the target file. The DecodeFile method takes two input arguments—the secret key and the name of the encoded file—and verifies that the file has not changed since it was written by EncodeFile.

LISTING 30.10   Compute a Keyed Hash for a Source File; Create a Target File with the Keyed Hash Prepended to the Contents of the Source File

```
public static void EncodeFile(byte[] key, String sourceFile,
➥ String destFile) {
  // initialize the keyed hash object
  HMACSHA1 hmacsha1 = new HMACSHA1(key);
  FileStream inStream = new FileStream(sourceFile, FileMode.Open);
  FileStream outStream = new FileStream(destFile, FileMode.Create);
  // Statically compute the hash of the input file
  byte[] hashValue = hmacsha1.ComputeHash(inStream);
  // Reset inStream to the beginning of the file
  inStream.Position = 0;
  // Write the computed hash value to the output file
```

LISTING 30.10   Continued

```
outStream.Write(hashValue, 0, hashValue.Length);
// copy the contents of the sourceFile to the destFile
int bytesRead;
byte[] buffer = new byte[1024]; // read 1K at a time
do {
  // read from the wrapping CryptoStream!
  bytesRead = inStream.Read(buffer,0,1024);
  outStream.Write(buffer, 0, bytesRead);
} while (bytesRead > 0);
// Done encrypting, close the streams
inStream.Close();
outStream.Close();
return;
}
```

This function is somewhat simpler than the EncryptFile method of Listing 30.8 in that it does not use any CryptoStreams. Because we chose to put the keyed hash value at the beginning of the encoded file, there is no advantage in setting up a CryptoStream to compute the keyed hash value. We will always have to read the input file twice—once to compute the hash value and a second time to write the contents of the input file to the output file. The code for the corresponding DecodeFile method is similarly straightforward.

LISTING 30.11   Verify the Integrity of a File Associated with a Keyed Hash Value

```
public static bool DecodeFile(byte[] key, String sourceFile) {
  // initialize the keyed hash object
  HMACSHA1 hmacsha1 = new HMACSHA1(key);
  // Create an array to hold the keyed hash value read from the file:
  byte[] storedHash = new byte[hmacsha1.HashSize/8];
  // create a FileStream for the source file
  FileStream inStream = new FileStream(sourceFile, FileMode.Open);
  // Read in the storedHash
  inStream.Read(storedHash, 0, storedHash.Length);
  // Compute the hash of the remaining contents of the file
  // The stream is properly positioned at the beginning of the content,
  // immediately after the stored hash value
  byte[] computedHash = hmacsha1.ComputeHash(inStream);
  // compare the computed hash with the stored value
  for (int i=0; i< storedHash.Length; i++) {
    if (computedHash[i] != storedHash[i]) {
```

LISTING 30.11   Continued

```
    Console.WriteLine("Hash values differ!
➥ Encoded file has been tampered with!");
      return false;
    }
  }
  Console.WriteLine("Hash values agree -- no tampering occurred.");
  return true;
}
```

DecodeFile is implemented as a Boolean function that returns true when the keyed hash value matches the calculated hash value; a message is also displayed on the console reporting the result of the hash comparison.

This concludes our discussion of the differences between (nonkeyed) hash functions and keyed hash functions. Except for the secret key, a KeyedHashAlgorithm object behaves the same as any other HashAlgorithm object. If you have an established shared secret between two parties, a keyed hash value is often the simplest way to convey data origin authentication (that is, who hashed the file) and integrity protection (tamper-resistance).

Random Number Generation and Key Derivation

In all of the examples so far in this chapter, when a secret key was necessary, it has been specified as an input parameter to the method. This is all well and good in the abstract, but somewhere in your program you will need to generate a good sequence of bytes to use as a random key for an encryption or keyed hash algorithm. How one generates good values to use as secret key material is the subject of this section. We now discuss two smaller portions of the cryptographic object hierarchy that are still extremely important to writing crypto-aware applications—random number generators and secret key derivation classes.

Generating Pseudo-Random Numbers

The ability to generate a random number, or a random sequence of bytes, is core to almost every cryptographic protocol. If Alice and Bob want to share a secret key so that they can later exchange encrypted information, they need to generate a random sequence of bytes to use as the secret key. An adversary that is able to predict the sequence of bytes Alice and Bob generate with high accuracy would later be able to eavesdrop on their encryption conversation. Obviously, we want our sources of random numbers to generate values that defy prediction by an adversary.

The random number generators included in the .NET Framework are properly classi-fied as pseudo-random number generators (PRNGs). We say that a function is a *pseudo-random number generator* if it is computationally unfeasible to predict the next number the function will output given all the previous numbers that have been output. More precisely, if a function f(x) outputs a sequence of bits x_0, x_1, x_2, and so on, we say that f(x) is a pseudo-random bit generator if the probability of correctly determining x_n given x_0, x_1, and so on, x_{n-1} is within an infinitesimally small amount of ?. That is, a computationally feasible process can do no better than random guess-ing to predict the next output bit of the function f.

The .NET Framework PRNGs work by collecting seed information from various portions of the operating system and then using this seed information to generate a cryptographically strong sequence of random numbers that cannot be predicted with better-than-guessing accuracy. Generating truly random numbers is quite difficult; the best sources of random bits are special-purpose devices that use physical systems to produce randomness. Some computer processors now include on-chip circuitry for generating random bits, and the PRNG provided in the .NET Framework will leverage this hardware when it is available to the operating system.

In the .NET Framework cryptographic object model, classes implementing random number generators descend from the abstract `RandomNumberGenerator` class. Every subclass of the `RandomNumberGenerator` class implements two methods for getting sequences of random bytes from the generator—`GetBytes` and `GetNonZeroBytes`. These routines accept an array of bytes as input and fill the array with random bytes or random non-zero bytes, respectively. It will almost always be the case that you will want to use the `GetBytes()` method to generate your random sequences of bytes; only exclude zero bytes if you have an application-specific reason for needing to eliminate randomly chosen zeros. The following is a code snippet for generating a random 256-bit Rijndael key using the .NET Framework's `RandomNumberGenerator` class:

```
// Create a new instance of the default implementation of the
// RandomNumberGenerator abstract class.
RandomNumberGenerator rng = RandomNumberGenerator.Create();
// Create an array that will hold the random values
byte[] rbytes = new byte[32]; // 256 bits/8 bits per byte = 32 bytes
// Fill the array with random bytes
rng.GetBytes(rbytes);
```

The default implementation class for `RandomNumberGenerator` is the `RNGCryptoServiceProvider` class, which is a wrapper on top of the PRNG provided in Windows by CryptoAPI. Unlike other random number generators with which you may be familiar, such as the `rand()` or `random()` functions in the C language library or even the `System.Random` class in the .NET Framework, the CryptoAPI PRNG does not produce reproducible sequences. That is, it is not possible to generate multiple instances of RNGCryptoServiceProvider that will reproducibly return the same sequences of random numbers.

> **CAUTION**
>
> Never use numbers derived from the System.Random class for cryptographic purposes. The System.Random class generates reproducible sequences of "random" numbers, and they are not sufficiently random to be used in a cryptographic protocol.

Deriving Keys from User Input

The RandomNumberGenerator class is great for generating pseudo-random numbers to use as cryptographic keys, but long strings of random digits are difficult for users to remember. For many applications, users want to be able to perform cryptographic operations using a password or passphrase as the encryption "key." In general, passwords make lousy cryptographic keys because to be memorable, passwords are generally not sufficiently random. Also, passwords tend to be composed of characters that are easy to type on a keyboard, so they do not uniformly use all possible values. To bridge the gap between user-friendly passwords and crypto-friendly sequences of bytes, cryptographic algorithms have been developed to derive key material from a password. This section describes one such algorithm that is included in the .NET Framework cryptography classes.

The DeriveBytes abstract class in the cryptographic object hierarchy represents any algorithm that derives bytes suitable for use as key material from another input. The PasswordDeriveBytes class implements one such algorithm that is an extension of the PBKDF1 algorithm defined in the PKCS #5 v2.0 standard and is documented in IETF RFC 2898. This algorithm accepts four values as input—a password, a salt value, an iteration count, and a cryptographic hash algorithm. The algorithm repeatedly applies the hash algorithm to a combination of the password and the salt, ultimately returning a sequence of bytes after running for the specified number of iterations.

> **CAUTION**
>
> We strongly recommend using randomly generated salt values when using PasswordDeriveBytes to create a random session key from a password. Salt values are random values mixed into the key-generation process to make a dictionary attack more difficult. (A dictionary attack is a brute force attack that iterates through a dictionary of likely passwords and precomputes the output of the algorithm applied to each individual password. This database can be searched very quickly once generated.) Salt values need not be kept secret; they must be known to all parties that are expected to derive the same key from the same input password.

By default, the `PasswordDeriveBytes` class uses SHA-1 as the hash algorithm and an interation count of 100. These defaults are appropriate for most applications, but if you are interoperating with another implementation of RFC 2898, you may have to use other hash algorithms or iteration counts to match those used by other applications.

The following code snippet shows how to derive an array of 16 bytes from a password string:

```
String password = "MySecretPassword";
// use no salt (second argument is a zero-length array)
PasswordDeriveBytes pdb = new PasswordDeriveBytes(password, new byte[0]);
byte[] derivedBytes = pdb.GetBytes(16);
```

In this example, no salt is used for simplicity. Using salt makes attacks against the algorithm harder, but like initialization vectors for symmetric ciphers, you have to know the salt to be able to derive the same sequence of key bytes from a given password. Salt values need not be kept secret. As the next example shows, we can persist salt in an encrypted file just as we do with initialization vectors.

For our last example of stream-based cryptography, we combine symmetric ciphers, random number generation, and a key derivation function to create a robust, password-based file encryption and decryption program. The program shown in Listing 30.12 takes four command-line arguments:

- A string argument, either -e or -d, to indicate whether to encrypt or decrypt

- A password

- The name of the source file to encrypt or decrypt

- The name of the output file in which to store the encrypted or decrypted contents

For each file, a 128-bit random salt value is generated that is combined with the password to create a 256-bit Rijndael encryption key. A 128-bit random initialization vector is also used. The IV and salt values are stored at the beginning of the encrypted file, before the encrypted content, so that they can be recovered and used when decrypting the contents.

LISTING 30.12   Password-Based Encryption and Decryption of Files

```
using System;
using System.IO;
using System.Security.Cryptography;
```

LISTING 30.12 Continued

```
public class Encrypt {

  public static void EncryptFile(String password, String sourceFile,
➡ String destFile) {
    // Derive a 256-bit Rijndael key from the password
    // We first have to generate a random salt value
    RandomNumberGenerator rng = RandomNumberGenerator.Create();
    byte[] salt = new byte[16]; // 16 bytes == 128 bits
    rng.GetBytes(salt);
    // Now compute the Rijndael key
    PasswordDeriveBytes pdb = new PasswordDeriveBytes(password, salt);
    byte[] key = pdb.GetBytes(32); // 32 bytes == 256 bits
    // Create a new Rijndael object, it'll have a random key and IV
    Rijndael aes = Rijndael.Create();
    // set the key to be the derived key
    aes.Key = key;
    // create FileStreams for source and dest
    FileStream inStream = new FileStream(sourceFile, FileMode.Open);
    FileStream outStream = new FileStream(destFile, FileMode.Create);
    // We want to write the salt and IV out to the destFile unencrypted,
    // so in this case we can wrap a CryptoStream around the *sourceFile*
    // and read encrypted bytes from it
    CryptoStream encryptedInStream = new CryptoStream(inStream,
➡ aes.CreateEncryptor(), CryptoStreamMode.Read);
    // Write the salt out
    outStream.Write(salt, 0, salt.Length);
    // Write the IV out
    outStream.Write(aes.IV, 0, aes.IV.Length);
    // Now we're ready to encrypt. Read the bytes from the CryptoStream
    // in a loop until there aren't any more (end-of-file), writing to
    // the output file as we go. We need a buffer to hold what we're going
    // to read, and bytesRead tells us how many bytes in buffer are
    // valid ciphertext.
    int bytesRead;
    byte[] buffer = new byte[1024]; // read 1K at a time
    do {
      bytesRead = encryptedInStream.Read(buffer,0,1024);
      outStream.Write(buffer, 0, bytesRead);
    } while (bytesRead > 0);
    // Done!
    inStream.Close();
```

LISTING 30.12   Continued

```
    outStream.Close();
    return;
  }


  public static void DecryptFile(String password, String sourceFile,
➡ String destFile) {
    // Create a new Rijndael object
    Rijndael aes = Rijndael.Create();
    // Create an array to hold the IV read from the file:
    byte[] IV = new byte[aes.IV.Length];
    // Create an array to hold the salt read from the file:
    byte[] salt = new byte[16];
    // create FileStreams for source and dest
    FileStream inStream = new FileStream(sourceFile, FileMode.Open);
    FileStream outStream = new FileStream(destFile, FileMode.Create);
    // We want to read the IV out to the sourceFile unencrypted,
    // so in this case we can wrap a CryptoStream around the *destFile*
    // and write encrypted bytes into it.
    // The output bytes will be decrypted.
    // First, read the salt and IV
    inStream.Read(salt, 0, salt.Length);
    inStream.Read(IV, 0, IV.Length);
    // Compute the Rijndael key
    PasswordDeriveBytes pdb = new PasswordDeriveBytes(password, salt);
    byte[] key = pdb.GetBytes(32); // 32 bytes == 256 bits
    // set the key and IV of the aes object
    aes.Key = key;
    aes.IV = IV;
    // Create the CryptoStream
    CryptoStream decryptedOutStream = new CryptoStream(outStream,
➡ aes.CreateDecryptor(), CryptoStreamMode.Write);
    // Now we're ready to decrypt.
    int bytesRead;
    byte[] buffer = new byte[1024]; // read 1K at a time
    do {
      bytesRead = inStream.Read(buffer,0,1024);
      decryptedOutStream.Write(buffer, 0, bytesRead);
    } while (bytesRead > 0);
    // We've read everything, so now call FlushFinalBlock() to write out
    // any remaining bytes
    decryptedOutStream.FlushFinalBlock();
    inStream.Close();
```

LISTING 30.12   Continued

```
      decryptedOutStream.Close();
      return;
    }

  public static void Main(String[] args) {
    if (args.Length < 4) {
      Console.WriteLine("Usage: [-d | -e] password infile outfile");
      return;
    }
    switch (args[0]){
      case "-e":
        EncryptFile(args[1], args[2], args[3]);
        break;
      case "-d":
        DecryptFile(args[1], args[2], args[3]);
        break;
      default:
        Console.WriteLine("Usage: [-d | -e] password infile outfile");
        break;
      }
      return;
    }
}
```

The source code for the EncryptFile and DecryptFile routines is very similar to that
of the corresponding routines in Listings 30.3 and 30.4, the major difference being
the explicit addition of key derivation and the addition of the salt as a second parameter written out to the encrypted file.

Using Asymmetric Algorithms

The final portion of the core cryptographic object model to discuss is the set of
classes that implement asymmetric algorithms and associated formatting/
deformatting functions. Asymmetric algorithms are represented in the .NET
Framework by the AsymmetricAlgorithm class and its subclasses. Like their symmetric
counterparts, individual asymmetric algorithms are represented in the object model
as subclasses of the abstract AsymmetricAlgorithm class and specific implementations
of an algorithm are subclasses of those subclasses. For example, the RSA algorithm is
represented by the RSA class, which is a subclass of AsymmetricAlgorithm. An implementation of the RSA algorithm is provided by the RSACryptoServiceProvider class,
which is a subclass of the RSA class.

The .NET Framework includes support for two asymmetric algorithms—RSA and DSA. RSA (named after its inventors, Ron Rivest, Adi Shamir, and Len Adelman) is a public key algorithm that supports both encryption and digital signatures. DSA, the Digital Signature Algorithm specified by the U.S. government in Federal Information Processing Standard (FIPS) 186-2, supports only digital signatures. Table 30.5 shows the abstract algorithm and implementation classes included in the .NET Framework that support RSA and DSA, as well as default and allowed key sizes.

TABLE 30.5 Asymmetric Algorithms in the .NET Framework

Cipher	Default Implementation Class	Legal Key Sizes	Default Key Size
RSA	RSACryptoServiceProvider	384–16384 bits (in 8 bit increments)	1,024 bits
DSA	DSACryptoServiceProvider	512–1024 bits (in 64 bit increments)	1,024 bits

NOTE

As is the case with any algorithm in the .NET Framework implemented on top of CryptoAPI, you may need to explicitly install a "high encryption" update to your operating system to use some key lengths. Platforms that do not have the "high encryption" option installed will not be able to generate RSACryptoServiceProvider public encryption keys greater than 512 bits in length.

An instance object of a class descendant from AsymmetricAlgorithm represents a particular algorithm, choice of operating parameters, and a public/private key pair. Every AsymmetricAlgorithm object supports two key-related properties—KeySize and LegalKeySizes. These properties are similar to those of the same name on SymmetricAlgorithm. KeySize returns the size (in bits) of the public key associated with the object. The LegalKeySizes property returns an array of KeySizes structures that declares what key sizes are valid for this algorithm.

AsymmetricAlgorithm objects are created using static Create() methods, just like other cryptographic objects in the .NET Framework. For example, to create a new instance of an RSA object, simply call RSA.Create():

```
RSA rsa = RSA.Create();
```

This will create a new instance of the default implementation of the RSA algorithm and generate a random key pair to use with RSA.

In the "Using Symmetric Algorithms" section, we were able to set the value of an encryption or decryption key on a SymetricAlgorithm object simply by assigning the key's byte[] value to the Key property on the object. The situation is a little more complicated for AsymmetricAlgorithm objects, because an asymmetric key pair typically consists of a set of related values and, furthermore, exactly what values need to be defined vary by algorithm. For these reasons, the .NET Framework has chosen to use stringified XML structures to *import* key values *into* an algorithm object and *export* key values *from* an object. (Importing a key or key pair into an AsymmetricAlgorithm is akin to setting the Key property on a SymmetricAlgorithm. Exporting is equivalent to retrieving the value of the Key property.) For public key values, the XML structures used by the .NET Framework are equivalent to KeyValue structures defined by the XML Digital Signature Standard. For private key values, the XML structures extend the KeyValue definitions by adding fields for the private key components.

The AsymmetricAlgorithm class defines two methods that deal with importing and exporting key values—ToXmlString and FromXmlString. The ToXmlString method creates a stringified XML structure for the public key value stored in the object. ToXmlString takes one argument as input, a Boolean value that specifies whether to also include private key components in the XML string. The following code snippet shows how to create XML string representations of public keys and public/private key pairs from any AsymmetricAlgorithm. (The sample uses an RSA object, but any subclass of AsymmetricAlgorithm can be used.)

```
RSA rsa = RSA.Create();
String publicKeyOnly = rsa.ToXmlString(false);
String publicAndPrivateKeys = rsa.ToXmlString(true);
```

The following are the XML string values for an actual random RSA public/private key pair. First is the string value stored in the publicKeyOnly variable as a result of calling rsa.ToXmlString(false):

```
<RSAKeyValue>
<Modulus>yB8PydTa4ka4CRXeoGzHO7MS7DDiuIhjgKFM23i83IbvwraLae2XvRzyXFj7
rz/C7nwK9MYqwFksTtSOhV3M1J96cPMuDMIcNJp/NIeODl08972idvVZivh0e35NpsQg3
ohxXVekN4LIqMmE9bkVmtPwX36xWai7Ws/TgMtNQEU=</Modulus>
<Exponent>AQAB</Exponent>
</RSAKeyValue>
```

For the RSA algorithm, a public key consists of a modulus and exponent. A private key contains this information and more, as shown next in the value stored in the publicAndPrivateKeys variable:

```
<RSAKeyValue>
<Modulus>yB8PydTa4ka4CRXeoGzHO7MS7DDiuIhjgKFM23i83IbvwraLae2XvRzyXFj7
rz/C7nwK9MYqwFksTtSOhV3M1J96cPMuDMIcNJp/NIeODl08972idvVZivh0e35NpsQg3
ohxXVekN4LIqMmE9bkVmtPwX36xWai7Ws/TgMtNQEU=</Modulus>
<Exponent>AQAB</Exponent>
<P>5njbrh6xncLf/VF/Uyeux7zxlUNdYjHedQq0rh5kt57Y7SLxsMhLqB9MFHwRgBGTmb
```

```
dj87+6kic2R54YwgdjhQ==</P>
<Q>3kmX+dFUe69Llt+P1xOJ9/Sp/1oJLZIg0G3LEEQW+gMEcxkZvo5aDk81ss3QPaDmGI
kDNkonNrIjzZxqecUlwQ==</Q>
<DP>TqhK2WcyWVRsG8mXueqeNR8gGEAwe9XnRWzM82v+FckJ4gz+DcaeQ5fC4G7jjiDxj
hHP9B2ocD8fwFuNuZLJ/Q==</DP><DQ>CHkBo/IIqFY8KVoIH4iNH7hhqmwCIYyKV6d3r
/0IaysmRkTUqGDAqf726wPRRigV3SWLy8vzxq/vkWy+2jlbgQ==</DQ>
<InverseQ>NQuTfOM7BHx9Uh2uPwOkvpMztbC1/2gs7Z9juJrg0B+6KA6+INe93hmQUm3
YdXpqpmAPke3nOGWqjA7ZlrNPdg==</InverseQ>
<D>XIH3U25gzE6yjgidA/2kz5UE/0fN1k296V0m4SFb9Hkv5gtqQMpC5Xm3EzdTCPzpiE
Kw8duVMZtHHx2k0EO/Bg1zFdStVHitOUS/5QfR3ctY+34+yAida5mOYB6kgCGpsgg7NaS
0DtyvI+8lDiSb+1nONXY0f/ZvS7T2OegXMQE=</D>
</RSAKeyValue>
```

To import a public key (or public/private key pair) from an XmlString generated by a prior call to ToXmlString, simply call the FromXmlString method on the object into which you want to import the key value. FromXmlString will correctly parse and handle XML representations of both public keys only as well as public/private key pairs.

```
RSA newRsa = RSA.Create();
newRsa.FromXmlString(publicAndPrivateKeys);
```

After importing the public and private keys into the newRsa variable, newRsa will be a clone of the rsa variable that originally generated the key.

NOTE

When using an asymmetric algorithm to encrypt data, you typically only have the public key of the intended recipient. AsymmetricAlgorithm objects are designed to accept as valid key imports either a functional public/private key pair or a lone public key value. If the object contains only a public key value, you can only use it to encrypt data or verify digital signatures (the operations that depend on the public component of the key pair). Attempting to export private key components (using ToXmlString(true)) when the object only contains a public key value will throw an exception.

XML string representations of public and private keys work great in general, but sometimes it can be inefficient to have to convert key data into an out of XML if you simply want to move it around within your program. In particular, sometimes it is useful to be able to move key parameters around as a structured object instead of as a string. Thus, in addition to the ToXmlString and FromXmlString methods on AsymmetricAlgorithm, the .NET Framework has adopted a further design pattern in which each direct subclass of AsymmetricAlgorithm implements algorithm-specific ImportParameters and ExportParameters functions. These functions consume and return a structured object that is specific to the algorithm represented by the subclass. For example, the abstract `RSA` class exposes an `ExportParameters` method that returns an `RSAParameters` object:

```
RSA rsa = RSA.Create();
RSAParameters publicKeyParameters = rsa.ExportParameters(false);
RSAParameters publicAndPrivateKeyParameters = rsa.ExportParameters(true);
```

By convention, for each abstract algorithm class such as `RSA` or `DSA`, there is a corresponding structure for holding key parameters whose name is the concatenation of the algorithm classname and `Parameters`. So the `DSAParameters` structure matches `DSA` and its subclasses, and any implementation subclass of `DSA` will be able to produce and consume `DSAParameters` objects. After you hold an instance of a `*Parameters` object, individual parameter values can be readily accessed. By convention, large integers (sometimes called "bignums") are stored as byte arrays in "big endian" format with the highest byte of the number stored in the first (lowest index) element of the array. Consequently, if `publicKeyParameters` is an instance of `RSAParameters`, `publicKeyParameters.Modulus` is the public key modulus, and `publicKeyParameters.Modulus[0]` is the high-order byte of the entire modulus value.

> **NOTE**
>
> The .NET Framework does not provide a generic service for persisting private keys securely; that task is left up to the algorithm implementation classes or the application using cryptography. Later chapters discuss how you can access CryptoAPI's various persisted key stores when using the `RSACryptoServiceProvider` and `DSACryptoServiceProvider` classes.

Now that you have an instance of your favorite asymmetric algorithm object configured with a key pair, you probably want to sign or encrypt some other data with it. Public key encryption and digital signature computations are easy to do, but the particular methods you will need to use vary by algorithm. We first discuss `RSA`-related methods and then move on to those for `DSA`. If you have other asymmetric algorithms available on your system, you will need to check the documentation that came with them to see what methods are supported.

The abstract `RSA` class defines two abstract methods for encryption and decryption—`EncryptValue(byte[] data)` and `DecryptValue(byte[] data)`. These classes do exactly what their respective names imply—they perform raw RSA computations on the large integer value represented by the `data` byte array. `EncryptValue` and `DecryptValue` perform no padding on the data. Implementations of the RSA algorithm implement `EncryptValue` and `DecryptValue` so that various encryption and signature formatters and deformatters can access the underlying raw RSA operations.

CAUTION

It is very unlikely that you will actually want or need to use the `EncryptValue` and `DecryptValue` methods in your programs. In general, you need to combine the RSA algorithm with a good padding function to pad the to-be-encrypted data out to the size of the modulus. Weak or nonexistent padding can seriously reduce the security of your program's use of RSA. The various `Asymmetric*Formatter` and `Asymmetric*Deformatter` classes, described later on in this chapter, make available combinations of RSA and padding algorithms. Finally, note that if you are using the `RSACryptoServiceProvider` class, which is the default implementation of RSA in the .NET Framework, you *cannot* call `EncryptValue` and `DecryptValue` because these methods are not implemented by `RSACryptoServiceProvider`. The CryptoAPI implementation of RSA does not expose the raw RSA operations at the Win32 layer; the only exposed signature and encryption functions always add some type of padding.

The RSA implementation class `RSACryptoServiceProvider` exposes a number of methods for performing padded encryption, decryption, signature generation, and signature validation. Encryption and decryption services are provided by the `Encrypt` and `Decrypt` methods. These methods take as input two arguments—the data to be encrypted or decrypted and a Boolean flag that indicates which padding algorithm should be used. The to-be-encrypted/decrypted data is passed as a `byte[]` array. If the Boolean flag is `true`, then OAEP padding will be used (a newer standard); PKCS#1 v1.5 padding will be used if the flag is `false`.

NOTE

At the time this book went to press, only Windows XP includes support for OAEP padding. Attempting to use OAEP padding on an earlier version of Windows will generate a `CryptographicException`.

Listing 30.13 contains sample code that shows how to encrypt the integer value 0x1f3f5f using RSA:

LISTING 30.13   Encrypting a Data Value with an RSA Public Key and PKCS#1 v1.5 Padding

```
RSACryptoServiceProvider rsa = new RSACryptoServiceProvider();
byte[] data = new byte[3]{ 0x1f, 0x3f, 0x5f };
byte[] enc = rsa.Encrypt(data, false);
```

This code sample used PKCS#1 v1.5 style padding (the `fOAEP` flag is `false`). The size of the encrypted value `enc` will, in general, be the same as the size of the public key modulus, which defaults to 1024 bits on "high encryption" platforms. Decrypting `enc` is similarly straightforward:

```
byte[] dec = rsa.Decrypt(enc, false);
```

You must use the same padding algorithm for both encryption and decryption; padding algorithms are not interchangeable.

> **CAUTION**
>
> If you are debugging an application that uses RSA encryption, beware that both the PKCS#1 v1.5 and OAEP padding algorithms for RSA generate and use random numbers as part of the padding. This means that if you encrypt the same value twice, using the same RSA public key, you will get two different encrypted outputs. The randomness that is explicitly used in the RSA padding makes debugging more difficult, especially if you are not aware of it!

RSACryptoServiceProvider includes a number of methods and overloads for computing and verifying digital signatures. The core operations, signing a hash value and verifying a signed hash value, are provided by the SignHash and VerifyHash methods. SignHash requires two arguments—the hash value to be signed (as a byte array) and a String value containing the ASN.1 Object Identifier (OID) for the hash algorithm used to generate the hash value. SignHash needs the OID value because it is a required input to the PKCS#1 signature padding function (which is always used). There are only two OID values you need to know, the values for the SHA-1 and MD5 hash algorithms, and Table 30.6 lists these values.

TABLE 30.6   Hash Algorithm ID Values

Algorithm	OID Value as a String
SHA-1	"1.3.14.3.2.26"
MD5	"1.2.840.113549.2.5"

Listing 30.14 shows a code fragment that creates an RSA object (with random public key), a SHA1 hash object, and then computes the RSA signature over the SHA1 hash of our three-byte sample data:

LISTING 30.14   Signing a Hash Value with an RSA Private Key

```
RSACryptoServiceProvider rsa = new RSACryptoServiceProvider();
SHA1 sha1 = SHA1.Create();
byte[] data = new byte[3]{ 0x1f, 0x3f, 0x5f };
byte[] signature = rsa.SignHash(sha1.ComputeHash(data), "1.3.14.3.2.26");
```

Verifying the sample signature is similarly easy; simply call VerifyHash with the hash of the data to compare to the signature, the OID of the hash function, and the signature. The Boolean return value will be true if the signed hash value corresponds to the input hash value:

```
bool signatureIsGood = rsa.VerifyHash(sha1.ComputeHash(data),
➥ "1.3.14.3.2.26", signature)
```

The `RSACryptoServiceProvider` class also includes methods that will compute a
hash of some input data and sign that hash value in a single operation. The three
`SignData` methods accept as input respectively a `Stream`, a buffer, or a portion of a
buffer (indicated by a starting offset and count); this input is the to-be-hashed data.
`SignData` also requires an `Object` argument that specifies the type of hash value to
generate. `SignData` is more forgiving than `SignValue` in that you need not pass in
the OID string to identify a hash algorithm. You can call `SignData` with any of the
following types of `Object`s:

- A `String`—If you pass a `String` to `SignData` to identify the hash function,
  `SignData` will use the cryptography configuration system to map that `String`
  value to an OID. Built-in definitions exist for the friendly names MD5, SHA1,
  SHA256, SHA384, and SHA512.

- A `HashAlgorithm`—You can pass `SignData` a subclass of `HashAlgorithm`, and it
  will attempt to automatically figure out the proper OID string to use based on
  the specific type of `HashAlgorithm` passed in.

- A `Type`—You can also pass `SignData` a `System.Type` object corresponding to a
  subclass of `HashAlgorithm`. Again, `SignData` will attempt to automatically figure
  out the proper OID that corresponds to this `Type`.

The same signature that was computed in Listing 30.14 using an explicit hash
computation and a call to the `SignHash` method can equivalently be computed by
the following call to `SignData`:

```
byte[] signature = rsa.SignData(data, "SHA1");
```

There is a corresponding `VerifyData` method that hashes the contents of an input
buffer and compares the computed hash with a signed hash value. However, there
are no corresponding `VerifyData` methods for `Stream` or partial buffer inputs; you
will need to hash these types of inputs yourself and call `VerifyHash` to check signatures.

Using the DSA signature algorithm is very similar to performing signing operations
with the RSA-related classes. Because DSA does not support encryption or decryption
functions, the DSA interfaces do not expose `EncryptValue`, `DecryptValue`, `Encrypt`,
or `Decrypt` methods. Rather, the abstract `DSA` class defines two methods common to
all DSA implementations for creating and verifying DSA digital signatures—
`CreateSignature` and `VerifySignature`. They are essentially equivalent to the RSA
`SignHash` and `VerifyHash` functions, except that they do not require an OID string

as input because by definition, DSA always uses the SHA-1 hash functions to compute to-be-signed hash values. The following is a code snippet for computing a DSA signature over the same sample three-byte data value used in Listing 30.13 and the other RSA samples:

```
SHA1 sha1 = SHA1.Create();
DSACryptoServiceProvider dsa = new DSACryptoServiceProvider();
byte[] data = new byte[3]{ 0x1f, 0x3f, 0x5f };
byte[] signature = dsa.CreateSignature(sha1.ComputeHash(data));
```

The signature can be verified by calling the VerifySignature method:

```
bool sigVerifies = dsa.VerifySignature(sha1.ComputeHash(data),signature);
```

CAUTION

If you are debugging an application that uses DSA signatures, beware that part of the DSA algorithm generates and uses a random number. This means that if you compute two DSA signatures over the same data/hash values with the same DSA keys, you will get two different signature values.

In addition to the CreateSignature and VerifySignature methods defined on the abstract DSA class, the DSACryptoServiceProvider class defines the same SignHash, VerifyHash, SignData, and VerifyData methods that RSACryptoServiceProvider does. The only difference between the DSACryptoServiceProvider and RSACryptoServiceProvider versions is that the DSACryptoServiceProvider methods never require information about the type of hash algorithm to use, because the hash algorithm is always by definition SHA-1.

Although the RSACryptoServiceProvider and DSACryptoServiceProvider classes automatically pad data to be signed or encrypted using an appropriate padding algorithm, other RSA and DSA implementations may not provide those functions. The .NET Framework assumes only that an RSA or DSA implementation class will implement the raw encryption and signature functions—RSA.EncryptValue, RSA.DecryptValue, DSA.CreateSignature, and DSA.VerifySignature—and provides separate "helper" functions to perform padding, formatting, deformatting, and depadding. The padding- and formatting-related classes that are included in the .NET Framework are as follows:

- `AsymmetricKeyExchangeFormatter`—An abstract class representing padding-and-formatting algorithms associated with encrypting a data value with a public encryption key

  - `RSAPKCS1KeyExchangeFormatter`—Subclass of `AsymmetricKeyExchangeFormatter` that implements PKCS#1 v1.5 padding for RSA encryption

  - `RSAOAEPKeyExchangeFormatter`—Subclass of `AsymmetricKeyExchangeFormatter` that implements OAEP formatting for RSA encryption

- `AsymmetricKeyExchangeDeformatter`—An abstract class representing deformatting and depadding algorithms associated with decrypting a public key encrypted data value

  - `RSAPKCS1KeyExchangeDeformatter`—Subclass of `AsymmetricKeyExchangeDeformatter` that implements PKCS#1 v1.5 depadding for RSA decryption

  - `RSAOAEPKeyExchangeDeformatter`—Subclass of `AsymmetricKeyExchangeDeformatter` that implements OAEP depadding for RSA decryption

- `AsymmetricSignatureFormatter`—An abstract class representing a signature algorithm's padding and formatting function

  - `RSAPKCS1SignatureFormatter`—Subclass of `AsymmetricSignatureFormatter` that implements PKCS#1 v1.5 padding for RSA signatures

  - `DSASignatureFormatter`—Subclass of `AsymmetricSignatureFormatter` that implements DSA signature padding (defined in [DSS])

- `AsymmetricSignatureDeformatter`—An abstract class representing a signature verification algorithm's deformatting and depadding function

  - `RSAPKCS1SignatureDeformatter`—Subclass of `AsymmetricSignatureDeformatter` that implements PKCS#1 v1.5 depadding for RSA signatures

  - `DSASignatureDeformatter`—Subclass of `AsymmetricSignatureDeformatter` that implements DSA signature depadding (as defined in [DSS])

Using these various formatters is straightforward. First, create an instance of the formatter you want to use. All of the implemented formatter classes included in the .NET Framework support a constructor that takes an `AsymmetricAlgorithm` object as its lone argument. The AsymmetricAlgorithm instance you pass to the constructor should hold the public key or key pair you want to use. (You can also create an instance of the formatter object using its null-argument constructor and associate an AsymmetricAlgorithm object with the new formatter instance using its SetKey method.) If you are using an RSAPKCS1SignatureFormatter or an RSAPKCS1SignatureDeformatter, you will also need to set or change the associated hash algorithm using the SetHashAlgorithm methods. (SetHashAlgorithm takes as input the a String name for a hash algorithm, such as MD5 or SHA1.) Finally, each formatter object has one method to actually "turn the crank" and perform the operation (for example, RSAPKCS1SignatureFormatter.CreateSignature). Call that method with the value to be signed or encrypted and the return value will be the desired signature or encrypted value.

To illustrate the use of formatter objects, we will now show how to perform the encryption operation in Listing 30.13 using a formatter object instead of a direct call to RSA.Encrypt. In Listing 30.13, we encrypted the hexadecimal values 0x1f3f5f using an RSA key and PKCS#1 v1.5 padding. Listing 30.15 shows how to perform the same computation using an RSAPKCS1KeyExchangeFormatter and any RSA key (not necessarily an RSACryptoServiceProvider).

LISTING 30.15   Encrypting a Data Value Using an RSAPKCS1KeyExchangeFormatter

```
RSA rsa = RSA.Create();
byte[] data = new byte[3]{ 0x1f, 0x3f, 0x5f };
RSAPKCS1KeyExchangeFormatter keyExchangeFormatter =
➡ new RSAPKCS1KeyExchangeFormatter(rsa);
byte[] enc = keyExchangeFormatter.CreateKeyExchange(data);
```

To decrypt the encrypted value enc, use a corresponding RSAPKCS1KeyExchangeDeformatter object and its DecryptKeyExchange method. Continuing the code in Listing 30.15, the decrypted value is computed as follows:

```
RSAPKCS1KeyExchangeDeformatter keyExchangeDeformatter =
➡ new RSAPKCS1KeyExchangeDeformatter(rsa);
byte[] dec = keyExchangeDeformatter.DecryptKeyExchange(enc);
```

AsymmetricSignatureFormatter and AsymmetricSignatureDeformatter objects work similarly, using the methods CreateSignature and VerifySignature as they are named. When using the RSAPKCS1SignatureFormatter and matching Deformatter, you must explicitly set the hash algorithm so that the formatter will know what OID to insert into the padding and signature computation.

NOTE

When combined with an `RSACryptoServiceProvider` or `DSACryptoServiceProvider` object, the formatters simply use CryptoAPI's implementation of the padding algorithms to generate the padding. (This is necessitated by the fact that CryptoAPI does not expose the raw encryption and digital signature methods but only combination methods that also perform padding.) This means, for example, that you can only use the `RSAOAEPSignatureFormatter` with an `RSACryptoServiceProvider` on Windows XP, because earlier versions of Windows do not expose OAEP functionality.

Summary

The .NET Framework contains a rich and extensible collection of classes that make it very easy to use cryptography within your own programs. As shipped, the cryptography classes include support for the most common algorithms for performing symmetric key encryption, public key encryption, public key digital signatures, and hash computations, including the new Advanced Encryption Standard algorithms Rijndael (encryption) and SHA-256, SHA-384, and SHA-512 (hash functions). You can also add your own algorithms to the system through subclassing.

In this chapter, we have demonstrated only the most common and basic cryptographic operations. Chapter 31 builds on this chapter and discusses advanced topics, including interacting with the Win32 CryptoAPI directly, as well as how to use the cryptographic configuration system to change default algorithms and make new algorithms "known" to the system.

31

Using Cryptography with the .NET Framework: Advanced Topics

By Brian A. LaMacchia

This chapter continues our discussion of cryptographic support in the .NET Framework, focusing on advanced topics and interoperability with the Windows CryptoAPI. On completion of this chapter, you should be able to

- Demonstrate use of the `CspParameters` structure to make use of CryptoAPI-based keys from within the .NET Framework

- Demonstrate use of the .NET Framework's platform invoke feature to access X.509v3 certificate-related functions available via CryptoAPI

- Demonstrate proper use of the `Clear()` methods on .NET Framework cryptography objects to erase sensitive data after completing a cryptographic operation

- Demonstrate how to define and add new cryptographic algorithms and implementations to the .NET Framework

In this chapter, we present information on a collection of advanced cryptographic topics for .NET Framework developers. We assume throughout this chapter that you have successfully completed Chapter 30, "Using Cryptography with the .NET Framework: The Basics;" if you are not reading the book straight through and have not yet read Chapter 30, you need to do so before proceeding on in this chapter.

The topics covered in this chapter can be roughly divided into three separate areas:

- Working with CryptoAPI from within the .NET Framework
- Cleaning up sensitive data after finishing a cryptographic operation
- Configuring the Framework to use new algorithms and implementations

Working with CryptoAPI 1.0

Microsoft's CryptoAPI consists roughly of two related sets of APIs—a low-level set of functions (CryptoAPI 1.0) that perform core cryptographic operations, such as basic encryption and digital signature operations, and a higher-level set of functions (CryptoAPI 2.0) designed to work with X.509v3/PKIX Part 1 digital certificates and S/MIME (CMS) signed messages. This section discusses interoperating with CryptoAPI 1.0 functions and data structures from the .NET Framework; CryptoAPI 2.0 functions are addressed in the next section.

The CryptoAPI Provider Model: Cryptographic Service Providers and Key Containers

CryptoAPI 1.0 contains a *pluggable-provider* model that permits third parties to implement cryptographic algorithms and "plug" them into the CryptoAPI architecture. At a high level, CryptoAPI's extensibility model is similar to that of the .NET Framework cryptographic object model; both architectures allow developers to write their own implementations of algorithms and make them available to other developers through common abstractions. CryptoAPI's unit of extension is called a *cryptographic service provider* (CSP); a CSP consists of implementations of one or more cryptographic algorithms. Developers using CryptoAPI can ask for a specific CSP when they begin performing cryptographic operations, or they can use the "default" CSP on the system for the particular algorithm that they want to use.

Cryptographic service providers are organized within CryptoAPI by *Types*; each Type of CSP defines a collection of algorithms that are implemented by all CSPs of that Type. (CSP Types are integer values defined by Microsoft within the wincrypt.h header file in the Win32 Platform SDK.) The most common provider type is Type 1, the PROV_RSA_FULL provider, that implements the RSA asymmetric algorithm and the DES, TripleDES, and RC2 symmetric algorithms. Table 31.1 lists the commonly used CryptoAPI provider Types. Typically, if you are interested in performing RSA operations, you will want to use a Type 1 CSP; if you are performing DSA operations, you will want to use a Type 13 CSP. Types tend to align closely with asymmetric algorithms, so, for example, both Type 1 and Type 13 CSPs include implementations of the MD5 and SHA1 hash algorithms, but you cannot use a Type 1 CSP to create or verify a DSA signature.

TABLE 31.1   CryptoAPI Provider Types

Provider Type (`wincrypt.h` Symbol)	Provider Type Numeric Value	Description
PROV_RSA_FULL	1	RSA implementations
PROV_DSS	3	DSA implementations
PROV_RSA_SCHANNEL	12	An RSA-based CSP with additional key derivation algorithms required by the SSL/TLS standard
PROV_DSS_DH	13	DSA/Diffie-Hellman implementations
PROV_DH_SCHANNEL	18	A DSA/Diffie-Hellman CSP with additional key derivation algorithms required by the SSL/TLS standard
PROV_RSA_AES	24	An expanded version of the PROV_RSA_FULL provider with additional support for the AES/Rijndael symmetric block cipher

Within a particular Type, individual CSPs are identified by a *name* that is simply an implementation-defined string. The default CSPs that ship with Windows XP for each Type are shown in Table 31.2. CSPs of the same Type implement the same algorithms (or, at least, are supposed to implement the same algorithms), but will implement those algorithms in different ways and perhaps using different resources (for example, hardware accelerators).

TABLE 31.2   Windows XP Default Cryptographic Service Providers

Provider Type Numeric Value	Windows XP Default CSP
1	Microsoft Strong Cryptographic Provider
3	Microsoft Base DSS Cryptographic Provider
12	Microsoft RSA SChannel Cryptographic Provider
13	Microsoft Enhanced DSS and Diffie-Hellman Cryptographic Provider
18	Microsoft DH SChannel Cryptographic Provider
24	Microsoft Enhanced RSA and AES Cryptographic Provider (Prototype)

Within each CSP are one or more cryptographic key pairs, stored in individual *key containers*. A key container is a named key pair; each CSP manages its own keys, including how those keys are persisted and the mapping between keys and key containers. The number of key containers that can be filled within a CSP at any given point in time is a property of the CSP implementation (typically, the limiting factor is key storage space, such as on a hardware token or smartcard). Thus, to access a specific key pair in CryptoAPI, you need to know the Type of the CSP it is stored within, the name of that CSP, and the name of the key container within the CSP that holds the key.

Accessing Specific Providers and Key Containers from the .NET Framework Using the `CspParameters` Structure

In general, the .NET Framework classes that use CryptoAPI—the classes with names ending in `CryptoServiceProvider`—do a good job of hiding the details of CryptoAPI's own architecture from the developer. Constructors for classes such as `RSACryptoServiceProvider` and `DSACryptoServiceProvider` automatically use the default CSPs on the machine when they need to perform RSA or DSA operations (the default Type 1 and Type 13 providers, respectively). To use a particular CSP or key container within a CSP with these classes, we simply need to identify the CSP or key container when constructing a new instance of the class. We can specify this data by including a `CspParameters` structure in the calls to the `RSACryptoServiceProvider`, `DSACryptoServiceProvider`, and `RNGCryptoServiceProvider` constructors.

The `CspParameters` structure is our method of communicating to CryptoAPI from managed code information identifying the CSP and key container we want to use for a cryptographic operation. The `RSACryptoServiceProvider`, `DSACryptoServiceProvider`, and `RNGCryptoServiceProvider` classes each have one or more constructor overloads that accept a `CspParameters` object as an argument to identify what specific CSP and/or key container holds the key we want to use. An instance of the `CspParameters` class contains four public fields and a single public property, as summarized in Table 31.3. The `ProviderType` and `ProviderName` fields specify which Cryptographic Service Provider to use for cryptographic operations and key storage. The `KeyContainerName` and `KeyNumber` fields, together with the value of the `Flags` property, identify the key storage location to use within the Cryptographic Service Provider.

NOTE

The `KeyContainerName` and `KeyNumber` fields and the `Flags` property within a `CspParameters` object are relevant only to the `RSACryptoServiceProvider` and `DSACryptoServiceProvider` classes, because there are no keys (and thus no key containers) used when requesting random numbers from an instance of the `RNGCryptoServiceProvider` class. It is possible to direct the `RNGCryptoServiceProvider` class to use another CSP, so the constructors on that class do use the information in the `ProviderType` and `ProviderName` fields. `CspParameter` information is not used with the other CSP-related classes in the .NET Framework (`MD5CryptoServiceProvider`, `SHA1CryptoServiceProvider`, `DESCryptoServiceProvider`, `TripleDESCryptoServiceProvider` and `RC2CryptoServiceProvider`). (CryptoAPI does not allow symmetric keys to be persisted directly in key containers, so there is no way to point an instance of, for example, `TripleDESCryptoServiceProvider`, to use a specific key that is already loaded into CryptoAPI.)

TABLE 31.3   Fields and Properties of the `CspParameters` Structure

Field/Property Name	Contents	Default Value
ProviderType	Cryptographic Service Provider Type (integer)	1
ProviderName	Cryptographic Service Provider Name (string)	Null
KeyContainerName	Key Container Name (string)	Null
KeyNumber	AT_KEYEXHCANGE or AT_SIGNATURE	Varies by class
Flags	CspProviderFlags	0

To use a specific cryptographic service provider or key container, simply create a corresponding `CspParameters` object and pass it as an argument to the `RSACryptoServiceProvider`, `DSACryptoServiceProvider`, or `RNGCryptoServiceProvider` constructor.

NOTE

Depending on the configuration of the operating system on which the CLR is running, some CryptoAPI-based cryptographic operations, CSPs, or key containers may not be available to your program. If you specify invalid values in the `CspParameters` object (for example, the name of a CSP that is not installed on the platform), one or more `CryptographicExceptions` may be thrown. It is especially important to program defensively, catching errors and handling them gracefully, when using `CspParameters` to access specific CSPs or key containers because it may not be possible for CryptoAPI to satisfy your request.

Let's now look at some practical examples of using the `CspParameters` object to access specific CSPs and key containers. Consider the following statement:

```
RSACryptoServiceProvider rsa = new RSACryptoServiceProvider();
```

This line of code creates a new `RSACryptoServiceProvider` object and assigns it to the rsa variable. Because no `CspParameters` object was specified in the constructor, the `RSACryptoServiceProvider` class uses the default Type 1 CSP installed in Windows and a randomly generated key container name. This is exactly equivalent to the following code snippet that makes the use of an explicit `CspParameters` object:

```
CspParameters cspParams = new CspParameters();
RSACryptoServiceProvider rsa = new RSACryptoServiceProvider(cspParams);
```

By default, when you create a `CspParameters` object using its `null` constructor, it indicates that you want to use a random, temporary key container in the default Type 1 CSP. Thus, the following two statements are equivalent:

```
CspParameters cspParams = new CspParameters();
CspParameters cspParams = new CspParameters(1);
```

The second argument to the `CspParameters` constructor, if present, is a `String` containing the name of the cryptographic service provider to use. A value of `null` indicates that the default provider on the platform for the specified provider type should be used. The default cryptographic service provider for a given provider type varies, depending on the specific version of the Windows operating system that is installed on the machine. For versions of Windows earlier than Windows XP, the default provider may also depend on whether a "strong cryptography" update has been installed. On Windows XP, the default Type 1 provider is called the `Microsoft Strong Cryptographic Provider`, so the following statements are equivalent:

```
CspParameters cspParams = new CspParameters(1);
CspParameters cspParams = new CspParameters(1, null);

CspParameters cspParams = new CspParameters(1,
➥ "Microsoft Strong Cryptographic Provider");
```

The third argument to the `CspParameters` constructor specifies the name of the key container to access within the cryptographic service provider. The key container name is also a `String` value. A value of `null` (the default value) indicates that the .NET Framework should generate a random key container name. If a non-`null` value is provided, the .NET Framework will look for a key container with that exact name. If present, the key within that container will be used. If the named key container does not already exist, a new key container with the specified name will be created and a random key will be generated within the key container.

The following code snippet shows how to use a key stored in a specific key container with the `RSACryptoServiceProvider` class. The name of the key container is `"My RSA Key"`, and we assume it is stored within the default Type 1 cryptographic service provider on the platform:

```
CspParameters cspParams = new CspParameters(1, null, "My RSA Key");
RSACryptoServiceProvider rsa = new RSACryptoServiceprovider(cspParams);
```

In most cases, you will not need to worry about the `KeyNumber` field within a `CspParameters` object (also the fourth argument to the `CspParameters` constructor), but we describe it here for completeness. Each CryptoAPI key container is actually capable of storing two pairs of keys, one pair for "key exchange" use and a second pair for "signature" use. Many production systems that use public key cryptography for both encryption and digital signatures issue a separate key pair for each function to each user of the system. (Separating encryption keys from signature keys allows the encryption key to be escrowed with a central authority—in case data needs to be recovered—but never duplicates the signature key to reduce the likelihood of signature repudiation.) By default, the `RSACryptoServiceProvider` class attempts to use the key pair in the "key exchange" slot of the key container when creating or acquiring keys. You can override this behavior by explicitly setting the value of the `KeyNumber` to indicate which slot within the key container you want to use. Table 31.4 shows the legal values for the `KeyNumber` field; these values correspond to constant values defined in the `wincrypt.h` header file for the Win32 CryptoAPI functions.

> **NOTE**
>
> While the `RSACryptoServiceProvider` class may be used with either "key exchange" or "signature" slot keys within a key container, the `DSACryptoServiceProvider` class will only operate with keys located in the "signature" slot of the container. This restriction is due to the fact that the DSA algorithm can only be used to create digital signatures, not perform general public key encryption operations. The `DSACryptoServiceProvider` class uses the "signature" slot of the specified key container by default, and attempting to use a "key exchange" slot key pair will generate a `CryptographicException`.
>
> Unless you explicitly need to access the "signature" slot of a key container to use with `RSACryptoServiceProvider`, we strongly suggest leaving the `KeyNumber` field as its default value and letting the .NET Framework figure out the proper value to use when communicating with the underlying cryptographic service provider. The following is sample code for accessing the "signature" slot of the `"My RSA Key"` key container:
>
> ```
> CspParameters cspParams = new CspParameters(1, null, "My RSA Key");
> cspParams.KeyNumber = 2; // 2 = AT_SIGNATURE
> RSACryptoServiceProvider rsa = new RSACryptoServiceprovider(cspParams);
> ```

TABLE 31.4   Legal Values for the `CspParameters` `KeyNumber` Field

KeyNumber **Value**	**Key Container "Slot"**	**Corresponding WinCrypt.h Constant**
-1	Default for class (key exchange for RSACryptoServiceProvider, signature for DSACryptoServiceProvider)	N/A
1	"key exchange" (RSACryptoServiceProvider only)	AT_KEYEXCHANGE
2	"signature" (RSACryptoServiceProvider or DSACryptoServiceProvider)	AT_SIGNATURE
0x0000A400	"key exchange" (RSACryptoServiceProvider only)	CALG_RSA_KEYX
0x00002400	"signature" (RSACryptoServiceProvider only)	CALG_RSA_SIGN
0x00002200	"signature" (DSACryptoServiceProvider only)	CALG_DSS_SIGN

Key container selection is also influenced by the value of the `Flags` property on a `CspParameters` objects. The `Flags` property contains an enum of type `CspProviderFlags`; there are two defined values for `CspProviderFlags` in version 1 of the .NET Framework—`UseMachineKeyStore` and `UseDefaultKeyContainer`. Either or both of these flags can be specified in an instance of `CspProviderFlags` (they can be `OR`'d together).

The `UseMachineKeyStore` flag is used to tell CryptoAPI to look for the key container in the set of per-machine keys instead of per-user keys. Within CryptoAPI, every logged-on user has access to an independent, isolated key storage database, and there is an additional database that holds "machine keys" that do not belong to any particular user. Typically, access to "machine key" storage is restricted to machine administrators. The `UseMachineKeyStore` flag is useful if you are performing crypto-graphic operations in a context in which there is no logged-on user account (and thus no per-user key storage associated with the process ID of the running process).

CryptoAPI also defines a "default" key container within each cryptographic service provider. The default key container is a persistent key container that is used by CryptoAPI when no explicit key container is requested. In the .NET Framework, you can access the default key container within a CSP by setting the `UseDefaultKeyContainer` flag on `Flags` property of the `CspParameters` object. When set, this flag instructs CryptoAPI to access the default key container. Like any other key container, if the default key container is empty, the .NET Framework will auto-matically generate a random key and insert it into the default container. The follow-ing example shows how to access the default key container when using the default Type 1 CSP with the `RSACryptoServiceProvider` class:

```
CspParameters cspParams = new CspParameters(1);
cspParams.Flags = CspProviderFlags.UseDefaultKeyContainer;
RSACryptoServiceProvider rsa = new RSACryptoServiceprovider(cspParams);
```

It is possible to combine both the `UseDefaultKeyContainer` and `UseMachineKeyStore` flags if you want to access the default machine key container:

```
CspParameters cspParams = new CspParameters(1);
cspParams.Flags = CspProviderFlags.UseDefaultKeyContainer |
➥ CspProviderFlags.UseMachineKeyStore;
RSACryptoServiceProvider rsa = new RSACryptoServiceprovider(cspParams);
```

NOTE

Within the .NET Framework, a key container is considered either *transient* or *persistent*. A transient key container (and the key material stored within it) is deleted when the .NET Framework object corresponding to the object is disposed or garbage collected. A persistent key container is not deleted when the corresponding managed object disappears; key material stored in a persistent key container will remain in the cryptographic service provider and can be accessed again in the future.

When the .NET Framework is asked to generate a random key container name, the corre-sponding key container is marked as a transient container. If an explicit key container name is specified in the `CspParameters` object passed to an `RSACryptoServiceProvider` or `DSACryptoServiceProvider` constructor, the corresponding key container is marked persis-tent. The state of a key container can be switched from transient to persistent by setting the value of the `PersistKeyInCsp` property to `true`.

> Creating or accessing a persistent key container is a protected operation. Callers must have the right to call unmanaged code, `SecurityPermission(SecurityPermissionFlag.UnmanagedCode)`, whenever explicitly requesting a specific key container name or setting the value of the `PersistKeyInCsp` property. (Setting the value to `true` is the equivalent of requesting that a new key container be created within CryptoAPI. Setting `PersistKeyInCsp` to `false` causes the key container to be deleted when the related managed object is garbage collected. Both of these operations are equivalent to direct calls to CryptoAPI, so they are protected with the same permission demand.) Requesting the default key container within a CSP (setting the `Flags` property to an enum value including `CspProviderFlags.UseDefaultKeyContainer`) is also a protected operation.

In addition to specifying where a cryptographic key pair is stored via a `CspParameters` object, you can also specify the size of the public key pair to be generated when filling a new key container. Two of the constructors on each of the `RSACryptoServiceProvider` and `DSACryptoServiceProvider` classes allow for explicit specification of the key size. They are

```
RSACryptoServiceProvider(int size);
RSACryptoServiceProvider(int size, CspParameters parameters);
DSACryptoServiceProvider(int size);
DSACryptoServiceProvider(int size, CspParameters parameters);
```

The `size` parameter in these constructors specifies the desired size in bits of the public key modulus. For `RSACryptoServiceProvider`, the requested key size must be supported by the underlying cryptographic service provider. As specified in Table 30.5 of Chapter 30, the default key size for `RSACryptographicServiceProvider` is 1024 bits if supported by the platform, and 512 bits if not. (Prior to Windows XP, the "high encryption" update is required to support RSA encryption key sizes in excess of 512 bits.) The default key size when using `DSACryptoServiceProvider` is always 1024 bits (the maximum permitted by the algorithm). The following example generates a 2048-bit RSA key in a new key container (`"My bigger RSA key"`):

```
CspParameters cspParams = new CspParameters(1,null,"My bigger RSA key");
RSACryptoServiceProvider rsa = new RSACryptoServiceProvider(2048,cspParams);
```

Calling CryptoAPI 1.0 Functions Directly Using Platform Invoke

The .NET Framework cryptography classes expose the most common CryptoAPI 1.0 functions cleanly through its object hierarchy. However, not all CryptoAPI functions or options are easily available through the managed classes, so sometimes you may need to call some CryptoAPI functions directly via the .NET Framework's platform invoke mechanism. The platform invoke feature allows managed code to call unmanaged functions that are exported from DLLs, such as the Win32 APIs.

To demonstrate the use of the .NET Framework's platform invoke feature, we will consider how to create a CryptoAPI key container that contains a non-exportable private key. Recall from earlier that the key pairs generated by the .NET Framework's RSACryptoServiceProvider and DSACryptoServiceProvider classes are *exportable* by default—the private key components of the key pair may be extracted from the key container and distributed. When a new public/private key pair is created by CryptoAPI, the private components are marked with one of three states—exportable, non-exportable, or user interface-protected (UI-protected). Non-exportable private keys can never be extracted from the cryptographic service provider that generated them. A UI-protected key can be exported from the cryptographic service provider, but attempting to use the private key or exporting it from the CSP will result in a dialog window being shown to the user requesting confirmation (and perhaps a password to unlock access to the key, depending on the type of UI protection desired by the user).

The exportability of a key, as well as whether confirmation from the user is required to use the key, is specified at the time the key is created by the CryptGenKey function within CryptoAPI. Because the .NET Framework cryptographic classes do not expose a mechanism for setting flags on its calls to CryptGenKey, we need to create the key in the proper key container ourselves. Creating the key will occur in two steps. First, we will need to acquire a handle on the desired key container in the cryptographic service provider where we want the key to live. Second, after we have a handle on the correct key container, we will create a new key in that container with the appropriate properties. After the key has been properly generated in its key container, we can access the container normally through the .NET Framework.

The CryptAcquireContext method is the function in CryptoAPI for acquiring a handle on a specific key container within a cryptographic service provider. The API definition for CryptAcquireContext is as follows:

```
BOOL WINAPI CryptAcquireContext(
  HCRYPTPROV* phProv,     // handle to a key container (out parameter)
  LPCTSTR pszContainer,   // name of the key container to access
  LPCTSTR pszProvider,    // name of the cryptographic service provider to use
  DWORD dwProvType,       // type of cryptographic service provider to use
  DWORD dwFlags           // flags (e.g. create or delete container)
);
```

To access this API from managed code, we use the DllImport attribute (part of platform invoke) to define a managed entry point for the external function. The CryptAcquireContext function is defined in the advapi32.dll library DLL (part of Windows), so the declaration to access this method from managed code is as follows:

```
[DllImport("advapi32.dll",EntryPoint="CryptAcquireContext",
➥ CharSet=CharSet.Auto, SetLastError=true)]
public static extern bool CryptAcquireContext(ref IntPtr hCryptProv,
➥ String containerName, String providerName, int providerType, uint provider-
Flags);
```

This piece of code defines a managed static method in our class, also called `CryptAcquireContext`, that is essentially a proxy for the unmanaged Win32 `CryptAcquireContext` API. The other arguments to the `DllImport` attribute are optional but useful. The `CharSet` attribute defines how we want the platform invoke mechanism to differentiate between Unicode and ANSI versions of APIs and marshal `String` objects to unmanaged code. (The `CharSet.Auto` setting tells the CLR to use Unicode on Windows NT, Windows 2000, and Windows XP and ANSI on Windows 98 and Windows ME.) The `SetLastError` attribute tells the platform invoke mechanism that we want Win32 error information maintained when we call through the proxy. (Error codes can be retrieved with a call to `Marshal.GetLastWin32Error()`, and they are quite useful when debugging CryptoAPI-based applications.)

> **NOTE**
>
> The `IntPtr` structure is a platform-specific type that is used to represent a pointer or handle. We use `IntPtr` objects for HCRYPTPROV and HCRYPTKEY handles in CryptoAPI.

`CryptAcquireContext` allows us to obtain a handle on a key container within a specific cryptographic service provider, but we also need to be able to call `CryptGenKey` to generate a key pair within a key container. The API definition for `CryptGenKey` is as follows:

```
BOOL WINAPI CryptGenKey(
  HCRYPTPROV hProv,      // handle to key container
  ALG_ID Algid,          // algorithm ID (uint)
  DWORD dwFlags,      // Flags (uint)
  HCRYPTKEY* phKey      // handle to key (out parameter)
);
```

The `DllImport` declaration for accessing `CryptGenKey` from managed code is as follows:

```
[DllImport("advapi32.dll",EntryPoint="CryptGenKey",CharSet=CharSet.Auto,
➥ SetLastError=true)]
public static extern bool CryptGenKey(IntPtr hProv, uint AlgID,
➥ uint dwFlags, ref IntPtr phKey);
```

With defined managed entry points for both `CryptAcquireContext` and `CryptGenKey`, we are now ready to proceed. Our goal is to write a method `CreateRSAKey` that allows us to specify whether the created key should be exportable and/or UI-protected. The signature for our desired method is as follows:

```
public static void CreateRSAKey(int size, String containerName,
➥ bool exportable, bool uiProtected)
{
    ...
}
```

For the purposes of this example, we always create the key within the default Type 1 cryptographic service provider. The `size` and `containerName` arguments allow us to determine key size and location. The Boolean values `exportable` and `uiProtected`, if set to `true`, will cause appropriate flags to be passed to CryptoAPI.

The first step to accomplish in our method is to obtain a handle (in an `IntPtr` structure) to the key container in which the key is to be generated. The following two lines of code create a new `IntPtr` structure and then invoke `CryptAcquireContext` to obtain a handle on the key container:

```
IntPtr hCryptProv = new IntPtr(0);
bool acquireSucceeded = CryptAcquireContext(ref hCryptProv,
➥ containerName, null, 1, 0);
```

The arguments to `CryptAcquireContext` are a reference to the `IntPtr` where the handle will be returned, the `String` value of the desired container name—`null` to indicate we want the default cryptographic service provider, 1 to indicate that we want a Type 1 provider, and 0 to indicate that we are not passing any additional flag (at this time) to `CryptAcquireContext`. The return value `acquireSucceeded` will be `true` if the call completed successfully; otherwise, `false`.

The previous code snippet works if the desired key container already exists, but it will fail if we have to create the key container within the CSP. If the container does not exist, the Win32 error code returned from `CryptAcquireContext` will be `NTE_BAD_KEYSET` (defined to be the value `0x80090016` in `winerror.h`). We can detect and handle this specific failure case as follows:

```
uint CRYPT_NEWKEYSET = 0x00000008;
IntPtr hCryptProv = new IntPtr(0);
// We assume the key container already exists.  If not, we'll catch the
// error and try again with CRYPT_NEWKEYSET specified
bool acquireSucceeded = CryptAcquireContext(ref hCryptProv, containerName,
➥ null, 1, 0);
if (!acquireSucceeded) {
```

```
    uint error = (uint) Marshal.GetLastWin32Error();
    // 0x8009000F = NTE_BAD_KEYSET, which means the key container
    // probably doesn't exist, so we'll try to create it
    if (error != 0x80090016) {
      throw new CryptographicException((int) error);
    }
    acquireSucceeded = CryptAcquireContext(ref hCryptProv, containerName,
➥ null, 1, CRYPT_NEWKEYSET);
    if (!acquireSucceeded) {
      throw new CryptographicException(Marshal.GetLastWin32Error());
    }
  }
}
```

This code snippet attempts to open the key container as though it already exists within the provider and, upon failure, attempts to create a new container with the desired name. The `CRYPT_NEWKEYSET` flag value is defined in the `wincrypt.h` header file, and we copy that definition into our managed source code for easy reference. The line

```
uint error = (uint) Marshal.GetLastWin32Error();
```

returns to us the Win32 error generated by the call to `CryptAcquireContext` because we set the `SetLastError` attribute to `true` on the `DllImport` attribute that defined the proxy to `CryptAcquireContext`. We have to cast the error value from `int` to `uint` so we can compare it with the `uint` value of `NTE_BAD_KEYSET` (defined in `winerror.h` as `0x80090016`). If the error we received from CryptoAPI is indeed `NTE_BAD_KEYSET`, we simply try calling `CryptAcquireContext` again by specifying the `CRYPT_NEWKEYSET` flag to cause the key container to be generated. On any other error, or if the second call to `CryptAcquireContext` fails, we throw a `CryptographicException`.

After we have successfully called `CryptAcquireContext`, the `IntPtr hCryptProv` will contain a handle to the desired key container, and we are ready to generate a new key pair within it. The `flags` argument to `CryptGenKey` tells CryptoAPI whether we want the key to be exportable and whether there should be a pop-up dialog shown to the user on every key access; we construct `flags` by ORing together the `CRYPT_EXPORTABLE` and `CRYPT_USER_PROTECTED` values as appropriate. The result of calling `CryptGenKey` is a Boolean value indicating success or failure and, if successful, the `hCryptKey IntPtr` argument will contain a handle to the generated key. The following is sample code for creating the key in the `hCryptProv` container:

```
uint flags = 0;
if (exportable) flags |= CRYPT_EXPORTABLE;
if (uiProtected) flags |= CRYPT_USER_PROTECTED;
IntPtr hCryptKey = new IntPtr(0);
```

```
bool genKeySucceeded = CryptGenKey(hCryptProv, 0x0000A400, flags,
➥ ref hCryptKey);
```

The second argument to the CryptGenKey call, the value 0x0000A400, is the value of the wincrypt.h constant CALG_RSA_KEYX, which indicates that the key to be generated is an RSA key suitable for "key exchange" and it should be stored in the "key exchange" slot of the key container. (CALG_RSA_KEYX also appears in Table 31.4.) In this example, we assume that we always want to create "key exchange" keys because they can be used both for signature and encryption operations.

There is one additional piece of information we need to process—the desired size of the resulting key pair. In CryptoAPI, the desired size of the public modulus is stored as the high 16 bits of the flags argument to CryptGenKey; with our current code, we always pass a 0 value that is interpreted as "use the default key size" (usually 1024 bits). To handle any valid key size between 384 and 16384 bits (the sizes supported by the Microsoft Strong Cryptographic Provider), we need to add that information into the flags field. The following code checks that the requested key size is valid and modifies flags accordingly:

```
// The desired size of the modulus is contained in the upper 16 bits of
// the flags field.  First we check that size is between 384 and 16384 (the
// size range allowed for Type 1 providers, and then we OR in the bits
if ((size < 384) || (size > 16384))
{
  throw new ArgumentException("Invalid size parameter.");
}
flags |= ((uint) size << 16);
```

We now have all the pieces necessary to create RSA keys with optional exportability of the private component and UI key protection. Listing 31.1 contains a small utility program for creating random keys built from the code snippets we have just discussed. The Main() routine processes command line arguments of -s <size>, -e, and -u to indicate the desired size of the public key modulus (in bits), exportability of the private key, and whether UI protection should be added to the key. The final command line argument is always the name of the key container in which to store the newly generated key.

LISTING 31.1   Creating a New RSA Encryption Key Pair Optional Exportability and UI Protection

---

```
using System;
using System.Security.Cryptography;
using System.Runtime.InteropServices;
```

LISTING 31.1 Continued

```
public class CreateNonExportableKeyClass
{
  private static uint CRYPT_NEWKEYSET = 0x00000008;

  [DllImport("advapi32.dll",EntryPoint="CryptAcquireContext",
➥ CharSet=CharSet.Auto, SetLastError=true)]
  public static extern bool CryptAcquireContext(ref IntPtr hCryptProv,
➥ String containerName,
    String providerName, int providerType, uint providerFlags);

  private static uint CRYPT_EXPORTABLE = 0x00000001;
  private static uint CRYPT_USER_PROTECTED = 0x00000002;

  [DllImport("advapi32.dll",EntryPoint="CryptGenKey",CharSet=CharSet.Auto,
➥ SetLastError=true)]
  public static extern bool CryptGenKey(IntPtr hProv, uint AlgID,
➥ uint dwFlags, ref IntPtr phKey);

  public static void CreateRSAKey(int size, String containerName,
➥ bool exportable, bool uiProtected)
  {
    IntPtr hCryptProv = new IntPtr(0);
    // We assume the key container already exists.  If not, we'll catch the
    // error and try again with CRYPT_NEWKEYSET specified
    uint flags = 0;
    if (exportable) flags |= CRYPT_EXPORTABLE;
    if (uiProtected) flags |= CRYPT_USER_PROTECTED;
    // The desired size of the modulus is contained in the upper 16 bits of
    // the flags field.  First we check that size is between 384 and 16384
    // (the size range allowed for Type 1 providers), and then we
    // OR in the bits
    if ((size < 384) || (size > 16384))
    {
      throw new ArgumentException("Invalid size parameter.");
    }
    flags |= ((uint) size << 16);
    bool acquireSucceeded = CryptAcquireContext(ref hCryptProv,
➥ containerName, null, 1, 0);
    if (!acquireSucceeded)
    {
      uint error = (uint) Marshal.GetLastWin32Error();
```

LISTING 31.1   Continued

```
    // 0x8009000F = NTE_BAD_KEYSET, which means the key container
    // probably doesn't exist, so we'll try to create it
    if (error != 0x80090016)
    {
      throw new CryptographicException((int) error);
    }
    acquireSucceeded = CryptAcquireContext(ref hCryptProv, containerName,
 null, 1, CRYPT_NEWKEYSET);
    if (!acquireSucceeded)
    {
      throw new CryptographicException(Marshal.GetLastWin32Error());
    }
  }
  IntPtr hCryptKey = new IntPtr(0);
  bool genKeySucceeded = CryptGenKey(hCryptProv, 0x0000A400, flags,
 ref hCryptKey);
  if (!genKeySucceeded)
  {
    throw new CryptographicException(Marshal.GetLastWin32Error());
  }
}


public static void Main(String[] args)
{
  if (args.Length < 1)
  {
    Console.WriteLine("Usage: createkey [-s size] [-e] [-u]
 keyContainerName");
    return;
  }
  String keyContainerName = null;
  bool exportable = false;
  bool uiProtected = false;
  int i = 0;
  int size = 1024;
  while (i < args.Length)
  {
    if (args[i].Equals("-s"))
    {
      i++;
```

LISTING 31.1   Continued

```
      size = Int32.Parse(args[i]);
      i++;
      continue;
    }
    if (args[i].Equals("-e"))
    {
      exportable = true;
      i++;
      continue;
    }
    if (args[i].Equals("-u"))
    {
      uiProtected = true;
      i++;
      continue;
    }
    keyContainerName = args[i];
    break;
  }
  CreateRSAKey(size, keyContainerName, exportable, uiProtected);
  }
}
```

NOTE

The program shown in Listing 31.1 has a couple of obvious limitations. First, as a result of the way the command line arguments are processed, it is not possible to use this program to access a key container called -s, -e, or -u, and, in fact, trying to do so will end up accessing the default key container (null string value). Second, there is no provision for creating keys in the "signature" slot of a key container, although that could easily be added by adding another command line argument, another Boolean flag to the CreateRSAKey method and, depending on the value of that flag, changing the algorithm ID value from 0x0000A400 to 0x00002400. Finally, there is no provision in this program for accessing key containers stored in the machine key store, but again, an option could be easily added by ORing in the CRYPT_MACHINE_KEYSET flag to the flags passed to the CryptAcquireContext call.

Cleaning Up: Deleting Keys and Key Containers

Our final comment on working with CryptoAPI 1.0 has to do with deleting keys and key containers. The .NET Framework does not provide a static method for deleting keys; keys are deleted only if they are stored in a transient key container and then only when a managed object bound to that key container is disposed of (via an explicit call to Clear() or implicitly by the garbage collector). If you want to explicitly delete a key container, you have two options. First, you could create a managed object bound to the key container (by specifying the name of the key container in a CspParameters object), force the key container to be considered transient by setting the PersistKeyInCsp property on the managed object to false, and then explicitly disposing of the managed object through a call to Clear(). The other method of deleting a key container is to explicitly call CryptAcquireContext and with the CRYPT_DELETE_KEYSET flag (value 0x00000010). Both mechanisms demand "unmanaged code" permission (an instance of SecurityPermission(SecurityPermissionFlag.UnmanagedCode)) of their call stack.

This concludes our discussion of working with CryptoAPI 1.0 (base cryptography) from within the .NET Framework. In the next section, we move to CryptoAPI 2.0 functions that relate to digital certificates and signed messages.

Working with CryptoAPI 2.0

We turn our attention now to the set of Win32 functions commonly known as CryptoAPI 2.0—functions that deal with digital certificates and signed messages. CryptoAPI includes support for handling and processing digital certificates based on the X.509 version 3 standard as profiled by the IETF's PKIX working group. CryptoAPI 2.0 also includes functions that generate cryptographically signed messages in the Cryptographic Message Syntax (CMS) format, which is the format used by the S/MIME secure mail standard to send and receive signed and encrypted e-mail messages. In this section, we assume that the reader is familiar with X.509/PKIX Part 1 certificates and CMS-format messages.

The .NET Framework includes minimal support for X.509/PKIX certificates and no support for CMS messages, so if you want to use these features of CryptoAPI in your programs, you have two choices:

- Use the CLR's platform invoke mechanism to call CryptoAPI functions directly.

- Use the COM interop capabilities built into the CLR to talk to the CAPICOM library, a COM wrapper distributed by Microsoft for accessing certain CryptoAPI functions.

We will focus initially on direct invocation of CryptoAPI 2.0's Win32 APIs from the .NET Framework, and how those APIs can be used with the Framework's X509Certificate class. Later examples in this section show how CAPICOM can be used from within the .NET Framework.

The X509Certificate class (located in the System.Security.Cryptography.X509Certificates namespace) is the .NET

Framework's representation of an X.509v3/PKIX Part 1 digital certificate. An instance of X509Certificate can be created in any of the following five ways:

- From a byte array containing the ASN.1 binary encoding of a certificate via the X509Certificate(byte[]) constructor.

- Cloned from an existing X509Certificate via the X509Certificate(X509Certificate) constructor.

- From a file containing an ASN.1 binary encoding of a certificate via the static method CreateFromCertificateFile(String) (the String argument is the name of the file containing the certificate data).

- From a file containing a CMS-format signed message via the static method CreateFromSignedFile(String) (the String argument is the name of the file containing the CMS-format message). The certificate obtained from the file is the one associated with the key pair used to sign the message.

- From a pointer to a CryptoAPI CERT_CONTEXT data structure, which is the unmanaged (native Win32) representation of a certificate.

This last constructor provides an interface between Win32 CryptoAPI certificate functions and the X509Certificate class in the .NET Framework. Using platform invoke, we can call CryptoAPI 2.0 functions to manipulate certificate stores (such as the per-user and per-machine certificate stores that exist in Windows) and then import individual certificates into the .NET Framework.

The program shown in Listing 31.2 demonstrates how the X509Certificate class works with the CryptoAPI certificate functions. This program enumerates the contents of one of the user's certificate stores (the "MY" store by default, where end-entity certificates for the user are normally stored). The program uses platform invoke to call three CryptoAPI functions—CertOpenStore, CertEnumCertificatesInStore, and CertCloseStore. Repeated calls to CertEnumCertificatesInStore iterate through the contents of the store (each iteration of the while loop causes the currentCertContext variable to point to a new certificate). When currentCertContext is equal to IntPtr(0), the underlying PCERT_CONTEXT is NULL and there are no more certificates to enumerate.

LISTING 31.2   Enumerating the Contents of a Certificate Store

```
using System;
using System.IO;
using System.Security.Cryptography;
using System.Security.Cryptography.X509Certificates;
using System.Text;
```

LISTING 31.2   Continued

```
using System.Runtime.InteropServices;

public class Test
{
  // magic constants from wincrypt.h
  private static int CERT_STORE_PROV_SYSTEM = 10;
  private static int CERT_SYSTEM_STORE_CURRENT_USER = (1 << 16);

  [DllImport("CRYPT32.DLL", EntryPoint="CertOpenStore",
➥ CharSet=CharSet.Auto, SetLastError=true)]
  public static extern IntPtr CertOpenStoreStringPara( int storeProvider,
➥ int encodingType, int hcryptProv, int flags, String pvPara);

  [DllImport("CRYPT32.DLL", EntryPoint="CertOpenStore",
➥ CharSet=CharSet.Auto, SetLastError=true)]
  public static extern IntPtr CertOpenStoreIntPtrPara( int storeProvider,
➥ int encodingType, int hcryptProv, int flags, IntPtr pvPara);

  [DllImport("CRYPT32.DLL", EntryPoint="CertEnumCertificatesInStore",
➥ CharSet=CharSet.Auto, SetLastError=true)]
  public static extern IntPtr CertEnumCertificatesInStore(
➥ IntPtr storeProvider, IntPtr prevCertContext);

  [DllImport("CRYPT32.DLL", EntryPoint="CertCloseStore",
➥ CharSet=CharSet.Auto, SetLastError=true)]
  public static extern bool CertCloseStore(IntPtr storeProvider, int flags);

  public static void Main(String[] args)
  {
    String store = "MY"; // default system store to search is the MY store
    if (args.Length > 0)
    {
      store = args[0]; // first argument, if any, overrides default value
    }
    IntPtr storeHandle = CertOpenStoreStringPara(CERT_STORE_PROV_SYSTEM,
➥ 0, 0, CERT_SYSTEM_STORE_CURRENT_USER, store);
    X509Certificate cert;
    IntPtr currentCertContext = CertEnumCertificatesInStore(storeHandle,
➥ (IntPtr) 0);
    while (currentCertContext != (IntPtr) 0)
    {
```

LISTING 31.2 Continued

```
        cert = new X509Certificate(currentCertContext);
        // Do something with the certificate...
        Console.WriteLine(cert.ToString(true));
        currentCertContext = CertEnumCertificatesInStore(storeHandle,
➥ currentCertContext);
    }
    CertCloseStore(storeHandle, 0);
  }
}
```

This program uses platform invoke to access Win32 APIs in a similar manner to that we saw in Listing 31.1. We use the IntPtr structure to represent handles to certificates and certificate stores, and of course there are some "magic constants" that we have to import manually from the wincrypt.h header file. Every call to CertEnumCertificatesInStore that succeeds returns a pointer to a new CERT_CONTEXT. Using the X509Certificate(IntPtr) constructor, we turn the CERT_CONTEXT pointer into a X509Certificate object, which we can then use as desired. (In this example, we just pretty-print the contents of the X509Certificate to the console.)

> **NOTE**
>
> Often, the APIs in CryptoAPI use void* arguments to pass context-dependent structures. CertOpenStore is an example of one such API; the last argument, pvPara, can be a pointer to a string, a file handle, a registry key handle, an HCRYPTMSG handle, or even a pointer to a CRYPT_DATA_BLOB. The CLR marshaler (which is responsible for converting managed objects into unmanaged objects during platform invoke calls) obviously cannot automatically distinguish among these various types of arguments, because it does not have the knowledge inherent in the CryptoAPI implementation concerning what type of argument to expect for each possible set of API arguments. Thus, we need to provide platform invoke with some additional information so that it can marshal arguments properly. In Listing 31.2, we chose to explicitly define multiple managed proxies for the CertOpenStore function, CertOpenStoreStringPara and CertOpenStoreIntPtrPara, where each managed proxy requires a different Type for its pvPara argument. In this example, all the calls to CertOpenStore required string arguments, so we always used CertOpenStoreStringPara, but if we had wanted to pass a file or registry key handle to CertOpenStore, we would have to have used the CertOpenStoreIntPtrPara proxy.

You can always use platform invoke to access any CryptoAPI 2.0 function you want, but it often may be easier for you to use CAPICOM to accomplish your task. CAPICOM is a set of classic COM wrappers for common CryptoAPI 2.0 functions; it is available for download from the Microsoft Developer Network (MSDN) as part of the Platform SDK. CAPICOM consists of a single DLL, `CAPICOM.dll`, which must be present at runtime if your application uses CAPICOM. If you do not already have the Platform SDK installed you can download just the redistributable version of CAPICOM from Microsoft's Download Center by visiting the URL `http://www.microsoft.com/downloads/release.asp?releaseid=30316`.

After you have obtained the CAPICOM library, you must first register it with Windows. Type the following command at the command prompt to register the CAPICOM library and make its COM interfaces available for use by other COM objects:

```
regsvr32 CAPICOM.dll
```

To use a COM component from managed code, we must first generate metadata for the COM interfaces the component exposes. If you are using Visual Studio.NET to write your programs, the metadata generation happens automatically when you add a reference to the COM component to your project. To use CAPICOM from within a Visual Studio.NET project, simply

1. Select Project, Add Reference from the Visual Studio.NET menu.

2. Select the COM tab on the Add Reference dialog.

3. Scroll down until you see `CAPICOM 1.0 Type Library`.

4. Click CAPICOM 1.0 Type Library to highlight it and click the Select button.

5. Click the OK button.

You will now see an additional reference to CAPICOM in the References section of the Solution Explorer. By default, the metadata generated by Visual Studio.NET for an imported COM object lives in a namespace identical to the name of the library DLL that was imported, so the metadata generated for `CAPICOM.dll` resides in the `CAPICOM` namespace. You will want to add a

```
using CAPICOM;
```

statement to your program so that you can automatically reference the types defined in `CAPICOM.dll`.

If you are not using Visual Studio.NET to author your programs, you need to generate the metadata for `CAPICOM.dll` manually. The .NET Framework SDK includes a utility called `tlbimp.exe` that will construct a managed proxy assembly with appropriate metadata for a COM object type library. The `CAPICOM` type library is contained within `CAPICOM.dll`, so you can generate the CLR metadata for CAPICOM by typing the following command at the command prompt:

```
tlbimp CAPICOM.dll /out:CAPICOMCLR.dll /namespace:CAPICOM
```

NOTE

The `Tlbimp.exe` program will issue some warning messages when used to generate metadata for `CAPICOM.dll`. These warnings can be safely ignored.

The assembly created by `tlbimp` is normally named the same as the input `.tlb` file, except that the file extension is changed from `.tlb` to `.dll`. Because the type library we imported was contained within a DLL already, we have to rename the output assembly to something else. We use the `/out` argument to name the output file `CAPICOMCLR.dll`, but you can use any name you like. The `/namespace` argument overrides `tlbimp`'s default namespace choice (the output DLL name, `CAPICOMCLR` in our case) and forces the metadata namespace to be just `CAPICOM`. To use the CAPICOM metadata in your program, you will need to explicitly reference the metadata assembly when compiling your programs. The exact method of referencing another assembly varies from compiler to compiler; the C# compiler `csc.exe` uses a `/r` command line argument, so you will want to add `/r:capicomclr.dll` to your other arguments to `csc.exe`. You will also probably want to add a `using CAPICOM;` statement to your C# source code (or equivalent syntax for the source language you are using) so you can more easily reference objects in the `CAPICOM` namespace.

Now that you have configured CAPICOM for use with the .NET Framework, let's look at some examples. Listing 31.3 contains a program that dumps the contents of the `"MY"` certificate store using `CAPICOM`; it performs the same function as the program in Listing 31.2 but without calling any Win32 APIs directly.

LISTING 31.3   Enumerating the Contents of a Certificate Store Using CAPICOM

```
using System;
using System.Security.Cryptography.X509Certificates;
using CAPICOM;
using System.IO;

public class ReadCertificateStore {
  public static void Main(String[] args) {
    Store store = new Store();
    store.Open(CAPICOM_STORE_LOCATION.CAPICOM_CURRENT_USER_STORE, "MY",
➥ CAPICOM_STORE_OPEN_MODE.CAPICOM_STORE_OPEN_READ_ONLY);
    foreach (Certificate cert in store.Certificates) {
      String certString = cert.Export(
➥ CAPICOM_ENCODING_TYPE.CAPICOM_ENCODE_BASE64);
      byte[] decodedcert = Convert.FromBase64String(certString);
      X509Certificate certificate = new  X509Certificate(decodedcert);
      Console.WriteLine(certificate.ToString(true));
```

LISTING 31.3   Continued

```
    }
  }
}
```

CAPICOM `Store` objects represent CryptoAPI 2.0 certificate stores. In this program, we create an empty `Store` object and then call its `Open` method to bind the object to a particular certificate store. Here, we ask CAPICOM to open up the user's `"MY"` store just as we did in Listing 31.2. CAPICOM provides a number of enumerations that correspond to the flags we would normally pass to the Win32 APIs; the `CAPICOM_STORE_LOCATION.CAPICOM_CURRENT_USER_STORE` enumeration used here corresponds to the `CERT_SYSTEM_STORE_CURRENT_USER` flag used previously. When open, the `Store`'s `Certificates` property returns a collection of all the certificates within the store that we can step through using the C# `foreach` language construct.

The most complicated portion of this program is the three lines of code needed to convert CAPICOM's representation of a certificate into an `X509Certificate` managed object. CAPICOM does not directly expose the `CERT_CONTEXT` associated with its `Certificate` objects, so to convert a certificate from CAPICOM to the .NET Framework, we need to export the certificate from CAPICOM in a common format and re-import it into an `X509Certificate` object. CAPICOM provides an `Export` method on the `Certificate` class that allows us to convert the certificate into a Base64 encoding of its ASN.1 binary representation. We convert the encoded form back into an array of bytes and construct a new `X509Certificate` object from the byte array.

CAPICOM also contains functions that build and verify chains of certificates; the program shown in Listing 31.4 is a sample application of these functions. This program opens the `"MY"` user certificate store, extracts the first certificate it finds in the store, and then asks CryptoAPI to build a certificate chain from that certificate to a trusted root certificate. Assuming that a chain exists, the program then walks the chain from end-entity certificate to root certificate, converting each certificate encountered along the way into an `X509Certificate` object using the export/import-as-Base64 technique used previously. The resulting `X509Certificate` objects are printed to the console.

LISTING 31.4   Building a Certificate Chain Using CAPICOM

```
using System;
using System.Security.Cryptography.X509Certificates;
using CAPICOM;
using System.IO;
```

LISTING 31.4   Continued

```
public class ReadCertificateStore {
  public static void Main(String[] args) {
    Store store = new Store();
    store.Open(CAPICOM_STORE_LOCATION.CAPICOM_CURRENT_USER_STORE, "MY",
➥ CAPICOM_STORE_OPEN_MODE.CAPICOM_STORE_OPEN_READ_ONLY);
    // Check to make sure there's at least one cert in the MY store
    if (store.Certificates.Count > 0) {
      Certificate cert = (Certificate) store.Certificates[0];
      Chain chain = new Chain();
      chain.Build(cert);
      foreach (Certificate chainCert in chain.Certificates) {
        String certString = chainCert.Export(
➥ CAPICOM_ENCODING_TYPE.CAPICOM_ENCODE_BASE64);
        byte[] decodedcert = Convert.FromBase64String(certString);
        X509Certificate certificate = new  X509Certificate(decodedcert);
        Console.WriteLine(certificate.ToString(true));
      }
    }
  }
}
```

As you can see, both platform invoke and CAPICOM make certificate-based operations relatively easy to perform from within the .NET Framework. For very simple, straightforward applications, CAPICOM will generally be the easier of the two mechanisms to use. However, because CAPICOM exposes only a subset of CryptoAPI 2.0 functionality, it is likely that as your application requirements increase you will need to use platform invoke to call the CryptoAPI 2.0 APIs directly.

Finalization Versus Explicit Destruction via IDisposable

Normally, when you are finished using an object in the .NET Framework, the memory allocated by the object will be reclaimed by the Framework's garbage collector on an as-needed basis. However, in the case of cryptographic objects, implicit garbage collection is generally not appropriate. By their very nature, cryptographic objects contain sensitive data, such as secret key values, which must be explicitly destroyed after they are no longer needed.

Every cryptographic object within the .NET Framework implements the IDisposable() interface to support proper disposal of sensitive data. Types within the .NET Framework implement the IDisposable interface to provide a programmable way for user code to indicate that its use of an object is finished. When called, an object's Dispose() method normally releases all the resources that are held by the object and recursively calls the Dispose() method of its parent type. In the case of cryptographic objects, however, simply releasing the internal resources is generally not sufficient, because sensitive data might still remain in the free portion of the managed memory heap. We must additionally destroy the sensitive data before releasing the memory it occupies.

All cryptographic classes that hold sensitive data within the .NET Framework implement a Clear() method to properly erase and dispose of instances of the class. When called, the Clear() method on a cryptographic object will first overwrite all sensitive data within the object with zeros and then release the now-zeroed object so that it can be safely garbage-collected. Listing 31.5 demonstrates how to use Clear() to prepare a cryptographic object for release.

LISTING 31.5   Encrypting an On-Disk File to a Second File with Random IV Generation

```
public static void EncryptFile(byte[] key, String sourceFile,
➡ String destFile) {
  // initialize with random key and IV
  Rijndael aes = Rijndael.Create();
  // set the key to the passed-in arg
  aes.Key = key;
  // create FileStreams for source and dest
  FileStream inStream = new FileStream(sourceFile, FileMode.Open);
  FileStream outStream = new FileStream(destFile, FileMode.Create);
  // We want to write the IV out to the destFile unencrypted,
  // so in this case we can wrap a CryptoStream around the *sourceFile*
  // and read encrypted bytes from it
  CryptoStream encryptedInStream = new CryptoStream(inStream,
➡ aes.CreateEncryptor(), CryptoStreamMode.Read);
  // Write the IV out to the ciphertext file as the first bytes in the file.
  outStream.Write(aes.IV, 0, aes.IV.Length);
  // Now we're ready to encrypt. Read the bytes from the CryptoStream
  // in a loop until there aren't any more (end-of-file), writing to
  // the output file as we go. We need a buffer to hold what we're going to
  // read, and bytesRead tells us how many bytes in buffer are
  //valid ciphertext.
  int bytesRead;
  byte[] buffer = new byte[1024]; // read 1K at a time
  do {
      bytesRead = encryptedInStream.Read(buffer,0,1024);
      outStream.Write(buffer, 0, bytesRead);
  } while (bytesRead > 0);
  // Done!  Close() the streams we used.
```

LISTING 31.5   Continued

```
inStream.Close();
outStream.Close();
// Clear the Rijndael and CryptoStream objects to zero out
// sensitive data (e.g. key and IV in Rijndael)
encryptedInStream.Clear();
aes.Clear();
// Clearing the buffer is not strictly required since it only holds
// ciphertext, but is good practice also.
Array.Clear(buffer,0,buffer.Length);
return;
}
```

The code shown in Listing 31.5 is based on the file encryption sample in Listing 30.3, except for the addition of the following lines immediately before the return; statement:

```
// Clear the Rijndael and CryptoStream objects to zero out
// sensitive data (e.g. key and IV in Rijndael)
encryptedInStream.Clear();
aes.Clear();
// Clearing the buffer is not strictly required since it only holds
// ciphertext, but is good practice also.
Array.Clear(buffer,0,buffer.Length);
```

This code snippet explicitly calls the Clear() methods on the CryptoStream and Rijndael objects created within the EncryptFile method, thus making them safe to free and release to the garbage collector. Notice that we also explicitly zero the contents of the internal buffer variable; because buffer contains only ciphertext, it is not strictly necessary to zero out its contents, but it is good practice to do so.

CAUTION

It is not sufficient to simply force a garbage collection after you have finished using a crypto-graphic object, you must explicitly call the Clear() method on the object to zero out and release all sensitive data within the object. The garbage collection does not zero the contents of the collected objects but simply marks the memory as available for reallocation. Thus, the data contained within a garbage collected object may still be present in the memory heap (in unallocated memory); in the case of a cryptographic object, that data could contain sensitive information, such as key data or a block of plain text. Whenever you finish using a crypto-graphic object, follow best practices and call the object's Clear() method before releasing it.

Additionally, as previously noted, the Clear() methods on .NET Framework cryptographic objects make it easier for conscientious developers to properly dispose of sensitive information, but they are not cure-alls. Any variable you create that subsequently holds sensitive information, especially encryption or decryption keys, must be explicitly zeroed by the developer before the last reference to the object is released.

Extending the .NET Framework's Cryptography Classes and the Cryptographic Configuration System

You will recall from our discussion in the "The Cryptographic Object Model of the .NET Framework" section of Chapter 30 that the .NET Framework's cryptographic object model was designed to be easily extended by third parties. While the .NET Framework includes implementations of common symmetric and asymmetric algorithms, hash functions, and keyed hash functions, it may be necessary or desirable for various reasons to add new algorithms or algorithm implementations to the object hierarchy. For example, you might have a cryptographic hardware accelerator that you want to perform RSA decryptions from within the .NET Framework, or you might want to use a symmetric encryption algorithm not included "in the box." In this section, we briefly describe the process of extending the cryptographic object model and modifying the cryptographic configuration system to be aware of new algorithms and implementations.

Extensions to the cryptographic object model fall into one of two categories

- Additions of new implementations of algorithms already defined in the .NET Framework

- Additions of new algorithms

An example of the first category would be the addition of a new implementation of the AES/Rijndael algorithm, because the .NET Framework already includes the `RijndaelManaged` implementation of that algorithm. The addition of an implementation of the hash function RIPEMD-160 is an example of the second category of extension. In both cases, you will need to subclass portions of the cryptographic object model and potentially update the runtime configuration files. We'll walk through an example of the first category first, adding a new implementation, and then show the additional work required for the second category.

Adding a new implementation of a pre-existing algorithm to the .NET Framework is easy—simply subclass the abstract class that represents the algorithm, supplying concrete implementations for abstract methods in the parent classes. For example, to extend the Framework with your own implementation of the Rijndael algorithm, you would subclass the abstract `Rijndael` class with your own implementation class (`MyRijndaelImplementation`). Your new class would have to provide implementations for the following abstract `SymmetricAlgorithm` methods—`CreateEncryptor(byte[], byte[]) CreateDecryptor(byte[], byte[])`,

GenerateKey(), and GenerateIV(). After your new class is verified to properly implement Rijndael, you might want to make it the default implementation of Rijndael on the system. By modifying the cryptography portion of the runtime configuration files, you can reconfigure the abstract Rijndael class so that Rijndael.Create() returns an instance of your new MyRijndaelImplementation class instead of the RijndaelManaged class that ships as part of the .NET Framework. (The cryptographic configuration system is discussed in detail in the "Administering Cryptography Settings" section of Chapter 22, "Administering Isolated Storage and Cryptography Settings in the .NET Framework.")

Extending the .NET Framework cryptography classes to support a new algorithm is almost as easy as adding a new implementation of an existing algorithm. The additional work involved to add a new algorithm is to create an abstract subclass that represents all implementations of the new algorithm, similar to the role the Rijndael abstract class plays in the cryptographic object model. Your new abstract class should subclass one of SymmetricAlgorithm, AsymmetricAlgorithm, or HashAlgorithm as appropriate. By convention, the name of your new abstract class should be a short name for the algorithm it represents. For example, if you were adding an implementation of the RC6 block cipher to the .NET Framework, you would first define an abstract subclass of the SymmetricAlgorithm class called RC6. Your abstract subclass should include definitions of property values that would be constant across all implementations of the algorithm. Continuing our example, the RC6 abstract class should include definitions for the LegalKeySizesValue and LegalBlockSizesValue fields because their values are properties of the RC6 algorithm and not any individual implementation of the algorithm. Your class implementing the new algorithm should now subclass this abstract class as in the first category of the previous bulleted list. Changes to the runtime configuration file (where cryptographic configuration information is stored) can also be necessary, depending on your specific requirements.

Summary

This concludes our discussion of the cryptographic capabilities present in the .NET Framework. We have seen in this chapter how cryptographic features of the Win32 API set and CAPICOM can be accessed from the .NET Framework through the Common Language Runtime's platform invoke and COM interoperability mechanisms, respectively. In most cases, though, you will probably not need to access these APIs because the managed classes in the System.Security.Cryptography namespace provide support for the common cryptographic operations.

32

Using Cryptography with the .NET Framework: Creating and Verifying XML Digital Signatures

By Brian A. LaMacchia

In Chapter 30, "Using Cryptography with the .NET Framework: The Basics," you saw how to use a cryptographic hash function and an asymmetric (public key) algorithm to compute a digital signature for some content. The digital signatures you generated were simply binary arrays that encoded the mathematical output of applying the asymmetric signing function to a hash value. In theory, any binary content can be signed using only the core techniques from Chapter 30, but in practice, the signature needs to be encoded in an interoperable format that includes information about the algorithms used to generate it. This chapter discusses how to create and use digital signatures that conform to the IETF/W3C joint standard for XML digital signature syntax and processing rules (commonly abbreviated as XMLDSIG), an interoperable format that expresses digital signature data as XML objects.

NOTE

You can find the IETF/W3C XML-Signature Syntax and Processing Model standard on the Web at `http://www.w3.org/TR/xmldsig-core/`. The W3C home page for the XML-Signature Working Group can be found at `http://www.w3.org/Signature/`.

You are probably already familiar with XML, the Extensible Markup Language, through its use in other portions of the .NET Framework. The XML standard is the fundamental data format on which .NET Web Services are built. Web Services are described by XML documents corresponding to the Web Services Description Language (WSDL) XML schema. Clients interact with Web Services using the Simple Object Access Protocol (SOAP); SOAP messages are also XML documents. Even configuration data for the Common Language Runtime and ASP.NET is stored as XML.

As use of XML grew across the Internet, the need for security services specific to XML objects was quickly realized. Standards for providing message integrity and authentication for XML documents were obviously needed. While there were pre-existing standards for providing these security services to arbitrary data, there was no standard for expressing a digital signature itself as an XML object. In 1999, the Internet Engineering Task Force (IETF) and the World Wide Web Consortium (W3C) chartered a joint working group within their organizations to create a standard for XML digital signatures. The resulting standard, XMLDSIG, defines the XML format for representing a digital signature. The standard can be used to sign both XML and non-XML objects, although many of the features of the standard only apply to digital signatures over another XML object.

This chapter discusses the support included in the .NET Framework for creating and verifying digital signatures of XML documents and document fragments. The classes in the `System.Security.Cryptography.Xml` namespace implement the XMLDSIG standard and allow you to easily manipulate signatures that conform to the standard. After completing this chapter, you should be able to

- Describe the contents of the `System.Security.Cryptography.Xml` namespace in the .NET Framework and the fundamental model of an XMLDSIG `Signature` element

- Demonstrate how to create the three styles of XML signatures—wrapped, detached, and enveloped

- Demonstrate how to create XMLDSIG signatures over XML content using an asymmetric (public-key) algorithm, including both RSA and DSA

- Demonstrate how to verify an XMLDSIG signature

- Demonstrate how to add key-related information to an XMLDSIG `Signature` element via the `KeyInfo` element

This chapter covers both the theory and practice of XML digital signatures. We begin in the next section, "XMLDSIG Design Principles and Modes of Use," with a discussion of the design principles underlying the XMLDSIG standard and its various modes of operation. Even if you are familiar with other signature standards, such as PGP or S/MIME, we recommend that you read through this section completely because XMLDSIG has options not included in PGP or S/MIME. In "The Structure of an XMLDSIG Signature" section, we describe the XML structure of an XMLDSIG object in detail. Later sections demonstrate how the `System.Security.Cryptography.Xml` classes can be used to create and verify XMLDSIG-compliant signatures in each of these modes.

XMLDSIG Design Principles and Modes of Use

To begin our discussion of the XMLDSIG signature standard, we focus on the design principles and specification requirements that guided the work of the IETF/W3C XML Signature Working Group. These requirement and design principles were published in the original charter for the working group and expanded upon in IETF Informational RFC 2807— "XML Signature Requirements." Readers interested in the detailed requirements are advised to download the Requirements document from the IETF or W3C Web sites.

> **NOTE**
>
> The "XML-Signature Requirements" document can be found on the Web at `http://www.w3.org/TR/xmldsig-requirements` or `http://www.ietf.org/rfc/rfc2807.txt`.

The following is a list of the key requirements and design principles:

1. The specification must describe how to sign digital content, and XML content in particular. The XML syntax used to represent a signature (over any content) is described as an XML signature.

   This is the core requirement for XML digital signatures and it states the overall goal of the standard—provide a means of digitally signing any content and representing that signature in an XML structure. The requirement that it must be possible to sign non-XML content with an XMLDSIG signature meant that XMLDSIG must support a "detached" mode of operation in which the XML object containing the signature is physically separate from the signed content.

   There are three ways in which an XMLDSIG signature can be associated with some signed content; each method is depicted graphically in Figure 32.1.

   - First, the digital signature can be *wrapped* around the signed content. A wrapped digital signature carries the signed content embedded within it, as shown in Figure 32.1(A). Readers familiar with the S/MIME and OpenPGP secure mail standards will recognize that these standard always (S/MIME) or often (OpenPGP) use wrapped signatures with embedded content. Wrapped signature formats have the advantage that they put the signature and signed content together in a single recognizable package, but necessarily obscure the original format of the signed data.

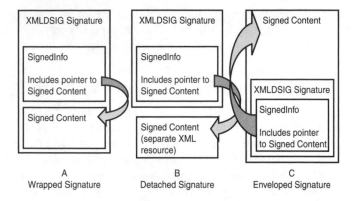

FIGURE 32.1   Three types of signatures—wrapped, detached, and enveloped.

- An example *detached* signature is shown in Figure 32.1(B). Detached signatures are carried in objects physically separated from the signed content. The detached signature may or may not carry an explicit reference to the signed content. In XMLDSIG, detached signatures always contain a reference pointer (URI) to the signed content (part of the `ds:Reference` element described in detail in "The Structure of an XMLDSIG Signature" section later in this chapter). In contrast, OpenPGP detached signatures do not contain an explicit reference pointer to the signed content.

- The third and final mode of operation supported by XMLDSIG is the *enveloped* or *embedded* signature, shown in Figure 32.1(C). Enveloped signatures embed the digital signature object within the signed content. An enveloped signature can be used only when there exists a mechanism for adding the signature data to the signed content without changing the hash of the signed content. XMLDSIG defines a mechanism (a type of `ds:Transform` element) that allows signature data to be embedded within another XML document yet ignored when that document is hashed. Enveloped signatures cannot be used with non-XML signed content.

2. The Working Group is not chartered to specify trust semantics, but syntax and processing rules necessary for communicating signature validity (authenticity, integrity, and non-repudiation).

Another difference between prior signature standards like S/MIME and XMLDSIG is that XMLDSIG defines *only* the mechanics of creating and verifying signature cryptographic values and explicitly does not specify a trust model. The S/MIME and OpenPGP standards specify how a verifying application should determine whether the key pair used to create the signature is "trusted" for some purpose. For example, in the case of S/MIME, these semantics are inherited from S/MIME's underlying reliance on PKIX certificates. XMLDSIG explicitly leaves all trust-related questions to the verifying application, recognizing that every application may have different policies concerning what evidence is required to prove a key pair trustworthy.

NOTE

Readers familiar with the concepts of trust management will recognize that by taking this approach, XMLDSIG chose to specify the process of verifying a piece of signed evidence input to an application's trust management engine, but did not specify the behavior of that engine. There were two main reasons for XMLDSIG to take this approach. First, based on the experiences of the IETF PKIX Working Group, it was clear that no fixed standard for policy evaluation could possibly satisfy all customer needs. Second, by explicitly delegating the policy evaluation tasks to the application, XMLDSIG makes clear the difference between cryptographic signature validation and making policy decisions based on the receipt of a signature.

3. The specification must only require the provision of key information essential to checking the validity of the cryptographic signature. For example, identity and key recovery information might be of interest to particular applications, but they are not within the class of required information defined in this specification.

   The third major requirement of XMLDSIG is a prohibition on requiring any sort of key validation information to be included within the `Signature` objects. Furthermore, key-related information provided in the `Signature` is present only to provide "hints" to the verifying application. This requirement flows naturally from requirement 2; if XMLDSIG is not required to follow any specific trust model, by extension information related to making a policy determination about a key pair cannot be required to be present. XMLDSIG does define XML structures for carrying commonly used key validation information within a `Signature`; these are the various child elements of the `KeyInfo` element and are discussed in "The Structure of an XMLDSIG Signature" section later in this chapter.

4. The specification must define or reference at least one method of canonicalizing and hashing the signature syntax.

5. XML signatures are generated from a hash over the canonical form of a signature.

The previous two requirements deal with *canonicalization algorithms*. Recall from Chapter 31, "Using Cryptography with the .NET Framework: Advanced Topics," that digital signatures over digital content are generally computed by signing the hash of the digital content. That is, the to-be-signed content is converted into a sequence of bytes, the sequence of byte is hashed by a cryptographic hash function, and the output hash value is the input to the digital signature function. Because the output hash value is sensitive to changes in each and every bit of the content, changing any bit of the content will yield a different hash value and invalidate the digital signature. Canonicalization deals with the first step in the process, the conversion of an XML document into a sequence of bytes.

At first, you would probably think that converting an XML document in a sequence of bytes would be easy. After all, XML documents are text documents containing Unicode characters (or a subset of Unicode characters, such as ASCII characters), and each Unicode character can be encoded as a sequence of bytes using standard encodings (for example, UCS-2 or UTF-8). The problem with this straightforward approach is that there are often multiple ways of writing the same XML object and, ideally, we want XML documents with the same semantic content to have the same hash value. For an illustrative example, consider the simple XML fragment shown in Listing 32.1.

LISTING 32.1   A Simple XML Fragment

```
<MyElement attribute1=foo attribute2=bar>
  MyValue
</MyElement>
```

This XML fragment shows a single XML element, `MyElement`, with two attributes (`attribute1` and `attribute2`) and one enclosed text value (the string `"MyValue"`). Now compare this fragment with the fragment shown in Listing 32.2.

LISTING 32.2   Another Simple XML Fragment

```
<MyElement attribute2=bar attribute1=foo>
  MyValue
</MyElement>
```

The only difference between the XML fragments in Listings 32.1 and 32.2 is the order in which attributes are listed after the opening `MyElement` element tag; both fragments represent the same abstract XML object, but their textual representations are quite different. If we naively convert an XML document (or fragment) into a byte sequence without taking into account equivalent semantic forms of an XML object, we will end up computing two different hashes for the objects in Listings 32.1 and 32.2, and thus two different signature values. Once signed, semantic-neutral processing of the signed XML content will potentially break the digital signature, yet XML processors are allowed to rewrite XML as much as they want as long as the rewrites are semantically neutral.

The answer to the problem illustrated in Listings 32.1 and 32.2 is to define for each XML expression a *canonical form* for that expression. The canonical form of an XML document has the same semantic content as the original document, and there is one and only one canonical form for every set of semantically equivalent XML documents. An *XML canonicalization algorithm* converts any XML document (or document fragment) into its corresponding canonical form. Thus, the hashes computed from the canonical forms of Listings 32.1 and 32.2 will be equal because their semantic content is identical. Returning to requirements 4 and 5, we now see why it was critical for the standard to include a canonicalization algorithm for XML. To the extent possible, signatures over XML objects needed to be resistant to permissible (semantically neutral) rewrites of the signed content as it moves around the network.

In parallel to the development of the XMLDSIG standard, the Working Group also defined a standard for Canonical XML and the algorithm for computing the canonical form of any XML object. The detailed operation of the Canonical XML algorithm is beyond the scope of this book; interested readers can download the specification from the IETF and W3C Web sites. The .NET Framework includes an implementation of the Canonical XML algorithm for internal use by the XMLDSIG-related classes.

NOTE

The Canonical XML algorithm is often abbreviated C14N because there are 14 letters between the initial "c" and final "n" in the word canonicalization.

6. XML signatures must be able to apply to a part or totality of an XML document.

Another major requirement for XML digital signatures necessitated a design that allowed digital signatures to be computed over subsets of an entire XML document. Previous digital signature standards, including both S/MIME and OpenPGP, always computed signatures over the entire content that they wrapped. While sufficient for e-mail application, always signing the entire document content blocks key workflow and online forms scenarios. Consider, for example, an online form that will be partially filled out by Alice and then completed by Bob, as illustrated in Figure 32.2. Alice wants to be able to sign the incomplete document at the time she finishes her portion of work to attest to her contribution to the document. After Alice finishes and passes the signed, partially completed document on to Bob, Bob will add additional information to the document. As long as Bob doesn't modify any of Alice's contributions, we want Alice's signature to continue to verify. At the same time, we do not want Alice's signature to cover the portions of the document that Bob will fill in. Thus, Alice needs to be able to specify exactly which portions of the compound document she is signing. Bob also has the choice of signing just the portion of the document he completed, or Bob may want to sign the combination of Alice's content and his own. These two possibilities are illustrated in Figure 32.3.

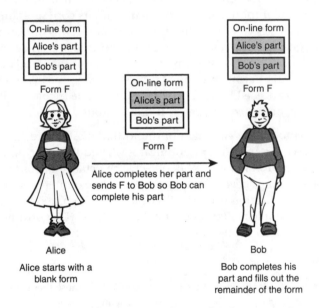

FIGURE 32.2   Sample online form scenario: Alice and Bob must each complete portions of the form.

In Figure 32.3(A), Alice and Bob each sign their respective portions of the document, and Alice's signed content does not overlap any portion of Bob's signed content. In contrast, Figure 32.3(B) shows Alice's signature over part of the document and Bob's subsequent signature over both Alice's content and his own additions.

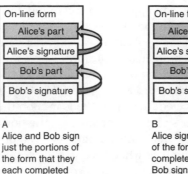

A
Alice and Bob sign
just the portions of
the form that they
each completed

B
Alice signs the portion
of the form she
completed.
Bob signs both Alice's
part and his own.

FIGURE 32.3   Two ways for Alice and Bob to sign the form.

NOTE

A brief digression about *time* is in order here, specifically the signing time of the four signatures illustrated in Figure 32.3. Unless there is specific evidence included within the digital signature, it is not possible to tell in either scenario A or scenario B which signature was created first.

In Figure 32.3(A), Alice's signature is completely disjoint from Bob's signature, and it is quite possible that the two signatures were computed without any knowledge of the overall document or any relationship between the two signed contents. Alice's and Bob's signatures may have been created in different locations and only merged together into a single document after all the pieces of the document were brought together.

The situation depicted in Figure 32.3(B) is a little more subtle. Here, we know that the content signed by Bob strictly includes the content signed by Alice. However, we do not know when Bob created his signature relative to Alice creating her signature. At the time Bob creates his signature, he sees Alice's content and his own content, but he is not required to see Alice's signature because he is not signing Alice's signature. Therefore, it is actually possible in this scenario for Bob to sign in parallel with Alice, or even before Alice, because their respective signatures are added after the fact. Because there is no temporal relationship between Alice's signature and Bob's signature, the two signatures are independent—they could have been made in any order.

7. XML signatures are first class objects themselves and consequently must be able to be referenced and signed.

In some scenarios, such as document workflow or online forms applications, it is often desired to represent a chain of processing steps by a series of "chained" signatures, where subsequent signatures sign previous signatures in the chain.

For example, consider the loan application scenario depicted in Figure 32.4. In this scenario, Alice applies for a loan through an online loan application form. She fills in some fields on the application, such as her current income and assets, signs the partially completed application, and submits it. The application is then routed to Bob, a loan officer. Bob performs two tasks with the application—he verifies the information Alice submitted, and he also adds information about Alice's credit rating to the loan. Bob then signs the entire document, including Alice's original signature on the portion she completed. Bob's signature explicitly includes Alice's signature as a piece of content, because Bob wants to commit to what Alice signed, not just what information she provided. Bob's signature is, in effect, a counter-signature on Alice's signature. Counter-signatures (sometimes also called a *cascaded signature*) are signatures over other signatures, and they are easy to create in XMLDSIG because every `Signature` element is also content that can be signed.

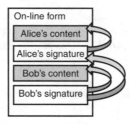

Alice signs the content she added to the form.

Bob signs both the new data he added to the form as well as Alice's signature. Bob indirectly signs Alice's form content by signing her signature over that content.

FIGURE 32.4   Cascaded signatures: Bob's signature over Alice's signature implicitly signs Alice's content.

8. The specification must permit arbitrary cryptographic signature and message authentication algorithms, symmetric and asymmetric authentication schemes, and key agreement methods.

9. The specification must specify at least one mandatory to implement signature canonicalization, content canonicalization, hash, and signature algorithm.

The last major design requirement for XML Digital Signatures deals with the underlying cryptographic algorithms that must be supported by the standard. The requirement has two components. First, XMLDSIG was required to be algorithm-neutral; it must be possible to use any digital signature algorithm or cryptographic hash function with the structures defined in the standard.

Second, for interoperability purposes, the standard had to define a set of mandatory-to-implement algorithms that would be guaranteed to be present and supported in every conforming implementation. The cryptographic algorithms specified in XMLDSIG are listed in Table 32.1. Required algorithms are mandatory-to-implement in all conforming applications; it is guaranteed, for example, that an XMLDSIG processor will be able to parse and understand a `Signature` block made using a DSA signature key. Recommended algorithms are not guaranteed to be present but are expected to be implemented in most implementations. RSA-SHA1 digital signatures are generally supported by implementation (including the .NET Framework) but is not a mandatory-to-implement algorithm.

TABLE 32.1   XMLDSIG Required and Recommended Algorithms

Algorithm Type	Algorithm	Status
Digest (hash function)	SHA1	Required
Signature	DSA with SHA1	Required
	RSA with SHA1	Recommended
MAC	HMAC-SHA1	Required
Canonicalization	Canonical XML (C14N)	Required
	Canonical XML with Comments	Recommended

This concludes our overview of the requirements that led to the final design of the XML Digital Signature standard. In the next section, we will see how each of these requirements impacts and is reflected in the actual structure of an XMLDSIG `Signature` element.

The Structure of an XMLDSIG Signature

We turn our attention now to the structure of an XMLDSIG signature object and its various subcomponents. Our goal in this section is to provide a comprehensive guide to an XMLDSIG `Signature` element and its various subcomponents. We will walk through the `Signature` structure in a top-down fashion, first describing the high-level components of a signature and then describing the various subcomponents in more detail.

Figure 32.5 shows a graphical block diagram of the major components that together comprise an XMLDSIG signature object, and the corresponding XML structure is shown in Listing 32.3.

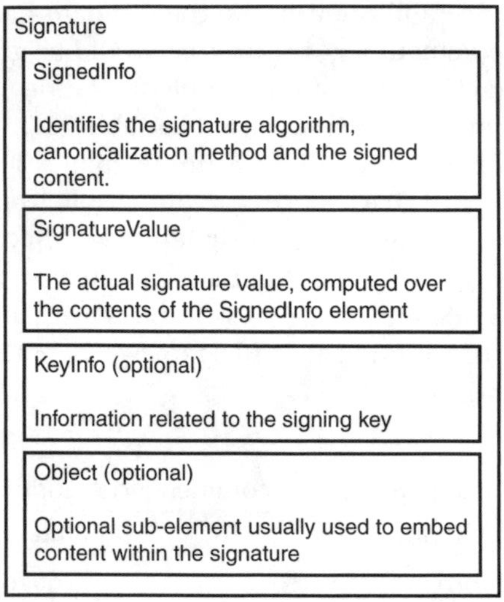

FIGURE 32.5   Block diagram of the top-level components of an XMLDSIG signature.

LISTING 32.3   A High-Level Representation of an XMLDSIG Signature

```
<Signature xmlns="http://www.w3.org/2000/09/xmldsig#">
  <SignedInfo>
    <CanonicalizationMethod
➥ Algorithm="URI identifier for canonicalization algorithm" />
    <SignatureMethod Algorithm="URI identifier for signature algorithm" />
    <Reference URI="URI pointing to the signed content">
      <DigestMethod Algorithm="URI identifier for hash algorithm" />
      <DigestValue>hash value of the signed content</DigestValue>
    </Reference>
  </SignedInfo>
  <SignatureValue>
    Signature computed over the hash of the canonicalized SignedInfo element
  </SignatureValue>
  <KeyInfo>
    optional key-related information goes here
  </KeyInfo>
  <Object Id="ID value so this object may be referenced via fragment URI">
    optional embedded objects go here
  </Object>
</Signature>
```

In Listing 32.3, every XMLDSIG signature is represented by an XML element tag named `Signature` in the XMLDSIG namespace. By definition in the specification, the XMLDSIG namespace is identified by the URL `http://www.w3.org/2000/09/xmldsig#`, so the top-level element of an XMLDSIG signature will look as follows:`<Signature xmlns="http://www.w3.org/2000/09/xmldsig#">…</Signature>`

or, alternatively, the namespace will be bound to some prefix and look like the following, where `ds` is the local prefix bound to the XMLDSIG namespace:

```
<ds:Signature xmlns:ds="http://www.w3.org/2000/09/xmldsig#">
…
</Signature>
```

> **NOTE**
>
> The XMLDSIG standard assumes that readers and implementers have a good background with core XML specifications, including the base XML specification, XML namespaces, and XML Schema. Understanding core XML processing and namespaces is vital to understanding some of the nuances of the XMLDSIG standard.

For ease of reference, we will subsequently assume that this namespace URL is defined as the `ds` namespace, which allows us to use XML prefix qualification for all XMLDSIG tag names. For example, from now on, we will write the XMLDSIG `Signature` element as `<ds:Signature>...</ds:Signature>` to represent the fact that `Signature` is defined in the XMLDSIG namespace.

Our descriptions of each of the elements in an XMLDSIG signature will adhere to the following pattern. First, we will show the XML Schema description for the element and a sample of how the element is used. We will then identify attributes and child elements that can appear within the structure.

> **NOTE**
>
> Many elements in the XMLDSIG standard are defined with optional `Id` attributes that can be used to name and reference the element elsewhere within the document. Except where specifically interesting, such as the use of `Id` elements to reference a `ds:Object` within a `ds:SignedInfo` for a wrapped signature, we will ignore the presence of the `Id` attributes in the schema.

The ds:Signature **Element**

We begin our tour of XMLDSIG elements at the top, with the ds:Signature element itself. Listings 32.4 and 32.5 show the XML Schema for the ds:Signature element and an example ds:Signature element, respectively. (The detailed contents of the child element have been omitted for readability.)

LISTING 32.4   XML Schema for the ds:Signature Element

```
<element name="Signature" type="ds:SignatureType"/>
  <complexType name="SignatureType">
    <sequence>
      <element ref="ds:SignedInfo"/>
      <element ref="ds:SignatureValue"/>
      <element ref="ds:KeyInfo" minOccurs="0"/>
      <element ref="ds:Object" minOccurs="0" maxOccurs="unbounded"/>
    </sequence>
    <attribute name="Id" type="ID" use="optional"/>
  </complexType>
```

LISTING 32.5   Sample ds:Signature Element

```
<Signature xmlns="http://www.w3.org/2000/09/xmldsig#">
  <SignedInfo>
    <!-- SignedInfo contents -->
  </SignedInfo>
  <SignatureValue>46qK2Zz3FuyXkjN5jDkrU947hX18BwMQjC8qS+pzt4JOouHWva
    CKUY8E7SaxeRnnDaWlBCOHWK7XIA1o8j2CtlZvjrv5itNEBcAOIZejtoSucEYIf7UM
    cZUgtVX4ORlNuhSygJVbSwggkLPVwkdBATdKULAF2Pz+bRCUpYyOgUE=
  </SignatureValue>
  <KeyInfo>
  </KeyInfo>
  <Object Id="object">
    <!--Object contents -->
  </Object>
</Signature>
```

Every ds:Signature element contains at least two child elements—a ds:SignedInfo element and a ds:SignatureValue element. The ds:SignatureValue element is exactly as it is named; it is a text node whose value is a Base64-encoded binary value corresponding to a digital signature computation. The ds:SignedInfo element specifies the XML content that was signed to produce the ds:SignatureValue. These two elements, ds:SignedInfo and ds:SignatureValue, hold the two core pieces of information carried in every XMLDSIG signature—what was signed and the value of the signature.

Table 32.2 lists the defined child elements of a ds:Signature element.

TABLE 32.2　Children of the ds:Signature Element

Element/Attribute Name	Contents	Mandatory or Optional	Number Appearing
SignedInfo (element)	Pointers (hash references) to the signed content	Mandatory	1
SignatureValue (element)	The actual digital signature value, Base64-encoded	Mandatory	1
KeyInfo (element)	Information related to the key used to generate the digital signature	Optional	Exactly 1 if present
Object (element)	Any XML content, but generally used with wrapped signatures to include signed content within the Signature element	Optional	Any number may be present

A ds:Signature element can optionally contain two additional types of elements in addition to the ds:SignedInfo and ds:SignatureValue elements. The first optional component, the ds:KeyInfo element, can only occur once in the ds:Signature block if present. The ds:KeyInfo element holds information that is intended to help the signature verifier find the public key needed to verify the signature. Essentially, ds:KeyInfo is a container for carrying any and all key-related information that the signature constructor thinks will be helpful to the verifier. For example, ds:KeyInfo can contain elements that specify the actual values of the public verification key. The ds:KeyInfo element could contain certificates for the verification key, intended to be used by the recipient (signature verifier) to validate that the key pair used to sign the message should be trusted to make the statements it did. It is also possible (and in many scenarios likely) to embed within the ds:KeyInfo element pointers (URIs) to structures that contain key-related information, so a signature verifier can find the information if necessary. We will see detailed examples of the various uses of ds:KeyInfo in the "Creating XMLDSIG-Compliant Signatures Using the .NET Framework" section later in this chapter.

Finally, a ds:Signature can optionally include one or more ds:Object elements. The ds:Object element is a wrapper element that is used to include any desired additional data within a ds:Signature. Usually ds:Object elements are used to embed to-be-signed content when creating "wrapped" signatures, in which case, the ds:Object will be explicitly referenced by one or more components of its sibling ds:SignedInfo element. However, the ds:Object element can also be used to carry unsigned information along with the signature if that is desired by the application.

The ds:SignatureValue Element

The ds:SignatureValue element is the child element of a ds:Signature that contains the actual digital signature value. It is always the second child of the ds:Signature element; we describe it here first because its structure is simple compared to ds:SignedInfo. Listing 32.6 shows the XML Schema for ds:SignatureValue elements and a sample element is shown in Listing 32.7. A ds:SignatureValue element contains only text content, and that text content must be of type base64Binary, which means simply that it is the Base64-encoding of an arbitrarily large binary value. The interpretation of the contents of the ds:SignatureValue element varies depending on the exact algorithm used to create the signature, so it is impossible to parse or understand the contents of the ds:SignatureValue element without first looking in the ds:SignedInfo element to see what algorithm was used to compute the signature.

LISTING 32.6   XML Schema for the ds:SignatureValue Element

```
<element name="SignatureValue" type="ds:SignatureValueType"/>
<complexType name="SignatureValueType">
  <simpleContent>
    <extension base="base64Binary">
      <attribute name="Id" type="ID" use="optional"/>
    </extension>
  </simpleContent>
</complexType>
```

LISTING 32.7   Sample ds:SignatureValue Element

```
<SignatureValue>46qK2Zz3FuyXkjN5jDkrU947hX18BwMQjC8qS+pzt4JOouHWva
  CKUY8E7SaxeRnnDaWlBCOHWK7XIA1o8j2CtlZvjrv5itNEBcAOIZejtoSucEYIf7UM
  cZUgtVX40R1NuhSygJVbSwggkLPVwkdBATdKULAF2Pz+bRCUpYyOgUE=
</SignatureValue>
```

The ds:SignedInfo Element

The ds:SignedInfo element identifies the exact content signed by the digital signature and is always the first child element of every ds:Signature element. The content contained within a ds:SignedInfo element answers three questions: what content is signed by the digital signature, how is the ds:SignedInfo element to be canonicalized, and what signature algorithm was used to generate the signature. Listings 32.8 and 32.9 show the XML Schema for the ds:SignedInfo element and a sample instance, respectively.

LISTING 32.8   XML Schema for the ds:SignedInfo Element

```
<element name="SignedInfo" type="ds:SignedInfoType"/>
 <complexType name="SignedInfoType">
   <sequence>
     <element ref="ds:CanonicalizationMethod"/>
     <element ref="ds:SignatureMethod"/>
     <element ref="ds:Reference" maxOccurs="unbounded"/>
   </sequence>
   <attribute name="Id" type="ID" use="optional"/>
 </complexType>
```

LISTING 32.9   Sample ds:SignedInfo Element

```
<SignedInfo>
  <CanonicalizationMethod Algorithm="http://www.w3.org/TR/2001/REC-xml-c14n-
➥20010315" />
  <SignatureMethod Algorithm="http://www.w3.org/2000/09/xmldsig#rsa-sha1" />
  <Reference URI="http://tempuri.org/">
    <!--Reference content goes here -->
  </Reference>
</SignedInfo>
```

Recall from the "XMLDSIG Design Principles and Modes of Use" earlier in this chapter the requirement that XMLDSIG signature be applied to entire XML documents, partial XML documents, and even non-XML content. This requirement forces XMLDSIG to support detached signatures (signatures separate from the signed content), and, as a result, XMLSIG uses a detached signature model for creating all of its signatures. In an XMLDSIG signature, the digital signature is computed over the contents of just the ds:SignedInfo element, and the ds:SignedInfo element in turn contains cryptographic references to the actual content. That is, a ds:SignedInfo element is really a collection of "hash references" to the to-be-signed content, where each reference identifies the to-be-signed content and the value obtained by applying a cryptographic hash function to the content. When the ds:SignedInfo element is hashed and signed, these hash references are implicitly included in the signature. Changing a single bit in the signed content will change its hash value, which will change the hash of the ds:SignedInfo element and cause the digital signature of the ds:SignedInfo element to change.

A ds:SignedInfo element contains at least three child elements, as shown in Table 32.3. The first child is the ds:CanonicalizationMethod element, which indicates how the ds:SignedInfo element itself was canonicalized before being signed. The second child element is the ds:SignatureMethod element, which identifies the digital signature algorithm used to sign the canonical form of the ds:SignedInfo element. Remaining child elements are ds:Reference elements that are hash references to the to-be-signed content.

TABLE 32.3   Children of the ds:SignedInfo Element

Element/Attribute Name	Contents	Mandatory or Optional	Number Appearing
CanonicalizationMethod	Algorithm to use to canonicalize the ds:SignedInfo element	Mandatory	1
SignatureMethod	Algorithm to use to compute the signature of the ds:SignedInfo element	Mandatory	1
Reference	Structure that identifies to-be-signed content along with its cryptographic hash value	Mandatory	At least 1

While it is possible to specify and use any canonicalization algorithm to canonicalize ds:SignedInfo, it is almost always the case that the mandatory-to-implement Canonical XML algorithm is used. The schema for ds:CanonicalizationMethod is shown in Listing 32.10. The schema specifies one mandatory attribute—a URI identifying the canonicalization algorithm—and optional substructure for specifying any parameters of the canonicalization algorithm.

LISTING 32.10   XML Schema for the ds:CanonicalizationMethod Element

```
<element name="CanonicalizationMethod" type="ds:CanonicalizationMethodType"/>
  <complexType name="CanonicalizationMethodType" mixed="true">
    <sequence>
      <any namespace="##any" minOccurs="0" maxOccurs="unbounded"/>
    </sequence>
    <attribute name="Algorithm" type="anyURI" use="required"/>
  </complexType>
```

When canonical XML is used as the canonicalization method, the resulting ds:CanonicalizationMethod contains only an algorithm identifier and looks as follows:

```
<CanonicalizationMethod Algorithm=
➡ "http://www.w3.org/TR/2001/REC-xml-c14n-20010315" />
```

The `ds:SignatureMethod` element is structurally very similar to the `ds:CanonicalizationMethod` element in that it specifies the signature algorithm by URI in an attribute and allows optional algorithm parameters to be embedded as substructure. For DSA and RSA signatures, the `SignatureMethod` elements will appear as follows:

```
<SignatureMethod Algorithm="http://www.w3.org/2000/09/xmldsig#rsa-sha1" />
```

```
<SignatureMethod Algorithm="http://www.w3.org/2000/09/xmldsig#dsa-sha1" />
```

An HMAC-SHA1 `ds:SignatureMethod` will appear in one of two forms depending on whether the optional parameter is used. The following are sample HMAC-SHA1 `SignatureMethod`s using 160 bits (full output) and 40 bits (truncated):

```
<SignatureMethod Algorithm="http://www.w3.org/2000/09/xmldsig#hmac-sha1" />
```

```
<SignatureMethod Algorithm="http://www.w3.org/2000/09/xmldsig#hmac-sha1">
  <HMACOutputLength>40</HMACOutputLength>
```

Listing 32.11 shows the entire schema for `ds:SignatureMethod`. Notice that the only difference between this schema and the schema for `ds:CanonicalizationMethod` shown in Listing 32.10 is the specification of an optional parameter that is used with HMAC-SHA1 "signatures."

LISTING 32.11   XML Schema for the `ds:SignatureMethod` Element

```
<element name="SignatureMethod" type="ds:SignatureMethodType"/>
  <complexType name="SignatureMethodType" mixed="true">
    <sequence>
      <element name="HMACOutputLength" minOccurs="0" type="ds:HMACOutput
➥LengthType"/>
      <any namespace="##other" minOccurs="0" maxOccurs="unbounded"/>
      <!-- (0,unbounded) elements from (1,1) external namespace -->
    </sequence>
   <attribute name="Algorithm" type="anyURI" use="required"/>
  </complexType>
```

NOTE

Recall from Chapter 31 that a keyed MAC function, such as HMAC-SHA1, can be used to provide integrity protection between two parties that share a secret key. XMLDSIG allows HMAC-SHA1 (and any other keyed MAC) to be used as a "signature" algorithm between parties sharing secret key material by simply using the output of the keyed MAC as the signature value. The optional parameter for HMAC-SHA1 is a desired output length that tells

XMLDSIG to use only a portion of the computed HMAC-SHA1 value as the actual signature value. Unless specifically required, you will always want to use the full length (160 bits) output by HMAC-SHA1 when it is your signature algorithm.

The `ds:Reference` Element

The remaining children of a `ds:SignedInfo` element are `ds:Reference` elements that identify the actual content signed by the signature. At least one `ds:Reference` element must be present in a `ds:SignedInfo`, because the signature must protect some content. Multiple distinct pieces of to-be-signed content can be jointly protected by a single signature by including multiple `ds:Reference` elements within a `ds:SignedInfo`.

The schema for a `ds:Reference` element is shown in Listing 32.12 and its child elements and attributes are summarized in Table 32.4. Each hash reference needs to contain information exactly identifying the to-be-signed content, the hash algorithm used to hash the content, and the actual hash value. The hash algorithm and hash value are contained in child elements `ds:DigestMethod` and `ds:DigestValue`, respectively. The schema for `ds:DigestMethod` (shown in Listing 32.13) is basically the same structure used previously for `ds:CanonicalizationMethod`—an Algorithm attribute whose value is a URI identifying the hash algorithm to use and optional open substructure that can be used to hold algorithm parameters. The `ds:DigestValue` is simply another Base64-encoded binary value, so its schema (Listing 32.14) is essentially the same as that of `ds:SignatureValue`.

LISTING 32.12   XML Schema for the `ds:Reference` Element

```
<element name="Reference" type="ds:ReferenceType"/>
<complexType name="ReferenceType">
  <sequence>
    <element ref="ds:Transforms" minOccurs="0"/>
    <element ref="ds:DigestMethod"/>
    <element ref="ds:DigestValue"/>
  </sequence>
  <attribute name="Id" type="ID" use="optional"/>
  <attribute name="URI" type="anyURI" use="optional"/>
  <attribute name="Type" type="anyURI" use="optional"/>
</complexType>
```

TABLE 32.4   Children of the ds:Reference Element

Element/Attribute Name	Contents	Mandatory or Optional	Number Appearing
URI (attribute)	URI for the source of the to-be-signed content	Optional	At most 1
Type (attribute)	Optional attribute used to identify the type of content to be retrieved from the URI in the URI attribute	Optional	At most 1
Transforms (element)	If present, contains a sequence of algorithms that transform content obtained from the URI before signing	Optional	At most 1
DigestMethod	The hash algorithm to use when calculating the hash of the to-be-signed content	Mandatory	1
DigestValue	The hash value of the to-be-signed content	Mandatory	1

LISTING 32.13   XML Schema for the ds:DigestMethod Element

```
<element name="DigestMethod" type="ds:DigestMethodType"/>
<complexType name="DigestMethodType" mixed="true">
  <sequence>
    <any namespace="##other" processContents="lax" minOccurs="0"
➥maxOccurs="unbounded"/>
  </sequence>
  <attribute name="Algorithm" type="anyURI" use="required"/>
</complexType>
```

LISTING 32.14   XML Schema for the ds:DigestValue Element

```
<element name="DigestValue" type="ds:DigestValueType"/>
<simpleType name="DigestValueType">
  <restriction base="base64Binary"/>
</simpleType>
```

The basic idea behind the Reference Processing Model is that to-be-signed content is defined as the *result* of taking some *input content* and processing that content through a series of *transformations*. A graphical depiction of the Reference Processing

Model is shown in Figure 32.6. The input content to be processed is specified via the URI attribute; the value of this attribute is the URI of the content to be retrieved and input for processing. The ds:Transforms element contains one or more individual transformations—each specified by a single ds:Transform element—that define a stage of processing to be performed on the input. The transforms are chained together, so the output from the first transform in the chain is the input to the second transform in the chain, the output from the second transform is the input to the third transform, and so on, until the chain is completed. The output from the final transform in the chain is the to-be-signed content that needs to be hashed.

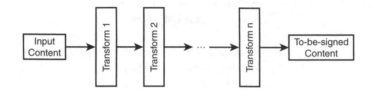

FIGURE 32.6   The Reference Processing Model.

Let's now look at some examples of the Reference Processing Model in action and see how it allows us to easily specify entire documents and portions of document. Referencing an entire document is easy—we put the URI to the document in the URI attribute. No transforms need to be specified if we want to sign the entire contents of a URI, so we omit the entire ds:Transforms element. The following is an example of a full-document reference:

```
<Reference URI="http://www.farcaster.com/document.xml">
  <DigestMethod Algorithm="http://www.w3.org/2000/09/xmldsig#sha1" />
  <DigestValue>XoaHIm+jLKnPocR7FX0678DUOqs=</DigestValue>
</Reference>
```

The ds:Reference element simply contains the URI of the document to be signed. Because no transforms are specified, the to-be-signed content is exactly the input content retrieved from URI http://www.farcaster.com/document.xml. (Note that in this example, we have not explicitly specified the default namespace and have assumed it has been specified at a higher level. In general, namespace declarations will appear only on the top-level ds:Signature element and be automatically inherited by child elements.) The content is then hashed with SHA1 (identified by the Algorithm attributed on the ds:DigestMethod element) and the result of hashing the content is the Base64-encoded value in the ds:DigestValue element.

Now let's look at how we sign only a portion of a document. If the portion of the document we want to sign is a single element within the document that has an Id attribute, we can reference that single element using a fragment URI. For example, if the document at http://www.farcaster.com/document.xml contains three

MyDocumentForm elements, identified as Form1, Form2, and Form3 as shown in the following

```
<MyDocumentForm Id="Form1">
  <!--complex form data goes here -->
</MyDocumentForm>


<MyDocumentForm Id="Form2">
  <!--complex form data goes here -->
</MyDocumentForm>


<MyDocumentForm Id="Form3">
  <!--complex form data goes here -->
</MyDocumentForm>
```

then we can sign just the content in the Form2 element by using a URI fragment reference as follows:

```
<Reference URI="http://www.farcaster.com/document.xml#Form2">
  <DigestMethod Algorithm="http://www.w3.org/2000/09/xmldsig#sha1" />
  <DigestValue>XoaHIm+jLKnPocR7FX0678DUOqs=</DigestValue>
</Reference>
```

The # character is the URI fragment separator; it indicates that the URI references just the sub-element of the document with Id attribute equal to the portion of the URI occurring after the separator.

We could also indicate that the to-be-signed content is just the contents of the Form2 by referencing the entire document in the URI attribute and then selecting the portion we want using a transform. Listing 32.15 shows our first example of using a ds:Transforms element with a URI attribute to invoke the full Reference Processing Model:

LISTING 32.15   Sample XMLDSIG Signature Using a Transform

```
<Reference URI="http://www.farcaster.com/document.xml>
  <Transforms>
    <Transform Algorithm="http://www.w3.org/TR/1999/REC-xpath-19991116">
      <XPath>
        ancestor-or-self::node()[@Id="Form2"]
      </XPath>
    </Transform>
  </Transforms>
  <DigestMethod Algorithm="http://www.w3.org/2000/09/xmldsig#sha1" />
  <DigestValue>XoaHIm+jLKnPocR7FX0678DUOqs=</DigestValue>
</Reference>
```

This ds:Reference says that the to-be-signed content is the result of applying an XPath transform to the content obtained from http://www.farcaster.com/document.xml. XPath (short for XML Path Language) is a W3C Recommendation that defines a language for addressing parts of an XML document. The XPath expression ancestor-or-self::node()[@Id="Form2"] says to select from the input document all elements that have an Id attribute with a value of Form2.

> **NOTE**
>
> The XPath language is very rich and complex, and we do not have space in this chapter to properly show off all the neat tricks you can perform with XPath expressions. The combination of XPath transforms and XMLDSIG references is very powerful and allows you to sign complicated subsets of XML documents. Support for XPath transforms is RECOMMENDED in the XMLDSIG standard, which means most XMLDSIG implementations will support XPath transforms, but support is not guaranteed. The .NET Framework implementation of XMLDSIG does support XPath transforms through the XmlDsigXPathTransform object, as described in the "Creating XMLDSIG-Compliant Signatures Using the .NET Framework" section later in this chapter.

So far, we have only used a single transform on the content retrieved from the URI in the URI attribute, but the Reference Processing Model permits an unlimited number of transformations to be applied in sequence to the retrieved content. The following is an example showing how multiple sequential transforms can be used. Continuing the previous example, suppose that each MyDocumentForm element contains within it a Picture element, and that the content of the Picture element is a Base64-encoded binary image of some sort. An example MyDocumentForm element would look something like the following (we've omitted other portions of the element that are not relevant to this example):

```
<MyDocumentForm ID="Form2">
  <!-- some form data goes here -->
  <!-- here is an image -->
  <Picture>
    SSBhbSB0a.......
    .......GUgdGV4dC4=
  </Picture>
  <!-- some more form data goes here -->
</MyDocumentForm>
```

Now, suppose we want to sign just the binary content of the Picture element in the MyDocumentForm with ID Form2. We need to construct a chain of transforms that will select the Picture element of the MyDocumentForm in which we are interested and then Base64-decode the encoded image data. XMLDSIG defines a Base64 decoding transform, so we can accomplish this task by combining an XPath transform with a Base64 decoding transform, as shown in the following:

```
<Reference URI="http://www.farcaster.com/document.xml>
  <Transforms>
    <Transform Algorithm="http://www.w3.org/TR/1999/REC-xpath-19991116">
      <XPath>
        ancestor-or-self::Picture/../self::node()[@Id="Form2"]
      </XPath>
    </Transform>
    <Transform Algorithm="http://www.w3.org/2000/09/xmldsig#base64" />
  </Transforms>
  <DigestMethod Algorithm="http://www.w3.org/2000/09/xmldsig#sha1" />
  <DigestValue>XoaHIm+jLKnPocR7FX0678DUOqs=</DigestValue>
</Reference>
```

The input content to the chain of transformations is the entire document retrieved from `http://www.farcaster.com/document.xml`. This document is input into the first transform (the XPath transform). Notice that we changed the expression in the XPath transform slightly from the previous example to extract just `Picture` elements with parent nodes that have an `Id` attribute with value `Form2`. The output of the XPath transform becomes the input to the Base64 decoding transform. By definition (see Section 6.6.2 in the XMLDSIG standard, "XML-Signature Syntax and Processing"), when passed an XML node set, the Base64 decoding transform operates on the text contained within the node, so the Base64 transform will strip off the enclosing `<Picture>...</Picture>` tags and just decode the encoded content. The resulting decoded bytestream is the to-be-signed content that is then hashed with SHA1.

XMLDSIG defines identifiers for two other types of transformations, which we mention here briefly for completeness. The Extensible Stylesheet Language (XSL) is another W3C Recommendation for describing XML document transformations. XMLDSIG allows any XSL transformation to be used as a `ds:Transform` by simply including the `<xsl:stylesheet>` content within a transform as follows:

```
<Transform Algorithm="http://www.w3.org/TR/1999/REC-xslt-19991116">
  <xsl:stylesheet xmlns:xsl="http://www.w3.org/1999/XSL/Transform"
    xmlns="http://www.w3.org/TR/xhtml1/strict" version="1.0">
    <!-- XSL expression goes here -->
  </xsl:stylesheet>
</Transform>
```

The other transform defined within the XMLDSIG Recommendation is the *Enveloped Signature Transform*, which is used when an XMLDSIG signature is to be embedded within the signed content (an "enveloped signature" as defined previously in the "XMLDSIG Design Principles and Modes of Use" section). Examples showing uses of the enveloped signature transform are provided in the "Creating XMLDSIG-Compliant Signatures Using the .NET Framework" section later in this chapter.

To conclude our discussion of the `ds:Reference` element, we need to make two final notes about URIs and the processing model of transform chains. First, in our previous examples, we have also used fully qualified URIs to identify content, but XMLDSIG also allows relative URIs to be used with specific meaning. The following is a list of the special forms of URLs that can appear in a `ds:Reference URI` attribute:

- The URI `""`, the empty-string URI, is always interpreted as the content of the XML resource containing the `ds:Reference` node. This is typically used with enveloped signatures; the empty-string URI is interpreted to mean the enclosing XML document that contains the embedded signature. (XML comment nodes are excluded from the content of the enclosing document when referenced with an empty-string URI.)

- A fragment URI, such as `#Form2`, is interpreted to mean the element with the unique ID matching the fragment appearing in the enclosing document that contains the embedded signature.

- Because the URI attribute is optional, it is possible to omit the attribute entirely from the `ds:Reference` element. If the URI attribute is omitted, it is assumed that the receiving application verifying the signature has implicit knowledge of the to-be-signed content. Obviously, omitting the URI attribute means that the resulting `ds:Reference` will only have meaning to those applications with implicit knowledge and will not, in general, be interoperable.

The other closing comment on `ds:Reference` concerns implicit conversions that occur between transforms in the transform chain. In XMLDSIG, an individual transform (that is, something defined by a `ds:Transform` element) can accept as input either an octet stream (a stream of arbitrary bytes) or an XML node-set (a parsed XML object), and their output can be either an octet stream or a node-set. When chaining transforms, if the output format of a transform does not match the input format of the next transform in the chain, an implicit conversion is performed automatically by the XMLDSIG implementation. One of two conversions is possible, depending on whether the necessary conversion is octet stream to node-set or node-set to octet stream:

- To convert an octet stream to a node-set, the octet stream is parsed by an XML parser. The octet stream must contain a well-formed serialization of an XML object.

- To convert a node-set to an octet stream, the node-set is canonicalized using the Canonical XML algorithm. (The output of the Canonical XML algorithm is always an octet stream because it is intended to be cryptographically hashed.)

Because the to-be-signed content (the final output of the chain of transformations) is intended to be hashed by the hash algorithm specified in `ds:DigestMethod`, XMLDSIG implementations force the output of the last stage of the transformation chain to be an octet stream. If the output of the last stage of the chain is a node-set, that node-set will be canonicalized with Canonical XML to create the octet stream to hash. Thus, when the `ds:Reference` shown in Listing 32.15 is processed, the following steps occur:

1. The content of `http://www.farcaster.com/document.xml` is retrieved over the network as an octet stream.

2. The octet-stream is implicitly converted, via XML well-formed processing, into a node-set for input into the XPath transform.

3. The XPath transform is applied to the input node-set yielding an output node-set.

4. The node-set output by the XPath transform is implicitly converted into an octet stream by application of the Canonical XML algorithm.

5. The resulting octet stream is input to the SHA1 hash algorithm to compute a hash value.

The implicit conversion rules have the effect of significantly shortening the size and complexity of the `ds:Transforms` elements in a `ds:Reference`.

The `ds:KeyInfo` Element

We now turn our attention to the last major type of child element that can be present in a `ds:Signature` element. The `ds:KeyInfo` element is an optional child of `ds:Signature` that contains information intended to help applications receiving an XMLDSIG signature find the keys necessary to validate that signature. This statement of purpose for the `ds:KeyInfo` element is somewhat vague because lots of different types of information can appear within a `ds:KeyInfo` element. For example, a single `ds:KeyInfo` element might contain one or more of the following types of information:

- An explicit copy of the public key needed to validate the signature

- A symbolic name that identifies the validation key to a receiving application

- A pointer to a URI where a copy of the validating key may be obtained

- A digital certificate (in one or more formats) for the public key that validates the signature

- Revocation information for digital certificates for the validating public key

- Trust management information about the key that generated the signature that will help convince an application receiving the signature that it should take some action

Although many different types of information can appear within a ds:KeyInfo element, the goal of all such information is the same—to provide hints to a signature verifier as to how to find the key necessary to cryptographically validate the signature and convey additional trust information that may be appropriate to the particular application. A copy of the XML schema for the ds:KeyInfo element is shown in Listing 32.16.

CAUTION

It should be stressed that the information provided in a ds:KeyInfo element is advisory in nature and should *never* be implicitly trusted by a signature verifier. In particular, the presence of some information within the ds:KeyInfo element does not in and of itself imply agreement with the content signed by the signature. Normally, the contents of the ds:KeyInfo element are not covered by the signature, although it is possible to do so by using an Id attribute on the ds:KeyInfo element and referencing the element through a fragment URI in a ds:Reference.

LISTING 32.16   XML Schema for the ds:KeyInfo Element

```
<element name="KeyInfo" type="ds:KeyInfoType"/>
<complexType name="KeyInfoType" mixed="true">
  <choice maxOccurs="unbounded">
    <element ref="ds:KeyName"/>
    <element ref="ds:KeyValue"/>
    <element ref="ds:RetrievalMethod"/>
    <element ref="ds:X509Data"/>
    <element ref="ds:PGPData"/>
    <element ref="ds:SPKIData"/>
    <element ref="ds:MgmtData"/>
    <any processContents="lax" namespace="##other"/>
    <!-- (1,1) elements from (0,unbounded) namespaces -->
  </choice>
  <attribute name="Id" type="ID" use="optional"/>
</complexType>
```

The child elements of the ds:KeyInfo element defined within the XMLDSIG standard fall into three broad categories—direct inclusion of key material, indirect pointers to key material, and trust management information related to signature keys. A summary of all of the defined child elements of the ds:KeyInfo element is contained in Table 32.5.

NOTE

Note that as the entire ds:KeyInfo element is optional, the presence of any specific type of child element is also optional. Conforming implementations of the XMLDSIG standard are required to recognize only the ds:KeyInfo element, the ds:KeyValue child of ds:KeyInfo, and the ds:DSAKeyValue child of ds:KeyValue. Support for all other children of ds:KeyInfo is implementation dependent.

TABLE 32.5   Children of the ds:KeyInfo Element

Element/Attribute Name	Contents	Mandatory or Optional	Number Appearing
KeyValue	A single public key value that may be useful in validating the signature.	Optional	Any number
KeyName	A string value intended to identify a key to the recipient of the signature.	Optional	Any number
RetrievalMethod	A reference to KeyInfo information stored external to the signature itself.	Optional	Any number
X509Data	One or more identifiers of keys, X.509v3 certificates, or X.509v2 certificate revocation lists (CRLs) related to the key necessary to validate the signature.	Optional	Any number
PGPData	Information related to PGP public key pairs and signatures.	Optional	Any number
SPKIData	Information related to SPKI public key pairs, SPKI certificates, or other SPKI data.	Optional	Any number
MgmtData	In-band key distribution or agreement data. No longer recommended for use as it is being superceded by work done as part of the XML Encryption standard.	Optional	Any number

The most commonly used child element of ds:KeyInfo is the ds:KeyValue element, which is used to directly include a copy of a public key in a signature. For example,

Listing 32.17 shows a `ds:KeyInfo` element, that includes an RSA public key (presumably the public key necessary to validate the signature), and Listing 32.18 shows the equivalent structure for including a DSA public key. Public keys related to a signature are always included as child elements of a `ds:KeyValue` element, which itself is a child of `ds:KeyInfo`. The XMLDSIG standard defines structures for holding DSA and RSA public keys (the `ds:DSAKeyValue` and `ds:RSAKeyValue` elements, respectively), but public keys for other algorithms can also appear under a `ds:KeyValue` element.

LISTING 32.17   Sample ds:KeyInfo/ds:KeyValue/ds:RSAKeyValue Element

```
<KeyInfo>
  <KeyValue xmlns="http://www.w3.org/2000/09/xmldsig#">
    <RSAKeyValue>
      <Modulus>qpkTNcNBXONxOCW+WPlNFeniABN8tkJYa2Y2IhcHfY3Qy3v01SeEWe
        CRYYPcli24CKml1DU1dEE/jqNWF/8eypJakyztz1xFSrNp+12o5KsmCWmLzcc
        940Fcb9I1eDffUm++GM0+FHARDEA9DZzFoJTLblyGd9XQS0rb4AVvnGc=
      </Modulus>
      <Exponent>AQAB</Exponent>
    </RSAKeyValue>
  </KeyValue>
</KeyInfo>
```

LISTING 32.18   Sample ds:KeyInfo/ds:KeyValue/ds:DSAKeyValue Element

```
<KeyInfo>
  <KeyValue xmlns="http://www.w3.org/2000/09/xmldsig#">
    <DSAKeyValue>
      <P>3vd/2Pj3yZbWjgO1PLh2ebVIem0nwjPYUcq+1qbDBz42xa5KEug6
        wIwVXUe+It3c1i1yt5uLZmdTFiYwI8v8QVGiG9+MH1hOVH3vmArcwEuHy
        SG/BmEYZD2Iivsi3iabzKI82C7RgIkSn9dMeQyDAHEkfYqNXy/aDldgEkTDvHs=
      </P>
      <Q>7djIzh61c7hJ2dfDVyGy47Zrbn0=</Q>
      <G>zpbWQ7ZHqb59WobUgTzXarfH0jxBw6ZdqFbGBGnHePXUYLLBSZADuZGzSf9cZnx2Pr
        n8unzcSVHi4V1VWpl0c8Y6cyN6zbPlixHBfhfEB2iBq5rE5s24KHUQJ4QyelTJUm1frdpy
        OPC5qGrlUWCONTPS6X6u4LH6zNY1fyX8mT0=
      </G>
      <Y>uFFFYABM7c4XQ6qjxtFYihGy+y8X6aplcTA6F0pc2iQssm99AKQ1ceody+9uZ1t
        BaItsMkGT2xqTZGMNAccb8BQ4a9emRwqvSOlufac40CPcIbuNtkLpnrU2Nr2kL1dO
        Cw6jYhoq9TWHVW7/nwceyR/MRRDakM7u6ZMtQqhcSpY=
      </Y>
      <J>7/v6mMmxG6/TJuzKu1ue0Iiz/KXzdfbQrlKFxedUJtqRJ/xobwCITelA/yIB
        Kc5pqURCkeyx7jlBZq6bx97qqW3cdi9XgwcOwB+ThnE7G4F5Dz2KLEDicRjPDLr
```

LISTING 32.18   Continued

```
        /Wmyw4TKbjGFBuwd42PWC
    </J>
    <Seed>6cyvB3e5AUAZ9dNQVxF8acDQeD0=</Seed>
    <PgenCounter>Eg==</PgenCounter>
   </DSAKeyValue>
  </KeyValue>
</KeyInfo>
```

NOTE

Note that the .NET Framework uses the same XML format as the ds:RSAKeyValue and
ds:DSAKeyValue structures for representing RSA and DSA public keys. For example, calling the
ToXmlString(false) method on an RSA key in the .NET Framework will produce a string serialization of the appropriate ds:RSAKeyValue structure. See the "Using Asymmetric
Algorithms" section in Chapter 30 for more details on the use of the FromXmlString and
ToXmlString methods on AsymmetricAlgorithm objects to import and export public keys in
ds:KeyValue-compatible formats.

XMLDSIG defines two elements to support indirect pointers to key material—the
ds:KeyName and ds:RetrievalMethod elements. The ds:KeyName child element of
ds:KeyInfo is intended to communicate a key identifier to the application verifying
the digital signature. The content of a ds:KeyName element is always just a string,
and the interpretation of that string is left unspecified by XMLDSIG and must be
determined by application context. Typically, ds:KeyInfo is used as part of a series of
communications between two parties where public keys were exchanged initially and
then simply referenced by name in later signed messages. The following is an
example use of ds:KeyName within ds:KeyInfo:

```
<KeyInfo>
  <KeyName>Alice's public key created on 9/26/2001</KeyName>
</KeyInfo>
```

The ds:RetrievalMethod child element of ds:KeyInfo allows a signature constructor
to include a reference to a ds:KeyInfo element stored elsewhere. The schema for
ds:RetrievalMethod is shown in Listing 32.19. The schema is very similar to the
schema for the ds:Reference element; in fact, ds:RetrievalMethod elements are
processed using the same Reference Processing Model described earlier, except that a
ds:RetrievalMethod is not a hash reference and thus does not contain hash algorithm and value sub-elements like ds:DigestMethod and ds:DigestValue. (Also, the
URI attribute must be present in a ds:RetrievalMethod.)

LISTING 32.19   XML Schema for the `ds:RetrievalMethod` Element

```
<element name="RetrievalMethod" type="ds:RetrievalMethodType"/>
<complexType name="RetrievalMethodType">
  <sequence>
    <element ref="ds:Transforms" minOccurs="0"/>
  </sequence>
  <attribute name="URI" type="anyURI"/>
  <attribute name="Type" type="anyURI" use="optional"/>
</complexType>
```

There are three defined elements in the XMLDSIG standard for carrying trust
management information related to signature keys within a `ds:KeyInfo` element—
the `ds:X509Data`, `ds:PGPData`, and `ds:SPKIData` elements. These three elements
correspond to the three separate trust models that have been standardized by the
IETF—X.509v3 certificates (standardized in the PKIX Working Group within the
IETF), PGP messages (based on the "Open Specification for Pretty Good Privacy"
developed by the OpenPGP Working Group), and Simple Public Key Infrastructure
certificates (based on the work of the SPKI Working Group), respectively. By far, the
most complex of the three elements is the `ds:X509Data` element; it is also the only
one of the three that is natively supported in the initial release of the .NET
Framework. The `ds:X509Data` element can contain X.509v3 certificates, identifiers
for certificates, and even entire certificate revocation lists (CRLs). The schema for the
`ds:X509Data` element is shown in Listing 32.20, and a summary of the possible child
elements of `ds:X509Data` is provided in Table 32.6. Notice that the `ds:X509Data`
element is extensible; other element types can be included in an instance of
`ds:X509Data`, but only the element types listed in Table 32.6 are defined by the standard.

LISTING 32.20   XML Schema for the `ds:X509Data` Element

```
<element name="X509Data" type="ds:X509DataType"/>
<complexType name="X509DataType">
  <sequence maxOccurs="unbounded">
    <choice>
      <element name="X509IssuerSerial" type="ds:X509IssuerSerialType"/>
      <element name="X509SKI" type="base64Binary"/>
      <element name="X509SubjectName" type="string"/>
      <element name="X509Certificate" type="base64Binary"/>
      <element name="X509CRL" type="base64Binary"/>
      <any namespace="##other" processContents="lax"/>
    </choice>
  </sequence>
</complexType>
```

LISTING 32.20   Continued

```
<complexType name="X509IssuerSerialType">
  <sequence>
    <element name="X509IssuerName" type="string"/>
    <element name="X509SerialNumber" type="integer"/>
  </sequence>
</complexType>
```

TABLE 32.6   Children of the `ds:X509Data` Element

Element/Attribute Name	Contents	Mandatory or Optional	Number Appearing
`X509IssuerSerial` (element)	An issuer name/serial number pair, which is one way to reference an X.509v3 certificate	Optional	Any number
`X509SKI` (element)	An X.509v3 Subject Key Identifier, which is an extension that may appear in a certificate	Optional	Any number
`X509SubjectName` (element)	An X.509v3 subject distinguished name (the subject name bound to the public key in a certificate)	Optional	Any number
`X509Certificate` (element)	A Base64-encoded X.509v3 certificate	Optional	Any number
`X509CRL` (element)	A Base64-encoded certificate revocation list (CRL)	Optional	Any number

The first three elements in Table 32.6—`ds:X509IssuerSerial`, `ds:X509SKI`, and `ds:X509SubjectName`—all represent different mechanisms for referencing a certificate or set of certificates. The `ds:X509IssuerSerial` element always names exactly one certificate; it contains a simple structure holding a pair consisting of an X.509v3 issuer distinguished name (a string) and a serial number. When a certificate issue creates a new certificate, it is required to generate a new, unique serial number for that certificate, so an issuer name/serial number pair is a unique identifier for a single certificate. The `ds:X509SubjectName` element contains a string value that is a subject distinguished name of one or more certificates (because multiple certificates can be issued to the same subject entity). The `ds:X509SKI` element contains the Base64 encoding of the subject key identifier (SKI) extension in a certificate, which is usually derived from the subject public key through some mathematical operation (such as hashing the public key value). Because multiple certificates can be issued for the same subject public key, there can be multiple certificates that share the same `ds:X509SKI` extension.

The XMLDSIG standard imposes three restrictions on the types of certificates that can be referenced by ds:X509IssuerSerial, ds:X509SKI, and ds:X509SubjectName and how that data must be organized within a ds:KeyInfo element. First, all references to certificates within these three types of elements must be to certificates that contain the signature validation key as its subject public key. Second, all instances of these three elements that refer to the same single certificate must be grouped together within a single ds:X509Data element. Third, all instances of these three elements that refer to the same subject public key but different certificates must appear within the same ds:KeyInfo but can appear within different ds:X509Data elements inside that ds:KeyInfo element.

It is also possible to directly encode X509v3 certificates in a signature by using the ds:X509Certificate child of ds:X509Data. All certificates appearing within a ds:X509Data element must either contain the validation key as its subject public key or be part of a chain of certificates whose end-entity certificate has the validation key as its subject. Thus, it is possible to include an entire X.509v3 certificate chain within a single ds:X509Data element by simply using multiple ds:X509Certificate elements.

NOTE

The .NET Framework does not contain explicit support for the other types of KeyInfo elements that are defined in the XMLDSIG standard: ds:PGPData, ds:SPKIData, and ds:MgmtData. When encountered in an XMLDSIG ds:Signature element, these three types of KeyInfo will be represented in the .NET Framework as KeyInfoNode objects. The Value property of a KeyInfoNode contains the entire XML content of the element that was not explicitly recognized.

This concludes our tour of the ds:Signature element and the sub-elements that can appear within it. In the next section, we discuss the objects and methods included in the .NET Framework for creating and validating XMLDSIG signatures.

Creating XMLDSIG-Compliant Signatures Using the .NET Framework

The .NET Framework includes a comprehensive set of object classes and methods for creating and verifying XMLDSIG digital signatures. All of these classes are located in the System.Security.Cryptography.Xml namespace. In general, there is a .NET Framework class for each defined XMLDSIG element plus the utility class SignedXml that provides high-level signature generation and verification functions. Table 32.7 provides a summary of the classes in the System.Security.Cryptography.Xml namespace. This section demonstrates how SignedXml and the other XMLDSIG classes can be used to construct XMLDSIG signatures.

NOTE

The classes in the System.Security.Cryptography.Xml namespace are contained in the System.Security.dll assembly, so to use these classes in your own programs, you will need to explicitly reference this assembly when compiling your programs. These classes also depend on the .NET Framework XML classes contained within the System.XML.dll assembly. For Visual Studio .NET, perform the following steps to add a reference to the System.Security assembly to your project:

1. In the Solution Explorer, select References, right-click, and select Add Reference.
2. Select System.Security from the selection list.
3. Either double-click the System.Security or highlight System.Security and click the Select button.
4. Select OK to complete the addition of System.Security to your Visual Studio .NET project.

(A reference to System.XML.dll is already included by default when you create a Visual Studio .NET project.)

If you are compiling your programs by invoking the compiler from the command line, you will need to explicitly reference both System.Security.dll and System.XML.dll. For example, when using the Visual C# .NET or Visual Basic .NET compiler, you will need to add the command-line arguments /r:System.Security.dll and /r:System.XML.dll.

TABLE 32.7 Classes in the System.Security.Cryptography.Xml Namespace

System.Security.dll Object	Description
SignedXml	Utility class for creating and verifying XMLDSIG signatures
Signature	Represents the ds:Signature element
SignedInfo	Represents the ds:SignedInfo element
Reference	Represents the ds:Reference element
TransformChain	Represents the content of a single ds:Transforms element, which is an ordered sequence of ds:Transform elements
Transform	Represents the ds:Transform element
KeyInfo	Represents the ds:KeyInfo element
RSAKeyValue	Represents the ds:RSAKeyValue element
DSAKeyValue	Represents the ds:DSAKeyValue element
KeyInfoName	Represents the ds:KeyName element
KeyInfoRetrievalMethod	Represents the ds:RetrievalMethod element
KeyInfoX509Data	Represents the ds:X509Data element
KeyInfoNode	A generic handler for child elements of ds:KeyInfo that do not have specific object representations in the .NET Framework
DataObject	Represents the ds:Object element

The .NET Framework object model for XMLDSIG mirrors the layout of XML elements in the standard. In general, there is a class present in the `System.Security.Cryptography.Xml` namespace for each complex type (for example, `ds:SignedInfo`) defined in XMLDSIG. Simple types, such as the `Algorithm` attribute on `ds:SignatureMethod`, are represented as typed properties on the classes representing their parent elements. The top-level `SignedXml` class provides high-level functions for generating and verifying signature (the `ComputeSignature` and `CheckSignature` methods, respectively) and for combining together `Reference`, `KeyInfo`, and `DataObject` objects to represent an overall `ds:Signature` object. Table 32.8 provides a summary of the important properties and methods available on a `SignedXml` object.

TABLE 32.8   Properties and Methods of the `SignedXml` Class

Property/Method Name	Description
SigningKey (property)	Gets/sets the key or key pair used to generate and/or verify the digital signature.
SignatureMethod (property)	Gets the URI identifying the digital signature algorithm.
SignatureValue	Gets the binary value of the digital signature.
KeyInfo	Gets/sets the `KeyInfo` object associated with this XMLDSIG signature, representing the entire contents of the `ds:KeyInfo` element.
Signature	Gets the `Signature` object that represents the contents of the `ds:Signature` element.
SignedInfo	Gets the `SignedInfo` object that represents the contents of the `ds:SignedInfo` element within the `ds:Signature` element.
AddObject	Adds an `Object` to the list of `Objects` to be embedded within the signature.
AddReference	Adds a `Reference` object to the list of `References` in the `SignedInfo` portion of the signature.
ComputeSignature	Calculates the digital signature value using the `SigningKey`.
CheckSignature	Attempts to verify the digital signature.
CheckSignatureReturningKey	Attempts to verify the digital signature. Returns the verification key in its out parameter if successful.

Our first set of examples demonstrates how to construct detached, wrapped, and enveloped XMLDSIG signatures. The procedures for creating XMLDSIG signatures all follow the same general set of steps:

1. Create a new `SignedXml` object to hold the signature information and associate it with a signing key.

2. Associate the signing key with the `SignedXml` object by setting its `SigningKey` property. This key will be either an `AsymmetricAlgorithm` or a `KeyedHashAlgorithm`.

3. Create a `Reference` object for each piece of content to be signed by the signature and add the `Reference` to the `SignedXml` object (via the `AddReference` method on `SignedXml`). Creating the `Reference` will generally require specifying the value of its `Uri` property and may also require defining a `TransformChain` for the `Reference`.

4. Optionally, add a `KeyInfo` object to the `SignedXml` object to communicate key-related information to the recipient of the signature.

5. Compute the XMLDSIG signature by calling one of the overloads of the `ComputeSignature` method on `SignedXml`.

6. Retrieve the completed `ds:Signature` object by calling the `SignedXml.GetXml()` method.

Individual scenarios may require slight modifications to these steps, but the general outline is the basis for all signature computation in the .NET Framework.

To see these steps in action, consider our first signature construction scenario—a detached signature construction method for URI-addressable content using RSA or DSA key pairs. Our goal is to create a subroutine that takes two input arguments—an `AsymmetricAlgorithm` signing key and a `String` URI—and returns a detached signature for the contents of that URI using the specified key. Listing 32.21 shows the code for such a subroutine.

NOTE

Source code in electronic form for all code listings in this chapter can be downloaded from the publisher's Web site for this book.

LISTING 32.21   Compute a Detached Signature Using an `AsymmetricAlgorithm`

```
public static XmlElement CreateDetachedSignature
➥ (AsymmetricAlgorithm signingKey, String uri) {
  // Create the SignedXml message
  SignedXml signedXml = new SignedXml();
  signedXml.SigningKey = signingKey;
  // Create a Reference to point to the to-be-signed content
  Reference reference = new Reference(uri);
  // Add the Reference to the SignedXml message
  signedXml.AddReference(reference);
  // Compute the XML Digital Signature
  signedXml.ComputeSignature();
  // Return the XmlElement containing the XMLDSIG signature
  return signedXml.GetXml();
}
```

The sample code in Listing 32.21 directly follows steps 1–6 outlined earlier. Input arguments to the `CreateDetachedSignature` method are the `signingKey` (an `AsymmetricAlgorithm`) and a `uri` (a String) identifying the contents to be signed. The first thing the method does is create a new `SignedXml` object using its null constructor; the null constructor form can be used when creating detached or wrapped XMLDSIG signatures. After the `SignedXml` object is created, its `SigningKey` property must be set to the `AsymmetricAlgorithm` object that is to be used to perform the signature function. The third step is to create a `Reference` object identifying the to-be-signed content. In this particular case, no `Transforms` are required, so we can create the necessary `Reference` object using the one-argument constructor that accepts a `String` containing the URI of the to-be-signed content. We then add the `Reference` to the `SignedXml` object using the `AddReference` method; this adds the `Reference` to the list of `References` maintained within a `SignedInfo` object inside a `Signature` object, which is itself stored inside the `SignedXml` class. Finally, the call to the `ComputeSignature()` method calculates the hashes of all referenced content, canonicalizes the XML element representation of the `SignedInfo` object, hashes the resulting XML element, signs this hash, and constructs the overall XMLDSIG `ds:Signature` element. The actual XML element is obtained by calling `SignedXml`'s `GetXml()` method.

NOTE

By default, the .NET Framework XMLDSIG classes use SHA1 wherever a hash algorithm is needed, so the `DigestMethod` of a `Reference` is initialized to the URI identifier for SHA1. Another hash algorithm can be used by setting the `DigestMethod` property on the `Reference` appropriately.

The XMLDSIG signature generated by the `CreateDetachedSignature` method in Listing 32.21 is generally the most compact signature possible because it contains only the URI of the content, the content's hash, and the digital signature value itself. Listing 32.22 contains a sample XMLDSIG signature created using a random RSA key for the content located at the URI `http://www.farcaster.com/index.htm`.

LISTING 32.22   Sample Detached XMLDSIG Signature Using RSA

```
<Signature xmlns="http://www.w3.org/2000/09/xmldsig#">
  <SignedInfo>
    <CanonicalizationMethod
➥ Algorithm="http://www.w3.org/TR/2001/REC-xml-c14n-20010315" />
    <SignatureMethod Algorithm="http://www.w3.org/2000/09/xmldsig#rsa-sha1" />
    <Reference URI="http://www.farcaster.com/index.htm">
      <DigestMethod Algorithm="http://www.w3.org/2000/09/xmldsig#sha1" />
      <DigestValue>XoaHIm+jLKnPocR7FX0678DUOqs=</DigestValue>
```

LISTING 32.22   Continued

```
    </Reference>
  </SignedInfo>
  <SignatureValue>
    M5BhlrxPaOEYcCwSZ3WEDR6dfK5id/ef1JWK6OO5PEGHp9/JxrdA2xT5TYr5egArZGdVURpM
    VGUeViWoeHcGAyMNG9Cmc/I56sYd/TSV/MjLgb/mxq+6Fh/HWtVhjHIG+AdL4lA+ZxxEi147
    QVVzgC14+dvIZaGo7oAFneDKv0I=
  </SignatureValue>
</Signature>
```

> **CAUTION**
>
> The XMLDSIG example signatures presented in this section have been "pretty-printed" (nicely formatted with line breaks and indentation) for easy reading by humans. Unfortunately, the Canonical XML algorithm does not properly handle pretty-printing, so if you want to verify any of these signatures yourself, you will need to remove all the line breaks and insignificant whitespace from the XML before verifying.

Detached signatures work well when the to-be-signed content can be easily addressed and retrieved by URI, but for signing small or dynamically generated XML fragments forcing the content to be Web addressable is overkill. For these scenarios, wrapped signatures work particularly well because the to-be-signed content can be easily embedded within the overall structure of a ds:Signature element. Creating a wrapped signature is very similar to creating a detached signature; the main difference is that the to-be-signed content must be added to the SignedXml object by wrapping the content within a DataObject, and the DataObject's Id property must have a value that can be referenced from a Reference object. As a concrete example, consider the following XML element, which is a simple element with text content:

```
<MyElement xmlns="">MyElement's Text Value</MyElement>
```

This MyElement element contains a single child node holding the text content MyElement's Text Value. An XML element corresponding to this structure could be constructed using the classes in the System.Xml namespace as follows:

```
XmlDocument doc = new XmlDocument();
XmlElement elem = doc.CreateElement("MyElement");
XmlNode child = (XmlNode) doc.CreateTextNode("MyElement's Text Value");
elem.AppendChild(child);
```

Listing 32.23 contains source code for an exemplary CreateWrappedSignature subroutine that can be used to sign our XmlElement. CreateWrappedSignature requires two arguments—a signing key and an XmlElement containing the to-be-signed data. The method embeds and then generates a wrapped XMLDSIG signature around the provided XmlElement.

LISTING 32.23   Compute a Wrapped Signature Using an AsymmetricAlgorithm

```
static XmlElement CreateWrappedSignature
➥ (AsymmetricAlgorithm signingKey, XmlElement contentToSign) {
    // Create the SignedXml message
    SignedXml signedXml = new SignedXml();
    signedXml.SigningKey = signingKey;
    // Create a DataObject to encapsulate the to-be-signed content
    // We use the string "ID1" as the internal reference ID for the object
    // Second and third arguments are null because we don't wish to specify
    // the optional MIME-Type and Encoding attributes.
    DataObject dataObject = new DataObject("ID1", null, null, contentToSign);
    // Add the new DataObject to the SignedXml object so it'll be included
    // in the output signature
    signedXml.AddObject(dataObject);
    // Create a Reference to point to the to-be-signed content
    Reference reference = new Reference();
    // Use a URI fragment to point to the same Id we used in the DataObject
    reference.Uri = "#ID1";
    // Add the Reference to the SignedXml message
    signedXml.AddReference(reference);
    // Compute the XML Digital Signature
    signedXml.ComputeSignature();
    // Return the XmlElement containing the XMLDSIG signature
    return signedXml.GetXml();
}
```

As expected, the code in Listing 32.23 is similar to that for a detached signature (Listing 32.21); the only differences are in the creating and inclusion of a DataObject and the link between that DataObject and a Reference. After assigning the signing key, a DataObject is created to encapsulate the to-be-signed content. If the to-be-signed content consists of a single XmlElement, it can be specified by providing the element as an argument to the DataObject's constructor, as shown here. Alternatively, if the to-be-signed content is a collection of independent XmlNodes held in an XmlNodeList, the embedded content can be added by using the DataObject's Data property. In either case, a value for the DataObject's Id attribute must be specified so that that ds:Object element can be referenced in a ds:SignedInfo element. In this example, the string "ID1" is used to identify the embedded object. After being created, the DataObject is added to the overall signature structure via the AddObject method on the SignedXml class. The AddObject method adds the DataObject to an internal list of DataObjects that must be included in the resulting XML represention of the signature. Next, a Reference object is created that points to the DataObject via a URI fragment. Because the DataObject's Id attribute was assigned a value of "ID1", the corresponding URI fragment value for the Reference's Uri property is "#ID1". The Reference object is then added as before, and signature calculation is performed by a call to ComputeSignature().

NOTE

There are a few points to be aware of when constructing wrapped signatures in your programs. First, notice that the XMLDSIG classes will not automatically generate Id values for DataObjects and corresponding fragment URIs for References; you must generate these values yourself and guarantee that there are no conflicts (multiple Id attributes with the same value) within the entire SignedXml object. If you are only including a single DataObject within your signature, this generally isn't a problem, but if you are combining data from multiple sources, you need to resolve any Id conflicts before computing signatures. This is especially true if you ever merge signed content from multiple documents; two signatures may be valid in independent document contexts but become invalid when combined into a single document because of Id conflicts.

Another important point is to remember to add DataObjects to your signatures using the AddObject method on the SignedXml class. The AddObject method not only adds a DataObject to the list of ds:Object elements that must be created at signature serialization time, but also adds the DataObject to the list of potential targets for fragment URIs found in References. When computing the DigestValue of a Reference that uses a fragment URI, the XMLDSIG classes know to look for corresponding embedded objects in a few places, including the list of DataObjects. If the DataObject is not added via AddObject, it will not be possible to resolve the fragment URI in the Reference and compute the corresponding hash value.

An example wrapped signature for our test element is shown in Listing 32.24. Notice how the output XML differs from that in Listing 32.22 only in the inclusion of the <Object>...</Object> element and the use of a URI fragment in the Reference to indicate that the element with Id attribute value "ID1" will be found in the same document as the document containing the <Signature>...</Signature> element.

LISTING 32.24   Sample Wrapped XMLDSIG Signature Using RSA

```
<Signature xmlns="http://www.w3.org/2000/09/xmldsig#">
  <SignedInfo>
    <CanonicalizationMethod
➥ Algorithm="http://www.w3.org/TR/2001/REC-xml-c14n-20010315" />
      <SignatureMethod Algorithm="http://www.w3.org/2000/09/xmldsig#rsa-sha1" />
      <Reference URI="#ID1">
        <DigestMethod Algorithm="http://www.w3.org/2000/09/xmldsig#sha1" />
```

LISTING 32.24   Continued

```
      <DigestValue>zrMsnr3MPXc/fFzYXYqrQtHDTH4=</DigestValue>
    </Reference>
  </SignedInfo>
  <SignatureValue>BNqo9l2cOjHMdgvcLz0y893JJlrO5zzPDeNIltUcExCjfhNoc8hH5Rs1Q
      gKi4WC9iIfStzBPu3wi213nU6JNRD/oZ80VICal6OSKpZT39sMvCkcqV5OMcfhOjupZ5k
      aTVDGVWrm1sPfDNgcEB+jTeeiTOysfLZHmbE8I4bJdZrY=
  </SignatureValue>
  <Object Id="ID1">
    <MyElement xmlns="">MyElement's Text Value</MyElement>
  </Object>
</Signature>
```

These two examples contain the minimum amount of information necessary to convey a digital signature from signer to verifier. In particular, there is no information or other indication in either example as to what key was actually used to sign the content. Thus, a party attempting to verify either of these signatures would have to have *a priori* knowledge of the verification key to use to validate the signature (or perhaps simply knowledge that one of a small set of keys was used). Generally, though, we cannot assume that *a priori* information exists between two communicating parties; we need to add information to the signature that will help verifiers find and use appropriate verification keys. In XMLDSIG terms, we need to add a `ds:KeyInfo` element to our signatures that contain one or more "hints" to help out verifiers receiving our signatures. The most basic form of the `ds:KeyInfo` element contains just a `ds:KeyValue` sub-element holding the public key that corresponds to the private signing key used to create the signature. In Listing 32.25, we have modified the wrapped signature code from Listing 32.23 to include a `ds:KeyInfo` element with an appropriate `ds:KeyValue` clause.

LISTING 32.25   Compute a Wrapped Signature Including a `KeyInfo` Element

```
static XmlElement CreateWrappedSignature
➥ (AsymmetricAlgorithm signingKey, XmlElement contentToSign) {
    // Create the SignedXml message
    SignedXml signedXml = new SignedXml();
    signedXml.SigningKey = signingKey;
    // Create a DataObject to encapsulate the to-be-signed content
    // We use the string "ID1" as the internal reference ID for the object
    // Second and third arguments are null because we don't wish to specify
    // the optional MIME-Type and Encoding attributes.
    DataObject dataObject = new DataObject("ID1", null, null, contentToSign);
    // Add the new DataObject to the SignedXml object so it'll be included
```

LISTING 32.25   Continued

```
    // in the output signature
    signedXml.AddObject(dataObject);
    // Create a Reference to point to the to-be-signed content
    Reference reference = new Reference();
    // Use a URI fragment to point to the same Id we used in the DataObject
    reference.Uri = "#ID1";
    // Add the Reference to the SignedXml message
    signedXml.AddReference(reference);
    // Add a KeyInfo element to the SignedXml message
    KeyInfo keyInfo = new KeyInfo();
    if (signingKey is RSA) {
        keyInfo.AddClause(new RSAKeyValue((RSA) signingKey));
    } else if (signingKey is DSA) {
        keyInfo.AddClause(new DSAKeyValue((DSA) signingKey));
    }
    signedXml.KeyInfo = keyInfo;
    // Compute the XML Digital Signature
    signedXml.ComputeSignature();
    // Return the XmlElement containing the XMLDSIG signature
    return signedXml.GetXml();
}
```

As you can see, adding `KeyInfo`-related information to an XMLDSIG signature is easy; all we had to do was create an empty `KeyInfo` object, add the `KeyInfo` clauses (sub-elements) we desired, and assign the object to the `KeyInfo` property on our `SignedXml` object. When the XML representation of the signature is created by the call to `GetXml()` at the end of the subroutine, the contents of the `KeyInfo` object are automatically serialized and added as a sub-element of the overall `ds:Signature` element. The .NET Framework natively understands both the `ds:RSAKeyValue` and `ds:DSAKeyValue` elements (via the `RSAKeyValue` and `DSAKeyValue` classes), so the seven lines of code we added to create Listing 32.25 suffice for all RSA and DSA keys. Listings 32.26 and 32.27 show two example wrapped signatures using RSA and DSA keys, respectively, that include corresponding `KeyInfo` elements with `KeyValue` sub-elements.

LISTING 32.26   Sample Wrapped XMLDSIG Signatures Using RSA and a `KeyInfo` Element

```
<Signature xmlns="http://www.w3.org/2000/09/xmldsig#">
  <SignedInfo>
    <CanonicalizationMethod
➥ Algorithm="http://www.w3.org/TR/2001/REC-xml-c14n-20010315" />
```

LISTING 32.26 Continued

```
      <SignatureMethod Algorithm="http://www.w3.org/2000/09/xmldsig#rsa-sha1" />
      <Reference URI="#ID1">
        <DigestMethod Algorithm="http://www.w3.org/2000/09/xmldsig#sha1" />
        <DigestValue>zrMsnr3MPXc/fFzYXYqrQtHDTH4=</DigestValue>
      </Reference>
    </SignedInfo>
    <SignatureValue>
      DtFNTsE7o4IJkVxB2/xNsQvkftRg02WM2mH/nxqNtbaFhlxJ9hCbOjvakM87QxbIRdZpr7Lnm
      N1H0IWTOxZiuYItLAyeXMLVwir9PHaPMFBp4QmSGrG983uZleGbnQ3oz536BGSYn4UVV7xhoY
      bjV/+lxXha++W9XzRN1KKaN6w=
    </SignatureValue>
    <KeyInfo>
      <KeyValue xmlns="http://www.w3.org/2000/09/xmldsig#">
        <RSAKeyValue>
          <Modulus>
            s0cVjgVj7rzRulP1148kHBaeEafbhmPrMbpkFT854HHu9tYp2DEP2f/VPxNtv6Hlk8g
            dDXHey6w4x5GBHUotQWix7XJC9xwa308duCCUnO1fV08+PchAfTaP7rNTZWXqJLiecO
            D0TPcvnxzK1NbQmYb9H4hY+XRu5yVFynoN8WM=
          </Modulus>
          <Exponent>AQAB</Exponent>
        </RSAKeyValue>
      </KeyValue>
    </KeyInfo>
    <Object Id="ID1">
      <MyElement xmlns="">MyElement's Text Value</MyElement>
    </Object>
  </Signature>
```

LISTING 32.27 Sample Wrapped XMLDSIG Signatures Using DSA

```
<Signature xmlns="http://www.w3.org/2000/09/xmldsig#">
  <SignedInfo>
    <CanonicalizationMethod
➥ Algorithm="http://www.w3.org/TR/2001/REC-xml-c14n-20010315" />
    <SignatureMethod Algorithm="http://www.w3.org/2000/09/xmldsig#dsa-sha1" />
    <Reference URI="#ID1">
      <DigestMethod Algorithm="http://www.w3.org/2000/09/xmldsig#sha1" />
      <DigestValue>zrMsnr3MPXc/fFzYXYqrQtHDTH4=</DigestValue>
    </Reference>
  </SignedInfo>
```

LISTING 32.27   Continued

```
<SignatureValue>
  64YrMQdC2wOAd7X/HwbJpC/fVM4J+ce01eguwYSmro8H82/mAsPdJA==
</SignatureValue>
<KeyInfo>
  <KeyValue xmlns="http://www.w3.org/2000/09/xmldsig#">
    <DSAKeyValue>
      <P>
        mJxJ7mx2sweRCvD0LJXraxE1oHPfh9A/qvdFoptX3NYIK7+Q6zsPKjmC+3xVA4F/nbx
        pjzjcxe8NAU6kIcALlbb+Are9bGAn1T6iX1vSX5yuag2uY9eetUxPZ+zBag7St7WbxE
        cJ2CnbFJy7MfKh1o1h5Lp44i9lY85nVAH1z6s=
      </P>
      <Q>7BSubUVUSrfwphIe28k1rCIaxbU=</Q>
      <G>
        S3AXH1iY2eKZc/J6qDmZZ9s8iPsiLFi4VuU8d4NaHkfvoVMMH2+0RQnpvLJisHBVNR5
        Rc9lumKJAwO6+bEqJxqWS2i6b+wJC9rAnm7MQzjc0tTOB5i0Ta1jDZjfHixDzNhvqe7
        mj93O6GiNkEIbRWNq2Gr3sKERqo4VidJjqCcc=
      </G>
      <Y>
        b05XXi7Pom5IYmSCgEFyq6+p89nnC/YNFq75FIxZZf7poVbSw1SeAQa1fvylPv3jqJ9
        ZQH/BKXCS/EIgcKai2RXVk82K5qpq1LyhmJRIZ7zXr38sL0NpPuGdAAyka30jlOQJf5
        jhDAKfpB9PRmXL243ENn8eT4964d7yDGVHOFs=
      </Y>
      <J>
        pXyonBRdcalnwbGtF6CY1PkLrvDxmtNJe4pYtYn2/4lsgVdrkvN/mKCJ0MbH+84889Z
        g3P51eDLwelF0+5pY+E4EBxMPYnhvOJMIy3e20RmPVqQncfHZo6wO/oU9WI9LmrgC2I
        4tEFXEWdtC
      </J>
      <Seed>cIUUPuDB7etAzIVGC3woIWnE/14=</Seed>
      <PgenCounter>oQ==</PgenCounter>
    </DSAKeyValue>
  </KeyValue>
</KeyInfo>
<Object Id="ID1">
  <MyElement xmlns="">MyElement's Text Value</MyElement>
</Object>
</Signature>
```

NOTE

Notice that the structure of the two examples differ not only in KeyInfo components but also in the size of the SignatureValue. This is due to the way the RSA and DSA signing algorithms operate. The output of the RSA signature function is comparable in size to the size of the RSA modulus (1,024 bits in these examples, or 128 bytes). A DSA signature, in contrast, always consists of two 20-byte values; the SignatureValue for DSA is simply the Base64 encoding of a 40-byte array formed by concatenating the two signature values.

Multiple types of KeyInfo sub-elements can be added to a signature by simply calling the AddClause method repeatedly for each additional sub-element. The KeyInfoClause abstract class is the parent class for RSAKeyValue, DSAKeyValue, and other KeyInfo sub-elements, and any number of KeyInfoClause elements can be added to a single KeyInfo object. For example, we can easily change the six lines of code in Listing 32.25 that create the KeyInfo object to also add a KeyName sub-element. Listing 32.28 shows the resulting code that adds a KeyName sub-element that says the key belongs to Alice. A sample RSA signature generated with this subroutine is shown in Listing 32.29.

LISTING 32.28   Using a KeyInfo Element with Multiple Sub-Elements

```
static XmlElement CreateWrappedSignature
➥(AsymmetricAlgorithm signingKey, XmlElement contentToSign) {
    // Create the SignedXml message
    SignedXml signedXml = new SignedXml();
    signedXml.SigningKey = signingKey;
    // Create a DataObject to encapsulate the to-be-signed content
    // We use the string "ID1" as the internal reference ID for the object
    // Second and third arguments are null because we don't wish to specify
    // the optional MIME-Type and Encoding attributes.
    DataObject dataObject = new DataObject("ID1", null, null, contentToSign);
    // Add the new DataObject to the SignedXml object so it'll be included
    // in the output signature
    signedXml.AddObject(dataObject);
    // Create a Reference to point to the to-be-signed content
    Reference reference = new Reference();
    // Use a URI fragment to point to the same Id we used in the DataObject
    reference.Uri = "#ID1";
    // Add the Reference to the SignedXml message
    signedXml.AddReference(reference);
    // Create a KeyInfo element to hold key-related information
    KeyInfo keyInfo = new KeyInfo();
    // Add an appropriate KeyValue sub-element
    if (signingKey is RSA) {
        keyInfo.AddClause(new RSAKeyValue((RSA) signingKey));
    } else if (signingKey is DSA) {
        keyInfo.AddClause(new DSAKeyValue((DSA) signingKey));
```

LISTING 32.28   Continued

```
    }
    // Create a KeyInfoName (representing a KeyName sub-element)
    KeyInfoName keyName = new KeyInfoName();
    // Set the text value for the KeyName element
    keyName.Value = "Alice's Signing Key";
    // Add the KeyInfoName object to the KeyInfo
    keyInfo.AddClause(keyName);
    // Assign the KeyInfo object
    signedXml.KeyInfo = keyInfo;
    // Compute the XML Digital Signature
    signedXml.ComputeSignature();
    // Return the XmlElement containing the XMLDSIG signature
    return signedXml.GetXml();
}
```

LISTING 32.29   Sample Wrapped XMLDSIG Signatures Using RSA

```
<Signature xmlns="http://www.w3.org/2000/09/xmldsig#">
  <SignedInfo>
    <CanonicalizationMethod
➥ Algorithm="http://www.w3.org/TR/2001/REC-xml-c14n-20010315" />
    <SignatureMethod Algorithm="http://www.w3.org/2000/09/xmldsig#rsa-sha1" />
    <Reference URI="#ID1">
      <DigestMethod Algorithm="http://www.w3.org/2000/09/xmldsig#sha1" />
      <DigestValue>zrMsnr3MPXc/fFzYXYqrQtHDTH4=</DigestValue>
    </Reference>
  </SignedInfo>
  <SignatureValue>
    tgSS9Zjd+/fLMx5CEKvzxPcMwWMvH1Jld331Ci3zmVf06l2DXI5lYuiehBUtvuBKaRaqB+Y
    8bAb9zKkyqaT0Yc9Fj6ftiFnrqj0pXCjc8x/1X/50vRzVcIANfgjHOzFnLNmA0+4t7eBdIi
    Ei9CQ0ktCXJ1kS0SE5ZyjwFEdNzho=
  </SignatureValue>
  <KeyInfo>
    <KeyValue xmlns="http://www.w3.org/2000/09/xmldsig#">
      <RSAKeyValue>
        <Modulus>
          tmsw2NKSFGgeJ2JBWM4I3OgFA7Q0O7A0aYugtdGWf60smOGNWegocQjQEzy1qmXM3
          UPxMTQZV4F5O28VLmTKtDn3F1QUa42XP0Oi7Rnvm0UApiNW39stauhg9/XwBH/myw
          I4SGiU1HjN8voYJe6xIZfUGanRXORIjIYMCGXpkgE=
        </Modulus>
        <Exponent>AQAB</Exponent>
```

LISTING 32.29   Continued

```
    </RSAKeyValue>
   </KeyValue>
   <KeyName>Alice's Signing Key</KeyName>
  </KeyInfo>
  <Object Id="ID1">
   <MyElement xmlns="">MyElement's Text Value</MyElement>
  </Object>
</Signature>
```

CAUTION

When constructing ds:KeyInfo elements, you must make sure that you abide by XMLDSIG restrictions concerning allowed combinations of sub-elements. In particular, when creating X509Data sub-elements, you must adhere to the restrictions detailed at the end of the last section, such as the requirement that all instances ds:X509IssuerSerial, ds:X509SKI, and ds:X509SubjectName that refer to the same single certificate be grouped together within a single ds:X509Data element. These semantic restrictions cannot be captured within the XMLDSIG schema, and the .NET Framework classes will allow you to construct KeyInfo elements that do not adhere to them.

So far, all of our examples have used simple references to identify to-be-signed content—content has always been completely identified by a full URI or fragment, same-document URI. In the next two examples, we show how to use the full power of the Reference Processing Model to sign just a portion of an XML document. We will add Transform objects to Reference objects to create chains of transformations to apply to the input content identified by a URI. As a result, we will be able to selectively sign any desired portion of the input content.

Creating Reference objects that include a chain of transformations is easy. All we need to do is create the Transform objects that represent each stage of the transformation chain and add them, in order, to the Reference object by calling that object's AddTransform method. Listing 32.30 shows a sample detached signature that includes a Base64 transformation in its Reference element; the content signed by this signature is not the content directly obtained from the URI http://www.farcaster.com/index.b64, but rather is the result of Base64-decoding that content. Listing 32.31 contains sample code for the method that created the exemplary signature; notice that the only difference between Listing 32.31 and Listing 32.21 is the explicit addition of an XmlDsigBase64Transform object to the Reference.

LISTING 32.30   Sample Detached XMLDSIG Signature with a Base64 Transform

```
<Signature xmlns="http://www.w3.org/2000/09/xmldsig#">
  <SignedInfo>
    <CanonicalizationMethod
➥ Algorithm="http://www.w3.org/TR/2001/REC-xml-c14n-20010315" />
    <SignatureMethod Algorithm="http://www.w3.org/2000/09/xmldsig#rsa-sha1" />
    <Reference URI="http://www.farcaster.com/index.b64">
      <Transforms>
        <Transform Algorithm="http://www.w3.org/2000/09/xmldsig#base64" />
      </Transforms>
      <DigestMethod Algorithm="http://www.w3.org/2000/09/xmldsig#sha1" />
      <DigestValue>XoaHIm+jLKnPocR7FX0678DUOqs=</DigestValue>
    </Reference>
  </SignedInfo>
  <SignatureValue>
    M9tyhbB05xUY0oB+EhFRt2IxdrY15mKdbKJphYA5RGSrU/7/oqEPWo0q02uig5lp9CBHeb5
    iIT6JOlLNaUgmUTF5gIcnB9NT62EWVBAIlr2N5o4NCpY/Q44kYH1Oq7wgYkmCvJpYDumpjJ
    DFao4cj7vDi/YouS0iDW9B/EcTKzk=
  </SignatureValue>
  <KeyInfo>
    <KeyValue xmlns="http://www.w3.org/2000/09/xmldsig#">
      <RSAKeyValue>
        <Modulus>
          othk0XJTRpeIsD4u4qGAcVebbAe9NCNCsTMBCcZhoniWm4AJeWIWAHgL0xCxoK5df
          iQhTk8YWkWt+lJcTmKUdx0/duDMpGLt6o7anfVs8xmeX3o5zwGg5EEZs8FKED8pvc
          bWsTorVGUpG2HgpqhNzbsFfrsgZsC10CGNe0G7qKE=
        </Modulus>
        <Exponent>AQAB</Exponent>
      </RSAKeyValue>
    </KeyValue>
  </KeyInfo>
</Signature>
```

LISTING 32.31   Creating a Detached Signature That Uses a Base64 Transform

```
static XmlElement CreateDetachedSignature
➥(AsymmetricAlgorithm signingKey, String uri) {
    // Create the SignedXml message
    SignedXml signedXml = new SignedXml();
    signedXml.SigningKey = signingKey;
    // Create a Reference to point to the to-be-signed content
    Reference reference = new Reference(uri);
```

LISTING 32.31   Continued

```
    // Create a Base64 transform: the input content retrieved from the
    // uri should be Base64-decoded before hashing
    Transform base64 = new XmlDsigBase64Transform();
    // Add the transform to the Reference object
    reference.AddTransform(base64);
    // Add the Reference to the SignedXml message
    signedXml.AddReference(reference);
    // Create a KeyInfo element to hold key-related information
    KeyInfo keyInfo = new KeyInfo();
    // Add an appropriate KeyValue sub-element
    if (signingKey is RSA) {
        keyInfo.AddClause(new RSAKeyValue((RSA) signingKey));
    } else if (signingKey is DSA) {
        keyInfo.AddClause(new DSAKeyValue((DSA) signingKey));
    }
    // Assign the KeyInfo object
    signedXml.KeyInfo = keyInfo;
    // Compute the XML Digital Signature
    signedXml.ComputeSignature();
    // Return the XmlElement containing the XMLDSIG signature
    return signedXml.GetXml();
}
```

Compare the Reference element in Listing 32.30 to that in Listing 32.22. The two References are obviously different in that the one in Listing 32.22 specifies the direct hash of content obtained from a URI, whereas the one in Listing 32.30 specifies the hash of Base64-decoded content. Notice, however, that the DigestValues in the two elements are identical! They are equivalent because the content stored at http://www.farcaster.com/index.b64 is the Base64 encoding of the content stored at http://www.farcaster.com/index.htm, so the to-be-signed content in Listing 32.30, the Base64-decoded content, is identical to the to-be-signed content in Listing 32.22. Identical to-be-signed content yields identical hashes (using the same hash algorithm), which is why the DigestValues are equal. Of course, the hash values of the canonicalized SignedInfo elements are not equal (they are structurally different) and so even if both signatures were created with the same signing key, the signature values would be different.

Perhaps the most powerful feature of Reference transformations is their ability to select for signing a subset of the input content. In particular, the XPath transformation allows a signer to precisely select a subset of input XML content and sign just that subset. Consider the XML fragment shown in Listing 32.32. This fragment represents a simple element, MyElement, with two child elements, MyFirstChild and MySecondChild. Each child element further contains some text content.

LISTING 32.32   Sample XML Fragment for XPath Transform Example

```
<MyElement xmlns="">
  <MyFirstChild>First Child's Text</MyFirstChild>
  <MySecondChild>Second Child's Text</MySecondChild>
</MyElement>
```

We saw in Listings 32.21 and 32.25 how we could create a wrapped signature for an entire XML object like this one. Suppose, however, that instead we want to sign only the content of the MyFirstChild sub-element; we want to commit to exactly the XML structure

```
<MyFirstChild>First Child's Text</MyFirstChild>
```

while still sending the entire content of the MyElement element. We can select just the MyFirstChild element (and all its descendants) by using the XPath expression:

```
ancestor-or-self::MyFirstChild
```

This XPath expression matches every node in an XML document that either a MyFirstChild element or has a MyFirstChild element as an ancestor node. For the fragment shown in Listing 32.32, the XPath expression ancestor-or-self::MyFirstChild will match exactly the content we want to sign. Thus, by modifying the sample code in Listing 32.25 to include an XPath transformation of ancestor-or-self::MyFirstChild, we can create a wrapped signature around the entire MyElement with a signature that only protects the MyFirstChild element.

The .NET Framework include a class, XmlDsigXPathTransform, that represents an XPath transformation in the Reference Processing Model. Unfortunately, the Framework neglected to include a simple constructor for building XmlDsigXpathTransform objects from a String XPath expression; the only way to set the internal state of an XmlDsigXPathTransform is to construct the object from the internal XML state of a ds:Transform node. Listing 32.33 contains the source code for a simple utility class that creates an XmlDsigXPathTransform from a String argument containing a valid XPath expression; you'll want to cut-and-paste this utility class into your own programs if you ever need to construct XPath transformations.

LISTING 32.33   Source Code for the `CreateXPathTransformFromString` Method

```
// This utility function creates an XmlDsigXPathTransform
// from an XPath string like "self::text()". It's necessary
// because XmlDsigXPathTransform doesn't have a constructor that
// takes a String argument, so we have to build it by importing
// an appropriate XmlNodeList!
static Transform CreateXPathTransformFromString(String xpathString) {
    XmlDsigXPathTransform xpathTransform = new XmlDsigXPathTransform();
    // We need a document to create nodes
    XmlDocument document = new XmlDocument();
    document.LoadXml("<XPath xmlns:dsig=\"http://www.w3.org/2000/09/xmldsig#\">"
➡ +xpathString+"</XPath>");
    xpathTransform.LoadInnerXml(document.ChildNodes);
    return xpathTransform;
}
```

With the `CreateXPathTransformFromString` method in our toolbox of useful functions, we can now easily construct a `Reference` with an embedded `Transform` that selects just the content we want to sign. Because we know that the XPath expression for selecting the to-be-signed content is `ancestor-or-self::MyFirstChild`, the only change we need to make to the code in Listing 32.25 is to change the construction of the `Reference` object from

```
// Create a Reference to point to the to-be-signed content
Reference reference = new Reference();
// Use a URI fragment to point to the same Id we used in the DataObject
reference.Uri = "#ID1";
// Add the Reference to the SignedXml message
signedXml.AddReference(reference);
```

to

```
// Create a Reference to point to the to-be-signed content
Reference reference = new Reference();
// Use a URI fragment to point to the same Id we used in the DataObject
reference.Uri = "#ID1";
// Create an XPath transform for the portion of the content we wish to sign
Transform xpath = CreateXPathTransformFromString("ancestor-or-self::MyFirstChild");
// Add the transform to the Reference object
reference.AddTransform(xpath);
// Add the Reference to the SignedXml message
signedXml.AddReference(reference);
```

The resulting signature, shown in Listing 32.34, contains the entire MyElement object embedded within an Object element. The Reference points to the entire Object via a fragment URI (#ID1), and the XPath transformation selects the to-be-signed content. For reference, Table 32.9 contains a complete listing of all XMLDSIG transforms included in the .NET Framework.

LISTING 32.34 Sample Wrapped Signature Using an XPath Transform

```
<Signature xmlns="http://www.w3.org/2000/09/xmldsig#">
  <SignedInfo>
    <CanonicalizationMethod
➥ Algorithm="http://www.w3.org/TR/2001/REC-xml-c14n-20010315" />
    <SignatureMethod Algorithm="http://www.w3.org/2000/09/xmldsig#rsa-sha1" />
    <Reference URI="#ID1">
      <Transforms>
        <Transform Algorithm="http://www.w3.org/TR/1999/REC-xpath-19991116">
          <XPath>
            ancestor-or-self::MyFirstChild
          </XPath>
        </Transform>
      </Transforms>
      <DigestMethod Algorithm="http://www.w3.org/2000/09/xmldsig#sha1" />
      <DigestValue>Hvipq88vrQCK4zYZsnpncslOiog=</DigestValue>
    </Reference>
  </SignedInfo>
  <SignatureValue>
    nBATUMs7Fev2kyiPD5k5/JgcQ4Fbk7SPoHrzctETw6Hgw0STAWFhZ+jvUXsFzcjU6zCHQug
    GEuDHh7bWIdknkmJjwnXQOU3UozBURRVu/nBJZo3UAWJAEC0FHO7FpkquGTxFHb/Nw3DrBx
    HtJXPDxijyjNM9vYVDwnBsfBrFtTk=
  </SignatureValue>
  <KeyInfo>
    <KeyValue xmlns="http://www.w3.org/2000/09/xmldsig#">
      <RSAKeyValue>
        <Modulus>
          txbfRFQ9fCxZWk4sbFZ1kSbpFt4RedOd6PS2+jOF44J5CX+DuY1mzhTY5HOW63fW7
          8OoGLwrITDcpXGD3mAmHqc1BzbO0Coulvu8o6G9sYthFkYFnfRTuwOM67C42eUlTU
          6E1ZjyOOxr3ONh+iu+zZiy7ff83svzstfwtR92rqE=
        </Modulus>
        <Exponent>AQAB</Exponent>
      </RSAKeyValue>
    </KeyValue>
  </KeyInfo>
```

LISTING 32.34   Continued

```
<Object Id="ID1">
  <MyElement xmlns="">
    <MyFirstChild>First Child's Text</MyFirstChild>
    <MySecondChild>Second Child's Text</MySecondChild>
  </MyElement>
</Object>
</Signature>
```

TABLE 32.9   Transform Classes and Algorithms Included in the .NET Framework

Class	Description
XmlDsigBase64Transform	The Base64 decoding transformation
XmlDsigC14NTransform	The Canonical XML canonicalization transform (comment nodes are excluded from the output in this algorithm)
XmlDsigC14NWithCommentsTransform	The Canonical XML canonicalization transform (comment nodes are preserved in the output in this algorithm)
XmlDsigEnvelopedSignatureTransform	The enveloped signature transform
XmlDsigXPathTransform	The XPath transform
XmlDsigXsltTransform	The XSLT transform

NOTE

Readers familiar with the XPath standard may wonder why we chose to use the XPath expression `ancestor-or-self::MyFirstChild` to select the to-be-signed content rather than a more direct path selection from the document root, such as `//MyFirstChild` or `/MyElement/MyFirstChild`. The answer has to do with the way the XPath transform is defined in Section 6.6.3, "XPath Filtering," of the XMLDSIG specification. XPath transforms in XMLDSIG are always treated filters on sets of XML nodes. An XML node is included in the output of an XPath transform if the result of the XPath expression, when evaluated in the context of the node and converted to a Boolean, is `true`. For XPath expressions that return node sets like `//MyFirstChild`, the Boolean result is `true` if the returned node set is non-empty. In practice, what this means is that an XML node is included in the output of the XPath transform if the XPath expression matches the content of the node *or any children recursively of the node*. So, if we had used the XPath expression `//MyFirstChild` in the previous example, we would have ended up signing more than just the `MyFirstChild` sub-element.

Our final example in this section demonstrates how to construct an *enveloped signature*, which is also sometimes called an *embedded signature*. An enveloped signature is an XMLDSIG `ds:Signature` that, after construction, is embedded within the signed content. A common use of embedded signatures is to sign documents where the outer XML structure of the document must be preserved; the signature is added to the document but does not obscure the overall structure of the document. This is the reverse situation from wrapped signatures where the ds:Signature element was the "outer" XML element, and the signed content was embedded within the signature elements. Now we want to perform the operation the other way, wrapping the signed content around the signature data. As a concrete exemplary scenario, we will embed an XMLDSIG ds:Signature element for the content of the MyElement of Listing 32.32 inside the element itself as a third child element of the root node.

Creating an enveloped signature differs from other signatures in three ways. First, we must specify the XML document into which the signature will be embedded at the time we create the SignedXml object. The SignedXml object needs to know the XML context in which the signature will exist so that XML canonicalization can be carried out properly. In particular, part of the Canonical XML specification requires that XML namespace nodes be propagated from parent nodes into child nodes automatically, so we must declare the node that will be the parent of the ds:Signature node before we can calculate the canonical form of the ds:SignedInfo element. The eventual parent node of the to-be-generated ds:Signature is declared in an argument to the SignedXml constructor using one of the following two constructor overloads:

```
public SignedXml(XmlElement);
public SignedXml(XmlDocument);
```

In the first constructor overload, the XmlElement argument is the parent element of the ds:Signature element about to be computed; the signature will be valid only when made a child of the specified XmlElement. The second constructor overload can be used when the ds:Signature is going to be a child of the top-level document element of an XmlDocument.

The other two differences between enveloped signatures and other forms of XMLDSIG signatures have to do with the construction of References. Enclosing content (that is, content that includes the Signature element) is indicated by creating a Reference object as using the empty string "" as the value of the Reference's URI property. The URI "" has special meaning in the XMLDSIG standard; it identifies the XML resource containing the Reference (with comment nodes removed from the XML). So, to reference the enclosing document, we construct the Reference object as follows:

```
// Create a Reference to point to the to-be-signed content
Reference reference = new Reference();
// Use an empty-string URI to indicate that the signed content is
// the document containing the Signature element
reference.Uri = "";
```

In addition to specifying an empty-string URI, we also need to add a `Transform` to the `Reference` that will exclude the contents of the `ds:Signature` element from the other content in the document. XMLDSIG defines a special-purpose transform for this particular purpose, the "enveloped signature transform" (see Section 6.6.4, "Enveloped Signature Transform" of the XMLDSIG specification, "XML-Signature Syntax and Processing"). In the .NET Framework, the `XmlDsigEnvelopedSignatureTransform` class represents this transform and when constructing enveloped signatures, we need to make an instance of this transform be the first member of the `Reference`'s transform chain:

```
// Create an enveloped signature transform to reference the entire document
// minus the Signature we're about to embed
XmlDsigEnvelopedSignatureTransform envSigTransform =
➡ new XmlDsigEnvelopedSignatureTransform();
// Add the transform to the Reference object
reference.AddTransform(envSigTransform);
```

Now we can perform any other transformations we want on the to-be-signed content, and signature verifiers will automatically ignore the information in the Signature element. Listing 32.35 contains a complete sample program for generating an enveloped signature around the `MyElement` sample text (using a randomly generated RSA key), and the resulting signature (pretty-printed) is shown in Listing 32.36.

LISTING 32.35   Creating an Enveloped Signature for the `MyElement` XML Element

```
using System;
using System.Security.Cryptography;
using System.Security.Cryptography.Xml;
using System.IO;
using System.Text;
using System.Xml;


// Enveloped signature example

public class RSAEnvelopedSignature {

    static XmlElement CreateEnvelopedSignature
➡(AsymmetricAlgorithm signingKey, XmlElement signatureParent) {
        // Create the SignedXml message
        SignedXml signedXml = new SignedXml(signatureParent);
        signedXml.SigningKey = signingKey;
        // Create a Reference to point to the to-be-signed content
        Reference reference = new Reference();
```

LISTING 32.35   Continued

```
            // Use an empty-string URI to indicate that the signed content
            // is the document containing the Signature element
            reference.Uri = "";
            // Create an enveloped signature transform to reference the entire
            // document minus the Signature we're about to embed
            XmlDsigEnvelopedSignatureTransform envSigTransform =
➡ new XmlDsigEnvelopedSignatureTransform();
            // Add the transform to the Reference object
            reference.AddTransform(envSigTransform);
            // Add the Reference to the SignedXml message
            signedXml.AddReference(reference);
            // Create a KeyInfo element to hold key-related information
            KeyInfo keyInfo = new KeyInfo();
            // Add an appropriate KeyValue sub-element
            if (signingKey is RSA) {
                keyInfo.AddClause(new RSAKeyValue((RSA) signingKey));
            } else if (signingKey is DSA) {
                keyInfo.AddClause(new DSAKeyValue((DSA) signingKey));
            }
            // Assign the KeyInfo object
            signedXml.KeyInfo = keyInfo;
            // Compute the XML Digital Signature
            signedXml.ComputeSignature();
            // Return the XmlElement containing the XMLDSIG signature
            return signedXml.GetXml();
        }

    public static void Main()
    {
            // Create a random RSA key
            RSACryptoServiceProvider rsa;
            rsa = new RSACryptoServiceProvider();
            // Create a new XmlDocument with the to-be-signed content
            XmlDocument doc = new XmlDocument();
            doc.LoadXml("<MyElement xmlns=\"\"><MyFirstChild>First Child's Text
➡</MyFirstChild><MySecondChild>Second Child's Text</MySecondChild>
➡</MyElement>");
            // Get the root document element
            XmlElement elem = (XmlElement) doc.DocumentElement;
            // Create an enveloped signature using the root document element as
            // the parent of the signature
            XmlElement xmlDigitalSignature = CreateEnvelopedSignature(rsa, elem);
```

LISTING 32.35   Continued

```
        // Add the computed Signature element to the root document element
        elem.AppendChild(xmlDigitalSignature);
        // Create an XmlTextWriter to write out the XML content to the Console
        XmlTextWriter xmltw;
        xmltw = new XmlTextWriter(Console.Out);
        // Write out the document
        doc.WriteTo(xmltw);
        // Close the XmlTextWriter
        xmltw.Close();
    }
}
```

LISTING 32.36   Sample Enveloped Signature

```
<MyElement xmlns="">
  <MyFirstChild>First Child's Text</MyFirstChild>
  <MySecondChild>Second Child's Text</MySecondChild>
  <Signature xmlns="http://www.w3.org/2000/09/xmldsig#">
    <SignedInfo>
      <CanonicalizationMethod Algorithm=
➥"http://www.w3.org/TR/2001/REC-xml-c14n-20010315" />
      <SignatureMethod Algorithm=
➥"http://www.w3.org/2000/09/xmldsig#rsa-sha1" />
      <Reference URI="">
        <Transforms>
          <Transform Algorithm=
➥"http://www.w3.org/2000/09/xmldsig#enveloped-signature" />
        </Transforms>
        <DigestMethod Algorithm="http://www.w3.org/2000/09/xmldsig#sha1" />
        <DigestValue>rKs5Gxt3IxfjGnT6yGPK9RrGeac=</DigestValue>
      </Reference>
    </SignedInfo>
    <SignatureValue>
      YyyQHXVsO1YPmfK9fBGoHHTMoq+5q9O8IoGD7XE/fArldgKfdVQ9z2EWQZBr6fzUhI4Yo
      LY1XHXNHIDKCNI72gcPr34BocVh/YQ5yF3pZRK3aeD32cRPcDmSfL569Yd02QgXvL67UQ
      dWIuJEABeXo9QvLyPiYZ6j+XERjB/MqZ0=
    </SignatureValue>
    <KeyInfo>
      <KeyValue xmlns="http://www.w3.org/2000/09/xmldsig#">
        <RSAKeyValue>
```

LISTING 32.36   Continued

```
        <Modulus>
            vUIbOs+9MVk/h5YdhruZzMM+aQ3T8mHKz1EkHWadJFofUC06/68Hu6YhrLIO7s2
            kDLws5ZckHW0yr1FSYWvf0xc6a+DsoEin+S9TvFMQ+MahoKs4/ckQxlpi6+u/2n
            yE2RpDmt5PX1eQQDK1z7hqhDMjnGtFupC8elCC5Q9gX6s=
        </Modulus>
        <Exponent>AQAB</Exponent>
      </RSAKeyValue>
    </KeyValue>
  </KeyInfo>
  </Signature>
</MyElement>
```

One closing note before concluding our section on creating XMLDSIG signatures: All of the examples in this section have used AsymmetricAlgorithm objects (RSA or DSA keys) to generate digital signatures. XMLDSIG also allows two communicating parties to authenticate information using a message authentication code (MAC); "signing" with a MAC consists simply of computing the MAC over the canonicalized form of the ds:SignedInfo using the shared secret. You can create these types of XMLDSIG signatures using the .NET Framework by calling the special overloaded form of SignedXml.ComputeSignature that takes a single KeyedHashAlgorithm input argument. Only the HMAC-SHA1 algorithm is supported for use with XMLDSIG in the first release of the .NET Framework.

Verifying an XMLDSIG Signature

We turn our attention now to the process of verifying an XMLDSIG digital signature using the .NET Framework. Signature verification is much easier in general than signature generation, because the only variable in the verification process is finding the correct verification key. The general procedure for verifying an XMLDSIG signature consists of the following steps:

1. Obtain the XMLDSIG ds:Signature you want to verify as an XmlElement object by using the XML-related classes in the System.Xml namespace. Depending on the method in which your application receives the XMLDSIG signature, you may have to scan an XmlDocument for the ds:Signature element, read the document containing the signature from an on-disk file, or parse a network stream for the relevant data. Ultimately, you need to have the signature available as an XmlElement.

2. Create a new SignedXml object. If the signature you want to verify is an enveloped signature, you will need to use one of the one-argument constructors for the SignedXml class to pass the document context for the signature.

3. Load the contents of the signature into the `SignedXml` object by using the `LoadXml` method.

4. Use one of the `CheckSignature` or `CheckSignatureReturningKey` methods available on the `SignedXml` object to validate the digital signature. All of these methods have Boolean return values and return `true` if and only if the signature validates correctly.

Depending on your particular situation, you may need to explicitly specify the verification key in step 4. If your application is handed the `ds:Signature` element as an `XmlElement` and includes sufficient `KeyInfo` to find the public verification key, the entire verification procedure is as simple, as shown in the following method:

```
public static bool VerifySignature(XmlElement signatureElement) {
    SignedXml signedXml = new SignedXml();
    signedXml.LoadXml(signatureElement);
    return signedXml.CheckSignature();
}
```

Of course, this method performs no error handling; various exceptions (usually of the `CryptographicException` class) will be thrown by the XMLDSIG classes if the `signatureElement` does not contain a well-formed XMLDSIG signature, or the verification key cannot be located.

Listing 32.37 contains sample code for a program that will attempt to find and verify an XMLDSIG signature in an on-disk file. The basic steps used to verify the signature are the same as in the previous code snippet, but the program demonstrates some additional routines that you may find useful in your own programs. Given the name of a file on-disk that contains XML content in `args[0]` (the first command-line argument to the program), we can read the contents of the file into an `XmlDocument` object as follows:

```
// Create a new XmlDocument object
XmlDocument xmlDocument = new XmlDocument();
// Tell the XmlDocument to preserve white space in the input
xmlDocument.PreserveWhitespace = true;
// Load the contents of the file into the XmlDocument
xmlDocument.Load(new XmlTextReader(args[0]));
```

CAUTION

It is very important that you configure the `XmlDocument` to preserve whitespace before loading signed XML content and XMLDSIG objects. Normally, the XML classes in the .NET Framework ignore "insignificant whitespace," such as the whitespace occurring between two XML tags not in mixed content. However, the Canonical XML algorithm used by XMLDSIG cannot distinguish between significant and insignificant whitespace, and therefore assumes that *all* whitespace is significant. If you do not tell the XML classes to preserve whitespace, they will automatically omit insignificant whitespace, which will likely lead to a different canonicalized form, different hash values, and ultimately break the digital signature.

After we have the XML containing the signature in an XmlDocument, the next step is to locate the top-level ds:Signature element. One convenient way to find the signature element is to perform an XPath query for it from the root element of the document. The following is a code snippet that locates the first ds:Signature element located anywhere within the xmlDocument:

```
// Our XPath query is going to look for a Signature tag in the
// XMLDSIG namespace, so we have to initialize an XmlNamespaceManager
// and tell it about the URI that identifies the XMLDSIG namespace
// The next two lines of code do that.
XmlNamespaceManager nsm = new XmlNamespaceManager(xmlDocument.NameTable);
nsm.AddNamespace("ds", SignedXml.XmlDsigNamespaceUrl);
// Now call the XPath query method on XmlDocument
// This will return the first XmlNode that matches the
// "//ds:Signature" query. That query will search the entire XML
// tree underneath the document root looking for an element with
// tag name "Signature" in the namespace bound to "ds" in the
// XmlNamespaceManager.
XmlNode node = xmlDocument.SelectSingleNode("//ds:Signature", nsm);
```

This code fragment works by searching the XmlDocument for elements that have the tag name Signature in the XMLDSIG namespace. (The static String variable SignedXml.XmlDsigNamespaceUrl holds the namespace URI defined by the XMLDSIG standard.) If multiple ds:Signature elements exist in the document, this routine finds the first such element in XPath document order; if you want to find all ds:Signature nodes, use the SelectNodes method to return them as an XmlNodeList.

The final step to perform before attempting signature validation is to populate a SignedXml object with the contents of the ds:Signature element:

```
SignedXml signedXml = new SignedXml();
signedXml.LoadXml((XmlElement)node);
```

Now we are ready to try to validate the signature. The SignedXml class contains four methods for checking the cryptographic validity of the signature information contained within it; three of the methods are overloads on CheckSignature and the fourth method is CheckSignatureReturningKey. The following is a detailed description of each of the methods; all return Boolean values:

- CheckSignature(AsymmetricAlgorithm key)—This is the most basic method available for validating an XMLDSIG signature. Each Reference in the SignedInfo is validated by independently obtaining the input content, applying the Reference Processing Model, and computing the hash of output of the chain of transforms. If the computed hash value of any Reference differs from the specified hash value, the signature is immediately declared invalid and CheckSignature returns false. After the References have been processed, the SignedInfo element is canonicalized, hashed, and compared to the result of validating the SignatureValue using the input key argument. The signature validates (and the method returns true) only if the computed hash of SignedInfo matches the hash value inside the SignatureValue.

- CheckSignature(KeyedHashAlgorithm macAlg)—This method works identically to CheckSignature(AsymmetricAlgorithm) except that it validates XMLDSIG signatures protected with a message authentication code, such as HMAC-SHA1.

- CheckSignature()—This method uses the information contained within the KeyInfo section of the signature to discover the validation key. The GetPublicKey() method on the SignedXml object is called repeatedly to produce candidate public keys, and each candidate is tried in turn to validate the signature. The GetPublicKey() method on SignedXml recognizes only the RSAKeyValue and DSAKeyValue types of KeyValue within KeyInfo, but, as described in the "Extending System.Security.Cryptography.Xml for Custom Processing" section later in this chapter, you can subclass SignedXml to define your own GetPublicKey() method to look at application-specific data or other types of KeyInfo to find the validation key.

- CheckSignatureReturningKey(out AsymmetricAlgorithm signingKey)—This method works exactly like CheckSignature() except that when successful, it assigns the actual key used to validate the signature to the signingKey argument.

Our task is complete when we have the result of checking the signature. In the program shown in Listing 32.37, we use the fourth method, CheckSignatureReturningKey, so that we can print out the actual key used to verify the signature. If we were verifying an enveloped signature, we would have to modify only the initial construction of the SignedXml object, passing the XmlDocument as an argument to set the proper verification context.

LISTING 32.37   Verifying an XMLDSIG Signature Stored in an On-Disk File

```
using System;
using System.Security.Cryptography;
using System.Security.Cryptography.Xml;
```

LISTING 32.37   Continued

```
using System.IO;
using System.Xml;
using System.Text;

public class VerifySignature {

  static void Main(String[] args) {
    // Create a new XmlDocument object
    XmlDocument xmlDocument = new XmlDocument();
    // Tell the XmlDocument to preserve white space in the input
    xmlDocument.PreserveWhitespace = true;
    // Load the contents of the file into the XmlDocument
    xmlDocument.Load(new XmlTextReader(args[0]));

    // Our XPath query is going to look for a Signature tag in the
    // XMLDSIG namespace, so we have to initialize an XmlNamespaceManager
    // and tell it about the URI that identifies the XMLDSIG namespace
    // The next two lines of code do that.
    XmlNamespaceManager nsm = new XmlNamespaceManager(xmlDocument.NameTable);
    nsm.AddNamespace("ds", SignedXml.XmlDsigNamespaceUrl);
    // Now call the XPath query method on XmlDocument
    // This will return the first XmlNode that matches the
    // "//ds:Signature" query. That query will search the entire XML
    // tree underneath the document root looking for an element with
    // tag name "Signature" in the namespace bound to "ds" in the
    // XmlNamespaceManager.
    XmlNode node = xmlDocument.SelectSingleNode("//ds:Signature", nsm);

    // Create a new SignedXml object
    SignedXml signedXml = new SignedXml();
    // Load in the Signature element
    signedXml.LoadXml((XmlElement)node);

    AsymmetricAlgorithm key;
    // Use CheckSignatureReturningKey so we get a handle
    // back on the key object that was discovered to
    // be the validation key
    if (signedXml.CheckSignatureReturningKey(out key)) {
      Console.WriteLine("Signature check OK");
      Console.WriteLine(key.ToXmlString(false));
    } else {
```

LISTING 32.37   Continued

```
    Console.WriteLine("Signature check FAILED");
  }
  return;
 }
}
```

Extending System.Security.Cryptography.Xml for Custom Processing

Our last major topic for this chapter is a brief discussion of the extensibility mechanisms supported by the XMLDSIG classes. Extensibility takes two distinct forms in the System.Security.Cryptography.Xml namespace:

- Support for new algorithms, including signature functions, hash algorithms, canonicalization algorithms, and XML transforms

- Support for extending the KeyInfo and Reference processing behavior of the SignedXml class

Recall from the "XMLDSIG Design Principles and Modes of Use" section earlier in the chapter that XMLDSIG was architected to support the use of arbitrary cryptographic algorithms. This requirement is reflected in the XMLDSIG schema in the use of URIs to identify algorithms throughout the defined element structures. The XMLDSIG classes handle arbitrary algorithms by leveraging the cryptographic configuration system described in the "Administering Cryptography Settings" section in Chapter 22. Whenever an XMLDSIG class needs to resolve a URI into an algorithm object, the resolution is performed by calling the CryptoConfig.CreateFromName method. Additionally, the CryptoConfig class is also used to resolve transform URIs into Transform subclasses and ds:KeyInfo sub-elements into subclasses of KeyInfoClause. A complete list of the default mappings from URIs to objects relevant to XMLDSIG is included in Table 32.10.

TABLE 32.10   Default CryptoConfig.CreateFromName Mappings Related to XMLDSIG Objects

Name:	http://www.w3.org/2000/09/xmldsig#dsa-sha1
Class:	System.Security.Cryptography.DSASignatureDescription
Name:	http://www.w3.org/2000/09/xmldsig#rsa-sha1
Class:	System.Security.Cryptography.RSAPKCS1SHA1SignatureDescription
Name:	http://www.w3.org/2000/09/xmldsig#sha1
Class:	System.Security.Cryptography.SHA1CryptoServiceProvider

TABLE 32.10   Continued

Name:	http://www.w3.org/TR/2001/REC-xml-c14n-20010315
Class:	System.Security.Cryptography.Xml.XmlDsigC14NTransform
Name:	http://www.w3.org/TR/2001/REC-xml-c14n-20010315#WithComments
Class:	System.Security.Cryptography.Xml.XmlDsigC14NWithCommentsTransform
Name:	http://www.w3.org/2000/09/xmldsig#base64
Class:	System.Security.Cryptography.Xml.XmlDsigBase64Transform
Name:	http://www.w3.org/TR/1999/REC-xpath-19991116
Class:	System.Security.Cryptography.Xml.XmlDsigXPathTransform
Name:	http://www.w3.org/TR/1999/REC-xslt-19991116
Class:	System.Security.Cryptography.Xml.XmlDsigXsltTransform
Name:	http://www.w3.org/2000/09/xmldsig#enveloped-signature
Class:	System.Security.Cryptography.Xml.XmlDsigEnvelopedSignatureTransform
Name:	http://www.w3.org/2000/09/xmldsig# X509Data
Class:	System.Security.Cryptography.Xml.KeyInfoX509Data
Name:	http://www.w3.org/2000/09/xmldsig# KeyName
Class:	System.Security.Cryptography.Xml.KeyInfoName
Name:	http://www.w3.org/2000/09/xmldsig# KeyValue/DSAKeyValue
Class:	System.Security.Cryptography.Xml.DSAKeyValue
Name:	http://www.w3.org/2000/09/xmldsig# KeyValue/RSAKeyValue
Class:	System.Security.Cryptography.Xml.RSAKeyValue
Name:	http://www.w3.org/2000/09/xmldsig# RetrievalMethod
Class:	System.Security.Cryptography.Xml.KeyInfoRetrievalMethod

To add support for a new signature, hash, or transformation algorithm, simply add a mapping between the algorithm's URI identifier and the class implementing the algorithm to the cryptographySettings section of the machine-wide .NET Framework configuration file. KeyInfo sub-element handlers are identified by concatenating the XMLDSIG namespace URI http://www.w3.org/2000/09/xmldsig#, a space character, and then the tag name of the sub-element. So, for example, to add support for the PGPData sub-element of KeyInfo, you would need to add a mapping from the string value

http://www.w3.org/2000/09/xmldsig# PGPData

to a subclass of KeyInfoClause that handles PGPData elements. For sub-elements of the KeyValue element, the tag name must begin with KeyValue/ and then is followed by the tag name of the sub-element. (See the entries for RSAKeyValue and DSAKeyValue in Table 32.10 for details.)

In addition to new algorithm definitions, it is possible to subclass the `SignedXml` class and modify some of its default behaviors. Two methods on the `SignedXml` class are declared virtual—the `GetPublicKey` and `GetIdElement` methods. These classes are used to generate candidate verification keys (usually based on `KeyInfo` information) and to resolve fragment URI references, respectively. The `GetPublicKey()` method is called by `CheckSignature()` and `CheckSignatureReturningKey()` to scan the contents of the `KeyInfo` element and suggest potential public keys to use to verify the signature. The implementation of `SignedXml.GetPublicKey()` enumerates the `KeyInfo` sub-elements looking for `RSAKeyValue` and `DSAKeyValue` elements. When it finds an RSA or DSA key in a `KeyValue` sub-element, it suggests that key be tried for verification. The method returns `null` to signal the end of its own enumeration when it runs out of keys to suggest.

The `MySignedXml` class shown in Listing 32.38 demonstrates how you can subclass `SignedXml` and define your own mechanism for suggesting possible verification keys. The `GetPublicKey()` method on `MySignedXml` uses information in `KeyName` elements in addition to `RSAKeyValue` and `DSAKeyValue` to try to find verification keys. In this sample, we assume that the signer and verifier have agreed that the string value contained in a `KeyName` element is the CryptoAPI key container name for a key located in the default `"Type 1"` Cryptographic Service Provider (CSP), and we use the techniques introduced in Chapter 31 for accessing and using CryptoAPI-based keys to find the key referenced in the `KeyName` element. When our new `GetPublicKey()` method finds a `KeyInfoName` object within `KeyInfo`, it extracts the `Value` property and calls `CheckForPresenceOfKeyContainer` to see if a key container of that name exists within the default CSP. If the container exists, a new `RSACryptographicServiceProvider` object is created referencing the specified key container by passing the container name within a `CspParameters` object. This new candidate verification key is then used by the other methods inherited from the `SignedXml` class to attempt verification of the digital signature.

LISTING 32.38   Subclassing `SignedXml` to Change the Behavior of `GetPublicKey()`

```
using System;
using System.Security.Cryptography;
using System.Security.Cryptography.Xml;
using System.IO;
using System.Xml;
using System.Text;
using System.Collections;
using System.Runtime.InteropServices;

public class MySignedXml : SignedXml {

  IEnumerator m_keyInfoEnum = null;
```

LISTING 32.38 Continued

```
public MySignedXml() : base() {
}

[DllImport("advapi32.dll", EntryPoint="CryptAcquireContext",
➥ CharSet=CharSet.Unicode)]
public static extern bool CryptAcquireContext(IntPtr phProv,
➥ String pszContainer, String pszProvider, int dwProvType, int dwFlags);

// Utility method for checking whether a specific key container
// is present in the default Type 1 CSP
private static bool CheckForPresenceOfKeyContainer(String keyContainerName) {
  IntPtr phProv = new IntPtr(0);
  bool result = CryptAcquireContext(phProv, keyContainerName, null, 1, 0);
  return result;
}

protected override AsymmetricAlgorithm GetPublicKey() {
  RSAKeyValue tempRSA;
  DSAKeyValue tempDSA;
  KeyInfoName tempName;

  if (m_keyInfoEnum == null)
    m_keyInfoEnum = KeyInfo.GetEnumerator();

  // In our implementation, we move to the next KeyInfo clause
  // which is an RSAKeyValue or a DSAKeyValue
  while (m_keyInfoEnum.MoveNext()) {
    tempRSA = m_keyInfoEnum.Current as RSAKeyValue;
    if (tempRSA != null) return(tempRSA.Key);
    tempDSA = m_keyInfoEnum.Current as DSAKeyValue;
    if (tempDSA != null) return(tempDSA.Key);
    tempName = m_keyInfoEnum.Current as KeyInfoName;
    if (tempName != null) {
      // Use the string value of the KeyInfoName as the public key container
      // Check to see if the container is present
      // We assume the key is an RSA key in this example
      if (CheckForPresenceOfKeyContainer(tempName.Value)) {
        // Create a new CspParameters referencing the key container
        CspParameters cspParams = new CspParameters();
        cspParams.KeyContainerName = tempName.Value;
```

LISTING 32.38   Continued

```
        // Create an RSACryptoServiceProvider referencing the key container
        RSACryptoServiceProvider rsa =
➡ new RSACryptoServiceProvider(cspParams);
        return(rsa);
      }
    }
  }
  return(null);
 }
}
```

By subclassing the SignedXml class, you can also override the default behavior of the GetIdElement method. GetIdElement is used by Reference objects to resolve fragment URI references, such as #ID1. The default behavior of this method is to first attempt to resolve an ID value using the GetElementById method on the XmlDocument class. If that should fail, a secondary attempt is made to resolve the ID value by searching the document for nodes with an Id attribute equal to the supplied value. If you use an attribute other than Id to identify elements and do not include an XML Schema for your documents, you may have to override the default behavior of this method to make in-document references succeed.

Summary

The System.Security.Cryptography.Xml namespace within the .NET Framework contains a comprehensive implementation of XMDLSIG, the XML digital signature standard. In this chapter, we have demonstrated how these classes can be used to create and verify detached, wrapped, and enveloped XMLDSIG signatures. Signatures can be generated for any type of content, whether or not it is expressed as XML resources.

Index

A

access control, 251

Access Control Entry (ACE), 251

Active Directory objects, 258-259

Dynamic Access Control List (DACL), 251, 254-256

examples, 252-254

how it works, 248-249

permission settings, 250-259

printers, 257-258

registry, 256-257

security descriptors, 248, 250-252

services, 258

System Access Control List (SACL), 251

Access Control Entry (ACE), 251

Access Control Lists (ACLs), 222-223

Active Directory objects, 258-259

Active Directory Users and Computers applet, 222

ActiveX controls, 14, 410-411

Adjust Security Wizard, 272, 274, 285-289, 408

AES (Advanced Encryption Standard), 622

Allaire JServ, 585

AllowPartiallyTrustedCallersAttribute (System.Security namespace), 592-594

anonymous access, 199

anonymous authentication, 561

Apache Tomcat Server, 585

Apple Web site, 15

I

P

Q – R

T